Protecting What's Yours

ALSO BY ANDREW D. WESTHEM

Winning the Wealth Game (with Donald Jay Korn)

ALSO BY DONALD JAY KORN

Audit-Proof Tax Shelters
Your Money or Your Life
High-Powered Investing (with Gary Goldberg)
Winning the Wealth Game (with Andrew D. Westhem)

Protecting What's Yours

How to Safeguard Your Assets and Maintain Your Personal Wealth

Andrew D. Westhem
and
Donald Jay Korn

A Birch Lane Press Book
Published by Carol Publishing Group

A Birch Lane Press Book
Published by Carol Publishing Group
Birch Lane is a registered trademark of Carol Communications, Inc.
Editorial Offices: 600 Madison Avenue, New York, N.Y. 10022
Sales and Distribution Offices: 120 Enterprise Avenue, Secaucus, N.J. 07094
In Canada: Canadian Manda Group, P.O. Box 920, Station U, Toronto, Ontario M8Z 5P9
Queries regarding rights and permissions should be addressed to Carol Publishing Group, 600 Madison Avenue, New York, N.Y. 10022

Carol Publishing Group books are available at special discounts for bulk purchases, sales promotions, fund-raising, or educational purposes. Special editions can be created to specifications. For details, contact Special Sales Department, Carol Publishing Group, 120 Enterprise Avenue, Secaucus, N.J. 07094

Manufactured in the United States of America
10 9 8 7 6 5 4 3 2 1

Library of Congress Cataloging-in-Publication Data

Westhem, Andrew D.
   Protecting what's yours : how to safeguard your assets and maintain your personal wealth / by Andrew D. Westhem and Donald Jay Korn.
       p.   cm.
   "A Birth Lane press book."
   ISBN 1-55972-258-4
   1. Finance, Personal.   2. Financial security.   I. Korn, Donald Jay.   II. Title.
HG179.W475   1994
332.024—dc20
                                                      94-16683
                                                        CIP

To all the honest, reliable,
service-oriented financial professionals
who are dedicated to helping
their clients protect hard-won assets

Contents

Contents

Acknowledgments

Since helping people protect assets, property, and themselves comes first, I would like to thank my partners and associates at Wealth Transfer Planning, Inc. This would include, Paul W. Colflesh, Susan G. Hiller, Susan G. Joyce, William A. Storum, Charles V. Douglas, and Lea Anne Storum.

Western Capital Financial's hardworking specialists who have spent the last ten years helping their clients, on a national basis, protect themselves against income taxes.

Thank you to Wealth Transfer Planning, Inc.'s nationally affiliated attorneys who have played such an important role in assisting us in the asset protection portion of this book. They are: Steven Sciarretta, William George, Stephen Margolin, Herb Guston, Larry Bell, Robin Klomparins, and Jack Charney.

Our newsletter editor friends who are greatly responsible for the general idea of the book. These editors are Mark Skousen, Richard Band, Peter Dickenson, William Donoghue, and Joseph Bradley.

Those whose seminars have enabled us to bring these ideas to the public: Kim and Charles Githler of Investment Seminars Incorporated and James Blanchard of Blanchard Seminars.

Samantha Hudson whose public relations expertise opens new avenues to travel.

Bambi Holzer whose expertise in the qualified retirement plan field has been extremely valuable to us.

Martin M. Shenkman, attorney at law, Teaneck, N.J.

A special thank you to my ever understanding and loving wife,

Emily; to my daughter, Lisa, my son David, and my daughter-in-law, Alicia. To my first grandchild, Ashley, the apple of my eye.

I would like to especially acknowledge my father, David S. Westheim (1890–1976), whose teachings and philosophies on protecting your sales territory and clients were invaluable to me.

Introduction

Keeping What We Have

Not everybody is driven by ambition to become wealthy. For every person who works one hundred hours a week, fifty-two weeks a year, to further a career, there are many who are content to put in their forty hours and devote leisure time to friends and family.

However, there is one thread that binds us all, no matter how we pursue wealth: We want to keep what we have. No one likes the idea of losing capital, whether to a thief or a con artist or an act of nature. What's more, we're all concerned with the well-being of our loved ones, as well as of ourselves.

Today, though, keeping what's yours isn't easy. You can be physically attacked in your house or your car or on the street where you live. A hurricane or an earthquake (for example) can destroy your home. If you stretch for extra yield, in today's puny three-percent environment, you have to take on more risks and expose yourself to unscrupulous predators.

Threats to your wealth can generate more perils. When an earthquake shook southern California in early 1994, Paula W. suffered considerable damage to her house. Moreover, her chimney was left at a perilous angle, leaning over the driveway of her next-door neighbor who was pregnant. Desperate, she hired a contractor to tear down the chimney, paying $1,500. The job, performed by three men, took only twenty minutes. Later, Paula learned that some of her neighbors had paid as little as $100 for similar work. She had been taken as well as shaken.

Some inroads into your wealth can be larger—*much* larger. George K., a Pittsburgh executive, decided to buy shares in a video store company for three cents per share, investing a total of $600. Over the next three years, encouraged by press releases, a broker's reassurances, and phone conversations with the company's president, George and members of his family built up a $100,000 stake. The stock, it turned out, was no blockbuster. Share prices moved up for a while, but then collapsed. After the company filed for bankruptcy in 1991, George and his fellow investors held virtually worthless stock. What's more, after he paid another $5,000 to an arbitration firm, the hearing went against him, adding financial insult to injury.

There seems to be no end to the ways in which promoters can separate investors from their money. In April 1994, one issue of the *Wall Street Journal* contained articles on an eight-state roundup of fraudulent wireless-communications deals, on federal charges against a firm selling movie posters as collectors' items, and on federal action against a company offering "guaranteed" annual returns of 10 percent–14 percent to investors who would make auto loans. In southern California alone, state regulators estimated that thirty phone-scam artists were ripping off investors to the tune (or tone) of $30 million per month.

Of course, "keeping what we have" means more than wealth preservation, in today's increasingly violent world. In 1992 (the latest year for which statistics were available as of this writing), over 1,000 Americans were murdered on the job, 32 percent higher than the rate in the not-exactly-pacific 1980s. In a 1994 survey by the American Management Association (AMA), nearly a quarter of the companies responding said that at least some employees had been murdered or attacked since 1990. Not only are you not safe at home, in your car, or walking on the streets, but you can't let your guard down at work, either.

With all the risks out there, your margin of error is slim. One serious illness can wipe out an uninsured family. One adverse judgment, handed down by an increasingly capricious legal system, can literally take away your life's work.

We all saw how Hurricane Andrew destroyed thousands of homes. There's not much you can do when you're in the path of an awesome storm, but (especially with the help of this book) at least you can make sure beforehand that you have the *right* kind of insurance coverage, with the *right* company, so that your house will be replaced.

The *wrong* kind of insurance company can cause irreparable damage in other areas of your life, also. For example, thousands of investors were victimized when both Executive Life and Mutual Benefit Life (and others) were seized by state regulators. Many people had suffered heavy losses on annuities and guaranteed investment contracts. If you pick a *healthy* insurance company, you won't be vulnerable to such disasters.

Today you need to play defense, whether or not you play offense. That's why we've written this book. We want to show you what you can do—*must do*—to protect yourself against catastrophic losses. Our advice is practical rather than theoretical, with many examples to help you see what kind of action to take in which sort of situation.

In this book, we begin by showing you how to invest profitably, yet safely. From there, we explain how to buy the right kind of insurance for your house and your car. We go on to show how to protect your career, how to keep your guard up while you travel, how to buy health insurance without getting sick from the bills, how to preserve your wealth in retirement, how to avoid disastrous lawsuits, how to keep your assets intact in case of a divorce, and how to pass on what you've earned to your family. Finally, we show you how to protect the most important things you have—yourself and your family. Our aim in this book is to provide guidance for everyone with something to protect—and that means *everyone*.

Part I

Get Rich Slowly

1

No Gains Without Potential Pain

Invest Profitably Without Taking Undue Risk

There was a time when school revolved around the "three R's": reading, 'riting, and 'rithmetic. Although those days are long gone, investing still depends on the "two R's": risk and reward.

Low-risk investments offer low rewards. A Treasury bill issued by the federal government, for example, pays a low interest rate. If T-bills paid high rates, investors would scramble to buy them and the increased demand would drive up the price. As the price went up, the yield would keep dropping until it was in line with the low level of risk.

Conversely, the stock of a start-up biotech company must offer the potential of high returns to lure investors into a risky venture. Once the stock price goes too high, further rewards will seem unlikely and investors will stop buying. Eventually, the price will drop to a level where there's the potential for huge gains.

No matter what anyone tells you, you can't escape the risk–reward matrix. After all, if you seek high returns, you'll have to take *some* risks. The trick is to keep the risks manageable while making investments that truly *have* potentially high returns.

Keep a Stash of Cash

Most investors play it too safe. That is, they keep too much of their money in bank accounts or money-market funds. These vehicles are extremely low-risk because you're not likely to suffer from defaults or trading losses associated with them. Therefore, they offer low returns. In early 1994, for example, six-month certificates of deposits (CDs) paid an average of 2.7 percent, the same as money-market funds. After-tax, you'd likely wind up with less than 2 percent—not enough to keep up with inflation.

Most people should keep a minimal amount in "cash equivalents": bank accounts, money-market funds, or T-bills. Besides low risk, they offer easy access to your cash in case of an emergency. Generally, you should keep one-third to one-fourth of a year's income in cash equivalents, where you can get at your money quickly. The rest you should hold in longer-term investments, where the potential rewards are greater.

Bank Notes

Some people prefer to keep more of their money in cash equivalents. They're so averse to taking any risks that they're willing to accept the low returns. That's fine when it comes to T-bills, which have the full backing of the U.S. government. Also, money-market funds have proven to be super-safe investments over their relatively short history. For safety's sake, use a money fund offered by a well-established brokerage firm or mutual-fund family.

Bank accounts, though, are a different story. From 1987 through the writing of this book, over 1,000 U.S. banks, holding a total of more than $150 billion in assets, failed. What happens when your bank fails? Deposits *of any size* are insured up to only $100,000.

That wasn't enough for Jerold and Judith S., who wired a maturing $99,000 CD to their joint account at Atlantic Financial Savings in

Pittsburgh, bringing their balance to $147,000—most of the money they had managed to save on Jerold's salary as a college professor. Jerold and Judith planned to invest $100,000 in municipal bonds within a week. Before they could act, though, Atlantic failed. They got back their $100,000, but it was still uncertain, as of last report, whether they'd ever get back the other $47,000.

Even if you stick to the $100,000 limit, you can get burned by a bank closing. Judy T., a third-grade teacher in Wilton, Connecticut, kept $145,000 in Resource Savings of Denison, Texas, selected for its high, federally insured rates. She put $100,000 in her own name, and the other $45,000 in joint accounts with her children.

When Resource went under in 1990, federal regulators stepped in, and Judy had to wait five weeks before she could get her money out. She didn't lose any of the principal, but she lost all the earnings on her $100,000 CD (because those earnings were over the limit), plus five weeks' interest on her other CDs. Altogether, she lost more than $2,000.

Be careful with your bank accounts. For example, *never* keep more than $100,000 in the same bank under the same name: You need to spread your money among several accounts (perhaps one in your name and one in the name of your spouse or a "significant other")— even several banks. And try to avoid banks in shaky financial condition. For an evaluation of your bank, call Veribanc (800-442-2657) or Bauer Financial Reports (800-388-6686).

Take an Interest in Bonds

After you have your emergency money in a money-market fund and/ or safe bank, you can start thinking about potentially higher-yield investments. The first step up from cash equivalents is the bond market. The principle is the same—you're lending your money in return for interest. When you invest in bonds, though, you're lending money for longer time periods, perhaps as long as thirty years.

The bond market actually breaks down into two categories: Treasuries, and everything else. Treasury notes (maturing in two to ten years) and bonds (out to thirty years) are do-it-yourself investments. You can buy Treasuries on your own, with little or no fee, from banks or brokers or the Federal Reserve. The only real risk is market risk: If interest rates go up, the value of your bonds will fall. But if you hold your bonds until maturity, this risk disappears. So stick to Treasuries maturing in eight years or less, to get a decent yield with minimal risk.

Other types of bonds pay higher yields, but they're not for most investors. That is, investors shouldn't buy these bonds directly. There is a great deal you need to know about—credit risk, market risk, call risk, reinvestment risk—and relatively little information available about each issue. In the related area of mortgage-backed securities, such as Ginnie Maes and collateralized mortgage obligations (CMOs), there's even more you need to know, such as the assumed speed of prepayments and the amortization of discounts or premiums.

In general, the only people who should invest in non-Treasury bonds are those with at least $50,000 to spread around ten different issues. Thus, your portfolio can survive a disaster that strikes any one issue. In addition, you should either be financially sophisticated about the bond market, or work with a broker or financial planner who is.

Few investors can meet those criteria. Fortunately, other investors have another path to investing in the bond market: no-load mutual funds. You may give up some potential reward when you turn to funds instead of investing directly in bonds, but you greatly reduce your risk.

Mutual funds can invest in dozens of different issues, so the risks are spread widely. Bonds are selected by full-time investment professionals who know the market. Mutual funds are particularly good vehicles for Ginnie Maes and CMOs because all prepayments are automatically reinvested, sparing you the headache thereof. Generally, you can invest in mutual funds for as little as $2,500 or $3,000.

Best Bond Buys

When you invest in bond mutual funds, you have hundreds to choose among. How can you pick the ones that will protect you from loss even while generating a substantial return?

• *Buy funds that have no sales charge and no redemption fee.* If you do your own research, you might as well buy a no-load. If you rely on a broker for advice, you'll have to pay a commission, reducing the amount you have working for you.

• *Buy the right type of fund.* It doesn't make sense to buy Treasuries through a mutual fund. Corporate bond funds and Ginnie Mae funds are most appropriate for investors in a low tax bracket, or for holding in a tax-sheltered retirement plan. If you're in a high bracket, investing outside of a retirement plan, municipal bond funds may be your best choice.

• *Look carefully at a fund's holdings.* If you buy a fund holding long-term bonds (average maturity of twenty years or more), you're vulnerable to interest-rate swings. Funds with average maturities under ten years are safer.

• *Buy seasoned funds with a good record.* Why buy a new fund when you can buy one that's been around five years or longer and has shown what it can do? Pick a fund based on total return rather than current yield: A high yield doesn't help if the share value of your bond fund goes down.

Perhaps the safest bond fund you can own, yet still earn high yields, is Vanguard Bond Index Fund (800-662-7447), which aims to duplicate the total return of Salomon Brothers Broad Investment-Grade Bond Index. The fund's expenses are extremely low. From its inception at the end of 1986 through 1993, the price stayed between $9 and $10.25 per share; average maturity is about ten years. The fund's total return was over 10 percent a year during this period.

A slightly better performance (over 11 percent per year) was registered by Harbor Bond Fund (800-422-1050). This fund holds a mix of bonds, everthing from Federal National Mortgage Association (Fannie Mae) to Chrysler. Again, the average maturity is around ten years, and share-price volatility has been moderate.

As mentioned, mortgage-backed securities go particularly well in mutual funds because *all* prepayments are reinvested. Managers Intermediate Mortgage Securities (800-835-3879) generated the top return in the 1989–93 period, nearly 14 percent per year, despite keeping maturities to an average of only six years, thus holding down risk. If you're looking for a straight Ginnie Mae fund (Ginnie Maes are extra-safe because they're fully backed by the federal government), Vanguard Fixed-Income GNMA (800-662-7447) has an excellent record, with *no* down years since its founding in 1980.

Among municipal bond funds, both Scudder Medium-Term Tax-Free Fund (800-225-2470) and USAA Tax-Exempt Intermediate-Term Fund (800-382-8722) have splendid records, protecting investors from loss of principal. Average maturities typically range between eight and nine years, so fluctuations in share prices have been modest.

No matter which bond fund you choose, ask for *dividend reinvestment*. Over the years the share value likely will stay fairly constant, yet your balance will grow as the reinvested dividends compound. With a diversified, intermediate-term bond fund, you're not likely to see your investment slip away from you.

Stock Answers

Investing in stocks is similar to investing in bonds. You should buy stocks directly only if you have the patience to do thorough research and the means to hold shares in ten or more companies. To protect your portfolio, those companies should be spread among different sectors of the economy rather than concentrated in one or two industries.

The safest investments are in companies that pay substantial dividends and have done so for many years—those companies consistently generate more cash than they need. Don't invest in the hot tip you've heard about in the locker room unless you already have a portfolio of blue-chips.

One possible strategy is to emphasize companies with a long history of increasing dividends. In early 1994, for example, Bic Corp., North America's largest maker of ballpoint pens and disposable lighters, increased its dividend for the eighth time in nine years; Bic has paid dividends every year since going public in 1971. When you invest in a company like this, you're fairly certain that your ownership stake will retain value and probably grow.

If you don't want to pick stocks yourself, there are mutual funds from which you can choose. There are many types of stock funds, everything from international funds to small-company funds to funds that specialize in one sector of the economy. Although some specialty funds may have excellent results, your principal probably is safest if you buy diversified funds that invest in a cross-section of U.S. stocks. Moreover, you want to look for a solid, long-term track record. The following no-loads fit that description, having posted average total returns of 16–17 percent per year for the ten years that ended in 1993:

- Berger 100 (800-333-1001)
- SteinRoe Special Fund (800-338-2550)
- Twentieth Century Ultra Investors (800-345-2021)

Again, if you *reinvest* dividends, your fund balance likely will grow over the long term, overriding any market losses.

Some discount brokers, such as Charles Schwab, will handle orders for no-load mutual funds. You may be able to buy more than 200 funds without paying transaction costs, and you'll enjoy the convenience of having your no-load funds summarized on a single statement.

Discount brokers may offer to let you buy mutual funds *on margin*—which is to say that you may be able to buy funds with up to 50 percent borrowed money. For most investors, however, buying on margin isn't a good idea. The same goes for buying individual stocks on margin. Investing in stocks is risky enough without investing with money that's not even yours.

Grow Now, Pay Tax Later

There's yet another investment option if you want asset growth and protection: buying deferred annuities. You give money to an insurance company or another financial institution, in one large payment or a series of payments. The earnings can grow, tax-deferred, until you withdraw your funds.

Deferred annuities can be either *fixed* or *variable*. With a *fixed* annuity, your money will earn a bondlike return each year, yet your principal won't shrink if the bond market declines. You have upside, but no downside.

Variable annuities give you a choice of investment vehicles, usually including several mutual funds. You can invest in the stock market if you want, with a shot at superior long-term results. Your account may fall, it's true, but variable annuities pay a death benefit to your beneficiaries that's guaranteed to be no lower than the money you invested.

How can you pick safe annuities? With a *fixed* annuity, start with the financial strength of the insurance company issuing it. The insurer should be rated A+ by A. M. Best, and AA or better by Standard & Poor's, Moody's, or Duff & Phelps. If you invest with a weak insurer, lured by the appeal of high interest rates, you risk the fate of those who bought Baldwin-United annuities: After the company became insolvent in 1983, annuity investors had to wait as long as four years to get any money out of their contracts. To find out how an insurer is rated, ask at your local library for insurance industry reference books.

The other key criterion is the company's history of renewal rates. You don't want an insurer that lured investors with an 11 percent yield several years ago, then gradually reduced renewal rates to 4 percent while continuing to use high come-on rates for new buyers. Ask to see the renewal record, and check on whether old investors are getting approximately the same deal as new ones.

Safe Harbors

As we have to some extent already demonstrated, variable annuities are different from fixed annuities. You don't need to be as concerned about insurance company safety because variable-annuity money goes into separate accounts, not into the insurance company's general account. Thus, if the insurance company runs into trouble, variable-annuity investors will not be lumped with other creditors—their funds will remain separate.

With a variable annuity, the big concern is the quality of the people managing your money. You should be looking for "name brand" mutual-fund managers, such as John Templeton and Martin Zweig and the people who manage funds for Fidelity, Janus, T. Rowe Price, and so on. Then you know you'll enjoy first-rate money management. Some variable annuities, in fact, are so confident of their managers' abilities that they'll guarantee paying a 5 percent or 7 percent annual profit to your beneficiaries if you die while holding a deferred annuity.

What if you're already in an annuity (fixed *or* variable) and become disenchanted? If you simply pull out of the contract, you'll owe surrender charges, income taxes, *and* possible penalties.

For example, Miles and Ann J. of Los Angeles invested $26,000 in a Pacific Standard Life Insurance annuity in 1988. In 1989, the troubled insurer was taken over by the state of California. Miles and Ann asked for their money back, and got a refund—after seven months of correspondence. However, even though their account had grown to nearly $30,000, they got back only $27,000—they lost $2,600 in surrender charges. Plus, they owed taxes and penalties on their $1,000 gain.

Miles and Ann would have been better off if they had acted sooner. They could have contacted an agent specializing in annuities, and switched to a better contract: You can execute a "1035 exchange" from one annuity (or life-insurance policy) to another and owe *no* income tax. You might pay a surrender charge, but that's better than staying with a subpar annuity.

Assuming you find a good contract to begin with, are annuities right for you? They should be considered supplementary retirement plans, to be purchased *after* you have funded your deductible IRA, Keogh, 401(k), etc. If you have excess money to invest, and you can keep your hands off that money until you reach age 59½, then deferred annuities are a tax-advantaged way to enjoy asset growth as well as safety.

SUMMING UP

• The key to investment success is to take measured risks while putting your money into vehicles with real growth potential.

• Don't keep more than a few months' worth of income in cash equivalents, such as bank accounts or money-market funds.

• Stick with financially strong banks and keep your accounts under $100,000, the limit for federal insurance.

• Although Treasury bonds may be bought directly, other types of bonds should be bought through no-load mutual funds (unless you're an extremely sophisticated investor).

• If you're a diligent investor, you can pick your own stocks, emphasizing established, dividend-paying companies.

• Most investors are better off buying stocks through mutual funds.

• Look for funds with solid, long-term records, and *reinvest* your dividends.

• Deferred annuities can provide investment safety *and* tax-advantaged growth.

• Look for a financially strong insurer when you buy a *fixed* annuity, and for first-class mutual-fund managers when you buy a *variable* annuity.

• Annuities should be a supplementary source of retirement funds, most appropriate for those who can do without the money until age 59½ (and thus avoid a tax penalty).

2

Getting Churned Is Getting Burned

How to Keep Your Broker Honest

Back in the late 1980s, Joseph F. was worried. He was a retired construction supervisor in Phoenix who had been treated for cancer. He and his wife had saved their money but were concerned about how long it would last. So when he received a call from a broker, he listened.

The broker, after all, worked for one of the top brokerage firms in the country, one that spends millions of dollars on TV ads touting its investment savvy. He told Joseph to pull all of his money out of insured bank accounts and get "more safety," along with high yields, in a "Triple-A rated" junk-bond fund.

The result? In just over a year, Joseph's $115,000 nest egg was worth less than $40,000.

Unfortunately, Joseph's story is hardly unique. William and Donna B. of California went to the Century City office of another big-name brokerage firm, where they were referred to one of the "star" brokers.

This broker even appeared regularly on local TV, giving investment advice. What more could they ask?

A few years later, William and Donna had lost $200,000 in a series of worthless limited partnerships.

Such horror stories could make up a book of their own. There are about 200,000 licensed brokers in the United States, most of whom are law-abiding citizens. Even a small percentage of bad apples, however, means hundreds, even thousands of brokers you need to watch out for, at large firms as well as small ones. One broker, in fact, moved some losing options investments from his personal account to clients' accounts, so his clients would pay for his losses.

Pieces of the Action

Most broker abuses involve the practice of *churning*. Brokers work on commission—every time you buy or sell securities, you pay a sales fee. So some brokers are *not* satisfied by telling you to buy AT&T and hold on until you retire. Instead, they'll tell you that what you have now is *wrong*—no matter *what* it is. You *must* sell, and buy something else!

A few months later, after their "sure thing" is down sharply, you're again told to sell, and to buy something else. This "churning" goes on and on, from one flaky investment to the next, while your portfolio value shrinks and the broker's commission income expands. (Some investors even sign discretionary agreements giving brokers the authority to trade their accounts *without* prior approval—an open invitation to churning.)

What can you do to avoid being victimized? Start by writing down your financial goals. You might, for example, say that preservation of capital is your primary objective, followed by long-term growth. Have your broker sign a copy. Once someone puts his or her name on a document, there's a marked tendency to live up to the stated terms.

Don't sign discretionary trading agreements. Rather, keep your eye on your monthly statements, to see how much trading activity is taking place. If more than 25 percent of your stocks turn over each year, you should find out why your account is so active.

What if you don't have the time or inclination to ride herd on your broker and approve all trades in advance? Most firms now offer "wrap" accounts, even to small investors. Here, you turn over your portfolio's management to a professional, paying a fee of around 3 percent of funds under management. That is, a $100,000 investor would pay around $3,000 per year for all brokerage costs, including commissions. That's a substantial amount, but it's far better than falling victim to a broker who churns your account.

If you do maintain control over your own investing, exercise caution. Don't believe in get-rich-quick schemes—no stock is "guaranteed" to double in a month, or even a year. New offerings and very small stocks are speculative, so don't overload. Build a solid base of proven stocks and investment-grade bonds before allocating a portion of your holdings to more-speculative issues.

Don't Call Us

If you suspect you've been victimized by your broker, how should you proceed? One thing you *shouldn't* do is call the Securities and Exchange Commission (SEC). But that's precisely what Lawrence V., a Glendora, California, building contractor, did. Proceeding on the advice of one SEC staffer, Lawrence wrote up a thirty-page report detailing his $100,000 loss. A month later, he received a two-page *form* letter saying that the SEC couldn't help him.

Your best bet is probably to go through channels at your brokerage firm. Complain to your broker, the branch manager, and the firm's compliance department. If all of that doesn't help, see a lawyer who specializes in securities law. (Your local bar association probably will be able to recommend someone.) Don't delay, because you may miss out on a deadline for bringing an action. Such deadlines vary from state to state, but the general rule is that you must act within a year or so of discovering that you've been defrauded.

You may be able to file a lawsuit, but in many cases you'll then be forced to go through arbitration, under the terms of your brokerage agreement. *Arbitration* is an expedited process during which your case is heard by a panel of experts. Chances are, you'll wind up with a partial recovery in far less time than would be the case if you brought a lawsuit. Arbitration hearings usually last one or two days, with resolution expectable within a year of filing.

Even though it's not required, you're best off retaining a securities lawyer if you go through arbitration. If your dispute involves $30,000 or more, you'll likely be able to find and hire an experienced securities lawyer. Even if you have a smaller claim, you probably can get a consultation with a lawyer for either a token fee or no fee at all.

What you're looking for is an indication that you'll have a good chance of succeeding, should you press your case. For example, if your broker misled you about expected results, you probably are in a strong position to win some restitution. The same holds if the broker sold you unsuitable securities—as would be shares in a start-up gold-mining company, if you're a widow depending on fixed income, for example.

Stake Your Claim

If you decide to proceed on your own, the National Association of Securities Dealers (NASD) offers arbitration. Call 212-858-4400 for an arbitration kit.

Whichever way you go for arbitration, do-it-yourself or with a lawyer, you'll need to file a *statement of claim*, which will become the basis of your case. In this statement, you'll explain what happened, and why you think you should get your money back.

Give as much detail as possible. If you say your account was churned, tell how many trades were executed and in what time period. Attach copies of the brokerage statements to support your allegations.

If you're claiming that the broker made misrepresentations, tell exactly (to the best of your recollection) what he or she said, and when. Attach any correspondence or promotional materials you received that made inflated claims.

Usually, disputes of $10,000 or less will be decided *without* a hearing, but rather based on the paperwork you submit. Disputes concerning between $10,000 and $30,000 will be heard by a single arbitrator. However, for smaller claims you have the right to request a hearing with *three* arbitrators. The stronger your case, the better off you are with a trio, because you risk losing, should the lone arbitrator take an unreasonable position.

If you do request a hearing, you also can request a location that's more convenient than otherwise for you. Obviously it doesn't pay for an Oklahoma City investor to travel to New York to resolve a dispute over $1,000.

Your broker should respond to your claim within a month. If silence prevails, prodding the NASD is more likely than not to result in waking him or her up. If the NASD remains inactive, you'll have to keep calling the association or hire an attorney.

After you get a response from the brokerage firm, write to the firm, requesting certain documents—the individual broker's disciplinary history, and a record of all commissions received on transactions for your account. Also ask for the firm's compliance manual, which may in fact *prohibit* the types of trades made on your behalf.

Send a copy of your letter to the NASD, and keep pressing for a complete response. If necessary, write to the NASD Director of Arbitration, 33 Whitehall Street, New York, NY 10004. Also, call your state securities regulator and ask for the NASD's Central Registration Depository report on your broker. If you can show that the broker has a blemished past, you'll increase your chances for a recovery.

Eventually you'll be assigned an arbitration date and a list of arbitrators. Before consenting, ask the NASD for a summary of the arbitrators' past decisions. If you see one who consistently has favored the brokerage industry, insist upon a replacement. On average, over half of investors get an award in arbitration, generally amounting to about half of the losses they claim.

SUMMING UP

- Although most brokers are honest, there are many unscrupulous ones out there, working for large and small firms alike.
- Brokers earn commissions when you buy or sell securities, so they may urge you to trade more often than necessary, or to buy unsuitable investments; and they may even make false promises about the expected results.
- To protect yourself, make your goals clear to your broker, and monitor your statements regularly.
- *Don't* give your broker unrestricted authority to make trades on your account.
- As soon as you see signs of what might be improper behavior, complain emphatically to both your broker and the firm.
- If the situation isn't resolved, consult with an experienced securities lawyer.
- If your case is too small to interest an attorney, you can represent yourself in arbitration proceedings before the National Association of Securities Dealers.
- Before going to arbitration, get as much information as possible about both your transactions and your broker.

3

Pro Power

Finding a First-Class Investment Manager

Brokers aren't the only financial advisers who can rip you off. There are thousands of people calling themselves "financial planners" today, and they occupy a wide spectrum of ability and honesty. Some planners are hardworking, knowledgeable pros who perform a needed role, but others are incompetent or unscrupulous (or both). Reportedly, poor financial planning costs clients at least $300 million per year.

One twenty-four-year-old, for example, set himself up as a financial planner in Phoenix. He promised clients 4 percent–7 percent growth per *month* from stocks and commodities futures. Working a "Ponzi scheme," he used money from new investors to pay off old ones, build favorable word-of-mouth, and attract more money. By the time the whole venture collapsed, investors had lost over $5 million.

The message, of course, is to keep your expectations reasonable. If top money managers shoot for 12 percent or 15 percent annual returns, why should anyone be willing to promise you 50 percent or more?

17

Even if you avoid out-and-out rip-offs, you may fall prey to poor advice. That's what happened to Milton and Betty M., who took early retirement and moved to Florida. They consulted a "certified financial planner," who advised them to put almost $90,000 into limited partnerships and junk-bond funds.

The investments weren't washouts, but neither were they very good. After seven years, $90,000 had shrunk to $83,000—and that sum includes distributions received in that time frame. If Milton and Betty had simply kept their money in a bank account or money-market fund, they'd have had $130,000 or more.

Now, no one is saying you should put all of your money into bank accounts and money funds. For a fifty-five-year-old couple, growth is important—even critical. And, considering the strength of the stock and bond markets in the late 1980s and early 1990s, there were plenty of ways that growth could have been obtained.

Unfortunately, their "financial planner" didn't come up with a very good plan. So Milton and Betty had not only a sizable loss—they also had an even greater *opportunity cost*, the money they might have made but didn't.

Information, Please

How can you separate real financial planners from the scam artists and the second-raters? You can tell a lot from even your first meeting. If your planner recommends a particular investment right away, watch out. Chances are, every "plan" offered involves the same thing: life insurance or a deferred annuity or a growth-stock fund, on *any* of which the planner will collect a commission.

Because there's no perfect investment that's right for all clients, a good planner should ask you questions—lots of questions—before recommending *anything*. How old are you? How much do you earn? What assets do you have? What's your family situation? What are your goals? How comfortable are you with investments that can go down as well as up?

Only after you've answered these (and other) questions should the adviser come up with a thorough plan—insurance, tax planning, retirement planning, investing. He or she may even suggest ways to cut your spending so you'll be able to increase savings.

At this point, you probably *will* know whether you have a real planner or a commission-hungry salesperson. There's nothing wrong with buying financial products (or paying commissions for services rendered), but those products should make sense in the context of an *overall* plan.

The Checking Game

Before you waste time trying to discover who's a real planner and who isn't, here's a screening process you can use:

• *Find out if a planner is registered.* Planners usually must register with the federal Securities and Exchange Commission as well as with state regulators. If a planner can't show you proof of registration, ask why not. If that challenge doesn't bring the desired reaction, call the SEC (202-272-7450) *and* the state's securities department as soon as you can, to find out if that planner has ever been subjected to disciplinary actions or arbitration proceedings.

• *Check into a planner's educational and financial background.* A degree in finance, business, or economics *usually* is evidence of a basic understanding of money matters. Also, *most* bona fide planners have passed an exam to become a CPA (accounting), a chartered life underwriter or chartered financial consultant (both in life insurance), a certified financial planner, or a registered financial planner. Such credentials show *some* competence, although they are *not* guarantees of excellence in financial planning.

• *Ask how your planner will get paid.* A typical arrangement is fee-plus-commission. That is, you'll pay a fee for a plan, by the hour, or for an annual retainer. You'll also pay a commission for buying life insurance, mutual funds, and other products that the planner recommends. Some planners are "fee-only," but their fees tend to be higher than those charged by planners who accept commissions.

Fee-only planners portray themselves as unbiased, but the truth is that the world of financial advisers doesn't break down so neatly into saints and sinners. The important thing is full disclosure—you want to know exactly how much of your money goes to a planner, so you can decide whether he or she is worth it.

Take your own inclinations into account, too. If you're an active investor, the kind who likes to select stocks and mutual funds on your own, you don't need a commission-based planner who'll put you into mutual funds with a sales load: You can buy your own no-load funds.

But if you really want your planner to make all the decisions for you, such as picking specific mutual funds, you may be better off with a planner who'll do the work and receive a commission therefor.

• *Ask for references.* A good planner will have satisfied clients, those who have been relying on him or her for years. Get the names of some, and call to find out which services the planner has performed for them.

You also should ask the planner to show examples of plans he or she prepared in the past (with names deleted), along with follow-up reports. If each plan contains very similar recommendations, be cautious.

• *Use common sense.* One planner advised his clients, a married couple, to refinance their house, thereby increasing their mortgage from $17,000 to $90,000. Then he advised them to sell five blue-chip stocks, to raise another $80,000. The combined proceeds went into four limited partnerships and four mutual funds (with sales commissions for the planner).

Before going through with any such portfolio conversion, ask your planner for a written explanation of what all this is meant to accomplish. Chances are it won't seem as brilliant, in black and white, as it does when the planner is glibly promising you riches. If the scheme seems bizarre, back off.

Don't Swing at the First Pitch

You can't rely on federal or state regulators to help you find a first-class planner, or to bail you out after you've lost money due to following poor advice. You need to protect yourself by aggressively checking on a planner before making any commitment. It's a good idea to interview *at least* three planners, to see how their different styles compare, before making your decision. And always get information *in writing* before investing any money—*don't* proceed solely on what the planner recommends.

The same advice holds true when you're dealing with other types of financial pros, including brokers or insurance agents. Find out their backgrounds, check references, and get everything in writing. Interview several before *choosing* one. Before *trusting* any of them with your life's savings, think about whether his or her advice really makes sense for someone in your position.

SUMMING UP

• Virtually anyone can claim to be a financial planner, so expect to find frauds and incompetents as well as helpful professionals in that business.

• A real (genuine) financial planner will want to hear all about your personal situation before recommending a comprehensive course of action, whereas the second-raters will primarily want to sell you something ASAP.

• Always check on a financial planner via federal and state regulators.

• The really good planners probably will have an impressive educational background as well as professional credentials.

• Before you make any commitments, be sure to find out how your planner expects to get paid.

• Ask to see copies of prior financial plans for other clients, and check on a planner's record with existing clients.

• Follow the same strategy when choosing such other types of financial professionals as brokers and insurance agents.

4

If the Phone Rings, Hang Up

Protect Yourself From Telephone Scams

As bank-account and money-market fund interest rates fell during the late 1980s and early 1990s, investors became more and more hungry for higher yields. Sometimes even desperately so.

Take the case of Gale S., of Thousand Oaks, California. She's a real-estate agent, so she's not a financial babe-in-the-woods. Yet she couldn't resist the appeal of yields in the 12 percent–16 percent range pitched to her by phone.

Supposedly, her money was going into second mortgages arranged by mortgage brokers for homeowners and developers whose credit ratings couldn't meet bank lending standards. Why lend to risky borrowers? Because your loan is secured by the property. When you hold a second mortgage, your claim on the property comes right behind the first-mortgage holder's.

Unfortunately, Gale invested with Phillips Financial Group, also of Thousand Oaks. Some Phillips properties had not just two mortgages but *hundreds*, according to press reports. Some mortgages were even unrecorded, so investors were totally unprotected when the properties went into foreclosure. Gale, for example, discovered she was in 176th position! The commercial property securing her investment was valued at $800,000, yet total loans on this building were $3.6 million. So Gale wound up losing her $60,000 investment.

But Gale was not alone. Hundreds of investors may have lost an estimated total of $30 million in such investments sponsored by Phillips, according to the *Wall Street Journal*. Jackie L., for example (a Malibu teacher married to a retired airline pilot), reported that her family lost a total of $400,000. Two Phillips executives were sentenced to jail for grand theft—but that didn't compensate for their victims' losses in any meaningful way.

Crime Ring

Even if the perpetrators get caught, that's little consolation to the victims of telephone scams. A survey by Louis Harris & Associates, conducted for the National Consumers League, found that 92 percent of American households have been solicited on behalf of phone-fraud schemes. Yet only one-third of the fraud victims report the scams, and only a tenth ever get any of their money back. The way to protect yourself is to avoid being bilked in the first place.

It helps to be familiar with the ploys you'll hear from telemarketing frauds. Second-mortgage scams, for example, are popular in California because that state has a large legitimate second-mortgage business.

Farther east, in Ohio, "air-time" pitches prevail. Investors are told that they can buy time on cable and low-powered TV stations which would be resold to advertisers—mainly people selling gadgets. Naturally, investors are told that they can double their money in sixty days.

Just as naturally, the investors who believed in Vision Television of Wooster, Ohio, wound up losing $13 million, according to regulators. A Wayne County judge called Vision Television a massive fraud and sentenced its president to thirty-seven years in jail.

Not only are investors vulnerable to these air-time swindles; there also are bogus investments in cable TV, wireless-cable TV, and low-powered TV stations. Wireless cable, for example, is a microwave-based technology that allows cable TV to be distributed via a minimum of equipment.

The Federal Communications Commission holds periodic lotteries of wireless-cable licenses. Scam artists charge $5,000 and more to prepare lottery applications, even though winning is not guaranteed, but the potential victims don't know that. These application mills often churn out hundreds of applications for the same market. Plus, this "lottery" is for the opportunity to run a business, not for an automatic cash payout.

Wireless communications figure in yet another type of scam, according to federal regulators. Some deals offering participation in wireless-phone franchises are fraudulent; moreover, since they're structured as "limited liability companies" (LLCs), the organizers don't register the offerings with securities regulators, claiming instead that all of the investors are active managers in an operating company. Shielded from securities law, the sponsors may tell investors that the money is going into an operating wireless system with customers and all necessary FCC licenses, touting returns of 400 percent in three years. Of course, *no* legitimate investment would make such claims.

Dirty Little Secret

Some swindles are "silent." You might, for example, be told that you can get a great buy on Florida real estate, but must keep the deal secret for a year. The story is that the current owners have a "right of redemption," if they find out that their property is being sold. Of course, the real reason for the imposed secrecy is to allow promoters sufficient time to make their getaway.

Stock-market boiler-room scams can *really* make investors sweat. Some disreputable brokerage firms bring out "hot" new companies, selling their shares to the public. Using phone scripts, hundreds of brokers make thousands of calls a day promising huge profits. Investors have been known to part with thousands—even tens of thousands—of dollars. Usually, this money goes into the pockets of the brokers and company insiders. After the initial offering the company stumbles along, not posting meaningful profits, and the stock falls to a fraction of its offering price.

Not all telephone scams involve investments; other schemes can take your money just as rapidly. Consider what happened to Cliff B., an Oakland, California, sheet-metal worker facing a layoff. He was already behind in his rent, desperately looking for a loan. In a local newspaper, he saw an ad offering loans to people with no job and no credit history. He followed up with a call and was told by the voice on the phone that he could get a $5,000 bank loan at prevailing rates. The company running the ads would act as cosigner. He'd get his money within ten days.

The catch? Cliff had to pay $200 up front to cover processing costs. As you might have guessed, he paid his $200 and never saw a penny from the "loan company."

Loan scams are widespread, and so are phony credit-card deals. Callers with poor or no credit history are offered cards that are not MasterCard or Visa. In fact, they're not affiliated with *any* banks. All they do is allow you to buy merchandise out of an overpriced catalog, and even then you can expect to pay half the price in cash.

No Contest

Variations on the above theme are seemingly endless. For example, you may be told you've won a "guaranteed" prize in a contest. However, to get your prize you must send cash. One elderly victim borrowed the $600 she was told she needed to "register" the $37,000 prize she supposedly won. When her son went to visit, he found that she had no food in the house—she had sent all of her cash to the promoter, who was still promising a huge cash award.

Some contest scams tell you that in order to win, you must call a costly 900 phone number. To reduce the risk that consumers will catch on to the 900 game, some scams involve similar phone lines in the Dominican Republic (area code 809) or the Netherlands Antilles (599). Or, you might be charged for information provided on calls to an 800 line, and also asked to accept "long-distance charges" on what is really a toll-free line.

Charitable frauds are prevalent, too. Usually, the only "charity" involved is the caller.

Increasingly, con men are using advanced computer and telecommunications technology to find likely victims—often people who have been cheated before. Swindlers also can buy lists of callers to sex-talk and easy-credit 800 and 900 lines who are considered easy marks.

Incredibly, once isn't enough for some fraud victims. Some scam artists posing as investigators or attorneys or bonding agents get hold of the names of telemarketing victims and promise to help them get their money back. For a fee, of course. Victims become double victims. Dixie L., for example, lost $900 in a phone contest. Then a telemarketing firm told her it would help obtain a refund. The seventy-four-year-old woman paid $670 in "investigative fees"; but the only help she received was a letter advising her to call the local state attorney general's office.

A new wave of telephone frauds aims to tap people who want to be caring and compassionate. In 1994, for example, the Attorney General of Massachusetts brought a suit against the National Awareness Foundation, which was raising money under the name "Hugs Not Drugs." The money was supposed to distribute workbooks in elementary schools, but neither funds nor books were distributed, according to state officials. Before you give money to *any* cause, no matter *how* worthy it sounds, *always* ask to see something in writing.

Pull the Plug

The best way to protect yourself against phone fraud is to hang up whenever *anybody* calls you and asks for money. You'll never lose a penny, and you'll save a lot of time you'd waste listening to come-ons. However, since some legitimate brokers, insurance agents, and financial planners also use the phone as a prospecting tool, you could be passing up an opportunity for genuine financial assistance by cutting them off too soon.

One way to tell the difference is to call 800-876-7060, a hotline sponsored by the National Consumers League in Washington, D.C. The people answering the phone can help you to evaluate proposals and steer you away from blatant frauds. Another resource you can use is your local Better Business Bureau. Call the BBB before making any purchases, to find out if there have been complaints registered against either the company or its management.

Better yet, use your own common sense to screen out scams. Whenever you hear extravagant promises, forget the deal. There's *no* investment guaranteed to double your money in sixty days. Be especially leery if there's some time pressure to send in money because the opportunity "won't last."

Always ask for something on paper before sending money. You can't really understand *any* investment from only a few sentences over the phone. Ask for something you can read at your leisure, such as a prospectus, in order to compare the risks with the potential rewards. If you're not comfortable with financial documents, ask for help from a friend or adviser you trust.

Ask for references, too: A legitimate financial professional will invariably work with a bank, a CPA, an attorney. Get names, and find out how long the people bearing them have been working with your caller. In other words, do your homework. Do everything you can to find out if this is a venture in which you want to get involved, and a person or group with whom you want to do business.

Even if all your investigations come up positive, crawl before you walk. *Don't* invest your life's savings in any one deal, no matter *how* alluring it seems. Invest a small amount, then see how things progress. You always can put more money in, if you're pleased—but it's nearly impossible to get money back after you've been ripped off.

SUMMING UP

- Almost all Americans are exposed to telephone scams. Victims rarely get their money back.
- Investment scams include second mortgages, hot stocks, TV systems, and TV air-time.
- Perhaps the most prevalent swindle in the U.S. today is the loan scam, requiring you to pay up-front fees in return for credit.
- Before you send any money to a voice you know only on the phone, check with organizations such as the National Consumers League and the Better Business Bureau.
- Do your own homework, looking carefully into both the legitimacy of the deal and the people offering it to you.

Part II

Natural (and Unnatural) Disasters

5

On the House

Protecting Your Home Against Fire, Theft, and Vandals

After Hurricane Andrew tore across Florida, creating a record $16.5 billion in damages, thousands of people ruefully inspected the wreckage of what used to be their homes. Other recent front-page disasters have included floods in the Midwest and fires and earthquakes in California. Everyone who buys homeowners insurance should learn a lesson from others' misfortunes.

Insurance should *really* be insurance: Buy protection against a *worst-case* scenario. Only after you're covered for catastrophes should you worry about whether to buy insurance for damage to your lawnmower and your CD player.

The most important question is how much insurance to buy. The answer: as much as it would cost to rebuild your house if it's completely wiped out. But *don't* buy insurance to cover the cost of your land. (Homeowners insurance should include liability, too, as described in Chapter 24.)

Shop for "replacement-cost" coverage, *not* "actual cash-value" coverage, because the latter pays replacement cost *minus* depreciation. In case of a natural disaster, actual cash-value coverage may fall far short of the amount needed to replace your house. As Hurricane Andrew demonstrated, your home might be totally destroyed in a major storm. In any case, you should insure your house for at least 80 percent of estimated market value—otherwise, your policy might not pay you in full for replacement.

Some policies state that they will *upgrade to code*. In Florida, for example, there were stories of houses put together with tacks; upgrade-to-code policies would pay for whatever screws or nails are required. Many localities now insist that destroyed homes be rebuilt to tougher, more expensive building-code standards. A variation on code policies, sold by many insurers, is "guaranteed replacement-cost" coverage, which pays to replace losses, no matter what the upper limits of the policy.

However, for many insurers, replacement cost excludes expenses for complying with building standards that did not exist when the home was built. For example, Charles P., a homeowner in Saga Bay, Florida, whose home suffered heavy damage from Hurricane Andrew, found that it had to be raised several feet to comply with new rules on flood plains. Even though Charles received $120,000 from his replacement-cost policy, he had to spend an additional $50,000 to raise his home. So always ask your insurance agent what your exposure would be to building-code-related expenses, and how much extra you'd have to pay for full coverage.

Don't buy insurance based on either what you paid for your house or what it might sell for today. Instead, insure against the cost of *completely* rebuilding it. That should include the cost of demolishing any wreckage left on-site, and carting the rubble to a dump. To get an estimate of probable rebuilding cost, ask a local bank for the name of a reliable appraiser. Underinsurance can be a problem in areas where inflation has driven up housing costs. Many of the homes destroyed in the Oakland Hills and southern California fires were inadequately insured.

The Cutting Edge

Full catastrophic coverage, of course, will cost more than partial coverage. If you can't afford to pay top dollar, don't skimp on the amount of protection you buy. Instead, take a higher deductible.

The standard deductible in a homeowners policy is $250. As a rough guideline, you can cut your premiums 5 percent–10 percent by choosing a $500 deductible. A policy with a $1,000 deductible will cost about 15 percent less than one with a $250 deductible, and going from a $50 to a $1,000 deductible can knock more than 40 percent off your annual premiums. With a higher deductible, you'll pay for $500 or $1,000 worth of damage but leave the insurance company on the hook in case of a disaster. That's the fundamental idea behind buying insurance.

You'll probably wind up ahead with a higher deductible. In 1993, one major insurer quoted a price of $746 per year to insure a $250,000 house on Long Island, near New York City. That policy would have a $250 deductible and provide up to $200,000 (80 percent) coverage. However, if the deductible were increased to $1,000, the annual premium would fall to $526 per year. What's more, if the deductible is maintained at $1,000, coverage could be increased to 100 percent and the annual premium would be only $675, considerably less than the cost of the $250-deductible, 80 percent-coverage policy.

Besides increasing deductibles, you also should install good burglar- and fire-alarm systems. You can get discounts on premiums up to 15 percent from many insurance companies. Add a fire-sprinkler system and your discount may go up to 30 percent. Additional discounts may be available to senior citizens, owners of new homes, and nonsmokers.

What sort of disasters should you insure against? The basic homeowners policy, HO1, covers damages from wind, fire, rain, lightning, explosions, and riots, the most likely causes of disasters. (In coastal areas, you may have to buy separate wind and hail coverage.)

Increasingly, state regulators are phasing out HO1 in favor of HO2 and HO3, which are broader. These latter policies also cover most other major hazards, such as leaks from frozen pipes, and damage from snow on your roof. Especially if you live in an area that suffers from cold winters, it's worth pricing the extra coverage.

Recommendation: Ask your agent to quote you prices for "all-perils" or "all-risk" policies, as opposed to the standard "named-perils" policy. The latter protects you against *specific* risks—vandalism, additional living expenses in case your house can't be occupied—while all-perils policies cover everything *except* risks specifically excluded, such as floods, earthquakes, war, and nuclear accidents.

One upstate New York homeowner, for example, had an unexpected visitor during his absence: a deer, which came and went through picture windows, stomped the furniture, and kicked holes in the walls. The $10,000 loss was *covered* in his all-perils policy, whereas a named-perils policy would have *excluded* it. All-perils policies may also cover chemical and paint spills, breakage, lock replacement, blood stains, and scorching without fire—all of which may be excluded by a named-perils policy.

If you rent, you should have basic tenants insurance, known as HO4, because your landlord's insurance won't cover your property. Depending on where you live, a policy covering $25,000 worth of possessions will cost $75 to $225 per year, with a $250 deductible.

No Day at the Beach

Some insurers are cutting back on coverage, particularly in waterfront areas. If you own a vacation house on the beach, or are shopping for one, you need to know the cost and availability of insuring it.

So far, Florida has been the hardest hit. At least twenty companies, including Allstate and Prudential, have announced plans to reduce their presence in Florida or pull out altogether. Many companies are avoiding Hawaii, while some are backing away from Northeastern coastal areas and Texas. On Long Island, for example, more than fifty insurance companies have stopped accepting new customers within 1,000 feet of the shore, while some companies won't sell insurance within 5,000 feet of the shoreline.

That doesn't mean you won't be able to buy homeowners insurance if you have beachfront property, however. You'll likely be able to get it from a company that has remained in the market, or from a state pool. However, you'll certainly pay dearly for the coverage. In Massachusetts, for instance, premiums in the state-run association can be 60 percent higher than the cost of private insurance.

For beachfront property owners, higher prices for insurance pack a *double* wallop. Not only will you have greater out-of-pocket costs each year, but also, higher insurance rates will lower the resale value of your home. For prospective property owners, the cost of buying insurance should be factored into other expenses (taxes, maintenance) before deciding how much to bid. In many coastal areas, you'll likely need to have homeowners insurance lined up in advance, in order to obtain a mortgage.

Besides buying the right kind of insurance, there are other steps you should take to preserve your waterfront property. Hire a reputable inspector to check on construction before you buy. (You can do the same for property you already own.) If there are structural flaws, see if they can be repaired economically.

A knowledgeable, reputable agent can help you buy the homeowners insurance you really need—no more, no less. Yes, there are agents like that, but you may have to search hard, asking friends for recommendations, before you find such an exemplar of intelligence and integrity. That's especially true if you're a condo owner: You'll likely need a savvy agent to tell you how much you can rely upon the condo association's policy, and how much individual coverage you'll need as a supplement.

USAA and Amica were the two top-rated homeowners insurers in a recent *Consumer Reports* survey of customer satisfaction; and USAA and State Farm have high levels of consumer satisfaction, according to complaint studies by state insurance departments. To check on an insurer, ask your state's department how it compares in terms of complaints versus complaints against other insurers of similar size. In addition, look for companies with good ratings from A. M. Best, Duff & Phelps, Moody's, and Standard & Poor's.

In 1994, a new type of homeowners insurance came to the market—*perpetual* insurance, sold by companies such as Mutual Assurance, Cincinnati Equitable, Baltimore Equitable, and Philadelphia Contributorship. With these policies, you pay one large lump sum up front. Say that your annual homeowner's premium presently is $500: You will pay (say) $5,000 to the insurer in one shot, and make *no* further payments. And your premium won't be increased unless you want more coverage.

You're effectively getting a 10 percent return on your money if you pay $5,000 and save a $500 premium each year. And if you sell your home or cancel your insurance, your deposit will be refunded. (Home buyers might want to increase their mortgage by $5,000 or so, using the extra money to pay for a perpetual policy.)

Beyond the Limits

Homeowners policies don't cover floods or earthquakes. If you live in a region that's vulnerable to earthquakes, you can buy appropriate coverage as an *endorsement* (added feature) to your homeowners policy. In California, where earthquake insurance is sold separately, insurers are required to offer it to residents every other year.

This coverage is expensive in quake-prone areas, even with high deductibles—which usually run to 2 percent–10 percent of the policy's limit. Lisa F., of Sherman Oaks, California, for example, paid $775 per year for $700,000 worth of earthquake insurance, with a 5 percent deductible. She suffered $50,000 worth of damage in the earthquake that struck southern California in 1994, and had to pay the first $35,000 worth of damages (5 percent of $700,000). Thus, her recovery was limited to $15,000. Joel G., of that state's Las Feliz, suffered $20,000 worth of damage in that quake, but recovered only about $5,000 because he had to pay the first $15,000 (10 percent of his $150,000 policy limit).

If your home was built recently and is bolted to the foundation, you may be able to reduce earthquake insurance costs by reducing coverage, taking a chance that your home won't be completely wiped out. If Joel had owned a $100,000 policy instead of a $150,000 policy, for example, he would have paid a smaller premium and collected $10,000, instead of $5,000.

Stinging From the Rain

Flood insurance is different from earthquake insurance. Coverage is available through the federal government's National Flood Insurance Program. However, you can buy flood insurance *only* if your community elects to participate in a program involving taking steps to reduce local flood dangers.

Although flood insurance is provided by the federal government, it's sold through agents affiliated with private insurance companies. If you suffer flood damage, you'll have to work with the company's reps to collect on claims. (Your standard homeowners policy, while it *won't* cover coastal or stream flooding, *should* cover water damage caused by heavy rains.)

Over 18,000 communities participate in the national flood insurance program. If you own property in these communities you're eligible to buy it; indeed, many mortgage lenders *require* you to carry it. Coverage is capped at $185,000 for the house, and another $60,000 for its contents.

Costs for flood insurance vary, depending on the house's location, age, and construction. If your house is above likely flood levels and built according to current standards, you might pay only a few hundred dollars a year. On the other hand, premiums for a high-risk house might cost $5,000 and up. Deductibles typically are $500–$750. Prices also will vary depending on how much your community has done to mitigate the risk of flooding. For information on the national flood insurance program, call 800-638-6620.

Since 1991 (and at least until the time this book went to press), Congress has attempted to pass new flood insurance legislation. Proposed legislation would require the Federal Emergency Management Agency to map thirty-year and sixty-year erosion zones. *No* federal flood insurance would be available for new buildings in the thirty-year zone, and insurance would be *limited* for new buildings in the sixty-year zone.

Existing structures would be eligible for federal flood insurance, but premium increases would be huge. Financial institutions would be prohibited from making loans unless flood insurance was in place. Owners would be allowed to buy private insurance, but such coverage, if available, would likely be quite expensive. If you're shopping for waterfront property, be aware that the cost of flood insurance might rise to scary heights within the next few years.

Taking a Rider

Besides buying insurance to protect your home, you'll also want to cover the contents. Replacing furnishings, appliances, and so on could add up to almost as much as replacing the house. Most homeowners policies set limits for what they'll pay to replace personal possessions—typically 50 percent–75 percent of the coverage on the house itself. For valuables such as furs, jewelry, and silver, you'll probably need separate policies ("floaters").

The more documentation you have regarding your possessions, the better will your insurance company be able to handle your claim. You might photograph your property in your home, with a still or video camera, and make up a floor plan of your house, showing where things are located. *Keep copies* of any films or maps or lists *off-premises*, so they won't be destroyed in case of disaster. A safe-deposit box may be the ideal place.

Here's a recommendation: Software packages for personal computers are increasingly popular. Personal Record Keeper and My-Treasures contain inventory programs. They organize your possessions by types and units and worth of furniture, appliances, collectibles, and so on. These programs will ask whether an item was bought or inherited, how much it cost, its replacement value, etc. Again, *keep a copy* of your computerized inventory *off-premises*.

Whatever your recording system, note the make, model, and serial number of every item whenever possible. Save your receipts (especially for expensive purchases). And update your list after every major purchase!

If you take these advance precautions, you'll be able to *prove* what you've lost. Your claim will will be processed more rapidly than otherwise, and you're more likely to collect in full. For more information on homeowners insurance, a free brochure, "Insurance for Your House and Personal Possessions," is available from the Insurance Information Institute, 110 William Street, New York, NY 10038. The Institute also runs a toll-free hotline (800-942-4242) to answer questions on homeowners insurance.

A Pound of Prevention

To *really* protect your possessions, take every possible step to keep thieves from seeing your home as an easy target. Make it difficult for burglars to break into your home. You can't totally burglar-proof your house, but you can get close to doing so. Here's how:

• Leave a radio or TV on when your house is empty. Automatic timers can turn lights on or off at irregular times while no one is home.

• If you're going on vacation, have someone pick up newspapers, shovel snow, and the like.

• Don't stop your daily newspapers, mail, garbage, recycling pick-ups, etc., when you're away from home, because such stop notices will be posted at the service providers' premises. Instead, ask friends or neighbors to pick up your mail and newspapers.

• Install outside lighting near all doors and windows. For $10–$20 apiece, you can buy photoelectric cells that turn outside lights on at dusk (and whenever else darkness occurs), and off at dawn (and at other times of equal natural illumination). Motion sensors can be hooked up to doorway lights, or to floodlights under the eaves.

• Post a sign warning that your house is protected by an alarm system. The sign can go by the front door, with copies at the back and on the sides.

• Put dog paraphernalia (water dish, large rawhide bone) outside by the back door, whether or not you have a dog.

• Join a Neighborhood Watch program sponsored by your local police. Such groups keep their eyes out for criminal activity in the neighborhood.

• Use metal or solid-core wood doors that open into the house, so hinges aren't exposed. If you have doors with outdoor hinges, get nonremovable pins from a hardware store.

• If you have a glass panel in a door, or a glass window near a door, replace the glass with an unbreakable material, or install a decorative grill over the panel.

• Install on all entry doors a deadbolt lock that operates with a key from the outside and a knob on the inside. Your dead bolt locks should have reinforced strike plates using 3-inch screws.

• Wedge sliding doors and windows shut; install metal pins on double-hung windows. A metal "Charley bar" that costs less than $10 spans the gap between the interior slider and the frame of a sliding door.

• Keep bushes trimmed below window level to expose would-be burglars.

• Install a chain lock and/or one-way, wide-angle "peep hole" viewer on your front door.

• Use an electric, self-locking garage-door opener, and put a lock on any door from your garage to your house. Put a heavy-duty padlock through the track just above the garage-door roller, in case burglars figure out how to bypass the electric opener.

• Keep your garage door closed at all times possible, and cover garage windows so nobody can see if your car is inside.

• Lock jewelry and valuables in a drawer, cabinet, or safe. Fire-resistant safes are not necessarily burglar-proof because they're made of light-gauge steel. For full protection, buy one made from steel and concrete. Such a safe, with one to three cubic feet of interior capacity, might sell for up to $350. Put it in a closet and anchor it to the floor.

• Install a home security alarm system that will be triggered by *any* tampering with doors or windows. A "central station" system transmits the alarm to a twenty-four-hour security staff, who will notify the police.

According to a Temple University study, having an alarm makes it nearly four times less likely you'll be hit. ADT Security Systems (800-238-4636) and Brinks Home Security (800-227-4657) offer basic systems that cost around $200 to install, plus $20–$25 per month for central-station monitoring. Wireless systems can cost as much as

$1,000—but with one of those systems, you won't have to drill holes and run wires all over your house.

Here's another recommendation: There are times when extra vigilance is needed. Professional burglars, for example, read wedding and death notices, then strike while you're out attending the service. If you're facing such a situation, make sure your alarm system is on, and ask a neighbor to keep an eye on your house. Hire a guard if you're particularly concerned.

Today, nearly 90 percent of all break-ins go unsolved. On average, burglars get away with over $1,000 worth of cash and valuables. A relatively few dollars spent on basic burglar-proofing now can spare you expensive losses in the future.

What's more, a few dollars spent today may also help you get your property back tomorrow. For example, Tom and Carol M. of Great Falls, Virginia, pay $6 a month to have a caller ID box connected to their home phone. Caller ID keeps a log of incoming calls, including the phone numbers from which they have been placed. When Tom and Carol came home from a vacation, they found that more than $10,000 worth of coins, stamps, and jewelry had been stolen. They checked the caller ID records, on the theory that a burglar might have been casing their house, and discovered several late-night calls from an unfamiliar phone number. The police followed up and found the phone calls were made by a young man in the neighborhood. He confessed, and Tom and Carol got back most of the stolen goods.

SUMMING UP

- Homeowners insurance should protect you from a castrophe that totally destroys your house—or nearly wrecks it.
- Policies should provide enough coverage to replace your house, upgrading to code if necessary, if disaster strikes.
- An all-perils policy will cover you for most occurences, even if such are not specifically cited in the policy.
- To cut the costs of catastrophic coverage, increase your deductible to $500 or $1,000.
- Policy discounts may be available for such various beneficial details as alarm systems, new homes, senior citizens, and nonsmokers.
- Special coverage is necessary to protect against earthquakes and floods.

• You can protect household possessions with extra insurance, called *riders*, especially if you maintain a thorough inventory of the items in your home.

• Always make sure your house appears occupied, and install safety devices to keep out intruders.

• Caller ID not only protects you against crank calls, but can indicate and record the phone number of a burglar who has been casing and calling your house.

6

Car Wars

Buying Auto Insurance That Won't Drive You Bankrupt

One or two thousand dollars—or even more—for auto insurance each year may seem like a lot, and in fact *is*. But suppose your car cost you $25,000 or more. Not many years ago, you could have bought a small *house* for that much. So it makes good sense to protect such a valuable asset.

In addition, when you drive your car (or another family member does), a potentially lethal weapon is put into operation. Should tragedy strike, and your car kill or injure someone, you could lose everything you own—unless you have the proper insurance.

So buying auto insurance is serious business, indeed. On the other hand, you don't need to buy the most expensive coverage just because your agent recommends it. Often, some aspect or another of insurance coverage is either redundant or unnecessary. If you know where to cut back, you can save hundreds of dollars a year, yet still enjoy full protection.

Playing Geography

There's one sure way to beat the cost of auto insurance: move. Insuring a Ford Taurus in Indiana might cost $750–$800 per year, as opposed to $1,500 in New York, and over $2,000 in Los Angeles. However, you may not want to live in Indiana, or be able to make a living there. You can, though, choose a car that's relatively inexpensive to insure. Typically, family-oriented, four-door cars such as the Taurus, Buick Century, Chevrolet Lumina, Oldsmobile Cutlass, and Pontiac Grand Prix cost a lot less to insure than the likes of the Chevrolet Camaro, Ford Mustang, and Pontiac Firebird.

Whether they're driving a Taurus in Topeka or a Camaro in Chicago, safe drivers pay less for auto insurance. The more moving violations you incur, and the more accidents in which you're involved, the faster you'll be downgraded from a "preferred" to a "standard" to a "nonstandard" risk. The lower your rating, the higher the premium you'll have to pay.

At some point, if your record continues to deteriorate, you may not be able to buy commercial insurance at all. If that happens, you may have to buy auto insurance from a state insurance pool, where your premium might be 300 percent higher than what "preferred" drivers pay. *So drive carefully.* And *don't* report minor accidents: The amount of your reimbursement likely will be less than you'll pay in higher premiums over the years!

More important, the benefits of safe driving go well beyond lower insurance premiums. When you avoid accidents, you protect yourself and your family. So *buckle up, keep within the speed limits,* and *don't drive after drinking.* Too, learn how to *correctly* operate your vehicle. For example: If you have antilock brakes, don't pump them when you skid—the proper technique is to apply steady pressure to the brake pedal and let the antilock system take over.

Moreover, you might want to consider "crashworthiness" when you choose a car. When the National Highway Traffic Safety Administration graded 1994 models, the Chevrolet Camaro and the Ford Bronco got top marks in test crashes into fixed barriers at thirty-five miles per hour. Both drivers and passengers had less than a 10 percent chance of being seriously injured, assuming they were wearing seat belts.

Shop Around

First, you should settle on exactly what kind of auto insurance you need—and on nothing beyond that. Then, get phone bids from several different insurers. When you do shop for coverage, here's what you should concentrate on:

• *Liability insurance.* The key coverage here is *bodily injury liability*, insurance that will pay medical expenses and legal fees for anyone hurt in an accident where you're at fault. At minimum, you should be covered up to $100,000 per person and $300,000 per accident.

You'll also need *property damage liability* coverage, which will pay for repairs on a vehicle you hit. Today, $10,000 in property liability coverage may not be enough—you probably should carry at least $50,000 worth.

Indeed, the basic liability coverage is known as 100/300/50, which is handy when you're comparison-shopping. However, if your net worth is over $300,000, you might want to increase liability coverage to $200,000 per person and $500,000 per accident. Usually, the cost of the added coverage is modest.

• *Collision and comprehensive insurance.* This coverage pays for damage to your own car, as well as for fire and theft. You're better off if you buy "pure" insurance: Protect against a catastrophe, but pay for your own *minor* repairs. In other words, take a higher deductible and pay a lower premium.

You might, for example, pay $350 per year to buy collision insurance, if you choose a $100 deductible. Raise that deductible to $500 and you might pay $250 per year. You save $100 per year by agreeing to pay for repairs up to $500. Similar savings can be achieved by taking a $500 or even a $1,000 deductible on comprehensive insurance, which covers theft and natural disasters.

Another way to cut insurance costs is to drop all collision coverage if your car is over five years old and collision insurance exceeds 10 percent of the car's value. If your car is worth less than $2,500, for example, why pay $250 per year for collision coverage? If your car is wrecked, buy a new one.

Moreover, even if you pay for insurance, you might not be able to collect. Most insurers won't cover a car for more than it's worth; they won't pay $5,000 worth of damages on a car worth $2,500. So get the "book value" of your old car from an auto dealer or your insurance agent, and drop the coverage when it's no longer worthwhile. Publications such as the *Blue Book* also will have this information.

• *Uninsured motorist coverage.* Do you really need this insurance, which kicks in only if you have an accident with a driver who's at fault *and* who doesn't have auto insurance? Some experts advocate buying it, while others say it merely duplicates your own health and liability insurance. *Our* position is to buy it, but don't go overboard—don't spend more than, say, $50 per year, for which you should be able to get $100,000 worth of coverage.

Where to Apply the Brakes

The coverages mentioned so far are those you'll need to protect your car(s) and your personal assets. Beyond them, there are a lot of coverages that you probably *don't* need:

• *Medical-payments insurance.* This coverage pays medical expenses when someone named in your policy or riding in your car is injured in an auto accident. Skip this coverage: Family members should be covered by health insurance, while liability insurance will pay for other people.

• *No-fault, or personal-injury protection (PIP).* In some states, this coverage for medical expenses, lost wages, etc., is optional. If so, decline it, because it duplicates other coverages you should have.

• *Miscellaneous coverages.* Adding coverage for road service, stolen audio equipment, car rentals if you can't use your own, and so on can drive up your insurance bill. In truth, these aren't such potential catastrophes that you should insure against them.

• *Extended-service contracts.* Auto dealers often push these contracts that will provide service for up to five years. But this insurance is expensive (as much as $1,200), and the problems it covers seldom appear in the first few years of ownership.

Dialing for Dollars

After you have decided which coverage you want and don't want, call *at least five* insurers and ask for quotes on this insurance—no more and no less. The spread between the highest and lowest quotes may be several hundred dollars per year—even as much as $1,000! To get quotes, call some independent agents, as well as companies (such as State Farm, Nationwide, and Amica) that sell directly to consumers.

Don't forget to ask for discounts, which can be quite sizable in auto insurance:

• *Out-of-towners.* If any child of yours is a college student who doesn't take your car to school, you're entitled to a discount.

• *Senior citizens.* Depending on the state and the company, drivers over age fifty may get 20 percent discounts.

• *Crime stoppers.* Discounts may be available if you install an alarm or some type of disabling device (see below).

• *Driver ed.* If you have—or a family member has—successfully completed a driver-education or defensive-driving course, you may be entitled to a discount of up to 15%.

• *Smoke out.* Some companies give discounts for nonsmokers.

• *Packaged deals.* Insuring both your house and your car with the same company may knock as much as 25 percent off your rate.

• *No-fault.* In about one-third of the states, you can cut your liability insurance premiums by up to 20 percent if you pass up your right to sue.

Also, some states *require* you to buy no-fault or PIP insurance, which covers your medical bills and at least *some* lost wages. If your health insurance company agrees to be the primary payer for these medical bills, you can cut PIP costs up to 40 percent. If you have an option, choose the highest possible deductible for PIP, which will reduce your cost.

For a free booklet, "Understanding Your Auto Insurance Policy and Get the Most for Your Money," send a stamped, self-addressed No. 10 envelope to The Society of Chartered Property and Casualty Underwriters, 720 Providence Road, P.O. Box 3309, Malvern, PA 19355-0709.

Stop, Thief!

Another way to cut auto insurance costs is to take crime-prevention measures: There's a car theft in the U.S. every twenty seconds. According to the latest available statistics (1992), 1.6 million cars were stolen in that year. Auto theft is increasing particularly fast in medium-sized suburbs (those with populations of 100,000 to 200,000).

Auto theft creates a huge expense for auto insurers—so they're willing to give you a discount if you take steps to foil car thieves. Discounts range from 5 percent to 35 percent of your policy's comprehensive insurance. Some states (New York and Texas, for example) require insurers to give discounts if certain anti-theft devices are installed.

Take the case of Al and Judy, a married couple in their thirties who live in Brooklyn and own a 1993 Ford Taurus. They pay $1,232 per year for comprehensive coverage from Aetna.

• They can etch the vehicle ID number onto their car windows, to facilitate the vehicle's return, at a cost of around $60. Aetna will in return give them a 5 percent discount—*more* than $60 per year.

• They can buy an alarm system with an "ignition killer" for about $300. The discount from Aetna would be 10 percent–15 percent, about $120–$180 per year, depending on whether the system is switched on manually (lower discount) or automatically. Established companies such as Excalibur, Alpine, Clifford Electronics, Crimestopper, Directed Electronics, and Audiovox offer lifetime warranties.

• They can buy an electronic tracking system, such as LoJack, Code-Alarm, or PacTel's Teletrac, all of which cost $600 and up. Again, Aetna would offer a 15 percent discount, which means over $180 per year off the insurance bill.

If Al and Judy install multiple anti-theft devices, Aetna will give discounts of up to 25 percent (over $300) per year.

Although Aetna gives no discount for steering-wheel bar locks, such as The Club, *some* insurers will give a 5 percent discount. These bars usually cost $20–$75. Not only do anti-theft precautions lower your auto insurance premiums; they also help you to avoid the expense and aggravation of having your car stolen.

You can insist upon anti-theft protection when you buy a new car. General Motors, for example, has a PASS-KEY system, in which a microchip embedded in the ignition key must match a code in an on-board computer before the car will start. For some GM models, the car-theft rate has dropped sharply since PASS-KEY was introduced.

No matter how much or how little you spend on anti-theft devices, don't ignore some basic precautions, the principal one of which is: *Always lock your car and take your keys with you.* Half of all stolen cars aren't locked, and one in five has a key in the ignition!

Peter Dickinson, editor of *The Retirement Letter*, offers these other tips for thwarting auto thieves:

• *Have your car dealer or locksmith punch out the ID numbers printed on your car keys so they can't be easily duplicated.* Keep your own record of those numbers in a safe place.

• *Keep a spare set of car keys in your wallet.* Don't put spare keys in one of those magnetic boxes that fasten to metal car parts, because thieves look for them—and find them.

• *Conceal car stereo equipment, cellular phones, radar detectors, etc.* Black cardboard taped over the dashboard can be effective. You also can buy a "Lasso Lock" that wraps around and secures stereo equipment.

• *Buy gas-tank locks and interior hood locks for further protection.*

Rent Checks

If you rent cars, watch out. Historically, your auto insurance would travel with you when you rented a car. Carless big-city residents (for example) who carried *no* auto insurance could nevertheless rely on the rental company's coverage. But increasing costs have caused cutbacks—often at *your* expense. Today your personal auto insurance may *not* apply to rental cars, and the car-rental company may not offer built-in coverage, either.

So check before you rent a car. Ask your agent if your auto insurance applies to rentals, and if you're employed by a sizable organization, find out whether your employer's insurance will cover your business rentals. If you *don't* carry auto insurance, check to see whether your homeowners or excess liability (*umbrella*) coverage will protect you.

If you find out your coverage *won't* cover auto rentals, there nevertheless are a few steps you can take. For example, you can use a major credit card to rent from a major car-rental company: American Express cards or Gold Visa or MasterCard often will provide collision insurance. For liability coverage, though, you may have to spend an extra $5–10 per day to buy special insurance when you rent the car.

Be especially careful when you rent outside the United States or Canada, because most auto insurance policies won't reach that far. Try to rent in advance, preferably through a knowledgeable travel agent—and buy whatever auto insurance is necessary.

The Fix Is In

Whether your car has been in an accident or needs repairs for some other reason, you have to be careful about getting your car fixed. You can easily wind up overpaying, with your car *still* not running well.

Your safest bet is to take your car to an independent repair shop, rather than to your dealership—because independents tend to charge less (as much as 50 percent less). The only exception might be in case of a problem that only a dealer would know how to handle, such as a flaw in your car's electronic dashboard.

Whenever you can, talk directly to the mechanic who'll be working on your car. If you talk to the manager who talks to the clerk who writes up the repair order, chances are your message will lose something in the translation. When you speak to the mechanic yourself, you can be more sure than otherwise that he or she really understands the problem.

In a way, getting your car repaired is like seeing a doctor or a lawyer: You want to be sure you're working with a reputable professional. So get references, and mention your mutual contact's name when you call for your first appointment. If you find a mechanic you can rely upon, especially long-term, you'll avoid the scams that unfortunately are too common in the auto repair industry.

SUMMING UP

• Auto insurance rates vary widely, with the highest prices often found in urban areas of the Northeast and California.

• There's a great variance in rates from one model of car to another, with family-type cars often costing less to insure.

• No matter where or what you drive, a record without accidents or moving violations is vital to maintaining low insurance premiums.

• You need to carry liability insurance amply covering both people and cars you might injure in an accident.

• Collision insurance is important with a new car, but increasingly less so as it ages and loses value.

• Raising your deductibles can cut your costs for collision insurance.

• Once you have liability, collision, and comprehensive insurance, other coverage may not be necessary.

• Call several different agents for bids before buying insurance, mentioning all the factors that entitle you to discounts.

• If you install anti-theft devices, you can reduce your insurance bill while you deter would-be thieves.

• Before renting a car, check to see if you need to buy additional insurance coverage on it.

7

When You Buy Big, Buy Right

Keep High-Priced Lemons Out of Your Shopping Cart

A hurricane can rip the roof right off your house (or the house off its foundation). A burglar can snatch your irreplaceable jewelry. And you can also suffer a huge house-related loss by purchasing the wrong home at the wrong price.

When you're shopping for a house, don't rush. Take a good look to see what's on the market, and what the asking prices are. Then, when you find a house you like, make a bid lower than the asking price. *Then* negotiate. Chances are, both parties will meet halfway between push and shove.

But your greatest risk isn't that you'll pay a few thousand dollars more than you might have, had you done sharper negotiating. Your house may truly become a money pit if it needs extensive repairs that you hadn't bargained on. So hire a professional inspector to look at the place, after your bid has been accepted. If you don't know of an inspector, your mortgage lender probably does. Inspectors affiliated with the American Society of Home Inspectors are required to pass qualifying exams, and should be expected to have enough professional experience to match their marks.

Typically, an inspection will cost less than $300. For that, you should get a written report and follow-up recommendations. You're better off spending the money on an inspection rather than relying upon—or buying—a home warranty, which may prove of little value in case you later have huge repair expenses. (A home warranty is a nice "throw-in" when you're buying a house, but you shouldn't pay extra for one. If a warranty *is* included, you're better off if it's backed by an independent warrantor rather than by the builder, who may not be around to honor it.)

Dealing With Defects

Your inspection may turn up only minor flaws, or it may reveal serious water damage, termites, and so on. In the latter case, reconsider whether you really want the house. At the least, reduce your offering price significantly, or insist that the seller pay for any needed repairs before the house changes hands. If the seller performs the repairs, the "fixed" items should be reinspected.

Make sure your inspector checks for radon, an odorless, cancer-causing gas found in unsafe concentrations in about 12 percent of U.S. houses, according to the federal Environmental Protection Agency (EPA). Besides the health risk, high levels of radon will reduce the resale value of your home. Excess radon levels generally can be corrected for $500–$2,500. The EPA publishes a "Home Buyer's and Seller's Guide to Radon," which costs $1.50 from the U.S. Government Printing Office, Superintendent of Documents, P.O. Box 371954, Pittsburgh, PA 15250 (202-783-3238). Ask for stock number 055-000-00428-5.

More prevalent than radon is lead-based paint, found in potentially dangerous levels in about 75 percent of homes built before 1980, the U.S. Department of Housing and Urban Development has reported. Ingestion of lead-based paint chips can result in brain damage, so young children should be kept from them.

If your inspector finds relatively small areas of lead-based paint, the problem can be easily solved, either by scraping the paint and vacuuming the lead dust or by covering the painted surface with plastic. A large-scale lead-paint abatement job, though, may take weeks and cost $5,000–$10,000. Again, if the house you're buying is loaded with lead paint, either find another house or slash your offering price.

Avoid Interest-Rate Roulette

While you're shopping for a home, you'll probably be shopping for a mortgage, too. Speak with several prospective lenders, to see what terms they'll be willing to offer. Your first choice probably should be a *fixed-rate* mortgage, because you'll have level payments for the life of the loan; but sometimes *adjustable-rate* mortgages (ARMs) are attractive. If you choose an ARM, make sure there's a lifetime cap— a maximum rate that the lender can charge, no matter what happens to interest rates.

When mortgage rates are volatile, finding the right mortgage rate can be tricky. Will you pay the rate in effect at the time of your application, at the time of loan approval, or when the real-estate closing takes place? A difference of 0.5 percent or 0.75 percent can mean thousands of dollars, over the life of the mortgage.

You may be able to "lock in" a rate by paying a fee ranging from a few hundred dollars up to 1 percent of the loan amount. If you pay a large fee, make *sure* you're getting a win-win deal, in which case your mortgage rate can go *down*, if rates fall before the deal closes, but not *up*.

Security—at a Price

When you buy a house with a mortgage, you'll have to decide about mortgage insurance. That is, should you buy a policy that will pay off the mortgage if you die and continue making payments if you become disabled?

If your lender insists upon such coverage, there's little you can do but buy it. However, if you have the option, you're better off passing up this coverage. Instead, increase your *regular life* and *disability* insurance by enough to handle this obligation. You'll wind up paying much less.

For example: a thirty-year-old man might pay $350–$400 per year for $100,000 worth of mortgage insurance. That same home buyer likely can purchase $100,000 worth of *term life* insurance for under $200 in the first year. It's true that the gap will narrow as the home buyer grows older, but it will be many years before the term insurance is more expensive than mortgage insurance. By that time, the insured might have bought a new house.

Also, by buying the added life insurance, instead of mortgage insurance, this man gives his spouse an option. When she collects the life-insurance proceeds, she can decide whether to pay off the mortgage or continue the tax-deductible payments.

Similarly, disability insurance bought especially to pay off a lender is usually more expensive than ordinary disability coverage. The same reasoning holds for any type of credit insurance: You're better off increasing your basic coverage. That's true also for "gimmick" insurance, such as policies that will make mortgage payments in case you lose your job. Rather than buy overpriced policies, protect yourself by increasing your savings or establishing lines of credit.

Default Lines

Another type of mortgage insurance is *default* insurance: If you buy a house with a down payment of less than 10 percent, you'll likely have to buy an insurance policy that protects the lender if you don't make the mortgage payments. Such insurance is expensive, effectively adding 4 percent to 5 percent per year to a mortgage rate. Thus, a 7.5 percent mortgage becomes a 12 percent mortgage. To add insult to injury, the insurance premiums aren't deductible.

The *good* news is that the insurance can be dropped once your equity reaches 20 percent, generally because the value of the house has appreciated. However, lenders are not always required to *tell* you that the insurance can be dropped. It may be up to *you* to have the house appraised, so that you can stop paying the insurance premiums.

Say you buy a $100,000 house with a $10,000 down payment. You might have to pay an extra $350 up front, plus $300 per year for mortgage insurance. If your home increases in value to $110,000, then 80 percent of its value is $88,000. As long as your mortgage balance has fallen below $88,000, you have more than 20 percent equity. (That is, your mortgage debt is less than 80 percent of the home's value.) You can then stop paying mortgage insurance.

Your best strategy is to make a down payment of at least 20 percent, so you can avoid mortgage insurance in the first place. If at all possible, *don't* buy a house until you *have* a 20 percent down payment! (If that's *not* possible, then keep track of your home's appreciation, and have the place appraised once your equity goes over the 20 percent mark.)

Lemon Aid

You should exercise as much caution when buying a car as when buying a house, especially now that the kind of car you want may cost at least $20,000. Shop tough—take your time, compare features and prices, and discount baloney. If you're inclined to look for bargains, services such as AutoAdvisor (800-326-1976), Carbargains (800-475-7283), and Consumers Automotive (703-631-5161) claim to be able to deliver the car of your choice at *thousands* of dollars below sticker price, even *after* their fees are included. They assert, for example, that a $20,000 Ford Taurus would cost you around $16,250.

When you buy a *used* car, you need to exercise extra caution. Unless you're a first-rate mechanic, have a knowledgeable friend (or someone from your service station) check out a used car before you buy. Or pay $50–$100 to have someone from a franchised inspection service give the car a thorough going-over.

Should you finance a car purchase? Probably not, if you can avoid that. Why borrow at 8 percent (1994 rates) when you can't deduct the interest? You're better off paying cash, even if you have to pull money from a bank account paying 3 percent.

Increasingly, people are deciding not to buy their cars at all, but rather to *lease*. Leasing means a much smaller up-front outlay and smaller monthly payments. The problem is that all those payments don't *buy* you anything. If you're the type of person who isn't concerned about ownership but does want a late-model car every few years, leasing may just be for you. But if you're in the habit of keeping cars for six to ten years (or longer), buying is easily the better deal.

Lease at Leisure

Whether buying or leasing, beware of scam artists. Some unscrupulous auto dealers will "sell" a car to a consumer, then write up the contract as if it were a lease. The buyers wind up not owning the car. This fraud is often perpetrated on older consumers.

One elderly Florida couple fell victim to another scam. They wanted to lease, but they used a trade-in to knock down the price of the car to be leased from $20,000 to $18,000. The lease documents, however, were based on the $20,000 price. In effect, this elderly couple traded in their old car for nothing.

The way to protect yourself is to negotiate a price for a car, whether or not you intend to buy or lease. If you're going to lease, demand to see, in writing, the "capitalized cost" of the car, the price that's built into the lease.

Another approach is to first negotiate a lease without a trade-in. Then offer your old car and see how the monthly lease rate comes down. On a three-year lease, for example, a $7,000 trade-in should reduce your monthly payments by around $200 apiece. In any event, get more than one lease quote and take the time to read any contract carefully before signing.

Passwords to Privacy

Increasingly, computers are becoming part of our households. You certainly won't spend as much on a computer as on a house or car, but a computer's value goes well beyond the hardware alone. If you keep financial records on a computer, if you run your own business, or even if you're self-employed, it's vital that you protect your computer data. You don't want to lose them, and you certainly don't want anyone else to have access to them.

Unfortunately, there are many computer-wise thieves out there, and the number is sure to increase. To protect your hard disk, diskettes, and e-mail, you may want to use *encryption*. In essence, encryption is the process of taking your standard computer file and modifying it with a *key*, or *password*. Then your files and your transmissions can be read only by those to whom you entrust the key.

A number of programs are available that provide computer privacy, and more undoubtedly are on the way. (As of this writing, encryption programs were to some extent being held up by federal government demands for a standard system that the government will be able to access.) The following are some rules to keep in mind when choosing passwords—as well as access numbers to bank cash machines and long-distance phone services:

1. Don't use standard words. Some high-tech criminals run automated dictionary programs that test virtually every word in the language in which the document is written as a possible password.
2. Use a mix of letters, numbers, and oddball keyboard symbols— @, #, $, and so on.
3. Use long passwords (at least eight characters).
4. Don't use passwords that might be easy to guess, such as your initials, your home address, or your kids' birth dates.
5. Never write down your password and then leave it where some-

one might find it—especially near your computer. If you *must* write it down, write it backwards, or begin with the third character, or find some other method of camouflage.

6. Change passwords frequently.

7. Never tell anyone else your password, especially over the phone—and never let anyone watch you enter it.

Computer Cautions

In addition to using passwords, some other basic precautions should be followed. Use surge protecters (plug strips) to guard against sudden changes in the power supply known as "spikes." "Save" your work frequently, and store copies on diskettes as well as on a hard drive. Keep labeled diskettes in a secure storage case.

When you travel, carry your laptops, palmtops, etc., with you rather than check them with your baggage. Use a padded case, preferably one that's anonymous enough not to tell the world "A computer lives here." Many portable computers come with security cables—which should be used.

Your personal computer may not be covered by your standard homeowners policy, especially if you use it for business. If that's the case, you generally can buy specialized insurance to protect a PC from fire, theft, accidents, and other hazards. The annual cost is usually modest—$75 or less per year.

Card-Sharp

Whenever you're buying computers or other electronic items, home furnishings, clothing, jewelry, and so on, use a credit card if possible. You may find it a lot easier to straighten out subsequent problems if you buy on your plastic.

In certain circumstances, the federal Fair Credit Billing Act protects you in cases of defective goods or services. Generally, your protection is greatest for charges over $50, especially if the sale took place within 100 miles of your home address, or elsewhere in your home state. You can withhold payment for goods or services in question, offering instead a full explanation in writing. Now you have a heavyweight (the credit-card issuer) on your side as you try to seek satisfaction from the merchant. For a brochure on "Solving Your Credit Card Billing Questions," send $1 to Bankcard Holders of America, 560 Herndon Parkway, Suite 120, Herndon, VA 22070.

SUMMING UP

• Not only should you shop thoroughly for a house, but also you should insist on an independent inspection before buying.

• If the inspection turns up major defects, you should find another house, drop your bid accordingly, or insist that the flaws be satisfactorily repaired before the sale.

• Fixed-rate mortgages usually make the best sense because you avoid the risk of sharply higher payments if rates rise.

• Credit life and credit disability insurance tend to be extremely expensive, so you're probably better off covering those risks by increasing your standard life and disability insurance.

• If you're buying a used car, have someone who's knowledgeable check it over carefully first.

• Auto leasing is increasingly popular, but scam artists are moving in, so you should take time to read any lease carefully before deciding whether to sign.

• Computer files and transmissions may contain valuable data, so you should protect them with backups and savvy password strategies.

• Whenever you make a big-ticket purchase, try to pay for it with a credit card, which may give you added leverage if a problem arises with the item.

Part III

Strictly Business

8

Inc. Spots

Trim Your Liability When You
Operate a Business

If you're a business owner, it's not hard to think up ways in which you can get wiped out by a huge award against you for damages, such as can be levied if, for example, a customer falls down in your parking lot, your store, or your office; the delivery person driving your van causes an accident; or the tomatoes you've sold cause an entire family to become seriously ill. The list could go on and on. Just one misstep, followed by an adverse court decision, and *all* of your personal assets could be lost.

Therefore, if you run a business, you should incorporate. In effect, you will form a new entity—let's say the ABC Corporation. The customer who falls down might sue ABC Corp. and possibly win a substantial award, but your *personal* assets might be protected—perhaps even fully.

But corporate status isn't an *absolute* barrier against claims. In some cases, courts have been willing to "pierce the corporate veil," allowing suits to proceed against a corporation's owners—especially if their own negligence led to the problem. Moreover, many lenders require a *personal* guarantee on loans to small companies, so you're effectively putting your own assets behind corporate debt. Nevertheless, you have considerably more protection with a corporation than you have without it.

Real Time

Incorporating your business isn't difficult. Most lawyers will handle the paperwork for a modest fee of perhaps a few hundred dollars. However, if you want to enjoy all the protection that incorporation can provide, you have to observe all the formalities—your corporation must be a real one.

The document you receive when you incorporate, the *certificate of incorporation* (or *articles of incorporation*) should be reviewed regularly. If any information is not up-to-date, the certificate should be amended.

Many states permit corporations to indeminify their officers and directors from certain lawsuits. If your corporation's certificate does *not* include such a provision, you may wish to add one. Martin M. Shenkman, an attorney in Teaneck, New Jersey, provides the following example:

> The directors and officers of the Corporation shall be indemnified by the Corporation, to the maximum extent permitted under state law, against reasonable costs, expenses, and counsel fees paid or incurred in connection with any action, suit, or proceeding in which the director or officer or the legal representative of the director or officer is a party by reason of being or having been a director or officer of the Corporation. This indemnification shall be subject to any conditions, limitations, and restrictions as may be imposed by law and shall be, in addition to, and not in restriction or limitation of, any other privilege which the Corporation may otherwise have with respect to the indemnification or reimbursement of officers.

Up to the Minutes

Corporations should meet at least once a year to elect officers and directors, adopt certain agreements, and approve important contracts.

Formal minutes should be kept. In addition, you should keep complete books and records, have a separate corporate bank account, and file corporate tax returns. You'll thus be able to show that the corporation either does or did exist as a legal entity, and enjoy the benefits of limited shareholder liability.

However, just because you've incorporated, don't neglect simple prudence. You should carry business liability insurance, and adopt policies (e.g., shovel snow in the parking lot, check driving records of employees who operate company vehicles) to reduce the risk of accidents. Such precautions will help bolster your case if a mishap occurs and a lawsuit is brought.

Two Paths to Protection

When you decide to incorporate, you also have to decide which type of corporation to use:

• *C corporation.* This is a regular corporation, subject to a corporate income tax. Thus, profits probably will be taxed twice—at the corporate level, and again on your personal return—when you take the money out. Also, C corporation losses can't be deducted on your personal return.

C corporations have other advantages. Health insurance, as well as some other fringe benefits, can prove deductible. Lenders often prefer dealing with C corporations because this is the traditional form. Plus, C corporations offer considerable flexibility when you want to pass them on to family members or employees. In general, if you expect to pay out virtually all of your earnings as compensation to employees (including yourself), you can operate a C company and *not* have to pay corporate income tax—because the company will have little or no income.

• *S corporation.* This is the alternative corporate form. You can elect S corporation status if your company meets certain criteria, such as having no more than thirty-five shareholders and only one class of stock.

If you qualify, S corporations can be great tax shelters because they're exempt from the corporate income tax. All corporate earnings are taxed on your personal tax return. If the company operates at a loss, that loss likely can be deducted on your personal tax return.

S corporations offer relief from many other tax headaches that plague C corporations, including the unreasonable compensation tax, the excess accumulated earnings tax, the personal holding company tax, and the corporate alternative minimum tax. On the other hand, fringe benefits aren't deductible if they're enjoyed by the primary shareholders, and the restrictions on ownership may interfere with estate planning. So check with a tax pro before electing S status.

For S corporations as well as C corporations, shareholders enjoy *limited* liability.

Staying Within the Limits

Besides incorporating, there are two other ways to run a business and still limit your liability for business-related claims:

• *Limited partnership.* In most partnerships, all partners are liable for all obligations of the partnership. Several law and accounting firms have felt the pinch in recent years, when hit by large awards for damages.

Limited partnerships, on the other hand, have two classes of partners: *limited* and *general.* Whereas general partners share full liability, limited partners' liability is limited to the cash they contribute and notes they sign. In some cases the general partner may be a corporation with limited liability, while most of the money flows to limited partners who also enjoy protection.

Often the limited partnership structure is used for investment real estate and other types of ventures wherein passive investors don't want to incur the risks of running a business.

• *Limited liability company (LLC).* This is a relatively new vehicle, but it's rapidly gaining popularity: In 1994, over half the states recognized LLCs, with more certain to join in.

In essence, an LLC is a cross between an S corporation and a partnership. Just as in the case of an S corporation, LLC owners enjoy limited liability. Again, there is no corporate income tax, so all income or loss is passed through to the owners' personal tax returns.

However, LLCs are not subject to the same restrictions as S corporations. For example, there is no limit to the number or type of owners, the latter of which might include trusts or corporations. Too, profits and losses can be divided disproportionately, if desired, which isn't so for an S corporation.

If your state recognizes the LLC, consider adopting it for your business. You can get limited liability, tax benefits, and flexibility. As

LLCs become more widely accepted, they likely will become the standard structure for small businesses.

Exit Laughing

If you're a co-owner of a business or investment venture, you should always have an up-to-date buy–sell agreement, no matter what type of business structure you use. A buy–sell agreement protects you and your family in case of retirement, death, or disability. If you don't have one, or if it's obsolete, the result can be disastrous.

Take the case of Wally W., who formed a partnership back in 1968 with Jack J. They bought investment property in Manhattan for $150,000 and signed a buy–sell. If one partner died, the survivor would buy the decedent's share for $75,000. After eighteen years of a real-estate boom, Wally died and Jack bought Wally's half of the property from Wally's estate for $75,000. Then he turned around and sold the building for over $1.6 million!

Wally's estate sued, but the New York County Surrogate Court upheld the transaction. The old buy–sell, which never had been updated, was ruled still valid. Wally's heirs got $75,000 instead of $800,000. So be sure your buy–sell agreement is revised regularly.

SUMMING UP

- Small-business owners are vulnerable to financially crippling lawsuits resulting from accidents or other causes.
- Incorporating your business doesn't give you absolute protection, but it can help, particularly in cases where you haven't been personally negligent.
- Even if you incorporate, you should carry business liability insurance and take precautions to avoid disasters.
- To enjoy limited liability from incorporating, your corporation should be a real one, complying with all the paperwork requirements.
- Corporations should hold meetings at least once a year, and formal minutes should be kept.
- Regular C corporations permit you to deduct fringe benefits, but they're subject to the corporate income tax.
- S corporations offer many tax advantages, including exemption

from the corporate income tax, but there are strict requirements for S status.

• Limited partnerships can be structured so that passive investors are limited partners, without exposure to partnership liability.

• Limited liability corporations, new vehicles that offer the best features of S corporations and partnerships, may become the preferred form of small-business ownership.

9

Territorial Imperative

Salespeople, Protect Your Livelihood

Plastic comes, software goes. There's always some "sure" sector of the economy that's bound to prosper in the coming years, an industry in which men and women can build secure careers. Then, after young strivers have become middle-aged middle managers, the bottom falls out and the companies cut back, assigning a lot of hard-to-employ white-collar workers to the jobless statistics columns.

There is one line of work where this isn't likely to occur, however—a profession most people can enter without going through years of medical or law school (or any other). You can *sell*. If you like to work with people and you're willing to put in long hours, you *can* succeed as a salesperson. In today's lingo, you'll become a "producer," bringing in business. As long as you produce, there will always be a way for you to earn a living, either as an employee or as an independent contractor.

For salespeople, the biggest threat is the loss of a *territory*—in this case perhaps a geographical region, an industry, or any grouping of customers. If your employer or principal takes away the customer base you've helped to build, you've lost your greatest asset.

How can you protect yourself? Demand a contract up front. Naturally, if you're an independent rep, you'll want a contract with each principal, spelling out the terms of each relationship. And salespeople who are employees should have contracts, too. Yours may not be easy to get when you're starting out, but after you've become a producer and employers are vying for your services, you should be able to negotiate a formal contract.

Sellers Keepers

The most important point in a sales contract is your ability to keep your customers after the contract terminates. If the contract says that the customers belong to the company, you can be in trouble. In sales, prospecting is 90 percent of the effort; you go to a lot of trouble to find customers and convince them to rely on you. If you can't take your clients with you, no matter where you go, your prior efforts will be wasted.

Some contracts do in fact contain what's known as a *noncompete clause* stating that after you break off a relationship, you won't be able to work in the same field as your former employer—generally for a specified time period. Such clauses may amount to restraint of trade, and if they do, they can be overturned in court. Nevertheless, you want to avoid costly litigation, if possible. So beware of such provisions when considering signing a contract.

Of course, you may think you're perfectly happy with your employer, and that your employer is happy with you, so why bother with a contract? However, few people—especially salespeople—stay with one employer during their entire career. At some point, a parting of the ways is likely. You'll be in a much better position if you have a formal contract, and especially one that a knowledgeable lawyer has looked over (*not* overlooked) before advising you to sign.

Loyalty Test

Aside from a formal contract, the key to self-preservation for salespeople is having a loyal customer base. Your customers *must* trust you and believe in your integrity. Those benefits being the case, if you move from one company to another your customers will find a way to move with you. But if you're just an order taker, your customers won't make the slightest effort to stay with you.

You must in effect bind your customers to you. You want them to have confidence in you, to be comfortable with you. The best way to accomplish this is to listen to what your customers have to say—really *listen*. They'll tell you, in one way or another, what they want and what they need. And if you supply what they ask for, they'll be *your* customers, not your company's.

Beyond this basic exercise in salesmanship, people appreciate thoughtfulness. When you meet with a new client, ask for some personal information—name, address, family members, dates of birth. Then, make it a point to send birthday cards each year. You might want to add an inexpensive gift: an inspirational book, a pen, a pocket calculator. Everybody likes to be remembered, and everybody likes to receive gifts (as long as it's clear that no bribe is intended).

While you're making an effort to think about your customers, think about your support staff, too—whether they're your employees, or coworkers. Their cooperation can make a world of difference to your professional success. For example, suppose you know that one of your support people has been working hard and is going to take a break by going out to dinner with his or her spouse. If you can, find out which restaurant they'll be dining at, call the place, and ask to have the meal charged to your credit card. Your efforts will be greatly appreciated and, for a fairly modest amount, you'll earn the loyalty of colleagues as well as customers.

Fireproof

Whether or not you're in sales, you have a "territory" to protect. That territory might be your job, your rung on the corporate ladder, or your niche in a sideline business. If someone else takes over that territory, your future income is in trouble. So take some basic steps to protect your livelihood. Keep learning new skills, and new applications for your existing ones. Find out what your particular strengths are (you're a whiz at soothing ruffled customers, for example), and focus on those areas.

No matter how safe or happy you are at your current position, don't be complacent. The job that you hold for forty years, from school until retirement, just about doesn't exist anymore. Conditions change, managements change, and you could find yourself on the wrong end of a "restructuring." So keep your eyes and ears open at all times. Attend industry meetings and make your presence known. Swap business cards. Find out who's expanding and where the job opportunities are likely to be. And keep your options open.

Now here's the one to memorize right away: At the first sign that your employer might be in trouble (the first rumor, even), start networking in earnest, looking for a more secure position.

The situation you want to avoid, if possible, is one in which your income depends on one person's good graces. No matter how well you get along with your boss, and how terrific he or she seems to be, don't hitch your wagon to just that star. Your boss might get sick, get fired, or have a change of heart. *Always* have a fallback position—at least instantly in mind.

The same principle applies if you have your own company or a sideline business: Don't focus all of your efforts on *one* customer. That one might find another supplier or, even worse, stick you with a large pile of unpaid receivables.

If you *must* rely on just one customer (or even a few of them), protect yourself by hedging your risks. One way to reduce your exposure is to work with an experienced *factor* (broker, money lender, etc.) who might advance you 70 percent to 75 percent of the face value of your invoice as soon as they're generated, with the balance sent to you when the bill is paid. Besides minimizing your exposure to bad debts, factors can provide you with immediate working capital, enabling you to expand your business.

Factors may also check the credit of prospects before they become customers, then accept invoices from approved accounts. This type of factoring is often done on a "nonrecourse" basis: You have *no* credit risk, even if the customer defaults. In effect, a factor can act as your credit *and* collection department, freeing you up to spend full time building your business.

SUMMING UP

• Although successful salespeople can make money in all economic circumstances, they need to diligently protect their customer base.

• You should have a contract that permits you to take your customers with you, upon your termination, with no restrictions on your future ability to compete against your present employer.

• The more customer loyalty you can build, the more likely you'll keep those customers as you move from job to job.

• You should make every effort to be on good terms with your support people, who can provide considerable help to your career.

• No matter what you do for a living, you need to cultivate other people, inside and outside of your company, so you'll have easier access to a new job in case you're laid off.

• Never put your future in the hands of one person or one company (other than yourself, of course).

• Hedge your risks by developing skills that are in wide demand, and by serving a variety of customers.

10

Wine 'Em and Dine 'Em

Get a Payoff From Your Business Entertainment Dollars

In some businesses you have to entertain: Clients expect to be taken out to lunch, to dinner, to sports events. If you don't entertain them, your competitors will. Effective entertaining is absolutely necessary to protect your business interests. However, effective entertaining is more than just spending money on customers and prospects. You have to make sure you get *value* for your money.

If most of your business entertainment takes place in one area—near your home or your office—you should focus on only one or two restaurants. Be a galloping gourmet on your own time. When it comes to business entertaining, be strictly business.

Pick restaurants that make sense for your industry. If you're in fashions, for example, or in advertising, you probably will want to select a trendy spot where people go to see and be seen.

In most businesses that's not the case. You should choose restaurants with a basic American menu from which virtually every client can choose something good to eat. Also, there should be ample (but not overpowering) lighting, so you can take notes if need be. Tables should be far apart, and the noise level should be low, so you and your clients can talk business without hearing everyone else's business.

Once you have found one or two places that meet these criteria, go back again and again. You'll know what you're getting, with no surprises (which often turn out to be unpleasant). The restaurant's management will get to know you well, and value you all the more as a customer. You'll be given good tables, and personalized service that will impress your clients.

No Check, Please

You can establish a private line of credit with such restaurants, or give them your credit card number. Leave instructions that all of your meals be charged to that account, along with a 20 percent service fee. No bill need be brought to the table. Thus, you'll avoid awkward sparring with clients as to who picks up the check.

Spread a little money around—it doesn't have to be a lot. Give a $20 bill to the owner or maître d', or to the chef. Your clients certainly will be impressed when you're greeted by name at the door, or when the chef comes out of the kitchen to say hello.

Pay attention to the doorman, too, when you're at a hotel or another establishment that employs such a person. Give him $10 to "watch" your car for you, and it likely will be sitting there waiting for you when you come out (whereas many other patrons will have to wait for valet parking to get theirs).

If you *must* use valet parking, be careful to turn over your ignition key, and no others. You don't want someone else having access to your trunk, where you might keep samples, papers, and other valuables. And you certainly don't want to put your house keys in the hands of a stranger.

Beyond maître d's, chefs, and doormen, be reasonably generous with waiters, waitresses, and bartenders: Tip 20 percent rather than 15 percent of the bill. The extra money isn't great ($2 on a $40 meal), and the goodwill you'll earn will be considerable. No salesperson should *ever* be known as a poor tipper.

Note-Worthy

There's one more step you need to take to get the most from your business entertainment dollars: Keep thorough records. If you *do*, you can deduct those bucks. (Actually, you can deduct 50 percent of them, under the 1993 tax law.) If you *don't* have records, you're apt to find yourself entertaining an IRS auditor.

The tax laws in this area are complicated, but entertaining is deductible if you make a genuine effort either to get new business or to maintain business you already have. There should be a reasonable prospect of a profitable return, too. If you take someone to a $100 dinner for the chance to make a one-time sale of $10 worth of housewares, the IRS might reject your deduction on the ground that it wasn't "ordinary and necessary." (You don't have to land a big deal in order to write off a meal, but you do at least need to make a real effort to obtain *some* amount of lucrative business.)

A daily diary or pocket notebook can substantiate your deductions. Just write down all the details—whom you entertained, where, how much you spent. Add a few words about the business purpose of the meal, and what you discussed. If you pay with a credit card, fasten your receipt to that page in the diary. Your accountant will appreciate your diligence, the IRS will focus its attention instead on taxpayers who try to re-create expenses, and you'll get the tax deductions to which you're entitled.

SUMMING UP

- If business entertaining is vital to your career, you should make the most of the money you spend.
- Limit yourself to one or two good restaurants as settings for most of your entertaining.
- At your regular business-meal restaurants, tip a little bit extra— and spread some money around—so you'll get personalized service whenever you entertain there.
- By keeping careful records, you'll be able to deduct 50 percent of your bona fide business entertainment costs.

Part IV

Foreign Affairs

11

Travel Smart

Keep Your Guard Up While You're on the Road

Vacations should be carefree but not careless. There are virtually no safe havens today, either in the United States or abroad. Wherever you go, you need to protect your property—not to mention your life. That's true whether you're on a solo business trip or a family holiday.

What can go wrong? Let us count the ways:

• *You could lose your luggage.* U.S. airlines report over two million instances of lost, damaged, or stolen baggage per year. Even if you get your luggage back, your trip could be ruined.

• *Your rental car could be stolen—or worse.* Florida, in particular, has experienced horrendous instances of carjackings and tourist murders.

• *You can be robbed or assaulted in your hotel.* Year after year, over 10,000 lawsuits are filed against U.S. hotels for negligent security.

• *Your credit cards might be stolen.* Hundreds of millions of dollars are lost each year to fraudulent use of credit cards. If you're ripped off, your own losses might be limited, but you'll suffer considerable aggravation and loss of time.

• *Your passport could be stolen.* Over 10,000 Americans reported passport theft during 1993.

• *Your telephone bill could skyrocket.* When you make a phone call from a hotel lobby or an airport, using your long-distance card, make sure no one else can see the buttons you push, or hear the number you give the operator. Thieves have been known to use telephoto lenses and mirrors as spy devices. If you can, use a phone with an electronic eye, permitting you to slide your card past it to get a reading.

In other words, never let your guard down. No matter if you're traveling on the world's finest airline, staying at a luxury hotel, or eating at a gourmet restaurant, you need to be constantly on your guard.

Too Good to Be True

Travel fraud starts even before you do. You might, for example, get a letter or a phone call announcing that you've won a "free trip," or a special packaged deal. All you need to do is give the "travel agent" your credit card number and expiration date.

Naturally, there isn't any free or bargain trip. You'll never receive the promised tickets. You *will* receive, though, credit card statements showing large charges for items you never purchased or ordered. (In a variation on this scheme you'll be asked to make a deposit—which you'll never get back.)

Don't fall for these illusory deals. *No one* is going to send you to Hawaii for $100. *Don't* give your credit card information to strangers! Instead, deal only with reputable travel agents. Book your trip through someone you know personally, or with an agent who has been recommended to you. The first time around, you might want to visit the agent in person, so you can size up the operation. No agent will be able to get you free trips, but a reliable one will have access to a computer system that can find the best available values for you.

Now You See Them . . .

Pay for travel with a credit card. Herta F., of New York City, wishes she had. Herta booked a tour of Southeast Asia and sent a certified check for $5,900 to her travel agency. The money never was forwarded to the airline and, by the time Herta discovered the omission, her travel agent was in bankruptcy, with $2 million in debts and $20,000 in assets. Herta didn't even bother to sue. If she had paid for the tour with a credit card, she might have been able to refuse to pay the charge, or even receive a refund from the card issuer.

Gail M., of Piscataway, New Jersey, had somewhat better luck when she lost $10,000 on a tour to Egypt in 1989, after the tour operator collapsed. She sued her travel agent and got back around $2,000, which the agent had received as a commission. She also was able to get back the $2,000 deposit she had put on her American Express card, although it took a year-long struggle. She was out the rest of the money, which she had paid by check—but at least it wasn't a total loss.

When a retiree like Herta or a secretary like Gail loses $6,000, that can be a heartbreaking disaster. Multiply them by the thousands and you get the $12 billion that consumers lose each year on busted tours, according to the National Consumers League.

So, how can *you* avoid being victimized? You should always pay with a credit card if your tour operator or travel agent will accept one. As mentioned, the federal Fair Credit Billing Act gives you sixty days from the date of the bill to contest a charge. For trips, MasterCard extends the deadline to 120 days, while Visa allows 120 days from the date of travel. American Express is even more flexible, sometimes allowing you a year to dispute payment. Sometimes a credit card issuer will even provide travel insurance if you pay with its card.

Whether or not you pay by credit card, however, check on the tour operator before paying. Call the airline or the main hotel you'll be using, and find out if the tour operator has lived up to its promises on previous trips. Call the U.S. Tour Operators Association (USTOA) (212-750-7371) and the National Tour Association (NTA) (800-682-8886) to find out if the operator is a current member in good standing. If so, there will be a guarantee fund you can tap in case a member tour operator fails; the USTOA guarantee generally is stronger.

Risky Business

There are many types of specialized travel insurance you can buy before you go. On the whole, you should save your money. For example, some airlines will sell you additional baggage insurance, but such coverage is expensive and loaded with exclusions—buy it only if your luggage contains something of great value. You're much better off not packing real valuables in baggage that you'll check with the airline.

Don't buy life or dismemberment insurance from an airport vending machine, the kind that pays off only in a plane crash. (In Part V of this book, we'll show you how to buy the right kind of health, life, and disability insurance. If those are all in place, you don't need special accident insurance.)

Trip-cancellation insurance has its place, but it isn't for everyone. If you have to cancel because a previously existing medical condition flares up, the policy may not pay. You won't have this problem if you buy a refundable ticket, or one in exchange for which the airline will reissue a ticket for a different date, charging you only a modest fee.

However, if you get a fabulous deal on a nonrefundable ticket, you might *want* to put some of your savings into trip-cancellation and interruption insurance. When Hugo M., a New Jersey retiree, had to miss a vacation in New Orleans because of an unexpected heart-bypass operation, he and his wife got back $2,400 from Travel Guard International. Such insurance (sold by most travel agents) typically costs $5.50 per $100 of coverage. Thus, it would cost about $135 to protect a $2,400 trip. Besides personal illnesses, such insurance should entitle you to a refund under other circumstances, such as the death of a family member.

Trip-cancellation insurance may protect you if a tour operator goes out of business, but some policies provide coverage only if the operator files for bankruptcy protection—which isn't always the case. If you're going on a packaged tour and you're considering trip-cancellation insurance, buy only if you'll be reimbursed for *all* tour operator failures. The trip-cancellation offered by American Express (800-234-0375), Access America (800-284-8300), and Travel Guard International (800-826-1300) is stronger than the insurance sold by tour operators, which would be worthless in case of a business failure.

If you're going on a cruise, be wary of "cancellation waivers" offered by some cruise lines. These waivers, which cost $60–$80, allow you to escape cancellation penalties if an accident or illness occurs. However, some of these waivers *won't* protect you if you cancel within seventy-two hours of departure time. Try to find a waiver that lets you cancel closer to sailing time.

Leave Home Without It

You don't need to take all your credit cards when you travel. Leave any *local* cards at home. Generally, all you'll need is an American Express card, and either a Visa or a MasterCard, plus an ATM card and a telephone calling card. If you have AT&T's Universal Card, for example, it serves not only as a Visa or MasterCard but also as a phone card and an ATM access card.

Just as you should leave some of your credit cards at home when you're going on a business or pleasure trip, you also should leave your car at home, in a locked garage, and take a cab. Taking your own car and leaving it in a long-term parking lot is like putting a "take me" sign on the windshield. If your car isn't stolen, it could easily be vandalized by thieves breaking in to steal parts.

For instance: Your car's internal computer (the device that controls the fuel-injection system and other functions) is highly prized. It has no vehicle ID number on it, can be resold for hundreds of dollars, and is quickly removed through the dashboard or glove compartment. Once someone takes your electronic module, your car can't operate—so you'll need to have it towed to a repair shop.

Few long-term parking lots have the security necessary to thwart thieves. If you absolutely *must* leave your car in a long-term lot, park under a light, as near as possible to the booth where operators collect parking fees. Never leave *anything* of value in the car. And be especially wary when walking to and from your car—particularly after dark.

SUMMING UP

• Crime against travelers is widespread, so you must be vigilant whenever you're away from home.

• Book all trips through reputable travel agents rather than falling for telephone come-ons, and pay with a credit card if you can.

• To protect yourself against tour cancellations, check out the tour operator carefully.

• If you decide you need trip-cancellation insurance, buy from an established third party instead of from a tour operator.

• You generally should skip other types of specialized travel insurance, relying instead on standard health, life, disability, and home-owners insurance.

- When you travel, take only a few, necessary credit cards.
- Leave your car at home rather than expose it to thieves in an airport long-term parking lot.

12

An Ounce of Prevention

Property Protection Shouldn't Stop at Home

Many travelers view airports and hotels as sanctuaries. Everyone there is just like you—prosperous people determined to enhance their success on a business trip, or enjoy a needed respite while on vacation. There's no need to feel threatened.

Don't fall into that trap! Just as Willie Sutton robbed banks because that's where the money was, today's thieves go where the best pickings are: relaxed, guards-down travelers laden with cash, travelers checks, jewelry, cameras, and expensive clothes. Airports and hotels teem with predators—so you need to keep constantly vigilant to avoid becoming their prey.

Baggage Handling

For short trips, travel as lightly as you can, and carry your luggage onto the plane with you. Stow it in an overhead compartment or in the area allotted for hanging bags. That way, you'll *know* your bag will arrive with you. You'll save time, too, on arrival at your destination.

If you *must* check your luggage, make sure each piece is secured—perhaps even with a small padlock. To thwart thieves who may have keys that fit a variety of luggage or key-operated locks, use a *combination* lock.

Never put your home address on your baggage tag, because a sharp-eyed thief can spot your address and go immediately to your empty house, probably free to take whatever is in there. Instead, put your *office* address on the tag. Before each trip, also put your destination phone number on the tag, so you can be reached in case your bag goes astray—innocently or otherwise.

Put something distinctive on each piece of luggage, too—colored tape or yarn around the handles, for example—so no one takes your bags by mistake. Colorful luggage straps are widely available. Samsonite makes beige or gray luggage straps that even include built-in combination locks.

Partners in Crime

Not only may your luggage be sent to the wrong place by accident, but also, dishonest airline employees are capable of stealing it from under everyone else's nose. Sometimes a ticketing agent or curbside baggage handler will be working with a confederate who loads the planes. If you look particularly prosperous, or if there's some indication that your bags could be holding valuables, the baggage check-in people might mark them with a distinctive "tipoff" coding so they'll be separated out, and never reach the plane. Or, your bags may be intentionally misrouted to an airport where an accomplice will be waiting with itchy palms.

So don't do anything to draw attention to either yourself or your baggage. Dress down when you travel, and don't flash expensive jewelry. Your best bet is to buy midpriced rather than top-of-the-line luggage. Just to be on the safe side, don't put valuables in your luggage, either: Keep all cash, jewelry, cameras, and vital papers with *you* when you travel. (If you read your airline ticket closely, you'll learn that the carrier bears no responsibility for lost jewelry, furs, antiques, and electronic equipment.)

Whenever you have any problem with your luggage, act right away. If you don't file a claim *within four hours* of your flight's arrival, most airlines won't recognize *any* responsibility. And even within that time period, airlines are picky about what they'll pay—you're in a stronger position if you can prove what was in your baggage, generally with receipts. So, if you're returning from a trip on which you've done a great deal of shopping, keep your receipts *with* you, rather than in your checked baggage.

Road Warriors

For many people, the first stop after arriving at their destination is the airport car-rental lot. You need to get around, on a vacation or business trip, and that usually includes having to rent a car.

However, even the most casual watcher of TV news knows that carjacking has become a real scourge, and that airport car rentals are particularly vulnerable. Miami's airport may be the most notorious, but it's by no means the only danger spot for tourists. So be extra-cautious when you're renting a car!

If possible, avoid the airport car-rental scene altogether. When you make your travel plans, have your agent arrange for you to pick up a car at your hotel, or at a nearby rental outlet. Use a cab, or the hotel shuttle, to get both from and to the airport.

If you *must* rent at an airport, try to get there before dark. Your unfamiliarity with an area is accentuated, and thus your vulnerability is increased at night. Whichever way you handle the car-rental arrangement, always put your luggage in the trunk, not in the backseat—where the pieces are visible, like a beacon to thieves and carjackers.

Know Before You Go

Get your route down pat *before* you drive out of any car-rental lot. If you pull over to look at a map for directions, you might well be putting on a sheep costume in front of a lot of hungry wolves.

If you absolutely must ask for directions, be selective about whom you talk to. Your first choice should be someone in a uniform—police officer, mail carrier, utility worker. Those types probably will give you the best instructions, as well as not endanger you.

When you're riding on local streets, lock your doors and windows. If it's hot, run the air-conditioning and keep the car buttoned up. At stop lights, be ready for anything (including peeling rubber). If you feel threatened, hit the accelerator if that's at all possible—you can worry later about a ticket for running a light, or whatever.

Most of all, don't get out of your car if you have any doubts *at all* about your circumstances. A favorite trick of carjackers is to bump you enough to cause a minor accident, so you'll pull over. When you do, and get out of the car to check insurance cards, you'll find yourself looking straight into a barrelful of lead poison. Not only your car, but also your luggage and your personal possessions, will disappear— probably forever. Some carjackers even shoot first and take later.

If you're in a fender-bender, don't pull over right away. Drive slowly to a well-lit area, with lots of traffic, before getting out of your car. If you don't like the looks of the people in the other vehicle, just keep going until you reach your hotel or other destination.

Similarly, don't stop for hitchhikers or people in distress, no matter how forlorn or attractive. Don't take a chance that the helpless-looking soul on the highway isn't a decoy for well-armed pals. If you really want to help a stranded motorist, note the location and call the police later, from a safe locale.

A common variation on the entrapment theme is the one in which a pedestrian jumps what looks to be in front of your car, and then falls down, as if injured. If this happens, *stay in your car*. Otherwise, when you get out to check, you might be walking right into an armed robbery—your own.

No Room for Carelessness

Even when you arrive at your hotel, you're *still* not home free. Hotels are riskier places than you think—especially big-city convention hotels. Almost anybody can wander in and out, at any time—there are no security checks or metal detectors at the doors.

Don't use your official title when making reservations. But *do* ask for a room between the second and seventh floors; that will give you some protection from ground-level, walk-in thieves but still leave you low enough to evacuate easily in case of a fire or other emergency.

If you're staying at a bustling, large hotel, keep a wary eye on your bags when you check in. While you're worrying about your reservation, some sneak thief could be making off with your camera. The same caution is necessary when you check out and you're concentrating on your bill.

Better yet, choose a small hotel when you make your plans. Such hotels don't attract as many thieves, because people who don't belong there are more conspicuous.

When you check in, make sure the clerk doesn't blurt out your name and room number within earshot of a listener. If he or she does, whisper that you'd like a different room. *Never* give *anyone* you don't know your room number!

As for your room: Insist on at least double deadbolts and a peephole. (Coded electronic locks are even safer.) Those little chain locks won't stop a serious intruder.

Don't let into your room anyone you're not expecting. If someone says he or she is bringing you a gift of fruit or flowers from the management, call the front desk to confirm. It's better to feel a little foolish than to be victimized a lot.

Keep any valuables in a hotel's safe-deposit box, rather than leave them in your room. However, don't assume that even the box is burglarproof: If you store valuables in one, get an itemized receipt.

Trouble Spots

Whenever you can when you travel, keep bag and camera straps under your clothing, where they can't be grabbed. If someone does get a hand on your belongings, don't start a tug-of-war unless you're sure you'll win. Thieves don't think anything of dragging a victim into traffic, if necessary. In fact, you're better off without any kind of bag, keeping valuables in a zippered pouch you can wrap around your arm, leg, or waist.

Yes, the scams you see on TV really happen, so don't be fooled. If someone spills ketchup or mustard or taco sauce on you, secure your wallet or purse, and other money, in your pockets before worrying about the stain.

And don't fall for this one: You're walking along with your family, a camera around your neck loudly proclaiming your tourist status. Some nice-seeming guy offers to take a picture, using your camera. He backs up and backs up, to get a better shot, and—he's gone, without even asking you to say "cheese."

In some locations you need to be *extra* cautious. Here are some of the real danger zones, according to *Money* magazine:

• *New York City.* You might think you're relatively safe in midtown, but that's not always the case, especially on Fifth in the 50s, from Rockefeller Center to Trump Tower. A lot of pickpockets are around. Be wary of distractions, from loud arguments to jostling.

If you find yourself on the subway or bus, don't fall for the pickpocket scam: An accomplice hollers, "There's a pickpocket on this train [or bus]." Hearing this, the passengers all reach for their money, to see if it's still there. This shows the pickpocket, sitting where he can observe the passengers, exactly where to go to get the dough.

• *Los Angeles.* Be careful when you go to the beach. Thieves will smash your car windows and take anything they can from inside.

• *Miami.* Carjackers are always coming up with new tricks. Now they pull up alongside your car and yell "Fire." *Don't* pull over and get out of your car.

• *Las Vegas.* Women should watch their handbags, no matter how exciting the action in the casinos. One favorite thieves' ploy is to drop a few coins near a woman who has put her purse on a table or chair. When she reaches to help pick up the coins, her purse disappears.

SUMMING UP

• At every stage of your travels, vigilance is vital.

• Never put your home address on a luggage tag—instead, use your business address, and include the phone number at your destination.

• Don't pack valuables in checked baggage, and don't look conspicuously affluent while you travel.

• Try to avoid renting a car at an airport counter, especially after dark.

• Don't do anything to indicate you're a tourist, while in a rental car, and don't get out of the car unless you're in a well-traveled, well-lit area.

• In a hotel, watch your valuables at all times, and never let into your room anyone you're not expecting.

• While out sightseeing, be alert for scam artists who'll distract you and then rob you.

13

At Sea, Overseas

Coping With Foreign Catastrophes

The list of dangerous vacation destinations doesn't stop with New York, Los Angeles, Miami, and Las Vegas. Foreign thugs are just as eager to relieve you of your possessions as are their domestic counterparts. Here are a few places where you *must* travel with care:

• *Cancun, Mexico.* Beware of violent street thieves.

• *Kingston, Jamaica.* If you're offered a great deal on currency exchange, walk away: The money may be illegal. Stick with banks and authorized exchange offices. Similarly, if a youngster offers to show you around, for a low price, don't go along; related robberies and assaults have been reported. Pickpockets operate freely in the main streets of Jamaica's cities.

• *Europe.* Keep copies of all credit card transactions—small shops often add zeros to increase the amount.

One trouble spot for street crime is Paris, especially near the American Embassy and the American Express office. Gangs of kids waving newspapers will rip you off after you've been distracted.

• *Hong Kong.* Here's another place where credit card fraud is common, so keep your charge slips. Some merchants will sell you one thing, then put a cheap substitute in your parcel. Pickpockets are a problem here, too.

• *Egypt.* Reportedly, tourists have been targeted by Islamic radicals.

• *Rio de Janeiro.* Ipanema and Copacabana beaches have become infested with muggers, especially around twilight. If you must go surfward, make sure you're in a large group.

• *Moscow.* Dress inconspicuously, and travel in pairs everywhere. Even cab drivers will rob you! Also, don't see local doctors if you can possibly avoid doing so, because many are not up to western standards.

• *Nigeria.* As of this writing, the only airport in the world where the U.S. government explicitly warns of security risks is in Lagos, the capital. If you *must* go, fly on American Trans Air, which provides its own security to help protect passengers.

In 1994, the International Airline Passengers Association issued a list of dangerous destinations: China, South Korea, India, Central Africa, the former Soviet Union, Colombia, and the Andes region of South America. If you *must* fly to these areas, use only the best-known, safest airlines—generally, U.S. airlines or foreign national carriers.

China, for example, was reported to lack the infrastructure and trained personnel to handle that country's air traffic, as well as to have the worst air piracy record in the world. Similarly, air travel in central Africa is marred by hijackings, unsafe airports, and poor air-traffic control systems, the association reported.

For an updated report on high-crime areas, call the State Department at 202-647-5225; the modem number is 202-647-9225. In general, for security as well as safety reasons, you're better off flying on a heavily regulated American airline (although some foreign carriers, such as Israel's El Al, are comfortingly vigilant about security).

By the Numbers

When you're traveling outside the United States, someone at home should have the numbers of both your passport and your traveler's checks, as well as a list of the credit cards you take with you, along with phone numbers usable to report lost or stolen cards. If you don't want to impose on a friend or relative, your credit card issuer may offer automatic cancellation service (generally costing $20–$30 per year).

Foreign travelers should take additional phone numbers with them. Wherever you go, *make sure* you have the number of the local U.S. Embassy, Consul, or regional security offices, as well as the twenty-four-hour number of the U.S. Mission. You can get these numbers from the State Department (202-647-4000) before you leave.

If anything happens to you while abroad, call those local numbers. You can get started right away to replace a lost or stolen passport, for example. In the meantime, *never* carry your passport or visa in a purse or wallet: If your pocket is picked or your bag is snatched, you'll lose your documents as well as your credit cards and money. Instead, carry your passport in a separate pocket. Better yet, get a zippered leg wrap or waist wrap that goes under your clothing.

Magellan's, a mail order company (call 800-962-4943), sells security wallets that can be tucked inside your clothing, through a belt loop, and neck pouches that hang by a cord. (Always wear such neck pouches *inside* your clothing.) Prices range from $10 to $20.

In Case of Emergency

If you're in an accident or are taken ill while you're out of the United States, you may need cash up front. Your health insurance card may not be accepted; Medicare generally won't pay for hospital or medical services outside the United States and its territories. Managed-care providers, such as health maintenance organizations (HMOs), and preferred provider organizations (PPOs) may in fact offer either *partial* or *no* coverage in foreign countries! Check with your insurer before you go. You might be able to buy, at a modest cost, a short-term rider that will cover you while you're traveling.

Also check with your credit card issuers. Many of them provide a phone number you can call to reach a "travel assistance company," if necessary. These companies fill a variety of roles: They might help you find a lawyer while overseas, or straighten out a dispute over a damaged rental car, for example.

Perhaps most important is the fact that travel assistance companies offer medical consulting service twenty-four hours a day. They can help find a doctor, or arrange for medical evacuation. Who'll pay?

That will depend on both your own health insurance and on the specific offer of the credit card company.

You should know too that if there are gaps in your foreign healthcare coverage, several companies can offer you travel insurance that's recognized around the world:

• TravMed/Medex Assistance (800-732-5309). Founded in 1977, this company sells coverage by the day for medical and hospital expenses. As of this writing, $3 per day was the standard fee, while students paid $2 and people over seventy paid $5. There are however limits on coverage for *preexisting conditions*—i.e., conditions that required treatment sometime in the previous ninety days are *not* covered.

• Europ Assistance Worldwide Services/Travel Assistance International (800-821-2828). Founded in 1963, this company sells evacuation coverage, local ambulance service, and emergency care. Individual and family coverage is priced per trip, depending upon the length. For example, a family vacation for up to fifteen days would be covered for $75, at last report. Again, there *are* restrictions on preexisting conditions. Travel agents frequently sell this coverage.

• International SOS Assistance (800-523-8930). Founded in 1975, it specializes in medical emergencies and evacuation, with *no* exclusions for preexisting conditions. For a couple on a fourteen-day trip, coverage is $60. Medical expense insurance is available for an extra charge.

• USAssist (800-756-5900). Founded in 1988, it specializes in medical evacuation; medical expenses are not covered. Annual membership cost $95 as of this writing, with *some* restrictions on preexisting conditions.

• Access America (800-284-8300). Founded in 1985, it offers services that include emergency medical and dental benefits. A family taking a two-week trip would pay $69 for a package of legal, medical, and trip-cancellation insurance; for an extra $30, baggage- and travel accident insurance can be included.

Generally, these services also will provide emergency cash, translation services, medical referrals, and links to U.S. doctors. These companies usually maintain twenty-four-hour hotlines. Callers will reach a staff member who, in turn, will make doctors' appointments, hospitalization arrangements, and (if necessary), air evacuation reservations to the nearest approved medical facility.

Deep Trouble

Consider what happened to Robert B., a Virginia-based consultant to the defense industry who went scuba diving in the Cayman Islands. Even though he observed the recommended safety rules, he wound up with a case of the "bends," a potentially fatal buildup of nitrogen bubbles in the bloodstream.

Fortunately, Robert had purchased catastrophe coverage from Access America. When informed of his sickness, the company arranged for him to be flown in a specially pressurized plane with a doctor and nurse to Duke University (in North Carolina) for emergency treatment. The cost for the air evacuation alone was $14,000: if Robert hadn't been covered by Access America, he would have had to find that much cash, up front, before the plane would take off.

A similar success story was told by Samuel T., who suffered an intestinal perforation and infection while spending the winter with his wife at their condo in St. Croix, in the U.S. Virgin Islands. Two operations were needed which could not be handled at the local hospital.

Sam was covered by a contract bought from Medical Air Services Association (MASA), through their condo development. He was able to fly first to Florida, then back to his home in New York, where he received the treatment he needed. The insurance policy not only helped him to get treatment, but also saved him nearly $8,000 in travel costs.

MASA (800-989-6272) specializes in expatriates and long-term foreign travelers, selling policies that are a bit more expensive than those offered by other emergency services (Sam and his wife paid $240) but last for at least one year. Family policies cover both spouses, as well as dependent children up to the age of twenty-three.

No matter what your insurance situation, call the Center for Disease Control & Prevention's hotline at 404-332-4559 before you travel outside the United States. The Center will tell you what food- and water precautions you need to take, which vaccinations are required, the diseases you might encounter, and type of preventive medicine recommended.

If you need a special vaccine, and your own physician is not familiar with it, you can seek out a travel-medicine practitioner. To get a list of over 100 specialists, send a large, self-addressed envelope and 98 cents in postage to Travelers Health & Immunization Service, 148 Highland Ave., Newton, MA 02165.

SUMMING UP

• Although no area of the world is perfectly safe, remember that some are extremely dangerous. The U.S. State Department maintains a phone hotline to inform travelers about which destinations are the most perilous.

• Before you leave the United States, make sure someone at home has the numbers of your passport, visa, credit cards, etc., to help you replace them in case of loss or theft.

• Always keep travel documents in a secure pocket, away from your cash or traveler's checks.

• Your domestic health insurance may not cover you outside the United States, but several services offer short-term insurance that can provide emergency medical service while you're in a foreign country.

• The Center for Disease Control & Prevention provides a hotline to tell travelers about special health hazards, but you may have to consult a travel-medical specialist to get the proper vaccinations and preventive treatment.

Part V

Healthy, Wealthy, Wise

14

Be Dollar-Wise, Not Penny-Foolish

The Sensible Way to Cope With Skyrocketing Health Insurance Costs

As of this writing, national health-care legislation was still very much up for debate—but likely in the end to take effect only on a state-by-state basis, with full implementatjon not required until the late 1990s, if then. In the meantime, don't neglect coverage for yourself and your family. Medical bills continue to soar, and one major illness or accident could wipe you out. Chances are, your employer now offers (or eventually will) *several* plans to choose among. (If you're self-employed, or if your employer doesn't provide health insurance, you'll have to buy your own coverage.)

Focus First on HMOs

Health maintenance organizations (HMOs) offer prepaid health care—you pay so much per person or per family, in return for virtually unlimited care, at little or no extra cost. Generally, HMOs are the least expensive choice for patients. For example, a 1992 study by the federal Bureau of Labor Statistics estimated that a family of four with an employer-paid premium and health-care expenses of around $7,000 would pay about $1,200 in out-of-pocket costs with traditional health insurance. That same family would pay less than $200 in an HMO.

But don't sign up for an HMO until you have looked at:

• *Doctors.* Are you willing to use the HMO's doctors? Are they mostly board-certified and well-regarded, with all specialties represented?

• *Hospitals.* Find out where you'll be sent in case of an operation or an emergency.

• *Locations.* If you have to go to one central HMO office, find out if it's convenient for you. Other HMOs use doctors who practice in their own offices, but make sure some of those physicians are near where you live or work.

• *Flexibility.* Some HMOs will let you go out of the network to see physicians, *if* you're willing to pay more of the cost. Instead of a $10 HMO visit, you might have to pay 20 percent of the doctor's bill.

• *Communications.* HMO patients who want answers to questions may face a daunting obstacle course of telephone transfers. See if there's a separate phone line for customer service.

• *Reach.* If your children are college students or future collegians, will the HMO provide coverage while they're away at school? Ideally, your kids should be able to get emergency care, then file a claim with your HMO.

• *Appointment time.* In a typical HMO, patients must first see a family doctor, or "gatekeeper," who'll make a referral to a specialist, if necessary. Unfortunately, family doctors are in short supply, so getting an appointment can be difficult. And when you're sick, you want to be able to see a doctor *immediately.*

• *Referral time.* You may be required to call a central office to clear referrals to specialists, schedule appointments, and discuss coverage. You're better off if your gatekeeper can make arrangements directly, saving you the hassle.

• *Physician screening.* Some HMOs aggressively keep tabs on doctors' performance, disciplining or even dropping those who receive a lot of patient complaints, fail to give patients the proper immunizations, and so on. *Don't* take an HMO's word for physician quality or patient service; ask some patients. If you don't know any, ask the HMO for names of patients who'll be willing to talk with you.

• *Grievances.* There should be a formal procedure for resolving patient disputes, and the plan should report that over 75 percent are settled within a month.

• *Accreditation.* Out of more than 500 HMOs in the United States, as of this writing, fewer than 100 were accredited by the National Committee for Quality Assurance, an independent organization that checks physicians and patient records. Find out if a prospective HMO has this credential.

HealthPlan Management Services, a consulting firm, rates over 400 HMOs on price and quality. Here were the top ten for 1993:

1. Kaiser Foundation Health Plan, San Francisco
2. Kaiser Foundation Health Plan, Los Angeles
3. Harvard Community Health Plan, Boston
4. Group Health, Minneapolis
5. TakeCare Health Plan, San Francisco
6. HMO PA—U.S. Healthcare, Philadelphia
7. Group Health Cooperative, Seattle
8. PacifiCare of California, Los Angeles
9. Pilgrim Health Care, Boston
10. MedCenters Health Plan, Minneapolis

Preferred-Provider Network News

Preferred provider organizations (PPOs) offer more flexibility. If you can't find an HMO that offers adequate service, or if you don't like the physicians on the list, a PPO may be a viable choice.

PPO structures vary, but the idea is to steer you to certain "providers" who have joined the network. If you see *those* providers, your financial exposure (deductibles, copayments) is less than if you go outside the network. Fees may be lower, too.

Again, there's an accrediting board—this time the American Accreditation Program—which has approved over 100 of the estimated 500 PPOs in the U.S.

Flying First Class

If you're willing to pay the price, the traditional "indemnity" system offers the most flexibility in choosing doctors. You can use *any* doctor and be reimbursed by the insurance company—paid back, that is, *after* you have satisfied your deductible and copayment requirements.

When you choose an indemnity plan (also called *fee-for-service*), choose real insurance rather than prepaid health care. That is, buy high-deductible insurance—$1,000 or $2,500 per person. With such plans, you pay most of your own doctor bills. You can even shop around and negotiate fees in advance. *Only* if you have a serious illness or injury will the insurance kick in.

The cost of this kind of real insurance is much less than the cost of low-deductible insurance—perhaps thousands of dollars less. If you and your family are reasonably healthy, you'll come out way ahead. Plus, you'll avoid the hassles of trying to get reimbursed for every $300 office visit. Be sure your fee-for-service plan has a stop-loss and a high cap on benefits. That is, after you pay $5,000 or so in any year, the insurance should take over and pay *all* your ongoing costs, up to at least $1 million.

Your employer may offer you a great deal on a low-deductible fee-for-service plan. But if you're buying your own insurance, such plans are out of reach.

For example, John H. was a corporate employee with first-rate health insurance: After he paid a $250 deductible, the plan picked up all the costs for his family of four. Then he left the company to start his own business, and found himself responsible for his own health insurance, too.

Even paying group rates—federal law forced his employer to let him continue coverage for sixteen months—he was paying $480 a month, nearly $6,000 per year. Individual coverage would have been even more expensive. So John raised his deductible to $2,000 and agreed to a 50 percent copayment, which means that after $2,000 he still pays half the bills. After paying a total of $7,000 per year, though, the stop-loss kicks in and the insurance takes over. The cost for this coverage was $350 per month in 1993, or $4,200 per year.

The bottom line: John and his family save at least $2,000 per year in insurance premiums, and probably much more. As long as they stay healthy, they're ahead of the game. The most they can be out of pocket is $7,000 per year, and they have protection against a catastrophic illness or disease.

Short-term fee-for-service plans are available for people who are between jobs, and for young adults no longer eligible for parental coverage but not yet entitled to employer coverage. Six-month plans, sold by insurers such as Golden Rule and Time Insurance, might cost only half as much as a standard plan. The catch: They generally don't cover preexisting conditions, so you're basically buying coverage only for new health problems that occur during this specific time frame.

In the Mainstream

Find out whether your physicians' fees are considered "usual and customary" before signing up for a fee-for-service plan. If a surgeon charges $125 for a consultation and your insurance company says it considers $75 to be a reasonable fee, you'll owe the extra $50, over and above any deductible or copayment and regardless of any stop-loss.

For $2–$4 per minute, you can call the Health Care Cost Hotline (900–225-2500) to learn the median fee, and range of fees, nationwide for more than 7,000 medical procedures. Two magazines, *Medical Economics* (201-945-9058) and *Health Pages* (212-929-6131), report on doctor fees by specialty, region, and type of service. You can compare your doctor's fees with the norm.

If your physicians' fees are way over the norm, they may be over your insurer's payment schedule, too. You may be better off in an HMO, with different physicians.

Relief in Sight

There may be low-cost alternatives if you're in a fee-for-service plan. For minor illnesses, X-rays, etc., consider seeing a Nurse Practitioner (NP)—typically a nurse with a master's degree. More than 30,000 NPs practice in the United States, either in their own offices, in clinics, or in doctors' offices. NPs charge rather less than doctors (perhaps 40 percent less, in some cases). Twenty states require insurers to reimburse NPs; in other states, many insurers cover NP services without a mandate to do so.

In addition to NPs, Physician Assistants (PAs) can handle most routine medical functions, thanks to a two-year training program. They earn about half what MDs earn, so their fees are commensurately lower.

Therefore, if you're in a fee-for-service plan, and you want to reduce your out-of-pocket expenses, ask your doctor if you can see an NP or PA, if available—concerning checkups, colds, and other non-critical appointments. If your doctor doesn't use NRPs or PAs, consider hunting for a doctor who does.

SUMMING UP

• Although federal health-care coverage may be in your future, for now you still have to provide your own protection—particularly if you're self-employed or work for an employer that does not provide health insurance.

• Your lowest-cost choice is probably a health-maintenance organization (HMO), which provides unlimited care for a predetermined fee.

• Before signing up for an HMO, be sure that it has a full range of doctors, convenient to where you live and work, and that it enjoys a good reputation among the patients who are enrolled.

• Traditional health insurance, in which you can go to any doctor, is increasingly expensive, so to lower premiums you should choose a high deductible—perhaps $2,000 or higher.

• Be sure your fee-for-service plan has a stop-loss that limits your out-of-pocket costs per year.

• If you're in a fee-for-service plan, you can cut costs by seeing Nurse Practitioners or Physician Assistants for routine services.

15

The Feds Fill the Medigap

Health Insurance for the
Social Security Set

When you reach age sixty-five, you qualify for *Medicare*, a federal health-insurance program, *regardless* of your health. It covers most medical bills—but not all. For example, patients are responsible for 20 percent of their doctors' bills. And, on long hospital stays, patients must (after 60 days) pay up to hundreds of dollars per day. Other exposures exist, too—usually modest, but occasionally catastrophic. To fill the gaps, *Medigap* insurance, sold by many insurers, was created. Over twenty-three million Americans spend more than $15 billion per year on Medigap insurance!

However, there was a great deal of confusion in the market. Insurers were offering a blizzard of different policies with relatively meaningless distinctions among them. They were difficult for buyers to compare and evaluate. Because the commission structure (naturally) rewarded agents for new sales much more than for renewals, many consumers bought policies when they already *had* adequate coverage. In fact, some consumers wound up with *several* policies.

Congress, gracious under pressure, finally passed a law calling for reform of the entire industry—which therapy took effect in 1992. Under the new law, the National Association of Insurance Commissioners (NAIC) came up with ten policies (see below). Every company that wants to sell Medigap insurance must offer A, the low-cost "core" policy. Insurers also can sell any or all of the other nine policies, B through J. No other Medigap policies can be sold, except in a few states with slightly different rules.

Standardized Medigap Policies

Medigap Policies

Benefits	A	B	C	D	E	F	G	H	I	J
Basic benefits	x	x	x	x	x	x	x	x	x	x
Part A hospital deductible		x	x	x	x	x	x	x	x	x
Skilled nursing home copayment			x	x	x	x	x	x	x	x
Part B deductible			x			x				x
Excess doctor charges (Part B)						(1)	(2)		(1)	(1)
Foreign travel emergency			x	x	x	x	x	x	x	x
At-home recovery				x			x		x	x
Outptient prescription drugs								(3)	(3)	(4)
Preventive screening					x					x

(1) 100%   (3) maximum benefit $1,250
(2) 80%   (4) maximum benefit $3,000

Note: Not all benefits are sold in every state.

Spelling Protection, A to J

Policy A covers the most common exposures:
• Such policies must pay the big hospital bills not covered by Medicare. Patients are liable for $174 per day (in 1994) for days 61 through 90, and $348 per day for a further 60 "lifetime reserve days." Core policies cover these costs plus full payments for an additional 365 days.
• Such policies must pay the 20 percent coinsurance for medical

expenses—especially doctor's bills—that Medicare requires from patients.

Policy B adds coverage for the Medicare Part A deductible, set at $696 per benefit period in 1994. That is, if you have this coverage, the policy pays the first $696 for hospital stays in each benefit period; with Policy A, the patient is responsible for the first $696.

All other policies, *C through J*, pay the Medicare Part A deductible. Also, each of these policies pays benefits for skilled nursing homes and for medical expenses incurred while traveling outside the United States. Medicare picks up *all* costs for the first twenty days in an approved nursing facility, but patients owe $87 for each of the next eighty days (1994 rate). This exposure, nearly $7,000, is worth covering. Also, foreign travel is a major exposure for Medicare recipients. If you're traveling out of the country, even only to Canada or Mexico, your medical expenses there probably *aren't* covered by Medicare. Therefore, you probably should go beyond policy A if you can afford a few hundred dollars more per year.

Some of the other optional benefits, such as preventive care and the $100 doctor-bill deductible, relate to meager exposures that needn't be covered. The at-home recovery feature has somFe value, but there's a benefit cap: Reimbursement is pegged at up to $40 per visit, up to $1,600 per year. You may have to buy some of these features, though, in order to get more valuable protection.

Prime Choices

How should you choose from among policies C through J? There are two key screens: *prescription drugs* and *balance billing*.

Are you likely to need several thousand dollars' worth of prescription drugs a year? With policies H and I you pay the first $250, then the policy pays 50 percent, up to a $1,250 annual limit. Policy J works the same, except that the upper limit is $3,000.

Balance billing is more complicated. Medicare sets limits on certain medical procedures and pays 80 percent; all ten Medigap policies pay the other 20 percent coinsurance. If the Medicare limit on hip replacements is $2,000, for example, Medicare will pay $1,600 while a Medigap policy will pay $400.

However, not all doctors stick with the Medigap limits. Any excess is called *balance billing*, which is the patient's responsibility. Although federal legislation caps balance billing for Medicare patients, a hip replacement (for example) might cost $2,200, leaving a $200 hole to fill.

This may not be a problem. Some Northeastern states have banned balance billing, or are moving in that direction. In some other areas of the country, medical fees usually are low, so balance billing isn't a significant problem.

Here's how to play the Medigap game:

• If you likely will spend much more than $3,000 on prescription drugs a year, buy J. No matter *what* sort of health condition you're in, you can take advantage of the open enrollment period and buy this policy within six months of signing up for Medicare Part B. Then, the Medigap policy will pay for up to $3,000 worth of prescription drugs a year.

• If your drug need is smaller, but still well over $1,000 per year, H or I may be the best bet. Choose I if there's likely to be a balance billing problem, H if balance billing isn't a concern.

• If you don't anticipate a heavy reliance on prescription drugs and you may run into a balance billing problem, G looks like the best choice because at-home recovery is included. (Remember, the difference between 80 percent and 100 percent of balance billing might be only 2 percent of the total bill.) Policy F might be worthwhile if it's well-priced.

• If you're neither a heavy user of prescription drugs nor vulnerable to balance billing, you can choose from the cheapest policies, C through J, and provide good catastrophic protection.

Some experts have indicated that D, F, and H may be good value-for-money choices. When you compare prices among policies, check the insurer's *premium schedules*, which are also known as the *outlines of coverage*. Find out if premiums will remain relatively stable, or will rise each year (due to your increasing age). You might be better off with a policy that's more expensive now, rather than one whose premiums will escalate in the future. Some worthwhile lower-cost group policies may be available through social or professional organizations you might do well to become more familiar with.

Ask if an insurer offers electronic billing, which could save you money and reduce aggravation. Also, some insurers offer *crossover billing*—automatic claims handling via which Medicare bills go directly to the Medigap insurance company. With this system, policyholders won't pay bills and then forget to file for reimbursement—which, strange to say, frequently happens.

Window of Opportunity

Another aspect of these Medigap rules is a *six-month window*, open for that long after one enrolls in Medicare Part B (generally at age 65). During this grace period, any qualified person can buy any of the new policies, regardless of his or her health. Even if you have a medical problem, you'll *still* be able to choose the *most* comprehensive policies. This "adverse selection," as the insurance companies put it, will most benefit the most severely ill—*if* they act wisely in the given time period. Coverage of preexisting conditions *can't* be excluded on new policies, and *must* be covered on replacement policies.

A few other features are built into the system. For example: Medigap policies must be *guaranteed* renewable (except because of non-payment of premiums, or misrepresentation), which means they *can't* be cancelled willy-nilly. This rule limits the spread between commissions on new and replacement policies, with rewards to encourage persistency—consumers renewing policies for many years. In some states, selling a replacement policy will generate a renewal commission, *not* a new-policy commission. The aim is to stop "churning," which we ran into earlier on.

Here's another built-in feature: The *minimum loss ratio* has been raised from 60 percent to 65 percent. Thus, at least 65 percent of premiums received *must* be paid out in claims. In addition, the guidelines prescribe a specific formula for arriving at the loss ratio, which will make it easier to enforce this requirement and harder for insurance companies to play around with their numbers. (Figures can't lie, but liars can figure.) If an insurance company doesn't meet the 65 percent test, its policyholders will get a credit equivalent to the shortfall.

Finally, disclosure forms have been reworked which explain how the policies compare. All buyers *must* receive these forms. They show (e.g.) that *duplicate* policies are now *illegal*: Companies and agents can't sell them, so won't unless they're willing to risk fines of up to $25,000 per policy.

Price Isn't Everything

Now that policies are standardized, how can you best choose from among Medigap insurers? On *price*, of course. Why buy a Policy A for say $600 when you can buy the same coverage for perhaps $375? (Actual prices may vary widely from company to company.) But don't shop on price *alone*. You might for instance want to spend a little more to buy from an insurer with an excellent reputation and extraordinary financial strength. You'll also want an insurer who emphasizes service, including speedy approval of applications, swift responses to customer questions, and rapid claims processing.

Most insurers will honor old, prestandard policies *as long as you are thereafter willing to renew*. In some cases these older policies offer greater benefits or better all-around values. So go over both the old and new policies carefully before deciding on changing.

In about a dozen states—prominently including California, Florida, and Texas—you can mix HMOs with a Medigap policy. You get the same coverage as any Medigap policy, but you pay about 15 percent– 20 percent less because you sign up for Medicare Select, and thus agree to use only certain doctors and hospitals. In Florida, for example, a sixty-eight-year-old man buying a standard Medigap policy from Blue Cross and Blue Shield might pay $85 per month, but only $70 a month with the Blue Cross/Blue Shield Medicare Select policy.

If you shop hard enough, you can find above-average health-insurance protection for below-average costs!

Recovery Room

No matter *what* kind of health insurance you have, if you wind up in a hospital, you'll wind up paying *some* part of your bills. Sometimes your out-of-pocket expenses, for example, will be modest, while some other patients will end up owing thousands of dollars on them. At least that's what the *hospitals* say. According to insurance company auditors, more than 90 percent of all hospital bills contain errors, and two-thirds of those miscues are in the hospitals' favor! It's a lot easier to double-charge a patient for certain items than to forget to bill for something.

You don't have to take hospital overcharges lying down—or in whatever other position they've left you. *Always* ask for a completely itemized bill, and question doubtful entries. Be *aware* of duplicate charges—two catheters rather than one, for example. To help your memory, either you or someone responsible to (or for) you can keep a log during your hospital stay.

If you spot any errors, complain at *once*. That's what Karen S. of Tampa did after she was billed $8,700 for a jaw operation that had an "estimated maximum cost" of $7,000. She objected to paying $28 for liquid protein she never received, $75 for two tubes of ointment selling in drugstores for $5 each, and so on.

She protested to the hospital's billing department, which knocked more than $400 off her bill. *Still* not satisfied, she wrote a formal complaint letter to the Florida Health Care Cost Containment Board, which leaned on the hospital to forgive another $1,300. Karen saved $1,700 altogether, bringing her total cost back down to the $7,000 estimate.

If you're going to be hospitalized, spend a few dollars to join the People's Medical Society (215-770-1670). Not only will you get help deciphering your bill, but you'll receive leads about where to complain if you spot overcharges.

Hospital patients scheduled for surgery have an even more important concern: contaminated blood transfusions. If possible, stock your own blood in a blood bank before any operation. Another option is to select a hospital that uses a "cell saver," which circulates your own blood back into your body during surgery.

SUMMING UP

• Americans over age sixty-five are covered by Medicare, but Medicare has gaps.

• To fill Medicare gaps, seniors should have Medigap insurance, which now is strictly regulated by federal law.

• Although low-cost core policies provide basic coverage, some more-expensive Medigap policies offer such valuable benefits as prescription drugs and coverage while traveling abroad.

• Be sure to apply for a Medigap policy soon after you become eligible for Medicare Part B, at age sixty-five, because you'll be able to buy *any* policy, *regardless* of your health.

• Hospital bills frequently contain overcharges, but you can win reductions with persistent protests.

16

Dealing With Disability

How to Protect Your Income Stream
If You Can't Work

James R. wasn't worried. He was thirty-six, in perfect health, and running his own construction business. Then, with no warning, he suffered a major heart attack and had to close his company. He applied for other construction jobs, but couldn't pass the physical exam. He and his wife went through their $70,000 savings account in a few years.

Unhappily, James's experience is all too common. According to Price Waterhouse, workers between ages thirty-five and sixty-five are six times as likely to be disabled as they are to die; the U. S. Housing and Home Finance Agency reports that 48 percent of mortgage foreclosures result from disability, versus 3 percent from death. Although you probably won't be comfortable thinking about it, disability is a risk you need to face.

If you get sick or hurt, your health insurance will pay the doctor and hospital bills. But who'll pay *you* if you can't work for a long time period? For that you need *disability insurance.*

Disability insurance paid off for Durwood W., who owned half of a computer distributorship whose annual sales were around $1 million. Back in 1981, when Durwood was forty-two, an aneurism in his brain burst. The surgeons removed a blood clot and gave him a 50 percent chance of survival. He survived, but his reading acumen had dropped from college level to second grade—so his career as an executive was over.

Since then, Durwood has been turned down for Social Security disability benefits three times. Fortunately, however, he and his company had purchased *disability income policies.* The company policy replaced his salary for a year, after which his personal policy kicked in. In addition, the company policy paid Durwood's partners a lump sum, so they could buy out his share of the firm. Thanks to these policies, income kept coming in, and Durwood's wife was able to stay home with their three daughters—all of whom were able to go through college.

Similarly, Dr. David R., a neurologist in Massachusetts, lost his ability to practice medicine in 1991, after he was struck by a van while riding his bike on a short, normally safe trip to a store. He suffered severe head injuries, and spent thirteen days in a coma.

David's disability insurance allowed him to maintain his mortgage payments while his wife finished her medical residency. His family continues to live comfortably. Moreover, David had a *business overhead disability policy*, which paid the rent as well as employee salaries, keeping his practice intact until he could sell it.

A Friend in Need

The premise of disability insurance is simple: If you can't work because of illness or injury, your income will drop, and perhaps disappear altogether. Nevertheless, you'll still have ongoing expenses. In such cases, disability insurance will pick up either some or all of the slack. A disability policy will pay you a certain amount *each month* if you can't work. When you buy disability insurance, you pay a smaller or larger premium in order to buy a commensurately smaller or larger monthly benefit.

You may think you already have disability coverage from your employer. Check on it! Many group disability policies last only six months or so. That won't save you from a financial catastrophe if you can't work for a year or more.

If you have no employer coverage, or if your group coverage is inadequate, you need to buy disability insurance on your own. You may find it difficult to afford the increased premiums, especially if you're struggling to meet all your other bills. The answer, in many cases, is to cut back on coverage—especially the "extras" that often are sold with such policies.

To hold costs down, insure only against *catastrophic* risks. Here, the real risk is that you'll have a lengthy disability that destroys your earning power. Focus on that protection, and ignore unnecessary options.

Your first task is to determine how much coverage you need. Insurers usually say to cover 60 percent–70 percent of your income. If you make $60,000 per year, which is $5,000 per month, you're advised to buy a policy that pays $3,000–$3,500 per month.

But do you really need that much coverage? A policy that pays $2,000 per month will be much cheaper. Your living standard may decline, but you won't starve if you collect $24,000 per year, tax-free, in addition to investment income, other family members' earnings, and the like. Buying a low-benefit policy is better than buying a more expensive policy you won't be able to keep in force.

Trimming the Fat

There's more to disability insurance than wrenched backs, strokes, and heart attacks. Claims for "mental and nervous" disorders, including drug and alcohol addictions, are increasingly common. And disability insurers, forced to foot the bill for all manner of stress-related claims, are becoming increasingly skeptical—looking harder than ever at applicants these days. For example, poor health risks are being either rejected or asked to pay higher premiums. You're likely to find that disability insurance, always pricey, is more and more so.

Whether you're buying a stand-alone disability policy or a supplement to group coverage, you'll find that disability insurance is expensive, costing 2 percent–3 percent of your income per year, or even more. A forty-year-old who wants to buy disability coverage with a $5,000 monthly benefit probably will pay premiums of around $2,000 per year, depending on policy features.

To keep your costs down, *don't* buy all the costly extras your agent may recommend. These add-ons could prove valuable, but you can do without them and still achieve your goal of financial security in case of long-term disability. For example, you can cut your premium by loosening up on the definition of disability. The basic policy is "any occupation" (any-occ), covering conditions under which you can't do the work you're suited for by reason of education and training.

Recently, disability insurers have been pushing more-expensive "own occupation" coverage (own-occ) that will pay if you can't perform your specific job duties. The classic example is a surgeon who hurts his hand, so takes a less lucrative job teaching: He'd collect under an own-occ policy, but not under an any-occ policy.

However, most people don't have such special circumstances. Own-occ, which is much more expensive, is "really a marketing-driven thing," a life-insurance executive told the *Wall Street Journal*. People feed their egos by buying own-occ and telling themselves that they're worth it.

In truth, most white-collar professionals are well-served by a disability policy that will pay if they can't perform suitable work. Make sure you go over a policy's definition of disability before you consider buying!

Choose a ninety-day waiting period before benefits begin. Your true risk is long-term disability, not three months without pay. Going from a thirty-day to ninety-day waiting period might save you 45 percent in premiums!

At the other end of the spectrum, buy a policy that pays until age sixty-five, not for your lifetime. Buying lifetime benefits can increase your premium by 75 percent because insurance companies are worried about the length of their exposure. Even if you're still disabled at sixty-five, and your insurance benefits stop, you'll be able to collect Social Security and other retirement benefits.

If you have a disability policy that pays after a 90-day waiting period, until age sixty-five, you're protected against disasters.

Offers You Can Refuse

Another option you can avoid is a *return-of-premium* feature. With this option, you'll get all or part of your money back, ten or twenty years from now, depending on the extent of the benefits you have received.

This "money-back" offer sounds great, but such policies may in fact cost 50 percent more. And they don't address the *key* reason for buying this insurance: protecting yourself against long-term disability.

Similarly, you probably can do without a *cost-of-living* rider. Say you buy a $5,000-a-month disability insurance policy with a COLA. If you're disabled, your monthly benefit will go up to $5,300, $5,500, etc., in sync with increases in inflation.

Again, this certainly is desirable, but the cost may be excessive. For someone in their forties, a COLA can increase the annual premium by 40 percent. Is that worth an extra 5 percent or 10 percent per year, as of some unknown future date?

Moreover, if you are disabled for a long period, your biggest headache may be making your mortgage payments so you can keep your house. You won't need a COLA for that because mortgage payments will usually be fixed, or at least will not rise above the cap on an adjustable-rate mortgage.

Rather than paying up for a COLA, you're better off adjusting your coverage every few years, as your circumstances change. Some companies will sell you a low-cost rider that enables you to buy extra coverage without a medical exam.

There is another option that generally is worth buying: *residual disability*. With this feature, you'll get a partial disability benefit if you can work only part-time.

Suppose, for example, you buy a disability insurance policy paying $5,000 per month. You suffer a heart attack that cuts in half your ability to work, and trims your income by 50 percent. The policy would pay you $2,500 per month, in addition to what you earn. With a good residual disability rider, you won't need own-occ coverage, because you're protected against loss of income.

Another wrinkle worth buying is a "Social Security" rider. If you don't qualify for Social Security disability benefits (most applicants are rejected), this rider will increase your benefit by, say, $1,000 per month. The cost of this rider is far less than buying an extra $1,000 in basic monthly benefits.

If you're a business owner, ask about special coverage. Some insurers have policies that will fund a buy–sell agreement if you're disabled, or the company's overhead expense may be covered while you're not working and not bringing in business.

Always be sure that disability insurance, like health- or life insurance, is "guaranteed renewable." This means that your coverage can't be dropped as long as you keep paying the premiums, even if your health deteriorates.

Discounts on Demand

Most insurers quote lower rates for nonsmokers than for nicotine enthusiasts. That's one way to cut premiums. Ask if an insurer also offers *annual renewable disability insurance* (ARDI), a little-publicized form of disability insurance in which premiums start out low—perhaps 50 percent of the basic price—and increase each year. This makes the most sense if you expect your annual income to increase. Agents don't push ARDI, perhaps because commissions are lower, but it may be a good way to buy disability insurance at a price you can afford, so perhaps you should check it out.

When you shop for disability insurance, you may discover that underwriting criteria are being toughened up in terms of finances, too. Previously, many companies would accept your word about your income. Increasingly, insurers are insisting on seeing tax returns and other financial documents. Some have hired CPAs to assist in underwriting, while others offer discounts to buyers who provide full financial disclosure.

Why is this so important? Disability insurers will offer benefits up to around only 60 percent of income. If you report $10,000 in monthly income, for example, you might be able to buy a policy paying $6,000 in monthly disability benefits. However, if you actually have $5,000 in monthly income, you could be sorely tempted to pay the premiums for a while, discover a "disability," and collect increased income while not working at all.

The tax consequences of disability benefits are straightforward. If *you* paid the premiums, benefits are tax-free. If your *employer* paid the premiums, benefits are taxable. In case of a split-dollar arrangement, a pro rata share will be taxed.

Some corporations offer employees "cafeteria" or "flex" benefit programs incorporating a selection of fringe benefits. If you have the opportunity to participate in such a plan, choose to have the *company* fund other fringes while *you* pay disability costs. Any disability benefits you receive will then be tax-free.

Now for the Hard Part

Buying the right policy at the right price isn't everything. You need to buy from a reputable insurer, and you need to pay attention to the exact terms of the policy.

Trial lawyer Lawrence H., for example, was stricken with multiple sclerosis, which made it difficult for him to speak—and so he couldn't try cases. He had disability coverage, but when he filed his initial claim, he didn't include a medical certificate from a physician. The insurance company refused to pay because of this technicality, forcing Lawrence to sue for benefits.

Similar difficulties faced Larry Z., a fifty-seven-year-old engineer who suffered severe head injuries when he was hit by a car in his company parking lot. For the next year and a half, Larry tried to work, even though his short-term memory was so bad that he had to tape-record instructions from his boss. Eventually he had a bout of vertigo, fell in a stairwell, and sustained brain damage. By the time Larry applied for disability benefits, his insurer turned him down because he had worked for 180 days after the auto injury. Again, his claim wound up in litigation.

Sometimes, however, disability claimants prevail in court. Pamela B., for example, a forty-one-year-old accountant who lost income after neck surgery, had her disability claim rejected. The insurer said she hadn't disclosed headaches, fatigue, allergies, back pain, sinus problems, and athlete's foot when she applied for a policy. She went to court, and a jury agreed that the insurance company should not have rescinded her policy over such trivial and irrelevant conditions. Pamela got her benefits, her attorney's fees, and a $25,000 award.

But you can't rely on a court victory, and you don't want to subject yourself to that trouble and expense unnecessarily. So check into the insurance company before buying: Companies with top ratings from A. M. Best, Moody's, and Standard & Poor's are more likely to pay claims without a hassle. Even with reputable companies, though, you should make full disclosure on your disability insurance application, and follow the claims-filing procedures carefully.

SUMMING UP

• If you can't work, your income will shrink while your ongoing expenses continue.

• Disability insurance will pay you a monthly benefit to help you meet your living expenses.

• Disability insurance is expensive, so buy only as much coverage as you'll need to ward off disaster.

• To cut costs, stipulate a long waiting period before benefits begin, and an end of benefits at age sixty-five—when you'd be retiring even if not disabled.

• You can do without such expensive options as specialized "own-occupation" coverage, cost-of-living adjustments, and money-back offers in case benefits aren't claimed.

• Some features are worthwhile—for example, a residual disability option that pays you partial benefits while your income is reduced.

• If you pay for a disability insurance policy yourself, any benefits you receive will be tax-free, so you should ask your employer to pay for other fringe benefits rather than for disability insurance.

• Deal with top-rated disability insurers, fill out applications honestly and thoroughly, and follow claims-filing procedures exactly.

17

Make Sure Your Money Doesn't Run Out Before You Do

Coping With the Crippling Costs of Long-Term Care

The cost of nursing-home stays has increased dramatically, reaching nearly $100,000 per year in some areas. Your wealth (or your inheritance from your parents or whomever) can be wiped out by a long spell in a nursing home. Therefore, *long-term care* (LTC) insurance, which will pay policyholders in case they're confined to a nursing home, has grown in popularity. From nowhere, in 1987, such policies now account for around $3 billion in premiums per year.

However, more that just a few buyers don't stick around: Consumer groups report that as many as 80 percent of all buyers allow LTC policies to lapse before they even receive any benefits! That's an astonishing lapse rate, considering that these policies are only a few years old.

118

Why the incredible dropout rate (which stat insurance companies challenge)? Because these policies are quite expensive. The average price of a policy purchased at age sixty-five is about $1,700 per year; for a topflight policy, the annual cost might be around $3,000. A married couple, of course, need to pay for *two* policies.

Apparently LTC policies are being oversold—to people who can't afford the ongoing premiums. After a few years, they let the coverage lapse. The National Association of Insurance Commissioners (NAIC), the umbrella group of state insurance commissioners, has agreed to *force* insurers to pay *some* benefits to consumers, even *after* policies lapse. The NAIC's Long-Term Care Insurance Model Act holds that "No long-term care insurance policy or certificate may be delivered . . . unless such policy or certificate provides for nonforfeiture benefits."

Better than Nothing

As of this writing, nonforfeiture benefits seemed destined to become standard in the mid- to late 1990s. Judging from the NAIC report, the most likely form of nonforfeiture benefit will be the *shortened benefit period.* That is, suppose a consumer buys an LTC policy that will pay $100 per day for up to three years. After a certain number of years, the consumer lets the policy lapse. With a shortened benefit period provision, the consumer might retain an LTC policy that will pay $100 per day for one or two years.

Another possible approach is to offer a *reduced paid-up* policy as a nonforfeiture provision. The holder of a policy with $100,000 in maximum benefits might get a $40,000 or $50,000 policy instead.

Insurance companies now offering these types of coverage generally charge 10 percent–30 percent higher premiums, compared with policies that do not have these features. According to the NAIC long-term care task force, providing nonforfeiture benefits could increase premiums by 7 percent–13 percent at issue age seventy-five, and 64 percent–232 percent (!) at issue age thirty-five. Although the task force implies that premium hikes might be reduced, it's clear that the costs of LTC coverage are going even higher.

Strength in Numbers

How can you hold down the costs? Buy through your employer's group policy, if one is offered. Such policies, which have to be approved by corporate benefits managers, often have better coverage than do individual policies. Typically, you can buy LTC insurance for your parents as well as for yourself and your spouse.

In a group plan, employees pay the premiums. Because prices are negotiated, premiums may be 20 percent–30 percent lower than for individual policies. And group LTC policies are *portable*, meaning that you can take yours with you if you leave your employer.

If you're not covered by a group plan, you *have* to buy individual LTC coverage. Here are some ways to hold down the costs of an LTC policy you buy on your own:

• *Buy young.* A policy bought at age forty-five might cost around $375 per year, whereas the same policy costs $1,700 per year if bought at age seventy. Your annual premium can't be raised unless the insurer raises it for *all* of its local policyholders.

• *Choose a lengthy waiting period.* Pay for the first 90 or 100 days in a nursing home yourself, before benefits kick in.

• *Limit your benefit period to three years.* That will give you enough time to transfer assets and qualify for Medicaid. Make sure you execute a durable power of attorney so your assets can be transferred if you're not capable of doing that (see Chapter 23).

• *Avoid home-care coverage.* Home-care coverage seems to be everybody's favorite: Who *wouldn't* prefer to spend his or her last days at home, covered by insurance (as well as given lots of personal attention), rather than in a nursing home? As a practical matter, though, your greatest risk of expensive custodial care is a long nursing-home stay rather than home health care.

Should you need year-after-year care, it's unlikely you'll be staying at home. You'll probably have to go into an institution. While home-care benefits frequently are bought in LTC policies, they're seldom used. Most people prefer to pay the $50 per day out of their own pocket, and save the $100 LTC insurance for the nursing home. So you may be better off skipping this expensive coverage, which could add 40 percent or more to your annual premium.

• *Don't buy a policy that will provide increasing benefits to protect against inflation.* You're paying in today's dollars for a benefit you may or may not receive years in the future.

Buy coverage that doesn't skimp on the essentials. An LTC policy should pay for custodial care, in any type of facility, with no prior hospitalization necessary. Benefits should be triggered if you can't perform such activities of daily living as bathing, dressing, and so on.

And there should be specific coverage for Alzheimer's and other organic-based mental illness.

If you're shopping for long-term care insurance, be sure to buy from a company that uses "front-end underwriting," screening applicants' health histories diligently. Such companies tend to insure healthier people so they'll be better able to hold down costs.

Back-end underwriters don't do much screening, so it's easier to get a policy. However, they likely will cover riskier clients, driving up costs, and they're more motivated to find inaccuracies in your initial application, so they can reject claims.

SUMMING UP

• As nursing home costs increase, LTC policies have become increasingly popular.

• Such policies pay a benefit if you need care in a nursing home, an expense not covered by Medicare or by private health insurance.

• Many LTC policies are allowed to lapse by consumers who don't keep up with the premiums.

• Insurance regulators have announced they'll *force* insurers to pay some benefits, even on lapsed policies.

• To cover this mandated expense, the cost of LTC policies will rise—perhaps substantially.

• You can keep LTC policies affordable by avoiding such extras as home-care coverage, inflation-adjusted benefits, and lifetime benefits.

• No matter how stringently you cut back, buy a policy from a reputable insurer that will cover stays in any type of nursing home, even without a prior hospital stay.

18

Winning the Endgame

How to Protect Your Parents' Savings— and Your Inheritance

Federal government statistics indicate that 4 percent of all men and 13 percent of all women can expect to spend at least five years in a nursing home. Having an aging parent confined to a nursing home is bad enough. Even worse is the prospect of seeing your family's assets evaporate, month after month, year after year. That modest inheritance you had hoped would help pay for your kids' college education or your own retirement may wind up in the pockets of a nursing-home operator.

An increasingly popular choice for financing nursing-home care is Medicaid, a federal–state welfare program. Nearly half of all U.S. nursing-home costs are paid by Medicaid.

To qualify for Medicaid, your aging parents must virtually impoverish themselves. They can have only a very limited income, and less than $2,000 in assets—plus (fortunately) a house, a car, and some personal possessions. Married couples can have nearly $75,000 in assets (as of 1994), plus the exclusions noted above. After they strip themselves down to that level, Medicaid will pay medical expenses, including nursing-home bills.

For these reasons, Medicaid "transfers" have become common. Your parents first give away enough assets (if they have enough to start with) to get down to the poverty line, *then* apply for Medicaid. Transfers may be outright—usually they're to relatives. Then those relatives will be responsible for supporting their elders for as long as no nursing-home care is needed. Or, Medicaid transfers can be to *trusts*. Then, the trustee (perhaps a child, perhaps a family friend or adviser) could pay out trust assets as necessary.

Wait Loss

You might think, "I'll wait until a parent goes into a nursing home, then arrange to transfer enough assets to the next generation to meet the Medicaid limits." That's certainly one strategy, but it has its costs.

Transferring assets creates a waiting period. A complicated formula (involving the amount transferred, and local nursing-home rates) is used to determine the length of the waiting period. During this time, someone else—probably the recipients of the transferred assets—has to pay nursing-home bills.

Suppose your father—let's say a widower—gives away $100,000 worth of assets in order to come down to the Medicaid limit. In his state, the average nursing-home cost is $4,000 per month. Thus, your father would have to wait twenty-five months ($100,000 ÷ $4,000) before Medicaid paid his medical expenses.

Until 1993, the waiting period was capped at thirty months. Whether your father gave away $150,000 or $1,000,000, he'd still be eligible after thirty months. Nowadays, the waiting period may be thirty-six months, or even longer (see below).

Besides the waiting period, there's another problem with using a wait-and-transfer strategy. Suppose your parent has to go into a nursing home because of a stroke or Alzheimer's, or some other ailment that renders him or her incompetent. An asset transfer might not be possible, and *all* your parent's assets will be on the line for nursing-home bills.

A different approach, then, is to transfer assets while your parents are still of sound body and mind. If they later are confined to a nursing home, the waiting period may have expired, and they'll be eligible for Medicaid immediately.

That may make good financial sense, but it's often not practical. Few elderly parents want to give away all of their assets so they can live out their lives in poverty, dependent on their children. If they never need to be institutionalized, they'll have gone through this turmoil for nothing.

Lack of Trust

Besides extending the waiting period from thirty to thirty-six months, the 1993 tax law changed the rules on Medicaid transfers in other respects:

• Anyone who sets up a trust fund must wait at least five years before applying to Medicaid.

• States may consider any distribution from a trust to be a transfer, starting a new waiting period. That applies even to trusts in existence before the law was passed.

• Premature Medicaid applications may wipe out the thirty-six-month cap. That is, if you apply after thirty-five months when you should have waited thirty-six months, your waiting period will be the full amount of assets divided by the monthly cost, even if that's 200 or 300 months.

• States are now required to recover outlays from the estates of Medicaid patients. This includes a principal residence, even if it was transferred to a spouse or a child.

Therefore, if you intend to do any Medicaid planning now, you're better off without using a trust. The new rules are clearly intended to put an end to the use of Medicaid trusts. If you have, or another family member already has, a trust in place, consult with an attorney before making any further distributions.

Deal From Strength

Medicaid planning is still viable if you're willing to make outright transfers and then wait up to thirty-six months. Of course, your parents must have absolute faith that the money will be provided as needed. Also: If you plan on having Medicaid pay for nursing-home expenses, be prepared to lose all or part of the sale proceeds from your parents' house, because your state likely will seek reimbursement.

The bottom line is that Medicaid planning should be used *only* as a last resort. Why should your aging parents impoverish themselves for the rest of their lives, giving up financial independence, on the chance that long-term nursing home care *might* be needed?

So—how can you keep your family wealth from this dilemma?

1. Have a frank talk with your parents. Discuss the costs of local nursing-home care, and the extent of their assets.

2. Hire an attorney who specializes in the emerging "elder law" area.

3. Have a durable power of attorney drawn up, giving someone in the next generation the authority to handle your parents' assets in case of their incompetency.

4. If long-term care insurance is available at a decent price, buy it. You want a policy that will cover custodial care in virtually all institutions. Choose a three-year benefit period, giving you time to transfer assets and outlast the waiting period. After the insurance runs out, Medicaid will take over.

5. If you can't buy insurance, plan a gradual, partial transfer of assets, beginning as soon as possible. The idea is to leave your parents enough so they maintain their independence, yet reduce the amount subject to nursing-home fees. The transfer might be to a trust, with a trustee in whom your parents have confidence. The trust *can* have the ability (but *can't* be required) to make distributions to your parents while they're not yet institutionalized.

6. Always leave your parents enough to enter a first-class nursing home as paying customers. Many good nursing homes won't take Medicaid patients, but few will actually discharge a patient who has been there for a while and run out of money. Check carefully on a nursing home before sending a parent there!

SUMMING UP

• Many people rely upon Medicaid to pay nursing home bills.

• Medicaid is a poverty program, so people have to impoverish themselves to qualify.

• If you wait to transfer assets, you'll run into a lengthy waiting period and have to pay nursing-home costs in the interim.

• If you arrange an asset transfer *beforehand,* when nursing-home care *isn't* required, you run the risk that the elderly person will have given up his or her independence needlessly.

• The 1993 tax law made it more difficult to transfer assets and qualify for Medicaid.

• You're better off buying a three-year, long-term care policy and executing a durable power of attorney, then arranging a Medicaid transfer only if a long nursing-home stay is inevitable.

Part VI

Keep Golden Years From Turning Leaden

19

Too Safe Can Be Sorry

Keep Your Retirement Funds
From Evaporating

There was a time when retirement planning was fairly simple. You might work until age sixty-five and then live off your savings for a little while longer, or if lucky until your death. Back in 1935, when Social Security was passed into law, the average life expectancy was around sixty-one years. That's not the case anymore. People increasingly live for many years after they retire. Early retirement is becoming common, at age sixty-two, sixty, or even younger.

At the same time, life expectancy is steadily lengthening. In early 1994, *Fortune* magazine reported that the average life expectancy was 72.7 years for American men and 79.6 years for American women. According to mutual-fund sponsor T. Rowe Price, an individual who retires at age fifty-five has an average life expectancy of twenty-eight years. If that individual has a spouse, also age fifty-five, the combined life expectancy is thirty-four years.

Even if you wait until age sixty-five to retire, you can expect to live for another twenty years. If your spouse is also sixty-five, the combined life expectancy is twenty-five years. (Naturally, if your spouse is younger, the combined life expectancy is even greater.)

Remember, those are averages. Dr. Edward Schneider, head of the Andrus Gerontology Center at the University of Southern California, has predicted that "At least half the baby boomers [today's middle-aged people] might expect to live into their late eighties and nineties."

The Long Goodbye

After you retire, you're likely to spend *many* years with little or no earned income. You need to plan for twenty, twenty-five—even thirty—years of not working, or of working part-time. And that will take lots of money, if you're looking forward to a *comfortable* retirement.

How can you gauge what amount of money you'll need to maintain your standard of living after you stop working? If you're only a few years from retirement, you can use the *itemized budget analysis* method: Review your current expenses and see which ones you'll keep up after retirement, which you'll drop, which you'll increase, and so on. You'll get a pretty good idea of what your actual expenses will be.

But what if you're five or ten years from retirement? Or even farther away? The longer the time period until retirement, the more you'll have to estimate future cash needs.

Booke & Co., an employee benefits firm, has determined that most people will need about 70 percent of their adjusted preretirement income for the kind of retirement they'd like. For example:

Your 1995 household income	$60,000
Minus savings	5,000
Minus taxes paid	15,000
Result = Total living expenses	40,000
Multiplied by suggested replacement ratio of 70%	28,000

As the table shows, you'd need about $28,000 a year to live comfortably. That's *after taxes*, of course. Assume a 25 percent income-tax rate, and you come out with around $37,000 gross income necessary for a comfortable retirement. But that's in 1994 dollars. And most assuredly you'll find that $37,000 in say 2015 won't buy you nearly as much as in (for example) 1995. You need to adjust for inflation, using a table such as this:

| | Inflation Adjustment Factors | | |
Years to Retirement	3%	4%	5%
5	1.159	1.217	1.276
10	1.344	1.480	1.629
20	1.806	2.191	2.653
30	2.427	3.243	4.322

SOURCE: American Society of CLU & ChFC

Suppose you're ten years from retirement and you expect inflation to increase 4 percent per year in the interim. Multiply the $37,000 gross income you'll need, in current dollars, by 1.480, the appropriate inflation adjustment factor. You'll wind up with $54,760. That's roughly the amount of gross income you'll need to maintain your current living standard in retirement.

Once you have this number, you can plan for making *sure* your retirement income will be adequate. You can, for example, expect to receive Social Security retirement benefits. Contact the Social Security Administration for an estimate of what your future benefits will be. Call 800-772-1213 for the appropriate form. You should check on your record every few years, since after three years you lose your right to correct errors.

In addition, either you or your employer may be contributing to a tax-deferred retirement plan on your behalf. Check with your company's benefits department, or a CPA, for an estimate of how much you can expect to receive in retirement.

The Dream Deferred

If you're relying on an employer's pension, take steps to make sure it will be there when you need it. At times, employers "borrow" from the plan and "forget" to repay the money. In other cases, they just steal it.

Consider the plight of James R., a shop foreman who worked for a small company in Irving, Texas, for twenty years. The owner of the company pleaded guilty to embezzling $103,000 from the employees' profit-sharing plans, including $33,000 that belonged to James—most of his life's savings. The employer convinced the judge that he was broke, so had to pay back only $100 per month. At that rate, it would take eighty-six years to reach $103,000. In the meantime, James had to forego retirement and find another job.

Such abuses can happen anywhere, but employees of small companies are particularly vulnerable because the authorities don't find it cost-effective to chase after every $103,000 swindle. You can't rely on someone else to watch over your nest egg; you have to do it yourself.

Your employer *must* supply you with a plan summary and annual reports. If you can't get these reports from your employer, or if you suspect you won't get the money you've been promised, write or call the Pension and Welfare Benefits Administration, Office of Program Services, Department of Labor, 200 Constitution Ave., N.W., Washington, DC 20210; 202-219-8776.

Increasingly, employers are terminating their pension plans, to avoid the regulatory burden and expense. If this happens to you, you're not necessarily wiped out: You likely will be entitled to a distribution of contributions already made on your behalf. You can find out by contacting the Pension Benefit Guaranty Corp., Participant Services Div., 1200 K St., N.W., Washington, DC 20005-4026; 202-326-4014. The Labor Department publishes "What You Should Know About Pension Law," available free from the U.S. Dept. of Labor, Division of Technical Assistance and Inquiries, 200 Constitution Avenue, N.W., Washington, DC 20216.

If you can't get satisfaction from these agencies, try the Pension Rights Center, 918 16th St., N.W., Suite 704, Washington, DC 20006-2902; 202-296-3776. This research group offers a booklet, "Where to Look for Help With a Pension Problem," for $8.50, that includes advice on how to proceed in cases of underfunding, mismanagement, and fraud. Another publication, "Protecting Your Pension Money," also is available.

Looking Out for Number One

Assuming you'll receive the full pension to which you're entitled, the total of your expected income from Social Security and retirement plans may still fall short of your retirement income needs. If so, it's up to you to make up the difference. Generally, that difference will come from a combination of earned income and investment income.

Say you expect to need $55,000 a year, in gross retirement income, with $30,000 per year likely from Social Security and retirement plans. You'd need another $25,000 a year, perhaps $10,000 from working part-time, and $15,000 a year in investment income.

Beyond Bonds

Once you know how much investment income you'll need in retirement, you can begin to accumulate an appropriate amount. A portfolio of $150,000–$200,000, for example, might be enough to generate the $15,000 per year in our example, depending on future interest rates.

The classic strategy for retirement investing is to concentrate on stocks while you're younger. As you get older, and thus closer to retirement, you then move into bonds, for higher income and less exposure to stock-market volatility. By the time you retire, you're fully invested in income-producing bonds.

Well—not *all* classics age gracefully. As mentioned, retirements last longer these days, and you've got to stay ahead of inflation to maintain purchasing power. You won't enjoy the inflation protection you'll need if your portfolio is *solely* in bonds and bond-type investments.

In the 1980s, retirees might have been able to justify loading up their portfolios with bonds. Interest rates were high enough so that double-digit yields were possible, with only moderate risk. In the mid-1990s, though, bonds were offering only modest returns. Therefore, you need to leaven your retirement portfolio with solid stocks for greater returns, so that your retirement will be comfortable, no matter how long you wind up living.

Stock Answers

In 1994, the Institute for Econometric Research (Fort Lauderdale, Florida) released one of the longest-term studies of investment returns ever attempted. It shows that from 1871 through 1993, common stocks gained 8.3 percent per year, after inflation. In other words, stocks have doubled every nine years, in real terms. If that doesn't impress you, consider that $1 invested in stocks in 1871 would have grown to nearly $18,000 by 1994.

By contrast, $1 invested in Treasury bills would have grown to $9, after inflation, and $1 in gold would have grown to $1.40 (that dollar would have lost ground, to 86 cents, if you assume a token storage and insurance fee). As the Institute points out, except for two 25 percent corrections (1929–33 and 1968–74), "Investors who bought stock at any time during the 123-year period—even at cyclical tops—made money if they simply held on for five or ten years."

If you're facing a lengthy retirement, put *at least half* of your money into stocks. Gold, T-bills, and money-market funds might preserve your principal, and bonds might beat inflation by a few points, but you need *stocks* in order to build wealth. Therefore, you should go into your retirement with a portfolio similar to the one you used to build a retirement fund, mixing stocks or stock funds with your bonds. As you grow older, you can shift from stocks to bonds. By the time you're in your eighties, your portfolio can be heavily weighted to income-producing vehicles.

Paltry Pensions

For some retirees, it's possible to put even more retirement money into stocks. They can turn down their longtime employer's pension, take the cash instead, and invest in stocks or stock funds.

Typically, when you retire you'll be offered an annuity from your employer. If you choose a *single-life annuity*, payments will continue until your death. If you opt for a *joint-and-survivor annuity*, the payments will continue for the lives of yourself and your spouse. Joint-and-survivor annuities provide lower monthly payments than single-life annuities, because the payments likely will go on for a longer time period. However, these annuities are based on current interest rates, which may lead to extremely low payout rates. In 1994, for example, employer-provided annuities typically assumed an investment return of only 5.1 percent.

Some employers will give you the option of taking a lump sum instead of a monthly pension. If you have the choice, take the lump sum and roll it into an Individual Retirement Account (IRA). The lower the assumed-interest rate, the higher the lump sum you'll receive.

When Lower Means Higher

Here's the reason for this seeming paradox. Say you're offered $1,000 per month, or $12,000 per year, from an employer annuity. If interest rates are high, that kind of an income may be possible with a lump sum of $100,000. But in a low-interest-rate environment you might need $150,000 to generate that $1,000 per month. So take your lump sum and roll it into an IRA. If you shop around among insurance companies, you'll likely find a much better deal on an annuity.

Take the example of George, age sixty-five, who's entitled to a $1,250 monthly pension. Using a 5.1 percent investment assumption, he'd be entitled to a $190,000 lump sum. With that parked in his IRA, George could easily get quotes from numerous insurance companies. *Kiplinger's Personal Finance* magazine has reported that every insurance company recently surveyed would pay more than $1,250 per month to a sixty-five-year-old with a $190,000 lump sum. Kansas City Life, a top-rated insurance company, offered 14 percent more— $1,430 per month. That's an extra $180 per month, or $2,160 per year, for one's entire retirement. To find the best deal on annuity payouts, you can buy a sample issue of *Annuity and Life Insurance Shopper* newsletter (800-872-6684) for $20.

While employers were paying out as if money earned 5.1 percent, insurers were basing payments on rates up to 6 percent. You can do still better if you hold on to your lump sum and invest on your own, mainly in stocks. If you earn 8 percent, say, you can pull out much more money, each and every year, than you can with an employer or an insurance-company annuity.

Spread Your Wealth

Whether you have an IRA rollover, an outside portfolio, or both, you can select your own stocks, as long as you diversify. Assuming an average $50 share price, you can buy a round lot of 100 shares for $5,000. You could invest in ten different issues for $50,000, and twenty issues for $100,000. For many retirees, that would be feasible, were they to receive a large distribution from an employer plan.

Just because you focus on stocks in your early retirement years, that doesn't mean you have to be reckless. If you emphasize blue-chip stocks, and especially those paying steady dividends, you can enjoy both income and growth potential.

Those blue-chip issues should be scattered among the key sectors of the economy: "Buy" a consumer-goods company, a high-tech company, a utility, an oil giant. Put some money into health care. Purchase a couple of multinationals. Besides your focus on proven, dividend-paying companies, grab some promising smaller companies, too.

If you're concerned about making stock-market commitments today, and your money is currently invested heavily in bonds, cash equivalents, and the like, you can use a *dollar-cost averaging approach* to move into the market: Each quarter, you can invest perhaps $10,000 or $20,000 in equities, until you have say $100,000 or $200,000 in stocks. By investing over an extended time period, you'll get the advantage of buying low, in case of a market downturn.

Feeling Mutual

If you'd rather not pick your own stocks, you can get professional management through mutual funds. Again, diversification is crucial—you'll want several funds rather than just one or two. You might as well buy *no-loads*, if *you're* going to do the work of researching and picking funds.

Morningstar, Inc., which tracks mutual-fund performance, has come up with an interesting approach to stock-fund diversification. If you buy, for example, a growth fund, an aggressive growth fund, a growth-and-income fund, and a small-cap fund, you may think you've diversified. However, you may have invested in four funds that all buy small companies, all using an earnings-growth approach to pick stocks.

If you select your funds based on top performance for the past few years, you may wind up with a bunch of small-growth stocks in the same industry—communications or financial services or whatever else has been hot recently. You're really not diversified, even if you own several funds holding hundreds of different companies. If one market sector suddenly goes out of favor, and many of your companies are in that sector, you could suffer a sizable loss of principal.

To avoid this problem, Morningstar has come up with "style boxes." In effect, these are grids showing which sizes of companies a fund holds (small, medium, or large), and what investment style it pursues (growth, value, or blend). By mixing style boxes, you can have a truly diversified mutual-fund portfolio.

Suppose, for example, you start out with Kaufmann Fund, a top-performing, aggressive growth fund. Its style box shows it's a small-cap fund looking for earnings growth.

For a growth fund, you might choose Crabbe Huson, another outstanding performer, with a style box that shows mid-cap stocks and a blended investment style. Round out your portfolio with Legg Mason Total Return Fund, a big-cap, value fund in the growth-and-income category. Once you have a foundation of three such funds in place, you can further diversify with a *sector fund, international fund, junk-bond fund,* and the like.

What if you don't want to make any decisions at all—no stockpicking, no mutual-fund selection? If your retirement fund is large enough (generally over $500,000 but sometimes as low as $100,000), you can ask your friends and relatives for references to a first-class stockbroker. Then, ask the broker to set you up in a *wrap account* with one or more money managers: with these accounts, you'll pay a stiff fee (usually 3 percent of assets under management) but you'll get professional management without having to worry about churning, because that 3 percent covers all fees, including brokers' commissions.

Whichever path you choose, be reasonable in your expectations. Remember, stocks have grown by around 8 percent per year, after inflation. With inflation running around 3 percent in the mid-1990s, you could expect to earn about 11 percent in stocks, including dividends.

So be skeptical about anyone who *promises* you 20 percent or 30 percent per year. That just can't be done—there's not enough money around. As the Institute for Econometric Research points out, if you had invested $1 in 1871 and earned 30 percent per year, you'd have $103 trillion—more than the Gross National Product of the entire world!

SUMMING UP

- As people retire earlier and live longer, it becomes vital for retirees to stretch out their retirement funds.
- In general, you'll need a retirement income that's around 70 percent of your preretirement income; and that retirement income should grow to keep pace with inflation.
- You can't enjoy growth and inflation protection if your retirement money is invested heavily in bonds, CDs, etc. Instead, you should invest most of your retirement funds in stocks, which have far outperformed bonds over virtually every time period.
- If you pick your own stocks, be sure to diversify among proven companies in a variety of industries.
- Rather than pick individual stocks, you can invest in mutual funds, as long as you make certain that your funds hold different types of companies and pursue different investment strategies.
- With a "wrap" account, your broker arranges for a money manager to handle your portfolio, in return for a flat fee that covers all expenses.

20

Let the Sun Shine In

In Retirement, Avoid Real-Estate Ripoffs and Ravening Tax Men

Most people see a "retirement dream-home" of their own at the end of the rainbow. Yours might well be located in a resort area, though perhaps a convenient urban one would be more practicable. Wherever you hope to wind up, your dream could turn into a nightmare if you choose the wrong kind of residence at the wrong time.

Take the case of Steve and Meg L., who moved from New York to Florida and quickly purchased a new home there. A year later, Steve had a stroke and was admitted to a nursing home for a long stay. Their income was squeezed, yet they couldn't sell their house to get at their capital, because of a weak housing market.

Or, consider what happened to Richard and Judy S., who moved from Milwaukee to Phoenix, where they bought a condo apartment. Unfortunately, the building sponsors weren't able to sell enough apartments, so they allowed the property to fall into disrepair. Now

Richard and Judy live in a building with failing services and virtually no hope to sell at a reasonable price.

To avoid such disasters, you need to be methodical and not let your emotions overwhelm your common sense. For example, *don't* buy a retirement home just because of a glossy sales brochure or a slick sales pitch. Instead, start out with a list of expectations—all the things you're *really* looking for in the place. Then search until you find a home that will satisfy as many of these preconditions as it will take to sell itself to you.

First Things First

Your first step should be to decide *where* you'd like to live in retirement, basing your choice on at least some of the following criteria:

• Are there family members—your children, perhaps—there whom you'd like to live near? (Or those whom you'd like to avoid?)

• If you've lived in or near a major metropolitan area all your life, you may not be ready to live out your life in a rural or semirural area. Conversely, if you have spent your life in a small town, you may not feel comfortable in Greater Phoenix or Miami.

• Unless you're a dedicated skier, you probably envision a retirement home free of overcoats and heating bills. But there's a continent's worth of difference between Florida's humidity and Arizona's blazing but dry heat. In fact, there's a huge difference between Florida's Keys, in the tropics, and the more moderate temperatures in the Panhandle region.

Your health might dictate an arid climate rather than a wet one. Also, don't forget allergies, if you have any. And if hay fever ruins your summers, choose a new location carefully.

• Certain states tax heavily, some lightly. Among popular retirement destinations, Florida, Nevada, and Texas are among the states that have *no personal income tax*.

Before you move, check with your new home's Chamber of Commerce or tax department for a complete picture: property tax, sales tax, and estate tax, *as well as* income tax. In some areas of Florida, for example, property taxes have risen tenfold in the past twenty-five years. Don't walk into any tax surprises!

• You probably want a lower cost of living in retirement. A couple who had been living in an $80,000 condo in New York City's outer boroughs recently bought a house of the same size in Delray Beach, Florida, for $40,000. Living on their Social Security and pension income of $24,000, this couple saved $5,000 per year in taxes, housing, heating, and clothing costs, compared to what they had been paying in New York.

Another couple living in a $300,000 home in New Jersey bought a smaller but still sizable home in Sarasota, Florida for under $100,000. With total income over $100,000 from Social Security, pensions, and investments, this couple wound up saving nearly $20,000 per year. You too can find retirement areas where you'll be able to live well for less money.

In general, the farther you get from large metropolitan areas and prime tourist spots, the lower your living costs will be. If you want to rent a one-bedroom apartment near Honolulu, for example, you'd pay over $1,000 per month, on average. In the next-most-expensive areas—San Francisco, Washington, D.C., New York City, Boston— apartment rents were over $700 per month, as of last report, while they topped $600 in metro Los Angeles and Chicago. These were *averages* for suburban apartments. You'll pay much more to live in a prime neighborhood in the city itself.

If you're content to retire in a small-town setting, you'll slash your living costs dramatically. Areas such as Corbin (Kentucky), Newport (Tennessee), Hennessey (Oklahoma), Scottsboro (Alabama), and Casper (Wyoming) offer one-bedroom apartments renting for $250 or less per month.

• Safety counts, too. There's nowhere you can go to avoid crime altogether these days, but some areas are safer than others. Again, urban and suburban areas tend to have more violent crime and more theft than do small towns.

• In social services, the reverse is true. If you need access to a particular type of service, you're more likely to find it in a metropolitan area. State and local agencies on aging may offer special programs for seniors.

• Health care is vital to most retirees, especially older ones. Make sure that proper health- and medical care will be available before you move.

Inspect local health facilities, and talk to residents about their doctors. The American Hospital Association publishes an annual "Guide to the Health Care Field" with state-by-state listings of every hospital in America, including specialties. Check into medical costs, too. Florida, for example, has surprisingly high health-care costs: A. Foster Higgins, a benefits consulting firm, found medical bills more than 50 percent higher in Florida than in New Jersey!

Get your health insurance and Medicare supplemental insurance lined up before you move, *especially* to Florida. Some insurers in other states will permit you to retain coverage even after you move to Florida—where premiums would be higher.

Little Things Mean a Lot

The factors listed above will be of prime importance to most retirees. However, after you feel comfortable with the major points, you can turn to seemingly minor considerations that can add up to a big difference in your retirement life style.

If access to cultural events is important to you, look into the entertainment offerings before relocating. Are there community theaters, dinner theaters, or major stage productions in the area? Will you find museums, ballet, opera, symphonies? Is there much night life? (You'll probably want convenient restaurants, movie theaters, and video-rental stores, too.)

You may choose a retirement setting because it permits you to pursue a favored activity, such as sailing, skiing, or golf. Or, you might pick a new home because you'll have access to big-league baseball, football, or whatever.

Many housing developments and apartment complexes offer exercise centers with pools, bicycle-type exercise machines, and classes in water aerobics or aerobic dancing. You'll also want to see if the area offers places for walking, especially if you walk regularly for exercise.

What will you do with your spare time in retirement? In Manhattan's Greenwich Village, you can take books out of a library, walk homeless dogs at a shelter, join political organizations, attend college courses, and so on (and on). In a small town, there might not be nearly as much to occupy your days and nights.

You may want to live near people your own age, who are more likely than others to share your interests. When you're surrounded by younger people with children, you may not have much in common with your neighbors anymore. You also may want to live in a certain ethnic neighborhood, or in an otherwise diversified community.

News Worthy

How do you find out about all the factors mentioned above—crime, sports, cost of living, etc?

One way to begin is by picking out a few areas where you might like to retire. Three or four cities on Florida's Gulf Coast, for example. Then, take out a subscription to the local newspapers in each city. There's no better way to get a feel for local issues. Too, *Editor and Publisher's International Yearbook*, which lists every newspaper in the United States, is available at most libraries. And many newspapers offer short-term subscriptions, mailing to your hometown.

Read these local papers with a particular eye to the police reports and crime stories. If a household robbery is big news, the community probably has a low crime rate. You'll also want to see if any new taxes have been proposed, whether residents are complaining about increased traffic congestion, and so on.

Pounding the Pavement

Reading newspaper articles about possible locations is a good way to begin, but *nothing* beats a visit to the area. To get this firsthand experience, take a vacation, or rent, in the vicinity before deciding on making a permanent move. When you're there, you can have face-to-face conversations with local police officers, storekeepers, and potential neighbors. You'll thereby learn what the newspapers *don't* cover.

While you're in town, call some local physicians, to get an idea of how much an office visit will cost. In fact, find out if local physicians *will* accept new Medicare patients. With Medicare fees capped, some physicians *won't* take on more seniors.

Ask some local residents who have moved from other areas how hard it is to get a driver's license. Some states require waiting periods for all new residents, but others have separate requirements for drivers over sixty-five, including more frequent driver tests and medical or vision exams.

Check into public transportation, too, to see if you can live comfortably in the neighborhood without a car. As you grow older, you may want to drive less—or even give up your car altogether. Strong bus service is a plus. Also, find out if cabs or car services are available (and reliable).

To get answers to all your questions, talk to people you meet at the post office, the gas station, the supermarket. Their personal experiences will more than likely be far more valuable than anything you read in brochures from the Chamber of Commerce or the Convention Bureau.

For a better look at how everyday life is for the average resident, do the everyday things. Visit the library to see what sort of books it carries. See how much variety there is among local restaurants, prices on their menus, and the hours they stay open. Find out whether or not stores stay open on Sunday.

If you're actively religious, check your choice of the local houses of worship there, to see which you'll be comfortable with. Attend both a service and a church function, to find out how you might relate to that congregation. Take with you a grocery receipt from home, so you can compare prices while you're away. You'll get a cook's-eye look (instead of a cockeyed one) at the nitty-grittiest cost of living in those prospective communities.

Patience Pays Off

After you've done your research and your on-site visits, you probably will have quite a good idea of where you'd like to live in retirement. One or another place will particularly appeal to you, for either tangible or intangible reasons—or both. Picking a city or town where you'd like to live is half the battle in choosing a retirement home.

There's *another* half, though: picking a specific house. You need to be absolutely certain you're getting value for your money. (In our next chapter, we'll have advice on choosing a retirement *community*. For now, we'll assume that you'll be living independently, outside of a *planned* development.) The best way to avoid a bad housing buy is not to buy at all! Instead, *rent* a house—or an apartment. At least, that's how you should dip your toe into any local housing market.

There are a few advantages to this approach. First, you preserve your capital: In case you need money for an emergency, you have it handy. (After you put your money into a house, it may not be easy to get it out, via either a sale *or* a loan.)

Second, no matter *how* much research you do, there's *no* way to really know a local housing market without living there for a time. If you *rent* for a while, you'll see what your expenses are, and know specifically where you want to live. You'll be able to make a savvier choice on the rent-versus-buy issue.

Shelter Plus Upside

Are there advantages to buying? Certainly. If you buy for all-cash, or with a fixed-rate mortgage, you lock in the purchase price. You won't have to worry about rents increasing, over ten or twenty years or longer. You may enjoy long-term appreciation, as well.

There also may be tax advantages to buying rather than renting. When you sell a house and move to a new area in retirement, a large capital gain may be triggered. By buying a retirement home, you may be able to defer the tax, or at least reduce it.

(Note, however, that homeowners over age 55 are entitled to a one-time tax exclusion of $125,000 worth of capital gains on the sale of a principal residence. Only if you have a larger gain will you need to pay tax. Thus, not every retiree will have to buy a retirement home in order to trim taxes on capital gains.)

In addition, buying a house may provide ongoing tax advantages. Property taxes and mortgage interest are deductible, whereas rent is not. Again, note that many people are in a lower tax bracket after retirement. The lower your tax bracket, the less valuable your tax deductions, including those for property taxes and mortgage interest.

So, buying a retirement home may offer tax benefits *and* the chance for appreciation. On the other hand, owning a house may mean more expense *and* responsibilities. Thus, many retirees prefer condo apartments, where one condo fee covers many of those expenses and responsibilities. Some housing developments, too, allow homeowners to pay a fee to cover upkeep of common areas.

Weigh all the alternatives before deciding to buy. Often, you'll be able to rent a house or condo with an *option* to buy. Even if you *need* to buy a house, to maintain tax deferral, you'll have two years to make a decision, after the sale of your prior residence.

The more you shop around, the more likely you'll avoid overpaying for a house, or buying a lemon. Pay a price that's comparable to real-estate transactions you see reported in the local newspaper, or to the price you hear about from friends and acquaintances. Hire an independent inspector to evaluate *any* house before you buy. If you're considering a condo project or a housing development, get financial statements and show them to a CPA of your choosing: You don't want to buy into a distressed project.

In short, don't rush into buying a retirement home. Move along carefully, consulting regularly with relatives and acquaintances you trust. It's much easier to make a mistake than to unmake one!

When You Move, Move

Some retirees like the idea of "doubling up." And why not? It's a great deal, if you can afford it. Half the year, you're in New York (for example), enjoying all the summertime cultural facilities. Then, when the weather turns cold, "snowbirds" head for Florida, where the livin' is easier.

But dual residency *can* be a tax trap: You don't want to pay *two* income taxes and *two* estate taxes. Therefore, take all steps necessary to establish what the lawyers call *domicile*, preferably in the lower-tax state.

How can you establish a domicile in, say, Florida rather than New York?

• Move your bank accounts.
• Change your auto registration.
• Change your driver's license.
• Establish relationships with a doctor, lawyer, accountant, and broker.
• Join a house of worship.
• Change your voter's registration.
• Pay your federal income tax from your Florida address.
• Change your address on all legal documents, including your passport.
• Write a new will.
• Perhaps most important, be sure you spend more time in Florida than in New York each year.

SUMMING UP

• When you choose a retirement home, you should do so methodically rather than emotionally.
• Start by choosing an area where you'd like to live in retirement—because of family relationships, low costs, or recreational opportunities—or some combination.
• Narrow your choice to specific communities by subscribing to local newspapers, making site visits, and talking to local residents.

• After you have selected a city or town, rent there *before* considering buying a house, so you won't tie up your capital.

• You may decide to buy, rather than rent, in order to prolong a tax deferral or to participate in housing appreciation.

• If you decide to buy, check carefully into the physical and fiscal condition of the development before making a commitment.

• After you make a retirement move to a low-tax state, take all steps necessary to sever your relationship with your old, high-tax state.

21

Community Sense

Pick a Retirement Development Without Getting Your Pocket Picked

As America has aged and the over-sixty-five population has expanded, the real-estate industry has been quick to address this growing market. Many *retirement communities* have been created, designed specifically to serve senior citizens. The variety is enormous, in amenities as well as in financial arrangements. Therefore, don't make a commitment to a retirement community until you've evaluated several alternatives.

When you first retire, relatively young and in reasonably good health, you'll probably want a community where you can live independently—in a house or an apartment. In a retirement community, you'll likely find yourself surrounded with neighbors who have common interests. Young married couples with children probably won't be around. Also, such a setting may offer you certain services that you wouldn't find in a standard apartment building or housing development. Start your search for the ideal community by looking at the

147

criteria mentioned previously: You'll want to live in a desirable location, in a physically sound home, among elements in solid financial condition.

But there are *other* factors you should look for in a retirement community. Perhaps most of all, you'll want to know about the people who live there. A "community" should be more than just a housing project with a lot of old residents. It should be the place where you look forward to spending much of your later life. You should if possible have close friends there, people you like to be around. On the down side, if you find yourself in a community with people you *don't* like, or with whom you have little in common, your retirement likely will not be very pleasant.

So visit a retirement community before making it your permanent residence (you may be able to rent there for a while). Look at the people already living there. If you and your spouse are in your early sixties, eager to play tennis and golf, you're not likely to be happy in a community where everyone else seems much older and generally infirm. On the other hand, you may be encouraged if you visit a community where everybody is zipping by on roller skates and bikes.

Be honest with yourself. If you feel most comfortable living among people of a certain ethnic or religious background, *make sure* that's who you'll find there.

Other features of a retirement community may influence your decision. You'll probably want good security, for example. And activities are important, too: Whether your passion is fishing or bridge or amateur theater, you'll want to be sure you can pursue it. (The same goes for your spouse.) You also may appreciate a retirement community that offers architecture that's pleasing to the eye, in a beautiful natural setting.

Cream of the Crop

In 1993, *New Choices* magazine picked the twenty top retirement communities in the United States, all of which accept residents without regard to race or religion but which have a minimum age requirement—generally around age fifty-five:

- Bayview Village at Port Ludlow, Washington; 800-872-1323.
- Bradford Village, Santee, South Carolina; 800-331-1457.

- The Fairways at Leisure World, Silver Spring, Maryland; 301-598-2100.
- Green Valley, in Green Valley, Arizona; 602-625-7575.
- The Harbours at Aberdeen Golf & Country Club, Boynton Beach, Florida; 800-749-9697.
- Heritage Village, Southbury, Connecticut; 203-264-7570.
- The Lakes at Gig Harbor, in Gig Harbor, Washington; 800-822-8875.
- Leisure Village Ocean Hills, Oceanside, California; 619-758-7080.
- The Maples at Old Country Road, Wenham, Massachusetts; 508-468-4950.
- Oakmont, Santa Rosa, California; 707-539-1530.
- Sonata Bay Club, Bayville, New Jersey; 800-952-9521.
- Sun City, Bermuda Dunes, California; 800-533-5932.
- Sun City, Las Vegas, Nevada; 800-843-4848.
- Sun City Center, in Sun City Center, Florida; 800-237-8200.
- Sun Lakes Country Club, Banning, California; 800-368-8887.
- Sun Lakes Country Clubs, Sun Lakes, Arizona; 800-321-8643.
- Swansgate, Greenville, South Carolina; 803-233-1107.
- The Villages Golf and Country Club, San Jose, California; 408-274-4400.
- Westbrook Village, Peoria, Arizona; 800-892-2838.
- Woodlake Village, Myrtle Beach, South Carolina; 800-651-0020.

Some of the standout communities are intimate: The Maples has only fifty-five co-op units in eight buildings, set on eight acres. At the other end of the spectrum, Green Valley has a mix of 10,000 housing units—apartments, attached clusters, townhouses, single-family houses—spread over 5,000 acres.

Amenities vary, too. The Villages Golf and Country Club, for example, has a 550-acre nature preserve, teeming with red foxes and wild turkeys. Florida's Sun City Center offers 126 holes of golf (seven eighteen-hole courses). The Fairways at Leisure World, near Washington, D.C., is frequently visited by current and former federal officials, while Heritage Village offers lectures by professors from three nearby universities. Depending on your interests, you may find your ideal retirement home in one of these places, or in some other community.

To find out which community is best for *you*, firsthand visits are necessary. Many communities offer short-term or seasonal rentals in unsold units. Or, you may be able to house-sit for a resident who's on vacation.

Only by living in a community will you learn what it's *really* like. Therefore, you're probably better off *not* moving into a startup retirement community. Wait until it's up and running, so you can see what you'd be getting into.

Money Matters

Although some of the retirement communities on the list offer rental apartments, most consist mainly of houses and condos for sale. Prices are literally all over the lot. Bradford Village is the least-expensive community on the list, with houses starting as low as $78,500, according to *New Choices*, while The Lakes at Gig Harbor includes only manufactured homes, selling in the $83,000–$105,000 range.

On the other hand, three of the California communities (Oakmont, The Villages, Leisure Village Ocean Hills) have *no* homes selling for *less* than $209,000, and going as high as $389,000 at Oakmont. Green Valley is so huge that it has houses in *all* price categories, ranging as high as $500,000.

If you're going to buy a house or condo in a retirement community, exercise normal real-estate prudence. Shop around so you don't overpay. And find out if there's an active resale market, so you'll be able to get your money out if you decide to move.

In Good Hands

Retirement communities such as those mentioned above appeal chiefly to younger, more-active retirees. But there's another type of retirement community, one aimed at older people, that is growing in popularity. With these developments—often known as *continuing care communities*—you may have to pay a huge up-front fee, so you need to be extremely cautious.

Take the case of William and Marilou M., who built a chain of pastry shops in Tulsa. In the 1970s, they took early retirement, sold their business, and purchased a house in Lake Placid, Florida. Twenty years later, at ages eighty and seventy-five, they sold their house, taking a $45,000 loss in a weak real-estate market. Then they paid a nonrefundable $276,000 "entrance fee" to live in a three-bedroom apartment. Plus, they agreed to pay an additional $3,000 per month as an ongoing fee.

What was the attraction? The apartment complex offers many amenities, from golf to local transportation. They're entitled to one meal per day in the main dining room. Perhaps most important, if either William or Marilou (or both) would have to go into a nursing home, there is one on the grounds—at no extra cost. And the other spouse may stay in their apartment. Thus, they're effectively buying catastrophic insurance as well as a place to live.

Price Points

Over 400,000 Americans lived in about 1,000 such continuing-care communities in 1993, up from 170,000 in 1983. Also known as *life-care communities*, they're especially attractive to retirees seventy-five and older, who may have concerns about their health. Residents may be in excellent health, as William and Marilou were. If residents are not quite as healthy, they may be able to live independently if they have *some* personal care, which is what these facilities provide. Or they may decline to the point where they need to live in a nursing home. (Some "assisted living facilities" are heavier on the care, lighter on the recreational facilities for active retirees.)

Today, with nursing-home costs anywhere from $30,000 to $100,000 per year, a long-term stay can impoverish a family and beggar the spouse who continues to live at home. Thus, continuing-care communities have enormous appeal.

They often have enormous costs, too. Entrance fees may be less than $100,000 but may reach $400,000. A complex with a low entrance fee may compensate with a high monthly fee, ranging up to $3,500 per person ($7,000 per couple). Fees may be based on age and health: Younger people may pay a higher entrance fee, while healthy people may have a lower monthly bill.

If the entrance fee is nonrefundable, a portion (usually 20 percent to 30 percent) may be tax-deductible as a prepayment of future health care. The healthier you are, and the more likely you are to outlive your life expectancy, the more attractive a nonrefundable entrance fee will be. They're based on age, so chances are that you'll get more housing for your money. However, paying an entrance fee *isn't* the same as buying a house. If you're deferring a gain from selling a principal residence, paying an entrance fee will trigger the tax, rather than maintain the deferral.

Money-Back Guarantees

Newer communities, particularly those established since 1985, offer partial refunds on entrance fees. Anywhere from 75 percent to 90 percent of the entrance fee will be returned, should you decide to move. Upon your death (or the death of your surviving spouse), the refund will go to your heirs. Thus, you're not locked into one community, and you will leave a larger inheritance.

There's a down side to refundable fees, though. They're often 10 percent to 25 percent higher than nonrefundable fees at comparable facilities. Also, there's a tax headache.

The IRS treats the refundable portion of the fee as a loan, and taxes you on the "interest" you don't actually receive. Say you pay a $200,000 entrance fee that's 90 percent refundable. That would be considered a $180,000 loan from you to the retirement community. Even though the community isn't paying you interest, the IRS will "impute" interest to you. At a 5 percent rate, for example, you'd have $9,000 in "phantom income" per year, on which you'd owe income tax.

So get all the facts before you spend $100,000, $200,000, or more on a retirement-community entrance fee. Read over the contract thoroughly. Consult with your lawyer *and* your CPA. Not only do you want to know all the financial and tax ramifications, but also, you want to know that the project is fiscally sound, before putting up your life's savings. If the complex goes under, you may find yourself without *any* money or *any* services, just when they're sorely needed.

Club Dues

Not all continuing-care communities demand huge up-front fees. Some are membership clubs: You buy a membership, which either you or your estate can sell.

This approach has risks. What happens if your membership brings a lower resale price, or if it can't be sold at all? Also, memberships generally cost 25 percent to 50 percent more than a nonrefundable entrance fee.

In other developments, apartments are sold as cooperatives or condos. Here, capital-gains deferral can be maintained. However, prices may be high, and owners bear resale risk. Also, if you've already taken the $125,000 capital-gains exclusion for home sellers over age fifty-five, the capital-gains deferral won't be meaningful.

Again, check carefully into the terms of the contract, and also into the financial health of the project, before making any major decisions. You might prefer a community with no entrance fees at all, paying monthly fees that depend on the level of services you require, and protecting yourself against long nursing-home stays by buying long-term care insurance (see Chapter 17).

Crunch the Numbers

Be wary of new developments, especially if the developer lacks a track record. For established projects, occupancy rates are crucial. If a community is less than 80 percent occupied and it's more than two years old, that may be a warning sign.

Always ask to see a community's most recent audited financial statement, which should be available from the management upon request. You (or a financial adviser) can check to see if the project is meeting its debt service and operating costs while maintaining sufficient reserves for emergencies. In some developments ski, golf, or tennis facilities are owned by a partnership of homeowners. If that's the case, you can request copies of federally mandated property reports, and other financial documents, to help you judge the project's financial health.

In addition, check the county clerk's office to see if liens have been filed against the property for nonpayment of taxes or secured debt. Also check with the local Better Business Bureau, to ascertain whether complaints have been made against the property.

The American Association of Retired Persons (AARP) has identified six "red flags" that can warn of potential trouble in a retirement community:

1. *Overbuilding.* There may be too many retirement facilities for the local population to support.

2. *Low value.* Seemingly low prices may indicate that the buildings are poorly designed, while services will be subpar.

3. *Overborrowing.* If the developer spent too much money on the project, mainly with borrowed money, the project's revenues might not cover the interest payments.

4. *Insufficient and depleted financial reserves.* Real-estate projects need a "rainy day" fund.

5. *Poor marketing.* Units may have been sold by inexperienced or uninformed sales staff using an inappropriate marketing strategy.

6. *Financial and operational mismanagement.* The owners may be using current income for misguided expansion.

These red flags may overlap. If occupancy is low, revenues will be below projections and the project will not provide the amenities that residents expect. Then, some residents may move out, making the problems even worse. Your best strategy is to look for troubles before you decide to buy, so you can avoid them altogether.

SUMMING UP

- Younger, more-active retirees may prefer to live in a community that offers a wide range of recreational and social opportunities.
- Besides the services that are available, evaluate the people who might be your neighbors, before deciding upon a retirement community.
- Topflight retirement communities come in all price ranges, in all areas of the United States, so shop carefully before buying.
- Retirees in poor health and those over age seventy-five may prefer an assisted-living or continuing-care community offering food, housekeeping, and nursing-home services, if necessary.
- Many of these communities charge a large up-front fee (which may however be nonrefundable), no matter how short your stay as a resident in the complex.
- Other communities have refundable fees, but they're often higher than nonrefundable fees—and they generate tax problems.
- *Don't* make a large initial outlay to get into a retirement community without first learning all the details and comparing the cost to a straight rental plus purchase of a long-term-care insurance policy.
- Be wary of new developments, and those that are less than 80 percent occupied after two years of operation.

22

Avoid Publicity as Well as Probate

Living Trusts Lead to Quiet Asset Transfers

Dr. John D., ninety-one years old, still practices medicine. He's a little hard of hearing, but most of his patients continue to come to him anyway. They all tell him the same sort of thing, and he just nods his head.

This may seem amusing—but some aspects of Dr. John's advancing age aren't so funny. He has misplaced $700,000 worth of bonds, for example. They were registered (rather than bearer) bonds, but it cost a significant amount to get them reissued. In addition, the doctor wasn't keeping track of dividend or interest income, so his income-tax records were a shambles.

Unfortunately, this story is not all that unusual. As America ages, more of us will fall prey to Alzheimer's disease and other forms of senility. You may not want to admit it, but the time may come when you're elderly, retired, the possessor of extensive assets you've accu-mulated all your life—and unable to exercise rational control over those assets.

In such circumstances, both your wealth and your family's wealth may be at risk. Who'll sign your Social Security or pension checks? Who'll sell your securities or real estate? Who'll handle all the finan-cial arrangements necessary to settle you into a nursing home?

Filling the Void

Unless the right steps are taken, *nobody* can do *anything* with an incompetent's assets. Someone—usually a spouse or a grown child—must apply to a court, in order to be named guardian. Only after the spending of a couple of thousand dollars on lawyer's fees and court costs (and after waiting until the court can schedule a hearing) can the guardian take over.

There's an even darker side to guardianship. As you get older, and perhaps frailer, *anyone* can petition the court to be named your guardian (sometimes called a *conservator*). If this does happen, *you* will get a written notice of a hearing. To object, you'll have to hire a lawyer and try to prove, in court, that you're in fact quite competent, thank you. The prospective guardian might then bring in friends or neighbors, however, to tell tales of seeing you walking around in your underwear, muttering to yourself—and so on.

What if you lose? You become a ward of the person who brought the petition! Indeed, in some jurisdictions you won't be able to do *anything* without the permission of your guardian.

In some states, it's relatively easy to become a guardian, even if the prospective ward protests. The subject's presence at the hearing may not even be required; medical proof of incompetence may not be at all necessary. To top it all off, a typical guardianship hearing lasts less than fifteen minutes—hardly enough time to convincingly demon-strate your lucidity, given your upset condition. And then afterward, it's extremely difficult to get a guardian removed.

On paper, guardians are required to operate under the supervision of a court. They're supposed to notify the court about what they're doing, and get permission for major expenditures. However, many probate courts (they're the ones that usually handle guardianships) have huge workloads, so judges often pay little attention to what guardians are doing. Therefore, if you receive a notice of a guardi-anship hearing, call a lawyer immediately. Hire one with some decent amount of experience in guardianship hearings. And ask your doctor or your accountant for references, if necessary.

Moreover, you should act *now*, while you're still competent, to avert future disaster. Even if you're a long way from your declining years, your *parents* may have assets you'd like to protect, for your sake as well as theirs. Their life's savings can be squandered, or lost to unscrupulous predators, if they reach the point where they no longer can manage their own affairs.

Put Your Trust in Living Trusts

Perhaps the best way to avoid such a disaster personally is to set up a trust while you're still in control of your faculties. Trusts aren't just for the Rockefellers and the DuPonts. If you have accumulated *any* meaningful wealth, trusts can help you to leave your property to your family with a minimum of trouble and expense.

A *trust* is a legal fiction created to own property. Virtually any attorney can set up a trust for you, but you should work with one who's experienced in this area, and preferably a member of the American College of Trust and Estate Counsel. For simple trusts, start-up costs should be relatively low—generally under $1,000.

A trust you create while you're still alive is called a *living trust*. One popular type is the *revocable* trust, which you can annul whenever you'd like. You, the creator of the trust, can act as the trustee who manages the trust funds, as well as the beneficiary who receives distributions from the trust. Therefore, you can transfer assets into a *revocable living trust*, keep control, and enjoy the income. You can sell assets from your trust, if you wish, and add new ones.

You'll probably want to transfer only a few assets into the trust at first, to hold down the cost and the paperwork. When you reach fifty-five or sixty (the age when health problems may become noticeable), selected assets can be transferred. The assets you transfer to the trust should be ones you'd want help in managing in case of incompetency, and ones that will be subject to probate after your death. Jointly owned property *shouldn't* go into a living trust.

Successor Stories

After you transfer assets into a trust, those assets no longer are owned by you, personally. If you become incapacitated, your chosen *successor trustee* can take control of those assets. Then there's continuity of management, so you won't have to worry about a family business, or investment property, or securities portfolio, being tied up in red tape.

With a living trust in place, you won't have to fear that a court will appoint a guardian or conservator in the event of disability or incompetence; control can be transferred in private, without any publicity. You can avoid the spectacle that surrounded Groucho Marx after he became incompetent and his family fought over his property.

There are two ways to plan for a change of control in case you do become incompetent: You can name your eventual successor as *cotrustee*, right from the beginning, or you can name what we've already identified as a successor trustee, to take over when necessary. Most people prefer to use a successor trustee. They thus control the trust assets without having to share power.

However, this all means that a specific action is necessary in order to change trustees. Most of the time, an incompetent person won't become obviously deranged overnight. Instead, from time to time he or she will begin to act irrationally. Who's to say where incompetence begins? Sometimes incompetence has to be certified by the family doctor, and at other times yet another doctor has to concur.

If you have absolute confidence in a spouse or grown child, you can name him or her as cotrustee and smooth the transition, because no trigger event is necessary. This strategy is especially attractive to professionals, and to others who won't want a written judgment that they're incapable.

The same issues cover your retirement plan (including an IRA or a Keogh), which may be your greatest asset. Generally, retirement plans must be held in a separate trust, not in your revocable living trust. Again, you can name a younger person as a cotrustee or a successor trustee, depending on whether you're willing to relinquish total control while you're still capable.

Negate Probate

A living trust also will help your family avoid probate after your death. Your successor trustee can quickly distribute trust assets according to your wishes.

On the other hand, assets you own personally *have* to go through probate, with few exceptions (jointly owned property, insurance policies, and pension plans with beneficiaries you've named). Probate can cost as much as 7 percent of your estate, and the lawyers get paid first, before anything goes to your family members. In some states, probate can take as long as two years, effectively tying up your assets. What's more, the probate process is on the public record. Thus, if you want to keep your affairs private, use a living trust.

With a living trust, you can accomplish most of your wealth-transfer goals, using a will only for those few assets not in the trust. In fact, a living trust is better than a will if you own property in more than one state, because your heirs won't have to go through probate in each state. A trust is easier to modify than a will if you relocate, or if your circumstances change significantly.

There are disadvantages, though. Here are two: Revocable living trusts are *not* tax shelters—while you're alive, the trust's income will flow through to your personal tax return. Also upon your death, trust assets *will* be included in your taxable estate.

If you want tax savings, you'll have to use another type of living trust: an *irrevocable living trust*. As the name suggests, such trusts remove assets from your control, with no turning back. However, you *can* name a reliable family member, friend, or financial adviser as trustee, and you *can* establish guidelines for the use of trust funds.

Whichever type of living trust you choose, you must take care to follow up. Assets must be retitled—from *your* name to the name of the trust. Otherwise, you and your family might not enjoy the benefits of protection, privacy, and probate avoidance.

SUMMING UP

- Some people will become incompetent as they grow older, jeopardizing their assets.
- You can protect your assets by putting them into a trust.
- A trust you set up while you're alive is called a *living trust.*
- A *revocable living trust,* which can be annulled, is useful for transferring assets without a guardianship hearing and for avoiding probate after your death.
- To provide tax shelter, a living trust *must* be irrevocable, which means you give up control over the trust assets.
- Assets must be retitled to the trust, if you are to receive full benefits from it.

23

Power Plays

Create an Impenetrable Paper
Barrier Against Incompetency

Living trusts provide excellent protection against incompetency, yet they have their shortcomings. For example, you won't be able to re-title all of your assets to trust ownership, and some assets you won't want to hold in trust. Therefore, a living trust can be supplemented by a *power of attorney*, a legal document that permits another party to act on your behalf. This document can cover assets *not* held in trust—such as automobiles or a checking account.

Even if you're not ready to title your assets to a living trust, a power of attorney can be invaluable. Dan M., for example, had a stroke while he was in his fifties, with no prior warning signals. He thereafter couldn't sign his name, a handicap which might have had serious financial consequences. Fortunately, however, he had executed a power of attorney—thus his son could sign checks and pay for private-duty nursing.

People with assets to protect should assign a power of attorney. In doing so, you can even name more than one party, specifying whether they can act singly or must act in concert. For example, you might nominate both of your children as *attorneys-in-fact*, stating that they must be in agreement in order to act on your behalf. Naturally, any person or persons you name must be from among those you trust fully. This usually means at least one close—and younger—family member.

General powers of attorney, though, terminate when the person whose assets are at stake (the *principal*) becomes incompetent. Therefore, you should use a *durable* power of attorney, a variation recognized by all fifty states. Such powers will contain language along the lines of, "This power of attorney shall not be terminated by the principal's disability or incompetence." You can change or cancel a power of attorney at any time. (At your death, a durable power will automatically be cancelled.)

If you wish, you can assign different attorneys-in-fact responsibilities to different people. You may name your spouse to make your housing decisions, for example, and your son to manage all your financial affairs.

A Touch of Spring

Understandably, you may not want to give power over your assets to a family member while you're still in command of your faculties. Fortunately, *springing* powers of attorney are recognized in about twenty states, including California and New York. These powers won't "spring" (become effective) until specified events take place, such as incompetency—certified by a doctor—or entry into a nursing home.

What if your state doesn't recognize springing powers? You often can achieve the same result with a durable power accompanied by a letter stating that the springing power will go into effect *if* certain events take place. An attorney should hold both documents until they're needed.

When you're ready to execute a power of attorney, retain a lawyer who's experienced in *estate planning*. Such a lawyer likely will spell out the powers that the agreement conveys: managing property, making gifts, establishing trusts, filing tax returns, making retirement-plan elections, and so on. You might want to restrict possible gift recipients (e.g., to family members) and limit such gifts to the $10,000 annual gift-tax exemption.

Some financial institutions require the use of their own power-of-attorney forms. Check with your banks, brokers, and such, after a power of attorney has been drawn up. Send a copy to *each* institution, asking if there's any problem with the form.

Just because you execute a durable power of attorney, *don't* ignore the need for a living trust also. Some banks and brokerage firms that balk at accepting powers of attorney won't have any problems dealing with a successor trustee. Revocable living trusts also may be better than powers of attorney for people with extensive assets spread over more than one state.

Why not just give assets to your children, or put them in a joint account? Joint ownership works, in some circumstances—but you need to be careful about gift taxes. Also, holding assets in joint ownership may rob you of flexibility when it comes to estate planning, because the property automatically passes to the other owner at your death! Gifts are fine, as part of an estate plan, but you probably need a power of attorney, too.

Once Is Not Enough

After you execute a power of attorney, you should update it every year or two, a move which will increase the likelihood that your power will be honored. Otherwise, a challenger with an adverse interest may claim that it's invalid. Each time it's renewed, have *several* original powers of attorney executed and notarized, because some institutions will insist upon keeping one of these in their files.

Expect to pay a lawyer $1,000–$1,500 to create a power of attorney in the first place; renewing it shouldn't cost more than a token fee. To hold down the costs, make your decisions *before* you consult with a lawyer. If you tell the attorney which assets you want managed, and what specific instructions you'd like to include, you'll reduce appreciably the hours for which you'll be billed.

Parent Protection

Even if you think you're years away from incompetency, you may have to worry about your parents—or your spouse's parents. If either set loses their ability to manage their affairs, assets could be misplaced or stolen. Many scam artists prey on the elderly, and you could wind up not only without an inheritance, but also supporting your elderly parents or in-laws.

To help protect your entire family, go over your parents' financial affairs. Check to see that they have Medicare supplement insurance, and that the premiums are paid regularly. (Have the bills sent to you, if necessary.) Find out how many bank accounts and safe-deposit vaults your parents have.

Have Social Security and pension checks deposited directly into your parents' bank account by means of electronic transfer. Many banks will permit senior citizens to sign a card authorizing it to let another relative know of any unusual account activity. If large checks are drawn against the account, you'll be informed, so you can see if they've been legitimately generated.

Final Thoughts

A durable power of attorney—which covers property—may not be enough. Today, a long-lasting illness may strain your family and drain your assets. You may want to draft a *medical* or *health-care* power of attorney, enabling someone else to make decisions when you no longer can. Similarly, you may want to draw up a living will. Living wills *don't* replace traditional wills, but *do* state the circumstances in which you'd want doctors to withhold or withdraw life-support systems.

Even if you've taken care of all the paperwork—trusts, powers of attorney, living will—you still haven't finished your incompetency planning. You need to explain your plan to your family, especially your spouse and children, or to a long-term companion for whom you wish to provide. Suppose you have three children and you're naming one as a successor trustee. You need to reassure the other two that the one who'll be trustee will have a fiduciary responsibility to watch out for their interests as well.

Planning for incompetency isn't pleasant to think about, but it's an absolute necessity. With luck, after you've taken all the essential steps, you'll live to see triple figures (in more than your checkbook), and still be in full command of your faculties. If so, this will be one plan you'll be *glad* turned out to be a waste of time.

SUMMING UP

- *Revocable* living trusts *don't* provide total asset protection, because it's unlikely you'll transfer all of your assets into a trust.
- Revocable living trusts *should* be supplemented by a power of

attorney that names trusted friends or relatives to handle your finances if necessary.

• *Durable* powers of attorney *will* remain in effect, even if you become incompetent.

• If you *don't* want to have a power of attorney in effect while you're still capable, you may be able to execute a *springing* power that will take effect in certain circumstances.

• Not only should you take steps to guard against *your* incapacity, but also you should make an effort to monitor your *parents'* affairs, to spot signs that they need help with their finances.

• A *medical* power of attorney and a *living* will can make it easier for your family to curtail futile life-support efforts.

Part VII

Courting Disaster

24

An Umbrella Can Let You Smile

Taking Liability Insurance to Excess

Whether or not you have any assets, you're a potential target for financial disaster. If your dog takes a nip at a neighbor's knee, or your teenage son bends a fender in the mall parking lot, you can expect to see a lot of your lawyer in the next few years. Americans love to file lawsuits, plenty of lawyers are willing to work for contingency fees, and juries seem to believe that life begins at seven figures.

In 1993, the *New York Times* published this list of common liability insurance claims paid by Aetna Life and Casualty:

	Percentage of All Claims
Slips and falls	34
Pet bites	19
Other injuries	13
Damage to others' property	13
Violence and altercations	10

Libel and slander	3
Accidental shooting	2
Swimming-pool accidents	1

You need to protect your assets in case any of these events happens on your property, or if a car you own is in an auto accident. Therefore, as mentioned previously, your homeowners and auto insurance both should include *liability coverage*.

Basic coverage for auto insurance is $100,000 worth of liability per person; $300,000 per accident. If you have substantial assets to protect, you might want to increase coverage to $200,000 and $500,000, respectively.

Standard homeowners insurance policies have a $100,000 limit for liability coverage, and that's what most people buy. However, for an extra $15–$25 per year, you can increase coverage to $300,000; for an extra $25–$50, you can increase liability from $100,000 to $500,000. If you have substantial assets, increasing liability insurance to $300,000 or $500,000 is well worth the modest extra cost.

Thanks a Million

Even though the average homeowner's liability claim is around $14,000, State Farm reports, million-dollar judgments have been awarded in cases where someone is severely injured, so $300,000 (or $500,000) worth of auto or homeowners liability coverage may not be enough. If you have $500,000 worth of coverage and lose a $1 million judgment, the extra $500,000 may have to come out of your savings, your pension plan, your house, and other personal assets.

People with assets to lose (or the prospect of sizable future earnings) should protect them with excess-liability insurance, commonly known as *umbrella coverage*. This type of policy kicks in after your *other* liability insurance reaches its limits.

Say that Bob B., a rising young executive, asks his boss over for dinner. His boss's wife becomes acutely ill from the meal, and has to be rushed to the hospital. Not only does she have a long, painful, and costly convalescence, but Bob's boss has to cancel a business trip, and winds up losing a key account. Bob is sued for all this, and the jury finds him at fault to the tune of $1.2 million.

Bob's homeowners policy will provide coverage up to $500,000.

Most fortunately, he is also covered by an umbrella policy—which provides the other $700,000, *plus* his legal costs.

Shelter From the Storm

In addition to increasing your liability coverage, an umbrella policy may expand it. For example, your homeowners policy might *not* cover you for libel or slander claims, but an umbrella policy will. Also, as we've seen in Bob's case, umbrella policies can pay for legal fees if you're sued for an amount in excess of the limits stated in your basic policies. However, some umbrella policies include legal-defense fees as part of their coverage. If you're buying a $1 million umbrella, for instance, look for a policy that covers $1 million worth of excess liability plus legal fees.

Umbrella coverage is surprisingly affordable—mainly because the insurer will be at risk only after your other coverage is used up. In most areas, you can buy $1 million worth of excess-liability insurance for less than $200 per year. If you want to buy instead $2 million worth of coverage, or $3 million, or more, the extra coverage is even less expensive, comparatively speaking, as it increases.

It pays to shop for umbrellas. Some insurers will issue umbrella policies *only* if you buy homeowners and auto insurance from them, too. Other companies will give you a better deal if you buy multiple policies (homeowners or auto insurance, or both, plus an umbrella).

Reaching Out

Not only will premiums vary from insurer to insurer, but coverage may be different, too. Some umbrella policies, for example, have very low limits for uninsured-motorist coverage (a $25,000 ceiling, for example).

Besides libel- and slander protection, an umbrella policy should cover claims of mental anguish, defamation of character, and invasion of privacy. They should cover you for liability associated with your residences, autos, watercraft, and recreational vehicles. If you travel abroad, be sure your umbrella gives you international protection— some policies are limited to the United States and Canada. If a policy *doesn't* have coverage you specifically want, ask for an amendment that will either add it or override the exclusion.

Unfortunately, umbrellas won't keep all the raindrops from falling on your head. They cover *personal*, rather than business or professional, liability. Thus, you may need even *more* liability coverage than you suspect you do, depending on how you earn your living.

SUMMING UP

• In recent years, million-dollar-plus judgments have become common in United States courts—especially in personal-injury cases.

• People with substantial assets are frequent targets of personal-injury suits.

• Ordinarily, homeowners' and auto insurance provide liability coverage, but seldom more than $300,000 or $500,000 worth.

• You can buy excess-liability insurance in order to provide coverage for larger amounts.

• Umbrella insurance, as it's known, generally starts at $1 million worth of coverage.

• The cost of excess-liability insurance probably will be only a few hundred dollars per year.

• Shop carefully for umbrella policies, paying special attention to what's covered and what's excluded.

• Even if you buy umbrella insurance, you *also* may need to carry business or professional (such as malpractice) liability insurance.

25

Sharing the Wealth

Joint Ownership Can Be a Wrenching Experience

If you're married, you probably own your home jointly. Officially, title is held in *joint tenancy* or *joint ownership with right of survivorship*. This may be comforting for you and your spouse—but in fact it might not be the best choice.

Technically, if you and your spouse or significant other are joint owners, you each own 100 percent of the property. When one dies, there is only one 100 percent owner left. And that's it. Nothing you state in either a will or a trust can override joint ownership.

Joint ownership has its virtues. At the death of the first spouse, transfer is fast and cheap: No probate, no lawyers, little paperwork. No taxes will be owed. If you have a simple family situation with a small estate, obviously joint ownership can make sense.

But (alas!) life isn't always simple. Suppose, for example, that you are divorced and remarried. You live with your second (or other succeeding) spouse in a house valued at $200,000. (In some parts of

171

California and the Northeast, you may very well live in a $400,000 house.)

If you die first, a jointly owned house goes entirely to your spouse—all $200,000 or $300,000 or $400,000 worth, or whatever. Any children you have, by any previous marriage, won't get any of that house—which may well have been your largest asset. Your spouse, then, is free to leave that house to his or her children, or indeed anyone else he or she chooses.

Suppose you own a vacation house, or investment real estate. If that's jointly owned, the same problems can arise. In fact, *anything* that's jointly owned, such as mutual-fund shares or a brokerage account, can lead to this trap.

Or, suppose you jointly own assets with someone who is not a relative, by blood or marriage. If you die first, those assets will automatically pass to your co-owner. If you want to make some other disposition, you're out of luck.

Out of Control

As you can see, joint ownership means both a loss of control and a lack of flexibility. This is a particular handicap if your estate is large enough to make estate taxes a concern.

Let's say, for example, that you and your spouse (a first marriage with children) have a total of $1.2 million in assets. You divide the assets equally, through spousal gifts, so that each spouse owns $500,000 worth, plus a $200,000 house in joint ownership. At the death of whichever spouse dies first, $500,000 is to pass to your children. Because of the $600,000 federal estate-tax exemption, *no* estate tax would be due.

The surviving spouse, though, now has $500,000 plus a $200,000 house. If he or she dies the next day, with a $700,000 estate, the children will owe $37,000 to the IRS. That's $37,000 that, with better planning, could have been in their pockets.

The larger the estate you have, and the more property held jointly, the greater the tax problems you're likely to run into. Those problems will be even more difficult to solve if you *also* have a sizable retirement plan with your spouse named as beneficiary—which usually *is* the case.

Tax Tactics

Besides estate-tax problems, joint ownership can cause income-tax problems. Take our example of the $1.2 million couple with the $200,000 house. Suppose the couple's "basis" (cost, for tax purposes) in the house is $50,000. After the death of the first spouse, the survivor sells the house for $200,000—the market price—because he or she intends to move to a small apartment.

Under current tax law, the half belonging to the spouse who died first is "stepped up" to $100,000, but the survivor still has a $25,000 basis for his or her half. Thus, he or she has a $75,000 taxable gain. (It's true that there's a $125,000 exclusion from these gains for homeowners over age fifty-five. But that won't help if either is under fifty-five, or if the jointly owned property is something other than a primary residence.)

By comparison, if the house had been owned entirely by the spouse who died first, and it was left to his or her survivor, the entire house would get a step-up. The widower could sell the house for $200,000 and owe *no* income tax on *any* capital gain.

Double Exposure

Another drawback to joint ownership is exposure to creditors. If *either* co-owner owes money, the *entire* property might be seized, even though the other co-owner doesn't! This drawback applies to any property owned jointly; if joint ownership is between *nonspouses*, the problems may be even *greater*.

Suppose you and your partner jointly own the building in which your garment business is located. If you die first, the building automatically passes to him or her. Your family is frozen out. Worse, half the value of the building is included in *your* taxable estate. Your family could wind up with a huge estate-tax bill for property that's going to your business partner!

Moreover, joint ownership between nonspouses may create a *gift-tax* obligation. (That won't be a problem for spouses, who can make unlimited gifts to each other, tax-free.) Suppose your spouse dies, so you sell the old family residence and buy a retirement home in Florida. Title is held jointly between you and your daughter. Assuming you paid the full $100,000 for the new house, you may have made a

$50,000 gift to your daughter—which would trigger a gift tax. Again, at your death, the house will automatically pass to your daughter, which may mean a smaller inheritance for your son. Plus, your daughter will get only a half step-up in basis (see above), which could lead to income taxes if she sells the house after your death.

Keep It Simple

If joint ownership is so fraught with perils, what can you do about that? First, you can always discuss title to a major asset (real estate, securities) with a local attorney. Different states have different rules—especially when it comes to taxes.

However, you may want to own property in *fee simple* (completely owned by one person) or in *tenancy in common*. In most states, the latter works just like joint ownership, except that each co-owner has the right to leave his or her share of the property to whomever he or she wishes. With either fee-simple or tenancy-in-common ownership, you generally have more control, more flexibility, and a greater opportunity to transfer your wealth in the way you prefer.

SUMMING UP

- Married couples often hold property jointly; joint ownership may be used by nonspouses as well.
- Joint ownership is simple, facilitating transfer of property after the death of one owner.
- Jointly owned property must however pass to the surviving owner, a move which can rob the deceased's estate and heirs of more than flexibility.
- Joint ownership may hamper tax planning, too.
- Unless your family situation is very straightforward, your property should be held in *fee simple* or in *tenancy in common* forms which give you more flexibility and more control.

26

Filing for the Future

Coping When Personal Bankruptcy Is Inevitable

What happens when your income plummets, yet you're stuck with debts from a happier time? When your liabilities exceed your assets, you're *insolvent*. You can try to negotiate with your creditors and consult with a "credit counselor." However, when all else fails, you may be forced to file for *personal bankruptcy*. In the United States, such filings are estimated at around one million per year.

Even though it's increasingly common, *don't* take a personal bankruptcy filing lightly. There are severe financial and psychological consequences. Bankruptcy is your last resort, not your first. But if you *are* forced into bankruptcy, go in with your eyes open. You may be able to retain substantial assets, and the damage to your credit rating may not be as severe as you'd expect.

The federal bankruptcy code contains several "Chapters" under which you can file. Many borrowers prefer Chapter 13, which can be filed as often as necessary. In Chapter 13, you're protected from creditors' demands while a court works out a repayment schedule—typically three to five years.

However, Chapter 13 is limited to debtors with less than $100,000 in *unsecured* debt and up to $350,000 in *secured* debt. (If your debts are larger, you can file under the more complicated Chapter 11, which usually is used by troubled businesses.)

The most common alternative to Chapter 13 is Chapter 7, which can be utilized no more than once every six years. When Chapter 7 is filed, all cosigners *must* make good on their promises to repay loans. Assuming there still are debts outstanding, you have to sell your assets and pay off the remaining creditors—who typically receive partial payments. If a Chapter 13 payment schedule isn't met, one's bankruptcy likely will be converted to Chapter 7.

If permitted by the six-year rule, you might consider (supposing that you're involved) a Chapter 20 filing—7 *plus* 13. First, you file under Chapter 7, and wipe out *most* of your obligations. Some debts (e.g., student loans, child support, alimony, certain taxes) *can't* be discharged in bankruptcy, however—so you can then file a Chapter 13, to stretch out the payments.

Holding On

Fortunately, even a Chapter 7 filing won't strip you completely: Even bankrupts are permitted to keep *some* assets. In fact, depending on your state, you may be able to keep a personal residence, life-insurance policies, annuities, IRAs, and other retirement plans, out of the reach of your creditors.

Some states are much more generous than others. Florida and Texas, for example, are known to be "debtor friendly." In some well-publicized cases, people have moved to these states and purchased large houses or annuities before filing for bankruptcy.

A New York court decision may afford yet *more* protection for bankrupts. Two restaurant owners filed for bankruptcy, owing $120,000 on bank loans they had personally guaranteed. Their main assets were their homes, jointly owned with spouses.

The usual practice in New York had been to sell the bankrupts' half-interests to their spouses at below-market prices. The proceeds could then be applied to the debt repayment. Instead, the bank asked the *bankruptcy trustee* to sell the houses on the open market, and deliver half the proceeds to the bank. However, a federal bankruptcy judge ruled that such a forced sale is unconstitutional, *even though* it's in the bankruptcy law, because it would jeopardize the spouses' property rights.

This decision, if followed by other courts, could provide nationwide protection to couples with jointly held property. As one lawyer has said, "There's no longer a reason to move to Florida in a bankruptcy situation."

In bankruptcy planning, remember the line between *transferring* and *shifting* assets. The former usually means giving your assets to a relative so they'll be protected from creditors. Such transfers, within a year or so of a bankruptcy filing, may well be disregarded by a bankruptcy court.

Shifting assets, on the other hand, means repositioning assets so they'll be safe within your *own* possession. Depending on your state, you might want to buy an annuity, or pay off a home mortgage, with cash in the bank. A certain amount of shifting is permitted—but pigs get slaughtered, as the saying goes.

Separation Pay

Even those who haven't been profligate may find themselves in a bankruptcy situation. Becky S. of Austin, Texas, for example, divorced her husband and wound up with a nasty postnuptial gift: her husband's $1 million tax obligation, payable to the IRS. Becky, who signed the joint tax returns, was on the hook. She offered to pay the IRS $100,000 over five years, but the IRS didn't accept. The only answer was a bankruptcy filing.

The first step to take if you're considering bankruptcy is to ask friends and associates for the name of a local lawyer who specializes in bankruptcy filings. Such a lawyer likely will help you shelter as much as possible *without* incurring the wrath of the bankruptcy court.

Is bankruptcy the end of the world? Not really. Officially, a bankruptcy filing stays on your credit rating for ten years. However, some lenders are willing to work with bankrupts after a year or two. One Purdue University study found that 16 percent of bankrupts get credit in *one* year, and 53 percent within *five* years. The best sources are consumer finance companies, retail stores, and auto dealers. You also might be able to obtain a *secured credit card*, backing up your credit line with a deposit in the issuer's bank.

One common ploy is to keep one credit card current, or to bring it current before the filing. That issuer, then, isn't listed as a creditor, and may not find out about the bankruptcy—so the card can still be used. (The legality of this maneuver is in doubt, to say the least, so we don't recommend it.)

Don't neglect the *personal* side of a bankruptcy filing. All of your family members will simply have to learn to do without even little luxuries—at least for a while. There also can be guilt feelings, blame-spreading, and loss of frienships. If you talk with everyone and explain the situation, however, conflicts usually can be brought out into the open and dealt with. In fact, some areas even have "insolvency support groups," to help with coping. A lawyer specializing in bankruptcy filings should be able to tell you if there's one nearby, and how to contact it.

SUMMING UP

• When your debts exceed your assets, you're *insolvent,* and you may find protection by filing for *bankruptcy.*

• Bankruptcy filings should be a last resort, because they cannot help but have severe repercussions.

• *Chapter 13* of the bankruptcy code is limited to small debtors, who are protected from creditors while they work out a repayment schedule—usually up to five years.

• In a *Chapter 7* filing, you have to sell off assets and repay creditors. They typically receive partial payments.

• Depending on the state of their residency, bankrupts are permitted to keep *some* assets (and rather valuable ones, at that), such as homes, retirement plans, and insurance policies.

• Shifting assets from an unprotected to a protected category before filing for bankruptcy may be acceptable, but transferring assets to friends or family members generally won't protect them.

• Although a bankruptcy stays on your credit rating for ten years, you may be able to get credit sooner—perhaps from a retailer or consumer finance company.

27

Family Value

Shelter Assets, Keep Control With a Family Limited Partnership

You don't have to be an avid newspaper reader to come across stories of outrageous court decisions in the United States in the late twentieth century. Reportedly, a ninety-one-year-old woman was found liable for $950,000 because she loaned money to her grandnephew, who bought a car with that money, wrecked it, and injured a passenger. Also, a man who tried to collect a $50,000 loan to a fellow church member was hit by a $2.7 million jury award. And a retailer lost a $1 million suit to a man who claimed he suffered a heart attack while pulling the starter cord on a lawn mower he bought at the other fellow's store. And so on.

If you have assets that mean anything at all, you're a target. Liability insurance, (described in Chapter 24 of this book) is a *must*, but it still won't cover everything. If you have substantial assets, you may need to take extraordinary measures to protect them. Moreover, people with the latter kind of assets face substantial estate-tax liability (which

we'll cover in Part IX). *Family limited partnerships,* increasingly popular these days, can enable you to reduce your taxable estate as well
as your exposure to creditors, yet retain control of your assets.

All in the Family

A *limited partnership* consists of two classes of partners: *general* (GP)
and *limited* (LP). The general partner makes all management decisions and bears liability for partnership debt. The limited partners,
who cannot participate in management, enjoy the same limited liability as corporate stockholders.

Suppose you form the Williams Family Limited Partnership, con-
sisting of a one percent GP interest and a 99 percent LP interest. A
newly formed corporation that you control (or that's controlled by
you and your spouse) might be the general partner, while the limited-
partnership interests also are held by you (and possibly your spouse).
As long as the corporation acting as general partner has some capital
and is more than a shell, it likely will shield you from liabilities incurred by the partnership.

Next, you retitle assets so that the Williams Family Limited Partnership owns your stocks and mutual funds, investment real-estate,
and other assets. There generally are no tax consequences for this
ownership transfer. Essentially, you're shifting assets from one pocket
to another.

A *family* limited partnership can hold just about anything except
retirement plans and shares of S corporations. However, if you transfer your family home into a limited partnership, you won't be able to
deduct mortgage interest on your personal tax return.

Depending on your situation, you might want more than one family
limited partnership. H&H Bagels of New York, for example, is owned
by the First Toro Family Limited Partnership. Founder Helmer Toro
created other limited partnerships in order to own his bakery and the
H&H trademark. Thus, if one of his assets is threatened, the others
will be insulated.

After the family limited partnership is in place, you can transfer
limited-partnership interests or partial interests. In most cases, the
transfers will be to your children or grandchildren.

With no gift-tax consequences, you can shift up to $10,000 worth
of assets per year, per recipient, to any number of recipients. For a
married couple, the limit is $20,000. In addition, you can give up to

$600,000, or $1.2 million worth of assets in larger chunks—this strategy *would not* trigger a gift tax but *would* reduce or eliminate your estate-tax exemption.

Less Equals More

Thanks to a 1993 IRS ruling on minority discounts, you may make even larger gifts—without owing tax—because the limited-partnership interests given away have *no control* over the assets. Suppose your family limited partnership contains a family corporation valued at $2 million, with 200,000 shares outstanding. Normally, each share would be worth $10, so a married couple could give away 2,000 shares per year ($20,000 worth), gift-tax-free.

However, if you transfer limited-partnership interests with no control over the business, a third-party appraisal might state that each of the transferred shares is worth *less* than $10. Thus, you can give away *more* shares. In many cases, the IRS will concede a 15 percent minority discount. If you have supporting evidence, such as an outside appraisal, you may even be able to sustain a 35 percent or 45 percent discount.

Say you have solid grounds for a 33.3 percent minority discount. Instead of giving away 2,000 shares per recipient per year, as in our example, you could give away 3,000 shares and still stay within the $20,000 gift-tax limit.

Number of shares	3,000
Nominal value per share	$10
Total	$30,000
Minority discount (33.3%)	($10,000)
Net value of gift	$20,000

By the same reasoning, you might transfer $1.8 million worth of shares (90 percent of your $2 million company), use a 33.3 percent discount to knock down the value to $1.2 million, and owe *no* gift tax.

Over time, you might transfer the entire 99 percent limited-partnership interest to your children and grandchildren, *free* of gift tax. And those assets *won't* be included in your taxable estate. Also, even though you give away as much as 99 percent of those assets, you're still in control of the general-partnership interest! You continue to manage the business, the real estate, the securities portfolio, and the like. In fact, you can pay *yourself* a salary for running your family limited partnership.

In addition, when you transfer interests to other family members, you may be able to retain *qualified preferred payments* (income that comes before anyone else gets paid) from partnership income. This will give you additional income which won't increase the tax on your Social Security benefits in retirement, while the value of the qualified preferred payments will reduce the taxable value of the transferred interests.

After your salary and any qualified preferred payments are accounted for, the remaining partnership income flows through to the partners. Your partnership agreement might even state that 99 percent of the income goes to the 99 percent limited-partnership interest. If your children and grandchildren own the limited-partnership interests, *they'll* owe the tax—hopefully in a lower bracket than yours. Yet, though you avoid both the income and estate taxes, you still have control over those assets!

Behind the Barricades

Moreover, your personal wealth is less vulnerable inside a family limited partnership. Or, you might want to set up a family limited partnership before you get married, as an alternative to a prenuptial agreement. You can thereby protect your assets against possible future divorce proceedings.

Suppose a carpenter hurts himself while working on your house, and sues you. He might win a huge judgment against you or your spouse that includes the rights to a share of the partnership. However, if your assets are in a properly structured family limited partnership, he generally won't be able to *seize* them, but rather will have to wait until assets or income are distributed. And, he can't either sell the asset he's been awarded, or borrow against it. Instead, the successful plaintiff likely will obtain a *charging order.*

You, in control of the general partner, can decide not to make distributions to the limited partners, even while you continue to receive a salary. Under the tax code, the limited partners (including your creditor) will have to pay taxes on any taxable income that the partnership generates, even though no cash is distributed. The thought of having to pay tax on phantom income, year after year, can be a powerful tool to force a creditor to settle for less—often pennies on the dollar.

If you already have a trust established, for estate-planning reasons, partnership interests *can* go into that trust, providing yet *another* layer of asset protection.

An Ounce of Prevention

What's the down side? Family limited partnerships are *expensive*. Expect to pay a lawyer around $3,000 up front, for legal drafting fees, plus up to $1,000 per year for ongoing administration, including tax preparation. If your affairs are more complicated, the legal costs may be even higher. Often, though, you can offset some of these costs by cutting back on your liability insurance.

Also, don't forget that the general partner bears partnership *liabilities*. If the assets you transfer into a family limited partnership are not likely to generate liability, you can be an individual general partner, or you and your spouse can be co-general partners. However, if there's either real estate or an operating business in the partnership, you *should* have a corporate general partner, for additional protection.

Another problem is the legal doctrine of *fraudulent conveyance*. To hold up, an asset transfer can't have the purpose of hindering, delaying, or defrauding creditors. You must be financially solvent both before and after the transaction.

If someone has a *claim* against you, it may not help to set up a family limited partnership: A judge most likely will say that you still own the assets. Similarly, establishing a family limited partnership to protect assets against an impending claim may not work. If an action is filed a few months after a partnership is created, the transaction probably won't pass the "smell test."

You need to strike *before* the iron gets hot. If you set up a family limited partnership now, you're not likely to be charged with fraud if a creditor comes after you several years from now. (One court decision has held that it is okay to transfer assets from the reach of *possible* creditors, but not from *probable* creditors.)

Document your reasons for setting up a family limited partnership. Estate-tax reduction will be accepted; creditor avoidance might not be. So get an opinion letter from your tax pro, saying you're setting up your family limited partnership as part of an estate plan.

A family limited partnership is *not* an absolute barrier against claims. For example, in one pertinent case, a creditor was allowed to attach and sell a limited partner's interest in order to satisfy an old judgment. Nor is a family limited partnership a license to steal with impunity, dodging legitimate creditors.

However, if your *personal* wealth is threatened, a family limited partnership *can* enhance your bargaining position. With most of your assets inside a limited partnership, beyond the easy reach of creditors, you'll be a smaller target. A claimant—and the claimant's lawyer—may be more willing to settle on reasonable, but *not* outrageous, terms.

SUMMING UP

- Family limited partnerships enable you to remove assets from your personal possession while retaining control.
- You can transfer assets to a limited partnership, then transfer the limited-partnership interests to family members—probably best your children and grandchildren.
- As long as you control the general-partnership interest, you control *all* the assets in the partnership.
- The assets you transfer to family members will be out of your taxable estate.
- Assets held inside a limited partnership will have substantial creditor protection, which may discourage claimants or lead to favorable settlements.
- You'll have to pay sizable legal fees to set up and maintain a family limited partnership, but it can allow you to enjoy advantages even beyond those discussed herein.
- If you're interested in setting up a limited partnership, you should act before you've been sued or face a likely suit.

28

Trusts, Un-Bustable

Protect Your Assets, Cut Taxes
With Irrevocable Trusts

How do you keep your assets from being consumed by divorce actions, lawsuits, business failures, catastrophic medical bills, or any of the many other means our society provides for others to put their hands into your pocket? Certain asset-protection steps are basic, such as buying liability insurance. Too, if you operate a business, you should use a corporate form to limit your liability. And family limited partnerships can help you reduce estate-tax liability while shielding your wealth.

Moreover, if you're really serious about asset protection, you should consider shifting assets into a trust. Property held in a properly drafted trust will belong to the trust, *not* to you—so it won't be vulnerable to assaults on your *personal* assets.

Revocable living trusts (covered in Chapter 22) are fine for transferring assets in case of your incompetency or after your death, without the time and expense of probate. However, such trusts generally *won't* work for asset protection. Since at any time you can revoke this type of trust and reclaim the assets, they are still considered *yours*.

For more asset protection, you'll need an *irrevocable trust*. As the name suggests, these trusts are for keeps. Once they're set up and funded, *you lose control* of the trust's assets—and you can't revoke the trust, or change its terms. Because the assets are beyond your control, they're generally beyond the reach of creditors, too—at times a most helpful limitation.

But isn't this cutting off your nose to spite your face? Your creditors can't get at your money, but you can't, *either*. Ah, but that's not necessarily the case! Working with an experienced attorney, you may be able to structure a trust that will protect your assets *even* as you continue to benefit. And you probably can set up a trust that will provide for your family—if not directly for yourself.

Hands Off

One possibility is a *charitable remainder trust*. You can get a lifetime income from this trust; appreciated assets you donate can be sold *without* generating a tax on the capital gains. Plus, assets in a bona fide charitable trust likely will be safe from creditors. However: After the death of the "income beneficiaries," *all* the assets will go to charity, rather than to your family.

A more common situation arises when you want to protect your own assets now and provide for your family later. (In some states, retirement funds, cash-value life insurance, or annuities are protected from creditors, so you might want to keep enough money in these vehicles for your own income, and transfer the rest to an irrevocable trust for safety.) You might establish a trust naming your spouse, or a grown child, or a trusted financial adviser as a trustee. Given such, although *you* won't have direct access to your money, friends or relatives can get their hands on it if necessary.

One asset-protection technique is the use of a *lifetime QTIP trust*. In such a trust, your *spouse* is entitled to all the income for life, while *you* can name the ultimate beneficiaries—usually your children. Naturally, the money that comes to your spouse can be used to buy groceries, make mortgage payments, etc.—so this may work well if you have a *strong* marriage.

Another approach is to set up a *spendthrift trust* whereby the trustee has a great deal of leeway in handling funds, and the beneficiaries can't transfer their interests, borrow against them, and the like. In general, the more discretionary the trustee's power, the more creditor-proof the trust will be.

Sprinkle With Care

Family circumstances can complicate any asset-protection plan. Let's say you want to protect your assets, but you're not sure whether you—and your spouse—will have enough to live on if you put most of your property into a trust. You're reluctant to part with assets you might need later.

Even if you decide to give away some assets, to whom would you give them? To the child who already has a family and a promising career, the child who is likely to have lifelong problems, or the child who is still too young to assess? And, once you give away assets, how can you be sure they'll be well conserved?

With a *sprinkle trust*, you can provide for each family member according to his or her needs, while you avoid gift- and estate taxes. You can name a number of trust beneficiaries, including your spouse, your children, and your grandchildren. The trust documents likely will state that the income from the trust assets, and possibly the trust assets themselves, can be used for the support and maintenance of the beneficiaries. *No* beneficiary is entitled to trust income as a matter of right. Instead, distribution of trust income and principal is *entirely* at the discretion of the trustee.

The key to a sprinkle trust, then, is the selection of a good trustee or trustees. You or your spouse *can't* be trustees, and neither can a child or grandchild. You may choose an *in-law*, a *friend*, a *professional adviser*, or an *institutional trustee*. Besides your absolute faith in the trustee's integrity, his or her common sense and knowledge of your family situation are the paramount qualifications.

If you choose cotrustees, try to pick people who are compatible, so that deadlocks can be avoided. Include a provision for selecting a successor trustee in case an original trustee dies or resigns.

Once assets are transferred to the trust, the trustee runs the show. He or she has a broad latitude in distributing trust assets to the beneficiaries. The trustee might, for example, distribute money to your son, say to help with a down payment on a house, or to finance his daughter's private schooling. If your daughter needs special medical care, the trustee can provide the necessary money. If your own fortunes suffer a reversal and you run short of retirement income, the trustee can distribute funds to your spouse.

Thus, if you have the right trustee, a sprinkle trust can give you the best of all such worlds. You protect your assets, you avoid gift- and estate taxes, you provide for your family's future needs, and you have a prudent trustee (*required* to act responsibly) rather than your family members handling the assets.

Tax Bracket Arbitrage

There may also be income-tax advantages to a sprinkle trust. Say you have a $600,000 securities portfolio, throwing off $30,000 a year in taxable income. In your possession, that $30,000 is added to all of your other income, and taxed at 40 percent or more, including state and local taxes. Your trustee, though, may be distributing the funds to lower-bracket recipients. Posit that your daughter, a banker, has a son in college. Money needed for education might be distributed to your grandson, who is in a lower tax bracket than your daughter and son-in-law.

Moreover, the trust itself has a tax bracket, which means that a surplus (income minus distributions) may be taxed at only 15 percent or 28 percent. In 1994, for example, trust income up to $1,500 qualified for a 15 percent rate, a threshold that will increase annually to keep up with inflation.

A sprinkle trust can solve a host of asset-protection, tax, and family problems. However, consider a sprinkle trust *only* if you're certain that your trustee will serve well, *and* if an experienced attorney handles the trust creation.

Little Words Mean a Lot

When you establish an irrevocable trust, one wrong word can ruin all your asset-protection time and expense. Suppose you create a trust that will provide lifetime income for your spouse, after your death. You want to keep the trust assets out of your spouse's estate, as well as out of yours. At his or her death, the assets either will pass to your children, or will stay in trust for the benefit of your children and grandchildren.

Your spouse is worried that the trust income won't be enough for him or her to live comfortably. Your spouse wants to be able to use the principal, if more money is needed. Therefore, some provision is made for him or her to have access to the trust assets. There's a trap here: If the survivor's access to trust principal is too broad, the assets will be considered under that person's control, and included in his or her taxable estate.

The Tax Court's 1991 decision in the Estate of Norman Vissering case illustrates what can happen. Vissering's mother set up a trust to pay lifetime income to herself. After her death, the trust was to pay lifetime income to her son, Norman Vissering. Other family members were also named as beneficiaries, eligible to receive trust distributions. Norman Vissering was cotrustee, along with a bank.

Many years after his mother's death, Norman Vissering developed Alzheimer's disease and was declared incapacitated. He died a few months later. The IRS asserted that the trust assets were part of his taxable estate.

The case went to Tax Court, where the IRS pointed to the trust provision giving the trustee the authority to use the principal for the "continued comfort, support, maintenance, or education" of the beneficiaries. This provision, it contended, gave cotrustee Vissering a "general power of appointment," meaning control over the assets. If this *general* power of appointment existed, the trust assets would be includible in his taxable estate.

Vissering's estate argued that the power of appointment was limited, *not* general. The tax code specifically states that the power to invade the trust for a beneficiary's "health, education, support, or maintenance" is a *limited* power, and thus does *not* result in inclusion.

An Un-Comfortable Decision

However, Vissering's estate lost solely because the word *comfort* was included in the trust. "Comfort" goes beyond "health, education, support, or maintenance." Because of the trust wording in this case, cotrustee Vissering could distribute the trust assets however he wanted for the comfort of beneficiaries. Therefore, said the Tax Court, the assets were under his control, and as such were includible in his taxable estate.

The IRS has specifically stated that the three words comfort, welfare, and happiness result in broader powers, and may result in inclusion. On the other hand, the IRS has *blessed* four *other* words—health, education, support, and maintenance—in the case of situations where the trust may need to be invaded. Those words are the legal equivalent of safe harbors. Any other words are invitations to disaster on the rocky shoals. In this case, that one no-no word—comfort—resulted in inclusion and cost the estate over $700,000 in estate taxes that needn't have been paid otherwise.

Moreover, the IRS has added the word *care* to the terms conveying broader powers than permitted. (Such words as *catastrophe* and *emergency* also should be avoided.) In truth, none of these words adds very much to the powers implied by the acceptable health-education-support-maintenance vocabulary list.

Vissering was officially incapacitated and could make no distributions at the time of his death. The court included the assets anyway, because Vissering had not been removed as trustee, and still technically retained the trustee's powers. Similarly, the fact that Vissering was cotrustee with a bank did not sway the court. The bank was not an "adverse" party having an interest in the trust assets opposed to Vissering's.

Whenever a trust beneficiary is also a trustee, the danger of inclusion is present. It may actually *help* to name a cotrustee with an adverse interest—such as another trust beneficiary. Even if a trust beneficiary is *not* a trustee, assets may be includible *if* the beneficiary can dismiss the trustee and name a replacement. That is, the beneficiary has control over the assets *because* he or she can appoint a friendly trustee.

Often, the beneficiaries' ability to remove trustees may be their sole leverage in assuring that they receive quality service. Therefore, if your estate planning calls for giving trust beneficiaries this leverage, you need to be sure that the power of appointment is limited rather than broad. Check the wording in existing trust documents and in your will, if it calls for a *testamentary trust* (a trust that goes into effect after death) to be created.

The Sooner, the Better

Creating an irrevocable trust won't protect your assets if they're *already* in jeopardy. If a worker falls off your roof today and you establish a trust tomorrow, the courts likely won't grant the trust assets any protection. But if you set up a trust *now* and run into a difficult situation in five years, the assets may well be out of creditors' reach. In any event, you should be able to show another reason for establishing the trust, besides asset protection—estate tax reduction, for example, or care for a family member.

Once you've made the decision to establish a trust, funding it can be a problem, however. Except for charitable trusts, gifts to irrevocable trusts are subject to gift-tax limitations. You can give away $10,000 per year per recipient ($20,000 from a married couple), but that won't do much if you want to protect *substantial* assets. Besides, you have to jump through a few hoops in order for gifts to trusts to qualify for the gift-tax exclusion.

Instead, you might want to use your *unified credit*. As of this writing, you can give away up to $600,000 worth of assets to such a trust, free of gift tax. If your spouse goes along with the gift, you can shift up to $1.2 million, tax-free. Making large gifts now *will* cut into (or use up) your $600,000 exemption from estate taxes, but doing so while it's still valid might just be a good idea: A revenue-starved Congress could trim this exemption at any time!

Once assets are shifted to an irrevocable trust, they're out of your taxable estate. If you transfer assets that may appreciate (stocks, real estate), any future growth *also* is out of your estate. Of course, "irrevocable" means that you can't change your mind: Once you make the transfer, the assets no longer belong to *you*.

Because such trust assets no longer belong to you, they should be protected—and probably can be, provided you work with a knowledgeable lawyer. At the very least, you'll be erecting a substantial barrier between your assets and the scavengers. When the contingency-fee lawyers come sniffing around, looking for easy prey, they may decide to pick on someone else if you have your assets snugly tucked away in an irrevocable trust.

SUMMING UP

- When you transfer assets into an irrevocable trust, they're out of your control, so they're also likely out of the reach of creditors.
- Transfers to irrevocable trusts also move assets out of your taxable estate.
- Such trusts can be structured so that your family members have access, even if *you* don't.
- Often, you'll need to rely on a trustee who'll make distributions where the money is needed.
- When you set up an irrevocable trust, take care that the trustee

can provide for the beneficiaries' "health," "education," "support," and "maintenance," but *not* for their "comfort," "happiness," "welfare," or "care."

• The sooner you set up an irrevocable trust, before there are real threats to your assets, the greater your protection will be.

29

Out of the Country, Out of Reach

Offshore Trusts May Provide the Ultimate in Asset Protection

For Dr. X, the trouble began with a story in the *Wall Street Journal*, announcing his plans to open a chain of bargain-priced clinics. After that article appeared, his not-so-professional colleagues put out a contract on him, Dr. X asserts. There was a lengthy exposé on a local TV station in the city where he practices, followed by a closetful of lawsuits. "I probably spent more time giving depositions than anyone else in America," he later recalled.

Whatever the cause, the doctor definitely faced a daunting calendar of days in court. Not only were more than 150 suits filed against him, but fifteen were uninsured. By his lights, they were nuisance suits. Still, the lawyers he first consulted took these claims seriously, telling him that he might wind up paying hundreds of thousands of dollars.

After years of fruitless expense and aggravation, Dr. X changed lawyers: He hired a law firm that specializes in shifting assets to idyllic isles, out of the reach of rapacious creditors. This firm helped Dr. X set up a trust in the Cook Islands, south of Hawaii. Into the trust went those assets which reasonable people might want: bank accounts, stocks, bonds. Remaining in Dr. X's name were mainly real-estate limited-partnership interests of uncertain value. If everything were to go well, they might pay off nicely for his children and grandchildren.

Once his liquid assets were in the South Pacific, Dr. X turned to the various plaintiffs. He told them to take their pick of the assets he had left. Or, they could take $1,000 in cash. Most of the claimants took the cash—he asserted that he settled all fifteen uninsured cases for under $20,000.

Strip Poker

You don't have to be an imperiled physician to love offshore trusts. One semiretired business owner, for example, had invested in a strip shopping center that defaulted on a $3.5 million mortgage. As a partner, this investor probably could have been held liable for the entire amount. But he set up a Cook Islands trust and transferred assets there—and eventually the lender settled for $150,000.

Today, it's not hard to think of ways in which you can be wiped out. If you're a professional or a business owner (or even a spouse in a shaky marriage), your personal assets may be vulnerable to large judgments. Traditional means of protection—liability insurance, incorporation—*aren't* fail-safe. The courts are continually recognizing new "rights" for plaintiffs, at the expense of people trying to hold on to their wealth.

For these reasons and more, affluent Americans are turning to a variety of preservation strategies, of which the offshore asset-protection trust (APT) may be the most formidable. In essence, by using this strategy, your assets are held in a trust set up *outside* the reach of the U.S. judicial system. A creditor must prevail in a *foreign* court before being able to lay his hands on those assets. In some overseas jurisdictions, you can retain control *and* enjoy the benefits of trust assets—even while they're protected.

One law firm that has become a leader in the field discovered the virtues of APTs when its own malpractice-insurance premiums skyrocketed. In 1984, despite a clean history, the firm's insurer raised the premium from $10,000 to $150,000 while reducing coverage from $10 million to $1 million. In response, the principals shifted personal assets to a trust on the Isle of Man, a British Commonwealth member in the Irish Sea. Many Americans like to deal with Manx trusts because they're comfortable with the location, the language, and the political and economic stability.

After the law firm (Engel & Rudman, based in Denver) began creating Manx trusts for wealthy clients, Cook Islands officials asked the firm to help create a state-of-the-art law on asset protection there, in the late 1980s. Since then, many jurisdictions have acquired enhanced-asset protection, including the Bahamas, Belize, the British Virgins, the Caymans, Cyprus, Gibraltar, Jersey, the Turks, and the Caicos—all from the onetime Tax Haven Hall of Fame and all now determined to become asset-protection havens. Nevertheless, the greatest protection may be available in the Cook Islands.

The Cook Islands International Trust Act prohibits the enforcement of foreign judgments, so litigants are forced to commence actions *de novo* ("from scratch") in a Cook Islands court. In the Cook Islands, therefore, judgments issued by U.S. courts *aren't* automatically recognized, as they are in most of the world. Instead, a claimant must hire an attorney who practices in the Cook Islands, and that attorney must be paid, win or lose—no contingency fees are permitted there. In court, the burden of proof rests on the creditor, who must satisfy a criminal standard (beyond a reasonable doubt) in order to prevail.

The Cook Islands law also addresses the aforementioned issue of *fraudulent conveyance*. If you transfer assets merely to put them out of the reach of creditors, the transaction will be considered fraud, and disregarded. The same outcome generally results if you transfer assets merely to thwart potential creditors—the visitor who's sure to sue you next week for the broken hip suffered while tripping on your dog's bone and falling down your steps.

Fraudulent conveyance is less likely to be a problem if you use an APT as a vaccine rather than as a cure. Establish a trust, and shift assets while you have no major claims outstanding, or likely claims pending. If you shift assets in 1995 and your visitor stumbles in 1999, it will be hard to make the case that assets were transferred to thwart future bone-trippers. Moreover, the Cook Islands has a statute of limitations on fraudulent conveyance: One year after the transfer of assets, or two years after the underlying cause of action (such as neg-

ligence), fraudulent conveyance can't be charged. By the time a plaintiff finds out where the money is and files an action, the statute of
limitations may prevent the suit.

However, most people procrastinate, so transfers are made *after*
creditors' actions are likely, or even are under way already. In these
situations, it's more difficult to avoid a fraudulent-conveyance claim.
You'll probably be better off if you stay solvent—at least on paper—
while moving the most tempting assets out of easy reach.

Pull Up the Drawbridge

Establishing an APT won't allow you to cheat or maim your fellows
with impunity. Instead, the idea is to reduce the financial profile you
present to would-be claimants. A lot of lawyers hit a brick wall when
they discover that anything foreign is involved. To press a suit successfully, a plaintiff has to overcome so many barriers, with no certainty of success, that frivolous suits will be abandoned while the
playing field is leveled for serious actions. Settlements will be reasonable instead of ridiculous.

Despite their advantages, Cook Islands APTs aren't likely to become as ubiquitous as VCRs. The price tag is too high, and shopping
around for discounts isn't recommended: You want a lawyer who
knows how the game is played.

Typically, the process starts by creating a family limited partnership
(see Chapter 27). Mom and/or Pop might control a 1 percent general-
partnership interest, as well as a 99 percent limited-partnership
interest. Then, the most tempting, most liquid personal assets are
transferred into this partnership, behind a protective barrier.

So far, so good. But you're still subject to the vagaries of the U.S.
judicial process. For belt-and-suspenders safety, the 99 percent limited-partnership interest (regardless of ownership) can be transferred
to an offshore APT. Transferred *on paper*, at least. Your brokerage
account, for example, still stays in New York or Dallas or wherever.

You may have a hard time convincing a court that the rental condo
you own near Seattle is held in the Cook Islands, but you can borrow
against your equity, and move the cash into the trust. In case of an
adverse decision, the trustee may be able to move trust assets to
Zurich or London. With today's technology, transactions with foreign
countries are no more difficult than conducting business from one
state to another.

For creating the limited partership and the APT, you'll probably pay a lawyer around $15,000, plus another couple of thousand a year to compensate the local trustee. That's expensive, but it's worth more for a really good job—you certainly don't want to spend thousands on a trust, only to have the whole process disregarded because your lawyer screwed up.

So far, relatively few law firms specialize in creating offshore APTs, but a number of major firms are in fact showing interest. And savvy lawyers will know the ins and outs: For example, you want a local trustee with *no* U.S. connections, but you also want the trust documents drawn up so he or she can't act (i.e., take your money) without your consent. Often you, the trust creator, can act as "protector," a watchdog with the power to veto distribution decisions and replace trustees.

Offshore trusts *won't* provide a tax haven—they're designed to be tax-neutral. And don't expect them to solve all of life's little problems. For example, you shouldn't set up a trust to avoid a $5,000 dispute with a landlord. Smart people don't swat flies with a sledgehammer.

When do you *need* a sledgehammer? When you're marrying late in life and don't want to discuss a prenuptial agreement with your spouse-to-be. When you've sold your business and don't want the buyer to come after the proceeds a few years later, should profits be disappointing. When you want to cut professional-liability insurance coverage, or even "go bare." When you want to protect assets while making sure they avoid probate.

In general, offshore APTs make sense for people with over $500,000 in personal wealth to protect. The more you're worth, and the greater the hazards you face, the more an APT can make sense. However, your legal position probably will be *stronger* if you keep some money in your *own* name, *within* reach of creditors, rather than move everything overseas.

SUMMING UP

• For extra asset protection, you can use an offshore trust.
• Typically, you set up a family limited partnership to hold assets, then transfer the limited-partnership interest into an offshore trust.
• Several jurisdictions have adopted laws to encourage asset protection.
• In the Cook Islands (for example), judgments by U.S. courts aren't automatically recognized, so some plaintiffs may have to start over.

• With an asset-protection trust in place, claimants may be willing
to settle for minor amounts, or not bother at all to bring suits.
• Even with all this protection in place, you may still be able to
keep your assets in the United States and merely shift title offshore.
• On the down side, offshore trusts are expensive to establish and
maintain, and may not be able to protect assets if creditors (or
potential creditors) already are in place.

30

Super Savers

Preserve Assets for Your Children
and Grandchildren

So far, we've shown you how to protect your own assets from lawsuits and divorce actions, as well as from estate taxes. You may want to go one step further and protect assets for your children and grandchildren as well. To do so, you can use a special "Wealth Trust" (a trademarked term), also called a "Super Trust" or "Mega Trust." All these names are for generation-skipping dynasty trusts with a great deal of flexibility.

Wealth Trusts are irrevocable living trusts, as we saw in Chapter 28. Unlike most trusts, though, they are designed to stay in force for *three generations*. That is, after your death, the trust will continue to exist during the lifetime of your children and their children. After the *last* of your grandchildren dies, the trust terminates—and *then* the assets will be distributed to your *great-grandchildren*.

As you can see, a Wealth Trust can stay in effect for many decades. For all this time, the assets in the trust are protected—they belong to the trust, *not* to you, your children, or your grandchildren. Thus, creditors can't get at those assets, nor can divorcing spouses or anyone bringing a lawsuit. The assets will be genuinely safe for your family.

Even though the assets aren't owned by your family, they *will* be available *if needed*. The usual practice is to name your child or children as trustee(s), with grandchildren as cotrustees or successor trustees (you, as creator, usually can't be the trustee for a Wealth Trust, except in special circumstances). Children and grandchildren also can be beneficiaries. Then, if an emergency comes up, the trustee can distribute or lend trust funds to the beneficiaries.

Therefore, money in the trust will be available for education, health care, business start-ups, and other situations where heavy funding is needed. If you personally face a critical need for cash, the money can be made available to you through your *family* members.

From the Jaws of the Tax Collector

A Wealth Trust also protects wealth by avoiding estate tax for two or three generations. A dollar subjected to the top estate-tax rate—55 percent—for two generations is reduced to around 20 cents. After three estate-tax bites, only 10 cents will be left. By putting assets into a long-lived Wealth Trust, out of the reach of the estate tax, the *entire dollar* is preserved and allowed to grow.

However (here it comes), there's a special *generation-skipping tax* that's meant to *prevent* such tax avoidance. As a result, you're limited as to how much you can contribute to a Wealth Trust—$1 million per donor, $2 million per married couple. Excess amounts are subject to the generation-skipping tax, levied at 55 percent.

Thus, amounts up to $1 million or $2 million can be transferred to a Wealth Trust, over a period of years. That's the *basic funding* of the trust, but there is no limit on the *growth* of this seed money. Once you move money into the trust, the trustees can invest any way they wish. In practice, three modes of investment are most common:

1. *Municipal bonds.* The interest will be tax-exempt and can be reinvested in still more tax-exempt securities. Thus the trust fund will grow, and not be diminished by income tax.

2. *Growth stocks.* Typically, growth stocks pay little or no dividends, so little or no tax will be payable each year. Under professional management, growth stocks can be expected to generate extremely high

returns over the decades during which the Wealth Trust will be in force.

3. *Life insurance.* Money going into the fund can be used to buy life insurance on yourself, your spouse, or both. When the insured individuals die, the trust will collect the proceeds, *tax-free*.

Which way works best? If the trust creators die soon after establishing the trust, life insurance will prove to have been the better use of trust funds. If the creators live for twenty, twenty-five, or more years, the trust likely will come out ahead with stocks and bonds.

In truth, no one knows when either you or your spouse will die. Therefore, you might want to diversify your trust funds among stocks, bonds, and life insurance. Your fund will be substantial no matter *when* its creators pass on.

How substantial? Suppose you and your spouse set up a trust with three children as beneficiaries. Under current law, you can give up to $60,000 per year to the trust ($20,000 joint gift-tax exclusion times three beneficiaries) with *no* tax consequences.

Over twenty years, you can contribute $1.2 million to the trust— well below the $2 million limit for the generation-skipping tax. Thanks to stock-market growth, reinvested bond interest, and life-insurance proceeds, your Wealth Trust could accumulate $2 million, $3 million, or more, after-tax. That money will be available for your children and grandchildren.

Also, you might want to transfer real estate—a house or a condo— into a Wealth Trust. A beneficiary would be able to use the real estate without actually owning it. Thus, the house or condo would not be subject to judgments or divorce settlements. Moreover, a valued home can stay in your family for decades without generating an estate tax as it passes from generation to generation.

Subdivide and Conquer

Wealth Trusts can be tailored to suit your individual circumstances. You might, for example, provide for the trust to divide into *new* trusts, one for each of your children, after the death of yourself and your spouse. Each of the new trusts can be created by you, in advance, with the trustees and beneficiaries you think most suitable. You even can provide for these new trusts to divide into still *more* trusts, for your individual grandchildren, after the deaths of your children. If you have a great deal of confidence in one of your children or grand-children, you can name him or her as a trustee with a *special power of appointment*—the option to treat various beneficiaries in different ways, according to their circumstances.

The Wealth Trust can be combined with other strategies. You might, for example, create a family limited partnership (Chapter 27) and transfer assets to a Wealth Trust, making the trust a limited part-ner. This will give you an extra layer of asset protection.

Thanks to some quirks in the tax code, you can sell assets to your Wealth Trust for a discount from their true value. (That's because you, as general partner, control all the limited-partnership assets.) The Wealth Trust could buy assets from you on an installment basis, effectively paying you with a note and making interest-only payments for many years. In the meantime, Wealth Trust assets can be invested in stocks, bonds, or life insurance, wherein they can grow, protected from creditors and estate taxes.

You also can use a Wealth Trust as an asset-protection-plus-private-pension plan for yourself, a retirement fund that's not subject to all the restrictions of ERISA, the federal pension law. In that case, as-suming you're the spouse with most of the income and the assets, you could transfer substantial assets to your spouse. (Transfers between spouses *won't* trigger a gift tax, no matter *how* large.) Then your spouse could establish a Wealth Trust, naming you as the initial trus-tee and a beneficiary. If life insurance is used for funding, the policy would cover your spouse's life.

Again, the trust will be structured with the idea that it will serve three generations. However, if you need money for yourself, you will have access to it—as both trustee and beneficiary. This money should be the last money you ever touch, because you intend it to provide for your children and grandchildren. But it's there, in case of emer-gency—and it will stay out of the reach of ordinary creditors, as well as of malpractice claimants. No one except your own family can touch those funds.

SUMMING UP

• Irrevocable trusts designed to serve your children and grandchil-dren can provide long-term asset protection.
• Wealth Trust trustees typically will be your children and grand-children, who may have access to trust funds if necessary.

• Because of tax laws, no more than $1 million per person can be contributed to a Wealth Trust, but there is no limit as to how much the money can grow.

• Trust funds may be allocated among growth stocks, municipal bonds, and life insurance for purposes of safety and wealth-building.

• For an extra layer of asset protection, without giving up control of the assets, you can establish a family limited partnership and use a Wealth Trust to hold assets, as a limited partner.

• By having your spouse establish the trust and name you as trustee as well as a beneficiary, you can use a Wealth Trust as a private pension plan.

Part VIII

Splitting Without Getting Fractured

31

His and Hers

Prenuptial Agreements Are for Everyone—Not Just Donald and Ivana

If you're addicted to reruns of "Cheers," you've probably seen the episode in which Frasier suggests that money comes before marriage. He tells Lilith they have an appointment to draw up a prenuptial agreement, she freezes him with a look, and he goes whimpering after her, promising to forget the whole sordid business.

Fast-forward a couple of seasons. Frasier and Lilith split, and he departs for another life in another venue. But who gets what? Who gets the condo, the cars, the pension funds, the savings? On TV, those questions aren't even raised, much less answered.

In real life, though, those questions *must* be answered, down to the last penny. Often that's what the divorce lawyers spar about—at great length and expense to *both* parties. If you've been in a "bad" marriage, you may walk away with very little left after your ex-spouse and both lawyers take their shares.

Long Division

Indeed, determining each party's "share" is the hard part. Virtually every state recognizes a legal tenet, known as *marital property*, requiring that assets acquired during a marriage be divided equitably in a divorce. But which property was acquired during the marriage, and what's an equitable division thereof? Deciding on those questions is, by and large, what keeps divorce lawyers in business—and fancy trappings.

This sort of grand mess is why prenuptial agreements make sense, despite what you might see on TV. A "prenup" is a document that spells out what's yours and what's your spouse's, in case of a divorce. (Often a prenup will cover asset division at death, *too*.)

A typical prenup will spell out the property that each party brings into the marriage, stating that such belongings will remain separate— as will any gains from reinvestment. Property acquired *during* the marriage will be considered *joint* property, subject to division. In the event of divorce, the wealthier spouse might agree to pay the other spouse a certain income after (say) three years, and a greater income after five years. These promised incomes might be fixed figures ($20,000 per year or $30,000 per year), or expressed as a percentage of the wealthier spouse's income.

Take the case of Steve G., who owned a small computer company when he got married in the mid-1980s. When he and his wife divorced in the 1990s, that company was worth several million dollars. According to their prenuptial agreement, Steve was entitled to keep the company, in case of a divorce. A court upheld his agreement, and he was able to hold on to his entire company.

Even though Steve had to give up *other* assets, he was able to keep his company alive—which might not have been the case without a prenup. If a sizable portion of the company had gone to his wife, as part of a property settlement, Steve would have had a major coshareholder who didn't know the business, and also might have been hostile. She could even have sold her share to a competitor, or some other adverse party.

In addition to middle-aged people concerned about asset protection in case of divorce, elderly people also are prenup candidates. People aged sixty-five or older who are getting married after being widowed or divorced may have assets from their previous marriage(s), and children to whom they want to leave those assets. However, many states give residents an *automatic* right to a substantial share (e,g., 30 percent in Florida) of a spouse's estate, and perhaps lifetime use of the marital residence as well! With a prenuptial agreement, however, both spouses can waive those rights, thus ensuring that their assets will pass to their children.

Not a Penny More

It is clear that prenuptial agreements are important for anyone who comes into a marriage with assets. However, for prenups to stand up in the future, care must be taken *when they're drawn up*. Some lawyers say that over half of all prenups are disregarded.

A well-drawn prenup, though, *will* be recognized. Even in the highly publicized Donald and Ivana Trump divorce, "Mrs. Trump eventually received precisely what was provided in the prenuptial agreement," attorney Raoul Lionel Felder asserted to the *New York Times*.

What's the key to a solid prenup? You need to play fair with your future spouse. Beyond that, the longer the time between the signing of the prenuptial agreement and the wedding, the better. If you wait until the night before the wedding, when the out-of-town guests have arrived and the reception is all arranged, then shove a prenup under your spouse's nose, it probably won't be considered valid later on, should it be contested. Because if the question of its validity eventually arises, a court likely will say that you obtained it by coercion.

Even if you go to a lawyer two weeks before the wedding and say you want a prenuptial agreement drawn up, an *honest* lawyer won't do that, even if only because there's really not enough time left to do it *right*. In some cases, people in fact have to postpone the wedding in order to properly execute a prenup! There's no safe harbor, really, in terms of length of time before the ceremony—but the courts *have* indicated that the more time between the agreement and the marriage, the better.

So you should get a prenup signed well in advance of the ceremony. But *how*? Few prospective brides *or* grooms like the idea of dividing property into "yours" and "mine" as a precondition to wedded bliss.

One approach you might use is to tell your future mate that you want to make sure he or she is properly taken care of. A new estate plan is needed. (Actually, *that* will be the truth, in *most* situations). As part of this estate plan you'll need a will, a review of life insurance, powers of attorney, probably a trust or two—*and* a prenup. In other words, make a prenup part of a total plan to protect yourself, your future spouse, and your combined assets.

Both Sides Now

Whether or not a prenup is part of a complete estate plan, both sides should have their own lawyers. If your attorney handles everything, a court likely will rule that your spouse wasn't adequately represented, so a prenup will be disregarded. Some lawyers recommend that the signing of a prenup be videotaped, to show that both parties were represented, and agreed willingly. Not a bad idea.

Similarly, a prenup can't be "unconscionable." If you're fairly well-off, you can't stipulate that your spouse will get nothing, in case of a divorce. By the very fact of your marriage, you're offering your spouse a certain lifestyle. A prenup *can't* cut that lifestyle off, even after long years of the "worse" part of the marriage vow.

The main sticking point in most prenups, though, is *full disclosure*. When you enter into a prenup, you must spell out *all* your assets and liabilities. (In case of hard-to-value assets, such as a small business or real estate, be sure to get an independent appraisal.) Both spouses should comply in this regard.

Generally, each side should submit a complete financial statement, and turn it over to the other side for inspection. Your CPA or other financial adviser can look over the other party's statements, and raise any questions that seem appropriate. If you don't have personal financial statements, your tax-return file may be sufficient. It's hard to hide assets from someone who can check *that* out.

The idea is to present an accurate snapshot of your respective financial positions *before* your marriage. Then, in case of a divorce, you'll both be able to track the asset gain or loss, and come to a fair division. If you leave anything meaningful out of a prenup, your spouse might successfully charge fraud or deception, thus invalidating the agreement.

Sometimes, prenuptial disclosure can be telling. Mary S., for example, planned to marry Andy C. Mary had her own business, and so did Andy. They decided upon a prenuptial agreement, so she could keep her company and he could keep his, no matter what happened.

At first glance, Andy's business was considerably larger. However, as the prenuptial negotiations proceeded, Mary discovered that Andy's company had considerable exposure to unpaid payroll taxes—which might be his personal responsibility, along with substantial penalties. As a result, the prenuptial agreement included a clause indemnifying Mary on this issue.

Tax Tips

Taxes often are overlooked when prenuptial agreements are executed. If an agreement spells out who'll pay which expenses, you should include a provision on who'll pay taxes—and it *shouldn't* be simply based on each party's gross income.

The agreement should cover who'll pay to defend a tax audit, if necessary, and also who'll pay any assessed taxes, interest, and penalties. Some prenuptial agreements stipulate that the couple will file as "married, filing separately," so that tax problems from one spouse won't spill onto the other—even though the couple will wind up paying more tax that way.

If joint returns are to be filed, both spouses should be entitled to receive copies of the return *and* supporting documents, each year. This will avoid future problems in case of divorce negotiations, if one spouse can't get hold of necessary tax records. If the prenup calls for a property division, either at death or upon divorce, recognition should be given to the fact that some assets are "low-basis," and thus carry a greater future tax liability than do "high-basis" assets.

Sign Now, Save Later

To say the least, prenuptial agreements aren't cheap. A lawyer might charge you $750 for a *simple* prenup; but most agreements are fairly complex and cost between $3,000 and $5,000. (The price might be less, however, *if* included in a package along with a new will and some trusts.)

But even if a prenup does cost a few thousand dollars to draw up, the price may be well worth it, because a contested divorce can be far more costly, in legal fees as well as emotional strain. Without a prenuptial agreement, you may also suffer an adverse property settlement, while a solid prenup can preserve your premarital property.

There are other steps you can take to protect your assets from a divorce settlement. For example, you should keep *all* of your assets in your *own* name, even after you're married. Changing them to joint ownership can make them marital property, subject to a property settlement. Similarly, if you inherit assets during your marriage, or receive assets as gifts, title them in your own name. And keep careful records to show where your assets came from. *Whenever* you commingle assets with your spouse's, you risk losing them in case of a divorce.

Strictly Business

Even if you're *not* getting married, you need to be vigilant about both prenups and property ownership. Suppose you have partners in a business venture or investment property. If one of your co-owners dies or gets a divorce, his or her share might pass to someone with whom you're not comfortable—and the value of the business property could be seriously damaged. So if one of your business partners is getting married, insist that a prenuptial agreement be executed— at least with reference to the assets with which you're involved. (This may give him or her a good reason to raise the issue with the betrothed.)

You'll probably want a *right of first refusal*, too. That is, in case of a partner's death or divorce, you (and the other surviving owners) will want the right to buy the assets in question, at a fair price. Generally, this will be acceptable to any partner's future spouse, too: He or she would be getting cash instead of an illiquid interest in a small business, or in investment real estate.

The same logic applies when you enter into a business arrangement. Make sure you have a right of first refusal, in case of someone's unfortunate death or messy divorce. Then you won't have to worry about taking on unwanted partners in the future.

Make Sense, Not War

Suppose you haven't been prescient enough to execute a prenup before you're married. If your marriage runs into trouble, what can you do to prevent an unmitigated disaster? Well—you can always follow the standard procedure and hire an attorney. Of course, your spouse can do likewise. Tit for tat, as it were.

Be aware that a typical *middle-class* divorce proceeding takes *at least* a year to work out before a decree is granted, often at a total cost of around $50,000. If you have *really* substantial assets, the cost could go ballistic. What's more, over 50 percent of conventional divorces *don't* work the first time, so there is "postjudgment litigation," as the lawyers put it. In layman's terms, you can anticipate more legal costs and much more aggravation.

There's a *better* way! (As long as you and your spouse are on decent terms, that is.) Instead of *two* lawyers, you hire *one* mediator. The mediator helps you and your spouse work out an asset division between yourselves. And mediation can take you through the whole process in just a few months, at a bargain cost of only $2,000–$5,000. Voilà!

What's more, mediation can be more flexible than a conventional divorce, adapting to unusual circumstances. Take the case of John D., a Wall Street whiz who built up a million-dollar net worth in the 1980s. After the 1987 crash, John lost his job. Using his capital, he started up a new health-care business. But the strain turned out to be unhealthy for his marriage, so he and his wife, Jane, decided to heal themselves through divorce, if possible.

In a conventional (adversarial) divorce, Jane would have been entitled to a certain level of child support, as well as a property settlement. However, the money would have come out of John's new business, hurting its chances for success. In a few years the business could go under, and John might not have been able to keep paying child support. Instead, John and Jane used mediation. As a result, Jane accepted a lower level of child support *and* passed up a property settlement, leaving the latter money in the business. In turn, she would gradually be entitled to a greater level of child support, *plus* a share of the company if it succeeded.

You and your spouse, should you face divorce, likely would want to hire your own lawyers, if only to approve a mediated settlement. Good move! Still, if you could keep your barristers from taking over the proceedings, you'd likely find that mediation would pay off rather better for you, and less well for them. For information and help in finding mediators, call the Academy of Family Mediatiors in Portland, Oregon, 503-345-1205.

SUMMING UP

• When people who have assets—or who expect to have assets at some point—get married, steps should be taken to protect those pluses.

- A *prenuptial agreement* (prenup) can spell out what will happen to each party's assets, in case of death or divorce.
- Prenups can help middle-aged people, as well as elderly people who remarry and want to protect the children of a prior marriage.
- A typical prenup will keep each party's assets separate while stipulating that assets acquired during a marriage are subject to a fair division.
- In order for a prenuptial agreement to be valid, it should be arrived at only after ample time for mutually satisfactory negotiation.
- Both sides should have their own lawyers, and fully disclose all their assets in order to draw up a valid prenuptial agreement.
- Either an attorney or a CPA should point out all the tax ramifications of a prenuptial agreement.
- After a marriage, it's easier to protect your property if you keep it in your own name, rather than attached to joint ownership.
- If you do find yourself in a divorce situation, mediation is faster and cheaper than the typical adversarial proceeding.

32

Send the Bill to the IRS

Structure a Divorce Agreement So
Both Sides Come Out Ahead

If you ever find yourself in the midst of a divorce, you'll face an overwhelming array of emotional, familial, and financial problems. (If you've been *through* one, just ride with this.) But don't forget the IRS—because divorce, like death, has tax consequences. With careful planning, you not only can reduce the tax bite, but you also can get the IRS to subsidize your family!

The prime tax issue in divorce is whether or not alimony is paid:

• Alimony payments *are* deductible, and the recipient thereof *must* admit to taxable income.

• Child-support payments and property settlements *are not* deductible, and the recipient thereof *does not* admit to any taxable income.

Naturally, if you're the spouse who'll be making the payments, you'd like to have them characterized as *deductible* alimony. Just as

215

naturally, the spouse who'll be receiving the payments wants *untaxed* property settlements and child support.

If you, the payer, are in a relatively high tax bracket (28 percent +), and your spouse stands to be in a 15 percent bracket (because there will be little or no other income for him or her), you can play a win-win game. In essence, you can increase the payment amounts by 20 percent or more, characterizing them as alimony rather than child support.

For example: Suppose you were to pay your spouse $2,000 a month in *child support*. You'd be out $2,000 and he or she would be ahead by $2,000. Instead, you pay $2,500 a month in *alimony*. Your spouse, in a 15 percent tax bracket, winds up with $2,125 a month. Assuming you're in a 40 percent tax bracket (counting state and local income taxes), your $2,500 deduction saves you $1,000 in taxes each month, bringing your net outlay down to $1,500. You *both* wind up ahead, and the IRS effectively subsidizes your divorce: You pay $1,500 a month, *after-tax*, and your spouse *nets* $2,125!

Of course, such magical results are not all that easy to achieve. Behind the magic is the reality that for a payment to qualify as deductible alimony, the following conditions must be met:

• Payments must be made in *cash*. There's little leeway here beyond checks and money orders.

• Payments must be made to or "on behalf of" the recipient. (At the written request of the recipient, payments can be made *directly* for rent, taxes, school tuition, home mortgages, or life-insurance premiums.)

• Payments must be *required* by a written divorce or separation agreement.

• Payments may *not* be designated as nondeductible or noninclu-dible in these agreements.

• The payor and the recipient *can't* live in the same household.

• The payments *must* terminate at the recipient's death.

• The payments *must not* be in the nature of child support.

Child Supporters

If payments terminate at the recipient's death, the children may be unprotected. So there should be other financial assets available for the children, or at least strong family support (including financial help) that you can rely upon. On the other hand, the payments may not need to go on at such high levels after the children are grown and the need is reduced. Some courts have okayed *finite-term alimony payments* when the term hasn't been directly tied to dependents' needs.

Today, many divorcing couples limit alimony payments to the amount of time it will take for the homemaker spouse to get back into the work force—generally from two to five years. If there are dependent children this might take longer—perhaps from six to ten years. Suppose you have two teenagers. You might want to pay $2,000 per month for as long as both kids are dependents, and $1,000 per month after the first child is on his or her own.

However, if you structure alimony payments in this manner, there are certain rules you must follow: You can't, for example, have the phaseout dates within six months of the children's reaching of age twenty-one, for example. Therefore, you need to work with a savvy divorce lawyer, to avoid tax traps.

Whether you're paying alimony or child support, you're often required to carry life insurance. That way, if you die before you've made all the agreed-upon payments, your ex-spouse will receive the insurance proceeds to make up the shortfall. (Generally, you'll buy term insurance, letting the insurance lapse after the obligation ends.)

But look what happens if you simply pay the premiums on that policy: If you die while the policy is in force, the proceeds will be included in your taxable estate, and your heirs (perhaps a second spouse) may owe an estate tax while your ex-spouse gets the insurance proceeds, tax-free!

To avoid this unhappy scenario, set up an irrevocable life-insurance trust, to hold the policy *outside of* your estate. Or, insist that your ex-spouse own the policy, using money you give to him or her to pay the premiums.

Property Rights and Wrongs

Tax considerations enter into property settlements, too. Suppose you have assets worth $300,000. In a property settlement, you agree to transfer $150,000. The question is: which $150,000?

In a property settlement, the recipient inherits the *cost basis*. Thus, if you transfer $150,000 worth of stock for which you've paid

$100,000, the built-in $50,000 capital-gain tax obligation goes with it. The same principle applies if you transfer your interest in the family home, or other real estate.

Often it's better to transfer assets (e.g., income-paying stocks and bonds) that are not likely to be sold. If your spouse holds on until his or her death, the capital gain will be wiped out. But if you transfer $150,000 worth of growth stocks, and your spouse sells those stocks to reinvest in interest-paying bonds, he or she will immediately incur a $50,000 capital gain. So, if a sale and reinvestment are inevitable, it's best to transfer *high-basis* assets, and to have the *lower-bracket* spouse bear the tax.

Of course, if you're strictly looking out for Number One, you're better off giving your spouse your *low-basis* assets and retaining the high-basis assets for yourself.

Finally, if you have dependent children, their personal exemptions may be negotiable. Taxpayers with adjusted gross income of over $110,000 lose the benefit of these exemptions (pegged at $2,450 per exemption in 1994). So, if you'll be in this situation, consider allocating these exemptions to your spouse, on IRS Form 8332, in return for concessions elsewhere in the divorce negotiations.

SUMMING UP

• In a divorce settlement, alimony is a taxable event—deductible for the payor and taxable for the recipient—whereas child support and property settlements aren't taxable.
• If one divorcing spouse will be in a much higher bracket than the other, both sides can come out ahead by focusing on alimony in the financial settlement.
• Although alimony may be necessary while the children still are dependents, it's increasingly common for alimony to stop after a certain time period—anywhere from two to ten years.
• If you have to carry term life insurance as part of a divorce settlement, keep the proceeds out of your taxable estate by holding the policy in an irrevocable trust, or have your ex-spouse hold it.
• When you transfer assets as part of a property settlement, giving away highly appreciated assets can reduce your future tax obligations.

Part IX

Exit Laughing

33

You Don't Need to Be a Millionaire . . .

to Have an Estate Plan

Your estate is, in essence, your life's work. If you have managed to acquire any assets, and you protect them against the perils we've described previously, you'll *have* an estate. To truly protect what's yours, however, you'll need to pass those assets on to your family—and to do that with a minimum of cost and confusion. You'll therefore need an *estate plan*.

When you think of estate planning, you may think of Rockefellers and Fords and DuPonts, with batteries of attorneys laboring to save millions in taxes through complex trust arrangements. But estate planning *isn't* just for the super-rich. If you have a house, a bank account, or a pension plan, you need an estate plan in order to ensure that those assets are transferred according to your wishes.

Will Power

The *sine qua non* of an estate plan is a will, since if you *don't* have a will, you *can't* have an estate plan. Your will should be drawn up by an attorney, and witnessed by unrelated parties. Make copies, but sign only the *original*, to avoid possible technical problems. (Your family needs to know the location of the original, which should be kept in a fireproof office safe or filing cabinet.)

Leaving your will in a bank safe-deposit box probably is *not* a good idea. In many states, your bank vault will be sealed right after your death, so that all the assets can be tallied—and possibly taxed. Thus, there may be delays in getting your will and distributing your assets according to its terms.

Don't worry too much about the form or contents of your will—that's your lawyer's job. Spell out for your lawyer as best you can how you want your assets distributed. Just be sure you name beneficiaries in full, and describe assets as completely as possible. Don't say, "the contents of my office desk," for instance—because you don't know what will be in there at the time of your death.

You probably won't want to list in your will every dish and desk ornament you own, so it's a good idea to have a separate *letter of instruction* as a supplement. As you acquire or dispose of possessions, this document can be updated.

You can explain your desired funeral and burial arrangements in your will. If you have minor children, you should name guardians, in case you and your spouse (if any) should die together. These guardians will be substitute parents, so you should name people most likely to fill that role. Cousins or siblings who have kids the same age as yours are good candidates.

Many people use trusts to hold title to their assets. However, it's unlikely that all of your assets, from your antiques to your zebra fish, will be owned by a trust. A *"pour over" will* can cover assets *not* held in trust, pouring them into a trust at your death, if desired.

Your will needs to be reviewed at least once every three years—perhaps more often. Federal tax laws change so rapidly that you should have an expert check your will frequently. Changes in family circumstances (births, deaths, marriages, divorces) are likely occasions for review. If you move to a different state, revise your will—because state laws differ. Depending on the magnitude of the change, you may need either a complete rewrite or just a simple addition called a *codicil*.

Courting Trouble

What if you die without a valid will in place? You'll be classified "intestate" and your property will be divided up according to a state formula, not your wishes.

For example, Solomon K. won $5 million in the New York State lottery in 1987. The fifty-four-year-old janitor became an ex-janitor and announced he'd take care of his family. He promised to help fix a sister's leaky roof; he told his handicapped niece he would buy her a van; other family members were told they would share in this good fortune.

Unfortunately, Solomon was killed in a car accident in 1988. Even worse (for them, at least), his family soon discovered that he had never made a will. For years, his two children and three surviving sisters and the Surrogate's Court of New York struggled to arrive at a fair distribution of Solomon's estate.

Much the same thing—though probably on a smaller scale—will happen to *your* "heirs" if *you* die without a will. Your family's fortunes will be in the hands of a court. No tax-reduction strategies will be pursued, and court-appointed outsiders may wind up telling your family what to do.

In some states, half of your assets will go to your children, not to your surviving spouse. Minor children may become wards of the state, so your surviving spouse will have to account to a court for every penny spent on their behalf. When your children come of age (eighteen, in many states), they may be entitled to *all* of their share of the assets, *no* strings attached. And if they're dissatisfied with the way your spouse has handled their assets, they can sue!

If your spouse remarries, the new husband or wife may be able to gain control over the assets you left to your spouse, with no guarantee they'll *ever* go to your children. And other family members, such as parents or siblings, may be cut out altogether. In essence, dying without a will deprives you of any say in the distribution of your estate.

Very likely, *none* of all this is what you have in mind for an estate plan. Therefore, it's well worth spending time and money on a professionally created will.

Probate's Not Great

In your will you'll also name an *executor* (sometimes called a *personal representative*). After your death, it's the executor's responsibility to handle all the paperwork and make sure the assets are distributed. Your executor needn't be a lawyer; your spouse, or even a grown child of yours, probably could fill that role. Patience and a sense of responsibility are the main requirements. Just make sure you get the executor's consent before naming him or her in the will.

After your death, many of your assets will go through *probate*—that's the process of "proving" your will and transferring your assets to your heirs. Depending on your state, the costs of probate might be as much as 7 percent of your assets. If you have a $200,000 brokerage account, transferring it to your heirs could cost your family $14,000 in attorney fees and court costs.

In some states, an estate can take two years to clear probate. *All* probate proceedings are part of the public record, so *anyone* can learn about your holdings, the debts you've incurred, and so on.

On the bright side, many types of assets are automatically exempt from probate: property that is held jointly, life-insurance proceeds (as long as you name a beneficiary who isn't a minor), retirement-plan assets (ditto), and certain bank accounts with "payable on death," or POD, provisions. If most of your assets fall into those categories, probate will be a nuisance—but at least not a disaster.

However, if you hold a significant amount of real estate in your own name, or an investment portfolio, or a closely held business, your family will have to contend with a great deal of nuisance in dealing with probate.

Out of Your Hands

Another way to avoid probate is to establish a *living trust*. In fact *any* trust established while you're alive is a living trust. Many people whose main goal is the avoidance of probate use *revocable* living trusts, which can be revoked or annulled by the trust creator.

Typically, the creator of the trust acts as trustee *and* as beneficiary. The ownership of your assets can be transferred to the trust. You still remain in control, as trustee, and you receive the trust income, as beneficiary. In case you change your mind, you can revoke the trust and take the assets back under your own name.

Every state recognizes *these* trusts, so you *don't* need to rewrite one if you move. Some updating may be necessary, as your personal situation changes, but revocable living trusts aren't hard to modify. You can amend the trust with only your signature, and witnesses aren't necessary.

Assuming you're pleased with the trust, you'll hold the assets in there until your death. Then, the revocable trust automatically becomes an *irrevocable* trust. A successor trustee, whom you have named, will distribute the trust assets according to the instructions you set out in your trust documents. Therefore, the trust assets pass to your heirs *without* going through probate. There's no time lag, and no public record.

This technique is versatile enough so that you can set up additional trusts, for special purposes, using assets from your living trust. These trusts are particularly helpful if you own real estate in more than one state, because your property doesn't have to go through probate in each of them.

Time and Money

There are, however, *disadvantages* to living trusts. For example, the money your family will save by going through probate will be offset by the money you pay to set up and administer the trust. Plus, the trust will work only if you take the time and effort to retitle your assets and change ownership.

Setting up a revocable living trust *won't* cut your taxes. You'll still owe tax on income from trust assets, which still will be included in your taxable estate. Indeed, if you want to make gifts in order to reduce your taxable estate, you probably shouldn't make them directly from the trust. To avoid IRS displeasure, it's better to take assets from the trust back into your own name, then give them away in order to reduce your estate.

Do revocable living trusts make sense? A lot depends on the shape of your portfolio. Several types of assets avoid probate: Jointly owned assets go directly to the surviving owners, while insurance proceeds and retirement plans (and some bank accounts) go directly to beneficiaries. If your assets chiefly fall into these categories, you won't have much probate to avoid.

So don't rush into a revocable living trust. Check around to see if your state has a reputation for being fast and cheap, or slow and costly, when it comes to probate. Ask your lawyer what the costs will be *before* you decide to make a commitment.

SUMMING UP

- Regardless of whether your assets are large or small, you should have a will.
- A bona fide will, drawn up by an experienced lawyer, can ensure that your assets will be distributed according to your wishes.

• If you die *without* a will, the distribution of your property will be determined by state law, and the results probably will not be what you would have wanted.

• Because you won't be able to mention all of your assets in your will, a separate *letter of instruction* should be used to specify how your possessions ought to be distributed.

• If you have minor children, you should name *guardians* in your will, in case you and your spouse both die.

• You should name an *executor,* who'll administer your estate and see to it that your property is transferred.

• A diligent family member can serve as executor, but you might want to name a financial institution as coexecutor if your estate is sizable.

• Assets left via a will go through *probate*, which can be expensive, time-consuming, and subject to public scrutiny.

• If you transfer assets to a *living trust*, they'll bypass probate after your death.

• Living trusts are worthwhile *when* you have substantial assets that would be subject to probate, and *if* you retitle those assets to the trust.

34

Life Goes On

What You Really Need to Know About Life Insurance

You need to protect your family as well as your physical possessions. From a financial point of view, if you're the main source of income in your household, you need to provide for your family in case you die while you still have dependents. To supply this protection, you need to buy enough life insurance to take care of your family—but to protect your assets, you should buy no more than what's truly necessary.

To determine the right amount of life insurance to carry, you and your spouse (presuming there is one) must decide how much money would be needed to cover basic living expenses for your immediate family in case of your sudden death. Let's say the number is $3,000 per month.

Next, estimate how much income your family could reasonably expect only from your spouse's job, investment income, Social Security benefits, etc. Suppose that number, after-tax, will be $1,800 per month. The shortfall would be $1,200 per month.

Then, determine which assets could be converted to income production. For example, your family might sell a vacation home and invest the proceeds in corporate bonds. Say they'd realize $120,000 and earn a 5 percent return, after-tax. That would be $6,000 per year, or $500 a month. *Now* the shortfall would be down to $700 monthly.

Estimated monthly expenses	$3,000
(Minus) expected monthly income	(1,800)
(Minus) income from other assets	(500)
Monthly shortfall	$ 700

If your shortfall *is* $700 per month, that would be $8,400 in just one year—quite a sum. Assuming a 5 percent return, after-tax, you'd then need $168,000 worth of life insurance. (You might buy $200,000 worth, just to be safe.)

Your $3,000 monthly budget probably wouldn't include money to put your kids through college. (Four years at a *top* private school now costs about $100,000.) If you plan to send your children to such a place, increase your total life insurance by $100,000 for *each* child. If you *don't* expect them to attend such a pricey college, increase life insurance by $50,000 apiece.

Every couple of years, go over your life-insurance needs. If your family has gradually gotten used to a richer lifestyle, you might increase the amount. On the other hand, after you've put your kids through college and you have a substantial amount in a retirement fund, you might well reduce your coverage—or eliminate it altogether.

One Year at a Time

How can you afford to buy up to $400,000 worth of life insurance? The least expensive type of life insurance is *term* insurance. You pay only so much in premiums for just so much insurance protection, for a stated time period (usually one year). After that, you pay another—and probably higher—premium for another term. Generally, premiums increase as you grow older. (You can buy term insurance where the premium will stay level for a number of years, but you're essentially shifting later costs to earlier years.)

You probably will be best served by buying *low-cost* term insurance. Be sure you buy *guaranteed renewable* term, because then the insurer can't cancel your coverage, as long as you pay the premiums. Also, you won't need to take any more physical exams, once you've passed the first one.

Term insurance *is* "pure" insurance, but be reminded that it comes with the catch we mentioned: The *older* you get, the *more* it may cost. If you're still carrying life insurance in your sixties and seventies, you're probably paying *huge* premiums for term insurance.

As an alternative, you can buy *permanent* life insurance. Here, you pay a *fixed* premium per year—the same one, year after year. However, permanent life is much more expensive than term in the *early* years. Depending upon your age, the same coverage you can buy for $300 per year for term insurance might cost up to $3,000 annually for permanent life!

Why pay $3,000 instead of $300? Because you get investment buildup and tax shelter. Most of your permanent life premium goes into an investment account, the "cash value," where it can compound, free of income tax. What's more, you can take out policy loans and withdrawals from the cash value (up to certain limits) without paying taxes. And you don't have to pay interest on any loans. However, outstanding policy loans and loan interest *will* be subtracted from the amount your beneficiaries receive upon your death.

Cash-value life insurance works only if you stay in for many years. Your first premium payments go largely to the sales agent, and there usually are a variety of early withdrawal penalties. If you need to get your cash back after only a year or two, you may wind up with even less than you paid in. Also, when you surrender a policy, you'll owe tax on all the investment income you've sheltered inside the policy. Buy permanent life *only* if you plan to hold the policy for at least fifteen years.

In for the Long Haul

When does *permanent* life insurance make better sense than term coverage? When your income is so great that you can pay the premiums without financial strain, and you welcome the tax shelter for investment income. Also, if you start a family late in life, you may prefer permanent life rather than term insurance because term premiums become relatively so expensive. Permanent life also makes sense for middle-aged and elderly people who have amassed a *great* deal of wealth. Your family may well need its proceeds to pay an estate tax.

Term insurance becomes extremely expensive as you go into your seventies and eighties, the time in many people's lives when they first realize how much they'll owe in estate taxes. A $500,000 policy, which might have cost you only $500 per year while you were in your thirties, might increase to $10,000 or $20,000 or more. (Some insurers won't even sell term insurance to the elderly.) Suppose the premium goes so high that you skip a payment—even your first ever. Despite your having carried the policy for years, it will lapse when you do that— and your heirs won't get a cent of the prospective insurance proceeds.

Obviously permanent life insurance makes the best sense when you're insuring to pay an estate tax. Unless you lose or spend most of your wealth, you'll *never* outgrow your need for cash to pay estate tax.

Some agents may offer you a policy which, to bring down the initial cost, mixes term with permanent insurance. That may be a good initial strategy, but (again) term insurance becomes tremendously expensive as you grow older. Find out how much term is included in the mix, and how high future premiums may go, before you consider buying.

Vanishing Acts

Actually, few people buy permanent life insurance with the idea that they'll pay premiums every year until they die. Suppose you want to buy a $500,000 policy. Your agent likely will suggest that instead of paying say $7,000 per year for the rest of your life, that you pay $10,000 per year. After perhaps eleven years, your obligation to pay premiums will "vanish."

The more money you pay up front, the greater the cash value will be. The cash value may even generate enough earnings to keep paying premiums, through the years, after *you* stop paying.

To back up the sales pitch, the agent likely will show you an "illustration," a computerized printout showing eleven years of $10,000 payments, a buildup of cash value, and a death benefit of around $500,000. It's hard not to be impressed by the columns of numbers.

Remember, though, that *all* permanent life insurance is a guessing game. An illustration merely puts those guesses on paper. There is *no way* the insurer can know how much it will earn, year after year, on the $110,000 you pay in. There is *no way* they can know things such as company expenses and mortality rates (how many policyholders will die each year).

Naturally, some insurers are more aggressive than others in their projections. They might predict a 10 percent compound growth on your invested premiums, while others project 7 percent. And they can make similarly optimistic assumptions about other factors, too. These companies' illustrations will of course tend to show higher cash values and lower premium payments for any given level of insurance than will the more reality-oriented ones.

If you buy a policy based on flawed projections, you might find that your cash value isn't growing as fast as expected, and thus also isn't generating enough income to pay future premiums. You may find that your premium vanishes not after just eleven years, but after an agonizing twenty. Instead of buying a $500,000 policy for $110,000, you might wind up paying over $200,000!

To avoid these pitfalls, you need to find out which assumptions are being used in the illustration. Ask about the *assumed rate for investment earnings*. If it seems unreasonable, ask to have the illustration rerun at a lower, more realistic rate. Even more important: Buy from *established* insurers. Look for a company with excellent ratings from two or more independent agencies (*at least* A+ from A. M. Best; AA from Standard & Poor's or Moody's; and B from Weiss Research), and at least fifty years of experience in the business.

Keeping Your Options Open

The most basic type of permanent life insurance is called *whole life*. An increasingly popular variation is *universal life*. The key difference is that with the latter you can vary your premiums from year to year. You can reduce your payments if you're short of cash, or you can increase payments as your income grows. As your payments vary, your death benefit and cash value will vary accordingly. Obviously the more you pay, the more coverage you'll have.

Yet another type of permanent life insurance is *variable life*. Your premium payments can be directed into various investment accounts—mainly mutual funds. Most variable life policies offer stock funds, bond funds, and money-market funds, while some also include real estate, international investments, zero-coupon bonds, and other categories.

Your death benefit and your cash value will reflect the success of the investments you choose. You may even lose money! However, the insurance company is required to guarantee a *minimum death benefit*: Your beneficiaries will receive *at least* as much as the amount you paid in premiums.

Generally, variable life insurance is suitable for younger investors—those with a long time to invest. Only those with sizable incomes and net worth should consider this coverage, because of the risks. If you're in this fortunate category, put most of your premiums into stock funds—and hold on for the long term.

For flexibility plus the chance for a large buildup, you can buy *universal variable* life, which (as you may have guessed) combines the features of universal life *and* variable life. However, if your main concern is simply insurance coverage, you may prefer to stick with plain vanilla *whole life*, which offers stronger guarantees than the variations cited.

Double Coverage

If you're married and buying life insurance for estate-planning purposes, you may want to buy *survivorship life*, commonly called *second-to-die* insurance. These policies insure two lives, and pay off only after *both* deaths.

Second-to-die life is increasingly popular because it's cheaper than buying policies on both spouses. The exact pricing will vary, depending on the age of the insured individuals, but this kind of policy might cut your cost by 20 percent or more of the cost of buying two single-life policies. Moreover, buying a second-to-die policy means no guessing games about who'll die first.

No matter which spouse does die first, *most* of the estate can go to the survivor—with little or no estate tax due. When the survivor dies, the money can pass to the children. The estate tax will be due *then*, but that obligation may be covered by the insurance proceeds.

You'll see policy illustrations for second-to-die life, too. Be careful of any potentially misleading projections! Some illustrations, for example, assume that both spouses will live for 100 years. Ask what would happen if one spouse were to die soon, and the other live for many years: Will premiums shoot up?

In Sickness and in Health

No matter *what* kind of life insurance you want to buy, you'll have to pass a physical to get it. Top-rated insurance companies are *very* choosy about whom they insure (that's how they get to be on top). Nevertheless, even the best insurers cover *some* less-than-healthy in- dividuals (they take moderate risks, in return for higher premiums).

Insurance companies base their rates on "standard" risks. These are people with no significant health problems, who can be expected to live to normal life expectancies. Some companies offer discounted rates to individuals (called "preferred" risks) in above-average health.

People with health problems are *rated*. Ratings start with Table 1, for slight problems—such as being only a little overweight. As your health problems increase, your rating goes to Table 2 (e.g., dia- betes), Table 4 (uncontrolled hypertension), Table 8 (liver problems), and Table 12 (abnormal EKG), for example. Some companies have sixteen tables. Although a few conditions (AIDS, advanced cancer) do make it impossible to buy *any* life insurance, most people will find a place *somewhere* on the tables.

In some cases, your rating will be determined by occupation (e.g., police officer) rather than by health condition, because some occu- pations are intrinsically hazardous.

Prices vary from company to company, but you can expect to pay 25 percent above the standard price for each rating level. A policy that would cost you $1,000 in standard health might cost you $1,250 in Table 1 and $1,500 in Table 2. Therefore, it's in your interest to get as *low* a rating as possible. (Some agents are experts on *impaired- risk* insurance. If your own agent says there's a health problem, ask for a referral to an agent who specializes in impaired risks.)

Remember that ratings vary from one insurer to another. For ex- ample, insurers believe that heart attacks are caused by smoking, by high blood pressure, and by high cholesterol levels. They differ, though, on how much weight they assign to each factor. If you apply to three companies, you'll get three medical exams and three evalu- ations. Also, there may be significant differences in what each com- pany charges for the same amount of life insurance.

Whenever you apply for life insurance, the company will ask for an attending physician's (AP) statement, as well as a physical exam. The AP statement is a report from your family doctor that gives an overall picture of your health. If your agent (or an impaired-risk specialist) gets the AP statement first, he or she can apply to the insurer that's best for people with hypertension, for example; or to the insurance company that's lenient with applicants who have had bypass opera- tions. If you're in excellent health, your agent can confidently apply to companies that are best for preferred risks.

No matter what anyone tells you, *don't* lie about your health on a life-insurance application. If you conceal a condition, and that omission is exposed, your policy eventually may be cancelled. Worse, the insurer may contest the claim after your death. After a policyholder dies, an insurer may refuse to pay, citing a misleading application.

You may in fact want to defer making an application until you've lost some weight, stopped smoking, or addressed some other health problem. The better condition you're in when you take your physical, the less you'll wind up paying for life insurance. When bought for the right purpose and at the right price, life insurance offers tax advantages unmatched by any other financial vehicles.

SUMMING UP

• If you have dependents, you need life insurance to provide income in case of your unexpected death.
• To determine how much insurance to buy, project the shortfall between ongoing income and expenses after your death, and cover yourself for about twenty times what your family will need each year.
• Buy *extra* life insurance in order to pay for your children's college education.
• Initially, the *least expensive* form of life insurance is *term* insurance, which however becomes more costly as you grow older.
• *Permanent* life insurance is initially *more* expensive, but may prove to be *less* costly, than term as you grow older.
• Permanent life insurance offers tax-free buildup *and* the ability to tap that buildup, tax-free.
• In order to realize the benefits of permanent life insurance, you need to hold the policy for *at least* fifteen years.
• Although an insurance policy illustration may promise that your responsibility for paying premiums will vanish after a certain number of years, such illustrations are only projections based on assumptions that may prove inaccurate.
• For estate-planning purposes, you may want to buy relatively inexpensive *second-to-die* life insurance, which will pay off after both spouses die and the estate tax is due.
• Most people are insurable, but healthy individuals will pay lower life-insurance premiums.

35

Disinheriting the Taxman

Basic Estate-Tax Reduction Strategies

Besides protecting your assets during your lifetime, you probably want to leave behind as much as you can for your family. You certainly don't want to leave hundreds of thousands of dollars to the IRS. Unfortunately, the federal government will become one of your *principal* heirs—unless you do some tax planning.

Everyone is entitled to a $600,000 estate-tax exemption. If your estate is valued at *less* than $600,000 when you die, *no* estate tax will be due. But that doesn't mean if you have $600,000 in the bank, period. At your death, your executor will be responsible for adding up *all* of your assets, and filing a tax return thereon. The value of your house, your retirement plan, your investments, and everything else you own must be accounted for.

If the executor's total is *over* $600,000, your estate *will* owe taxes—and at a breathtakingly steep rate. The very lowest bracket is 37 percent, so if you have a $700,000 estate, you'll owe $37,000 on the excess $100,000. From there, the tax escalates to 55 percent, with a special

60 percent bracket on estates ranging in value from $10 million to $21 million.

In most cases, the estate tax will be due—in full—within nine months of your death. If cash isn't readily available, your executor may have to sell real estate, stocks, or other assets (in a hurry) to raise the money.

The Joy of Giving

If you reduce the size of your estate, you'll automatically reduce your estate's tax obligation. One strategy is to give away assets. However, there's a gift tax that's "unified" with the estate tax: In essence, whatever assets you give away reduce your estate-tax exemption. Let's look at some examples of how this strange system works (or doesn't).

Say you give away $100,000 before you die. Now, your estate-tax exemption is $500,000, *not* $600,000. And if you give away $800,000, your executor will have to pay a gift tax on the "excess" $200,000, at estate-tax rates.

Suppose you make gifts frequently, sending for instance birthday presents to your grandchildren, and anniversary presents to your children. Does every $50 check you write come out of your estate-tax exemption? No. At least not yet. In fact, under current law, anyone can make gifts of up to $10,000 each year, to *any* number of recipients, *without* reducing your gift- or estate-tax exemption. Say you have two children, plus a son- and daughter-in-law, and six grandchildren. You could give each of them up to $10,000 worth of assets per year (annually $100,000 in all), with *no* tax consequences. You wouldn't even have to fill out any gift-tax returns!

If you're married, the allowance increases to $20,000 per recipient per year, as long as your spouse formally agrees to the gifts. Given the rest of the family in the above example, you could reduce your taxable estate by up to $200,000 per year.

In addition to gifts of up to $20,000 per year, you can use the "med-ed" exclusion. That is, you can make unlimited gifts of medical payments and tuition on behalf of someone else, providing the payments are made directly to the health-care provider or school.

Give While the Giving Is Good

You also can make larger lifetime gifts, in effect using up part or all of your $600,000 lifetime exemption from gift- and estate taxes. Why should you do this? Politicians are hungry to tax the rich, and what better way than to increase estate taxes? Because of them, the $600,000 threshold may be dropped to as low as $300,000. If you act now, you may be able to make a larger tax-free gift while this shelter is still available. Also, once you give away assets, any future appreciation will be excluded from your taxable estate.

If you make gifts in order to reduce your estate tax, they should be made in cash, if at all possible, to avoid tax complications. If you have securities with a loss position (they have fallen in value since you bought them), you can sell them, take the tax loss, and then give away cash. On the other hand, giving away appreciated securities saddles the recipient with a low tax basis—and a tax obligation when the securities are sold.

When you make sizable gifts, look for assets that are likely to *appreciate* before you die. The 1990s may be an excellent time to give away real estate, for example: The current value may be low, because of depressed market conditions, and *any* recovery in real-estate prices won't increase your taxable estate. The same reasoning applies if you own shares in a small business whose earnings have been depressed.

Gifts such as real estate, and shares in a private business, need a valuation that will stand up to possible IRS scrutiny—so an independent appraisal is recommended.

Capital Gain, No Pain

Your appreciated assets should be held until you die. Under current law, at that time all your assets get a *step-up in basis*. Let's look into this a bit.

Suppose you purchased mutual-fund shares ten years ago, for $100,000. By the time of your death, those shares have appreciated in value to $300,000. Whoever inherits those shares gets a *new basis*—$300,000 instead of $100,000. If he or she sells the shares right away, for $300,000, *no* income tax will be due. The $200,000 capital gain goes untaxed! And the same is true for your home, other real estate, business interests, and any appreciated assets.

Gift and estate taxes *don't* apply when you either give or leave assets to your spouse. No matter how large, such transfers aren't taxed. You can have a $2 million estate—even a $10 million estate. If you leave everything to your spouse at your death, *no* estate tax will be due.

However, when your spouse dies, and those assets pass to your children and grandchildren, everything over $600,000 *will* be subject to an estate tax.

Trusts Are a Must

Most estate planning involves the use of trusts, in order to hold title to assets. To avoid estate and income taxes, you can transfer assets to an *irrevocable trust*, so that the assets are definitely out of your control.

Suppose, for example, you're making $10,000 annual gifts to reduce your taxable estate. Minors can't hold assets legally, so gifts to your grandchildren may have to be either in a trust or in a custodial account. Even gifts to adults might be made to a trust, if you have doubts about that adult's ability to handle money carefully. When gifts *are* made in trust, the assets can be preserved from creditors, from divorce actions, and from general squandering alike.

You may be able to make large annual gifts to a trust, free of a gift tax, if you follow the trail blazed by Maria Cristofani, a widow with two children, Frank and Lillian. She set up a trust, naming her children as *primary* beneficiaries. Their five children (Maria's grandchildren), ages two through eleven, were named *secondary* beneficiaries. If either Frank or Lillian failed to outlive Maria by 120 days, that child's children would split his or her share.

After setting up the trust, Maria transferred assets valued at $70,000 to the trust in 1984, and again in 1985. But then Maria died—and the IRS demanded back-taxes. According to the IRS, $20,000 of the annual gifts could be excluded, but the other $50,000 per year was subject to a gift tax. The Cristofani estate contended, and the Tax Court agreed, that there were seven trust beneficiaries—Frank, Lillian, and the five grandchildren. Under the terms of the trust, each beneficiary had a "Crummey" power—so called by virtue of taking the name of a landmark case.

After each contribution, the grandchildren had the legal right to withdraw assets from the trust, during a fifteen-day period, and so they had a "present interest" in the gifts. Therefore, Maria was entitled to give $10,000 per year to each of them, and the $70,000 gifts incurred no gift tax.

The court actually approved a very cozy setup. Frank and Lillian, the primary beneficiaries, also were the trustees. The secondary beneficiaries all were minors who, were they to exercise their withdrawal rights, could do so *only* through their guardians. And who were those guardians? Their parents, including Frank and Lillian. So Frank and Lillian had control over *all* the trust assets. Maria Cristofani effectively transferred $140,000 worth of assets to her two children in two years, without owing a cent of gift tax.

Thanks a $1.2 Million

Putting together the pieces outlined above, here's an estate-tax plan suitable for most families: First, make sure that you and your spouse each have at least $600,000 in assets—held outright, *not* jointly. If one spouse has significantly greater assets than the other, tax-free spousal gifts can be used to make sure each spouse has at least $600,000.

Then, each spouse should have either a will or a living trust stating that $600,000 should pass to children or grandchildren at his or her death. No matter *which* spouse dies first, $600,000 will go to future generations, tax-free, because of the estate-tax exemption. The rest should be left to the other spouse, tax-free, because it's a bequest to a spouse. Therefore, no estate tax will be due at the first death.

In the interim period following the first death, the surviving spouse can make tax-free gifts, up to the $10,000 annual limit. At the second death, when all the remaining assets are passed down, another $600,000 will be sheltered. Thus, $1.2 million (plus any assets transferred through gifts) will escape the estate tax.

This strategy calls for $600,000 to pass to your children from the first spouse to die. This may not leave the surviving spouse with enough income to live in comfort. In that case, you can leave that $600,000 to a trust. As long as the surviving spouse lives, he or she receives the income from that trust. On $600,000 worth of assets, that could be $30,000 or $35,000 per year. At the death of the second spouse, the trust assets go to the trust beneficiaries—probably your children. So you see that you *can* save taxes and *still* provide for your surviving spouse.

Mission: Control

Could the strategy just envisioned have any potential flaws? Unfortunately, yes. For example: Your spouse might squander the money you leave to him or her, beyond the $600,000 that goes into the trust. Or, in the case of his or her second marriage, your spouse might leave this money to his or her children, rather than to yours. Or (also in the case of such a remarriage), your assets might wind up with a spouse's new mate.

These problems can *all* be averted with a QTIP (*qualified terminable interest property*) trust. With these trusts, *all* the income *must* go to the surviving spouse. In case of an emergency, the trustee can use the principal to support the surviving spouse. When the surviving spouse dies, though, the trust assets will go to the trust beneficiaries named by you—probably your own children. Therefore, a QTIP trust provides for your spouse yet lets you control the assets so that they wind up with your children. Plus, the estate tax is deferred through the unlimited marital deduction.

Getting Your Money's Worth

Another type of trust that may be a huge tax saver is a *life-insurance trust*. Often, an estate plan includes a policy covering your life (or your life *and* your spouse's life). At your death, the policy's beneficiaries collect the proceeds, which can be used to pay the estate tax. However, if that policy is owned by you, the proceeds will be *included in* your estate, and half the proceeds will be lost to estate taxes.

Suppose you expect to leave a $2 million estate, so you buy a $700,000 life-insurance policy to cover the expected tax bill. If you die holding the policy, your estate jumps up to $2.7 million, and your tax bill to $1.05 million. You'll have bought a $700,000 policy, but received only $350,000 in benefits.

Because of what we have seen can happen otherwise, life-insurance policies are commonly held in irrevocable trusts. As long as certain rules are followed, and you have no control over the trust that holds the policy, all of the money paid under the policy will be excluded from your taxable estate.

House Rules

If you own a valuable house, you might want to establish a *personal residence trust*, according to the terms of which you give your house to the trust while retaining the right to reside in it for a specified number of years. *After* the trust term, the house can pass to your children, and the delay will greatly reduce the gift tax.

Suppose you're fifty years old and you specify a twenty-year term. You may wind up owing almost a zero gift tax. This would permit you to exclude the house and all future appreciation on it from your taxable estate. You can also use such a trust to transfer a *vacation* house on a discounted basis.

Setting up the trusts mentioned in this chapter might cost a few thousand dollars, plus the ongoing expense of administration and tax preparation. However, this investment will be worthwhile if you wind up saving your family many times that much in estate taxes.

SUMMING UP

• At your death, all of your assets will be valued and the result will be reported to the IRS.

• If your assets total under $600,000, *no* estate tax will be due.

• Any amount *over* $600,000 will be steeply taxed, starting at 37 percent and going as high as 60 percent.

• You can reduce your taxable estate by giving away assets during your lifetime.

• On gifts up to $10,000 per year per recipient ($20,000 from a married couple), *no* gift tax will be due.

• Gifts and bequests between spouses *aren't* taxed, no matter how large.

• Gifts and bequests often are made in trust, to protect assets and to direct them toward certain beneficiaries.

• Married couples can leave up to $1.2 million, free of gift- and estate taxes, by making sure that their children receive up to $600,000 worth of assets at the death of each donor.

• A QTIP trust will permit an older, wealthier spouse to provide for a surviving spouse yet make sure that the estate winds up with designated beneficiaries.

• If you buy life insurance to help pay an estate tax, the policy should be held in an irrevocable trust, outside of your taxable estate.

Part X

At Last, Safety First

36

Protect Your Most Precious Assets

The Health and Well-Being of Yourself and Your Family

On a certain Thanksgiving morning Anne S., a seventy-four-year-old widow weighing a spare 105 pounds, put on her best jewelry as she finished getting ready to go to a friend's home to enjoy a festive Turkey Day celebration. She then drove her new Nissan from the Borough of Queens in New York's metropolitan area to the suburban area of Valley Stream, on Long Island. She was thinking happy thoughts when suddenly two men in a sedan bumped her car from behind, then sideswiped it, and finally drove in front of her, to slow her down.

Because Anne had heard about carjacking, she refused to even stop her car (no less get out of it). Instead, she kept going—over the lawns of private homes when necessary. At one point the men cut her off, and one got out of their car and ran directly at her. "I put the transmission in drive and aimed right at him," she later told the *New York Times*. "I was trying to kill him as the only way of saving my life."

He dodged her, and she threw the car into reverse. The attacker then thrust his arm into her window, which she'd left open—but she kept going in reverse, dragging him almost a block. After that little setback, the outwitted miscreants gave up. And Anne got to have her turkey dinner, *plus* keep the gems and wheels.

If an attempted carjacking can take place on Thanksgiving Day in Nassau County, it can happen anywhere, at any time. In upscale North Dallas, for instance, where Ross Perot and town Mayor Steve Bartlett live, two residents were murdered and twenty others were victims of gunpoint robberies in early 1994 alone. Residents felt forced to switch from Cadillacs to Hondas, to lower their profiles.

Nationwide, a 1991 survey by the National Opinion Research Council found that more than 42 percent of residents in suburbs of major cities are afraid to walk in their own neighborhood at night. Apparently you're never *totally* safe, and neither are your loved ones. Everyone in your family must know what they need to do in order to survive!

Proceed With Caution

In some ways, Anne was lucky. Her assailants had tried to use the old "bump and rob" technique, about which she'd heard. But carjackers have moved on to other tactics. Now, you might be held up—at gunpoint—while you're pumping gas at a self-service station, or perhaps followed home, to have your house looted and your car stolen.

Whenever you're in a car, the threat of carjacking can exist. The American Automobile Association (AAA) has published these tips that you and your family should know about, concerning how to thwart carjackers:

• When you're out in public, look around and get a good view of the entire area.

• If you stop to use a pay phone or buy gas, choose sites that are busy and well-lighted.

• When you're returning home, keep an eye out for pedestrians and other vehicles in the area. Beep your horn so someone in the house knows you've arrived.

• Make sure your driveway and garage area are well-lighted after dark.

• If your car is bumped from behind, don't stop and get out if you have *any* doubts. Drive slowly to the nearest populated service station, police station, hospital, or fire station.

• Always keep your car doors locked, and roll your windows up most of the way. If you're in a doubtful neighborhood, close your windows and use the air-conditioning, if necessary.

The AAA doesn't recommend it, but in some situations you're justified in running a red light or ignoring a stop sign—at that point, getting a ticket is the least of your problems. In addition, everyone in your family should have a first-class *car phone*. Not only can they call 911 for help, if they see someone following them, but also, they won't have to worry about being stranded in case of a flat tire, engine trouble, or such.

Ted L. Gunderson, a security consultant in Santa Monica, California, advises drivers to use well-traveled streets at night. Put any valuables *in the trunk*, rather than exposed inside your car, and never leave any important papers in the glove compartment. In case of a breakdown, place a white handkerchief on the antenna, and sit inside your *locked* car, Gunderson suggests. Also, never accept a lift from a stranger.

In addition to following these precautions, you can buy an *anticarjacking device*. These are becoming increasingly sophisticated. One, for example, comes with a hidden "kill switch." You throw the switch if a carjacker forces you to get out of your car. Three minutes later, after the thief has gone out of shooting range, the car dies. (If you miss the switch you'll miss your car, of course.)

Another device, called Lasso (which sells for $300–$400) begins talking to unauthorized drivers seventy-five seconds after the car is in motion. Thieves and carjackers are told "Get out of my vehicle" because the engine will shut off and loud sirens will turn on. Not only sirens *outside* the vehicle, but also a painful, high-pitched squeal will sound *inside* the car.

Even buying an "armored car" won't help. Well—actually, it might, but it costs at least $40,000 to armor a car (with fiber) and install 2½"-thick window glass so that a 9-mm bullet won't penetrate. If you want "full-metal jacket" protection capable of stopping an armor-piercing projectile, the cost would be around $100,000—plus the price of the car. Following the precautions previously mentioned would seem to be a much more practical approach.

Ultra-Bright

The aforementioned Gunderson, a twenty-seven-year FBI veteran, offers these tips for everyday personal care, which you should pass on to your entire family:

- Use well-traveled, well-lit streets.
- Be alert, and watch for shadows.
- If necessary, use any available object as a weapon, such as an umbrella, shoes, or even your keys.
- Don't be embarrassed to *scream*!
- If you are being followed, cross the street; and if the person also crosses, run to the nearest residence and phone the police.
- Be alert for pickpockets working in pairs, with one jostling you while the other extracts your wallet.
- Carry only small amounts of cash.
- If you carry a handbag, always walk with the clasp facing toward you.
- Never walk alone after dark.
- Avoid shortcuts through dark areas.
- Stay away from doorways, shrubbery, and clumps of trees.
- Never accept rides from strangers.
- Never open your wallet so a stranger can see your identification or how much money you're carrying.
- Never leave a handbag in an unattended location, or carry it open.
- Keep the phone numbers of your local fire and police department handy and, if applicable, the number of your apartment building's security office.

Should you or your family members carry a defensive spray? Mace is made from a chlorine-based tear-gas compound called CN, or chloroacetophenone. However, CN acts by irritating membrane tissues, so it's not always effective against attackers high on drugs or alcohol. Aficionados prefer Mace fortified with pepper.

What about stun guns? They deliver 200,000 volts of electricity (versus 120 volts for a typical home-wiring system), quite enough to stagger most attackers. But then, you have to *touch* your assailant in order for a stun gun to work. Although stun guns are illegal in many areas, if you live in one where they *are* legal, it may be worth paying around $60 to have one you can hold in your hand while you're taking a walk on the wild side.

Raise the Drawbridge!

Your home is supposed to be your castle, a fortress against intruders. But that's no longer automatically the case, so—if you can afford to—move into a secure community. Especially in Nevada and Texas, subdivisions are being built with gates, walls, and even moats.

Assuming you don't live in such a safe development, you and your family members should know what to do if a burglar is discovered in your house, perhaps at night while the family is asleep. The best strategy, in most cases, is to *get out*, along with the rest of the family. You never know what weapons a burglar might have, and how willing that intruder is to use them. If that's not practical, make noise—turn your radio on full volume, perhaps. If the burglar is actually in your room, play possum. You're really at a disadvantage, so you have to hope that the intruder will only take the money and run. Most burglars *won't* attack unless they're frightened.

If you arrive home to see that your house has been broken into, leave it. Get the police before going back in, just in case a burglar is still there. For insurance purposes, take a photo of any damage before cleaning up; then get a copy of the police report.

One way to alert yourself to an intruder is to do this (but first be sure to warn anyone living with you): Whenever you leave home, put (say) a $20 bill just inside the door. If that bait isn't there when you're back home, get out immediately. (You can do the same in a hotel room *if* you're not expecting maid or other service.) When you're at home, don't let door-to-door salespeople in.

Unsafe Deposit

When you leave your house, pick your shopping malls with care—favor those with visible security forces cruising through the parking lot. Even in such malls, park in well-lit areas, however.

For city dwellers especially, one of the most dangerous trips possible is to an automated teller machine (ATM). Marshall N., a New York banker, went to an ATM in mid-Manhattan at 10:30 on a summer night. A man with a knife met him there and "invited" Marshall to make a $200 withdrawal. It was an "offer" that Marshall couldn't refuse.

If you're an ATM user, follow some simple rules. Avoid ATMs in dark, remote places: If you can't get to a safe one at a bank, go to your *supermarket*. Don't go near an ATM if you see someone hanging around, either on foot *or* in a parked car. If you're driving up to an ATM, keep your doors and other windows locked:

Don't register and use a personal identification number (PIN) that someone might guess, such as the last four digits of your phone number. *Never* write down your PIN.

Have your ATM card ready, so you can get in and out of the ATM area as quickly as possible. Put the cash you receive in your pocket or purse right away, so you're not ambling along flashing a wad of bills. Make sure you have your *card* before you leave the ATM, and retain your *receipt*, to prevent anyone from getting your account information. Go with someone you know, if possible—and *don't* hold the door for strangers when entering an enclosed ATM.

Never make a *cash deposit* into an ATM. If there's a foul-up, you won't be able to prove you actually made the deposit!

Ready and Willing

If you're being mugged, should you fight back or give in? Put yourself in the shoes of Brian H., a Canadian businessman who had just finished dinner with a countryman in London. As they left the restaurant and headed back toward their hotel, they encountered five skinheads who were making martial-arts moves.

One of the skinheads asked them for money. According to the conventional wisdom, Brian should have handed over his wallet and been happy to escape without injury. However, in the hair-trigger 1990s, meekness may invite aggression. Frustrated criminals may injure you, even kill you, if you're too passive.

Brian, who had some martial-arts training himself, set himself for action, sending a subtle signal to the skinheads that he wouldn't be an easy mark. At the same time, he kept on walking and making conversation with the skinheads. "I've spent all my money," he told them. The skinheads wound up giving Brian a 50-pence coin!

If you're ever involved in anything even resembling *this* confrontation, you *also* may not be of a mind to give in docilely. If so, keep up a conversation with your would-be muggers. Tell them you're just an average working man (or woman), just as they are. While you're talking, though, look for a chance to get away or yell for help. If you *truly* know what you're doing, perhaps launch a preemptive strike. (If none of the above applies, you can try either running, or giving in.)

The best defense is offense: Avoid confrontations by staying alert. For example, never stop to look at your watch if someone asks you for the time. Make a guess, and keep walking.

What should you do if someone comes up behind you and puts an arm around your throat? Spin around and face the bugger. Now your opponent *can't* choke you because it's the muscles at the *back* of your neck that are being squeezed. Even if you have never had any martial-arts training whatsoever, you can still strike at his groin, kneecap, face, or throat, with whatever it takes to do that. (*Hint:* A man's groin is *extremely* sensitive, so give it your best shot. He more than likely will release you—and not be able to catch you when you flee. *Also:* you'll have two free arms, to his one or none.)

You may want to make sure that everyone in your family knows basic self-defense techniques. Many martial-arts instructors have special programs for people who *don't* care to earn a black belt but *do* want to know how to defend themselves.

Buddy System

If you come from a wealthy family, or even if you're only moderately wealthy, you're a potential kidnap victim. Hire a driver, if you can afford it. Not only will that give you less stress and more work time, but also it will provide a defender in case of a kidnap attempt. You might want to apply for a sidearm (gun) permit, too. Just make sure you take enough training so you know how to use it if you're threatened.

Vary your routine. *Don't* eat the same meal in the same restaurant every day; *don't* regularly jog the same route at the same time. Dress conservatively, and save any jewelry for private occasions.

Skip vanity license plates, because they draw attention to yourself. If you think you're being followed while in your car, *don't* drive home. Go somewhere public and official—such as a police station or hospital.

Kid Stuff

Of course, children, too, can be kidnap victims—but there are *some* devices that might well help protect your kids. The Child Guardian ($50 from Direkt Inc.) allows a parent to beep a child. And, if the child feels threatened, he or she can sound a loud alarm.

For around $30, you can buy a Personal Attack Alarm, sold by

Quorum International. These are hand-held devices that enable you to pull a pin and activate a 100-decibel alarm, roughly equal to the noise a commercial jet makes on takeoff and many New York subway trains create. (These so-called "panic buttons" also may be appropriate for adults who go out alone or stay home alone.)

Whether or not you go in for high-tech protection, make sure your kids know the basics: *Don't* talk with strangers, and *don't* go off with anyone. If an adult tries to abduct your child, that young one shouldn't just cry, since tears can make a confrontation seem like a normal parent–child altercation. Instead, your child should keep saying "I don't know you," over and over, *as loud as possible.* If anything will attract help from passersby, *that* will do it.

Also, don't buy any clothes for a child with his or her name on display, and don't sew on name tags where they're visible. Those clues make it all too easy for a stranger to call the child by name and say "Your Mom sent me to get you"—or some other come-on line.

For information on Child Lures Community Plan, a Vermont-based program that teaches children how to resist enticements from would-be abductors, call 802-985-8458.

Learn Your Lesson

Don't send your child off to college without checking on the crime climate there! The federal Crime Awareness and Campus Security Act (which took effect in late 1992), requires most colleges to annually publish crime statistics for the past three years, including on-campus and near-campus murders, rapes, robberies, assaults, and arrests for weapons possession.

In addition, colleges *must* describe their campus security programs. On a campus visit, when you check out the dorms and the academic facilities, stop by the admissions office and get a copy of the school's crime-prevention pamphlet. Also, go to its security office and talk with the officers there, to get a personal impression of the magnitude of the crime problem, and the effectiveness of the security department.

Shop Before You Drop

Many of the personal-security devices mentioned in this chapter, and elsewhere in this book, are available from Safety Zone (call 800-999-3030 for a catalog). Here's a sampling of the 1994 offerings:

• Water-resistant Electro Flares for use in case of highway emergencies (two for $15.95)

• A keychain alarm that emits a shrill noise meant to scare off attackers, and converts to a door-, window-, or fire alarm ($15.95)

• Peppergard, Mace, and Spray Stunner ($14.95–$22.95)

• Bubble Box Safe for travel ($39.95)

• "Leg Safe" and "Waist Safe" ($9.95) to hold valuables while traveling

• Door Jammer ($17.95), a steel brace that keeps intruders out of your home or hotel room

• Safe-T-Man ($119.95), a life-size simulated male meant to indicate you're not alone, whether at home or in your car

For free pamphlets such as "How to Be Streetwise and Safe," "Got a Minute? You Could Stop Crime," "How to Crimeproof Your Business," "How to Protect Your Home," and "How to Protect Your Children," write to the Superintendent of Documents, U.S. Government Printing Office, Washington, DC 20402.

SUMMING UP

• Today, *defensive* driving means keeping an eye out for carjackers, and using *offensive* measures to thwart them, if necessary.

• Wherever you go, stay in well-populated, well-lighted areas whenever possible.

• Instead of letting your guard down when you're home, make it a point *not* to open the door to strangers.

• Automated teller machines lure cash-hungry thieves, so be wary of people hanging around when you use an ATM.

• If you are approached by potential muggers, engage them in conversation *while* you seek a chance to escape.

• Teach your kids to keep away from strangers, and *don't* dress them in anything that reveals their name.

• Before you send a child to college, find out how many violent *crimes* have been committed there, and how serious the school is about physical *security*.

Index

‍EL™ for *Reading Literature and Writing Argument*

™ is Pearson's newest way of delivering our respected content. Fully digital ‍ly engaging, REVEL™ offers an immersive learning experience designed ‍way today's students read, think, and learn. Enlivening course content ‍dia interactives and assessments, REVEL™ empowers educators to in-‍engagement with the course and to connect better with students.

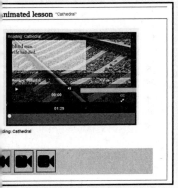

animated lesson "Cathedral"

Reading: Cathedral

blind man.
wife had died.

00:00   CC
01:29

ding: Cathedral

Video and Rich Multimedia Content

Videos, audio recordings, animations, and multimedia instruction provide context that enables students to engage with the text in a more meaningful way.

‍active Readings and Exercises

‍s explore readings through interactive texts. Robust annotation tools allow ‍s to take notes, and post-reading assignments let instructors monitor their ‍s' completion of readings before class begins.

‍n-Time Context

‍ime context—encompassing biographical, historical, and social insights—is ‍rated throughout, giving students a deeper understanding of what they read.

‍grated Writing
‍nments

‍-stakes, low-stakes, and high-stakes ‍ tasks allow students multiple ‍unities to interact with the ideas ‍ed in the reading assignments, ensur-‍ they come to class better prepared.

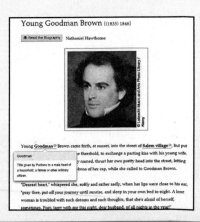

Young Goodman Brown [(1835) 1846]

Read the Biography   Nathaniel Hawthorne

© Lebrecht Music and Arts Photo Library / Alamy

Young Goodman ‍ Brown came forth, at sunset, into the street of Salem village ‍, but put

Goodman

Title given by Puritans to a male head of a household; a farmer or other ordinary citizen.

‍e threshold, to exchange a parting kiss with his young wife.
‍y named, thrust her own pretty head into the street, letting
‍bons of her cap, while she called to Goodman Brown.

'Dearest heart,' whispered she, softly and rather sadly, when her lips were close to his ear,
'pray thee, put off your journey until sunrise, and sleep in your own bed to-night. A lone
woman is troubled with such dreams and such thoughts, that she's afraid of herself,
sometimes. Pray, tarry with me this night, dear husband, of all nights in the year!'

Reading Literature and Writing Argument

Reading Literature and Writing Argument

SIXTH EDITION

Missy James
Tallahassee Community College

Alan P. Merickel
Tallahassee Community College
Emeritus

Greg Loyd
Tallahassee Community College

Jenny Perkins
Tallahassee Community College

Boston   Columbus   Indianapolis   New York   San Francisco   Amsterdam   Cape Town
Dubai   London   Madrid   Milan   Munich   Paris   Montréal   Toronto   Delhi   Mexico City
São Paulo   Sydney   Hong Kong   Seoul   Singapore   Taipei   Tokyo

Senior Editor: Brad Potthoff
Senior Development Editor: Anne Brunell Ehrenworth
Program Manager: Anne Shure
Product Marketing Manager: Nicholas T. Bolt
Field Marketing Manager: Joyce Nilsen
Digital Content Specialist: Julia Pomann
Senior Media Producer: Tracy Cunningham
Project Manager: Rebecca Gilpin

Project Coordination, Text Design, and Electronic Page Makeup: Integra Software Services Pvt., Ltd.
Design Lead: Heather Scott
Cover Designer: Tamara Newnam
Cover Illustration: Exdez/Getty Images
Senior Manufacturing Buyer: Roy L. Pickering, Jr.
Printer/Binder: Edwards Brothers Malloy
Cover Printer: Lehigh-Phoenix Color/Hagerstown

Acknowledgments of third-party content appear on pages 587–592, which constitute an extension of this copyright page.

Library of Congress Cataloging-in-Publication Data

James, Missy.
  Reading literature and writing argument/Missy P. James, Alan P. Merickel, Jenny Perkins, Greg Loyd.
    pages cm
Includes bibliographical references and indexes.
  ISBN 978-0-13-412013-3—ISBN 0-13-412013-2
  1. English language—Rhetoric. 2. Persuasion (Rhetoric)
3. College readers. 4. Report writing. I. Merickel, Alan.
II. Perkins, Jenny. III. Loyd, Greg. IV. Title.
  PE1408.J36 2015
  808'.0427—dc23

                            2015030063

10 9 8 7 6 5 4 3 2 1—EBM—19 18 17 16

www.pearsonhighered.com

ISBN 10:   0-134-12013-2
ISBN 13: 978-0-134-12013-3

Contents

7 Crime and Punishment   185

9 Power and Responsibility   435

Preface

Reading Literature and Writing Argument springs directly from our classroom experiences as teachers of two college composition courses: "Writing Argument and Persuasion" and "Writing about Literature." We want our students to experience the essence of these two courses. In both courses, students are enriched, as readers and as writers, through their active engagement with ideas in written text. *Reading Literature and Writing Argument* is based on the premise that writing is valued when it makes readers think. This premise implies, of course, that a person must have ideas—something to say—in order to put pen to paper or fingers to keyboard. However, the notion that these ideas must have value can be daunting to the individual who is staring at the blank page or screen. Here is where literature—stories, poems, plays, essays—can play a vital role.

Literature liberates thinking, and argument disciplines it. The combined forces of literature and argument are inspiring and empowering. Through their engagement with literature and application of the principles of argument, students practice the skills of analysis and evaluation and, in doing so, develop critical standards for judging ideas. Henry David Thoreau's essay "Civil Disobedience," for example, presents an explicit argument. Reading Thoreau's essay, students can examine his assertion that the individual's first responsibility is to maintain his or her own integrity. Similarly, students can examine the implied arguments in a poem by Gwendolyn Brooks, or in stories by Louise Erdrich, Sir Arthur Conan Doyle, and Ernest Hemingway.

To borrow from Robert Frost's statement on poetry, *Reading Literature and Writing Argument* is designed to bring both "delight" and "wisdom" to the first-year college student's composition experience. We believe that students will enjoy reading the literature pieces, practicing critical thinking skills, and exploring various perspectives on issues related to their own lives. And finally, students will discover that they have a wealth of ideas as well as the critical skills to enable them to compose written arguments that will compel their readers to think. The blank page or computer screen will present a welcome invitation to speak out and to be heard, to make choices, and to make a difference in one's own life and in the lives of others.

NEW TO THIS EDITION

- **New chapter on improving reading skills.** Chapter 2 ("Reading Litera-ture") covers the importance of learning how to read poetry, fiction, essays, and drama. Complete with helpful tips to improve reading skills, this chap-ter guides students in expanding critical thinking by identifying theme and recognizing ambiguity in literary works.
- **Revised chapter on analyzing argument.** Chapter 3 ("Analyzing Argu-ment") shows students the connection between argument and critical thinking and breaks down the components of an argument in a way that students will understand, with more on audience appeal and tone. The chapter culminates with an annotated argument essay that shows students the moves one writer makes in crafting a successful argument.
- **New chapter on researching and documentation.** Chapter 4 ("Research-ing and Documenting an Argument Essay") walks students through the pro-cess of finding and integrating sources into their argument essay with more information on finding credible sources and avoiding plagiarism. The chapter concludes with an annotated research essay that shows students how to suc-cessfully integrate paraphrase, direct quotation, and summary into an essay.
- **A revised chapter on creating an argument.** Chapter 5 ("Creating an Argument") guides students in planning and drafting their argument, with more on the writing process and more on constructing an academic argument. New strategy questions provide a helpful checklist to ensure the argument is sound—both structurally and grammatically. Annotated student essays in this chapter show the moves two writers made to produce sound argument essays.
- **New student writing.** Two new student papers show students models of well-crafted arguments. In addition, a new annotated bibliography provides a useful model for students conducting research for their argument essay.
- **New selections in Part 2.** Fiction by writers including Shirley Jackson, Katherine Mansfield, O Henry, Sir Arthur Conan Doyle, and Virgil Suarez; poetry by Joy Harjo and A.E. Housman; nonfiction by George Will; and dra-mas by William Shakespeare and Susan Glaspell.
- **A new thematic chapter in Part 2.** An entirely new Chapter 7 ("Crime and Punishment") brings together classic works by Kate Chopin and Edgar Allen Poe with contemporary pieces by Rhett Morgan and Kevin Crossley-Holland.
- **New and revised exercises throughout.** Activities in every chapter reinforce chapter concepts and provide practice for students to apply what they have learned in the form of both short and long writing assignments.

ORGANIZATION

Part I: Rhetoric

Chapter 1, The Literature and Argument Connection. This chapter intro-duces students to core concepts of the book: developing the habit of critical inquiry and reading literature as a way to open up thinking and thus discover their own questions and subjects for writing argument.

Chapter 2, Reading Literature. This chapter examines the reading process and offers suggestions for improving critical reading and, therefore, critical thinking. We include sample reading strategies and analysis of poetry, fiction, and drama. We define key literary terms and apply the terms to the sample literature.

Activities reinforce the chapter concepts by giving students a chance to practice applying the concepts to their reading of two literature pieces and a sample student essay.

Chapter 3, Analyzing Argument. This chapter explains academic argument—how we form opinions and arrive at conclusions—and introduces the terms and tools of argument. We challenge students to exercise critical inquiry by questioning the foundation of their opinions. In explaining logical fallacies, we take a lead from our experiences in the composition classroom and highlight hasty generalization, arguably the most common fallacy. Activities are provided to help students apply what they have learned in this chapter, thus far, about examining thinking.

Next, we introduce terms of argument structure as well as rhetorical concepts related to audience appeal and tone, applying these concepts to literature. In selecting terms and concepts to feature, we again chose the tools our classroom experiences have shown to be particularly useful for our students, both as readers and as writers. Activities featuring poetry, fiction, and visual argument give students opportunities to apply the terms and tools of argument analysis and to engage in creative and critical thinking.

Chapter 4, Researching and Documenting an Argument Essay. This chapter provides a detailed explanation of the research process for a research-based, academic argument. We address the challenges students face when working with sources, including properly documenting sources. We stress the essential skills of avoiding plagiarism and utilizing credible research material. We also offer suggestions for smoothly incorporating direct quotations, summaries, and paraphrases.

Again, learning from our students, we attempt to help students understand the *whys* of the research and writing processes and procedures. The chapter includes a section on the annotated bibliography and a sample student essay with notes.

Chapter 5, Creating an Argument. This chapter gives students the opportunity to practice their critical analysis and writing skills. We begin with suggestions for beginning the writing process. We offer an annotated argument so that students have yet another example of the use of terms explained in previous chapters. We explain the concept of the Rogerian argument with samples for illustration. Activities provide students an opportunity to plan an academic argument and practice applying Rogerian argument strategy, specifically, the skill of creative problem solving.

Part 2: Anthology

Chapters 6 through 9, Literature Selections Centered Around Four Enduring Themes: "Individuality and Community," "Crime and Punishment," "Family and Identity," and "Power and Responsibility." Following each reading selection are questions that invite students to apply the critical thinking concepts and argument terms and tools from Chapters 1 through 5. In this way, the literature pieces offer a practice field for students to hone the tools of critical thinking. Also, writing topics are provided to generate longer written responses and, thus, to prompt students' ideas for writing their own arguments.

For the anthology chapters, we purposefully selected broad cultural themes. To echo Katherine Anne Porter's testimony, we believe that students appreciate the opportunity to explore their own thinking processes within these contexts. Also, the themes invite students to draw connections, not only among the readings within a single chapter, but also among readings throughout the four chapters. For example, some family issues that students may identify in the Chapter 8 readings can be related to responsibility issues in the Chapter 9 readings. Chapter Activities are designed to stimulate students' thinking about their reading experiences and about potential issues for writing an argument. Moreover, we provide two global perspectives research/writing topics, a Rogerian argument student collaboration activity and sample issue, as well as topic connections among the literature within the chapter and across chapters.

ADDITIONAL RESOURCES

REVEL™ for James, *Reading Literature and Writing Argument*

REVEL™ is Pearson's newest way of delivering our respected content. Fully digital and highly engaging, REVEL™ offers an immersive learning experience designed for the way today's students read, think, and learn. Enlivening course content with media interactives and assessments, REVEL™ empowers educators to increase engagement with the course, and to better connect with students.

With an emphasis on critical thinking and argument, REVEL™ for *Reading Literature and Writing Argument* offers superior coverage of reading, writing, and arguing about literature enhanced by an array of multimedia interactives that prompt student engagement. Throughout REVEL's™ flexible online environment, the authors demonstrate that the skills emphasized in their discussions of communication are relevant not only to literature courses, but to all courses in which students analyze texts or write arguments.

Instructor's Manual

An accompanying online manual provides notes on teaching the rhetoric section, Chapters 1 through 5; suggestions for peer critiques; notes on Chapters 6 through 9, including teaching notes for each of the literature selections. Finally, the manual provides a list of argument terms paired with literature titles from the Anthology chapters and a list connecting Anthology chapter themes to films. ISBN-10: 0134134567

ACKNOWLEDGMENTS

First, we thank our students, who throughout our decades of teaching college composition have been the primary reason we have endeavored to write this book. We are grateful to Danielle Peacock, Holden Giles, Cale Blount, and Simone Weatherly for their generosity in sharing their essays and creativity.

For the changes in the sixth edition, the following colleagues provided helpful and constructive guidance: Forster Agama, Tallahassee Community College; Susan Arvay, Raritan Valley Community College; Annette Cole, Tarrant County College; Mildred A. Duprey, College of Southern Nevada; Melissa Edwards, Middlesex County College–Edison; Iris Nicole Harvey, Tarrant County College; Jonathan Harvey, Northern Virginia Community College; Burgsbee Lee Hobbs, Saint Leo University; Chalet Jean-Baptiste, Northern Virginia Community College–Manassas; Arlandis Jones, Tarrant County College; Ray Linville, Sandhills Community College; and Hilary Stillwell, Tallahassee Community College.

We thank editor-in-chief Joseph Terry, and we are most grateful to our development editor, Anne Brunell Ehrenworth. We appreciate the direction of Anne Shure, Program Manager, and Sue Nodine, Project Editor. We wish to offer a special thank you to Rebecca Gilpin for her oversight throughout the production process.

Our families encouraged and supported us as we worked on this edition; we are especially thankful to David and Geneva Loyd, Melanie Loyd, Todd Robinson, Terry and Linda Cole, Donna Mehr, Iain McHenry, and Cole Perkins.

Missy James
Alan Merickel
Greg Loyd
Jenny Perkins

Reading Literature and Writing Argument

PART 1

RHETORIC

CHAPTER 1

The Literature and Argument Connection

In this chapter, you will learn about

- defining academic argument.
- expanding thinking and taking a position on an issue.
- exploring issues to find the right topic for your argument.
- analyzing an argument.

When people join a confrontational argument, they often close their minds. Their emotions displace their reason as their desire for victory overcomes any inclination to listen to their opposition's point of view.

ACADEMIC ARGUMENT AND CRITICAL INQUIRY

In an academic setting, however, argument means more than confrontation. **Academic argument** implies a reasoned approach to issues. People also hold opposing viewpoints in an academic community, but they debate in order to modify and strengthen their positions. Rather than attempting to defeat an opponent, through the respectful exchange of viewpoints, each side "wins" by attaining a deeper understanding of the issue. After all, the purpose of the college experience is learning. Whether that learning comes through classroom discussion, through research, or through the general interaction of members in the academic community, academic argument is an integral part of the learning process.

Each semester, many contemporary social issues wash across a college campus, touching the academic disciplines both directly and indirectly: freedom of speech, cyberbullying, immigration, national health insurance, drones. Although in society at large, sharply focused debates emerge as people establish positions around these issues, while in a college setting, you have the opportunity to step back from the moment and create some emotional distance. The college experience enables you to probe the values and belief systems that underlie issues and ideas. Looking inward and outward, you develop and practice the habit of **critical inquiry**, which enables you to make independent choices, deliberately and thoughtfully, and to participate in shaping a free society.

In acknowledging that "[o]ne of the dangers in the White House, based on my reading of history, is that you get wrapped up in groupthink and everybody agrees with everything and there's no discussion and there are no dissenting views," it is clear that President Barack Obama understands the need for critical inquiry.[1] Through discussion and addressing dissenting views, thinking is strengthened rather than weakened. The academic community provides a place for you to participate in discussion with individuals who hold dissenting views and, thus, to practice critical inquiry.

Like the skills of repairing a motorcycle engine or playing guitar, critical thinking is not innate; however, just as through study and practice, you can learn to repair an engine and play guitar, you also can learn to become a proficient critical thinker. First, a critical thinker is one who is willing to question his or her own thinking. For example, consider the following scenario:

Your college has a mandatory class attendance policy, which you adamantly oppose. After all, you are the one who is paying to attend the class. Given your strong feelings, you decide to write a letter to the editor for publication in your college newspaper. You know that among your audience, besides your parents, who have taught you to speak up for yourself, will be administrators, professors, and, of course, fellow students—quite a diverse group. As you prepare to write your letter, here are some questions you might ask yourself: Besides the fact that I pay for my own classes, what other reasons do I have to support my position opposing the college's mandatory attendance policy? How might my different groups of readers—administrators, professors, students—respond to each reason I have listed? Why do others, including most, if not all, administrators and professors and even some of my fellow classmates, believe that the policy is necessary? What might happen if the policy were dropped? Would I continue to attend class regularly and would most of my peers? What would be some of the consequences—on our attitudes, our learning, our grades—of allowing us students to choose whether or not to attend class?

As you attempt to answer your questions, you may be surprised to discover that, while you have some strong personal opinions about the topic, you do not have a lot of solid information beyond your own viewpoint. After critically examining your thinking, you readily acknowledge that you need to seek out more information and viewpoints if you wish to develop an argument that will influence others, especially those who do not already share your viewpoint.

The following questions illustrate how you can apply your skills as a critical thinker:

---

[1] qtd. in Peter Baker and Helene Cooper. "Appointments Begin a New Phase for Obama." *The New York Times*. The New York Times, 2 Dec. 2008. Web. 10 June 2015.

Monitoring Yourself as a Critical Thinker

***Do I have solid information upon which to base
my judgment? Is that information enough
to stimulate my creative thinking?***

One example, no matter how powerful, is not sufficient to support a position: Certainly, cases of police brutality are common in the media, but that does not mean that all law enforcement officers are vicious and uncaring.

Do I recognize assumptions I hold that may influence my reasoning?

As one who has grown up in a society with high-tech advantages, I might assume that Western technology is superior. This assumption, however, could lead to missed opportunities to invest in start-up technology firms in India.

***Am I making a fair judgment by examining
all sides of the issue equally?***

Hoping to support the ecological advantage of alternative fuel vehicles, I might fail to take into account the environmental impact of the huge power plants required to generate the electricity coming into my garage where I plug in my electric car.

***Am I allowing my prejudices and goals to push me too
quickly toward a particular conclusion?***

If my uncle plays professional football, am I able to objectively assess his team's chances of making the Super Bowl?

***Have I taken the time to share my ideas with people who will give
me an honest assessment of their quality?***

My roommates won't take my argument seriously and my mother thinks I am the next Hemingway, but I have observed several classmates who are outspoken in voicing their viewpoints. I will arrange for us to share drafts with each other.

READING LITERATURE TO EXPAND THINKING

The study of literature and the study of argument are complementary and mutually empowering; both contribute to creative envisioning and critical thinking. Even as we hold fast to opposing viewpoints, we share the common ground of our humanity. Literature can lead us to this common ground. Through careful and close reading, we are better prepared to articulate a thoughtful position and to argue it with heartfelt emotion, clear logic, and valid reasoning. When we read, we discover our own interpretations of a text. Explaining the theme of a selection, the motivation of a character, or the significance of an ambiguous ending requires a specific thesis/claim, sufficient evidence, and clear organization. We create an argument when we articulate our position about a piece of literature.

READING LITERATURE TO EXPLORE AN ISSUE

Another connection between literature and argument can come from inspiration or emotion. One way to develop and practice the habit of critical inquiry is to explore ideas and experiences through different lenses. Imaginative literature provides readers with such an array of lenses. While reading literature, you are transported from the particular details of your life to the lives of other persons, to their places and their times. You may emerge from the pages of the literary work with fresh perspectives, new lenses for examining both the personal issues that sometimes cloud your daily life and the social issues that often divide communities.

Listening to stories as a young child, you were not only entertained but also informally instructed in values, such as honesty, competition, pride, loyalty, compassion, and empathy. As a reader in a first-year college writing course, you continue to learn from stories about your beliefs and ideas, the **value assumptions** that underlie your behavior and attitudes and inform your opinions and conclusions. Reading stories, poems, plays, and essays, you not only are entertained but also are prompted to explore your own thinking. This exploration can provide inspiration when generating ideas for an argument essay. Perhaps you would like to write an essay on the reception American soldiers receive when returning home from the Middle East. You have a valid claim and have conducted appropriate research on veterans' medical benefits and mental health, but you feel the essay lacks an emotional connection. You could consider Wilfred Owen's poem, "*Dulce et Decorum Est*," which provides a first-person account of World War I, and though this war began 100 years ago, the feelings of the narrator have a timeless, universal appeal. His poem may give you insight into the reactions of a soldier when you have not experienced the horrors of battle yourself.

READING LITERATURE TO ANALYZE ARGUMENT

Some literature is an argument itself. It might take a position or make a claim, either directly stated or implied. It might provide supporting details from personal experience, observation, or careful research. It might appeal to our emotions, challenge our assumptions, or prompt us to question respected institutions, such as the legal system. Evaluating the academic argument techniques within a piece of literature provides us with another opportunity for critical inquiry and logical reasoning. (Later in Chapter 3, after we have delved more deeply into academic argument, we will use "*Dulce et Decorum Est*" to articulate the elements of argument found in that poem.)

CHAPTER 2

Reading Literature

In this chapter, you will learn about
- improving analytical reading skills.
- expanding critical thinking by identifying theme and recognizing ambiguity.
- exploring issues to develop topics for an argument essay.

IMPROVING READING SKILLS

You've probably heard the expression, "reading for pleasure," and plenty of people do find enjoyment in reading. The problem with the concept of pleasure reading is the assumption of the opposite, that some reading is painful. There will be literature that does not appeal to everyone, of course, but reading that requires time and effort should not immediately be dismissed; careful reading can yield rewarding results.

Tips for Improving Your Reading Skills

Read the text more than once.   Some readers pick up a text and read it through one time, close the book, and declare they didn't understand it. That approach isn't fair to the reader or the text. Complex or unfamiliar literature requires a bit of work. Plus, practice makes all skills come more naturally.

Read the text in small sections.   Sometimes, trying to understand an entire piece can be overwhelming. Approach a poem by lines or stanzas or a story by paragraphs or pages. All tasks seem easier when attacked in manageable amounts.

Read the text aloud.   Something fascinating happens when you slow down and take the time to read out loud. Concentration improves. Emphasis shifts. You notice words, phrases, and sounds that you might have missed when reading visually. This simple shift can improve your understanding of the text.

Take notes.   Like reading out loud, writing notes can increase concentration and focus. The notes can follow your own style—maybe you like to write notes in the margin; maybe you prefer writing notes on paper; perhaps you are organized; perhaps you are visual. It doesn't matter how you approach note-taking. The key is to pay attention to what the author has written.

Look up unfamiliar words.   It may appear obvious, but many readers don't make the effort to learn new vocabulary or understand literary allusions to history, mythology, religion, or literature. The author expects you to understand the references and vocabulary. Use a dictionary or the Internet when you encounter an unfamiliar term or reference.

Prepare for multiple interpretations.   Life experiences, age, gender, and political preferences may all contribute to how you understand a certain text. While you may understand a text differently than a classmate, both interpretations can be valid.

Recognize ambiguity, tone, and subtext.   All writing is not straightforward in its presentation. Some writers may use humor or sarcasm, while others want the reader to understand ideas that are not directly written, the subtext. Sometimes, authors leave us wondering what happened, creating ambiguity. All of these complex situations require more effort from readers. We have to make judgments, decisions, and choices based on our understanding of the characters and our own perspective.

Identify the theme.   The theme of a selection is its main point, its central topic. Each piece of literature may have more than one theme. It is up to you to articulate the theme clearly and specifically. One poem, for example, may be about love. That theme is very broad because there are so many types of love: romantic, unrequited, familial, brotherly, obsessive, platonic, and so on.

William Carlos Williams's "The Red Wheelbarrow"

"The Red Wheelbarrow" by William Carlos Williams is an imagist poem, very brief with simple vocabulary. You might wonder how it can even be called a poem—it doesn't rhyme; it doesn't have meter. It *does* have structure: three words, one word, three words, one word. It also creates a very clear picture, a snapshot of a moment. We can use this poem to practice reading through a text and identifying a theme.

The Red Wheelbarrow (1923)

so much depends
upon

a red wheel
barrow

5   glazed with rain
water

beside the white
chickens.

The first step is to read the poem several times, including at least one time out loud. Even though the poem is short, it can still be analyzed in small sections.

You might begin by considering what words stand out. "Glazed"? What do you think of when you read that word? Donuts? A glazed donut is a beautiful thing! It is sweet and shiny and lovely. Perhaps you think of glazed pottery, which is also shiny and beautiful and a piece of art. So, why is the wheelbarrow shiny?

Perhaps the wheelbarrow is shiny because of the rainwater, the cleansing rainwater. Most wheelbarrows are used for carting dirt or fertilizer or debris around a yard or farm. A wheelbarrow can be a useful or utilitarian item. In this poem, at this moment, it is clean and bright and red—why red?

Consider the symbolism of colors. Red is powerful, passionate. It is a contrast to white, which typically symbolizes innocence or purity, perhaps simplicity. How does the color white connect to the chickens? Are they innocent? Pure? Simple?

Another item to consider is the first line's tiny word "so." The speaker doesn't tell us what depends on the red wheelbarrow, only that it is "so much." Why isn't he more specific; why is he ambiguous? Could it be that if he told us, we wouldn't use our imagination? Is it the lives of the white chickens that depend on the wheelbarrow? Is it the farm? Is it the livelihood of the farmer and his family?

Finally, consider the **theme** of the poem. What could a poem of eight short lines tell us? Is it only about a wet wheelbarrow? It might be about how practical tools are sometimes more than just useful; they might be attractive and have an appeal of their own. This poem's theme could be the beauty of utilitarian objects. You might find another theme, and that would be okay. You only have to support it with evidence from the poem.

EXPANDING THINKING

The challenge (and the fun) of reading complex literature often comes from the **ambiguity** in the piece, the ability to interpret the theme or the characters in more than one way. Sometimes ambiguity has a negative connotation; a lack of clarity is not what we want in our politicians, instructors, or parents. However, in literature, ambiguity can occur because of the differences of the readers or because of the author's intent. Ambiguity allows readers to analyze and interpret literature, helping to expand their thinking.

Theodore Roethke's "My Papa's Waltz"

"My Papa's Waltz," by Theodore Roethke, describes the relationship between a father and his son. Most readers will agree on this broad theme.

My Papa's Waltz (1942)

The whiskey on your breath
Could make a small boy dizzy;
But I hung on like death:
Such waltzing was not easy.

We romped until the pans   5
Slid from the kitchen shelf;
My mother's countenance
Could not unfrown itself.

The hand that held my wrist
Was battered on one knuckle;   10
At every step you missed
My right ear scraped a buckle.

You beat time on my head
With a palm caked hard by dirt,
Then waltzed me off to bed   15
Still clinging to your shirt.

When trying to make the nature of the relationship more specific, you might debate the significance of the language. You might see this poem as an adult reflection on the rough play of a working-class father with his son. Others might find the language more violent and see evidence of abuse in the relationship. One side, arguing that the interaction is typical roughhousing, might point out that the young boy "clings to [the father's] shirt" and emphasize the use of playful language like "romped" and "waltzed." Others, those who see potential abuse in the relationship, might argue that "whiskey," "death," "battered," "scraped," and "beat" indicate violence. Taking a position on this *debatable theme* or *ambiguous language* can become the focus of an argument essay.

From Raymond Carver's "Cathedral" (1983)

In reading Raymond Carver's short story, "Cathedral" (Chapter 9), we witness the narrator's personal growth through his reluctant interaction with his "wife's blind friend," Robert. As an active reader, you can track your evolving response to the narrator. Here is a passage from early in the story:

My idea of blindness came from the movies. In the movies, the blind moved slowly and never laughed. Sometimes they were led by seeing-eye dogs.

> At first glance, his [Robert's] eyes looked like anyone else's eyes. But if you looked close, there was something different about them. Too much white in the iris, for one thing, and the pupils seemed to move around in the sockets without his knowing it or being able to stop it. Creepy.

While the narrator shows himself to be observant, his comments probably strike you as simpleminded, crass, and insensitive. By the end of the story, however, the narrator reveals a softer, more serious, and thoughtful side of his character:

> He [Robert] found my hand, the hand with the pen. He closed his hand over my hand. "Go ahead, bub, draw," he said....
>
> So I began. First I drew a box that looked like a house. It could have been the house I lived in. Then I put a roof on it. At either end of the roof, I drew spires....

Despite the intimacy of the moment, critical readers will ask questions: Is the narrator's transformation authentic? Is it plausible for a one-night encounter with a blind man to change the narrator's outlook? By writing an analysis that explains your reaction to the narrator at various points in the story, you can create an argument essay that conveys your own conclusions in judging the character of the narrator.

William Shakespeare's "Sonnet 130"

During the English Renaissance, when Shakespeare lived, many poets wrote sonnets in which the speakers of the poems idealized the women they loved. Shakespeare, too, wrote many traditional love sonnets, but one of his most famous, "Sonnet 130," twists the conventional descriptions of beauty.

Sonnet 130 (1609)

My mistress' eyes are nothing like the sun;
Coral is far more red than her lips' red;
If snow be white, why then her breasts are dun;
If hairs be wires, black wires grow on her head.
5   I have seen roses damasked, red and white,
But no such roses see I in her cheeks;
And in some perfumes there is more delight
Than in the breath that from my mistress reeks.
I love to hear her speak, yet well I know
10   That music has a far more pleasing sound;
I grant I never saw a goddess go;
My mistress, when she walks, treads on the ground.
And yet, by heaven, I think my love as rare
As any she belied with false compare.

As in most Shakespearian sonnets, the speaker of the poem states his theme in the final two lines: "And yet, by heaven, I think my love as rare/As any she belied with false compare." The speaker seems to argue that he loves his mistress as much as other men love theirs, and he doesn't have to lie about her to prove it.

However, studying the comparisons in the first twelve lines, readers are led to scrutinize the speaker's tone and to question the sincerity of his declaration of his "love as rare." What does he mean by "rare"—rare as in precious or rare as in unusual? Why would one whose love is "rare" describe his mistress's breasts as "dun," her hair as "black wires," her breath as "reek[ing]"? Does the poet intend to compliment her or to poke fun at her? Many contemporaries of Shakespeare wrote poems idealizing women, describing them as beautiful objects admired from afar. Could this poem be a satire of other poems of the era? Could it be an acknowledgement that women are not goddesses yet still worthy of love? Because of the complexity of the poem, you should consider how you respond to the speaker. Do you admire him for his down-to-earth honesty and witty outlook, or do you fault him for a mean-spirited, sexist attitude? Debating the theme of the poem can spark lively classroom discussions and engaging essays that prompt you to examine your own attitudes and assumptions about men and women and relationships.

EXPLORING ISSUES

Another connection between literature and argument comes from the inspiration and understanding that powerful pieces can provide about social issues or political movements. When reading literature from a different perspective, from another time period or another culture, readers might recognize modern or personal struggles. This discovery of universal concerns can expand our thinking on relevant issues.

From *The Crucible* (1953)

Arthur Miller's twentieth-century play *The Crucible,* based on the Salem Witch Trials of 1692, illustrates how emotion (in this case, fear) can derail reasoning and clear thinking. In the play, as in historical Salem, Massachusetts, the townspeople jump to the conclusion that the women are witches, although their evidence, the testimony of young girls, is inadequate. At the close of Act 1, the girls, Abigail and Betty, begin their accusations, encouraged by Reverend Hale, an "expert" on witchcraft brought in for the trials, and two local men, Thomas Putnam and Reverend Parris:

Hale: Take courage, you must give us all their names. How can you bear to see this child suffering? Look at her, Tituba. *He is indicating Betty on the bed.* Look at her God-given innocence; her soul so tender; we must protect her Tituba; the Devil is out and preying on her like a beast upon the flesh of the pure lamb. God will bless you for your help.

Abigail rises, staring as though inspired, and cries out.

Abigail: I want to open myself! *They turn to her, startled. She is enraptured, as though in a pearly light.* I want the light of God, I want the sweet love of Jesus! I danced for the Devil; I saw him; I wrote in his book; I go back to Jesus; I kiss His hand. I saw Sarah Good with the Devil! I saw Goody Osburn with the Devil! I saw Bridget Bishop with the Devil!

As she is speaking, Betty is rising from the bed, a fever in her eyes, and picks up the chant.

Betty, *staring too:* I saw George Jacobs with the Devil! I saw Goody Howe with the Devil!
Parris: She speaks! *He rushes to embrace Betty.* She speaks!
Hale: Glory to God! It is broken, they are free!
Betty, *calling out hysterically and with great relief:* I saw Martha Bellows with the Devil!
Abigail: I saw Goody Sibber with the Devil! *It is rising to a great glee.*
Putnam: The marshal, I'll call the marshal!

Parris is shouting a prayer of thanksgiving.

Betty: I saw Alice Barrow with the Devil!

The curtain begins to fall.

Hale, *as Putnam goes out:* Let the marshal bring irons!

[The dialogue and stage directions depict the strong emotions that surround this situation. The men, who very much *want* to believe the girls' accusations, readily make the inductive leap to condemn the accused women. And once made, they secure exactly what they want: the accused women's guilty verdict. In contrast, at the start of Act 2, Miller shows us two people, John and Elizabeth Proctor, for whom the evidence is inadequate.]

Elizabeth: ...There be fourteen people in jail now. *Proctor simply looks at her, unable to grasp it.* And they'll be tried, and the courts have power to hang them too.
Proctor, *scoffing, but without conviction:* Ah, they'd never hang—
Elizabeth: The Deputy Governor promises hangin' if they'll not confess, John. The town's gone wild, I think. She speaks of Abigail, and I thought she were a saint, to hear her. Abigail brings the other girls into the court, and where she walks the crowd will part like the sea for Israel. And folks are brought before them, and if they scream and howl and fall to the floor—the person's clapped in the jail for bewitchin' them.
Proctor, *wide-eyed:* Oh, it is a black mischief.
Elizabeth: I think you must go to Salem, John. *He turns to her.* I think so. You must tell them it is a fraud.

[John Proctor does, indeed, go to Salem, but to no avail. The town has "gone wild," allowing emotion to overcome all reason. Based on inadequate evidence, the people of Salem have made a hasty generalization. As a result, fourteen people are hanged.]

Perhaps we are inclined to tell ourselves that these events in Salem took place more than three hundred years ago and, therefore, do not apply to our contemporary world. However, we need only to look back to the mid-twentieth century to see a series of events dominated by emotion rather than reason—the McCarthy hearings in which the House UnAmerican Activities Commission investigated persons accused of being communists. In fact, this occurrence inspired Miller to write *The Crucible*. Appealing to fear—the post–World War II threat of communism, the "Red Scare"—this group in Congress thwarted or ruined the careers of many journalists and actors in this country. Again, as in colonial Salem, reason was overcome by emotion. Indeed, the term "witch hunt" has as much viability today as it did in the late 1600s. Currently, western society is struggling to offer citizens protection from terrorist threats without infringing on individual rights. We must remain vigilant to avoid becoming victims of our own flawed reasoning, bound to purely emotional appeals. Examining literature such as *The Crucible* helps us to practice this vigilance.

ACTIVITIES

In order to practice analytical reading and critical thinking, as well as making connections to modern issues, read the following texts and answer the questions that follow.

POEM FOR ANALYSIS

Barbie Doll (1971)

This girlchild was born as usual
and presented dolls that did pee-pee
and miniature GE stoves and irons
and wee lipsticks the color of cherry candy.
Then in the magic of puberty, a classmate said: 5
You have a great big nose and fat legs.

She was healthy, tested intelligent,
possessed strong arms and back,
abundant sexual drive and manual dexterity.
She went to and fro apologizing.   10
Everyone saw a fat nose on thick legs.

She was advised to play coy,
exhorted to come on hearty,
exercise, diet, smile and wheedle.
Her good nature wore out   15

like a fan belt.
So she cut off her nose and her legs
and offered them up.

20
In the casket displayed on satin she lay
with the undertaker's cosmetics painted on,
a turned-up putty nose,
dressed in a pink and white nightie.
Doesn't she look pretty? everyone said.
Consummation at last.
25
To every woman a happy ending.

1. After reading Marge Piercy's poem, "Barbie Doll," several times, explain the action and events of the final two stanzas. What ambiguity and/or irony do you notice?

2. Write out a potential theme for this poem. Which lines from the poem support this theme? Give two to three specific quotations.

3. Look up the history of the Barbie doll. Why does Piercy use "Barbie Doll" as the title? Why does she not mention the doll again in the poem? What is the effect of this ambiguity?

4. Consider current images of women in pop culture and the media. How might this poem, first published in 1971, demonstrate an issue that still resonates today?

5. Read the following student essay, written as an in-class, timed writing assignment. What is the thesis (or claim)? Does her explanation of the theme of "Barbie Doll" match your understanding of the poem? Why or why not?

Simone Weatherly
Professor Perkins
ENC 1141
19 February 2015

Life as Plastic

In society's ever-judging eyes, there is no better measure of a woman's worth than her physical beauty. The ideal woman must be dainty and symmetrical, flawless of skin, and thin. The health of the woman does not matter; she can, and sometimes will, starve herself until she is able to count every rib and has to hide her gaunt, discolored face beneath layers of makeup in this pressured pursuit of perfection. Beauty is often painful: it is hunger and anxiety, uncomfortable clothing and surgeries. There is nothing beautiful about letting society mold a human being into a living Barbie doll, like what happens to the "girlchild" in Marge Piercy's poem, "Barbie Doll" (1).

The speaker of the poem introduces the protagonist as having been "born as usual" (1). She is a normal little girl with no obvious defects or flaws who dutifully plays with the traditional conditioning toys she is handed: babies, stoves, irons, and lipstick. Despite not mentioning Barbie dolls anywhere in the poem itself, the speaker implies these girl toys are the catalyst for the girlchild's inadequacies. While she first becomes just a "great big nose and fat legs" during puberty, she has spent her life until that point playing with toys that had already begun molding her into a dutiful, beautiful housewife (6). She has baby dolls that act like live babies, and she has been told she should want to play with them. She gets appliances because every woman should aspire to a life spent cooking and cleaning, and, of course, she gets lipstick, so that she can practice being beautiful. But her self-confidence is all shaken up by her classmate's cruel remark. No amount of cherry candy lipstick can fix a "great big nose" (6). No skill with a baby doll that urinates can make up for "fat legs"; the girlchild feels innately flawed and believes these flaws are all anyone notices (6).

She tries everything to get them to see her as beautiful; she follows society's advice to diet, exercise, and smile in the hope that she can finally make up for her flaws. She tries her hardest to fit in and fix herself, and yet the moment after the speaker tells the reader the girlchild "cut off her nose and her legs and offered them up," she is dead, lying in a casket, displayed like a doll for the world to admire (17-18). It is the direct action of conforming, of giving up, that leads to her death as a human being. She is dead now; she will never get a chance to show her other, natural traits, like her dexterity, strength, or intelligence. She is now beautiful, but it is an artificial beauty with "the undertaker's cosmetics painted on," having truly given up and let society do what it wants to her cold, unfeeling body (20).

The death may not even be a literal demise but a spiritual one, as the girlchild goes through the world as an unfeeling Barbie doll, beautiful but molded out of putty and plastic. Barbie dolls might not be mentioned by name, but at the end of the poem, this is clearly what she has become, and by extension, what society wants all women to become: toys, for the public to play with and admire, to pose and leave on a bedroom shelf, smiling and stiff, pliant to the hands of those who wish to control them. Piercy wrote "Barbie Doll" in the early 1970s, a time when equating women with men was still a hard concept for the world to grasp, and while attitudes regarding gender equality have certainly improved, her words still ring true today: one only has to go to a toy store and see those segregated aisles, those pink and purple gauntlets filled with Barbie dolls with more hair than body fat.

Works Cited

Piercy, Marge. "Barbie Doll." *Reading Literature and Writing Argument*. Ed. Missy James, et al. 6th ed. Boston: Pearson, 2017. 13-14. Print.

SHORT STORY FOR ANALYSIS

The Subliminal Man (1963)

J. G. Ballard

"The signs, Doctor! Have you seen the signs?"

Frowning with annoyance, Dr. Franklin quickened his pace and hurried down the hospital steps toward the line of parked cars. Over his shoulder he caught a glimpse of a thin, scruffy young man in ragged sandals and lime-stained jeans waving to him from the far side of the drive, then break into a run when he saw Franklin try to evade him.

"Dr. Franklin! The signs!"

Head down, Franklin swerved around an elderly couple approaching the outpatients department. His car was over a hundred yards away. Too tired to start running himself, he waited for the young man to catch him up.

5 "All right, Hathaway, what is it this time?" he snapped irritably. "I'm getting sick of you hanging around here all day."

Hathaway lurched to a halt in front of him, uncut black hair like an awning over his eyes. He brushed it back with a clawlike hand and turned on a wild smile, obviously glad to see Franklin and oblivious of the latter's hostility.

"I've been trying to reach you at night, Doctor, but your wife always puts the phone down on me," he explained without a hint of rancor, as if well used to this kind of snub. "And I didn't want to look for you inside the Clinic." They were standing by a privet hedge that shielded them from the lower windows of the main administrative block, but Franklin's regular rendezvous with Hathaway and his strange messianic cries had already been the subject of amused comment.

Franklin began to say: "I appreciate that—" but Hathaway brushed this aside. "Forget it, Doctor, there are more important things happening now. They've started to build the first big signs! Over a hundred feet high, on the traffic islands just outside town. They'll soon have all the approach roads covered. When they do we might as well stop thinking."

"Your trouble is that you're thinking too much," Franklin told him. "You've been rambling about these signs for weeks now. Tell me, have you actually seen one signaling?"

10 Hathaway tore a handful of leaves from the hedge, exasperated by this irrelevancy. "Of course I haven't, that's the whole point, Doctor." He dropped his voice as a group of nurses walked past, watching him uneasily out of the corners of their eyes. "The construction gangs were out again last night, laying huge power cables. You'll see them on the way home. Everything's nearly ready now."

"They're traffic signs," Franklin explained patiently. "The flyover has just been completed. Hathaway, for God's sake, relax. Try to think of Dora and the child."

"I *am* thinking of them!" Hathaway's voice rose to a controlled scream. "Those cables were 40,000-volt lines, Doctor, with terrific switch gear. The trucks were loaded with enormous metal scaffolds. Tomorrow they'll start lifting them up all over the city, they'll block off half the sky! What do you think Dora will be like after six months of that? We've got to stop them, Doctor, they're trying to transistorize our brains!"

Embarrassed by Hathaway's high-pitched shouting, Franklin had momentarily lost his sense of direction and helplessly searched the sea of cars for his own. "Hathaway, I can't waste any more time talking to you. Believe me, you need skilled help; these obsessions are beginning to master you."

Hathaway started to protest, and Franklin raised his right hand firmly. "Listen. For the last time, if you can show me one of these new signs, and prove that it's transmitting subliminal commands, I'll go to the police with you. But you haven't got a shred of evidence, and you know it. Subliminal advertising was banned thirty years ago, and the laws have never been repealed. Anyway, the technique was unsatisfactory; any success it had was marginal. Your idea of a huge conspiracy with all these thousands of giant signs everywhere is preposterous."

"All right, Doctor." Hathaway leaned against the bonnet of one of the cars. His moods seemed to switch abruptly from one level to the next. He watched Franklin amiably. "What's the matter—lost your car?"

"All your damned shouting has confused me." Franklin pulled out his ignition key and read the number off the tag: "NYN 299-566-367-21—can you see it?"

Hathaway leaned around lazily, one sandal up on the bonnet, surveying the square of a thousand or so cars facing them. "Difficult, isn't it, when they're all identical, even the same color? Thirty years ago there were about ten different makes, each in a dozen colors."

Franklin spotted his car, began to walk toward it. "Sixty years ago there were a hundred makes. What of it? The economies of standardization are obviously bought at a price."

Hathaway drummed his palm lightly on the roofs. "But these cars aren't all that cheap, Doctor. In fact, comparing them on an average income basis with those of thirty years ago they're about forty percent more expensive. With only one make being produced you'd expect a substantial reduction in price, not an increase."

"Maybe," Franklin said, opening his door. "But mechanically the cars of today are far more sophisticated. They're lighter, more durable, safer to drive."

Hathaway shook his head skeptically. "They bore me. The same model, same styling, same color, year after year. It's a sort of communism." He rubbed a greasy finger over the windshield. "This is a new one again, isn't it, Doctor? Where's the old one—you only had it for three months?"

"I traded it in," Franklin told him, starting the engine. "If you ever had any money you'd realize that it's the most economical way of owning a car. You don't keep driving the same one until it falls apart. It's the same with everything else—television sets, washing machines, refrigerators. But you aren't faced with the problem—you haven't got any."

Hathaway ignored the gibe, and leaned his elbow on Franklin's window. "Not a bad idea, either, Doctor. It gives me time to think. I'm not working a twelve-hour day to pay for a lot of things I'm too busy to use before they're obsolete."

He waved as Franklin reversed the car out of its line, then shouted into the wake of exhaust: "Drive with your eyes closed, Doctor!"

On the way home Franklin kept carefully to the slowest of the four-speed lanes. As usual after his discussions with Hathaway he felt vaguely depressed. He realized that unconsciously he envied Hathaway his footloose existence. Despite the grimy cold-water apartment in the shadow and roar of the flyover, despite his nagging wife and their sick child, and the endless altercations with the landlord and the supermarket credit manager, Hathaway still retained his freedom intact. Spared any responsibilities, he could resist the smallest encroachment upon him by the rest of

15

20

25

society, if only by generating obsessive fantasies such as his latest one about sub-liminal advertising.

The ability to react to stimuli, even irrationally, was a valid criterion of freedom. By contrast, what freedom Franklin possessed was peripheral, sharply demarked by the manifold responsibilities in the center of his life—the three mortgages on his home, the mandatory rounds of cocktail and TV parties, the private consul-tancy occupying most of Saturday which paid the installments on the multitude of household gadgets, clothes and past holidays. About the only time he had to himself was driving to and from work.

But at least the roads were magnificent. Whatever other criticisms might be leveled at the present society, it certainly knew how to build roads. Eight-, ten- and twelve-lane expressways interlaced across the continent, plunging from overhead causeways into the giant car parks in the center of the cities, or dividing into the great suburban arteries with their multi-acre parking aprons around the marketing cen-ters. Together the roadways and car parks covered more than a third of the country's entire area, and in the neighborhood of the cities the proportion was higher. The old cities were surrounded by the vast, dazzling abstract sculptures of the cloverleafs and flyovers, but even so the congestion was unremitting.

The ten-mile journey to his home in fact covered over twenty-five miles and took him twice as long as it had done before the construction of the expressway, the additional miles contained within the three giant cloverleafs. New cities were spring-ing from the motels, cafés and car marts around the highways. At the slightest hint of an intersection a shantytown of shacks and filling stations sprawled away among the forest of electric signs and route indicators, many of them substantial cities.

All around him cars bulleted along, streaming toward the suburbs. Relaxed by the smooth motion of the car, Franklin edged outward into the next speed lane. As he accelerated from 40 to 50 mph a strident, ear-jarring noise drummed out from his tires, shaking the chassis of the car. Ostensibly as an aid to lane discipline, the surface of the road was covered with a mesh of smaller rubber studs, spaced pro-gressively farther apart in each of the lanes so that the tire hum resonated exactly on 40, 50, 60 and 70 mph. Driving at an intermediate speed for more than a few seconds became physiologically painful, and soon resulted in damage to the car and tires.

30   When the studs wore out they were replaced by slightly different patterns, matching those on the latest tires, so that regular tire changes were necessary, increas-ing the safety and efficiency of the expressway. It also increased the revenues of the car and tire manufacturers, for most cars over six months old soon fell to pieces under the steady battering, but this was regarded as a desirable end, the greater turnover reducing the unit price and making more frequent model changes, as well as ridding the roads of dangerous vehicles.

A quarter of a mile ahead, at the approach of the first of the cloverleafs, the traf-fic stream was slowing, huge police signs signaling "Lanes Closed Ahead" or "Drop Speed by 10 mph." Franklin tried to return to the previous lane, but the cars were jammed bumper to bumper. As the chassis began to shudder and vibrate, jarring his spine, he clamped his teeth and tried to restrain himself from sounding the horn. Other drivers were less self-controlled and everywhere engines were plunging and snarling, horns blaring. Road taxes were now so high, up to thirty percent of the gross national product (by contrast, income taxes were a bare two percent) that any delay on the expressways called for an immediate government inquiry, and the major departments of the state were concerned with the administration of the road systems.

Nearer the cloverleaf the lanes had been closed to allow a gang of construction workers to erect a massive metal sign on one of the traffic islands. The palisaded area swarmed with engineers and surveyors, and Franklin assumed that this was the sign Hathaway had seen unloaded the previous night. His apartment was in one of the gim-crack buildings in the settlement that straggled away around a nearby flyover, a low-rent area inhabited by service-station personnel, waitresses and other migrant labor.

The sign was enormous, at least a hundred feet high, fitted with heavy concave grilles similar to radar dishes. Rooted in a series of concrete caissons, it reared high into the air above the approach roads, visible for miles. Franklin craned up at the grilles, tracing the power cables from the transformers up into the intricate mesh of metal coils that covered their surface. A line of red aircraft-warning beacons was already alight along the top strut, and Franklin assumed that the sign was part of the ground approach system of the city airport ten miles to the east.

Three minutes later, as he accelerated down the two-mile link of straight high-way to the next cloverleaf, he saw the second of the giant signs looming up into the sky before him.

Changing down into the 40 mph lane, Franklin watched the great bulk of the   35
second sign recede in his rear-view mirror. Although there were no graphic symbols among the wire coils covering the grilles, Hathaway's warnings still sounded in his ears. Without knowing why, he felt sure that the signs were not part of the airport approach system. Neither of them was in line with the principal airlines. To jus-tify the expense of siting them in the center of the expressway—the second sign required elaborate angled buttresses to support it on the narrow island—obviously meant that their role related in some way to the traffic streams.

Two hundred yards away was a roadside auto-mart, and Franklin abruptly remembered that he needed some cigarettes. Swinging the car down the entrance ramp, he joined the queue passing the self-service dispenser at the far end of the rank. The auto-mart was packed with cars, each of the five purchasing ranks lined with tired-looking men hunched over their wheels.

Inserting his coins (paper money was no longer in circulation, unmanageable by the automats), he took a carton from the dispenser. This was the only brand of cigarettes available—in fact there was only one brand of everything—though giant economy packs were an alternative. Moving off, he opened the dashboard locker.

Inside, still sealed in their wrappers, were three other cartons.

A strong fish-like smell pervaded the house when he reached home, steaming out from the oven in the kitchen. Sniffing it uneagerly, Franklin took off his coat and hat. His wife was crouched over the TV set in the lounge. An announcer was dictat-ing a stream of numbers, and Judith scribbled them down on a pad, occasionally cursing under her breath. "What a muddle!" she snapped. "He was talking so quickly I took only a few things down."

"Probably deliberate," Franklin commented. "A new panel game?"   40

Judith kissed him on the cheek, discreetly hiding the ashtray loaded with ciga-rette butts and chocolate wrappings. "Hello, darling, sorry not to have a drink ready for you. They've started this series of Spot Bargains, they give you a selection of things on which you get a ninety percent trade-in discount at the local stores, if you're in the right area and have the right serial numbers. It's all terribly complicated."

"Sounds good, though. What have you got?"

Judith peered at her checklist. "Well, as far as I can see the only thing is the infrared barbecue spit. But we have to be there before eight o'clock tonight. It's seven thirty already."

"Then that's out. I'm tired, angel, I need something to eat." When Judith started to protest he added firmly: "Look, I don't want a new infrared barbecue spit, we've only had this one for two months. Damn it, it's not even a different model."

"But, darling, don't you see, it makes it cheaper if you keep buying new ones. We'll have to trade ours in at the end of the year anyway, we signed the contract, and this way we save at least twenty dollars. These Spot Bargains aren't just a gimmick, you know. I've been glued to that set all day." A note of irritation had crept into her voice, but Franklin sat his ground, doggedly ignoring the clock.

"Right, we lose twenty dollars. It's worth it." Before she could remonstrate he said: "Judith, please, you probably took the wrong number down anyway." As she shrugged and went over to the bar he called: "Make it a stiff one. I see we have health foods on the menu."

"They're good for you, darling. You know you can't live on ordinary foods all the time. They don't contain any proteins or vitamins. You're always saying we ought to be like people in the old days and eat nothing but health foods."

"I would, but they smell so awful." Franklin lay back, nose in the glass of whiskey, gazing at the darkened skyline outside.

A quarter of a mile away, gleaming out above the roof of the neighborhood supermarket, were the five red beacon lights. Now and then, as the headlamps of the Spot Bargainers swung up across the face of the building, he could see the square massive bulk of the giant sign clearly silhouetted against the evening sky.

"Judith!" He went into the kitchen and took her over to the window. "That sign, just behind the supermarket. When did they put it up?"

"I don't know." Judith peered at him curiously. "Why are you so worried, Robert? Isn't it something to do with the airport?"

Franklin stared thoughtfully at the dark hull of the sign. "So everyone probably thinks."

Carefully he poured his whiskey into the sink.

After parking his car on the supermarket apron at seven o'clock the next morning, Franklin carefully emptied his pockets and stacked the coins in the dashboard locker. The supermarket was already busy with early morning shoppers and the line of thirty turnstiles clicked and slammed. Since the introduction of the "24-hour spending day" the shopping complex was never closed. The bulk of the shoppers were discount buyers, housewives contracted to make huge volume purchases of food, clothing and appliances against substantial overall price cuts, and forced to drive around all day from supermarket to supermarket, frantically trying to keep pace with their purchase schedules and grappling with the added incentives inserted to keep the schemes alive.

Many of the women had teamed up, and as Franklin walked over to the entrance a pack of them charged toward their cars, stuffing their pay slips into their bags and gesticulating at each other. A moment later their cars roared off in a convoy to the next marketing zone.

A large neon sign over the entrance listed the latest discount—a mere 5 percent—calculated on the volume of turnover. The highest discounts, sometimes up to 25 percent, were earned in the housing estates where junior white-collar workers lived. There, spending had a strong social incentive, and the desire to be the highest spender in the neighborhood was given moral reinforcement by the system of listing all the names and their accumulating cash totals on a huge electric sign in the supermarket foyers. The higher the spender, the greater his contribution to the discounts enjoyed by others. The lowest-spending were regarded as social criminals, free-riding on the backs of others.

Luckily this system had yet to be adopted in Franklin's neighborhood. Not because the professional men and their wives were able to exercise more discretion, but because their higher incomes allowed them to contract into more expensive discount schemes operated by the big department stores in the city.

Ten yards from the entrance Franklin paused, looking up at the huge metal sign mounted in an enclosure at the edge of the car park. Unlike the other signs and billboards that proliferated everywhere, no attempt had been made to decorate it, or disguise the gaunt bare rectangle of riveted steel mesh. Power lines wound down its sides, and the concrete surface of the car park was crossed by a long scar where a cable had been sunk.

Franklin strolled along, then fifty feet from the sign stopped and turned, realizing that he would be late for the hospital and needed a new carton of cigarettes. A dim but powerful humming emanated from the transformers below the sign, fading as he retraced his steps to the supermarket.

Going over to the automats in the foyer, he felt for his change, then whistled   60 sharply when he remembered why he had deliberately emptied his pockets.

"The cunning thing!" he said, loud enough for two shoppers to stare at him. Reluctant to look directly at the sign, he watched its reflection in one of the glass door panes, so that any subliminal message would be reversed.

Almost certainly he had received two distinct signals—"Keep Away" and "Buy Cigarettes." The people who normally parked their cars along the perimeter of the apron were avoiding the area under the enclosure, the cars describing a loose semicircle fifty feet around it.

He turned to the janitor sweeping out the foyer. "What's that sign for?"

The man leaned on his broom, gazing dully at the sign. "Dunno," he said. "Must be something to do with the airport." He had an almost fresh cigarette in his mouth, but his right hand reached unconsciously to his hip pocket and pulled out a pack. He drummed the second cigarette absently on his thumbnail as Franklin walked away.

Everyone entering the supermarket was buying cigarettes.   65

Cruising quietly along the 40 mph lane, Franklin began to take a closer interest in the landscape around him. Usually he was either too tired or too preoccupied to do more than think about his driving, but now he examined the expressway methodically, scanning the roadside cafés for any smaller versions of the new signs. A host of neon displays covered the doorways and windows, but most of them seemed innocuous, and he turned his attention to the larger billboards erected along the open stretches of the expressway. Many of these were as high as four-story houses, elaborate three-dimensional devices in which giant, glossy-skinned housewives with electric eyes and teeth jerked and postured around their ideal kitchens, neon flashes exploding from their smiles.

The areas of either side of the expressway were wasteland, continuous junkyards filled with cars and trucks, washing machines and refrigerators, all perfectly workable but jettisoned by the economic pressure of the succeeding waves of discount models. Their intact chrome hardly tarnished, the mounds of metal shells and cabinets glittered in the sunlight. Nearer the city the billboards were sufficiently close together to hide them, but now and then, as he slowed to approach one of the flyovers, Franklin caught a glimpse of the huge pyramids of metal, gleaming silently like the refuse grounds of some forgotten El Dorado.

That evening Hathaway was waiting for him as he came down the hospital steps. Franklin waved him across the court, then led the way quickly to his car.

"What's the matter, Doctor?" Hathaway asked as Franklin wound up the windows and glanced around the lines of parked cars. "Is someone after you?"

70 Franklin laughed somberly. "I don't know. I hope not, but if what you say is right, I suppose there is."

Hathaway leaned back with a chuckle, propping one knee up on the dashboard. "So you've seen something, Doctor, after all."

"Well, I'm not sure yet, but there's just a chance you may be right. This morning at the Fairlawne supermarket…" He broke off, uneasily remembering the huge blank sign and the abrupt way in which he had turned back to the supermarket as he approached it, then described his encounter.

Hathaway nodded slowly. "I've seen the sign there. It's big, but not as big as some that are going up. They're building them everywhere now. All over the city. What are you going to do, Doctor?"

Franklin gripped the wheel tightly. Hathaway's thinly veiled amusement irritated him. "Nothing, of course. Damn it, it may be just autosuggestion; you've probably got me imagining—"

75 Hathaway sat up with a jerk, his face mottled and savage. "Don't be absurd, Doctor! If you can't believe your own senses what chance have you left? They're invading your brain, if you don't defend yourself they'll take it over completely! We've got to act now, before we're all paralyzed."

Wearily Franklin raised one hand to restrain him. "Just a minute. Assuming that these signs are going up everywhere, what would be their object? Apart from wasting the enormous amount of capital invested in all the other millions of signs and billboards, the amounts of discretionary spending power still available must be infinitesimal. Some of the present mortgage and discount schemes reach half a century ahead, so there can't be much slack left to take up. A big trade war would be disastrous."

"Quite right, Doctor," Hathaway rejoined evenly, "but you're forgetting one thing. What would supply that extra spending power? A big increase in production. Already they've started to raise the working day from twelve hours to fourteen. In some of the appliance plants around the city Sunday working is being introduced as a norm.

Can you visualize it, Doctor—a seven-day week, everyone with at least three jobs?"

Franklin shook his head. "People won't stand for it."

80 "They will. Within the last twenty-five years the gross national product has risen by fifty percent, but so have the average hours worked. Ultimately we'll all be working and spending twenty-four hours a day, seven days a week. No one will dare refuse. Think what a slump would mean—millions of layoffs, people with time on their hands and nothing to spend it on. Real leisure, not just time spent buying things." He seized Franklin by the shoulder. "Well, Doctor, are you going to join me?"

Franklin freed himself. Half a mile away, partly hidden by the four-story bulk of the Pathology Department, was the upper half of one of the giant signs, workmen still crawling across its girders. The airlines over the city had deliberately been routed away from the hospital, and the sign obviously had no connection with approaching aircraft.

"Isn't there a prohibition on subliminal living? How can the unions accept it?"

"The fear of a slump. You know the new economic dogmas. Unless output rises by a steady inflationary five percent the economy is stagnating. Ten years ago increased efficiency alone would raise output, but the advantages there are minimal now and only one thing is left. More work. Increased consumption and subliminal advertising will provide the spur."

"What are you planning to do?"

"I can't tell you, Doctor, unless you accept equal responsibility for it."   85

"Sounds rather quixotic," Franklin commented. "Tilting at windmills. You won't be able to chop those things down with an ax."

"I won't try." Hathaway suddenly gave up and opened the door. "Don't wait too long to make up your mind, Doctor. By then it may not be yours to make up." With a wave he was gone.

On the way home Franklin's skepticism returned. The idea of the conspiracy was preposterous, and the economic arguments were too plausible. As usual, though, there had been a hook in the soft bait Hathaway dangled before him—Sunday working. His own consultancy had been extended into Sunday morning with his appointment as visiting factory doctor to one of the automobile plants that had started Sunday shifts. But instead of resenting this incursion into his already meager hours of leisure he had been glad. For one frightening reason—he needed the extra income.

Looking out over the lines of scurrying cars, he noticed that at least a dozen of the great signs had been erected along the expressway. As Hathaway had said, more were going up everywhere, rearing over the supermarkets in the housing developments like rusty metal sails.

Judith was in the kitchen when he reached home, watching the TV program on   90 the handset over the cooker. Franklin climbed past a big cardboard carton, its seals still unbroken, which blocked the doorway, kissed her on the cheek as she scribbled numbers down on her pad. The pleasant odor of pot-roast chicken—or, rather, a gelatine dummy of a chicken fully flavored and free of any toxic or nutritional properties—mollified his irritation at finding her still playing the Spot Bargains.

He tapped the carton with his foot. "What's this?"

"No idea, darling, something's always coming these days, I can't keep up with it all." She peered through the glass door at the chicken—an economy 12-pounder, the size of a turkey, with stylized legs and wings and an enormous breast, most of which would be discarded at the end of the meal (there were no dogs or cats these days; the crumbs from the rich man's table saw to that)—and then glanced at him pointedly.

"You look rather worried, Robert. Bad day?"

Franklin murmured noncommittally. The hours spent trying to detect false clues in the faces of the Spot Bargain announcers had sharpened Judith's perceptions, and he felt a pang of sympathy for the legion of husbands similarly outmatched.

"Have you been talking to that crazy beatnik again?"   95

"Hathaway? As a matter of fact, I have. He's not all that crazy." He stepped backward into the carton, almost spilling his drink. "Well, what is this thing? As I'll be working for the next fifty Sundays to pay for it I'd like to find out."

He searched the sides, finally located the label. "*A TV set?* Judith, do we need another one? We've already got three. Lounge, dining room, and the handset. What's the fourth for?"

"The guest room, dear; don't get so excited. We can't leave a handset in the guest room, it's rude. I'm trying to economize, but four TV sets is the bare minimum. All the magazines say so."

"*And* three radios?" Franklin stared irritably at the carton. "If we do invite a guest here how much time is he going to spend alone in his room watching television? Judith, we've got to call a halt. It's not as if these things were free, or even cheap. Anyway, television is a total waste of time. There's only one program. It's ridiculous to have four sets."

100 "Robert, there are *four* channels."

"But only the commercials are different." Before Judith could reply the telephone rang. Franklin lifted the kitchen receiver, listened to the gabble of noise that poured from it. At first he wondered whether this was some offbeat prestige commercial, then realized it was Hathaway in a manic swing.

"Hathaway!" he shouted back. "Relax, man! What's the matter now?"

"—Doctor, you'll have to believe me this time. I tell you I got on to one of the islands with a stroboscope, they've got hundreds of high-speed shutters blasting away like machine guns straight into people's faces and they can't see a thing, it's fantastic! The next big campaign's going to be cars and TV sets; they're trying to swing a two-month model change—can you imagine it, Doctor, a new car every two months? God Almighty, it's just—"

Franklin waited impatiently as the five-second commercial break cut in (all telephone calls were free, the length of the commercial extending with range— for long-distance calls the ratio of commercial to conversation was as high as 10:1, the participants desperately trying to get a word in edgeways to the interminable interruptions), but just before it ended he abruptly put the telephone down, then removed the receiver from the cradle.

105 Judith came over and took his arm. "Robert, what's the matter? You look terribly strained."

Franklin picked up his drink and walked through into the lounge. "It's just Hathaway. As you say, I'm getting a little too involved with him. He's starting to prey on my mind."

He looked at the dark outline of the sign over the supermarket, its red warning lights glowing in the night sky. Blank and nameless, like an area forever closed off in an insane mind, what frightened him was its total anonymity.

"Yet I'm not sure," he muttered. "So much of what Hathaway says makes sense. These subliminal techniques are the sort of last-ditch attempt you'd expect from an overcapitalized industrial system."

He waited for Judith to reply, then looked up at her. She stood in the center of the carpet, hands folded limply, her sharp, intelligent face curiously dull and blunted. He followed her gaze out over the rooftops, then with an effort turned his head and quickly switched on the TV set.

110 "Come on," he said grimly. "Let's watch television. God, we're going to need that fourth set."

A week later Franklin began to compile his inventory. He saw nothing more of Hathaway; as he left the hospital in the evening the familiar scruffy figure was absent.

When the first of the explosions sounded dimly around the city and he read of the attempts to sabotage the giant signs, he automatically assumed that Hathaway was responsible, but later he heard on a newscast that the detonations had been set off by construction workers excavating foundations.

More of the signs appeared over the rooftops, isolated on the palisaded islands near the suburban shopping centers. Already there were over thirty on the ten-mile route from the hospital, standing shoulder to shoulder over the speeding cars like giant dominoes. Franklin had given up his attempt to avoid looking at them, but the slim possibility that the explosions might be Hathaway's counterattack kept his suspicions alive.

He began his inventory after hearing the newscast, and discovered that in the previous fortnight he and Judith had traded in their

> Car (previous model 2 months old)
> 2 TV sets (4 months)
> Power mower (7 months)
> Electric cooker (5 months)
> Hair dryer (4 months)
> Refrigerator (3 months)
> 2 radios (7 months)
> Record player (5 months)
> Cocktail bar (8 months)

Half these purchases had been made by himself, but exactly when he could never recall realizing at the time. The car, for example, he had left in the garage near the hospital to be greased, that evening had signed for the new model as he sat at its wheel, accepting the salesman's assurance that the depreciation on the two-month trade-in was virtually less than the cost of the grease job. Ten minutes later, as he sped along the expressway, he suddenly realized that he had bought a new car. Similarly, the TV sets had been replaced by identical models after developing the same irritating interference pattern (curiously, the new sets also displayed the pattern, but as the salesman assured them, this promptly vanished two days later). Not once had he actually decided of his own volition that he wanted something and then gone out to a store and bought it!

He carried the inventory around with him, adding to it as necessary, quietly 115 and without protest analyzing these new sales techniques, wondering whether total capitulation might be the only way of defeating them. As long as he kept up even a token resistance, the inflationary growth curve would show a controlled annual 10 percent climb. With that resistance removed, however, it would begin to rocket upward out of control....

Then, driving home from the hospital two months later, he saw one of the signs for the first time.

He was in the 40 mph lane, unable to keep up with the flood of new cars, had just passed the second of the three cloverleafs when the traffic half a mile away began to slow down. Hundreds of cars had driven up onto the grass verge, and a large crowd was gathering around one of the signs. Two small black figures were climbing up the metal face, and a series of huge grid-like patterns of light flashed on and off, illuminating the evening air. The patterns were random and broken, as if the sign was being tested for the first time.

Relieved that Hathaway's suspicions had been completely groundless, Franklin turned off onto the soft shoulder, then walked forward through the spectators as the lights blinked and stuttered in their faces. Below, behind the steel palisades around the island, was a large group of police and engineers, craning up at the men scaling the sign a hundred feet over their heads.

Suddenly Franklin stopped, the sense of relief fading instantly. With a jolt he saw that several of the police on the ground were armed with shotguns, and that the two policemen climbing the sign carried submachine guns slung over their shoulders. They were converging on a third figure, crouched by a switchbox on the penultimate tier, a ragged bearded man in a grimy shirt, a bare knee poking through his jeans.

120   Hathaway!

Franklin hurried toward the island, the sign hissing and spluttering, fuses blowing by the dozen.

Then the flicker of lights cleared and steadied, blazing out continuously, and together the crowd looked up at the decks of brilliant letters. The phrases, and every combination of them possible, were entirely familiar, and Franklin knew that he had been reading them unconsciously in his mind for weeks as he passed up and down the expressway.

BUY NOW BUY NOW BUY NOW BUY NOW BUY NOW
NEW CAR NOW NEW CAR NOW NEW CAR NOW
YES YES YES YES YES YES YES YES YES YES YES

Sirens blaring, two patrol cars swung up onto the verge through the crowd and plunged across the damp grass. Police spilled from its doors, batons in their hands, quickly began to force back the crowd. Franklin held his ground as they approached, started to say: "Officer, I know the man—" but the policeman punched him in the chest with the flat of his hand. Winded, he stumbled back among the cars, leaned helplessly against a fender as the police began to break the windshields, the hapless drivers protesting angrily, those farther back rushing for their vehicles.

The noise fell away abruptly when one of the submachine guns fired a brief roaring burst, then rose in a massive gasp of horror as Hathaway, arms outstretched, let out a cry of triumph and pain, and jumped.

125   "But, Robert, what does it really matter?" Judith asked as Franklin sat inertly in the lounge the next morning. "I know it's tragic for his wife and daughter, but Hathaway was in the grip of an obsession. If he hated advertising signs so much why didn't he dynamite those we can see, instead of worrying so much about those we can't?"

Franklin stared at the TV screen, hoping the program would distract him.

"Hathaway was right," he said simply.

"Was he? Advertising is here to stay. We've no real freedom of choice, anyway. We can't spend more than we can afford; the finance companies soon clamp down."

"You accept that?" Franklin went over to the window. A quarter of a mile away, in the center of the estate, another of the signs was being erected. It was due east from them, and in the early morning light the shadows of its rectangular superstructure fell across the garden, reaching almost to the steps of the French windows at his feet. As a concession to the neighborhood, and perhaps to allay any suspicions while it was being erected by an appeal to petty snobbery, the lowest sections had been encased in mock-Tudor paneling.

Franklin stared at it numbly, counting the half-dozen police lounging by their 130 patrol cars as the construction gang unloaded prefabricated grilles from a couple of trucks. Then he looked at the sign by the supermarket, trying to repress his memories of Hathaway and the pathetic attempts the man had made to convince Franklin and gain his help.

He was still standing there an hour later when Judith came in, putting on her hat and coat, ready to visit the supermarket.

Franklin followed her to the door. "I'll drive you down there, Judith," he said in a flat, dead voice. "I have to see about booking a new car. The next models are coming out at the end of the month. With luck, we'll get one of the early deliveries."

They walked out into the trim drive, the shadows of the great signs swinging across the quiet neighborhood as the day progressed, sweeping over the heads of the people on their way to the supermarket like the dark blades of enormous scythes.

1. What might be a potential theme for this story? Which lines from the story support this theme? Give two to three specific quotations.

2. Consumers in "The Subliminal Man" no longer have the free will to make market choices. In fact, technology enables sellers to manipulate them into spending against their will. Does our reliance on technology today create any manipulation? Give specific examples.

3. J. G. Ballard wrote "The Subliminal Man" in 1963. While subliminal advertising is illegal today, advertisers do specifically target groups of consumers, and research shows such targeting to be quite successful. Can you offer examples of this targeting? Do you fit into groups that advertisers might target? Is such targeting unfair in any way? List contemporary examples that might support Ballard's theme.

CHAPTER 3

Analyzing Argument

In this chapter, you will learn about
- recognizing claims, evidence, assumptions, and counterarguments.
- identifying logical fallacies.
- understanding audience appeals.
- applying argument terms to visuals.

ARGUMENT/CRITICAL THINKING CONNECTION

The word *argument* might evoke images of a shouting match, where people call each other names, trade insults, and compete to see who can yell the loudest. When the emotional need to prove one's self correct overtakes an exchange between disagreeing parties, dialogue is not advanced, leaving most people angry and so emotionally charged that, often, the origin of the argument itself is forgotten amid the chaos. For our purposes, we want to suspend this definition of argument and instead, focus upon the word in its academic sense.

Academic argument considers all sides of an issue and implies willingness of participants in a conversation to listen to views that may differ from their own. When we enter into an academic argument, we work actively to cast aside all preconceived notions. For example, you may already have a strong view on health care reform, but as an academic arguer, you have a responsibility to acknowledge perspectives that vary from your own. To advance a conversation on a heated topic, you need to demonstrate a universal understanding of the issue. Doing so not only makes an arguer more informed, but helps him or her craft stronger rebuttals to opposing sides. A willingness to enter into a global view also promotes critical thinking skills.

Critical thinking skills involve analyzing all elements of a situation and considering possible outcomes. These skills are essential to developing professional academic arguments, which are exchanges that advance the discussion of issues or problems with the goal of offering thought-provoking points. In doing so, audience members are prompted to consider conflicting views and challenged to redefine or clarify their own stances on the issues in a method that focuses on logic instead of raw emotion.

By choosing to attend college, you have chosen to be a part of an academic community, one that thrives on conversation among its members. As a participant in this academic argument, you have the responsibility to bring your best thinking to this conversation: to read background information about the issues and to entertain diverse viewpoints, ideas, and beliefs, including those that may clash with your ideas and beliefs. Moreover, as a participant in the conversation, you have the responsibility to ask questions—ones that will compel you to examine your own ideas and thinking as well as those you encounter in your reading and discussion and through your writing.

COMPONENTS OF AN ARGUMENT

Claims

An academic argument requires a claim. The **claim** is the assertion made in an argument, the main point or thesis. We can also think of the claim as the conclusion the writer has drawn. A claim reveals a writer's purpose for addressing an audience. Say, for example, you were going to write a paper about rain forests. The topic sounds wonderful, but what exactly about the rain forests do you wish to convey? A solid argument is built when the writer takes time to identify his or her claim and then makes a plan for conveying that claim to the audience.

Depending upon the subject matter, you may decide to make an explicit claim; that is, you might feel that directly stating your purpose in a focused thesis statement early in the paper is the best method to convey your argument. Other times, however, you may choose to make an implicit claim, beginning your paper with an interesting scenario or subtle clues to lead and invite the reader to think deeply, perhaps attempting to steer the readers on a thought-provoking journey toward the claim.

Argument theorists identify several types of claims, including a claim of fact, a claim of policy, and a claim of value. Using our earlier example of the rain forest as a topic of an argument, let's look at how establishing one of these type of claims could help a writer plan his or her argument in a more focused manner.

If you state that the world loses ten acres of rainforest every minute, then you are making a **claim of fact**, which may be useful as evidence in an argument calling for new environmental laws to protect the rainforest. The call for new laws would be a **claim of policy** because it asks for a specific action to take place. If the argument makes a judgment labeling something good or bad, then you have a **claim of value**: Rainforests are an invaluable and irreplaceable natural resource.

Claims in Literature

Do you recall reading *The Scarlet Letter* by Nathaniel Hawthorne? Like many high school students, you probably encountered this novel sometime during your four years, but can you state the claim Hawthorne makes? Something about deception perhaps? Maybe something about values? Readers are not likely to find a single sentence in Hawthorne's novel equivalent to a thesis in an academic essay. However, in a classroom discussion, through the interplay of varying interpretations, readers can articulate a central claim or assertion for this novel.

Of course, some imaginative literature can be rather ambiguous, making it harder to identify a theme or claim. Look, for example, at a short poem by Kenneth Rexroth:

Cold before Dawn (1979)

Cold before dawn,
Off in the misty night,
Under the gibbous moon,
The peacocks cry to each other,
5   As if in pain.

Do you see a claim in this poem? You might sense the contrasts in this poem— the contrast between the cold of night and the warmth of morning; the darkness of the mist and the light from the almost full moon; the beauty of a peacock and the discord of its cry. This poem contains beauty and seems rather musical, but it would be harder to argue a claim because of its abstract qualities.

As a further example, look at this Ezra Pound poem, an imagist poem:

In a Station of the Metro (1926)

The apparition of these faces in the crowd,
Petals on a wet, black bough.

This poem is meant to create a precise image and a specific metaphor: the comparison of the people in the station to the petals on a tree. Of course, the poem could be analyzed and explained, its theme explored, but arguing a claim can be difficult.

Now look at the following poem by the eighteenth-century British poet William Blake:

London (1794)

I wander thro' each charter'd street,
Near where the charter'd Thames does flow,
And mark in every face I meet
Marks of weakness, marks of woe.

In every cry of every Man,   5
In every Infant's cry of fear,
In every voice, in every ban,
The mind-forg'd manacles I hear.
How the Chimney-sweeper's cry
Every black'ning Church appalls;   10
And the hapless Soldier's sigh
Runs in blood down Palace walls.

But most thro' midnight streets I hear
How the youthful Harlot's curse
Blasts the new born Infant's tear,   15
And blights with plagues the Marriage hearse.

What do you see as the claim in this poem? Is the claim about the young children used as chimney sweeps and doomed to early deaths? Is it about venereal disease? Yes, the poem says something about both of these subjects; indeed, a number of subclaims usually can be identified in any example of writing. In this poem, however, Blake indirectly accuses the religious, military, and legal institutions of being responsible for the human suffering endured by so many people in the late 1700s. No single line makes such a claim, but when you reread the poem, you will see that the indictment is certainly the poem's central focus, the conclusion the writer wishes the reader to draw.

Evidence

No matter how explicit or implicit a writer opts to make his or her claim, what must be present in the argument is evidence. **Evidence** is the body of information used to support claims. In building this body of evidence, the arguer draws on sources—both *primary* (firsthand examples, observations, interviews) and *secondary* (reported facts, information, authoritative testimonies). With relevant and substantive evidence to support the claim, the arguer earns credibility with an audience, and, regardless of their stance on the issue, the audience will seriously consider the arguer's viewpoint.

Evidence may be based on subjective personal experience, on objective facts, or on the authority of an expert. There are various types of evidence, but for our purposes, let's concentrate on three: personal experience, reports, and authority.

In an essay, a student claims euthanasia should be legalized and cites his experience of watching his grandmother suffer a prolonged and painful death from cancer. The student's choice of descriptive details, coupled with his sincere tone, create a strong, emotional response in his readers. His use of **personal experience** provides strong evidence for the validity of his argument, particularly among readers who have had similar experiences.

On the other hand, some readers may not have any experience with cancer and may never have experienced the death of a family member or loved one.

For these people, despite the obvious emotional pull of the evidence, further proof will be required. In this case, the writer might want to provide some statistics of the numbers of patients on life support in this country, as well as the costs to families and health care providers. Taking this approach, the writer is using **reports**, objective facts gathered from outside sources, to support his argument.

The student writer might take one further step toward validating his argument for legalizing euthanasia by citing an **authority**. In this case, a quote from a health care professional would be a good choice. In fact, any field has authorities, people recognized as experts. Citing Dr. Spock as an authority on babies, Bill Gates when discussing the computer industry, or Michael Jordan in relation to professional basketball, a writer could be certain readers would recognize these people as authorities. They have credibility.

In this way, academic argument is more than the mere expression of an opinion; instead, the writer's opinion must be reinforced by primary and secondary sources that lend credibility to the author's claims in the eyes of the audience. Depending upon the assignment, your instructor may allow you to use personal experiences to support your claims. At the same time, many college-level writing classes require students to incorporate outside research materials from print or online books, or articles to support their claims.

Evidence in Literature

Applying the concept of evidence to imaginative literature complicates and enriches our reading experience. To begin with, we must address the **dramatic context** of the writing itself, including the actions, words, and thoughts of the characters within that work. Examining the characters' arguments, their positions, framed within the dramatic context, we look beyond ourselves and ultimately gain a clearer perception of our own positions. For example, readers of Harper Lee's novel *To Kill a Mockingbird* not only see the transformation of attitudes within the characters as they confront the issue of racial discrimination, but they may also come away from that reading experience examining their own attitudes about prejudice. Thus, analyzing the evidence in the dramatic context of a particular work leads you to understand the position of the character within the work and to explore your own beliefs and values.

Moving beyond the dramatic context, we also can examine the **social context** of a story, poem, or play as evidence of the writer's claim. However, an understanding of that evidence often requires us to gather additional information.

Look back at the poem "London." If William Blake wants the reader to believe the social institutions of eighteenth-century England were to blame for much of the suffering endured by its citizens, he must offer us some evidence. At that time, poor families often sold one of their children to the chimney sweeps, who used them to slide down London's many tight chimneys. As they brushed the soot from those chimneys, the children's lungs filled with black dust, and they regularly died while still in their early teens. The fact that such an abuse of children was legal in London is clear evidence in support of Blake's claim. By acquainting yourself with this historical background, you enrich your understanding of Blake's implied argument.

Assumptions

Assumptions are general principles or commonly accepted beliefs that underlie an argument. Commonly, assumptions are based on values that an arguer believes his or her audience shares and, therefore, readily accepts. Although an assumption may be stated outright in an argument, it frequently is a hidden or an unstated assumption.

For example, in arguing for strict environmental regulation of rainforests (claim of policy), a writer may offer statistical data and scientific facts to show how rainforests are being destroyed (evidence). The assumption—rainforests are valuable resources—may be readily accepted by American readers and require no backing. However, for the Brazilian landowner, his property may seem more valuable as a clear-cut and plowed field than as a rainforest. Perhaps the writer should not assume all of her readers will accept her assumption. Depending on whom the writer envisions as her audience, she may need to back her assumption with evidence to show how rainforests are valuable. Of course, within our own boundaries, from the Pacific Northwest to the Everglades, similar disputes rage over how to use our wilderness areas. First, how do we define *wilderness*? And how is our view of wilderness affected by the economic or cultural factors in our lives? Responses will vary among individuals. Yet these responses are crucial to any discussion of wilderness issues. Our personal definition informs the value we assign to wilderness areas; this value assignment (the assumption) then shapes our viewpoint about specific land use issues. Similarly, in the case of euthanasia or physician-assisted suicide, the sanctity and dignity of human life are values that influence our positions. In articulating a claim for physician-assisted suicide, the assumption would be based on our degree of allegiance to each of these values.

Assumptions in Literature

Now that we have identified a claim (the social institutions of eighteenth-century England were to blame for much of the suffering of its citizens) and pointed out evidence (the practice of selling children to chimney sweeps) in Blake's poem, we can consider the assumptions of the argument. We learned that assumptions are general principles or commonly accepted beliefs that underlie an argument. What assumption can you identify binding the evidence to the claim? Interestingly, the assumption, a *value* assumption, is so readily accepted by contemporary readers that we don't think to question it: The use of child labor is an affront to the principles of compassionate people everywhere. In eighteenth-century England, however, children, especially children of poor families, were viewed as property; the selling and buying of children was not widely condemned. Fortunately, enlightened thinkers, such as Blake, stood apart and questioned social institutions that supported the exploitation and abuse of children.

But the child labor issue is still complicated for contemporary readers. What about those expensive athletic shoes or the smartphone we may have recently purchased? Where were they manufactured? And by whom? Recently, the employment practices of several well-known U.S. manufacturers of name-brand shoes and clothing have come under critical scrutiny. Many U.S. manufacturers have opened factories in foreign countries, where operating costs are far lower: Land is cheaper, and environmental and labor laws are often either nonexistent or far less stringent than in the United States. In some cases, boys and girls younger than sixteen work long hours in brutal working conditions for meager wages. Is this practice not abusive and exploitative, an affront to our principles of compassion? Even though we are not directly responsible for hiring the twelve-year-old girl who works in the factory where our designer jeans were manufactured, do we share some portion of responsibility? Reading Blake's poem as an argument and examining its assumption from this perspective, we bridge the centuries that seem to divide us from eighteenth-century London.

Counterarguments: Concessions and Refutations

In designing an argument strategy, a writer should determine which opposing views or **counterarguments** are significant and, therefore, merit attention. A writer can address counterarguments in two ways: through **concessions** (acknowledging an opponent's point) and through **refutations** (disproving an opponent's point). Often, writers make some concessions and also present refutations.

For example, in the case of climate change, an arguer might acknowledge that accurate climate records are relatively recent and, therefore, offer some credence to the argument that climate change is not man-made, but, in fact, is a naturally recurring climatic phenomenon. By acknowledging the merit of this opposing argument, the writer has offered a limited *concession*. However, the writer could answer this concession with a detailed *refutation*—compelling factual evidence that points to man-made factors such as the primary causes of climate change.

By addressing opposing arguments thoroughly and fairly, an arguer strengthens his or her position with a large and diverse audience, one that is likely to include persons who are undecided, who are skeptical, who are adamantly opposed, or who readily accept the arguer's claim. In this way, the arguer reinforces a bond of respect and trust between writer and audience, which is fundamental to affect successful communication.

Not only should argument writers look for areas of weakness in their opposition's logic, they must take inventory of their own. Truly successful argument writers take inventory of their own beliefs and ideas on any given subject to look carefully for any logical fallacies.

LOGICAL FALLACIES

Most of us would not knowingly choose to be flawed or prejudicial thinkers. One way we can develop our mental stamina as thinkers is to practice examining the logic in reasoning. An error or flaw in reasoning is called a **logical fallacy**. While there are many logical fallacies, we have chosen to feature ten of the more common ones.

As you read through the list and definitions, you will see that understanding fallacies directs you to practice clear thinking. Familiarizing yourself with common fallacies and practicing detecting them in arguments is not just an academic exercise. This study and application sharpen your critical thinking skills and, thus, empower you as an independent thinker.

Common Logical Fallacies

Ad hominem—(from the Latin for "against the person") using personal attack instead of addressing the issue. Ex.: Mrs. X has had an extramarital affair and does not deserve our vote.

Begging the question—assumes exactly what the argument attempts to prove. Ex.: Capital punishment deters crimes because it prevents criminals from committing crimes.

Either–or reasoning—characterized by oversimplification that presents an issue only in two ways. Ex.: Either you vote for this school bond, or we may as well shut down our public schools.

Equivocation—intentional use of a word that has more than one interpretation that confuses instead of clarifies an issue. Ex.: I am simply *adjusting* some figures; I am not cheating on my tax return.

False analogy—false or illogical comparison, "comparing apples to oranges." Ex.: Some people might say that like Rome, America is destined for destruction; however, modern America is quite unlike ancient Rome.

Hasty generalization—fallacy of induction in which someone jumps to a broad conclusion based on too little evidence. Stereotyping is an example. Ex.: English professors are nonathletic bookworms.

***Post hoc* fallacy**—(from the Latin for "after this") also called the false cause fallacy; incorrectly attributing a cause-and-effect relationship. Ex.: After Brock became a vegetarian, he lost his muscle tone.

Red herring—the fallacy of distraction; leading the reader astray by bringing up a different issue as bait to capture the reader's interest. Ex.: You must give me a "B" in this class; I need the grade to keep my scholarship.

Slippery slope—a false appeal to fear; suggesting that a single event will trigger a series of catastrophic effects. Ex.: If the drinking age is lowered to eighteen, we will end up with a nation of alcoholics.

Two wrongs make a right—justifying wrongdoing by pointing to another's wrongdoing. Ex.: So maybe I did fudge a bit when I reported my income to the IRS, but so do many of the nation's richest people.

AUDIENCE APPEAL AND TONE: *PATHOS, LOGOS, ETHOS*

Aristotle's Basic Argument Model

Rhetorical context is the conversation, both written and oral, surrounding an issue. As you develop an organizational strategy for your argument, you want to be cognizant of the rhetorical context surrounding the issue. An arguer needs to be aware of the diverse viewpoints and passionate feelings surrounding an issue.

The famous and revered ancient Greek philosopher Aristotle offered the world a model of argument that you might find helpful as you begin to plan a paper or a speech. Aristotle's model, though short and simple, offers us three fundamentals of persuasion useful to most writers and speakers:

- *pathos* (feeling):   Arguers can use emotion to connect with the audience.
- *logos* (logic):   An argument must be clear and sensible.
- *ethos* (credibility):   An arguer must bring credibility to his/her claims.

Perhaps you have noticed a television commercial asking you to support humane organizations that foster animals that have been subjected to horrible living conditions. True animal lovers are moved by mere tales of animal abuse, but when organizations use pictures of animals in their ads, the power of *pathos* is undeniable. By seeing the sweet faces of neglected animals, many who might not otherwise be motivated to give could decide to make contributions.

Whether or not you realize, you demand a certain amount of *logos* from the world around you. Have you ever watched guests on an interview show and found yourself frustrated not only because their beliefs differed from your own, but also because you could not understand their argument? If so, your need for logic was not satisfied.

Suppose one of your friends repeatedly lectured you about the ills of smoking. One day, you run into your friend at a party and see him in the back-yard smoking. Likely you will see his *ethos* as damaged. Credibility is paramount for an arguer to be taken seriously—and if he or she gives anyone reason to think he or she is less than honest, his or her chances of persuading others are marred.

Drawing on these three appeals, the writer of argument addresses the basic human characteristics of his or her audience: emotion and empathy (*pathos*), logic and reasoning (*logos*), credibility and trust (*ethos*). Today, any lawyer who expects to win over a jury understands the necessity for making these appeals.

Martin Luther King, Jr.'s essay, "Letter from Birmingham Jail," written in 1963 (Chapter 6), stands as a modern classic of argumentation, in part because of King's use of rhetorical appeals. Reading King's "Letter," you will see how King builds trust with his audience as a fellow clergyman (appeal to *ethos*), reasons deliberately and analytically about the just nature of law (appeal to *logos*), and evokes his audience's empathy and compassion as he writes about the pain of explaining racism to children (appeal to *pathos*). Although addressed more than forty-five years ago to a specific audience, eight Alabama clergymen, King's "Letter" speaks compellingly to a universal audience.

Using Aristotle's rhetorical appeals to examine several poems, we can appreciate the poems as argumentation, as well as deepen our understanding of the appeals as ways that writers connect with their readers.

Pathos

"Federico's Ghost," by Martín Espada, provides a striking illustration of appeal to *pathos*. The poem tells the story of a boy's defiant gesture of protest against the abusive treatment of workers by those in positions of power:

Federico's Ghost (1990)

> The story is
> that whole families of fruitpickers
> still crept between the furrows
> of the field at dusk,
> when for reasons of whiskey or whatever   5
> the cropduster plane sprayed anyway,
> floating a pesticide drizzle
> over the pickers
> who thrashed like dark birds
> in a glistening white net,   10
> except for Federico,
> a skinny boy who stood apart
> in his own green row,
> and, knowing the pilot
> would not understand in Spanish   15
> that he was the son of a whore,
> instead jerked his arm
> and thrust an obscene finger.
>
> The pilot understood
> He circled the plane and sprayed again,   20
> watching a fine gauze of poison

> drift over the brown bodies
> that cowered and scurried on the ground,
> and aiming for Federico,
25 leaving the skin beneath his shirt
> wet and blistered,
> but still pumping his finger at the sky.
> After Federico died,
> rumors at the labor camp,
30 told of tomatoes picked and smashed at night,
> growers muttering of vandal children
> or communists in camp,
> first threatening to call Immigration,
> then promising every Sunday off
35 if only the smashing of tomatoes would stop.
>
> Still tomatoes were picked and squashed
> in the dark,
> and the old women in camp
> said it was Federico,
40 laboring after sundown
> to cool the burns on his arms,
> flinging tomatoes
> at the cropduster
> that hummed like a mosquito
45 lost in his ear,
> and kept his soul awake.

Using sensory language and specific details, Espada pulls us inside—behind the words—to where we cannot avoid seeing the human faces of the tomato pickers, who are not unlike ourselves: "whole families," "a skinny boy," "old women." By acknowledging our common humanity, we must acknowledge the injustice and the oppression of the field laborers' lives.

Poetic structure also heightens appeal to *pathos*. Because we are accustomed to reading margin-to-margin prose, the poem's line breaks slow down our reading. We cannot rush or skip over words, as we may do in reading an essay. Espada isolates images in short lines, which surprise and shock us as readers:

> over the pickers
> who thrashed like dark birds
> in a glistening white net,
> ….
> leaving the skin beneath his shirt
> wet and blistered.

With these images alive in our imaginations, we are compelled to confront the reality of "man's inhumanity to man" and also to examine our own attitudes toward day laborers, migrant workers, and illegal aliens. Appealing to our emotions and moral values, Espada's poem makes a powerful statement about prejudice and power and about human dignity and heroism. "Federico's Ghost" may, indeed, keep our own "soul[s] awake."

Logos

Shakespeare's sonnets can exemplify the *logos* point of Aristotle's triangle. Compare the form of the English or Shakespearean sonnet itself, a logical, fixed structure (fourteen lines—three quatrains and a couplet) to Espada's free-verse (open-form) poetry, for example. The sonnet's structure reinforces the poem's argumentative emphasis. As noted earlier, Espada's free-form line breaks counter logical structure and dramatize emotion. In the case of a Shakespearean sonnet, however, its ordered structure and regular rhythm underscore its pattern of reasoning and logic, as illustrated in "Sonnet 18":

Sonnet 18 (1609)

> Shall I compare thee to a summer's day?
> Thou art more lovely and more temperate:
> Rough winds do shake the darling buds of May,
> And summer's lease hath all too short a date:
> Sometime too hot the eye of heaven shines,   5
> And often is his gold complexion dimmed;
> And every fair from fair sometimes declines
> By chance or nature's changing course untrimmed;
> But thy eternal summer shall not fade,
> Nor lose possession of that fair thou ow'st,   10
> Nor shall death brag thou wander'st in his shade,
> When in eternal lines to time thou grow'st:
>> So long as men can breathe or eyes can see,
>> So long lives this, and this gives life to thee.

In the sonnet, the poet's claim is explicitly stated in the final quatrain: For as long as men live, this poem shall live and so, too, shall his beloved. In the preceding twelve lines, the poet provides evidence for his claim. Beginning with "a summer's day," he lists comparisons, each of which he finds deficient: "Sometime too hot the eye of heaven shines,/And often is his gold complexion dimmed." As readers, we are invited to think and reason with the poet as he makes his case for his beloved's immortality.

Ethos

Questioning the speaker's reliability leads us to the final point of Aristotle's rhetorical triangle: appeal to *ethos*—the attitude the speaker or writer conveys through specific word choices. The opening of King's "Letter" (page 151) provides a clear example of a highly effective appeal to *ethos*. King offers his audience a verbal handshake as a gesture of respect and cordiality. In the case of King's "Letter," the writer's intent is clear. However, other writers are not always as transparent in their purposes. Thus, as critical thinkers, we cannot always readily agree upon a speaker's or a writer's credibility. The following short fiction piece, "Girl" by Jamaica Kincaid, offers a debatable perspective on *ethos:*

Girl (1983)

Jamaica Kincaid

Wash the white clothes on Monday and put them on the stone heap; wash the color clothes on Tuesday and put them on the clothesline to dry; don't walk barehead in the hot sun; cook pumpkin fritters in very hot sweet oil; soak your little clothes right after you take them off; when buying cotton to make yourself a nice blouse, be sure that it doesn't have gum on it, because that way it won't hold up well after a wash; soak salt fish overnight before you cook it; is it true that you sing benna in Sunday school?; always eat your food in such a way that it won't turn someone else's stomach; on Sundays try to walk like a lady and not like the slut you are so bent on becoming; don't sing benna in Sunday school; you mustn't speak to wharf-rat boys, not even to give directions; don't eat fruits on the street—flies will follow you; *but I don't sing benna on Sundays at all and never in Sunday school;* this is how to sew on a button; this is how to make a buttonhole for the button you have just sewed on; this is how to hem a dress when you see the hem coming down and so to prevent yourself from looking like the slut I know you are so bent on becoming; this is how you iron your father's khaki shirt so that it doesn't have a crease; this is how you iron your father's khaki pants so that they don't have a crease; this is how you grow okra—far from the house, because okra tree harbors red ants; when you are growing dasheen, make sure it gets plenty of water or else it makes your throat itch when you are eating it; this is how you sweep a corner; this is how you sweep a whole house; this is how you sweep a yard; this is how you smile to someone you don't like too much; this is how you smile to someone you don't like at all; this is how you smile to someone you like completely; this is how you set a table for tea; this is how you set a table for dinner; this is how you set a table for dinner with an important guest; this is how you set a table for lunch; this is how you set a table for breakfast; this is how to behave in the presence of men who don't know you very well, and this way they won't recognize immediately the slut I have warned you against becoming; be sure to wash every day, even if it is with your own spit; don't squat down to play marbles—you are not a boy, you know; don't pick people's flowers—you might catch something; don't throw stones at blackbirds, because it might not be a blackbird at all; this is how to make a bread pudding; this is how to make doukona; this is how to make pepper pot; this is how to make a good medicine for a cold; this is how to make a good medicine to throw away a child before it even becomes a child; this is how to catch a fish; this is how to throw back a fish you don't like, and that way something bad won't fall on you; this is how to bully a man; this is how a man bullies you; this is how to love a man, and if this doesn't work there are other ways, and if they don't work don't feel too bad about giving up; this is how to spit up in the air if you feel like it, and this is how to move quickly so that it doesn't fall on you; this is how to make ends meet; always squeeze bread to make sure it's fresh; *but what if the baker won't let me feel the bread?;* you mean to say that after all you are really going to be the kind of woman who the baker won't let near the bread?

Kincaid's narrator would seem to be a mother lecturing her daughter, "girl." The mother's advice and admonitions are salt-of-the-earth, basic survival skills for a girl or woman: from how to cook, how to clean, and how to spit or smile, to how to take care of a man, or to administer her own birth control. Clearly, the mother is intent on her daughter's listening; the daughter manages only two brief rebuttals: *"but I don't sing benna on Sundays…but what if the baker won't let me feel the bread?"* Furthermore, the mother's tone is authoritative and domineering; her lecture is spiked with imperative clauses: Do this, do that, don't do that, never do this, etc. Yet it also is a catalogue of practical information: "this is how…; this is how…." The mother is passing on to her daughter all of her own hard-earned knowledge. As readers, what is our attitude toward this mother? Is she a "good" mother? Do we respect her? Trust her? Why or why not? Finally, would we describe the tone as simple yet elegant, a message of "tough love," or crude and haranguing, a belittling message of misguided love? Kincaid's short fiction piece can provoke an energetic discussion among readers and prompt us to explore our underlying assumptions about the role of a parent or an authority figure.

VISUAL ARGUMENT

So far in this chapter we have illustrated the principles of argument in written examples. These principles also apply to visuals, such as political cartoons, advertisements, or **propaganda** (usually information spread by a government to support a political cause).

Advertisers want their audience to buy a particular product, so they often include assumptions and audience appeals to convince the audience that its product is needed. When analyzing visuals, we must consider what assumptions are present. For example, most of us believe wrinkles are bad and wealth is good. Visuals, like written arguments, often rely on appeals to *ethos*, *logos*, and *pathos* to persuade consumers to purchase these products. An appeal to *pathos* might include the use of adorable animals or small children in their ads; an appeal to *logos* in a car ad might include statistics such as low gas mileage or affordability; an appeal to *ethos* for medication might include a doctor's recommendation. Consider the following WWI poster:

The purpose of the poster is obviously to recruit new soldiers. The claim implies that there are positive (even fun?) reasons to join the Army. What assumptions are made about the connection between sports and the military? How does this poster appeal to *logos*, *ethos*, and *pathos*?

ACTIVITIES

1. If you were assigned to write on the topic of whether college students are too open with information concerning their private lives on social media such as Facebook or Twitter, which type of claim (fact, policy, value) would be best for approaching the assignment?

2. How might you offer evidence for your ideas on the use and/or abuse of social media? What sources would be best to support your stance?

3. Identify any underlying assumptions and judgments that your readers might hold regarding social media. How would it affect your approach to the topic?

4. After reading the following poem, "Those Winter Sundays," by Robert Hayden, write out the poet's claim in one sentence. Then list the poem's evidence that supports that claim. Is the claim valid only within the dramatic context of the poem, or is the claim

valid universally? Can you find evidence within your own personal experience that would support the claim? What assumption underlies the claim?

Those Winter Sundays (1966)

Sundays too my father got up early
and put his clothes on in the blueblack cold,
then with cracked hands that ached
from labor in the weekday weather made
banked fires blaze. No one ever thanked him.   5

I'd wake and hear the cold splintering, breaking.
When the rooms were warm, he'd call,
and slowly I would rise and dress,
fearing the chronic angers of that house,

Speaking indifferently to him,   10
who had driven out the cold
and polished my good shoes as well.
What did I know, what did I know
of love's austere and lonely offices?

---

5. Read the following poem by Wilfred Owen, "*Dulce Et Decorum Est.*" How does the poet use Aristotle's three rhetorical appeals to convince readers of his claim that the phrase "*Dulce et decorum est Pro patria mori*"[1] lacks merit? Is there a logical presentation of evidence? Is there an emotional presentation of evidence? Does the speaker seem to have credibility?

Dulce Et Decorum Est (1917)

Bent double, like old beggars under sacks,
Knock-kneed, coughing like hags, we cursed through sludge,
Till on the haunting flares we turned our backs
And towards our distant rest began to trudge.
Men marched asleep. Many had lost their boots   5
But limped on, blood-shod. All went lame; all blind;
Drunk with fatigue; deaf even to the hoots
Of tired, outstripped Five-Nines that dropped behind.
Gas! GAS! Quick boys!—An ecstasy of fumbling,
Fitting the clumsy helmets just in time;   10
But someone still was yelling out and stumbling
And flound'ring like a man in fire or lime—
Dim, through the misty panes and thick green light,

---

[1]Quotation from Horace, meaning, "It is sweet and dutiful to die for one's country."

As under a green sea, I saw him drowning.
15   In all my dreams, before my helpless sight,
He plunges at me, guttering, choking, drowning.
If in some smothering dreams you too could pace
Behind the wagon that we flung him in,
And watch the white eyes writhing in his face,
20   His hanging face, like a devil's sick of sin;
If you could hear, at every jolt, the blood
Come gargling from the froth-corrupted lungs,
Obscene as cancer, bitter as the cud
Of vile, incurable sores on innocent tongues,—
25   My friend, you would not tell with such high zest
To children ardent for some desperate glory,
The old Lie: *Dulce et decorum est*
Pro patria mori.

---

6. Some claims are easily seen. For example, in the following essay, "Truer to the Game," Randy Horick makes this statement: "The women play a superior brand of basketball." For readers, there can be no misunderstanding—in fact, every word in Horick's essay leads readers to accept his claim. Read his essay and answer the questions that follow it.

Truer to the Game (2000)

Randy Horick

Offering examples of plays establishes credibility of author's sports knowledge and appeals to fellow sports enthusiasts.

Out in our driveway, where my 12-year-old daughter dreams of becoming the next Chamique Holdsclaw, we have been working together on a few of the finer points of competitive basketball. Like how to use your elbow semi-legally to establish position (an old Don Meyer bit of wisdom). Or how to inbound the ball to yourself by thunking it off the buttocks of an unsuspecting opponent. Or the deep personal satisfaction, to say nothing of the psychological advantage, gained from setting a teeth-rattling screen.

As part of this regimen, I have tried to use games on TV as teaching tools. I point out, for example, a good blockout on a rebound, a properly executed pick and roll, or the way to run a two-on-one fast break (or, more often, the way *not* to run a break).

Being a quick study, my daughter has observed one of the game's truths just from viewing two telecasts: the women's Final Four games on Friday and the corresponding men's contests on Saturday evening. "Dad," she observed, "the guys can't shoot."

This is either basketball's deep, dark secret or a cause for excitement, depending on your point of view. The truth is that the women take better shots than their male counterparts. As their respective NCAA tournaments made it ever clearer this March, when it comes to putting the pill in the hoop, girls' basketball rocks. Boys' basketball, well, doesn't.

But not only that: The women play a superior brand of basketball.   5
These are not the tilted rantings of some addle-brained pot-stirrer, as
accustomed as you may profess to be to seeing such things on these   *Thesis*
pages. You can find a whole pantheon of old NBA stars—including no   *statement*
less of a luminary than Bill Russell his own bad shot-blocking self—
who proclaim that women's basketball is much truer to the game they
played than the men's version today.

Claims of superiority, of course, all depend upon your definitions. If you measure quality by physical measures—speed, play above the rim, dazzling one-on-one moves— it's still a man's world. (Don't imagine, however, that the women in the Final Four aren't superbly conditioned athletes.)

If you're looking for solid fundamentals and all-around team play,
well, um, fellas, y'all got next. Ironically, the relative physical inferior-   *Horick offers*
ity of today's women players provides the basis for a superior game.   *readers*
                                                                                          characteristics
The ability of men to complete acrobatic, soaring drives and   *he notices*
dunks increasingly has led them to become infatuated with "taking   *about male*
it to the tin"—regardless of which defenders are in the way or which   *basketball*
teammates may be open elsewhere. It's as if the guys have all gradu-   *players.*
ated from some funky basketball camp that teaches that style points
count for even more than real ones.

If you had $250 for every time during the men's NCAAs that a
player passed up a jump shot, faked with the ball, then put his head
down and headed toward the hole, they'd make you an honorary   *To support his*
member of the bar association. The predictable results of such reckless   *argument and*
driving, all too often, are offensive fouls, ugly collisions, and loads of   *offer balance,*
bricks. For every dunk, we are forced to witness several thunks. For   *Horick*
every electrifying play, there are several short-circuits. The literal rise   *transitions*
of countless would-be Jordans has corresponded with a steady fall in   *to note*   10
field goal and free throw percentages in the men's game.   *characteristics*
                                                                                          of female
Contrast that with the women's game, where the play is decidedly   *basketball*
below the rim and dunks are rarer than incorruptible state legislators.   *players.*

Because the girls aren't yet throwing it down, they're forced to
concentrate on the aspects of the game that many of the boys seem   *Horick*
to regard as beneath them. Like practicing free throws. Running pat-   *offers specific*
terned offenses. Looking for back-door cutters. Making routine shots.   *aspects of*
Executing the fundamentals.   *female*
                                                                                          basketball he
For all of these reasons, if you want to teach someone to play the   *finds superior*
game, women's basketball today is far more instructive. In part, that's   *to the male*
because their game runs at a slightly slower speed, allowing you more   *game.*
clearly to see plays develop. Much more, however, it has to do with
better shot selection, better ball movement, and more faithful adher-
ence to the concept of team play.

Off the court, of course, women's college basketball looks even better in comparison. At the Division I Level, men's hoops today less and less exemplifies the old ideals of amateur competition and more and more resembles a corporate leviathan.

In the way that drug cartels have corrupted the institutions in countries like Colombia and Mexico, those who control the money and labor supply have leeched into men's basketball. AAU coaches serve as talent brokers who wield inordinate influence. Shoe companies sponsor posh summer camps for top high school players and sign college coaches to cushy contracts, hoping to win future endorsements from those who become stars.

15

Horick adds support to his argument by examining reasons why men's basketball is not as loyal to the game as women's basketball.

Meanwhile, the pressures to win are so enormous upon coaches, and the financial allure of an NBA career so powerful to players, that almost any action can be rationalized in the name of winning. Top high school players with marginal grades may be shipped off to basketball trade schools that pass themselves off as institutions of academic learning.

Collegiate coaches recruit the nation's elite players knowing all too well that they will be gone within a year or two, and that their only real interest in the college experience lies in gaining experience that will prepare them for the pros.

Things are so whomperdejawed that the NCAA, which blithely presided over the creation of this mess, is now declaring that the entire culture of men's basketball is diseased and needs a radical cure. (Good luck, guys.)

Against this backdrop, the women's game looks like a fount of purity. Star players don't bug out early for the professional league; they stay and earn their degrees.

Coaches don't have to hire bodyguards to protect their athletes from contact by predatory agents. The recruiting process does not begin in the eighth or ninth grades. There are no televised McDonald's all-American games or dunk contests that teach the best players that they belong to some sort of celebrity elite.

20

Those days may be coming. As the popularity of women's basketball continues to increase (Sunday's championship between Tennessee and Connecticut was the most watched women's game ever), so too will the pressures.

The retirement last week of Louisiana Tech coach Leon Barmore is a reminder of where the game is going. Tech and Old Dominion are perhaps the last of the "little" schools that remain powers in women's basketball today. It's easy to forget that, barely two decades ago, the game was dominated by colleges you never heard of: Delta State, Immaculata, Stephen F. Austin, Wayland Baptist.

In recognizing that women's basketball has the potential to face the same issues as the men's game, Horick is acknowledging the complexity of the issue.

Women's basketball belongs to the big schools now. With the WNBA successfully established, it is conceivable that collegians might turn pro early if salaries become attractive enough. Coaches might cut corners and grease palms to lure the best high schoolers to their programs. A whole industry might rise up and enshroud the game, as it has with men's basketball.

Until then, though, I'll keep offering up as role models the kind of unspoiled, we-first players who were evident in the women's tournament.

Meanwhile, we won't forget at our house that the men's pro league still offers enormous entertainment value. Just last Sunday, during the Knicks-Lakers game, my daughter came rushing in breathlessly. "Dad, dad, come check it out. Kobe Bryant and Chris Childs are having a fight!"

DISCUSSION QUESTIONS

1. What type of claim—fact, policy, or value—would you attribute to Horick's article?

2. Do you think Horick makes a convincing argument that female players are "truer to the game" of basketball? Why or why not?

3. What evidence does Horick use to support his claim? What assumptions are present?

4. Suppose you were tasked with refuting Horick's assertions. What supporting claims would you offer to strengthen your position?

CHAPTER 4

Researching and Documenting an Argument Essay

In this chapter, you will learn about
- finding credible sources.
- avoiding plagiarism in your writing.
- using proper source citations in your essay.

WORKING WITH SOURCES

You certainly can write a college-level essay that expresses your opinions and insights on an issue by using personal experience or observations to support your claims. However, in an academic community, instructors often expect you to move beyond the use of personal experience as evidence. In these cases, you will make use of evidence from authoritative sources, such as books, periodicals, websites, and databases. When using this information, you have specific responsibilities as a writer.

First, you must make accurate and fair use of the material in your essay. This task involves taking good notes and then deciding whether to *quote* directly or *paraphrase* that information as you integrate it into your essay. Second, you must follow a *documentation system* to give credit to the original sources of your information and to allow your reader to see the sources of this information.

Finding Credible Sources

Although you may think that research can be done via an Internet search using Google or other popular search engines, much of the scholarly information that exists can only be found through your campus library.

Using a search engine will bring up multiple pages of links related to your subject, but you will be challenged to find credible and authoritative information. Beginning your research process with your school library—an *academic* library—allows you to use "presifted information," or source material that has already been deemed credible. An academic library houses thousands of peer-reviewed scholarly journals, both in print and online in academic library databases, including articles written by professionals in a specific discipline for both students and professionals. Thus, to find articles from *The Journal of the American Medical Association* (*JAMA*), from *Women's Studies*, or from *Film Journal International*, you would use an academic library database, such as Academic Search Complete.

Avoiding Plagiarism

Using someone else's ideas or facts without giving that person credit is **plagiarism**. Plagiarism is equivalent to theft, and thieves, when caught, are punished. While a few students knowingly take others' ideas and pass them off as their own, many more students unknowingly commit plagiarism because they do not understand how to make fair use of ideas and facts from outside sources. In particular, because information is so readily available through the Internet, some students do not realize that they still must document such sources throughout the essay and on the Works Cited page.

To avoid charges of plagiarism, begin by taking *accurate notes*. As you examine materials from your research, you will need to record useful facts and ideas. Whether you take your notes on index cards or in electronic format, one concept is particularly important to keep in mind: Make a clear distinction between your words and the words of the author. Always place quotes around any words or phrases that are the author's, and clearly note when you have paraphrased, or restated, someone else's ideas. Otherwise, you will be unable to distinguish your words or ideas from the author's when you write your essay.

Some information from sources may not require documentation; this information is called *common knowledge*. For instance, you may read that the U.S. military suffered many casualties during the worst battles of World War II; because that information is common knowledge, you are not required to document its source even though you also make that statement in your essay. On the other hand, if you read that 3,200 Americans were wounded or killed at the Battle of the Bulge—information that is not common knowledge—you would need to document the source of that statistic in your essay.

[*Hint:* Deciding what is or is not common knowledge can be confusing. When in doubt, cite the source and, if time allows, check with your campus writing center specialists or your instructor.]

Documentation Systems

All academic disciplines require a systematic approach to research and documentation. Whether your essay is in anthropology or chemistry, economics or English, geology or art history, you will need to learn how to use outside sources accurately and correctly. Academic disciplines make use of several documentation systems. Humanities typically use a system created by the Modern Language Association (MLA), while the social sciences often use a system devised by the American Psychological Association (APA). Other academic documentation systems include Turabian and the *Chicago Manual of Style*. However, because essays written for your English course will fall under the category *humanities*, the following explanation will center on the MLA documentation system.

[For information on using the other documentation systems, we suggest you consult your campus writing center, library, or the following websites: *apastyle.org; chicagomanualofstyle.org.*]

Although the primary purpose of documentation is to give credit to the originators of any material that is not your own, documentation also serves another important purpose: It enables your readers to locate the information you used and evaluate it for themselves. In effect, you are sharing the information you have found, a consideration that becomes increasingly important as you become an active participant in an academic community.

In order to fulfill these two purposes, your readers must be able to find the complete bibliographic information for each of your sources. To this end, within your essay, you provide the key name or title in a parenthetical citation, immediately after your use of the information. Now the reader can turn to the last page of your essay and locate the full bibliographic entry for each of your sources; therefore, you must create a Works Cited page.

The Preliminary Bibliography

As you begin to locate potential sources, you will want to maintain a list of the sources you examine; this list is called a *preliminary bibliography*. To create this list, get into the habit of recording as much bibliographic information as is available—author, title, publisher, date of publication, page or paragraph numbers, name of online database, etc. You will need this information when you compose the Works Cited page for your essay. Nothing is more frustrating than finishing an essay only to discover that you must try to locate the source of a quotation you found three weeks earlier when you began the project. In fact, when using Web or online sources, you will find it useful to save files of the sources or print copies so that you have the information you need, in hand, both for developing your argument and for citing sources.

[*Hint:* Articles accessed from academic databases, such as those to which your college library subscribes, often include source citations. When you open the link to an article, look to see if the article's citation is included, and, if so, make sure you select the format required for your assignment (for example, MLA or APA).]

The Annotated Bibliography

A bibliography is your list of sources of information, and to annotate a bibliography, you write notes about each source. Creating an annotated bibliography serves at least two valuable purposes:

1. It gives you an opportunity to review and assess the sources you have located: You can see what gaps you may have—for example, do you need more information on an aspect of the issue? You also may see overlaps among your sources, which can help you to identify noteworthy perspectives and information.

2. It helps you begin to synthesize the information from those sources and, thus, to move toward developing a preliminary or working claim for your argument; even though you are not, in fact, trying to write a claim when producing your annotated bibliography, the process of *thinking* about the information will move you in that direction.

To prepare an annotated bibliography, begin by writing out your sources in the style required for your Works Cited page. (This is a *third* advantage of creating an annotated bibliography: You already will have the task of putting together your Works Cited page virtually completed. All you will need to do is create a second Word file, renamed as Works Cited, which you can edit later.) To write the annotations for your sources, you write out a summary and/or evaluation—depending on the assignment requirements—of each source in paragraph form, immediately after each source citation. These sentences should be written *in your own words*. The length of the annotations depends on your assignment requirement as well as on the complexity of the source you are annotating.

In the following annotated bibliography sample, a student has written evaluation notes, which are particularly useful in preparing to write an argument. Reading through these annotations, you will see how the student is using this assignment to synthesize the different perspectives on the issue surrounding social media and networking.

Annotated Bibliography

Andrews, Lori B. *I Know Who You Are and I Saw What You Did: Social Networks and the Death of Privacy*. New York: Free Press, 2012. Print.

Andrews describes how America's love of social media has led to the widespread erosion of privacy. As social media users willingly surrender more personal information, the author examines ways information can be used against them in court cases, by spouses or employers, or even by illegal voyeurs.

Barnes, Julian E. "Spies Plugging into Social-Media Networks." *Wall Street Journal*. 7 Aug. 2014: A.4. *SIRS Issues Researcher*. Web. 1 Dec. 2015.

Technology combined with social media can offer the United States an advantage in monitoring global relations. American intelligence officials can gather useful information by utilizing new technologies to monitor posts on social media sites.

Brooks, Stoney. "Does Personal Social Media Usage Affect Efficiency and Well-Being?" *Computers in Human Behavior* 46 (2015): 26-37. *Social Sciences Full Text (H.W. Wilson)*. Web. 30 Nov. 2015.

Brooks examines the negative outcomes associated with social media users who multi-task work projects while simultaneously engaged in social networking. The findings include lower levels of productivity and happiness among some social media users.

Frison, Eline, and Steven Eggermont. "The Impact of Daily Stress on Adolescents' Depressed Mood: The Role of Social Support Seeking Through Facebook." *Computers in Human Behavior* 44 (2015): 315+. *Academic OneFile*. Web. 2 Nov. 2015.

Teens who seek positive affirmations and encouragement could likely be looking for it in the wrong place when they seek such sentiments from their favorite social networking sites. In examining adolescents' use of social networking to improve mood, Frison and Eggermont found that social media could fuel depression among teens.

Heser, Kathrin, Rainer Banse, and Roland Imhoff. "Affiliation or Power: What Motivates Behavior on Social Networking Sites?" *Swiss Journal of Psychology* 74.1 (2015): 37-47. *PsycARTICLES*. Web. 1 Dec. 2015.

The authors, studying the social networking habits of 59 subjects, make connections between the amount of time spent on social networking sites and motivation of social network users. Researchers studied how subjects promoted feelings of belonging, power, and achievement via social network connections. For example, individuals motivated by power usually post a greater number of pictures.

Mazur, Elizabeth, and Yidi Li. "Identity and Self-Presentation on Social Networking Web Sites: A Comparison of Online Profiles of Chinese and American Emerging Adults." *Psychology of Popular Media Culture* (2014): *PsycARTICLES*. Web. 4 Dec. 2015.

A group of 100 social media users from America and China between 18 to 25 years of age served as subjects in this exploration of cultural attitudes toward social networking. Young Americans are more likely to maintain positive self-images and less likely to explore negative moods online.

McLeod, Scott, and Chris Lehmann. *What School Leaders Need to Know About Digital Technologies and Social Media*. San Francisco, CA: Jossey-Bass, 2012. *eBook Collection (EBSCOhost)*. Web. 1 Mar. 2015.

This book examines how public school administrators can best showcase technology and social networking to promote learning. For example, some schools have found online blogs a creative way of demonstrating to parents what their children are learning in the classroom.

Padilla-Walker, Laura M., Sarah M. Coyne, and Ashley M. Fraser. "Getting a High-Speed Family Connection: Associations Between Family Media Use and Family Connection." *Family Relations* (July 2012): 426-440. *JSTOR*. Web. 30 Nov. 2015.

The families who text, watch movies, and play video games together maintain closer ties than those who rely on social networking for connection. In a study of 459 adolescents and parents, researchers discovered that children feel less connected to their parents when social networking is the primary form of family connection through media.

Think B4 U Post: Your Reputation and Privacy on Social Networking Sites. Films on Demand. Films Media Group, 2011. Web. 1 Dec. 2015.

Some young people are careless when it comes to listing personal information on the Internet. This film reminds social media users about the dangers of being too open with posts, including vulnerability to web predators and the possibility of employers using social media to make employment decisions.

INCORPORATING SOURCES

Paraphrasing and Summarizing

As you take notes, you may encounter passages that you want to record. To avoid the overuse of direct quotations, you can choose either to paraphrase or to summarize the passage from your source. To *paraphrase* the material, read and reread the original passage until you know what it is saying, and then, using your own words, express the ideas accurately in a passage of approximately the same length as the original. It is not enough for you simply to change or rearrange a few words here and there; indeed, such a practice is considered plagiarism. Also, although paraphrased material is not enclosed in quotation marks (because the wording is, in fact, your own), you still must document its source with an in-text parenthetical citation because the ideas, concepts, and information are not your own but your source's.

Similar to paraphrasing, in *summarizing*, you are rewriting a passage from a source in your own words. The important distinction, however, between paraphrasing and summarizing is that a summary is much shorter in length than the original passage, whereas a paraphrase is approximately the same length as the original. As with paraphrasing, when you summarize, you must document your use of the source with an in-text parenthetical citation.

Direct Quotations

A *direct quotation* is an exact, word-for-word restatement of a writer's or a speaker's words. A direct quotation must be documented in two ways: It must be enclosed in quotation marks, and it must be noted with an in-text parenthetical citation that refers to its source on the Works Cited page. Moreover, as the writer, you must weave the quotation smoothly into the text of your own writing. Provide an introduction to the quotation and follow it with a sentence or more of your own analysis and commentary. In the following example, notice how the student lets readers know who is being quoted (in this case, two researchers), and follows the quote with a sentence of the student's own commentary:

> Researchers Charles D. Weddle and Phillip Wishon state, "There are estimates of some twenty-eight million children of alcoholics in this country" (8). Children of alcoholics are challenged by their own development as well as their experiences of living in a dysfunctional home environment.

Longer direct quotations—more than four typed lines—are introduced with your own sentence, indented ten spaces from the left margin, and double-spaced. Because the indented format signals a direct quotation, the quotation marks are omitted; also, the parenthetical citation follows, rather than precedes, the quoted passage's closing period. In the following example, notice not only the format, but also the student's lead-in and follow-up sentences, which provide a smooth integration of the source material into the student's own text:

> If one is going to help a child of an alcoholic, one must know what alcoholism is. Alcoholism is defined as:
>
>> primary chronic disease with genetic, psychosocial and environmental factors influencing its development and manifestations. The disease is often progressive and fatal. It is characterized by continuous or periodic: impaired control over drinking, preoccupation with the drug alcohol, use of alcohol despite adverse consequences, and distortions in thinking most notably denial. ("Definition")
>
> This is a very clinical and detailed definition of the disease and its effects; however, aside from the effects on the consumer of alcohol, it fails to mention the other victims affected by this disease.

As you incorporate quotations into your writing, you will want them to flow smoothly into the context of what you have to say rather than dropping them in awkwardly. Introduce a paraphrase, summary, or quotation with a signal phrase, which may include the author's name and a verb, usually in present tense. Here are commonly used source signal verbs:

acknowledges	confirms	opposes
advises	contends	recommends
advocates	criticizes	refutes
affirms	declares	remarks
agrees	denies	reports
allows	disagrees	responds
answers	discusses	states
asserts	emphasizes	suggests
avows	expresses	thinks
believes	interprets	writes
charges	lists	
claims	objects	
concedes	observes	
concludes	offers	

[*Hint:* Direct quotations, of course, provide explicit evidence of your research efforts; however, maintain your responsibility as the author of your essay. Be selective in quoting and frame your use of quotations with lead-in sentences to provide context and follow-up sentences to provide commentary.]

IN-TEXT PARENTHETICAL CITATIONS

In MLA style, the in-text parenthetical citations usually include the author's last name—or if an author's name is not given with the source, the source's title—and a page number, all enclosed in parentheses. Again, remember this key principle: You must use in-text parenthetical citations for direct quotations; for paraphrases or summaries of another person's words; and for facts, figures, or concepts that originated in someone else's work. The *MLA Handbook for Writers of Research Papers* is an excellent source for documenting bibliographic information. For updates and further explanations, go to mla.org.

Print Sources

If you are citing information you found in an article by Danielle S. Furlich entitled "Field Studies" and published on page 54 of the magazine *Nature Conservancy* in its Spring 2009 issue, the parenthetical citation would look like this: (Furlich 54). It would be placed at the end of the sentence containing that information and before the ending punctuation. In cases where your source does not identify an author, use key words of the title, enclosed in quotation marks, to identify the source, as follows: ("Postmodern Culture" 398).

Electronic Sources

To document your use of an **electronic source**, you apply the basic two-step principle outlined earlier: Identify the source within the context of the writing and with an in-text parenthetical citation, followed by a full bibliographic entry for the source on the Works Cited page. The in-text parenthetical citation identifies the source either by the author's last name, if the source has an author, or by the first key words in the title: (Bishop) or ("Newsroom Integrity"). However, unlike hard-copy source citations that require page numbers, electronic source citations include the page number only if the source is formatted in "page display format" or PDF: (Johnson 5) or ("Fighting with Microbes" 11). If the electronic source includes paragraph numbers, you should include the paragraph number corresponding to the specific spot from which you took a quote, fact, or paraphrase: (Vickers, par. 14) or ("Finding Your Future," par. 23).

[*Hint:* As you type in your in-text parenthetical citations, keep this guideline in mind: The author's last name or the key words from the source's title in your in-text parenthetical citation should match the first word of the source citation on your Works Cited page (excluding articles—*A, An, The*). Think of the in-text citation as a "shorthand" guide for your readers that allows them to locate the source on your Works Cited page, where they can see the full bibliographical entry for that source.]

THE WORKS CITED PAGE

The final page of your essay is the Works Cited page, a list of the sources you directly cited in your essay. These citations are arranged alphabetically by the author's last name or by the first word in the source's title (excluding *A, An,* and *The*). The specific details to be included in each source entry vary, according to the type of source—book, article, website, interview, or electronic source. Following are sample source citations typically found in first-year college essays:

Book by one author

> Herzog, Hal. *Some We Love, Some We Hate, Some We Eat: Why It's so Hard to Think Straight About Animals.* New York: Harper, 2010. Print.

Story, poem, or essay from a collection in a book

> Owen, Wilfred. "*Dulce et Decorum Est.*" *Reading Literature and Writing Argument.* Ed. Missy James, et al. 6th ed. Upper Saddle River: Pearson/Prentice Hall, 2015. 152–63. Print.

Article from a print magazine

> Tidwell, Mike. "The Low-Carbon Diet." *Audubon* Feb. 2009. 46+. Print.

Personal interview

Pekins, John. Personal interview. 13 Dec. 2015.

Film on DVD

Gone Girl. Dir. David Fincher. Perf. Ben Affleck, Rosamund Pike, Neil Patrick Harris, and Tyler Perry. Twentieth Century Fox, 2014. DVD.

Article in an online journal

McQueen, Tena F., and Robert A. Fleck, Jr. "Changing Patterns of Internet Usage and Challenges at Colleges and Universities." *First Monday* 9.12 (2004)-.: N. pag. Web. 16 Feb. 2015.

[Note: Because this article is in html format, it does not include page numbers (which is indicated by "N. pag.").]

Hughes, John. "Owen's 'Dulce et Decorum Est.'." *Explicator* 64.3 (Spring 2006): 160-162. Rpt. in *Poetry Criticism.* Ed. Michelle Lee. Vol. 102. Detroit: Gale, 2010. *Literature Resource Center.* Web. 9 Dec. 2015.

Article with no author specified from an electronic database

"Being Stalked by Intelligent Design." *American Scientist* Nov./Dec. 2005: n. pag. *OmniFile Full Text Mega.* Web. 18 Jan. 2016.

Article with more than one author from an electronic database

Beard, Lawrence A., Cynthia Harper, and Gena Riley. "Online Versus On-Campus Instruction: Student Attitudes & Perceptions." *TechTrends: Linking Research & Practice to Improve Learning* Nov./Dec. 2004: 29–31. *Academic Search Premier.* Web. 1 Jan. 2016.

[Note: Because this article is in PDF format, this reference does include page numbers.]

A literary work from an electronic database

Yeats, W. B. "To a Wealthy Man." *Responsibilities and Other Poems.* New York: McMillan, 1916. *Bartleby.com.* Web. 20 Nov. 2015

Online magazine article

Ozols, Jennifer Barrett. "At Risk." *Newsweek* 15 Mar. 2005. N pag. *MSN.com.* Web. 10 Dec. 2015.

Websites

Chastain, James. "Marie von Ebner-Eschenbach." Encyclopedia of 1848 Revolutions. Ohio U., 13 Oct. 2004. Web. 3 Nov. 2015. <http://www.ohiou.edu/~chastain/dh/ebner.htm>. [Website addresses or URLs are omitted unless, as this example illustrates, the website may be difficult to locate without the URL.]

Documenting the American South. Lib., U of North Carolina at Chapel Hill, 19 Dec. 2005. Web. 19 Jan. 2016.

"Lincoln Wins: Honest Abe Tops New Presidential Survey." CNN.com. CNNPolitics.com., 16 Feb. 2009. Web. 6 Jan. 2016.

The Zora Neale Hurston Plays at the Library of Congress. Lib. of Cong., 7 Jan. 2004. Web. 18 Dec. 2015.

ANNOTATED STUDENT ESSAY

In the following essay, student Josh Griep presents a research-based argument centered on a *claim of policy* that is explicitly stated in the last sentence of paragraph two:

Josh Griep
Professor James
ENC 1102–028
3 Nov. 2015

Wild Captives: The Exotic Animal Trade

Lead-in

An estimated five thousand tigers live freely in the wild today; the number of tigers living in captivity is approximately the same (Brook). The latter figure, however, is only the tip of the animal-trading iceberg. Each year, approximately thirty thousand animals are taken from the wild to be sold to private owners (Elton). It has been estimated that fifty to ninety percent of these animals die before ever reaching the United States to be sold.

Rhetorical context

Clearly, the traders of these animals care only about profits; the animals' welfare is the least of their concerns. Jorge Risemberg, who heads up the Ecological Police's Animal Division in Peru, says, "On the global level, after drug trafficking and the contraband arms trade, the contraband trade of animals is the most profitable" (Elton). The animals that are strong enough to survive are sold for as little as fifty dollars in the United States. These animals were not put on this earth to be conversation pieces or to simply look exotic in someone's backyard in Ohio. These wild animals belong in their natural habitats where

Claim of policy

they can roam their native habitat freely. The United States Government must step in and outlaw the shipping of exotic animals into this country.

Twelve states currently have bans against large exotic animals, and seven have partial bans. There is no federal law, however, that restricts anyone from selling or owning nonendangered, exotic animals ("HSUS"). U.S. Representative George Miller has been the prime supporter of HR 5226, a bill which would halt private ownership of many exotic animals: "Wild animals, especially such large and uniquely powerful animals as lions and tigers, should be kept in captivity by professional zoological facilities" (Woolf, "Lions"). Opponents of the bill argue that some people have the resources to care for these animals as well as or even better than zoos. This may be true, but this justification also begs the central question: the humane treatment of the wild animals. If zoos are unable to provide sufficient habitat, they should not be allowed to house the animals. Furthermore, how would the animals' living conditions be evaluated and qualified as suitable or not? Who would continue to monitor these facilities to make sure living conditions remain sufficient? Partial bans, while suggesting a compromise solution, would only serve the selfish needs of the human owners, not the basic needs of the captive animals. Therefore, a complete federal ban must be established to protect these wild creatures and to preserve the natural balance of species of the native lands from which they have been stolen.

Not only is a total ban necessary to maintain the well-being of the animals and their native habitats, but it also is a prime factor in the safety of humans. The director of governmental affairs for the Humane Society states, "Each wild animal kept as a pet in a community is a time bomb waiting to go off. They're genetically programmed to kill" (Brook). Most people are not qualified to own wild animals. The United States Department of Agriculture "believes that only qualified, trained professionals should keep these animals, even if they are only to be pets" (Woolf, "Movie Stars"). However, owners of exotic animals disagree: "Ninety-nine percent of the people with exotic animals look after them properly. Of course, you only hear about that one percent that don't," claims Mark Killman, owner of the Killman Zoo which keeps exotic pets (Nikolovsky). One percent seems extremely low, so perhaps Killman has a point. However, that minute percentile includes the following: a Toronto man who was killed by one of his twenty Burmese pythons (Nikolovsky); the wild boar (Nikolovsky) and three lions found roaming around small towns that had to be executed (Brook); the leopard found in a freezing garage; and the two thousand exotic animals found in an animal breeder's home—all must be factored in to Killman's so-called "one percent" (Elton). Apparently, Killman and other opponents of the ban need a math lesson. Ten thousand fewer exotic animals survive being imported each year, and two thousand are found in

Opposing viewpoint

Refutation

Supporting evidence

Opposing viewpoint

Concession

Refutation

single homes. That adds up to one-fifth or twenty percent of the animals imported that, Killman claims, are "properly taken care of."

Supporting evidence

The problem extends far beyond the animals having to be put down when they are beyond rehabilitation. These animals are killing machines, and unpredictably they will return to their basic predatory instincts. For example, a three-year-old boy in Texas was killed by a "pet" tiger; another three-year-old had part of his arm ripped off; and a woman was bitten on the head by a 750-pound Siberian-Bengal tiger mix ("HSUS"). Cases such as these convincingly demonstrate that these wild creatures are not only dangerous to their owners, but to other people as well.

Authoritative testimony

Paris Griep, who has been a wildlife biologist for thirty years, believes that no one should be allowed to own these animals: "Well-regulated and monitored zoos are the only facilities with highly trained personnel who can truly care for these animals properly. They cannot be stuck in an 8′ by 8′ cage and expect to live any kind of a life." Not only does this importation of wild animals harm the individual animals, but it also endangers the ecosystem from which they are captured. "Whenever those animals are taken out of the wild, it depletes the natural diversity from the place where they are taken from," Griep points out. These animals already have a difficult time trying to maintain their species populations without humans' further interfering through the exotics trade.

Restatement of claim

Wild animals are called wild for a reason; they should be allowed to live freely in their native habitats. Furthermore, wild animals are by their natures unpredictable and cannot safely interact with people. A complete federal ban on the selling and housing of exotic animals is the only rational and humane policy. Such a ban would not remove these animals from the public eye; in fact, that is quite the contrary. If a complete ban is established by law, the populations of these animals can be returned to the flourishing populations they once were. These animals can still be loved and viewed in the safety of well-regulated zoos and licensed wildlife preserves. If owners of exotic pets truly care for their animals, as they insist, they will realize that keeping the animals in a cage or in an environment that they are not accustomed to is unreasonable, unsafe, and inhumane.

Written almost a century ago, the poem, "The Panther" by Rainer Maria Rilke, offers powerful support for a complete ban on the wild animal trade:

> His vision, from the constantly passing bars,
> has grown so weary that it cannot hold
> anything else. It seems to him there are
> a thousand bars; and behind the bars, no world. (1–4)

Let's not take away these animals' vision. We must make sure that they can roam freely in a world without bars.

Works Cited

Brook, Tom Vanden. "Exotic Pets Growing More Accessible in USA." *USA Today.* USA Today, Dec. 2002. Web. 26 Oct. 2015.

Elton, Catherine. "Peru's Eco-Police Make Barely a Dent in Trade of Exotic Pets." *Christian Science Monitor* 5 May 1998: n. pag. *Academic Search Premier.* Web. 24 Oct. 2015.

Griep, Paris. Personal interview. 20 Oct. 2015.

"HSUS Applauds Rep. George Miller for Introducing Legislation." *HSUS.org.* The Humane Society of the United States, July 2002. Web. 25 Oct. 2015.

Nikolovsky, Boris. "Critics Growl over Keeping of Exotic Pets: Zoo Animals Live in Basements and Backyards." *Zoocheck Canada Inc.* Aug. 1994. Web. 26 Oct. 2015.

Rilke, Rainer Maria. "The Panther." *Ahead of All Parting: The Selected Poetry and Prose of Rainer Maria Rilke.* New York: Random House, 1995. 31. Print.

Woolf, Norma Bennett. "Lions and Tigers and Bears, Oh No!" *Naiaonline.org.* National Animal Interest Alliance, July 2002. Web. 19 Oct. 2015.

– – –. "Movie Stars Want Federal Restrictions on Private Ownership of Exotic Animals." *Naiaonline.org.* National Animal Interest Alliance, Feb. 2000. Web. 16 Oct. 2015.

CHAPTER 5

Creating an Argument

In this chapter you will learn about
- implementing a plan to write your paper.
- writing a claim and providing evidence.
- utilizing Rogerian argument for controversial topics.

PLANNING AN ARGUMENT

When creating a plan to write an argument essay, the first step is to read the assignment carefully and to make certain you understand what the instructor expects. Some instructors will give you specific topics; some may give you more freedom. **Prewriting** is an essential step in the writing process. Prewriting means to focus your thoughts before you begin an essay. Some might like to make lists, some might attack a blank page with thoughts as they come, and some might use note cards. There is not a single, right way to begin. After some informal prewriting and gathering ideas, it is time to get focused. Before you start writing a draft, formulate a claim and look for evidence that will build the strongest support for your argument. You might find it helpful to start by making a list or perhaps an informal outline. Try to think of this task not as a dreaded activity, but as an investment in your writing project. Taking a few minutes to write down your ideas can lead to some wonderful discoveries about your own thinking. More than likely, such an enterprise will help you ultimately structure a more formal outline to map out your paper and assist you in formulating evidence.

Creating an Informal Outline

The following structure can be useful if you want specific organizational guidelines, or it can serve as a starting point if you want to devise your own organizational plan:

Basic Structure of an Informal Outline

Introduction

- Lead-in "hook" sentences
- Concise overview of issue/rhetorical context
- Explicit claim of fact, value, or policy

Opposition

- Concise summary of key points of opposing viewpoint
- Concession/acknowledgment of legitimacy of aspects of this viewpoint
- Refutation/counterargument to address weak aspects of viewpoint

Supporting Argument

- Specific proof of claim
- Evidence grouped under three or so key points
- Strongest point presented last

Conclusion

- Restatement of claim
- Resolution, compromise, or call to action

Many students feel getting started is the most intimidating part of a writing assignment. In order to kick start your writing, you might find answering the following strategy questions helpful.

Strategy Questions for Organizing Your Argument Essay

1. Do you have a lead-in to "hook" your reader? (an example, anecdote, scenario, startling statistic, or provocative question)
2. How much background is required to properly acquaint readers with your issue?
3. Will your claim be placed early (introduction) or delayed (conclusion) in your paper?
4. What is your supporting evidence?
5. Have you located authoritative (expert) sources that add credibility to your argument?
6. Have you considered addressing opposing viewpoints?

7. Are you willing to make some concessions (compromises) toward opposing sides?
8. What type of tone (serious, comical, sarcastic, inquisitive) best relates your message to reach your audience?
9. Once written, have you maintained a third person voice? (No "I" or "you" statements)
10. How will you conclude in a meaningful way? (Call your readers to take action, explain why the topic has global importance, or offer a common ground compromise that benefits all sides?)

CREATING A DRAFT

You have thought about your issue; discussed it with friends and classmates; and read about it in various periodicals, books, and electronic sources. You have a collection of notes, photocopies of sources, and an annotated bibliography. Now comes the time to sit down and create a draft.

Writing a Thesis/Claim Statement

The heart of an argument is its claim. Now is the time for you to make that heart come alive. To do so, you will engage in the higher-order critical thinking skill of *synthesis*. You will "cook down" the source information and your ideas to its essence—to one essential and arguable point.

Rereading the issue question, which has been the subject of your research efforts, you will now write your informed opinion in response to that question—the position or assertion for which you can create a compelling case. Although the claim should, finally, be a single, succinct yet specific statement, be prepared to spend some time—and many words—to discover your claim. You are cooking the pot of information and ideas down to its richest essence. This thinking and writing task should be hard—a process of writing, scratching out, writing, and rewriting as you write your way to discovering your claim. In the process of writing, you will be synthesizing information and ideas; concurrently, you will begin to see a claim emerge. Allow your first efforts in wording your claim to be rough, if not awkward and simplistic. You can revise the wording to be more specific and compelling once you can *see* on paper (or the screen) the point you want to argue. As you revise, keep in mind the chiseling tool for sharpening your claim: determining whether you want to focus your argument primarily as a claim of fact, value, or policy.

Following are examples of the three types of claims in response to this issue question: *Should the city place a moratorium on the construction of fast-food restaurants in lower-income neighborhoods?*

- *Claim of fact:* Residents of lower-income neighborhoods are targeted by the fast-food industry, and, as a result, they are particularly prone to health problems associated with high-fat and processed foods.
- *Claim of value:* A proposal to ban fast-food restaurant construction in lower-income neighborhoods unfairly stereotypes and discriminates against the residents of those neighborhoods.
- *Claim of policy:* The city should not implement a moratorium on fast-food restaurant construction in lower-income neighborhoods.

ACTIVITY

Practice writing claims based on the following issue question: *Should the college implement a mandatory attendance policy?* Write three versions of a claim: fact, value, and policy. Be prepared to share your three claim statements with several classmates for their review.

FROM CLAIM TO DRAFT

- With a claim in hand, you now are ready to map out your argument strategy—to create an outline of body paragraph topics, to jot down five or so details for each paragraph, and to lay out a logical order for your paragraphs. Using the strategy questions and outline (pages 63–64), you should be able to create a useful outline for your argument. Remember that your claim is your promise to your readers; it tells readers what they can expect you to deliver in the body paragraphs. Thus, write your claim out at the top of the first page of your outline, and keep your body paragraphs aligned with it. However, keep in mind that you are *planning*—nothing is yet set in stone, not even your claim. If you come across an essential topic or idea that your claim does not include, revise your claim to embrace this topic.
- Finally, with an outline in hand, you are ready to write that first draft. Here is how we suggest you proceed:

  1. Proclaim yourself an expert on the issue; most certainly, you are more informed than many other laypersons.
  2. Put your sources aside—*out of sight*—and write a first, fast-draft by using only your outline/planning pages and the knowledge in your head that you have gained through intensive study of the issue.

  By writing this first draft—*on your own*—you will avoid the common pitfall of overrelying on source material and, as a consequence, losing ownership of your writing. Once you have cranked out a first draft, you can return to your sources/notes and identify relative information to flesh out your draft and, thus, enhance the authoritative basis of your argument.

BASIC TOOLS FOR DESIGNING YOUR ARGUMENT

Constructing your academic argument will be much easier if you take the time to consider your subject, purpose, and audience.

Clarifying a Subject, Purpose, and Audience

The *subject* of an argument is, by definition, an *issue*, a debatable topic. You can test a subject to make sure that it is, in fact, an arguable topic by framing it as an *issue question*, one about which reasonable people might disagree. For example, a "college policy of mandatory class attendance" is a *subject*; "Should a college policy of mandatory class attendance be implemented?" is an *issue question*.

Let's further explore the idea of subjects as debatable topics. No one will argue that December 25 is Christmas or that the police have the authority to make arrests. Both of these items are accepted facts. However, a worthwhile conversation on these two topics can be advanced by carefully considering controversies surrounding these issues. Some people disagree as to whether a socially conscious society should abandon specific greetings such as "Merry Christmas" and instead stick with the more generic "Happy Holidays" due to religious differences. Further, police have the power to make arrests, but that authority is not arbitrary, and a good many people debate the merits of excessive force in police officers' interactions with suspects. Remember, often our ideas come to us as broad subjects, but a successful arguer is able to narrow the range of discussion by delving into specific areas of dissention with a chosen topic.

The **purpose** of your argument is found in your motivation for initiating a conversation on your chosen subject. Sure, most of us would not choose to write research papers if they were not assigned by our instructors. But in order to offer our best writing performance, we must move past this obligatory sense and search for what we can add to the dialog on our chosen subject. In writing an essay about holidays and political correctness, is your purpose to make the audience consider that we need to be more sensitive to religious differences or that political correctness is now extreme when a goodwill tiding is cause for offense? Merely reporting the facts on a recent case of alleged police misconduct is not enough to accomplish a purpose for an argument; instead, what points would you like to invite your audience to consider about the case? Establishing a sense of purpose will empower your writing.

Knowing your audience is a must in a successful argument presentation. When you are completing a college assignment, consider your audience as the global academic community. You are addressing an educated body of your peers. Educated members of your community bring a baseline of knowledge to their reading. Therefore, part of your audience consideration is realizing that your readers expect you to advance the subject and not merely fill a page with reporting summary information.

Consideration of subject, purpose, and audience are integral to successful academic argument. We know that academic writing is more formal and that usually, unless there is a rare need to quote such, profanities should be not used. Take a look at how student Cale Blount takes that assumption about academic writing and challenges it in the following essay.

Cale Blount
Greg Loyd
ENC 1102- Position Paper
18 Nov. 2015

The Last Words of Power

Language is powerful. From the first grunt shared between our cave-dwelling ancestors to the thoughts disseminated among the youth in our schools, this has always been true. Language brought its own magic to the world, giving man something no other creature before or since had: the power to conjure in the mind of another exactly what that person was thinking. Until the end of the Middle Ages, language was so powerful that to know the name of another person was to have a hold over their very soul. Ceremonies and wars could be stopped with a word or two, and all of Europe followed the words of the Pope. Storytellers of old would enthrall communities by the fireside at night, weaving whole tales into the minds of those listening, like a gentle breeze across their face, to bring joy to a mundane life.

Notice how the writer offers a broad chronicle of language's historical evolvement to contextualize his discussion of profanity.

Today, language has lost its luster. Where once a sentence or two could rile a nation, today that same passage would not even gain the attention of the random passerby. The traditions of old have become forgotten as the world modernized and cultures have come together. Individual words, even whole stories, have lost their power to move people. Only one group of words can still elicit the same strength as those of old. The actual words change for every language, yet all fall into the same group. They are the words of pure emotion: swear words.

The writer offers a thesis statement.

Many an academic would laugh at the proposition that swear words hold any power. It has long been the tradition of teachers and the academic community as a whole to shun such words as vulgar terms that debase language. The oft-told expression "Swearing is just the sign of an ignorant mind" is fairly common among teachers and intellectuals when talking to children or less educated peers. Many refrain from using them in certain formal settings for fear of seeming ignorant or rude. This mindset seems to be a warped mirror of the truth. Those who hear swear words tend to look at the reactions, the emotional state of those using the words and rationalize the outbursts as weakness. However, when has emotion been weakness? Have countless leaders and heroes not been idolized for such things? This argument is just an excuse to not look at the truth. When some people are at an emotional peak, they swear. Why they swear is not always easily discerned, but this argument refuses to answer that.

The writer transitions to offer support for his thesis.

In truth, cussing is an extension of pain because these groups of words are the closest any language has to pure emotion in written form. The definition of such words rarely matter as much as the feeling they give off, the cathartic release of pent up stimulus and an end to aggression (Joelving). We swear to do one of two things: either in the throes of pain or emotion, for our own benefit, or when lobbing them like loaded bombs to another person to rile them up or cause them harm. There is no wonder why curse words are viewed with such disdain; they are nothing but the manifestation of all the emotion put behind them (Burton). They are a forced unmasking of truly negative emotions, the very base nature of our race.

The writer's use of outside sources lends authority that swear words are not necessarily hallmarks of the uneducated.

Perhaps that is the truth behind the argument of curse words being only part of an ignorant mind. These words ally themselves with the very basic part of our brains: the part of our mind that we suppress in good society, the one that speaks to our true nature, the nature of what is left of our more bestial ancestors (Jay & Janschewitz). We fear this part of ourselves, what we cannot control. Society has always tried to reign in this beast, and yet this area of the lexicon of any language is part of that. Such words used in hushed tones between giggling children, or in the throes of passion, when the humors override our intellect, and we can only think of one thing to say to help ease our frazzled nerves.

The transition leads into a direct challenge of the opposition's point of view.

This offers academic research that supports the writer's thesis.

But those who wish to erase such utterances fail to grasp their true importance. Science has finally begun to delve into the why of swearing. They have found that using curse words has a real, physical benefit, especially with pain. When in pain, a person who cusses activates the human "Fight or Flight" response, which in turn releases adrenaline throughout the body (Burton). A study at the University of England found that subjects told to place their hands in ice water for as long as they could were able to keep the limbs in the water twice as long when allowed to swear (Burton). When someone stubs his or her toe or gets a paper cut in real life, one of the first reactions, if he or she does not force self-censorship, is to curse.

It is a natural reaction to such stimulus. The benefits extend far beyond just pain though. Swearing can increase circulation, elevate endorphin levels, and even bring about a sense of calm in a person (Burton). From the health benefits alone, swearing can be seen as a good thing.

Cursing is not limited to just being beneficial physically; there is a real social aspect that is only now being realized. Most English speakers learn to curse at around the age of 2 (Jay & Janschewitz). They also learn the implications society has given them. Swearing is a socialization tool for many young adults and children, as it shows a sense of comfort around members within a group to curse (Burton). It can also symbolize trust and honesty toward other people. These taboo words that society shuns are being spoken within this group. They must be close, we think, to not be offended by them. A person using a curse word is rarely joking or idly throwing it out there. We as a society view these words as serious, so to use them is to either harm a person, give oneself relief, or show comfort around one another.

There exists in many societies the idea of decency. In fact, many civilized nations have what are called anti-decency laws in place to prevent the corruption of youth. The corruption of youth has long been a rallying cry for censorship, the idea that a word or action is the cause of strife among the generational gap. Today we have censorship of curse words rampant in the media, as it is thought that the impressionable youth will easily absorb such material and use it as a gateway down a dark path. The truth is words alone rarely have an impact anymore (Jay & Janschewitz). It is the underlying emotions that children pick up on. But beyond that, most children enter school knowing from 30-40 vulgarities, and their lexicon of "filth" only grows as they do. Children begin learning to swear by about age 2, far before most have the opportunity to view any programs or movies that would utilize curse words. Thus, it seems that swearing is more than part of the environment (Jay & Janschewitz). It is innate, hidden deep within the brain in areas that are still primal (Joelving).

Society has always had a stigma when it came to the taboo lexicon. Whether for the idea of the ignorant, to the idea of corruption in some way, there has been a never-ending battle to rid the language of these monstrosities. Yet, despite their attempts, the language finds new words to use, new ways of expressing this innate nature. It has been so prevalent that science is now forced to look into the matter and is finding surprising results. Swearing is a part of humanity, and it goes beyond any kind of intellectual debate. There are words of power left, who with an utterance casts a spell on whomever they are directed. They are lost until we need them, and no matter what we do, they will

Here the author goes so far as to offer documented proof of health benefits of swearing, thus furthering credibility for his position.

Here the writer offers research suggesting that swearing promotes socialization in peer groups.

The author uses his ideas to blend with researchers who question conventional negative concepts regarding profanity.

Notice how this statement supports the author's title.

always be there. Perhaps one day humanity will learn to celebrate its baser nature, instead of condemning it. Until that day comes, however, we are left with these mighty pillars of the id, constant reminders of who we truly are.

Works Cited

Burton, Neel. "Hell Yes: The 7 Best Reasons for Swearing." *Psychology Today* "Hide and Seek" Blog Post-Published. 19 May 2012. Web. 20 Oct 2015.

Jay, Timothy, and Kristin Janschewitz. "The Science of Swearing." *Association for Psychological Science* RSS. May-June 2012. Web. 17 Oct. 2015.

Joelving, Frederick. "Why the #$%! Do We Swear? For Pain Relief." *Scientific American Global* RSS. 12 July 2009. Web. 18 Oct. 2015.

DISCUSSION QUESTIONS

1. What claim does the writer make about swear words? Do you agree or disagree with his stance?

2. What do you find to be the author's most compelling evidence to support his views on profanity?

3. Do you think any benefit would have been added to the writer's essay had he included examples of swear words? Why or why not?

In his paper, the author examines whether cursing, though frowned upon in academics, actually has physical and mental benefits. Though he conveys his opinion that curse words are no big deal, he does so without uttering a single profanity. Such results come from careful attention to the subject, purpose, and audience.

ROGERIAN ARGUMENT: CREATIVE PROBLEM SOLVING

Creating an academic argument, though designed to respect the diversity of viewpoints within an audience, can still incite controversial and emotional responses. When dealing with a highly charged issue, what is the best way to approach the subject in a matter that eases into the dissenting views and honors the opposing sides?

American psychotherapist and communication theorist Carl R. Rogers (1902–1987) is renowned for his promotion of empathetic listening and consensus-building dialogue. According to Rogers, constructive dialogue is more likely to occur if both parties demonstrate understanding of opposing arguments and, moreover, approach an issue as an opportunity to solve a mutual problem.

Rogerian argument strategy approaches a controversial issue through a dialogue that has a nonconfrontational structure and a consensus-building tone. The idea behind this strategy is that traditional Western argument structure, which begins with an assertive stance, often fosters resistance on the part of the "target" audience. To soften this resistance, the writer seeks out "common ground" among readers by adopting an outwardly neutral and objective stance toward the issue. In place of the traditional argument structure—claim, support, counterargument, reaffirmation of claim—Rogerian argument substitutes this structure: question, alternatives, consideration of alternatives, and advocacy of a compromise position.

As the writer of Rogerian argument, your purpose is to build bridges of communication among opposing sides in order to bring the sides together in support of a middle ground or compromise position. To develop a reasonable compromise position, you will apply the higher-order critical thinking skills of synthesis and creative problem solving.

Rogerian Argument Organizational Plan

Here is a basic structure for organizing a Rogerian argument essay. Of course, you may choose to adapt these guidelines to suit your material and individual writing style. Two principles, however, hold for all Rogerian arguments: (1) You should maintain a mask of neutrality/*persona* of fair-mindedness, and (2) you should conclude by advocating a compromise/middle-ground position.

Basic Structure of a Rogerian Argument Essay

Introduction

- Lead-in sentences ("hook" strategies: a scenario or an example, a related current event in the news, a startling statistic, a provocative question or statement)
- Synopsis of the discussion surrounding the issue/rhetorical context
- Issue stated as an issue question to set a tone of inquiry and investigation

Body

- Two or three paragraphs to examine key points that support one prominent position on the issue

---

- Two or three paragraphs to examine key points that support alternative positions (The writer's use of transitional "signal sentences"—*On the other hand, critics argue ...*; or *Despite these compelling arguments for ..., many persons strongly oppose*—helps prepare readers for the writer's switch from examining one position to examining an opposing position.)

Conclusion

- Paragraph that presents a balanced and concise summation of the most compelling points representing opposing sides of the argument
- Paragraph(s) that present(s) and advocate(s) the writer's middle-ground position, drawing on elements from the diverse positions examined earlier

The following student essay, "A Bull's Life" by Christian Garcia, presents a Rogerian argument.

Christian Garcia
Professor James
ENC 1102
10 April 2015

A Bull's Life

Note the writer's opinion is not known from his introduction. He simply raises the issues surrounding bullfighting.

Where does one draw the line in determining acts of animal cruelty? Is it punishing a domestic animal for not following a person's command? Is it training an animal to perform stunts to please the crowd in a circus? Or is animal cruelty the slow and painful killing of an animal simply to entertain the public?

The author acknowledges some cultures value bullfighting without attacking them as inhumane.

Approximately 1,100 bulls are killed by Matadors during bullfights in Southern France, which is a fraction of the number killed in Spain every year (Mulholland). Bullfighting has been around for centuries, and in Spain and most Latin American countries, it is considered a tradition. Bullfighting originated in Spain, where the best Matadors still come from today. Is bullfighting a cruel process of torture for the animal? Is it a respectful tradition, a way of living that should never cease or be forgotten?

Despite its value as a tradition, bullfighting clearly is not valued by all persons. However, if one thinks of a bullfight as a cruelty to the bull, then one also should think about the bull's first four to five years. Before a bull is sent to a bullfight, he is basically treated like a champion, sometimes even better than an average person. Raised on a well-tended farm, he receives top quality food and care. The bull runs freely in an open field, unlike captured exotic animals such as panthers, which are trapped in a cage whether they are located in a zoo or a circus. In the poem "The Panther," Rainer Maria Rilke states, "His vision, from the constantly passing bars,/has grown so weary that it cannot hold/anything else. It seems to him there are/a thousand bars; and behind the bars, no world" (269). In a zoo, some may acknowledge the cruelty to the panther, as it is locked in its cage, for the simple purpose of entertaining the public. As the poem implies, the panther might as well be dead.

Certainly, many persons may view bullfighting as cruelty to the bull because of the way this event is often publicized to feature the gore and blood. They, therefore, associate bullfights exclusively with the violence of the kill without understanding the art of bullfighting. In fact, it is hard to imagine a bullfight without the kill (Nash); it is like playing basketball without a basket. Meanwhile, animals die each day for the purpose of developing or testing new cosmetics or medicines for our personal benefit. This type of animal cruelty is not publicized; it is unlikely to see a company advertising its product by stating that thanks to testing on an animal we are healthier (or more beautiful) today. Millions of Americans readily swallow down a Nyquil when a cold is coming on, but few, if any, stop to wonder how many animals may have been sacrificed before this cold medicine hit the market.

If understood correctly, bull fighting is an art, similar to ballet. The moments of danger are beautiful, rather than simply thrilling, because the Matador controls them (Hannan, "Moments"). However, one may never understand this type of art until one experiences it by being in the stadium watching the bullfight. Words cannot describe the feeling and rush from watching how the Matador dodges and cheats death, time after time. No matter what anyone says, it takes a lot of guts for a man to stand alone in the middle of the stadium waiting for a 1,100-pound bull to charge. Also, there is an allotted time for a bullfight; the Matador has approximately 16 minutes to perform a series of passes with his cape and deliver the deathblow (Schwartz). After the event is completed, the bull is taken out of the stadium, butchered, and sold as meat. The bull is not wasted because it is following its "natural" course, the course that any other bull would go through of being sold as meat.

Nevertheless, opponents argue that bullfights are cruel to the bull because he goes through a slow and painful death. In a bullfighting event, there are three Matadors; each will kill two bulls (Hannan, "Bulls"). Before

The writer raises points that favor bullfighting as a sport.

The author incorporates literature, in this case a poem, to contrast a fighter bull's life with that of a caged zoo animal.

The writer acknowledges those opposed to bull fighting.

The author shifts politely to validate the opinions of pro-bull fighters.

The writer challenges the audience's views by an experience to which many people can relate.

More non-judgmental understanding of pro-bullfighting stance.

Research on the bullfighting process.

*The writer
smoothly
transitions to
offer valida-
tion to those
opposed to
bullfighting.*

the Matador faces the bull, the bull is weakened, and in most cases, one can find blood in the bull's mouth and on his back due to darts. The bull is weakened by men called banderillas, whose sole purpose is to approach the bull and pierce him with two, bright-colored darts on his back. The bull essentially has no chance of survival, once he meets the Matador at the end of the match. Furthermore, a Matador is supposed to kill a bull with one blow of the sword. Unfortunately, this is not always the case; there are incidents where the Matador missed or stabbed the wrong section of the bull. This serves to prolong his slow and painful death—all to entertain the public.

Even though the bull chosen for this event has been given the best care throughout his life, it does not justify the way he is killed. The bull does not have an option as to how to live or lose his life. In the story "May's Lion" by Ursula Le Guin, a mountain lion wanders into May's yard and lies down under a fig tree: "It just laid there looking around. It wasn't well" (230). Not knowing what to do, May called the sheriff, who sent out two carloads of county police. "I guess there was nothing else they knew how to do, so they shot it," May said (231). Likewise, matadors think that the only option for the bull is for it to die after the bullfight. Many people therefore claim that bullfighting is a barbaric and unethical tradition that should be abolished. The only purpose bullfighting serves is to show the Matador's manliness to the world and to feed people's appetite for blood and gore.

*The author
offers polite
understand-
ing of both
sides of the
issue.*

Although it is difficult for one to watch a bull being stabbed six times and eventually a sword penetrating his heart to end his life, it is equally hard to imagine a bullfight without the kill. Perhaps over time, this change could be effected, but it would take generations to bring about an end to this tradition. Meanwhile, many people depend on bullfights to make a living and consider it an honorable livelihood, one that is a strong family tradition and community bond. Given the contrasting perspectives, bullfighting as animal cruelty and bullfighting as an honorable tradition, an alternative to abolishing bullfights would be to reduce the numbers of bulls that are killed.

*The writer
transitions
into a
Rogerian
compromise.*

Specifically, the number of events should be limited to 500 bullfights per year. Also, as with many other sports, there should be a fine for the Matador if he does not kill the bull on his first attempt. This way will ensure that the Matador understands there is a lot at stake for his having the privilege to take the bull's life. The number of banderillas should be decreased to only four banderillas per bull, which would increase the bull's chance of survival. These terms will require the Matador to be strong and have the sufficient endurance to fight against a bull. If the bull is not killed by the Matador in his first opportunity, the match will end; the bull will be euthanized if he is badly hurt or be treated and earn his freedom if he has minor injuries. If the bull injures the Matador and the bull is in a decent condition, then that bull has earned his freedom, and he shall be allowed to live out his life on the farm where he was raised. Understanding these new regulations will help the Matador understand the value of the life of the bull and the privilege it is to take a bull's life. Furthermore, these regulations will increase the chances a bull has to win his freedom and minimize the animal cruelty in bullfighting.

The Rogerian paper ends with ways that both sides can find benefit.

Works Cited

Hannan, Daniel. "The Bulls Have It." *The Spectator Ltd*. 17 May 2003: 81. *InfoTrac OneFile*. 22 Mar. 2015.

– – –. "Moments of Truth." *The Spectator Ltd*. 19 July 2003: 44. *InfoTrac OneFile*. Web. 22 Mar. 2015.

Le Guin, Ursula. "May's Lion." *The Oxford Book of Women's Writing in the United States*. Ed. Linda Wagner-Martin and Cathy N. Davidson. New York: Oxford, 1995. 190-196. Print.

Mulholland, Rory. "Most French Disapprove, but Bullfighting Battles on in South." *Agence France*. 3 Aug. 2004. *NewsBank Online*. Web. 4 Apr. 2015.

Nash, Elizabeth. "A Bloody Fight to the Death." *The Independent*. 13 Dec. 2004. *NewsBank Online*. Web. 28 Feb. 2015.

Rilke, Rainer Maria. "The Panther." *Ahead of All Parting: The Selected Poetry and Prose of Rainer Maria Rilke*. New York: Random House, 1995. 31. Print.

Schwartz, Jeremy. "Super Bowl of Bullfighting." *American Statesman*. 6 Feb. 2005. *NewsBank Online*. Web. 28. Mar. 2015.

DISCUSSION QUESTIONS

1. Do you feel Garcia's essay is effective in promoting a fair exploration of bullfighting?

2. Did this essay change your opinion about bullfighting? If so, why? If not, did you find yourself considering viewpoints that countered with your own?

3. Was Garcia's compromise effective in allowing each side of the controversy to walk away with a "win"?

As you prepare to write your argument, approach your essay with the understanding that good academic writing requires practice and patience. Your favorite author, reporter, blogger, or instructor likely goes through a vigorous planning process and multiple drafts before formulating successful written pieces.

Because writing an argument is an investment of intellect, you are likely to produce your best work when you give yourself plenty of time to plan, write, and revise ahead of your deadline. Be sure to begin planning your work as soon as it is assigned by your instructor.

ACTIVITIES

FINDING IDEAS AND PLANNING AN ACADEMIC ARGUMENT

In order to gain an understanding of academic argument, create your own argument using the topic "knowledge and individual power." Think about how the amount of knowledge one holds relates to one's power. For this activity, rather than writing out the argument as an essay, follow the steps below to discover ideas, develop a claim, and outline the evidence you might use in support of that claim.

Exploration 1: Examine your own thinking on the subject of *knowledge and individual power*.
Try one of the following prewriting strategies:

- Write the words *knowledge and individual power* at the top of a page, and write nonstop for ten minutes or so just to see what ideas emerge.
- Write *knowledge and individual power*, and list all the ideas, concepts, and terms that are associated with the words. List, but do not edit; allow your creative mind to work.
- Write *knowledge and individual power* in the center of a page, circle the words, and cluster around the circle any ideas and concepts that come to mind.

Re-read your prewriting and write responses to the following questions:

- What **assumptions** or broad generalizations about *knowledge and individual power* are revealed in your prewriting?
- Can you identify specific, personal experiences that may have led you to make those generalizations?

Exploration 2: Explore ideas beyond your own.
Read three of the following selections and then respond to the questions that follow:

Randall Kenan, "The Foundations of the Earth" (Chapter 6)
Emily Dickinson, "Much Madness is divinest Sense" (Chapter 6)
Alma Luz Villanueva, "Crazy Courage" (Chapter 6)
Raymond Carver, "Cathedral" (Chapter 9)
Nathaniel Hawthorne, "The Birth-Mark" (Chapter 9)
Langston Hughes, "Theme for English 'B'" (Chapter 9)

a. What is an implied **claim** on the subject of *knowledge and individual power*?
b. What **evidence** is offered in support of that claim?
c. What **rhetorical appeals** (*ethos, logos, pathos*) move the reader toward acceptance of the claim?
d. Upon reflection, how might you defend, refute, and/or qualify each claim?

Exploration 3: Create a plan for an argument.

- *Develop your claim:* Based on Explorations 1 and 2, what do you think is true of the relationship between an individual's knowledge and his or her power? Write several sentences in response to the question and then synthesize the ideas to arrive at a single statement of a claim that states your perspective.
- *List evidence to support your claim:* Select specific examples from three (or more) literature pieces you have examined as well as from your own experience and observations. Write out your claim list and the examples (by title and author) you might use as evidence.
- *Small-group activity:* Share your argument plan—claim and list of examples—with several students. Discuss the similarities and differences among your plans.

In an academic community, you have the opportunity to advance knowledge and shape your own and others' thinking about ideas and issues. You, therefore, have the responsibility to move beyond discussing issues to expressing your informed opinion in an **academic argument**. The writing process for academic argument is neither simple nor fast; it requires a steadfast commitment to hard work—to reading, thinking, writing; to rereading, rethinking, rewriting.

In developing an academic argument, we suggest following these fundamental steps:

1. *Explore* multiple perspectives on a subject through reading, writing, and conversation in order to expand, deepen, and complicate your thinking.
2. *Analyze* and *evaluate* those perspectives in order to construct your own argument, centered on a clear claim that you can support with credibility and specificity.

3. *Design* an organizational plan, mapping out an argument strategy based on your specific goals with your audience.

4. *Draft* and *seek* feedback in order to "field-test" your argument with a live audience; by doing so, you will value your writing as "real" writing for "real" readers and, thus, will recharge your commitment to working further on it, asking new questions, and creating new knowledge.

5. *Rethink* and *revise, edit,* and *proofread* in order to present an argument that will compel your readers (an academic community) to respect your position and to rethink their own: *Good writing makes readers think.*

PART 2

ANTHOLOGY

CHAPTER 6

Individuality and Community

The goals of an individual sometimes conflict with the goals of the society in which he or she lives. People naturally want to live in an orderly environment and, as a result, generally choose to obey the rules of their society. For example, a person cannot choose to grow cabbages in a public park just because the park makes a convenient spot for a garden: Usurping public land for private enterprise is against the law. Similarly, although the temperature soars to 100 degrees on an August afternoon, a person cannot elect to walk the streets naked: Public nudity is usually prohibited by local law. And, of course, even beyond the authority of the law, society may enforce codes of behavior simply through the power of its approval or its disapproval.

In each selection in this chapter, we encounter the question of the individual's place in his or her society. However, finding our place as individuals in a complex society is always a struggle. Communities tend to base their values on the moral codes of the majority. In a democratic society such as ours, we are granted the privilege and obliged with the responsibility to articulate and defend our positions, our choices, to others. Thus, in creating an argument based on morals and values, we must define and clarify, explain and elaborate those principles that have guided our decisions. Literature often portrays an individual's struggle to justify a choice that conflicts with his or her community's standards. Before you begin reading the selections in this chapter, take a moment to consider the following questions.

PREWRITING AND DISCUSSION

1. What do we mean when we use the word *community*? Is a community merely a group of people joined by the fact that they live in the same small geographic area? Or are there other ways in which a group can be held together to form a community?

2. Consider both the positive and the negative effects of belonging to a community. What pressures are exerted on individuals by communities? Think about a community that you or a friend has experienced. How does this community describe itself, and is the description consistent with the way outsiders would describe it?

3. Write for a few minutes about what it means to be an individual in our contemporary society. What qualities signal one's individuality? List some people you consider to be strong, independent individuals. In small groups of four or five, discuss your ideas of individuality.

FICTION

Truman Capote

Jug of Silver (1945)

After school I used to work in the Valhalla drugstore. It was owned by my uncle, Mr. Ed Marshall. I call him Mr. Marshall because everybody, including his wife, called him Mr. Marshall. Nevertheless he was a nice man.

This drugstore was maybe old-fashioned, but it was large and dark and cool: during summer months there was no pleasanter place in town. At the left, as you entered, was a tobacco-magazine counter behind which, as a rule, sat Mr. Marshall: a squat, square-face, pink-fleshed man with looping, manly, white mustaches. Beyond this counter stood the beautiful soda fountain. It was very antique and made of fine, yellowed marble, smooth to the touch but without a trace of cheap glaze. Mr. Marshall bought it at an auction in New Orleans in 1910 and was plainly proud of it. When you sat on the high, delicate stools and looked across the fountain you could see yourself reflected softly, as though by candle-light, in a row of ancient, mahogany-framed mirrors. All general merchandise was displayed in glass-doored, curio-like cabinets that were locked with brass keys. There was always in the air the smell of syrup and nutmeg and other delicacies.

The Valhalla was the gathering place of Wachata County till a certain Rufus McPherson came to town and opened a second drugstore directly across the courthouse square. This old Rufus McPherson was a villain; that is, he took away my uncle's trade. He installed fancy equipment such as electric fans and colored lights; he provided curb service and made grilled-cheese sandwiches to order. Naturally, though some remained devoted to Mr. Marshall, most folks couldn't resist Rufus McPherson.

For a while, Mr. Marshall chose to ignore him: if you were to mention McPherson's name, he could sort of snort, finger his mustaches, and look the other way. But you could tell he was mad. And getting madder. Then one day toward the middle of October I strolled into the Valhalla to find him sitting at the fountain playing dominoes and drinking wine with Hamurabi.

5   Hamurabi was an Egyptian and some kind of dentist, though he didn't do much business, as the people hereabouts have usually strong teeth, due to an element in the water. He spent a great deal of his time loafing around the Valhalla and was my uncle's chief buddy. He was a handsome figure of a man, this

Hamurabi, being dark-skinned and nearly seven feet tall; the matrons of the town kept their daughters under lock and key and gave him the eye themselves. He had no foreign accent whatsoever, and it was always my opinion that he wasn't any more Egyptian than the man in the moon.

Anyway, there they were swigging red Italian wine from a gallon jug. It was a troubling sight, for Mr. Marshall was a renowned teetotaler. So naturally, I thought: Oh, golly, Rufus McPherson has finally got his goat. That was not the case, however.

"Here, son," said Mr. Marshall, "come have a glass of wine."

"Sure," said Hamurabi, "help us finish it up. It's store-bought, so we can't waste it."

Much later, when the jug was dry, Mr. Marshall picked it up and said, "Now we shall see!" And with that disappeared out into the afternoon.

"Where's he off to?" I asked.   10

"Ah," was all Hamurabi would say. He liked to devil me.

A half-hour passed before my uncle returned. He was stooped and grunting under the load he carried. He set the jug atop the fountain and stepped back, smiling and rubbing his hands together. "Well, what do you think?"

"Ah," purred Hamurabi.

"Gee…" I said.

It was the same wine jug, God knows, but there was a wonderful difference;   15
for now it was crammed to the brim with nickels and dimes that shone dully through the thick glass.

"Pretty, eh?" said my uncle. "Had it done over at the First National. Couldn't get in anything bigger-sized than a nickel. Still, there's losta money in there, let me tell you."

"But what's the point, Mr. Marshall?" I said. "I mean, what's the idea?"

Mr. Marshall's smile deepened to a grin. "This here's a jug of silver, you might say…"

"The pot at the end of the rainbow," interrupted Hamurabi.

"…and the idea, as you call it, is for folks to guess how much money is in   20
there. For instance, say you buy a quarter's worth of stuff—well, then you get to take a chance. The more you buy, the more chances you get. And I'll keep all guesses in a ledger till Christmas Eve, at which time whoever comes closest to the right amount will get the whole shebang."

Hamurabi nodded solemnly. "He's playing Santa Claus—a mighty crafty Santa Claus," he said. "I'm going home and write a book: *The Skillful Murder of Rufus McPherson*." To tell the truth, he sometimes did write stories and send them out to the magazines. They always came back.

It was surprising, really like a miracle, how Wachata County took to the jug. Why, the Valhalla hadn't done so much business since Station Master Tully, poor soul, went stark raving mad and claimed to have discovered oil back of the depot, causing the town to be overrun with wildcat prospectors. Even the poolhall bums who never spent a cent on anything not connected with whisky or women took to investing their spare cash in milk shakes. A few elderly ladies publicly disapproved of Mr. Marshall's enterprise as a kind of gambling, but they didn't start any trouble and some even found occasion to visit us and hazard a guess. The schoolkids were crazy about the whole thing, and I was very popular because they figured I knew the answer.

"I'll tell you why all this is," said Hamurabi, lighting one of the Egyptian cigarettes he bought by mail from a concern in New York City. "It's not for the reason you may imagine; not, in other words, avidity. No. It's the mystery that's enchanting. Now you look at those nickels and dimes and what do you think: ah, so much! No, no. You think: ah, *how* much? And that's a profound question, indeed. It can mean different things to different people. Understand?"

And oh, was Rufus McPherson wild! When you're in trade, you count on Christmas to make up a large share of your yearly profit, and he was hard pressed to find a customer. So he tried to imitate the jug; but being such a stingy man he filled his with pennies. He also wrote a letter to the editor of *The Banner*, our weekly paper, in which he said that Mr. Marshall ought to be "tarred and feathered and strung up for turning innocent little children into confirmed gamblers and sending them down the path to Hell!" You can imagine what kind of laughingstock he was. Nobody had anything for McPherson but scorn. And so by the middle of November he just stood on the sidewalk outside his store and gazed bitterly at the festivities across the square.

25   At about this time Appleseed and sister made their first appearance.

He was a stranger in town. At least no one could recall ever having seen him before. He said he lived on a farm a mile past Indian Branches; told us his mother weighed only seventy-four pounds and that he had an older brother who would play the fiddle at anybody's wedding for fifty cents. He claimed that Appleseed was the only name he had and that he was twelve years old. But his sister, Middy, said he was eight. His hair was straight and dark yellow. He had a tight, weather-tanned little face with anxious green eyes that had a very wise and knowing look. He was small and puny and high-strung; and he wore always the same outfit: a red sweater, blue denim britches and a pair of man-sized boots that went clop-clop with every step.

It was raining that first time he came into the Valhalla; his hair was plastered around his head like a cap and his boots were caked with red mud from the country roads. Middy trailed behind as he swaggered like a cowboy up to the fountain where I was wiping some glasses.

"I hear tell you folks got a bottle fulla money you fixin' to give 'way," he said, looking me square in the eye. "Seein' as you-all are givin' it away, we'd be obliged iffen you'd give it to us. Name's Appleseed, and this here's my sister Middy."

Middy was a sad, sad-looking kid. She was a good bit taller and older-looking than her brother: a regular bean pole. She had tow-colored hair that was chopped short, and a pale pitiful little face. She wore a faded cotton dress that came way up above her bony knees. There was something wrong with her teeth, and she tried to conceal this by keeping her lips primly pursed like an old lady.

"Sorry," I said, "but you'll have to talk with Mr. Marshall."   30

So sure enough he did. I could hear my uncle explaining what he would have to do to win the jug. Appleseed listened attentively, nodding now and then. Presently he came back and stood in front of the jug and, touching it lightly with his hand, said, "Ain't it a pretty thing, Middy?"

Middy said, "Is they gonna give it to us?"

"Naw. What you gotta do, you gotta guess how much money's inside there. And you gotta buy two bits' worth so's even to get a chance."

"Huh, we ain't got no two bits. Where you 'spec we gonna get us two bits?"

Appleseed frowned and rubbed his chin. "That'll be the easy part, just leave   35
it to me. The only worrisome thing is: I can't just take a chance and guess. ... I gotta *know*."

Well, a few days later they showed up again. Appleseed perched on a stool at the fountain and boldly asked for two glasses of water, one for him and one for Middy. It was on this occasion that he gave out the information about his family: "... then there's Papa Daddy, that's my mama's papa, who's a Cajun, an' on accounta that he don't speak English good. My brother, the one what plays the fiddle, he's been in jail three times.... It's on accounta him we had to pick up and leave Louisiana. He cut a fella bad in a razor fight over a woman ten years older'n him. She had yellow hair."

Middy, lingering in the background, said nervously, "You oughtn't to be tellin' our personal private fam'ly business thataway, Appleseed."

"Hush now, Middy," he said, and she hushed. "She's a good little gal," he added, turning to pat her head, "but you can't let her get away with much. You go look at the picture books, honey, and stop frettin' with your teeth. Appleseed here's got some figurin' to do."

This figuring meant staring hard at the jug, as if his eyes were trying to eat it up. With his chin cupped in his hand, he studied it for a long period, not batting his eyelids once. "A lady in Louisiana told me I could see things other folks couldn't see 'cause I was born with a caul on my head."

"It's a cinch you aren't going to see how much there is," I told him. "Why don't   40
you just let a number pop into your head, and maybe that'll be the right one."

"Uh, uh," he said, "too darn risky. Me, I can't take no sucha chance. Now, the way I got it figured, there ain't but one sure-fire thing and that's to count every nickel and dime."

"Count!"

"Count what?" asked Hamurabi, who had just moseyed inside and was settling himself at the fountain.

"This kid says he's going to count how much is in the jug," I explained.

Hamurabi looked at Appleseed with interest. "How do you plan to do   45
that, son?"

"Oh, by countin'," said Appleseed matter-of-factly.

Hamurabi laughed. "You better have X-ray eyes, son, that's all I can say."

"Oh, no. All you gotta do is be born with a caul on your head. A lady in Louisiana told me so. She was a witch; she loved me and when my ma wouldn't give me to her she put a hex on her and now my ma don't weigh but seventy-four pounds."

"Ve-ry in-ter-esting," was Hamurabi's comment as he gave Appleseed a queer glance.

50 Middy sauntered up, clutching a copy of *Screen Secrets*. She pointed out a certain photo to Appleseed and said: "Ain't she the nicest-lookin' lady? Now you see, Appleseed, you see how pretty her teeth are? Not a one outa joint."

"Well, don't you fret none," he said.

After they left, Hamurabi ordered a bottle of orange Nehi and drank it slowly, while smoking a cigarette. "Do you think maybe that kid's okay upstairs?" he asked presently in puzzled voice.

Small towns are best for spending Christmas, I think. They catch the mood quicker and change and come alive under its spell. By the first week in December house doors were decorated with wreaths, and store windows were flashy with red paper bells and snowflakes of glittering isinglass. The kids hiked out into the woods and came back dragging spicy evergreen trees. Already the women were busy baking fruit cakes, unsealing jars of mincemeat and opening bottles of blackberry and scuppernong wine. In the courthouse square a huge tree was trimmed with silver tinsel and colored electric bulbs that were lighted up at sunset. Late of an afternoon you could hear the choir in the Presbyterian church practicing carols for their annual pageant. All over town the japonicas were in full bloom.

The only person who appeared not the least touched by this heartwarming atmosphere was Appleseed. He went about his declared business of counting the jug-money with great, persistent care. Every day now he came to the Valhalla and concentrated on the jug, scowling and mumbling to himself. At first we were all fascinated, but after a while it got tiresome and nobody paid him any mind whatsoever. He never bought anything, apparently having never been able to raise the two bits. Some times he'd talk to Hamurabi, who had taken a tender interest in him and occasionally stood treat to a jawbreaker or a penny's worth of licorice.

55 "Do you still think he's nuts?" I asked.

"I'm not so sure," said Hamurabi. "But I'll let you know. He doesn't eat enough. I'm going to take him over to the Rainbow Café and buy him a plate of barbecue."

"He'd appreciate it more if you'd give him a quarter."

"No. A dish of barbecue is what he needs. Besides, it would be better if he never was to make a guess. A high-strung kid like that, so unusual, I wouldn't want to be the one responsible if he lost. Say, it would be pitiful."

I'll admit that at the time, Appleseed struck me as being just funny. Mr. Marshall felt sorry for him, and the kids tried to tease him, but had to give it up when he refused to respond. There you could see him plain as day sitting at the fountain with his forehead puckered and his eyes fixed forever on that jug. Yet he was so withdrawn you sometimes had this awful creepy feeling that, well, maybe he didn't exist. And when you were pretty much convinced of this he'd wake up and say something like, "You know, I hope a 1913 buffalo nickel's in there. A fella was tellin' me he saw where a 1913 buffalo nickel's worth fifty dollars." Or, "Middy's gonna be a big lady in the picture shows. They make lotsa money, the ladies in the pictures shows do, and then we ain't gonna never eat another collard green as long as we live. Only Middy says she can't be in the picture shows 'less her teeth look good."

Middy didn't always tag along with her brother. On those occasions when   60
she didn't come, Appleseed wasn't himself; he acted shy and left soon.

Hamurabi kept his promise and stood treat to a dish of barbecue at the café. "Mr. Hamurabi's nice, all right," said Appleseed afterward, "but he's got peculiar notions: has a notion that if he lived in this place named Egypt he'd be a king or somethin'."

And Hamurabi said, "That kid has the most touching faith. It's a beautiful thing to see. But I'm beginning to despise the whole business." He gestured toward the jug. "Hope of this kind is a cruel thing to give anybody, and I'm damned sorry I was ever a party to it."

Around the Valhalla the most popular pastime was deciding what you would buy if you won the jug. Among those who participated were: Solomon Katy, Phoebe Jones, Carl Kuhnhardt, Puly Simmons, Addie Foxcroft, Marvin Finkle, Trudy Edwards and a colored man named Erskine Washington. And these were some of their answers: a trip to and a permanent wave in Birmingham, a second-hand piano, a Shetland pony, a gold bracelet, a set of *Rover Boys* books and a life insurance policy.

Once Mr. Marshall asked Appleseed what he would get. "It's a secret," was the reply, and no amount of prying could make him tell. We took it for granted that whatever it was, he wanted it real bad.

Honest winter, as a rule, doesn't settle on our part of the country till late   65
January, and then it's mild, lasting only a short time. But in the year of which I write we were blessed with a singular cold spell the week before Christmas. Some still talk of it, for it was so terrible: water pipes froze solid; many folks had to spend the days in bed snuggled under their quilts, having neglected to lay in enough kindling for the fireplace; the sky turned that strange dull gray that it does just before a storm, and the sun was pale as a waning moon. There was a sharp wind: the old dried-up leaves of last fall fell on the icy ground, and the evergreen tree in the courthouse square was twice stripped of its Christmas finery. When you breathed, your breath made smoky clouds. Down by the silk mill where the very poor people lived, the families huddled together in the dark at night and told tales to keep their minds off the cold. Out in the country the farmers covered their delicate plants with gunnysacks and prayed; some took advantage of the weather to slaughter their hogs and bring the fresh sausage to town. Mr. R.C. Judkins, our town drunk, outfitted himself in a red cheesecloth suit and played Santa Claus at the five 'n' dime. Mr. R.C. Judkins was the father of a big family, so everybody was happy to see him sober enough to earn a dollar. There were several church socials, at one of which Mr. Marshall came face to face with Rufus McPherson: bitter words were passed but not a blow was struck.

Now, as has been mentioned, Appleseed lived on a farm a mile below Indian Branches; this would be approximately three miles from town; a mighty long and lonesome walk. Still, despite the cold, he came every day to the Valhalla and stayed till closing time, which, as the days had grown short, was after nightfall. Once in a while he'd catch a ride part way home with the foreman from the silk mill, but not often. He looked tired, and there were worry lines about his mouth. He was always cold and shivered a lot. I don't think he wore any warm drawers underneath his red sweater and blue britches.

It was three days before Christmas when out of the clear sky, he announced: "Well, I'm finished. I mean I know how much is in the bottle." He claimed this with such grave, solemn sureness it was hard to doubt him.

"Why, say now, son, hold on," said Hamurabi, who was present. "You can't know anything of the sort. It's wrong to think so: You're just heading to get yourself hurt."

"You don't need to preach to me, Mr. Hamurabi. I know what I'm up to. A lady in Louisiana, she told me…"

70 "Yes yes yes—but you got to forget that. If it were me, I'd go home and stay put and forget about this goddamned jug."

"My brother's gonna play the fiddle at a wedding over in Cherokee City tonight and he's gonna give me the two bits," said Appleseed stubbornly. "Tomorrow I'll take my chance."

So the next day I felt kind of excited when Appleseed and Middy arrived. Sure enough, he had his quarter: it was tied for safekeeping in the corner of a red bandanna.

The two of them wandered hand in hand among the showcases, holding a whispery consultation as to what to purchase. They finally decided on a thimble-sized bottle of gardenia cologne which Middy promptly opened and partly emptied on her hair. "It smells like…Oh, darlin' Mary, I ain't never smelled nothin' as sweet. Here, Appleseed, honey, let me douse some on your hair." But he wouldn't let her.

Mr. Marshall got out the ledger in which he kept his records, while Appleseed strolled over to the fountain and cupped the jug between his hands, stroking it gently. His eyes were bright and his cheeks flushed from excitement. Several persons who were in the drugstore at that moment crowded close. Middy stood in the background quietly scratching her leg and smelling the cologne. Hamurabi wasn't there.

75 Mr. Marshall licked the point of his pencil and smiled. "OK, son, what do you say?"

Appleseed took a deep breath. "Seventy-seven dollars and thirty-five cents," he blurted.

In picking such an uneven sum he showed originality, for the run-of-the-mill guess was a plain round figure. Mr. Marshall repeated the amount solemnly as he copied it down.

"When'll I know if I won?"

"Christmas Eve," someone said.

"That's tomorrow, huh?"

"Why, so it is," said Mr. Marshall, not surprised. "Come at four o'clock."

During the night the thermometer dropped even lower, and toward dawn there was one of those swift, summerlike rainstorms, so that the following day was bright and frozen. The town was like a picture postcard of a Northern scene, what with icicles sparkling whitely on the trees and frost flowers coating all windowpanes. Mr. R.C. Judkins rose early and, for no clear reason, tramped the streets ringing a supper bell, stopping now and then to take a swig of whisky from a pint which he kept in his hip pocket. As the day was windless, smoke climbed lazily from various chimneys straightway to the still, frozen sky. By midmorning the Presbyterian choir was in full swing; and the town kids (wearing horror masks, as if Halloween) were chasing one another round and round the square, kicking up an awful fuss.

Hamurabi dropped by at noon to help us fix up the Valhalla. He brought along a fat sack of Satsumas, and together we ate every last one, tossing the hulls into a newly installed potbellied stove (a present from Mr. Marshall to himself) which stood in the middle of the room. Then my uncle took the jug off the fountain, polished and placed it on a prominently situated table. He was no help after that whatsoever, for he squatted in a chair and spent his time tying and retying a tacky green ribbon around the jug. So Hamurabi and I had the rest to do alone: we swept the floor and washed the mirrors and dusted the cabinets and strung streamers of red and green crepe paper from wall to wall. When we were finished it looked very fine and elegant.

But Hamurabi gazed sadly at our work, and said: "Well, I think I better be getting along now."

"Aren't you going to stay?" asked Mr. Marshall, shocked.

"No, oh, no," said Hamurabi, shaking his head slowly. "I don't want to see that kid's face. This is Christmas and I mean to have a rip-roaring time. And I couldn't, not with something like that on my conscience. Hell, I wouldn't sleep."

"Suit yourself," said Mr. Marshall. And he shrugged, but you could see he was really hurt. "Life's like that—and besides, who knows, he might win."

Hamurabi sighed gloomily. "What's his guess?"

"Seventy-seven dollars and thirty-five cents," I said.

"Now I ask you, isn't that fantastic?" said Hamurabi. He slumped in a chair next to Mr. Marshall and crossed his legs and lit a cigarette. "If you got any Baby Ruths I think I'd like one; my mouth tastes sour."

As the afternoon wore on, the three of us sat around the table feeling terribly blue. No one said hardly a word and, as the kids had deserted the square, the only sound was the clock tolling the hour on the courthouse steeple. The Valhalla was closed to business, but people kept passing by and peeking in the window. At three o'clock Mr. Marshall told me to unlock the door.

Within twenty minutes, the place was jam full; everyone was wearing his Sunday best, and the air smelled sweet, for most of the little silk-mill girls had scented themselves with vanilla flavoring. They scrunched up against the walls, perched on the fountain, squeezed in wherever they could; soon the crowd had spread to the sidewalk and stretched into the road. The square was lined with team-drawn wagons and Model T Fords that had carted farmers and their families into town. There was much laughter and shouting and joking—several outraged ladies complained of the cursing and the rough, shoving ways of the younger men, but nobody left. At the side entrance a group of colored folks had formed and were having the most fun of all. Everybody was making the best of a good thing. It's usually so quiet around here: nothing much ever happens. It's safe to say that nearly all of Wachata County was present but invalids and Rufus McPherson. I looked around for Appleseed but didn't see him anywhere.

Mr. Marshall harrumphed, and clapped for attention. When things quieted down and the atmosphere was properly tense, he raised his voice like an auctioneer and called: "Now listen, everybody, in this here envelope you see in my hand"—he held a manila envelope above his head—"well, in it's the *answer*— which nobody but God and the First National Bank knows up to now, ha, ha. And in this book"—he held up the ledger with his free hand—"I've got written down what you folks guessed. Are there any questions?" All was silence. "Fine. Now, if we could have a volunteer…"

Not a living soul budged an inch: it was as if an awful shyness had overcome the crowd, and even those who were ordinarily natural-born show-offs shuffled their feet, ashamed. Then a voice, Appleseed's, hollered, "Lemme by…Outa the way, please, ma'am." Trotting along behind as he pushed forward were Middy and a lanky, sleepy-eyed fellow who was evidently the fiddling brother. Appleseed was dressed the same as usual, but his face was scrubbed rosy clean, his boots polished and his hair slicked back skintight with Stacomb. "Did we get here in time?" he panted.

95 But Mr. Marshall said, "So you want to be our volunteer?"

Appleseed looked bewildered, then nodded vigorously.

"Does anybody have an objection to this young man?"

Still there was dead quiet. Mr. Marshall handed the envelope to Appleseed who accepted it calmly. He chewed his under lip while studying it a moment before ripping the flap.

In all that congregation there was no sound except an occasional cough and the soft tinkling of Mr. R.C. Judkins' supper bell. Hamurabi was leaning against the fountain, staring up at the ceiling; Middy was gazing blankly over her brother's shoulder, and when he started to tear open the envelope she let out a pained little gasp.

100 Appleseed withdrew a slip of pink paper and, holding it as though it was very fragile, muttered to himself whatever was written there. Suddenly his face paled and tears glistened in his eyes.

"Hey, speak up, boy," someone hollered.

Hamurabi stepped forward and all but snatched the slip away. He cleared his throat and commenced to read when his expression changed most comically. "Well, Mother o' God …" he said.

"Louder! Louder!" an angry chorus demanded.

"Buncha crooks!" yelled Mr. R.C. Judkins, who had a snootful by that time. "I smell a rat and he smells to high heavens!" Whereupon a cyclone of catcalls and whistling rent the air.

Appleseed's brother whirled around and shook his fist. "Shuddup, shuddup 105 'fore I bust every one a your...heads together so's you got knots the size a muskmelons, hear me?"

"Citizens," cried Mayor Mawes, "citizens—I say, this is Christmas...I say..."

And Mr. Marshall hopped up on a chair and clapped and stamped till a minimum of order was restored. It might as well be noted here that we later found out Rufus McPherson had paid Mr. R.C. Judkins to start the rumpus. Anyway, when the outbreak was quelled, who should be in possession of the slip but me...don't ask how.

Without thinking, I shouted, "Seventy-seven dollars and thirty-five cents." Naturally, due to the excitement, I didn't at first catch the meaning; it was just a number. Then Appleseed's brother let forth with his whooping yell, and so I understood. The name of the winner spread quickly, and the awed, murmuring whispers were like a rainstorm.

Oh, Appleseed himself was a sorry sight. He was crying as though he was mortally wounded, but when Hamurabi lifted him onto his shoulders so the crowd could get a gander, he dried his eyes with the cuffs of his sweater and began grinning. Mr. R.C. Judkins yelled, "Gyp! Lousy gyp!" but was drowned out by a deafening round of applause.

Middy grabbed my arm. "My teeth," she squealed. "Now I'm gonna get my 110 teeth."

"Teeth?" said I, kind of dazed.

"The false kind," says she. "That's what we're gonna get us with the money—a lovely set of white false teeth."

But at that moment my sole interest was in how Appleseed had known. "Hey, tell me," I said desperately, "tell me how in God's name did he know there was just exactly seventy-seven dollars and thirty-five cents?"

Middy gave me this *look*. "Why, I thought he told you," she said, real serious. "He counted."

"Yes, but how—how?"   115

"Gee, don't you even know how to count?"

"But is that all he did?"

"Well," she said, following a thoughtful pause, "he did do a little praying, too." She started to dart off, then turned back and called, "Besides, he was born with a caul on his head."

And that's the nearest anybody ever came to solving the mystery. Thereafter, if you were to ask Appleseed "How come?" he would smile strangely and change the subject. Many years later he and his family moved to somewhere in Florida and were never heard from again.

But in our town his legend flourishes still; and, till his death a year ago last 120
April, Mr. Marshall was invited each Christmas Day to tell the story of Appleseed
to the Baptist Bible class. Hamurabi once typed up an account and mailed it
around to various magazines. It was never printed. One editor wrote back and
said "If the little girl really turned out to be a movie star, then there might be
something to your story." But that's not what happened, so why should you lie?

CRITICAL THINKING QUESTIONS

1. In what ways was Appleseed judged by the folks of Wachata County? What
   assumptions do you believe people made about Appleseed based upon his
   appearance, speech, and beliefs?

2. The story takes place at Christmas, a time each year when humanity is supposedly at its best. However, what do you make of the other customers'
   reactions to Appleseed's winning guess? Why would they not be happy for
   Appleseed and his family to win the jackpot? Does this speak to human
   nature or challenge your views on humanity and the holiday spirit? Explain
   your answer.

3. The fantastic ending of this story is nothing short of a legend in Wachata
   County. However, when Hamurabi sends out a written manuscript to various publications, the story is rejected for print. Capote writes, "One editor
   wrote back and said 'If the little girl really turned out to be a movie star, then
   there might be something to your story.'" Do you believe this response to be
   indicative of modern media? What does the rejection of the publication of
   this fantastic tale say about the value systems of our society?

WRITING TOPIC

The rivalry between Mr. Marshall's Valhalla drug store and Mr. Murphy's
more flashy and modern store epitomizes a consumer shift in recent years.
Modern and less expensive chain stores draw the majority of consumers versus the more personal, yet slightly more expensive, family-owned
operations. In fact, smaller business have dwindled as mega-stores replace
their popularity by offering customers savings. Explore some numbers for
yourself. Find research regarding the economic impact facing smaller businesses going against the Goliath mega-merchandise chains. You might even
research the history of a smaller town near where you grew up that has dwindled economically over the years. In what ways do local businesses reflect
communities in ways that chains do not? What is the motivation for customers to support smaller businesses if prices are cheaper at large retailers?

Louise Erdrich

The Red Convertible (1984)

Lyman Lamartine

I was the first one to drive a convertible on my reservation. And of course it was red, a red Olds. I owned that car along with my brother Henry Junior. We owned it together until his boots filled with water on a windy night and he bought out my share. Now Henry owns the whole car, and his youngest brother Lyman (that's myself), Lyman walks everywhere he goes.

How did I earn enough money to buy my share in the first place? My own talent was I could always make money. I had a touch for it, unusual in a Chippewa. From the first I was different that way, and everyone recognized it. I was the only kid they let in the American Legion Hall to shine shoes, for example, and one Christmas I sold spiritual bouquets for the mission door to door. The nuns let me keep a percentage. Once I started, it seemed the more money I made the easier the money came. Everyone encouraged it. When I was fifteen I got a job washing dishes at the Joliet Cafe, and that was where my first big break happened.

It wasn't long before I was promoted to busing tables, and then the short-order cook quit and I was hired to take her place. No sooner than you know it I was managing the Joliet. The rest is history. I went on managing. I soon became part owner, and of course there was no stopping me then. It wasn't long before the whole thing was mine.

After I'd owned the Joliet for one year, it blew over in the worst tornado ever seen around here. The whole operation was smashed to bits. A total loss. The fryalator was up in a tree, the grill torn in half like it was paper. I was only sixteen. I had it all in my mother's name, and I lost it quick, but before I lost it I had every one of my relatives, and their relatives, to dinner, and I also bought that red Olds I mentioned, along with Henry.

The first time we saw it! I'll tell you when we first saw it. We had gotten 5
a ride to Winnipeg, and both of us had money. Don't ask me why, because we never mentioned a car or anything, we just had all our money. Mine was cash, a big bankroll from the Joliet's insurance. Henry had two checks—a week's extra pay for being laid off, and his regular check from the Jewel Bearing Plant.

We were walking down Portage anyway, seeing the sights, when we saw it. There it was, parked, large as life. Really as *if* it was alive. I thought of the word *repose*, because the car wasn't simply stopped, parked, or whatever. That car reposed, calm and gleaming, a for sale sign in its left front window. Then, before we had thought it over at all, the car belonged to us and our pockets were empty. We had just enough money for gas back home.

We went places in that car, me and Henry. We took off driving all one whole summer. We started off toward the Little Knife River and Mandaree in Fort

Berthold and then we found ourselves down in Wakpala somehow, and then suddenly we were over in Montana on the Rocky Boy, and yet the summer was not even half over. Some people hang on to details when they travel, but we didn't let them bother us and just lived our everyday lives here to there.

I do remember this place with willows. I remember I laid under those trees and it was comfortable. So comfortable. The branches bent down all around me like a tent or a stable. And quiet, it was quiet, even though there was a powwow close enough so I could see it going on. The air was not too still, not too windy either. When the dust rises up and hangs in the air around dancers like that, I feel good. Henry was asleep with his arms thrown wide. Later on, he woke up and we started driving again. We were somewhere in Montana, or maybe on the Blood Reserve—it could have been anywhere. Anyway it was where we met the girl.

All her hair was in buns around her ears, that's the first thing I noticed about her. She was posed alongside the road with her arm out, so we stopped. That girl was short, so short her lumber shirt looked comical on her, like a nightgown. She had jeans on and fancy moccasins and she carried a little suitcase.

10   "Hop on in," says Henry. So she climbs in between us.

"We'll take you home," I says. "Where do you live?"

"Chicken," she says.

"Where the hell's that?" I ask her.

"Alaska."

15   "Okay," says Henry, and we drive.

We got up there and never wanted to leave. The sun doesn't truly set there in summer, and the night is more a soft dusk. You might doze off, sometimes, but before you know it you're up again, like an animal in nature. You never feel like you have to sleep hard or put away the world. And things would grow up there. One day just dirt or moss, the next day flowers and long grass. The girl's name was Susy. Her family really took to us. They fed us and put us up. We had our own tent to live in by their house, and the kids would be in and out of there all day and night. They couldn't get over me and Henry being brothers, we looked so different. We told them we knew we had the same mother, anyway.

One night Susy came in to visit us. We sat around in the tent talking of this and that. The season was changing. It was getting darker by that time, and the cold was even getting just a little mean. I told her it was time for us to go. She stood up on a chair.

"You never seen my hair," Susy said.

That was true. She was standing on a chair, but still, when she unclipped her buns the hair reached all the way to the ground. Our eyes opened. You couldn't tell how much hair she had when it was rolled up so neatly. Then my brother Henry did something funny. He went up to the chair and said, "Jump on my shoulders." So she did that, and her hair reached down past his waist, and he started twirling, this way and that, so her hair was flung out from side to side.

"I always wondered what it was like to have long pretty hair," Henry says.   20
Well, we laughed. It was a funny sight, the way he did it. The next morning we
got up and took leave of those people.

On to greener pastures, as they say. It was down through Spokane and across
Idaho then Montana and very soon we were racing the weather right along under
the Canadian border through Columbus, Des Lacs, and then were in Bottineau
County and soon home. We'd made most of the trip, that summer, without putting up the car hood at all. We got home just in time.

I don't wonder that the army was so glad to get my brother that they turned
him into a Marine. He was built like a brick outhouse anyway. We liked to tease
him that they really wanted him for his Indian nose. He had a nose big and sharp
as a hatchet, like the nose on Red Tomahawk, the Indian who killed Sitting Bull,
whose profile is on signs all along the North Dakota highways. Henry went off to
training camp, came home once during Christmas, then the next thing you know
we got an overseas letter from him. It was 1970, and he said he was stationed up
in the northern hill country. Whereabouts I did not know. He wasn't such a hot
letter writer, and only got off two before the enemy caught him. I could never
keep it straight, which direction those good Vietnam soldiers were from.

I wrote him back several times, even though I didn't know if those letters
would get through. I kept him informed all about the car. Most of the time I had
it up on blocks in the yard or half taken apart, because that long trip did a hard
job on it under the hood.

I always had good luck with numbers, and never worried about the draft
myself. I never even had to think about what my number was. But Henry was
never lucky in the same way as me. It was at least three years before Henry came
home. By then I guess the whole war was solved in the government's mind, but
for him it would keep on going. In those years I'd put his car into almost perfect
shape. I always thought of it as his car while he was gone, even though when he
left he said, "Now it's yours," and threw me his key.

"Thanks for the extra key," I'd said. "I'll put it in your drawer just in case I   25
need it." He laughed.

When he came home, though, Henry was very different, and I'll say this:
the change was no good. You could hardly expect him to change for the better, I know. But he was quiet, so quiet, and never comfortable sitting still anywhere but always up and moving around. I thought back to times we'd sat still
for whole afternoons, never moving a muscle, just shifting our weight along the
ground, talking to whoever sat with us, watching things. He'd always had a joke,
then, too, and now you couldn't get him to laugh, or when he did it was more
the sound of a man choking, a sound that stopped up the throats of other people
around him. They got to leaving him alone most of the time, and I didn't blame
them. It was a fact: Henry was jumpy and mean.

I'd bought a color TV set for my mom and the rest of us while Henry was
away. Money still came very easy. I was sorry I'd ever bought it though, because
of Henry. I was also sorry I'd bought color, because with black-and-white the

pictures seem older and farther away. But what are you going to do? He sat in front of it, watching it, and that was the only time he was completely still. But it was the kind of stillness that you see in a rabbit when it freezes and before it will bolt. He was not easy. He sat in his chair gripping the armrests with all his might, as if the chair itself was moving at a high speed and if he let go at all he would rocket forward and maybe crash right through the set.

Once I was in the room watching TV with Henry and I heard his teeth click at something. I looked over, and he'd bitten through his lip. Blood was going down his chin. I tell you right then I wanted to smash that tube to pieces. I went over to it but Henry must have known what I was up to. He rushed from his chair and shoved me out of the way, against the wall. I told myself he didn't know what he was doing.

My mom came in, turned the set off real quiet, and told us she had made something for supper. So we went and sat down. There was still blood going down Henry's chin, but he didn't notice it and no one said anything, even though every time he took a bite of his bread his blood fell onto it until he was eating his own blood mixed in with the food.

30   While Henry was not around we talked about what was going to happen to him. There were no Indian doctors on the reservation, and my mom couldn't come around to trusting the old man, Moses Pillager, because he courted her long ago and was jealous of her husbands. He might take revenge through her son. We were afraid that if we brought Henry to a regular hospital they would keep him.

"They don't fix them in those places," Mom said; "they just give them drugs."

"We wouldn't get him there in the first place," I agreed, "so let's just forget about it."

Then I thought about the car.

Henry had not even looked at the car since he'd gotten home, though like I said, it was in tip-top condition and ready to drive. I thought the car might bring the old Henry back somehow. So I bided my time and waited for my chance to interest him in the vehicle.

35   One night Henry was off somewhere. I took myself a hammer. I went out to that car and I did a number on its underside. Whacked it up. Bent the tail pipe double. Ripped the muffler loose. By the time I was done with the car it looked worse than any typical Indian car that has been driven all its life on reservation roads, which they always say are like government promises—full of holes. It just about hurt me, I'll tell you that! I threw dirt in the carburetor and I ripped all the electric tape off the seats. I make it look just as beat up as I could. Then I sat back and waited for Henry to find it.

Still, it took him over a month. That was all right, because it was just getting warm enough, not melting, but warm enough to work outside.

"Lyman," he says, walking in one day, "that red car looks like shit."

"Well, it's old," I says. "You got to expect that."

"No way!" says Henry. "That car's a classic! But you went and ran the piss right out of it, Lyman, and you know it don't deserve that. I kept that car in A-one shape. You don't remember. You're too young. But when I left, that car was running like a watch. Now I don't even know if I can get it to start again, let alone get it anywhere near its old condition."

"Well you try," I said, like I was getting mad, "but I say it's a piece of junk."   40

Then I walked out before he could realize I knew he'd strung together more than six words at once.

After that I thought he'd freeze himself to death working on that car. He was out there all day, and at night he rigged up a little lamp, ran a cord out the window, and had himself some light to see by while he worked. He was better than he had been before, but that's still not saying much. It was easier for him to do the things the rest of us did. He ate more slowly and didn't jump up and down during the meal to get this or that or look out the window. I put my hand in the back of the TV set, I admit, and fiddled around with it good, so that it was almost impossible now to get a clear picture. He didn't look at it very often anyway. He was always out with that car or going off to get parts for it. By the time it was really melting outside, he had it fixed.

I had been feeling down in the dumps about Henry around this time. We had always been together before. Henry and Lyman. But he was such a loner now that I didn't know how to take it. So I jumped at the chance one day when Henry seemed friendly. It's not that he smiled or anything. He just said, "Let's take that old shitbox for a spin." Just the way he said it made me think he could be coming around.

We went out to the car. It was spring. The sun was shining very bright. My only sister, Bonita, who was just eleven years old, came out and made us stand together for a picture. Henry leaned his elbow on the red car's windshield, and he took his other arm and put it over my shoulder, very carefully, as though it was heavy for him to lift and he didn't want to bring the weight down all at once.

"Smile," Bonita said, and he did.   45

That picture. I never look at it anymore. A few months ago, I don't know why, I got his picture out and tacked it on the wall. I felt good about Henry at the time, close to him. I felt good having his picture on the wall, until one night when I was looking at television. I was a little drunk and stoned. I looked up at the wall and Henry was staring at me. I don't know what it was, but his smile had changed, or maybe it was gone. All I know is I couldn't stay in the same room with that picture. I was shaking. I got up, closed the door, and went into the kitchen. A little later my friend Ray came over and we both went back into that room. We put the picture in a brown bag, folded the bag over and over tightly, then put it way back in a closet.

I still see that picture now, as if it tugs at me, whenever I pass that closet door. The picture is very clear in my mind. It was so sunny that day Henry had to squint against the glare. Or maybe the camera Bonita held flashed like a mirror, blinding him, before she snapped the picture. My face is right out in the sun, big and round. But he might have drawn back, because the shadows on his face are deep as holes. There are two shadows curved like little hooks around the ends of his smile, as if to frame it and try to keep it there—that one, first smile that looked like it might have hurt his face. He has his field jacket on and the worn-in clothes he'd come back in and kept wearing ever since. After Bonita took the picture, she went into the house and we got into the car. There was a full cooler in the trunk. We started off, east, toward Pembina and the Red River because Henry said he wanted to see the high water.

The trip over there was beautiful. When everything starts changing, drying up, clearing off, you feel like your whole life is starting. Henry felt it, too. The top was down and the car hummed like a top. He'd really put it back in shape, even the tape on the seats was very carefully put down and glued back in layers. It's not that he smiled again or even joked, but his face looked to me as if it was clear, more peaceful. It looked as though he wasn't thinking of anything in particular except the bare fields and windbreaks and houses we were passing.

The river was high and full of winter trash when we got there. The sun was still out, but it was colder by the river. There were still little clumps of dirty snow here and there on the banks. The water hadn't gone over the banks yet, but it would, you could tell. It was just at its limit, hard swollen, glossy like an old gray scar. We made ourselves a fire, and we sat down and watched the current go. As I watched it I felt something squeezing inside me and tightening and trying to let go all at the same time. I knew I was not just feeling it myself; I knew I was feeling what Henry was going through at that moment. Except that I couldn't stand it, the closing and opening. I jumped to my feet. I took Henry by the shoulders and I started shaking him. "Wake up," I says, "wake up, wake up, wake up!" I didn't know what had come over me. I sat down beside him again.

50   His face was totally white and hard. Then it broke, like stones break all of a sudden when water boils up inside them.

"I know it," he says. "I know it. I can't help it. It's no use."

We start talking. He said he knew what I'd done with the car. It was obvious it had been whacked out of shape and not just neglected. He said he wanted to give the car to me for good now, it was no use. He said he'd fixed it just to give it back and I should take it.

"No way," I says. "I don't want it."

"That's okay," he says, "you take it."

55   "I don't want it, though," I says back to him, and then to emphasize, just to emphasize, you understand, I touch his shoulder. He slaps my hand off.

"Take that car," he says.

"No," I say. "Make me," I say, and then he grabs my jacket and rips the arm loose. That jacket is a class act, suede with tags and zippers. I push Henry backwards, off the log. He jumps up and bowls me over. We go down in a clinch and come up swinging hard, for all we're worth, with our fists. He socks my jaw so hard I feel like it swings loose. Then I'm at his rib cage and land a good one under his chin so his head snaps back. He's dazzled. He looks at me and I look at him and then his eyes are full of tears and blood and at first I think he's crying. But no, he's laughing. "Ha, ha!" he says. "Ha! Ha! Take good care of it."

"Okay," I says. "Okay, no problem. Ha! Ha!"

I can't help it, and I start laughing, too. My face feels fat and strange, and after a while I get a beer from the cooler in the trunk, and when I hand it to Henry he takes his shirt and wipes my germs off. "Hoof-and-mouth disease," he says. For some reason this cracks me up, and so we're really laughing for a while, and then we drink all the rest of the beers one by one and throw them in the river and see how far, how fast, the current takes them before they fill up and sink.

"You want to go on back?" I ask after a while. "Maybe we could snag a   60
couple nice Kashpaw girls."

He says nothing. But I can tell his mood is turning again.

"They're all crazy, the girls up here, every damn one of them."

"You're crazy too," I say, to jolly him up. "Crazy Lamartine boys!"

He looks as though he will take this wrong at first. His face twists, then clears, and he jumps up on his feet. "That's right!" he says. "Crazier'n hell. Crazy Indians!"

I think it's the old Henry again. He throws off his jacket and starts spring-   65
ing his legs up from the knees like a fancy dancer. He's down doing something between a grass dance and a bunny hop, no kind of dance I ever saw before, but neither has anyone else on all this green growing earth. He's wild. He wants to pitch whoopee! He's up and at me and all over. All this time I'm laughing so hard, so hard my belly is getting tied up in a knot.

"Got to cool me off!" he shouts all of a sudden. Then he runs over to the river and jumps in.

There's boards and other things in the current. It's so high. No sound comes from the river after the splash he makes, so I run right over. I look around. It's getting dark. I see he's halfway across the water already, and I know he didn't swim there but the current took him. It's far. I hear his voice, though, very clearly across it.

"My boots are filling," he says.

He says this in a normal voice, like he just noticed and he doesn't know what to think of it. Then he's gone. A branch comes by. Another branch. And I go in.

By the time I get out of the river, off the snag I pulled myself onto, the sun   70
is down. I walk back to the car, turn on the high beams, and drive it up the bank. I put it in first gear and then I take my foot off the clutch. I get out, close the door, and watch it plough softly into the water. The headlights reach in as they go down, searching, still lighted even after the water swirls over the back end. I wait. The wires short out. It is all finally dark. And then there is only the water, the sound of it going and running and going and running and running.

CRITICAL THINKING QUESTIONS

1. The word *pariah* means "outcast or outsider." When Vietnam veterans returned to American society, some said they felt like pariahs. In what way does Henry demonstrate this attitude in Erdrich's story?

2. Read Louise Erdrich's biographical information (see Authors' Biographical Notes). In what ways do you think her heritage influences her story?

3. At the Red River, Henry and Lyman fight over their car, then laugh and joke—"pitch whoopee." When Lyman says, "Crazy Lamartine boys!", Henry responds, "Crazier'n hell. Crazy Indians!" Is Henry crazy? Does his final act suggest that he is in control or out of control? Use evidence from the story to discuss how you arrived at your **claim of value** in judging Henry.

WRITING TOPIC

Do you know any war veteran (of World War II; the Korean, Vietnam, Persian Gulf Wars; the wars in Iraq and Afghanistan)? If so, interview him or her to learn about his or her war and postwar experiences. Also, contact your local veterans' affairs office to find out information about the benefits for veterans who have sustained disabilities. Are disabled or wounded veterans receiving adequate treatment and fair compensation?

Shirley Jackson

The Lottery (1948)

The morning of June 27th was clear and sunny, with the fresh warmth of a full-summer day; the flowers were blossoming profusely and the grass was richly green. The people of the village began to gather in the square, between the post office and the bank, around ten o'clock; in some towns there were so many people that the lottery took two days and had to be started on June 26th, but in this village, where there were only about three hundred people, the whole lottery took less than two hours, so it could begin at ten o'clock in the morning and still be through in time to allow the villagers to get home for noon dinner.

The children assembled first, of course. School was recently over for the summer, and the feeling of liberty sat uneasily on most of them; they tended to gather together quietly for a while before they broke into boisterous play, and their talk was still of the classroom and the teacher, of books and reprimands. Bobby Martin had already stuffed his pockets full of stones, and the other boys soon followed his example, selecting the smoothest and roundest stones; Bobby and Harry Jones "Dellacroy"—eventually made a great pile of stones in one corner of the square and guarded it against the raids of the other boys. The girls stood aside, talking among themselves, looking over their shoulders at the boys, and the very small children rolled in the dust or clung to the hands of their older brothers or sisters.

Soon the men began to gather, surveying their own children, speaking of planting and rain, tractors and taxes. They stood together, away from the pile of stones in the corner, and their jokes were quiet and they smiled rather than laughed. The women, wearing faded house dresses and sweaters, came shortly after their menfolk. They greeted one another and exchanged bits of gossip as they went to join their husbands. Soon the women, standing by their husbands, began to call to their children, and the children came reluctantly, having to be called four or five times. Bobby Martin ducked under his mother's grasping hand and ran, laughing, back to the pile of stones. His father spoke up sharply, and Bobby came quickly and took his place between his father and his oldest brother.

The lottery was conducted—as were the square dances, the teen-age club, the Halloween program—by Mr. Summers, who had time and energy to devote to civic activities. He was a round-faced, jovial man and he ran the coal business, and people were sorry for him, because he had no children and his wife was a scold. When he arrived in the square, carrying the black wooden box, there was a murmur of conversation among the villagers, and he waved and called, "Little late today, folks." The postmaster, Mr. Graves, followed him, carrying a three-legged stool, and the stool was put in the center of the square and Mr. Summers set the black box down on it. The villagers kept their distance, leaving a space between themselves and the stool, and when Mr. Summers said, "Some of you fellows want to give me a hand?" there was a hesitation before two men, Mr. Martin and his oldest son, Baxter, came forward to hold the box steady on the stool while Mr. Summers stirred up the papers inside it.

The original paraphernalia for the lottery had been lost long ago, and the black box now resting on the stool had been put into use even before Old Man Warner, the oldest man in town, was born. Mr. Summers spoke frequently to the villagers about making a new box, but no one liked to upset even as much tradition as was represented by the black box. There was a story that the present box had been made with some pieces of the box that had preceded it, the one that had been constructed when the first people settled down to make a village here. Every year, after the lottery, Mr. Summers began talking again about a new box, but every year the subject was allowed to fade off without anything's being done. The black box grew shabbier each year; by now it was no longer completely black but splintered badly along one side to show the original wood color, and in some places faded or stained.

Mr. Martin and his oldest son, Baxter, held the black box securely on the stool until Mr. Summers had stirred the papers thoroughly with his hand. Because so much of the ritual had been forgotten or discarded, Mr. Summers had been successful in having slips of paper substituted for the chips of wood that had been used for generations. Chips of wood, Mr. Summers had argued, had been all very well when the village was tiny, but now that the population was more than three hundred and likely to keep on growing, it was necessary to use something that would fit more

5

easily into the black box. The night before the lottery, Mr. Summers and Mr. Graves made up the slips of paper and put them in the box, and it was then taken to the safe of Mr. Summers's coal company and locked up until Mr. Summers was ready to take it to the square next morning. The rest of the year, the box was put away, sometimes one place, sometimes another; it had spent one year in Mr. Graves's barn and another year underfoot in the post office, and sometimes it was set on a shelf in the Martin grocery and left there.

There was a great deal of fussing to be done before Mr. Summers declared the lottery open. There were the lists to make up—of heads of families, heads of households in each family, members of each househould in each family. There was the proper swearing-in of Mr. Summers by the postmaster, as the official of the lottery; at one time, some people remembered, there had been a recital of some sort, performed by the official of the lottery, a perfunctory, tuneless chant that had been rattled off duly each year; some people believed that the official of the lottery used to stand just so when he said or sang it, others believed that he was supposed to walk among the people, but years and years ago this part of the ritual had been allowed to lapse. There had been, also, a ritual salute, which the official of the lottery had had to use in addressing each person who came up to draw from the box, but this also had changed with time, until now it was felt necessary only for the official to speak to each person approaching. Mr. Summers was very good at all this; in his clean white shirt and blue jeans, with one hand resting carelessly on the black box, he seemed very proper and important as he talked interminably to Mr. Graves and the Martins.

Just as Mr. Summers finally left off talking and turned to the assembled villagers, Mrs. Hutchinson came hurriedly along the path to the square, her sweater thrown over her shoulders, and slid into place in the back of the crowd. "Clean forgot what day it was," she said to Mrs. Delacroix, who stood next to her, and they both laughed softly. "Thought my old man was out back stacking wood," Mrs. Hutchinson went on, "and then I looked out the window and the kids was gone, and then I remembered it was the twenty-seventh and came a-running." She dried her hands on her apron, and Mrs. Delacroix said, "You're in time, through. They're still talking away up there."

Mrs. Hutchinson craned her neck to see through the crowd and found her husband and children standing near the front. She tapped Mrs. Delacroix on the arm as a farewell and began to make her way through the crowd. The people separated good-humoredly to let her through; two or three people said, in voices just loud enough to be heard across the crowd, "Here comes your Missus, Hutchinson," and "Bill, she made it after all." Mrs. Hutchinson reached her husband, and Mr. Summers, who had been waiting, said cheerfully, "Thought we were going to have to get on without you, Tessie." Mrs. Hutchinson said, grinning, "Wouldn't have me leave m'dishes in the sink, now, would you, Joe?," and soft laughter ran through the crowd as the people stirred back into possition after Mrs. Hutchinson's arrival.

10   "Well, now," Mr. Summers said soberly, "guess we better get started, get this over with, so's we can go back to work. Anybody ain't here?"

"Dunbar," several people said. "Dunbar, Dunbar."

Mr. Summers consulted his list. "Clyde Dunbar," he said. "That's right. He's broke his leg, hasn't he? Who's drawing for him?"

"Me, I guess," a woman said, and Mr. Summers turned to look at her. "Wife draws for her husband," Mr. Summers said. "Don't you have a grown boy to do it for you, Janey?" Althrough Mr. Summers and everyone else in the village knew the answer perfectly well, it was the business of the official of the lottery to ask such questions formally. Mr. Summers waited with an expression of polite interest while Mrs. Dunbar answered.

"Horace's not but sixteen yet," Mrs. Dunbar said regretfully. "Guess I gotta fill in for the old man this year."

"Right," Mr. Summers said. He made a note on the list he was holding. 15 Then he asked, "Watson boy drawing this year?"

A tall boy in the crowd raised his hand. "Here," he said. "I'm drawing for m'mother and me." He blinked his eyes nervously and ducked his head as several voices in the crowd said things like "Good fellow, Jack," and "Glad to see your mother's got a man to do it."

"Well," Mr. Summers said, "guess that's everyone. Old Man Warner make it?"

"Here," a voice said, and Mr. Summers nodded.

A sudden hush fell on the crowd as Mr. Summers cleared his throat and looked at the list. "All ready?" he called. "Now, I'll read the names—heads of families first—and the men come up and take a paper out of the box. Keep the paper folded in your hand without looking at it until everyone has had a turn. Everything clear?"

The people had done it so many times that they only half listened to the 20 directions; most of them were quiet, wetting their lips, not looking around. Then Mr. Summers raised one hand high and said, "Adams." A man disengaged himself from the crowd and came forward. "Hi, Steve," Mr. Summers said, and Mr. Adams said. "Hi, Joe." They grinned at one another humorlessly and nervously. Then Mr. Adams reached into the black box and took out a folded paper. He held it firmly by one corner as he turned and went hastily back to his place in the crowd, where he stood a little apart from his family, not looking down at his hand.

"Allen," Mr. Summers said. "Anderson. … Bentham."

"Seems like there's no time at all between lotteries any more," Mrs. Delacroix said to Mrs. Graves in the back row. "Seems like we got through with the last one only last week."

"Time sure goes fast," Mrs. Graves said.

"Clark. … Delacroix."

"There goes my old man," Mrs. Delacroix said. She held her breath while 25 her husband went forward.

"Dunbar," Mr. Summers said, and Mrs. Dunbar went steadily to the box while one of the women said, "Go on, Janey," and another said, "There she goes."

"We're next," Mrs. Graves said. She watched while Mr. Graves came around from the side of the box, greeted Mr. Summers gravely, and selected a slip of paper from the box. By now, all through the crowd there were men holding the small folded papers in the large hands, turning them over and over nervously. Mrs. Dunbar and her two sons stood together, Mrs. Dunbar holding the slip of paper.

"Harburt. ... Hutchinson."

"Get up there, Bill," Mrs. Hutchinson said, and the people near her laughed.

30   "Jones."

"They do say," Mr. Adams said to Old Man Warner, who stood next to him, "that over in the north village they're talking of giving up the lottery."

Old Man Warner snorted. "Pack of crazy fools," he said. "Listening to the young folks, nothing's good enough for *them*. Next thing you know, they'll be wanting to go back to living in caves, nobody work any more, live *that* way for a while. Used to be a saying about 'Lottery in June, corn be heavy soon.' First thing you know, we'd all be eating stewed chickweed and acorns. There's *always* been a lottery," he added petulantly. "Bad enough to see young Joe Summers up there joking with everybody."

"Some places have already quit lotteries," Mrs. Adams said.

"Nothing but trouble in *that*," Old Man Warner said stoutly. "Pack of young fools."

35   "Martin." And Bobby Martin watched his father go forward. "Overdyke. ... Percy."

"I wish they'd hurry," Mrs. Dunbar said to her older son. "I wish they'd hurry."

"They're almost through," her son said.

"You get ready to run tell Dad," Mrs. Dunbar said.

Mr. Summers called his own name and then stepped forward precisely and selected a slip from the box. Then he called, "Warner."

40   "Seventy-seventh year I been in the lottery," Old Man Warner said as he went through the crowd. "Seventy-seventh time."

"Watson." The tall boy came awkwardly through the crowd. Someone said, "Don't be nervous, Jack," and Mr. Summers said, "Take your time, son."

"Zanini."

After that, there was a long pause, a breathless pause, until Mr. Summers, holding his slip of paper in the air, said, "All right, fellows." For a minute, no one moved, and then all the slips of paper were opened. Suddenly, all the women began to speak at once, saying, "Who is it?," "Who's got it?," "Is it the Dunbars?," "Is it the Watsons?" Then the voices began to say, "It's Hutchinson. It's Bill," "Bill Hutchinson's got it."

"Go tell your father," Mrs. Dunbar said to her older son.

45   People began to look around to see the Hutchinsons. Bill Hutchinson was standing quiet, staring down at the paper in his hand. Suddenly, Tessie Hutchinson shouted to Mr. Summers, "You didn't give him time enough to take any paper he wanted. I saw you. It wasn't fair!"

"Be a good sport, Tessie," Mrs. Delacroix called, and Mrs. Graves said, "All of us took the same chance."

"Shut up, Tessie," Bill Hutchinson said.

"Well, everyone," Mr. Summers said, "that was done pretty fast, and now we've got to be hurrying a little more to get done in time." He consulted his next list. "Bill," he said, "you draw for the Hutchinson family. You got any other households in the Hutchinsons?"

"There's Don and Eva," Mrs. Hutchinson yelled. "Make *them* take their chance!"

"Daughters draw with their husbands' families, Tessie," Mr. Summers said   50 gently. "You know that as well as anyone else."

"It wasn't *fair*," Tessie said.

"I guess not, Joe," Bill Hutchinson said regretfully. "My daughter draws with her husband's family, that's only fair. And I've got no other family except the kids."

"Then, as far as drawing for families is concerned, it's you," Mr. Summers said in explanation, "and as far as drawing for households is concerned, that's you, too. Right?"

"Right," Bill Hutchinson said.

"How many kids, Bill?" Mr. Summers asked formally.   55

"Three," Bill Hutchinson said. "There's Bill, Jr., and Nancy, and little Dave. And Tessie and me."

"All right, then," Mr. Summers said. "Harry, you got their tickets back?"

Mr. Graves nodded and held up the slips of paper. "Put them in the box, then," Mr. Summers directed. "Take Bill's and put it in."

"I think we ought to start over," Mrs. Hutchinson said, as quietly as she could. "I tell you it wasn't *fair*. You didn't give him time enough to choose. *Every-body* saw that."

Mr. Graves had selected the five slips and put them in the box, and he   60 dropped all the papers but those onto the ground, where the breeze caught them and lifted them off.

"Listen, everybody," Mrs. Hutchinson was saying to the people around her.

"Ready, Bill?" Mr. Summers asked, and Bill Hutchinson, with one quick glance around at his wife and children, nodded.

"Remember," Mr. Summers said, "take the slips and keep them folded until each person has taken one. Harry, you help little Dave." Mr. Graves took the hand of the little boy, who came willingly with him up to the box. "Take a paper out of the box, Davy," Mr. Summers said. Davy put his hand into the box and laughed. "Take just *one* paper," Mr. Summers said. "Harry, you hold it for him." Mr. Graves took the child's hand and removed the folded paper from the tight fist and held it while little Dave stood next to him and looked up at him wonderingly.

"Nancy next," Mr. Summers said. Nancy was twelve, and her school friends breathed heavily as she went forward, switching her skirt, and took a slip dain-tily from the box. "Bill, Jr.," Mr. Summers said, and Billy, his face red and his feet overlarge, nearly knocked the box over as he got a paper out. "Tessie," Mr. Summers said. She hesitated for a minute, looking around defiantly, and then set her lips and went up to the box. She snatched a paper out and held it behind her.

65   "Bill," Mr. Summers said, and Bill Hutchinson reached into the box and felt around, bringing his hand out at last with the slip of paper in it.

The crowd was quiet. A girl whispered, "I hope it's not Nancy," and the sound of the whisper reached the edges of the crowd.

"It's not the way it used to be," Old Man Warner said clearly. "People ain't the way they used to be."

"All right," Mr. Summers said. "Open the papers. Harry, you open little Dave's."

Mr. Graves opened the slip of paper and there was a general sigh through the crowd as he held it up and everyone could see that it was blank. Nancy and Bill, Jr., opened theirs at the same time, and both beamed and laughed, turning around to the crowd and holding their slips of paper above their heads.

70   "Tessie," Mr. Summers said. There was a pause, and then Mr. Summers looked at Bill Hutchinson, and Bill unfolded his paper and showed it. It was blank.

"It's Tessie," Mr. Summers said, and his voice was hushed. "Show us her paper, Bill."

Bill Hutchinson went over to his wife and forced the slip of paper out of her hand. It had a black spot on it, the black spot Mr. Summers had made the night before with the heavy pencil in the coal-company office. Bill Hutchinson held it up, and there was a stir in the crowd.

"All right, folks," Mr. Summers said. "Let's finish quickly."

Although the villagers had forgotten the ritual and lost the original black box, they still remembered to use stones. The pile of stones the boys had made earlier was ready; there were stones on the ground with the blowing scraps of paper that had come out of the box. Mrs. Delacroix selected a stone so large she had to pick it up with both hands and turned to Mrs. Dunbar. "Come on," she said. "Hurry up."

75   Mrs. Dunbar had small stones in both hands, and she said, gasping for breath, "I can't run at all. You'll have to go ahead and I'll catch up with you."

The children had stones already, and someone gave little Davy Hutchinson a few pebbles.

Tessie Hutchinson was in the center of a cleared space by now, and she held her hands out desperately as the villagers moved in on her. "It isn't fair," she said. A stone hit her on the side of the head.

Old Man Warner was saying, "Come on, come on, everyone." Steve Adams was in the front of the crowd of villagers, with Mrs. Graves beside him.

"It isn't fair, it isn't right," Mrs. Hutchinson screamed, and then they were upon her.

CRITICAL THINKING QUESTIONS

1. When Old Man Warner says that the younger generation in some villages is considering doing away with lotteries, he refers to proponents of such as "a pack of young fools." Do you feel this difference in ideology is reflective of the modern-day generation gap between the technologically savvy younger crowd and the slow-to-change older generation? In what ways do people clash generationally and over what issues?

2. When Tessie finds out the Hutchinson family will have to draw in the final round of the lottery, she expresses her belief that this action is unfair because she says her husband was rushed to draw a slip of paper. As she pleads, she mentions her own daughter and son-in-law were not counted among the Hutchinson clan. Are you shocked by her actions? Is this a knee-jerk reaction of a desperate woman not thinking clearly, or does it reveal deeper truths regarding Tessie's character?

3. Do you think that all the villagers passionately believe in the purpose of the lottery, or do you feel that most of them participate in an act they might otherwise deplore in order to maintain their identity in this particular community? Does this story speak to you on themes of peer pressure and hypocrisy? Explain your answer.

WRITING TOPIC

Can you think of a community that observes a peculiar custom, festival, or celebration? In what ways is the ritual strange, in your opinion? Once you have identified the community and event, research the origins of the custom. How did the observance start? Why do you believe it continues? In what ways does this event play into the identity of the community and the beliefs of its people?

Randall Kenan

The Foundations of the Earth (1992)

I

Of course they didn't pay it any mind at first: just a tractor—one of the most natural things in the world to see in a field—kicking dust up into the afternoon sky and slowly toddling off the road into a soybean field. And fields surrounded Mrs. Maggie MacGowan Williams's house, giving the impression that her lawn stretched on and on until it dropped off into the woods far by the way. Sometimes she was certain she could actually see the earth's curve—not merely the bend of the small hill on which her house sat but the great slope of the sphere, the way scientists explained it in books, a monstrous globe floating in a cold nothingness. She would sometimes sit by herself on the patio late of an evening, in the same chair she was sitting in now, sip from her Coca-Cola, and think about how big the earth must be to seem flat to the eye.

She wished she were alone now. It was Sunday.

"Now I wonder what that man is doing with a tractor out there today?"

They sat on Maggie's patio, reclined in that after-Sunday-dinner way— Maggie; the Right Reverend Hezekiah Barden, round and pompous as ever; Henrietta Fuchee, the prim and priggish music teacher and president of the First Baptist Church Auxiliary Council; Emma Lewis, Maggie's sometimes house-keeper; and Gabriel, Mrs. Maggie Williams's young, white, special guest—all look-ing out lazily into the early summer, watching the sun begin its slow downward arc, feeling the baked ham and the candied sweet potatoes and the fried chicken with the collard greens and green beans and beets settle in their bellies, talking shallow and pleasant talk, and sipping their Coca-Colas and bitter lemonade.

5   "Don't they realize it's Sunday?" Reverend Barden leaned back in his chair and tugged at his suspenders thoughtfully, eyeing the tractor as it turned into another row. He reached for a sweating glass of lemonade, his red bow tie afire in the penultimate beams of the day.

"I … I don't understand. What's wrong?" Maggie could see her other guests watching Gabriel intently, trying to discern why on earth he was present at Maggie MacGowan Williams's table.

"What you mean, what's wrong?" The Reverend Barden leaned forward and narrowed his eyes at the young man. "What's wrong is: it's Sunday."

"So? I don't …" Gabriel himself now looked embarrassed, glancing to Maggie, who wanted to save him but could not.

"'So?' 'So?'" Leaning toward Gabriel and narrowing his eyes, Barden asked: "You're not from a churchgoing family, are you?"

10   "Well, no. Today was my first time in … Oh, probably ten years."

"Uh-huh." Barden corrected his posture, as if to say he pitied Gabriel's being an infidel but had the patience to instruct him. "Now you see, the Lord has declared Sunday as His day. It's holy. 'Six days shalt thou labor and do all thy work: but the seventh day is the sabbath of the Lord thy God: in it thou shalt not do any work, thou, nor thy son, nor thy daughter, thy manservant, nor thy maidservant, nor thy cattle, nor thy stranger that is within thy gates: for in six days the Lord made heaven and earth, the sea, and all that in them is, and rested the seventh day: wherefore, the Lord blessed the sabbath day, and hallowed it.' Exodus. Chapter twenty, verses nine and ten."

"Amen." Henrietta closed her eyes and rocked.

"Hez." Maggie inclined her head a bit to entreat the good Reverend to desist. He gave her an understanding smile, which made her cringe slightly, fear-ing her gesture might have been mistaken for a sign of intimacy.

"But, Miss Henrietta—" Emma Lewis tapped the tabletop, like a judge in court, changing the subject. "Like I was saying, I believe that Rick on *The Winds of Hope* is going to marry that gal before she gets too big with child, don't you?" Though Emma kept house for Maggie Williams, to Maggie she seemed more like a sister who came three days a week, more to visit than to clean.

"Now go on away from here, Emma." Henrietta did not look up from her empty cake plate, her glasses hanging on top of her sagging breasts from a silver chain. "Talking about that worldly foolishness on TV. You know I don't pay that mess any attention." She did not want the Reverend to know that she secretly watched afternoon soap operas, just like Emma and all the other women in the congregation. Usually she gossiped to beat the band about this rich heifer and that handsome hunk whenever she found a fellow TV-gazer. Buck-toothed hypocrite, Maggie thought. She knew the truth: Henrietta, herself a widow now on ten years, was sweet on the widower minister, who in turn, alas, had his eye on Maggie.

"Now, Miss Henrietta, we was talking about it t'other day. Don't you think he's apt to marry her soon?" Emma's tone was insistent.

"I *don't know*, Emma." Visibly agitated, Henrietta donned her glasses and looked into the fields. "I wonder who that is anyhow?"

Annoyed by Henrietta's rebuff, Emma stood and began to collect the few remaining dishes. Her purple-and-yellow floral print dress hugged her ample hips. "It's that ole Morton Henry that Miss Maggie leases that piece of land to." She walked toward the door, into the house. "He ain't no God-fearing man."

"Well, that's plain to see." The Reverend glanced over to Maggie. She shrugged.

They are ignoring Gabriel, Maggie thought. She had invited them to dinner after church services thinking it would be pleasant for Gabriel to meet other people in Tims Creek. But generally they chose not to see him, and when they did it was with illconcealed scorn or petty curiosity or annoyance. At first the conversation seemed civil enough. But the ice was never truly broken, questions still buzzed around the talk like horseflies, Maggie could tell. "Where you from?" Henrietta had asked. "What's your line of work?" Barden had asked. While Gabriel sat there with a look on his face somewhere between peace and pain. But Maggie refused to believe she had made a mistake. At this stage of her life she depended on no one for anything, and she was certainly not dependent on the approval of these self-important fools.

She had been steeled by anxiety when she picked Gabriel up at the airport that Friday night. But as she caught sight of him stepping from the jet and greeted him, asking about the weather in Boston; and after she had ushered him to her car and watched him slide in, seeming quite at home; though it still felt awkward, she thought: I'm doing the right thing.

II

"Well, thank you for inviting me, Mrs. Williams. But I don't understand ... Is something wrong?"

"*Wrong*? No, nothing's wrong, Gabriel. I just thought it'd be good to see you. Sit and talk to you. We didn't have much time at the funeral."

"Gee ... I—"

25   "You don't want to make an old woman sad, now do you?"

"Well, Mrs. Williams, if you put it like that, how can I refuse?"

"Weekend after next then?"

There was a pause in which she heard muted voices in the wire.

"Okay."

30   After she hung up the phone and sat down in her favorite chair in the den, she heaved a momentous sigh. Well, she had done it. At last. The weight of uncertainty would be lifted. She could confront him face to face. She wanted to know about her grandboy, and Gabriel was the only one who could tell her what she wanted to know. It was that simple. Surely, he realized what this invitation meant. She leaned back looking out the big picture window onto the tops of the brilliantly blooming crepe myrtle trees in the yard, listening to the grandfather clock mark the time.

III

Her grandson's funeral had been six months ago, but it seemed much longer. Perhaps the fact that Edward had been gone away from home so long without seeing her, combined with the weeks and days and hours and minutes she had spent trying not to think about him and all the craziness that had surrounded his death, somehow lengthened the time.

At first she chose to ignore it, the strange and bitter sadness that seemed to have overtaken her every waking moment. She went about her daily life as she had done for thirty-odd years, overseeing her stores, her land, her money; buying groceries, paying bills, shopping, shopping; going to church and talking to her few good living friends and the few silly fools she was obliged to suffer. But all day, dusk to dawn, and especially at night, she had what the field-workers called "a monkey on your back," when the sun beats down so hot it makes you delirious; but her monkey chilled and angered her, born not of the sun but of a profound loneliness, an oppressive emptiness, a stabbing guilt. Sometimes she even wished she were a drinking woman.

The depression had come with the death of Edward, though its roots reached farther back, to the time he seemed to have vanished. There had been so many years of asking other members of the family: Have you heard from him? Have you seen him? So many years of only a Christmas card or birthday card a few days early, or a cryptic, taciturn phone call on Sunday mornings, and then no calls at all. At some point she realized she had no idea where he was or how to get in touch with him. Mysteriously, he would drop a line to his half-sister, Clarissa, or drop a card without a return address. He was gone. Inevitably, she had to ask: Had she done something evil to the boy to drive him away? Had she tried too hard to make sure he became nothing like his father and grandfather? I was as good a mother as a woman can claim to be, she thought: from the cradle on he had all the material things he needed, and he certainly didn't want for attention, for care; and I trained him proper, he was a well-mannered and upright young fellow when he left here for college. Oh, I was proud of that boy, winning a scholarship to Boston University. Tall, handsome like his granddad. He'd make somebody a good …

So she continued picking out culprits: school, the cold North, strange people, strange ideas. But now in her crystalline hindsight she could lay no blame on anyone but Edward. And the more she remembered battles with the mumps and the measles and long division and taunts from his schoolmates, the more she became aware of her true anger. He owes me respect, damn it. The least he can do is keep in touch. Is that so much to ask?

But before she could make up her mind to find him and confront him 35 with her fury, before she could cuss him out good and call him an ungrateful, no-account bastard just like his father, a truck would have the heartless audacity to skid into her grandchild's car one rainy night in Springfield and end his life at twenty-seven, taking that opportunity away from her forever. When they told her of his death she cursed her weakness. Begging God for another chance. But instead He gave her something she had never imagined.

Clarissa was the one to finally tell her. "Grandma," she had said, "Edward's been living with another man all these years."

"So?"

"No, Grandma. Like man and wife."

Maggie had never before been so paralyzed by news. One question answered, only to be replaced by a multitude. Gabriel had come with the body, like an interpreter for the dead. They had been living together in Boston, where Edward worked in a bookstore. He came, head bowed, rheumy-eyed, exhausted. He gave her no explanation; nor had she asked him for any, for he displayed the truth in his vacant and humble glare and had nothing to offer but the penurious tribute of his trembling hands. Which was more than she wanted.

In her world she had been expected to be tearless, patient, comforting to 40 other members of the family; folk were meant to sit back and say, "Lord, ain't she taking it well. I don't think I could be so calm if my grandboy had've died so young." Magisterially she had done her duty; she had taken it all in stride. But her world began to hopelessly unravel that summer night at the wake in the Raymond Brown Funeral Home, among the many somber-bright flower arrangements, the fluorescent lights, and the gleaming bronze casket, when Gabriel tried to tell her how sorry he was … How dare he? This pathetic, stumbling, poor trashy white boy, to throw his sinful lust for her grandbaby in her face, as if to bury a grandchild weren't bad enough. Now this abomination had to be flaunted.—Sorry, indeed! The nerve! Who the hell did he think he was to parade their shame about?

Her anger was burning so intensely that she knew if she didn't get out she would tear his heart from his chest, his eyes from their sockets, his testicles from their sac. With great haste she took her leave, brushing off the funeral director and her brother's wives and husband's brothers—they all probably thinking her overcome with grief rather than anger—and had Clarissa drive her home. When she got to the house she filled a tub with water as hot as she could stand it and a handful of bath oil beads, and slipped in, praying her hatred would mingle with the mist and evaporate, leaving her at least sane.

Next, sleep. Healing sleep, soothing sleep, sleep to make the world go away, sleep like death. Her mama had told her that sleep was the best medicine God ever made. When things get too rough—go to bed. Her family had been known as the family that retreated to bed. Ruined crop? No money? Get some shut-eye. Maybe it'll be better in the morning. Can't be worse. Maggie didn't give a damn where Gabriel was to sleep that night; someone else would deal with it. She didn't care about all the people who would come to the house after the wake to the Sitting Up, talking, eating, drinking, watching over the still body till sunrise; they could take care of themselves. The people came; but Maggie slept. From deeps under deeps of slumber she sensed her granddaughter stick her head in the door and whisper, asking Maggie if she wanted something to eat. Maggie didn't stir. She slept. And in her sleep she dreamed.

She dreamed she was Job sitting on his dung heap, dressed in sackcloth and ashes, her body covered with boils, scratching with a stick, sending away Eliphaz and Bildad and Zophar and Elihu, who came to counsel her, and above her the sky boiled and churned and the air roared, and she matched it, railing against God, against her life—*Why? Why? Why did you kill him, you heartless old fiend? Why make me live to see him die? What earthly purpose could you have in such a wicked deed? You are God, but you are not good. Speak to me, damn it. Why? Why? Why?* Hurricanes whipped and thunder ripped through a sky streaked by lightning, and she was lifted up, spinning, spinning, and Edward floated before her in the rushing air and quickly turned around into the comforting arms of Gabriel, winged, who clutched her grandboy to his bosom and soared away, out of the storm. Maggie screamed and the winds grew stronger, and a voice, gentle and sweet, not thunderous as she expected, spoke to her from the whirlwind: *Who is this that darkeneth counsel by words without knowledge? Gird up now thy loins like a man; for I will demand of thee, and answer thou me. Where wast thou when I laid the foundations of the earth? Declare if thou hast understanding* ... The voice spoke of the myriad creations of the universe, the stupendous glory of the Earth and its inhabitants. But Maggie was not deterred in the face of the maelstrom, saying: *Answer me, damn you: Why?*, and the winds began to taper off and finally halted, and Maggie was alone, standing on water. A fish, what appeared to be a mackerel, stuck its head through the surface and said: *Kind woman, be not aggrieved and put your anger away. Your arrogance has clouded your good mind. Who asked you to love? Who asked you to hate?* The fish dipped down with a plip and gradually Maggie too began to slip down into the water, down, down, down, sinking, below depths of reason and love, down into the dark unknown of her own mind, down, down, down.

Maggie MacGowan Williams woke the next morning to the harsh chatter of a bluejay chasing a mockingbird just outside her window, a racket that caused her to open her eyes quickly to blinding sunlight. Squinting, she looked about the room, seeing the chest of drawers that had once belonged to her mother and her mother's mother before that, the chairs, the photographs on the wall, the television, the rug thickly soft, the closet door slightly ajar, the bureau, the mirror atop the bureau, and herself in the mirror, all of it bright in the crisp morning light. She saw herself looking, if not refreshed, calmed and within her the rage had gone, replaced by a numb humility and a plethora of questions. Questions. Questions. Questions.

Inwardly she had felt beatific that day of the funeral, ashamed at her anger   45 of the day before. She greeted folk gently, softly, with a smile, her tones honey-flavored but solemn, and she reassumed the mantle of one-who-comforts-more-than-needing-comfort.

The immediate family had gathered at Maggie's house—Edward's father, Tom, Jr.; Tom, Jr.'s wife, Lucille; the grandbaby, Paul (Edward's brother); Clarissa. Raymond Brown's long black limousine took them from the front door of Maggie's house to the church, where the yard was crammed with people in their greys and navy blues, dark browns, and deep, deep burgundies. In her new humility she mused: When, oh when will we learn that death is not so somber, not something to mourn so much as celebrate? We should wear fire reds, sun oranges, hello greens, ocean-deep blues, and dazzling, welcome-home whites. She herself wore a bright dress of saffron and a blue scarf. She thought Edward would have liked it.

The family lined up and Gabriel approached her. As he stood before her—raven-haired, pink-skinned, abject, eyes bloodshot—she experienced a bevy of conflicting emotions: disgust, grief, anger, tenderness, fear, weariness, pity. Nevertheless she *had* to be civil, *had* to make a leap of faith and of understanding. Somehow she felt it had been asked of her. And though there were still so many questions, so much to sort out, for now she would mime patience, pretend to be accepting, feign peace. Time would unravel the rest.

She reached out, taking both his hands into her own, and said, the way she would to an old friend: "How have you been?"

IV

"But now, Miss Maggie ..."

She sometimes imagined the good Reverend Barden as a toad-frog or an   50 impotent bull. His rantings and ravings bored her, and his clumsy advances repelled her; and when he tried to impress her with his holiness and his goodness, well ...

"... that man should know better than to be plowing on a Sunday. Sunday! Why, the Lord said ..."

"Reverend, I know what the Lord said. And I'm sure Morton Henry knows what the Lord said. But I am not the Lord, Reverend, and if Morton Henry wants to plow the west field on Sunday afternoon, well, it's his soul, not mine."

"But, Maggie. Miss Maggie. It's—"

"Well,"—Henrietta Fuchee sat perched to interject her five cents into the debate—"but, Maggie. It's your land! Now, Reverend, doesn't it say somewhere in Exodus that a man, or a woman in this case, a woman is responsible for the deeds or misdeeds of someone in his or her employ, especially on her property?"

55   "But he's not an emplo—"

"Well,"—Barden scratched his head—"I think I know what you're talking about, Henrietta. It may be in Deuteronomy ... or Leviticus ... part of the Mosaic Law, which ..."

Maggie cast a quick glance at Gabriel. He seemed to be interested in and entertained by this contest of moral superiority. There was certainly something about his face ... but she could not stare. He looked so *normal...*

"Well, I don't think you should stand for it, Maggie."

"Henrietta? What do you ...? Look, if you want him to stop, *you go* tell him what the Lord said. I—"

60   The Right Reverend Hezekiah Barden stood, hiking his pants up to his belly. "Well, *I* will. A man's soul is a valuable thing. And I can't risk your own soul being tainted by the actions of one of your sharecroppers."

"My soul? Sharecropper—he's not a sharecropper. He leases that land. I— wait! ... Hezekiah! ... This doesn't ..."

But Barden had stepped off the patio onto the lawn and was headed toward the field, marching forth like old Nathan on his way to confront King David.

"Wait, Reverend." Henrietta hopped up, slinging her black pocketbook over her left shoulder. "Well, Maggie?" She peered at Maggie defiantly, as if to ask: *Where do you stand?*

"Now, Henrietta, I—"

65   Henrietta pivoted, her moral righteousness jagged and sharp as a shard of glass. "Somebody has to stand up for right!" She tromped off after Barden.

Giggling, Emma picked up the empty glasses. "I don't think ole Morton Henry gone be too happy to be preached at this afternoon."

Maggie looked from Emma to Gabriel in bewilderment, at once annoyed and amused. All three began to laugh out loud. As Emma got to the door she turned to Maggie. "Hon, you better go see that they don't get into no fist-fight, don't you think? You know that Reverend don't know when to be quiet." She looked to Gabriel and nodded knowingly. "You better go with her, son," and was gone into the house; her molasses-thick laughter sweetening the air.

Reluctantly Maggie stood, looking at the two figures—Henrietta had caught up with Barden—a tiny cloud of dust rising from their feet. "Come on, Gabe. Looks like we have to go referee."

Gabriel walked beside her, a broad smile on his face. Maggie thought of her grandson being attracted to this tall white man. She tried to see them together and couldn't. At that moment she understood that she was being called on to realign her thinking about men and women, and men and men, and even women and women. Together ... the way Adam and Eve were meant to be together.

V

Initially she found it difficult to ask the questions she wanted to ask. Almost   70
impossible.

They got along well on Saturday. She took him out to dinner; they went
shopping. All the while she tried with all her might to convince herself that she
felt comfortable with this white man, with this homosexual, with this man who
had slept with her grandboy. Yet he managed to impress her with his easygoing
manner and openness and humor.

"Mrs. W." He had given her a nickname, of all things. No one had given her a
nickname since … "Mrs. W., you sure you don't want to try on some swimsuits?"

She laughed at his kind-hearted jokes, seeing, oddly enough, something about
him very like Edward; but then that thought would make her sad and confused.

Finally that night over coffee at the kitchen table she began to ask what they
had both gingerly avoided.

Why didn't he just tell me?"   75
"He was afraid, Mrs. W. It's just that simple."
"Of what?"
"That you might disown him. That you might stop … well, you know, loving
him, I guess."
"Does your family know?"
"Yes."   80
"How do they take it?"
"My mom's fine. She's great. Really. She and Edward got along swell. My
dad. Well, he'll be okay for a while, but every now and again we'll have these
talks, you know, about cures and stuff and sometimes it just gets heated. I guess
it'll just take a little more time with him."
"But don't you want to be normal?"
"Mrs. W., I am. Normal."
"I see."   85

They went to bed at one-thirty that morning. As Maggie buttoned up her
nightgown, Gabriel's answers whizzed about her brain; but they brought along
more damnable questions and Maggie went to bed feeling betrayal and disbelief
and revulsion and anger.

In church that next morning with Gabriel, she began to doubt the wisdom
of having asked him to come. As he sat beside her in the pew, as the Reverend
Barden sermonized on Jezebel and Ahab, as the congregation unsuccessfully
tried to disguise their curiosity—("What is that white boy doing here with Maggie Williams? Who is he? Where he come from?")—she wanted Gabriel to go
ahead and tell her what to think: *We're perverts* or *You're wrong-headed, your church
has poisoned your mind against your own grandson; if he had come out to you, you would
have rejected him. Wouldn't you?* Would she have?

Barden's sermon droned on and on that morning; the choir sang; after the
service people politely and gently shook Gabriel and Maggie's hands and then
stood off to the side, whispering, clearly perplexed.

On the drive back home, as if out of the blue, she asked him: "Is it hard?"

90   "Ma'am?"

"Being who you are? What you are?"

He looked over at her, and she could not meet his gaze with the same intensity that had gone into her question. "Being gay?"

"Yes."

"Well, I have no choice."

95   "So I understand. But is it hard?"

"Edward and I used to get into arguments about that, Mrs. W." His tone altered a bit. He spoke more softly, gently, the way a widow speaks of her dead husband. Or, indeed, the way a widower speaks of his dead husband. "He used to say it was harder being black in this country than gay. Gays can always pass for straight; but blacks can't always pass for white. And most can never pass."

"And what do you think now?"

"Mrs. W., I think *life* is hard, you know?"

"Yes. I know."

VI

100   Death had first introduced itself to Maggie when she was a child. Her grandfather and grandmother both died before she was five; her father died when she was nine; her mother when she was twenty-five; over the years all her brothers except one. Her husband ten years ago. Her first memories of death: watching the women wash a cold body: the look of brown skin darkening, hardening: the corpse laid out on a cooling board, wrapped in a winding-cloth, before interment: fear of ghosts, bodyless souls: troubled sleep. So much had changed in seventy years; now there were embalming, funeral homes, morticians, insurance policies, bronze caskets, a bureaucratic wall between deceased and bereaved. Among the many things she regretted about Edward's death was not being able to touch his body. It made his death less real. But so much about the world seemed unreal to her these dark, dismal, and gloomy days. Now the flat earth was said to be round and bumblebees were not supposed to fly.

What was supposed to be and what truly was. Maggie learned these things from magazines and television and books; she loved to read. From her first week in that small schoolhouse with Miss Clara Oxendine, she had wanted to be a teacher. School: the scratchy chalkboard, the dusty-smelling textbooks, labyrinthine grammar and spelling and arithmetic, geography, reading out loud, giving confidence to the boy who would never learn to read well, correcting addition and subtraction problems, the taste and the scent of the schoolroom, the heat of the potbellied stove in January. She liked that small world; for her it was large. Yet how could she pay for enough education to become a teacher? Her mother would smile, encouragingly, when young Maggie would ask her, not looking up from her sewing, and merely say: "We'll find a way."

However, when she was fourteen she met a man named Thomas Williams, he sixteen going on thirty-nine. Infatuation replaced her dreams and murmured to her in languages she had never heard before, whispered to her another tale: *You will be a merchant's wife.*

Thomas Williams would come a-courting on Sunday evenings for two years, come driving his father's red Ford truck, stepping out with his biscuit-shined shoes, his one good Sunday suit, his hat cocked at an impertinent angle, and a smile that would make cold butter drip. But his true power lay in his tongue. He would spin yarns and tell tales that would make the oldest storyteller slap his knee and declare: "Hot damn! Can't that boy lie!" He could talk a possum out of a tree. He spoke to Maggie about his dream of opening his own store, a dry-goods store, and then maybe two or three or four. An audacious dream for a seventeen-year-old black boy, son of a farmer in 1936—and he promised, oh, how he promised, to keep Maggie by his side through it all.

Thinking back, on the other side of time and dreams, where fantasies and wishing had been realized, where she sat rich and alone, Maggie wondered what Thomas Williams could possibly have seen in that plain brown girl. Himself the son of a farmer with his own land, ten sons and two daughters, all married and doing well. There she was, poorer than a skinned rabbit, and not that pretty. Was he looking for a woman who would not flinch at hard work?

Somehow, borrowing from his father, from his brothers, working two, three 105 jobs at the shipyards, in the fields, with Maggie taking in sewing and laundry, cleaning houses, saving, saving, saving, they opened their store; and were married. Days, weeks, years of days, weeks of days, weeks of inventory and cleaning and waiting on people and watching over the dry-goods store, which became a hardware store in the sixties while the one store became two. They were prosperous; they were respected; they owned property. At seventy she now wanted for nothing. Long gone was the dream of a schoolhouse and little children who skinned their knees and the teaching of the ABCs. Some days she imagined she had two lives and she preferred the original dream to the flesh-and-blood reality.

Now, at least, she no longer had to fight bitterly with her pompous, self-satisfied, driven, blaspheming husband, who worked seven days a week, sixteen hours a day, money-grubbing and mean though—outwardly—flamboyantly generous; a man who lost interest in her bed after her first and only son, Thomas Jr., arrived broken in heart, spirit, and brain upon delivery; a son whose only true achievement in life was to illegitimately produce Edward by some equally brainless waif of a girl, now long vanished; a son who practically thrust the few-week-old infant into Maggie's arms, then flew off to a life of waste, sloth, petty crime, and finally a menial job in one of her stores and an ignoble marriage to a woman who could not conceal her greedy wish for Maggie to die.

Her life now was life that no longer had bite or spit or fire. She no longer worked. She no longer had to worry about Thomas's philandering and what pretty young thing he was messing with now. She no longer had the little boy whom Providence seemed to have sent her to maintain her sanity, to moor her to the Earth, and to give her vast energies focus.

In a world not real, is there truly guilt in willing reality to cohere through the life of another? Is that such a great sin? Maggie had turned to the boy—young, brown, handsome—to hold on to the world itself. She now saw that clearly. How did it happen? The mental slipping and sliding that allowed her to meld and mess and confuse her life with his, his rights with her wants, his life with her wish? He would not be like his father or his grandfather; he would rise up, go to school, be strong, be honest, upright. He would be; she would be ... a feat of legerdemain; a sorcery of vicariousness in which his victory was her victory. He was her champion. Her hope.

Now he was gone. And now she had to come to terms with this news of his being "gay," as the world called what she had been taught was an unholy abomination. Slowly it all came together in her mind's eye: Edward.

110   He should have known better. I should have known better. I must learn better.

VII

They stood there at the end of the row, all of them waiting for the tractor to arrive and for the Reverend Hezekiah Barden to save the soul of Morton Henry.

Morton saw them standing there from his mount atop the green John Deere as it bounced across the broken soil. Maggie could make out the expression on his face: confusion. Three blacks and a white man out in the fields to see him. Did his house burn down? His wife die? The President declare war on Russia?

A big, red-haired, red-faced man, his face had so many freckles he appeared splotched. He had a big chew of tobacco in his left jaw and he spat out the brown juice as he came up the edge of the row and put the clutch in neutral.

"How you all today? Miss Maggie?"

115   "Hey, Morton."

Barden started right up, thumbs in his suspenders, and reared back on his heels. "Now I spect you're a God-fearing man?"

"Beg pardon?"

"I even spect you go to church from time to time?"

"Church? Miss Maggie, I—"

120   The Reverend held up his hand. "And I warrant you that your preacher— where *do* you go to church, son?"

"I go to—wait a minute. What's going on here? Miss Maggie—"

Henrietta piped up. "It's Sunday! You ain't supposed to be working and plowing fields on a Sunday!"

Morton Henry looked over to Maggie, who stood there in the bright sun, then to Gabriel, as if to beg him to speak, make some sense of this curious event. He scratched his head. "You mean to tell me you all come out here to tell me I ain't suppose to plow this here field?"

"Not on Sunday you ain't. It's the Lord's Day."

"The Lord's Day?" Morton Henry was visibly amused. He tongued at the 125 wad of tobacco in his jaw. "The Lord's Day." He chuckled out loud.

"Now it ain't no laughing matter, young man." The Reverend's voice took on a dark tone.

Morton seemed to be trying to figure out who Gabriel was. He spat. "Well, I tell you, Reverend. If the Lord wants to come plow these fields I'd be happy to let him."

"You …" Henrietta stomped her foot, causing dust to rise. "You can't talk about the Lord like that. You're using His name in vain."

"I'll talk about Him any way I please to." Morton Henry's face became redder by the minute. "I got two jobs, five head of children, and a sick wife, and the Lord don't seem too worried about that. I spect I ain't gone worry to much about plowing this here field on His day none neither."

"Young man, you can't—"   130

Morton Henry looked to Maggie. "Now, Miss Maggie, this is your land, and if you don't want me to plow it, I'll give you back your lease and you can pay me my money and find somebody else to tend this here field!"

Everybody looked at Maggie. How does this look, she couldn't help thinking, a black woman defending a white man against a black minister? Why the *hell* am I here having to do this? she fumed. Childish, hypocritical idiots and fools. Time is just slipping, slipping away and all they have to do is fuss and bother about other folk's business while their own houses are burning down. God save their souls. She wanted to yell this, to cuss them out and stomp away and leave them to their ignorance. But in the end, what good would it do?

She took a deep breath. "Morton Henry. You do what you got to do. Just like the rest of us."

Morton Henry bowed his head to Maggie, "Ma'am," turned to the others with a gloating grin, "Scuse me," put his gear in first, and turned down the next row.

"Well—"   135

Barden began to speak but Maggie just turned, not listening, not wanting to hear, thinking: When, Lord, oh when will we learn? Will we ever? *Respect*, she thought. Oh how complicated.

They followed Maggie, heading back to the house, Gabriel beside her, tall and silent, the afternoon sunrays romping in his black hair. How curious the world had become that she would be asking a white man to exonerate her in the eyes of her own grandson; how strange that at seventy, when she had all the laws and rules down pat, she would have to begin again to learn. But all this stuff and bother would have to come later, for now she felt so, so tired, what with the weekend's activities weighing on her three-score-and-ten-year-old bones and joints; and she wished it were sunset, and she alone on her patio, contemplating the roundness and flatness of the earth, and slipping softly and safely into sleep.

CRITICAL THINKING QUESTIONS

1. If Reverend Barden and Henrietta can be said to represent the values of their community, Tims Creek, then Edward, Gabriel, and Morton Henry represent an implicit challenge to those values.

    a. List the values that the Reverend and Henrietta represent.

    b. List the values that Edward, Gabriel, and Morton represent.

    c. Identify specific passages that show Maggie as one who is caught between these two forces.

2. On page 114, Maggie understands she must "realign her thinking." Describe the stages of Maggie's realigned thinking as she navigates her way between the two forces you described in question 1.

3. Consider the following examples of **figurative language** (*see* Glossary) in Kenan's story:

- the flatness of the earth
- the angel Gabriel
- the dream and sleep

How do these images reveal aspects of Maggie's conflict?

WRITING TOPIC

"The Foundations of the Earth" presents an **implied claim** about the relationship between an individual's attitudes toward homosexuality and his or her religious values. Write an essay in which you first summarize the implied claim and then develop your own argument to defend, challenge, or qualify the claim. Use textual **evidence** as well as evidence from your own direct observations and experience to support your viewpoint.

Ernesto Quiñonez

from *Bodega Dreams* (2000)

Back in Julia de Burgos Junior High, back in the days of my growing up and all that Piri Thomas kinda crap that I will spare you from, there was the English teacher, Mr. Blessington. He kept telling us boys we were all going to end up in jail and that all the girls were going to end up hooking. He would say these things right out loud and the administration wouldn't do anything. I hated Blessington and he knew it. He looked at Blanca with the eyes of a repressed rapist. He thought he was smooth but what he came out looking was creepy. He'd come to school in a suit and tell us that a man with a suit is a man that is valuable and that a man without a suit has no worth. He always did Robert Frost poems with us, which were all right, but after a while we started to hate Robert Frost. Blessington thought he was doing us a service, and that was his error. He was one of those upper-middle-class people who think highly of themselves because they could be making money or something, but no, they have taken the high road and have chosen to "help" poor kids from the ghetto.

On the other hand the science teacher, Jose Tapia, was always lecturing us on how fortunate we were because we were young and Latin. His speeches were at times so fiery and full of passion that every year the principal would try to make Tapia the gym teacher, in hopes of cutting down Tapia's influence over us. But as a science teacher Tapia was state certified and was appointed to our school so there'was no way for the principal to get rid of him.

And he didn't want to be called Mr. Tapia, simply Tapia.

One day when Sapo and me were in the eighth grade, Tapia told us, "You speak two languages, you are worth two people." Sapo retorted, "What about the pope? He speaks like a hundred languages, but he ain't worth jack." The class was rolled.

"Sapo, do you think the pope would be the pope if he didn't know his hun-   5
dred languages?" Tapia asked after the laughter died down.

"Nah, if he didn't speak a hundred languages he'd still be pope, because he's white. All popes are white. I ain't never seen no black pope. I ain't seen a Spanish pope, either."

"Hey, Tapia," I said, "I never even seen a black nun." Of course we were just stalling. The truth was we hadn't done our homework and wanted to kill time.

"Or a Chinese nun. All I've ever seen are white nuns," Edwin jumped in, so I figured he hadn't done his homework either. "You can't have a black pope if there are no black nuns." I hated Edwin. When he borrowed a pencil he never gave it back and when school was almost over, he always borrowed loose-leaf paper because he didn't see the point of buying a new notebook.

"Yeah, a black nun!" Sapo shouted in agreement.

"Julio, can you shut him up?" Blanca whispered to me. I always sat next to   10
Blanca. I would leave my science book at home on purpose so I could use the excuse of sharing hers. Tapia understood this and, even though we had assigned seats, would always let me move.

"No," I whispered back at Blanca. "Sapo has a point."

"The point is Sapo hasn't done his homework."

"I haven't done mine, either," I said.

"Then this book"—she pulled the science text we were sharing toward her side of the desk—"does you no good."

"Look, forget about the pope," Tapia continued. "I don't care about the   15
pope. The pope is not one of my students. The pope has a good job and there

are black nuns and Chinese nuns, too, but that doesn't matter. All that matters is you. I care about you. And I played the same games when I was your age. If you haven't done your homework just tell me." Hands shot up.

Tapia sighed loudly. "Edwin, you didn't do your homework?"

"Yeah, I did."

"Well?"

"Well, I did it, I just didn't bring it." The class laughed and Tapia looked at his roll book.

20   "All right, Edwin, you live on 102nd and Third. That's three blocks from here. You better get your homework at lunchtime or you'd better have it done by then." Edwin nodded his head.

"Sapo, your homework?"

"I didn't do it."

"Why didn't you do it?"

"Because Mr. Blessington told me I was going to end up in jail, so why waste my time doing homework?" We all laughed.

25   "Sapo, don't you want to prove Blessington wrong?"

"Nah, I'd rather not do my homework."

Tapia got upset. He threw down the roll book and began to yell at us. "I don't care what Blessington's been telling you! If you are here it is because you want to be, right? Otherwise don't even come to school, just stay on the street. You can make more money selling pot on the stairwells than coming to my classroom, but if you come—and I want you to come, I like having you here—all I ask is that you make an effort! That's all I ask. Don't give me this nonsense about what Mr. Blessington is telling you. You guys are smart enough to know that it's up to you to become what you want to be. So why even listen to him? I've heard what he says. It's all nonsense." Tapia pointed at one of the girls. "Rita Moreno, she was once like you, is Rita Moreno hooking?" Tapia then pointed at one of the guys. "Reggie Jackson, he was once as young as you, he's half Puerto Rican, is Reggie in jail? They worked hard. That's what you have to do. Just do your work and don't pay attention to Blessington."

So we all quieted down and did our work, even Sapo, although he copied off me. Sapo always copied me but it was no big deal. The next period was English and we hated it because it was Blessington. I was in no mood for Robert Frost, that white-assed crusty old man from some cow state. But I couldn't say that to Blessington. Instead, as politely as I could, I asked, "Mr. Blessington, why do we always do Robert Frost, why can't we do someone else?"

"Because Robert Frost," he said, slowly shaking his head in disbelief as if I was asking something real stupid, "is a major American poet."

30   "Well, I heard that Julia de Burgos was a poet; why don't we do some of her poems?" I said, and the class jumped in with me.

"That's right," Lucy, Blanca's Pentecostal friend whom we used to call Chewbacca, chimed in, "why did they name the school after her? She must have been important."

"Yeah, they didn't name the school Robert Frost Junior High, why we always reading him?" someone else asked. Truth was, I was happy we were killing time. I wanted those forty-five minutes in his class to fly. I wanted to keep this discussion going for as long as possible.

"If any of you have noticed since September," Blessington pointed out, "this is English class, not Spanish. Julia-day-Burgos"—he pronounced her name with a thick accent—"wrote only in Spanish."

"But maybe she wrote in English too. I write in Spanish and in English sometimes," Blanca said to him. Every time Blanca spoke Blessington would leer. It was one of those cartoon monster smiles, where the monster rubs his hands as he thinks of something dastardly.

"Listen, you people"—he always called us you people—"Julia-day-Burgos 35 is so obscure it would be hard to find a single poem of hers. In any language." I turned to Blanca and, whispering, asked what *obscure* meant. Sapo was quietly drawing all this time. He drew terribly, but it never stopped him. He mostly did it because he was bored. But I knew he was listening and could jump in any minute.

"But if she is so unknown," I said confidently, emphasizing the word Blanca had provided to let Blessington know that I knew what *obscure* meant, "then I agree with Lucy, why did they name an entire school after her? Why not after someone famous?"

"Finally, a good question," Blessington said, adjusting his tie and buttoning up his blazer. "I'll tell you why: because the people in this district are simpletons, that's why. District Four has no idea what it's doing. The name they chose for this school was probably the worst name they could choose. Why, we teachers didn't even know who she was when they renamed this place."

"Mr. Tapia did," Sapo piped up, leaving his drawing for a minute. We all knew what Blessington was saying was that none of the white teachers knew who she was, and they were the only teachers that mattered.

"Oh, him," Blessington said in a tired voice. "Him again. Well, I heard he's a good science teacher," he said with a smirk, "but we're in English now. You people need to get on with today's work." And it was all right with me because we had chopped off at least fifteen minutes of the period. Blessington then went to the board and wrote, "Analogies Between Frost's Poems and New York City." I turned around and asked Blanca what *analogies* meant. She told me. I laughed. "What similarities?" I called out. Blessington was upset now. 40

"End of discussion," he said. "Get out your homework." Blessington walked over to Sapo's desk.

"Enrique, where's your homework?" Blessington asked.

"I'm going to jail, so why bother, right?" Sapo kept drawing. "Yo'r the smart guy here, right, can't you figure that out yo'self?" The class went "Oooooh," which Blessington took as a challenge.

"You'll be lucky to even make jail," he said to Sapo.

"Why you snapping at me? I said you were right." 45

"I know I'm right. I'm doing all you people a favor. I say these things to you so you can maybe prove me wrong. Now, it's sad to say, but I've yet to see one of my Puerto Rican students, just one, prove me wrong. And I know it's not going to be Sapo here." Blessington then leaned over and took Sapo's drawing from him and crumpled it in his hands. Sapo got so mad, he shot straight up from his seat and thrust himself at Blessington so they were face to face.

"Thass right, I won't prove you wrong b'cause I'm going to jail for jamming your wife." The class was silent because that wasn't a snap any longer but an insult. They stared each other down for a second or two before Sapo turned around and headed for the door. "Where do you think you're going?" Blessington yelled, and went after Sapo, grabbing him by the shoulder.

"Don't touch me, man!" Sapo yelled, but Blessington didn't listen. I got up from my seat and went over to Sapo.

"Yo, take a chill pill," I said to Sapo. Blessington yelled at me, "I can handle this. Sit back down!" He didn't let go of Sapo. Sapo started to pull himself away and that's when Blessington made the mistake of putting Sapo in a headlock.

50   "Yo, you choking him!" I yelled, but Blessington kept at it, all the while cursing at Sapo. Blanca and her friend Lucy started to run out of the room to get the teacher next door. Blessington released Sapo and went after Blanca. And that's when Sapo jumped him from behind. Sapo crawled on Blessington as if Blessington were going to give him a piggyback ride. Before Blessington could shake Sapo free, Sapo dug his teeth into the base of the teacher's neck. Blessington screamed; the blood spurted out, running down his back and staining his white shirt collar crimson. Sapo scrambled off Blessington's back as Blessington fell to his knees, pressing the wound with his hands. Then Sapo came around and grabbed Blessington's face in his hands and pulled it toward his own. Sapo spat out a chunk of Blessington's flesh, bouncing it off Blessington's left cheekbone. Covered in blood and saliva, Blessington's eyes were frozen in disbelief. He wasn't screaming. He was in shock. It was only when he saw a piece of his own flesh on the floor that he registered what had happened, and passed out.

Standing in front of the classroom Sapo smiled as only Sapo could; he slowly turned to the class, showing us his shining red teeth. He then calmly walked out of the room. Everyone was stunned. Blanca was the first one to shake herself and ran out of the room. "Help us, help us, Blessington's dying!" she kept yelling down the hall. A minute later the school nurse arrived. When she saw all that blood on the floor she took off her smock and put pressure on Blessington's neck. Meanwhile I went looking for Sapo. He had stopped by the bathroom to rinse his mouth and when he saw me he laughed.

"The nigga had that shit coming." He spat water.

"Sapo, bro, what you gonna do?"

"I could give two fucks," he said. "I never felt better. It's as if I let some fucken courier pigeon go free." At that minute Tapia walked into the bathroom, his face red with fury. It was the same anger he would show us when we let him down by not behaving, by not doing work or getting in trouble.

"Did he really have you in a headlock?" Tapia asked Sapo.   55

"Yeah, I saw it all, Ta—"

"Shut up! I'm asking Sapo!" I quieted down and backed away. Sapo nodded and Tapia paced the bathroom. He sighed loudly. He stopped in front of Sapo and placed both arms on top of Sapo's shoulders.

"Look at me," Tapia said. "Don't say that he had you in a headlock—"

I jumped in. "But he did, Tapia—"

"Shut up, Chino! *Coño*, just shut up!" This time I did for good. Tapia   60
breathed hard. His eyes were watery. "Sapo, look at me. If you say he had you in a headlock, when he recovers he will deny it. And it won't matter which of your friends backs you up, they will believe Blessington. Now, you listen to me and you listen good because I don't want you to go to Juvie. The police are on their way. When they ask you why you bit Blessington, you tell them you heard voices. You got that?" Sapo nodded. "You tell them the voices said to bite Blessington. You don't say Blessington said all this bullshit to you or that he had you in a headlock, you just say you heard voices. You got that?" Sapo understood and a slow smirk began to form on his big lips as he nodded. When he had completely registered what Tapia had told him, that smirk became a full-blown smile.

That whole year Sapo saw a shrink and thus avoided juvenile detention. He must have lied, and I bet for a while he loved the opportunity to have an audience for those stories he was so good at making up. It was like getting away with biting Blessington's neck all over again. But then he got tired of it, started blowing off sessions, and ultimately he dropped out of school and moved out on his own. That year something happened to Sapo. He had always been Sapo but that year, after biting Blessington, he started turning into someone who wasn't afraid to die. It was the beginning of the adult Sapo. His was the sneaker you wouldn't want to step on because "sorry" wouldn't cut it. He became that person you wouldn't want to cut off in traffic because he'd pull a knife and slice you. He became that person you wanted on your side so you could unleash him on your enemies. Like the rest of us, Sapo was still a kid, but he was already turning into something else. He had reached that point in existence where he wasn't afraid to hurt anyone who threatened his only source of meaning, his love for himself.

CRITICAL THINKING QUESTIONS

1. Identify the two opposing arguments Mr. Blessington and Mr. Tapia present regarding their students' potential.

2. Do negative arguments carry a stronger emotional impact than positive ones? Support your conclusion with evidence from the story, as well as examples from history.

WRITING TOPIC

Unfortunately, stories involving mass shootings in high schools and universities have become common news headlines in America. Often the shooter is an individual who seems to be someone who feels like an outsider, one who does not feel integrated into his or her community. Do some research on this topic, as well as recall and analyze your own experiences and observations as a high school and/or college student. Based on your research and analysis, what factors do you think push some students to the fringe? Advocate specific approaches and strategies high schools and colleges might take to reduce the anger within such individuals.

———————————————

POETRY

Michael Cleary

Burning Dreams on the Sun (1992)

LONG BEACH, Calif. (AP)—A truck driver with 45 weather balloons rigged to a lawn chair took a 45 minute ride ... up to 16,000 feet before he got cold, shot some balloons with a BB gun and crashed into a power line.

Were there too many turnaround loads,
distance measured by all-night diners,
hours yawning through too much coffee,
kidneys throbbing again at 3 a.m.?
Were there too many nights on your hands   5
that hung like chains from the wheel,
monotonous, humdrum motion
droning away the sound of your dream?
And did the darkness ever whisper,
it might not work, it might not,   10
nearly grounding you in mortal shame,
too foolish ever to dream again?
Icarus, too, must have felt like you,
restless with impudent wonder.
No labyrinth could hold him;   15
he flew on wings of feathers and wax
until he burned his dreams on the sun.
But no matter. For a time,
you dared to leave the darkful land,
rising high in wacky flight   20
like an uncouth god, purified by light.

CRITICAL THINKING QUESTIONS

1. What stereotypes are associated with truck drivers?

2. How does Cleary's poem refute those stereotypes?

WRITING TOPIC

Literary works often use allusions, meaning the author refers to characters and/or events from other works of literature for reasons of drawing comparisons and/or promoting assumptions between his or her work and the one mentioned. In this poem, the author does just that with his mention of Icarus, a character from Greek mythology. If you are unfamiliar with Icarus, research the character. After you understand the basic storyline of Icarus, consider the following: What is the poet's implied **claim of value** about Icarus's and the truck driver's flights? Are you convinced? Please explain.

Countee Cullen

Incident (1925)

> Once riding in old Baltimore,
>   Heart-filled, head-filled with glee,
> I saw a Baltimorean
>   Keep looking straight at me.
>
> Now I was eight and very small,
>   And he was no whit bigger,
> And so I smiled, but he poked out
>   His tongue and called me, "Nigger."
>
> I saw the whole of Baltimore
>   From May until December:
> Of all the things that happened there
>   That's all that I remember.

5

10

CRITICAL THINKING QUESTION

"Sticks and stones may break my bones, but words will never hurt me." This playground jingle suggests that name-calling is harmless, at least physically. But is it? What happens when we label certain individuals, as for example, "enviros," "right-wing Bible-thumpers," "illegal aliens"? To what degree, if any, are such labels harmful?

WRITING TOPIC

Sometimes an incident carries with it such emotional force that it blocks any positive experiences that might have been enjoyed. Intellectually, you might argue that it is best to ignore the negative and focus on the positive, but emotions are so powerful that they usually prevail. Can you recall and describe an incident when the power of your emotions overwhelmed all the rational arguments you knew to be correct?

Emily Dickinson

Much Madness is divinest Sense (1862)

> Much Madness is divinest Sense—
> To a discerning Eye—
> Much Sense—the starkest Madness—
> 'Tis the Majority
> In this, as All, prevail— 5
> Assent—and you are sane—
> Demur—you're straightway dangerous—
> And handled with a Chain—

CRITICAL THINKING QUESTIONS

1. What **value assumptions** about "Madness" does Dickinson's poem refute? To what extent do you agree or disagree with the poet? Cite evidence from your own observations and experiences to support your viewpoint. Consider how some people break the limits placed upon them by others who consider them different. For example, if you have seen the movie *The Theory of Everything* (2014), how does it affect your thinking?

2. Majority rule is a democratic principle that we value. As the antithesis of monarchical dictatorship, it is meant to guarantee a government that is "of the people, for the people, by the people." Dickinson's poem, however, implies that "Majority" is anything but liberating (lines 7–8). Do you agree or disagree with the poet's perspective on the majority?

WRITING TOPIC

Read "Crazy Courage" by Alma Luz Villanueva (page 148). Does Michael's "crazy courage" support Dickinson's viewpoint on madness? Build on your response to question 1, and create your own argument about individuality. Cite evidence from the poems, as well as your own experiences and observations.

T. S. Eliot

The Love Song of J. Alfred Prufrock (1915)

S o'io credesse che mia risposta fosse
A persona che mai tornasse al mondo,
Questa fiamma staria senza piu scosse.
Ma perciocche giammai di questo fondo
5 *Non torno vivo alcun, s 'i'odo il vero,*
Senza tema d'infamia ti rispondo.[1]

Let us go then, you and I,
When the evening is spread out against the sky
Like a patient etherised upon a table;
10 Let us go, through certain half-deserted streets,
The muttering retreats
Of restless nights in one-night cheap hotels
And sawdust restaurants with oyster-shells:
Streets that follow like a tedious argument
15 Of insidious intent
To lead you to an overwhelming question …
Oh, do not ask, "What is it?"
Let us go and make our visit.

In the room the women come and go
20 Talking of Michelangelo.

The yellow fog that rubs its back upon the window-panes,
The yellow smoke that rubs its muzzle on the window-panes
Licked its tongue into the corners of the evening,
Lingered upon the pools that stand in drains,
25 Let fall upon its back the soot that falls from chimneys,
Slipped by the terrace, made a sudden leap,
And seeing that it was a soft October night,
Curled once about the house, and fell asleep.

And indeed there will be time
30 For the yellow smoke that slides along the street,
Rubbing its back upon the window-panes;
There will be time, there will be time

---

[1] "If I believed that my reply were made / to one who could ever climb to the world again / this flame would shake me no more. But since no shade / ever returned—if what I am told is true— / from this blind world into the living light, / without fear of dishonor I answer you." *Dante Alighieri, The Inferno*, trans. Henry Wadsworth Longfellow *(The Divine Comedy of Dante Translated by Henry Wadsworth Longfellow,* August 1997) (27:61–66):etext.

To prepare a face to meet the faces that you meet;
There will be time to murder and create,
And time for all the works and days of hands 35
That lift and drop a question on your plate;
Time for you and time for me,
And time yet for a hundred indecisions,
And for a hundred visions and revisions,
Before the taking of a toast and tea. 40

  In the room the women come and go
Talking of Michelangelo.

  And indeed there will be time
To wonder, "Do I dare?" and, "Do I dare?"
Time to turn back and descend the stair, 45
With a bald spot in the middle of my hair—
[They will say: "How his hair is growing thin!"]
My morning coat, my collar mounting firmly to the chin,
My necktie rich and modest, but asserted by a simple pin—
[They will say: "But how his arms and legs are thin!"] 50
Do I dare
Disturb the universe?
In a minute there is time
For decisions and revisions which a minute will reverse.

  For I have known them all already, known them all:— 55
Have known the evenings, mornings, afternoons,
I have measured out my life with coffee spoons;
I know the voices dying with a dying fall
Beneath the music from a farther room.
  So how should I presume? 60

  And I have known the eyes already, known them all—
The eyes that fix you in a formulated phrase,
And when I am formulated, sprawling on a pin,
When I am pinned and wriggling on the wall,
Then how should I begin 65
To spit out all the butt-ends of my days and ways?
And how should I presume?

  And I have known the arms already, known them all—
Arms that are braceleted and white and bare
[But in the lamplight, downed with light brown hair!] 70
Is it perfume from a dress
That makes me so digress?

Arms that lie along a table, or wrap about a shawl.
  And should I then presume?
  75 And how should I begin?

*   *   *

Shall I say, I have gone at dusk through narrow streets
And watched the smoke that rises from the pipes
Of lonely men in shirt-sleeves, leaning out of windows? ...

  I should have been a pair of ragged claws
80 Scuttling across the floors of silent seas.

*   *   *

And the afternoon, the evening, sleeps so peacefully!
Smoothed by long fingers,
Asleep ... tired ... or it malingers,
Stretched on the floor, here beside you and me.
85 Should I, after tea and cakes and ices,
Have the strength to force the moment to its crisis?
But though I have wept and fasted, wept and prayed,
Though I have seen my head [grown slightly bald] brought
    in upon a platter,
I am no prophet—and here's no great matter;
90 I have seen the moment of my greatness flicker,
And I have seen the eternal Footman hold my coat, and snicker,
And in short, I was afraid.

  And would it have been worth it, after all,
    After the cups, the marmalade, the tea,
95 Among the porcelain, among some talk of you and me,
Would it have been worth while,
To have bitten off the matter with a smile,
To have squeezed the universe into a ball
To roll it toward some overwhelming question,
100 To say: "I am Lazarus, come from the dead,
    Come back to tell you all, I shall tell you all"—
  If one, settling a pillow by her head,

  Should say: "That is not what I meant at all.
  That is not it, at all."

105   And would it have been worth it, after all,

  Would it have been worth while,
  After the sunsets and the dooryards and the sprinkled streets,
  After the novels, after the teacups, after the skirts that trail along
    the floor—

And this, and so much more?—
It is impossible to say just what I mean!   110
But as if a magic lantern threw the nerves in patterns on a screen:
Would it have been worth while
If one, settling a pillow or throwing off a shawl,
And turning toward the window, should say:

   "That is not it at all,   115
   That is not what I meant, at all."

* * *

No! I am not Prince Hamlet, nor was meant to be;
Am an attendant lord, one that will do
To swell a progress, start a scene or two,
Advise the prince; no doubt, an easy tool,   120
Deferential, glad to be of use,
Politic, cautious, and meticulous;
Full of high sentence but a bit obtuse;
At times, indeed, almost ridiculous—
Almost, at times, the Fool.   125

   I grow old ... I grow old ...
I shall wear the bottoms of my trousers rolled.

   Shall I part my hair behind? Do I dare to eat a peach?
I shall wear white flannel trousers, and walk upon the beach.
I have heard the mermaids singing, each to each.   130

   I do not think that they will sing to me.

   I have seen them riding seaward on the waves
Combing the white hair of the waves blown back
When the wind blows the water white and black.

   We have lingered in the chambers of the sea   135
By sea-girls wreathed with seaweed red and brown
Till human voices wake us, and we drown.

CRITICAL THINKING QUESTIONS

1. In presenting the reader with J. Alfred Prufrock, Eliot is also presenting an argument about an individual's sense of self in modern society. Articulate a claim for this argument.

2. What specific evidence is offered in the poem to support the claim you wrote in question 1?

3. Add your voice to the vast array of interpretations for the poem's closing three lines. In doing so, apply your creative thinking skills: Think boldly and freely and without censuring your thinking.

WRITING TOPIC

Does the claim you articulated apply exclusively to Prufrock, or would you extend it to apply generally to persons today? Write your own argument that either limits or extends the poem's claim; use evidence from the poem and your own experience to support your claim.

Jack Gilbert

Trying to Sleep (2005)

> The girl shepherd on the farm beyond has been
> taken from school now she is twelve, and her life is over.
> I got my genius brother a summer job in the mills
> and he stayed all his life. I lived with a woman four
> 5   years who went crazy later, escaped from the hospital,
> hitchhiked across America terrified and in the snow
> without a coat, and was raped by most men who gave her
> a ride. I crank my heart even so and it turns over.
> Ranges high in the sun over continents and eruptions
> 10   of mortality, through winds and immensities of rain
> falling for miles. Until all the world is overcome
> by what goes up and up in us, singing and dancing
> and throwing down flowers as we continue north taking
> the maimed with us, keeping the sad parts carefully.

CRITICAL THINKING QUESTIONS

1. Gilbert lists examples of events that should be very discouraging, if not depressing, to anyone. However, he tell us, "I crank my heart even so and it turns over." What idea is he expressing through this metaphorical language? What does Gilbert mean by "crank" and "turn over"?

2. In a single sentence, state a claim the poet seems to be making about the human spirit. What are your thoughts about this perspective?

WRITING TOPC

Consider the last words of the poem: "taking the maimed with us, keeping the sad parts carefully." What do these words mean to you? In what ways does a person's past disappointment and heartaches positively develop his or her identify over time? Can you identify an experience in your past that taught you painful lessons that have ultimately made a positive impact upon who you have become?

Judy Grahn

Ella, In a Square Apron, Along Highway 80 (1971)

She's a copperheaded waitress,
tired and sharp-worded, she hides
her bad brown tooth behind a wicked
smile, and flicks her ass
out of habit, to fend off the pass   5
that passes for affection.
She keeps her mind the way men
keep a knife—keen to strip the game
down to her size. She has a thin spine,
swallows her eggs cold, and tells lies.   10
She slaps a wet rag at the truck drivers
if they should complain. She understands
the necessity for pain, turns away
the smaller tips, out of pride, and
keeps a flask under the counter. Once,   15
she shot a lover who misused her child.
Before she got out of jail, the courts had pounced
and given the child away. Like some isolated lake,
her flat blue eyes take care of their own stark
bottoms. Her hands are nervous, curled, ready to scrape. 20
The common woman is as common
as a rattlesnake.

CRITICAL THINKING QUESTIONS

1. Compare and contrast your response to the snake imagery in the poem's opening and closing lines.

2. What is the speaker's claim of value about Ella as "the common woman"?

3. On which rhetorical appeal (***ethos***, ***logos***, ***pathos***) is this poem's argument based? Is this an effective persuasive strategy? Why or why not?

WRITING TOPIC

How does Grahn's waitress attempt to maintain her individuality within her environment? Are her efforts successful? What pressure does your environment exert on your sense of individuality?

———————

Joy Harjo

Everybody Has a Heartache: A Blues (2013)

In the United Terminal in Chicago at five on a Friday afternoon
The sky is breaking with rain and wind and all the flights
Are delayed forever. We will never get to where we are going
And there's no way back to where we've been.
5 The sun and the moon have disappeared to an island far from
anywhere.

Everybody has a heartache-

The immense gatekeeper of Gate Z-100 keeps his cool.
This guardian of the sky teases me and makes me smile through
the mess,
Building up his airline by stacking it against the company I usually
travel:
10 *Come on over to our side, we'll treat you nice.*
I laugh as he hands me back my ticket, then he turns to charm
The next customer, his feet tired in his minimum wage shoes.

Everybody has a heartache-

Everyone's mouthing fried, sweet, soft and fat,
15 While we wait for word in the heart of the scrambled beast.
The sparkle of soda wets the dream core.
That woman over, there the color of broth, did what she was told.
It's worked out well as can be expected in a world
Where she was no beauty queen, and was never seen,
20 Always in the back of someplace in the back.
She holds the newest baby. He has the croup.
Shush, shush. Go to sleep, my little baby sheepie.
He sits up front of her with his new crop of teeth.

Everybody has a heartache-

The man with his head bobbing to music no one else can hear   25
speaks to no one, but his body does.
Half his liver is swollen with anger; the other half is trying
To apologize-
What a mess I've made of history, he thinks without thinking.
Mother coming through the screen door, her clothes torn,   30
Whimpering: *it's okay baby, please don't cry.*
Don't cry. Baby don't cry.
And he never cries again.

Everybody has a heartache-

Baby girl dressed to impress, toddles about with lace
on this and ruffle on that—
Her mother's relatives are a few hundred miles away poised to   35
welcome.
They might as well live on a planet of ice cream.
She's a brand new wing, grown up from a family's broken hope.
Smile girl, you carry our joy.
Just don't look down.   40

Everybody has a heartache-

Good-looking girl-woman taps this on her screen
to a stranger she has never seen:
Just before dawn, you're high again beneath a marbled sky,
I was slick fine leather with a drink in my hand.   45
Flying with a comet messenger nobody sees.
The quick visitor predicts that the top will be the bottom
And the bottom will flatten and dive into the sea.
I want to tell her:
You will dine with the lobster king, and   50
You will dance with crabs clicking castanets. You will sleep
Walk beyond the vestibule of sadness with a stranger
You have loved for years.

Everybody has a heartache-

This silence in the noise of the terminal is a mountain of bison skulls.   55
Nobody knows, nobody sees
Unless we're dancing powwow all decked out in flash and beauty
We just don't exist. We've been disappeared to an outlaw cowboy tale.
What were they thinking with all those guns, and those handcuffs,
In a size for babies?   60
They just don't choose to remember.
We're here.

In the terminal of stopped time I was unsteady in the beat,
Driven by a hungry spirit who is drunk with words and songs.
65 What can I do?
I have to take care of it.
The famished spirit eats fire, poetry and pain; it only wants love.

I argue:
You want love?

70 *Do you even know what it looks like, smells like?*

But you cannot argue with hungry spirits.

Everybody has a heartache.

I don't know exactly where I'm going; I only know where I've been,
I want to tell the man who sifted through the wreck to find us here
75 In the blues shack of history.
I feel weight of his heart against my cheek.
His hand is on my back pulling me to him in the dark, to a place
No soldiers can reach.

We will all find our way, no matter fire leaping through holes in
jump time,
80 No matter earthquake, or the breaking of love spilling over
the drek of matter
In the ether, stacking one burden
Against the other.

We have heartache.

Joy Harjo March 18, 2013 United Terminal C, Chicago and en
route between Chicago O'Hare and Newport, Virginia
Revised July 19, 2013 Taos, NM, and July 22, 2013 Glenpool, OK
Revised September 28, 2013 Blairstown, NY

CRITICAL THINKING QUESTIONS

1. In the opening stanza, how does Harjo use the airport terminal as a metaphor?

2. What is the claim of the poem?

WRITING TOPIC

How does the speaker connect the individuals she observes at the airport?
How are they different? How are they the same? Do the descriptions seem
negative or positive? Is there optimism in the connection of heartache? Give
examples for support.

Claude McKay

Outcast (1920)

For the dim regions whence my fathers came
My spirit, bondaged by the body, longs.
Words felt, but never heard, my lips would frame;
My soul would sing forgotten jungle songs.
I would go back to darkness and to peace,   5
But the great western world holds me in fee,
And I may never hope for full release
While to its alien gods I bend my knee.
Something in me is lost, forever lost,
Some vital thing has gone out of my heart,   10
And I must walk the way of life a ghost
Among the sons of earth, a thing apart.
For I was born, far from my native clime,
Under the white man's menace, out of time.

CRITICAL THINKING QUESTIONS

1. Use the rhetorical triangle of appeals to analyze and evaluate this poem as an argument:
   a. How does the speaker appeal to *ethos*?
   b. How does the speaker appeal to *logos*?
   c. How does the speaker use appeal to *pathos*?

2. In your view, which rhetorical appeal is most persuasive?

WRITING TOPIC

In your mind, what images does the term *outcast* evoke? In today's social climate, what attributes contribute to one being labeled "outcast"? Do you think that someone's accepting the label for himself or herself reveals a weakness or unwillingness to be confident in his or her originality? Contrarily, do you feel the very fact that people are labeled "outcasts" reveals a harshness of human nature in judging others? Have you ever felt like an outcast? Explain.

Dwight Okita

In Response to Executive Order 9066 (1992)

All Americans of Japanese Descent Must Report to Relocation Centers

Dear Sirs:
Of course I'll come. I've packed my galoshes
and three packets of tomato seeds. Denise calls them
"love apples." My father says where we're going
5   they won't grow.
I am a fourteen-year-old girl with bad spelling
and a messy room. If it helps any, I will tell you
I have always felt funny using chopsticks
and my favorite food is hot dogs.
10   My best friend is a white girl named Denise—
we look at boys together. She sat in front of me
all through grade school because of our names:
O'Connor, Ozawa. I know the back of Denise's head very well.
I tell her she's going bald. She tells me I copy on tests.
15   We're best friends.
I saw Denise today in Geography class.
She was sitting on the other side of the room.
"You're trying to start a war," she said, "giving secrets away
to the Enemy, Why can't you keep your big mouth shut?"
20   I didn't know what to say.
I gave her a packet of tomato seeds
and asked her to plant them for me, told her
when the first tomato ripens
to miss me

CRITICAL THINKING QUESTIONS

1. Why does the author choose a fourteen-year-old girl to write this letter? What does this persona or voice offer the reader?

2. Would the letter be more or less convincing if it were written by the girl's father? Explain your answer.

3. What evidence might the father select to prove that this order is unfair to innocent people?

4. The narrator in the poem is being relocated to a detention camp. At age fourteen, she does not understand what she has done to deserve this fate.

Look on the Internet for comments by young refugees living in camps today. How does the situation shape their attitudes?

WRITING TOPIC

During World War II, on February 19, 1942, President Franklin D. Roosevelt issued "Executive Order 9066," which authorized removing more than 100,000 Americans of Japanese descent from their homes and sending them to internment camps. The Civil Liberties Act of 1989 provided a settlement to these people for the mistreatment they had received. Research this topic and then write an argument defending or refuting such payments (reparations).

———————

Mary Oliver

Wild Geese (1986)

You do not have to be good.
You do not have to walk on your knees
for a hundred miles through the desert, repenting.
You only have to let the soft animal of your body love
    what it loves.
Tell me about despair, yours, and I will tell you mine.   5
Meanwhile the world goes on.
Meanwhile the sun and the clear pebbles of the rain
are moving across the landscapes,
over the prairies and the deep trees,
the mountains and the rivers.   10
Meanwhile the wild geese, high in the clean blue air,
are heading home again.
Whoever you are, no matter how lonely,
the world offers itself to your imagination,
calls to you like the wild geese, harsh and exciting—   15
over and over announcing your place
in the family of things.

CRITICAL THINKING QUESTIONS

1. What **assumptions** about being "good" does Oliver challenge in the poem's first four lines?

2. How does the phrase "family of things" create a distinct perspective on the idea of community? What implied claim does the poet make about an individual's place within his or her community?

3. On which rhetorical appeal—*pathos, logos, ethos*—does the poet rely? Cite examples and discuss their effect on you as a reader.

4. How might the calls of the wild geese be both "harsh and exciting" (line 15)?

WRITING TOPIC

Read Wallace Stevens's "Disillusionment of Ten O'Clock" (page 147). Compare and contrast the ideas about the value of imagination in Stevens's and Oliver's poems. What role does imagination play in your daily life? Create your own claim about the value of imagination, and support your argument with evidence from the two poems and your own experiences and observations. For a different perspective on imagination, you can read and cite evidence from Michael Cleary's "Burning Dreams on the Sun" (page 127).

———————————

Edwin Arlington Robinson

Richard Cory (1897)

Whenever Richard Cory went down town,
We people on the pavement looked at him:
He was a gentleman from sole to crown,
Clean favored, and imperially slim.
5   And he was always quietly arrayed,
And he was always human when he talked;
But still he fluttered pulses when he said;
"Good-morning," and he glittered when he walked.
And he was rich—yes, richer than a king—
10   And admirably schooled in every grace:
In fine, we thought that he was everything
To make us wish that we were in his place.
So on we worked, and waited for the light,
And went without the meat, and cursed the bread;
15   And Richard Cory, one calm summer night,
Went home, and put a bullet through his head.

CRITICAL THINKING QUESTION

What assumptions do the townspeople make about Richard Cory? On what evidence are those assumptions based?

WRITING TOPIC

The poem urges the reader to accept a generalization—that money does not make people happy. Does your experience cause you to support or reject that generalization? Can you identify any famous people who, either literally or figuratively, are modern-day Richard Corys? Please explain fully.

Muriel Rukeyser

The Lost Romans (1978)

Where are they, not those young men, not those young women
Who walked among the bullet-headed Romans with their roads,
their symmetry, their iron rule—
We know the dust and bones they are gone to, those young Romans
Who stood against the bitter imperial, their young green life with its poems—   5
Where are the poems made music against the purple
Setting their own purple up for a living sign,
Bright fire of some forgotten future against empire,
Their poems in the beautiful Roman tongue
Sex-songs, love-poems, freedom-songs?   10
Not only the young, but the old and in chains,
The slaves in their singing, the fierce northern gentle blond rhythms,
The Judean cantillations, lullabies of Carthage,
Gaul with her cries, all the young Roman rebels,
Where are their songs? Who will unlock them,   15
Who will find them for us, in some undiscovered painted cave
For we need you, sisters, far brothers, poems of our lost Rome.

CRITICAL THINKING QUESTIONS

1. Reading this poem as an argument—that is, as a "call to action"—to whom is the poet addressing and what action is she advocating?

2. On which **rhetorical appeal** does the poet's argument rely? Provide some examples and evaluate their persuasiveness.

WRITING TOPIC

Does Rukeyser's argument speak directly to you as an individual? Why or why not?

———————————

Cathy Song

Lost Sister (1983)

1

In China,
even the peasants
named their first daughters
Jade—
5   the stone that in the far fields
could moisten the dry season,
could make men move mountains
for the healing green of the inner hills
glistening like slices of winter melon.
10   And the daughters were grateful:
They never left home.
To move freely was a luxury
stolen from them at birth.
Instead, they gathered patience;
15   learning to walk in shoes
the size of teacups,
without breaking—
the arc of their movements
as dormant as the rooted willow,
20   as redundant as the farmyard hens.
But they traveled far
in surviving,
learning to stretch the family rice,
to quiet the demons,
25   the noisy stomachs.

2

There is a sister
across the ocean,
who relinquished her name,

diluting jade green
with the blue of the Pacific.   30
Rising with a tide of locusts,
she swarmed with others
to inundate another shore.
In America,
there are many roads   35
and women can stride along with men.
But in another wilderness,
the possibilities,
the loneliness,
can strangulate like jungle vines.   40
The meager provisions and sentiments
of once belonging—
fermented roots, Mah-Jong tiles and firecrackers—set but
a flimsy household
in a forest of nightless cities.   45
A giant snake rattles above,
spewing black clouds into your kitchen.
Dough-faced landlords
slip in and out of your keyholes,
making claims you don't understand,   50
tapping into your communication systems
of laundry lines and restaurant chains.
You find you need China:
your one fragile identification,
a jade link   55
handcuffed to your wrist.
You remember your mother
who walked for centuries,
footless—
and like her,   60
you have left no footprints,
but only because
there is an ocean in between,
the unremitting space of your rebellion.

CRITICAL THINKING QUESTION

The poet implies that the sister should have stayed in China. Do you agree? Why
or why not?

WRITING TOPIC

What value assumptions about the individual and freedom does this poem challenge? Do you agree or disagree with those assumptions? What do you feel the poem expresses about life in China as compared to America? Is the poet making a claim that one culture is superior to the other? Please elaborate.

Gary Soto

Mexicans Begin Jogging (1995)

At the factory I worked
In the fleck of rubber, under the press
Of an oven yellow with flame,
Until the border patrol opened

5   Their vans and my boss waved for us to run.
"Over the fence, Soto," he shouted,
And I shouted that I was American.
"No time for lies," he said, and pressed
A dollar in my palm, hurrying me

10   Through the back door.
Since I was on his time, I ran
And became the wag to a short tail of Mexicans—
Ran past the amazed crowds that lined
The streets and blurred like photographs, in rain.

15   I ran from that industrial road to the soft
Houses where people paled at the turn of an autumn sky.
What could I do but yell *vivas*
To baseball, milkshakes, and those sociologists
Who would clock me

20   As I jog into the next century
On the power of a great, silly grin.

CRITICAL THINKING QUESTION

Word choice or **diction** can be a strong element in a successful argument because words carry with them a range of subtle meanings beyond their literal meanings. Look up the terms **denotation** and **connotation** in the book's Glossary, and then in a paragraph explain the connotative meaning of the word *jogging* as Soto uses it in his poem. How do jogging, baseball, and milkshakes correlate to the world the Mexican workers experience? When, in fact, he is running away from the immigration authorities, why would Soto say, I "jog into the next century"? Why would Mexican immigrants want to begin jogging?

WRITING TOPIC

In the poem, Soto says he is an American; however, his coworkers are illegal immigrants and face deportation. These workers and their employers break the law, and yet our economy seems to depend on just such illegal immigrants to maintain productivity. After reading about immigration as it affects the U.S. economy, create your own **claim of policy** regarding this issue, and list at least three pieces of evidence you might use in its support.

Wallace Stevens

Disillusionment of Ten O'Clock (1954)

The houses are haunted
By white night-gowns.
None are green,
Or purple with green rings,
Or green with yellow rings,   5
Or yellow with blue rings.
None of them are strange,
With socks of lace
And beaded ceintures.
People are not going   10
To dream of baboons and periwinkles.
Only, here and there, an old sailor,
Drunk and asleep in his boots,
Catches tigers
In red weather.   15

CRITICAL THINKING QUESTION

Stevens seems to regret the fact that residents of these houses are lacking in imagination, hence, the key word in the title of the poem, "Disillusionment." Bring to mind a quiet, middle-class residential street in this country. Do you believe the people living on this street have traded their imaginations for the comfort of conformity?

WRITING TOPIC

The poet's underlying assumption here is that not having an imagination is a bad thing; he assumes you agree. Do you? Is it somehow better to be "an old sailor, Drunk and asleep in his boots," than to be someone living without an imagination? Read a definition of the term *imagination*; for this task, go beyond the dictionary and consult a psychology textbook or similar academic work. Write an essay in which you argue that a person can or cannot lead a fully productive life without imagination.

Alma Luz Villanueva

Crazy Courage (1998)

To Michael B.
Why do I think of Michael ...
He came to my fiction class
as a man (dressed in men's
5   clothes); then he came
to my poetry class
as a woman (dressed in women's
clothes; but he was still
a man under the clothes).
10   Was I moved in the face of
such courage (man/woman
woman/man) ...
Was I moved by the gentleness
of his masculinity; the strength
15   of his femininity ...
His presence at the class poetry
reading, dressed in a miniskirt,
high boots, bright purple tights,
a scooped-neck blouse, carrying
a single, living, red rose, in a
20   vase, to the podium (the visitors,
not from the class, shocked—
the young, seen-it-all MTV crowd—
into silence as he's introduced,
"Michael ...") And what it was, I think,
was his perfect dignity, the offering
25   of his living, red rose to the perceptive,

to the blind, to the amused, to the impressed,
to those who would kill him, and
to those who would love him.
And of course I remember the surprise   30
of his foamy breasts as we hugged
goodbye, his face blossomed
open, set apart, the pain of it,
the joy of it (the crazy courage
to be whole, as a rose is   35
whole, as a child is
whole before they're
punished for including
everything in their
innocence).   40

CRITICAL THINKING QUESTIONS

1. In judging Michael, what is the speaker's claim of value about courage? On what evidence is this claim based? Are you convinced?

2. What values underlie our attitudes about nonconformist or unconventional behavior? How do these value assumptions inform our judgments about those individuals who exhibit nonconformist behavior?

WRITING TOPIC

In the United States, we often say we value expressions of individuality, yet people who run counter to prevailing cultural norms sometimes face some degree of discrimination. Using at least two specific examples, argue that this discrimination is either justified or unjustified.

NONFICTION

John Hope Franklin

The Train from Hate (1994)

My pilgrimage from racial apprehension—read just plain confusion—to racial tolerance was early and brief. I was 7 years old, and we lived in the all-black town of Rentiesville, Oklahoma. My father had moved to Tulsa where he hoped to have a law practice that would make it possible for him to support his family. Meanwhile, my mother, sister, and I would occasionally make the journey to Checotah, six miles away, to shop for supplies.

One day, we went down, as usual, by railroad. My mother flagged the train and we boarded. It so happened that when the train stopped, the only place we could enter was the coach reserved for white people. We did not take notice of this, and as the train picked up speed, the conductor entered and told us that we would have to move to the "colored" coach. My mother explained that we were not responsible for where the coach stopped and we had no other alternative to climbing aboard and finding seats as soon as possible. She told him that she could not risk the possible injury of her and her children by going to the "colored" coach while the train was moving. The conductor seemed to agree and said that he would signal to the engineer to stop the train. When the train came to a halt, the conductor did not guide us to the coach for African Americans. Instead, he commanded us to leave the train. We had no alternative to stepping off the train into the woods and beginning the trek back to Rentiesville.

As we trudged along, I began to cry. Taking notice of my sadness, my mother sought to comfort me by saying that it was not all that far to Rentiesville. I assured her that I did not mind the walk, but that man, the conductor, was so mean. Why would he not permit us to ride the train to Checotah?

My mother then gave me my first lesson in race relations. She told me that the laws required racial separation, but that they did not, could not, make us inferior in any way. She assured me that the conductor was not superior because he was white, and I was not inferior because I was black. I must always remember that simple fact, she said. Then she made a statement that is as vivid and clear to me today as the day she uttered it. Under no circumstances, she said, should I be upset or distressed because someone sought to demean me. It took too much energy to hate or even to fight intolerance with one's emotions. She smiled and added that in going home we did not have far to walk.

It would be too much to claim that my mother's calm talk removed a burden 5 from my shoulders. But it is not too much to say that her observations provided a sound basis for my attitudes and conduct from that day to this. At that early age, I had made an important journey. In the future, I remembered that I should not waste my time or energy lamenting the inability of some members of society to take me as I was. Instead, I would use my energies to make me a better person and to distance myself from the perpetrators and purveyors of hate and misunderstanding. I shall always be happy that my mother taught me that the journey to understanding and tolerance was more important than the journey to Checotah.

CRITICAL THINKING QUESTIONS

1. Through his personal experience, Franklin argues for a claim of policy. Can you articulate that claim?

2. What assumptions underlie the thinking of those who put the mother and son off that train?

WRITING TOPIC

Do you recall a time as a child when you witnessed an injustice upon innocent people? In what ways did it change you and/or your views of the world and others? What did you learn from the experience? Was the lesson immediate, or did it take years for you to understand it fully?

Martin Luther King, Jr.

Letter from Birmingham Jail (1963)

April 16, 1963

My Dear Fellow Clergymen:

While confined here in the Birmingham city jail, I came across your recent statement calling my present activities "unwise and untimely." Seldom do I pause to answer criticism of my work and ideas. If I sought to answer all the criticisms that cross my desk, my secretaries would have little time for anything other than such correspondence in the course of the day, and I would have no time for constructive work. But since I feel that you are men of genuine good will and that your criticisms are sincerely set forth, I want to try to answer your statement in what I hope will be patient and reasonable terms.

I think I should indicate why I am here in Birmingham, since you have been influenced by the view which argues against "outsiders coming in." I have the honor of serving as president of the Southern Christian Leadership Conference, an organization operating in every southern state, with headquarters in Atlanta, Georgia. We have some eighty-five affiliated organizations across the South, and one of them is the Alabama Christian Movement for Human Rights. Frequently we share staff, educational and financial resources with our affiliates. Several months ago the affiliate here in Birmingham asked us to be on call to engage in a nonviolent direct-action program if such were deemed necessary. We readily consented, and when the hour came we lived up to our promise. So I, along with several members of my staff, am here because I was invited here. I am here because I have organizational ties here.

But more basically, I am in Birmingham because injustice is here. Just as the prophets of the eighth century b.c. left their villages and carried their "thus saith the Lord" far beyond the boundaries of their home towns, and just as the Apostle Paul left his village of Tarsus and carried the gospel of Jesus Christ to the far corners of the Greco-Roman world, so am I compelled to carry the gospel of freedom beyond my own home town. Like Paul, I must constantly respond to the Macedonian call for aid.

Moreover, I am cognizant of the interrelatedness of all communities and states. I cannot sit idly by in Atlanta and not be concerned about what happens in Birmingham. Injustice anywhere is a threat to justice everywhere. We are caught in an inescapable network of mutuality, tied in a single garment of destiny. Whatever affects one directly, affects all indirectly. Never again can we afford to live with the narrow, provincial "outside agitator" idea. Anyone who lives inside the United States can never be considered an outsider anywhere within its bounds.

5   You deplore the demonstrations taking place in Birmingham. But your statement, I am sorry to say, fails to express a similar concern for the conditions that brought about the demonstrations. I am sure that none of you would want to rest content with the superficial kind of social analysis that deals merely with effects and does not grapple with underlying causes. It is unfortunate that demonstrations are taking place in Birmingham, but it is even more unfortunate that the city's white power structure left the Negro community with no alternative.

In any nonviolent campaign there are four basic steps: collection of the facts to determine whether injustices exist; negotiation; self-purification; and direct action. We have gone through all these steps in Birmingham. There can be no gainsaying the fact that racial injustice engulfs this community. Birmingham is probably the most thoroughly segregated city in the United States. Its ugly record of brutality is widely known. Negroes have experienced grossly unjust treatment in the courts. There have been more unsolved bombings of Negro homes and churches in Birmingham than in any other city in the nation. These are the hard, brutal facts of the case. On the basis of these conditions, Negro leaders sought to negotiate with the city fathers. But the latter consistently refused to engage in good-faith negotiation.

Then, last September, came the opportunity to talk with leaders of Birmingham's economic community. In the course of the negotiations, certain promises were made by the merchants—for example, to remove the stores' humiliating racial signs. On the basis of these promises, the Reverend Fred Shuttlesworth and the leaders of the Alabama Christian Movement for Human Rights agreed to a moratorium on all demonstrations. As the weeks and months went by, we realized that we were the victims of a broken promise. A few signs, briefly removed, returned; the others remained.

As in so many past experiences, our hopes had been blasted, and the shadow of deep disappointment settled upon us. We had no alternative except to prepare for direct action, whereby we would present our very bodies as a means of laying our case before the conscience of the local and the national community. Mindful of the difficulties involved, we decided to undertake a process of self-purification. We began a series of workshops on nonviolence, and we repeatedly asked ourselves: "Are you able to accept blows without retaliating?" "Are you able to endure the ordeal of jail?" We decided to schedule our direct-action program for the Easter season, realizing that except for Christmas, this is the main shopping period of the year. Knowing that a strong economic-withdrawal program would be the by-product of direct action, we felt that this would be the best time to bring pressure to bear on the merchants for the needed change.

Then it occurred to us that Birmingham's mayoral election was coming up in March, and we speedily decided to postpone action until after election day. When we discovered that the Commissioner of Public Safety, Eugene "Bull" Connor, had piled up enough votes to be in the run-off, we decided again to postpone action until the day after the run-off so that the demonstrations could not be used to cloud the issues. Like many others, we waited to see Mr. Connor defeated, and to this end we endured postponement after postponement. Having aided in this community need, we felt that our direct action program could be delayed no longer.

You may well ask: "Why direct action? Why sit-ins, marches and so forth? Isn't negotiation a better path?" You are quite right in calling for negotiation. Indeed, this is the very purpose of direct action. Nonviolent direct action seeks to create such a crisis and foster such a tension that a community which has constantly refused to negotiate is forced to confront the issue. It seeks so to dramatize the issue that it can no longer be ignored. My citing the creation of tension as part of the work of the nonviolent-resister may sound rather shocking. But I must confess that I am not afraid of the word "tension." I have earnestly opposed violent tension, but there is a type of constructive, nonviolent tension which is necessary for growth. Just as Socrates felt that it was necessary to create a tension in the mind so that individuals could rise from the bondage of myths and half-truths to the unfettered realm of creative analysis and objective appraisal, so must we see the need for nonviolent gadflies to create the kind of tension in society that will help men rise from the dark depths of prejudice and racism to the majestic heights of understanding and brotherhood. 10

The purpose of our direct-action program is to create a situation so crisis-packed that it will inevitably open the door to negotiation. I therefore concur with you in your call for negotiation. Too long has our beloved Southland been bogged down in a tragic effort to live in monologue rather than dialogue.

One of the basic points in your statements is that the action that I and my associates have taken in Birmingham is untimely. Some have asked: "Why didn't you give the new city administration time to act?" The only answer that I can give to this query is that the new Birmingham administration must be prodded about as much as the outgoing one, before it will act. We are sadly mistaken if we feel that the election of Albert Boutwell as mayor will bring the millennium to Birmingham. While Mr. Boutwell is a much more gentle person than Mr. Connor, they are both segregationists, dedicated to maintenance of the status quo. I have hope that Mr. Boutwell will be reasonable enough to see the futility of massive resistance to desegregation. But he will not see this without pressure from devotees of civil rights. My friends, I must say to you that we have not made a single gain in civil rights without determined legal and nonviolent pressure. Lamentably, it is an historical fact that privileged groups seldom give up their privileges voluntarily. Individuals may see the moral light and voluntarily give up their unjust posture; but, as Reinhold Niebuhr has reminded us, groups tend to be more immoral than individuals.

We know through painful experience that freedom is never voluntarily given by the oppressor; it must be demanded by the oppressed. Frankly, I have yet to engage in a direct-action campaign that was "well timed" in the view of those who have not suffered unduly from the disease of segregation. For years now I have heard the word "Wait!" It rings in the ear of every Negro with piercing familiarity. This "Wait" has almost always meant "Never." We must come to see, with one of our distinguished jurists, that "justice too long delayed is justice denied."

We have waited for more than 340 years for our constitutional and God-given rights. The nations of Asia and Africa are moving with jetlike speed toward gaining political independence, but we still creep at horse-and-buggy pace toward gaining a cup of coffee at a lunch counter. Perhaps it is easy for those who have never felt the stinging darts of segregation to say, "Wait." But when you have seen vicious mobs lynch your mothers and fathers at will and drown your sisters and brothers at whim; when you have seen hate-filled policemen curse, kick and even kill your black brothers and sisters; when you see the vast majority of your twenty million Negro brothers smothering in an airtight cage of poverty in the midst of an affluent society; when you suddenly find your tongue twisted and your speech stammering as you seek to explain to your six-year-old daughter why she can't go to the public amusement park that has just been advertised on television, and see tears welling up in her eyes when she is told that Funtown is closed to colored children, and see ominous clouds of inferiority beginning to form in her little mental sky, and see her beginning to distort her personality by developing an unconscious bitterness toward white people; when you have to concoct an answer for a five-year-old son who is asking: "Daddy, why do white people treat colored people so mean?"; when you take a cross-country drive and find it necessary to sleep night after night in the uncomfortable corners of your automobile because no motel will accept you; when you are humiliated day in and day out by nagging signs reading "white" and "colored"; when your first name becomes "nigger," your middle name becomes "boy" (however old you are) and your last name becomes "John," and your wife and mother are never given the respected title "Mrs."; when you are harried by day and haunted by night by the fact that you are a Negro, living constantly at tiptoe stance, never quite knowing what to expect next, and are plagued with inner fears and outer resentments; when you are forever fighting a degenerating sense of "nobodiness"—then you will understand why we find it difficult to wait. There comes a time when the cup of endurance runs over, and men are no longer willing to be plunged into the abyss of despair. I hope, sirs, you can understand our legitimate and unavoidable impatience.

You express a great deal of anxiety over our willingness to break laws. This   15
is certainly a legitimate concern. Since we so diligently urge people to obey the Supreme Court's decision of 1954 outlawing segregation in the public schools, at first glance it may seem rather paradoxical for us consciously to break laws. One may well ask: "How can you advocate breaking some laws and obeying others?" The answer lies in the fact that there are two types of laws: just and unjust. I would be the first to advocate obeying just laws. One has not only a legal but a moral responsibility to obey just laws. Conversely, one has a moral responsibility to disobey unjust laws. I would agree with St. Augustine that "an unjust law is no law at all."

Now, what is the difference between the two? How does one determine whether a law is just or unjust? A just law is a man-made code that squares with the moral law or the law of God. An unjust law is a code that is out of harmony with the moral law. To put it in the terms of St. Thomas Aquinas: An unjust law is a human law that is not rooted in eternal law and natural law. Any law that uplifts human personality is just. Any law that degrades human personality is unjust. All segregation statutes are unjust because segregation distorts the soul and damages the personality. It gives the segregator a false sense of superiority and the segregated a false sense of inferiority. Segregation, to use the terminology of the Jewish philosopher Martin Buber, substitutes an "I-it" relationship for an "I-thou" relationship and ends up relegating persons to the status of things. Hence segregation is not only politically, economically and sociologically unsound, it is morally wrong and sinful. Paul Tillich has said that sin is separation. Is not segregation an existential expression of man's tragic separation, his awful estrangement, his terrible sinfulness? Thus it is that I can urge men to obey the 1954 decision of the Supreme Court, for it is morally right; and I can urge them to disobey segregation ordinances, for they are morally wrong.

Let us consider a more concrete example of just and unjust laws. An unjust law is a code that a numerical or power majority group compels a minority group to obey but does not make binding on itself. This is difference made legal. By the same token, a just law is a code that a majority compels a minority to follow and that it is willing to follow itself. This is sameness made legal.

Let me give another explanation. A law is unjust if it is inflicted on a minority that, as a result of being denied the right to vote, had no part in enacting or devising the law. Who can say that the legislature of Alabama which set up that state's segregation laws was democratically elected? Throughout Alabama all sorts of devious methods are used to prevent Negroes from becoming registered voters, and there are some counties in which, even though Negroes constitute a majority of the population, not a single Negro is registered. Can any law enacted under such circumstances be considered democratically structured?

Sometimes a law is just on its face and unjust in its application. For instance, I have been arrested on a charge of parading without a permit. Now, there is nothing wrong in having an ordinance which requires a permit for a parade. But such an ordinance becomes unjust when it is used to maintain segregation and to deny citizens the First-Amendment privilege of peaceful assembly and protest.

20   I hope you are able to see the distinction I am trying to point out. In no sense do I advocate evading or defying the law, as would the rabid segregationist. That would lead to anarchy. One who breaks an unjust law must do so openly, lovingly, and with a willingness to accept the penalty. I submit that an individual who breaks a law that conscience tells him is unjust, and who willingly accepts the penalty of imprisonment in order to arouse the conscience of the community over its injustice, is in reality expressing the highest respect for law.

Of course, there is nothing new about this kind of civil disobedience. It was evidenced sublimely in the refusal of Shadrach, Meshach and Abednego to obey the laws of Nebuchadnezzar, on the ground that a higher moral law was at stake. It was practiced superbly by the early Christians, who were willing to face hungry lions and the excruciating pain of chopping blocks rather than submit to certain unjust laws of the Roman Empire. To a degree, academic freedom is a reality today because Socrates practiced civil disobedience. In our own nation, the Boston Tea party represented a massive act of civil disobedience.

We should never forget that everything Adolf Hitler did in Germany was "legal" and everything the Hungarian freedom fighters did in Hungary was "illegal." It was "illegal" to aid and comfort a Jew in Hitler's Germany. Even so, I am sure that, had I lived in Germany at the time, I would have aided and comforted my Jewish brothers. If today I lived in a Communist country where certain principles dear to the Christian faith are suppressed, I would openly advocate disobeying that country's antireligious laws.

I must make two honest confessions to you, my Christian and Jewish brothers. First, I must confess that over the past few years I have been gravely disappointed with the white moderate. I have almost reached the regrettable conclusion that the Negro's great stumbling block in his stride toward freedom is not the White Citizen's Counciler or the Ku Klux Klanner, but the white moderate, who is more devoted to "order" than to justice; who prefers a negative peace which is the absence of tension to a positive peace which is the presence of justice; who constantly says: "I agree with you in the goal you seek, but I cannot agree with your methods of direct action"; who paternalistically believes he can set the timetable for another man's freedom; who lives by a mythical concept of time and who constantly advises the Negro to wait for a "more convenient season." Shallow understanding from people of good will is more frustrating than absolute misunderstanding from people of ill will. Lukewarm acceptance is much more bewildering than outright rejection.

I had hoped that the white moderate would understand that law and order exist for the purpose of establishing justice and that when they fail in this purpose they become the dangerously structured dams that block the flow of social progress. I had hoped that the white moderate would understand that the present tension in the South is a necessary phase of the transition from an obnoxious negative peace, in which the Negro passively accepted his unjust plight, to a substantive and positive peace, in which all men will respect the dignity and worth of human personality. Actually, we who engage in nonviolent direct action are not the creators of tension. We merely bring to the surface the hidden tension that is already alive. We bring it out in the open, where it can be seen and dealt with. Like a boil that can never be cured so long as it is covered up but must be opened with all its ugliness to the natural medicines of air and light, injustice must be exposed, with all the tension its exposure creates, to the light of human conscience and the air of national opinion before it can be cured.

In your statement you assert that our actions, even though peaceful, must 25 be condemned because they precipitate violence. But is this a logical assertion? Isn't this like condemning a robbed man because his possession of money precipitated the evil act of robbery? Isn't this like condemning Socrates because his unswerving commitment to truth and his philosophical inquiries precipitated the act by the misguided populace in which they made him drink hemlock? Isn't this like condemning Jesus because his unique God-consciousness and never-ceasing devotion to God's will precipitated the evil act of crucifixion? We must come to see that, as the federal courts have consistently affirmed, it is wrong to urge an individual to cease his efforts to gain his basic constitutional rights because the quest may precipitate violence. Society must protect the robbed and punish the robber.

I had also hoped that the white moderate would reject the myth concerning time in relation to the struggle for freedom. I have just received a letter from a white brother in Texas. He writes: "All Christians know that the colored people will receive equal rights eventually, but it is possible that you are in too great a religious hurry. It has taken Christianity almost two thousand years to accomplish what it has. The teachings of Christ take time to come to earth." Such an attitude stems from a tragic misconception of time, from the strangely irrational notion that there is something in the very flow of time that will inevitably cure all ills. Actually, time itself is neutral; it can be used either destructively or constructively. More and more I feel that the people of ill will have used time much more effectively than have the people of good will. We will have to repent in this generation not merely for the hateful words and actions of the bad people but for the appalling silence of the good people. Human progress never rolls in on wheels of inevitability; it comes through the tireless efforts of men willing to be co-workers with God, and without this hard work, time itself becomes an ally of the forces of social stagnation. We must use time creatively, in the knowledge that time is always ripe to do right. Now is the time to make real the promise of democracy and transform our pending national elegy into a creative psalm of brotherhood. Now is the time to lift our national policy from the quicksand of racial injustice to the solid rock of human dignity.

You speak of our activity in Birmingham as extreme. At first I was rather disappointed that fellow clergymen would see my nonviolent efforts as those of an extremist. I began thinking about the fact that I stand in the middle of two opposing forces in the Negro community. One is a force of complacency, made up in part of Negroes who, as a result of long years of oppression, are so drained of self-respect and a sense of "somebodiness" that they have adjusted to segregation; and in part of a few middle-class Negroes who, because of a degree of academic and economic security and because in some ways they profit by segregation, have become insensitive to the problems of the masses. The other force is one of bitterness and hatred, and it comes perilously close to advocating violence. It is expressed in the various black nationalist groups that are spring-ing up across the nation, the largest and best-known being Elijah Muhammad's Muslim movement. Nourished by the Negro's frustration over the continued existence of racial discrimination, this movement is made up of people who have lost faith in America, who have absolutely repudiated Christianity, and who have concluded that the white man is an incorrigible "devil."

I have tried to stand between these two forces, saying that we need emulate neither the "do-nothingism" of the complacent nor the hatred and despair of the black nationalist. For there is the more excellent way of love and nonviolent protest. I am grateful to God that, through the influence of the Negro church, the way of nonviolence became an integral part of our struggle.

If this philosophy had not emerged, by now many streets of the South would, I am convinced, be flowing with blood. And I am further convinced that if our white brothers dismiss as "rabble-rousers" and "outside agitators" those of us who employ nonviolent direct action, and if they refuse to support our nonviolent efforts, millions of Negroes will, out of frustration and despair, seek solace and security in blacknationalist ideologies—a development that would inevitably lead to a frightening racial nightmare.

30   Oppressed people cannot remain oppressed forever. The yearning for free-dom eventually manifests itself, and that is what has happened to the Ameri-can Negro. Something within has reminded him of his birthright of freedom, and something without has reminded him that it can be gained. Consciously or unconsciously, he has been caught up by the *Zeitgeist*, and with his black broth-ers of Africa and his brown and yellow brothers of Asia, South America and the

Caribbean, the United States Negro is moving with a sense of great urgency toward the promised land of racial justice. If one recognizes this vital urge that has engulfed the Negro community, one should readily understand why public demonstrations are taking place. The Negro has many pent-up resentments and latent frustrations, and he must release them. So let him march; let him make prayer pilgrimages to the city hall; let him go on freedom rides—and try to understand why he must do so. If his repressed emotions are not released in nonviolent ways, they will seek expression through violence; this is not a threat but a fact of history. So I have not said to my people: "Get rid of your discontent." Rather, I have tried to say that this normal and healthy discontent can be channeled into the creative outlet of nonviolent direct action. And now this approach is being termed extremist.

But though I was initially disappointed at being categorized as an extremist, as I continued to think about the matter I gradually gained a measure of satisfaction from the label. Was not Jesus an extremist for love: "Love your enemies, bless them that curse you, do good to them that hate you, and pray for them which despitefully use you, and persecute you." Was not Amos an extremist for justice: "Let justice roll down like waters and righteousness like an ever-flowing stream." Was not Paul an extremist for the Christian gospel: "I bear in my body the marks of the Lord Jesus." Was not Martin Luther an extremist: "Here I stand; I cannot do otherwise, so help me God." And John Bunyan: "I will stay in jail to the end of my days before I make a butchery of my conscience." And Abraham Lincoln: "This nation cannot survive half slave and half free." And Thomas Jefferson: "We hold these truths to be self-evident, that all men are created equal ..." So the question is not whether we will be extremists, but what kind of extremists we will be. Will we be extremists for hate or for love? Will we be extremists for the preservation of injustice or for the extension of justice? In that dramatic scene on Calvary's hill three men were crucified. We must never forget that all three were crucified for the same crime—the crime of extremism. Two were extremists for immorality, and thus fell below their environment. The other, Jesus Christ, was an extremist for love, truth and goodness, and thereby rose above his environment. Perhaps the South, the nation and the world are in dire need of creative extremists.

I had hoped that the white moderate would see this need. Perhaps I was too optimistic; perhaps I expected too much. I suppose I should have realized that few members of the oppressor race can understand the deep groans and passionate yearnings of the oppressed race, and still fewer have the vision to see that injustice must be rooted out by strong, persistent and determined action. I am thankful, however, that some of our white brothers in the South have grasped the meaning of this social revolution and committed themselves to it. They are still all too few in quantity, but they are big in quality. Some—such as Ralph McGill, Lillian Smith, Harry Golden, James McBride Dabbs, Ann Braden and Sarah Patton Boyle—have written about our struggle in eloquent and prophetic terms. Others have marched with us down nameless streets of the South. They have languished in filthy, roach-infested jails, suffering the abuse and brutality of policemen who view them as "dirty nigger-lovers." Unlike so many of their moderate brothers and sisters, they have recognized the urgency of the moment and sensed the need for powerful "action" antidotes to combat the disease of segregation.

Let me take note of my other major disappointment. I have been so greatly disappointed with the white church and its leadership. Of course, there are some notable exceptions. I am not unmindful of the fact that each of you has taken some significant stands on this issue. I commend you, Reverend Stallings, for your Christian stand on this past Sunday, in welcoming Negroes to your worship service on a nonsegregated basis. I commend the Catholic leaders of this state for integrating Spring Hill College several years ago.

But despite these notable exceptions, I must honestly reiterate that I have been disappointed with the church. I do not say this as one of those negative critics who can always find something wrong with the church. I say this as a minister of the gospel, who loves the church; who was nurtured in its bosom; who has been sustained by its spiritual blessings and who will remain true to it as long as the cord of life shall lengthen.

35   When I was suddenly catapulted into the leadership of the bus protest in Montgomery, Alabama, a few years ago, I felt we would be supported by the white church. I felt that the white ministers, priests and rabbis of the South would be among our strongest allies. Instead, some have been outright opponents, refusing to understand the freedom movement and misrepresenting its leaders; all too many others have been more cautious than courageous and have remained silent behind the anesthetizing security of stained-glass windows.

In spite of my shattered dreams, I came to Birmingham with the hope that the white religious leadership of this community would see the justice of our cause and, with deep moral concern, would serve as the channel through which our just grievances could reach the power structure. I had hoped that each of you would understand. But again I have been disappointed.

I have heard numerous southern religious leaders admonish their worshipers to comply with a desegregation decision because it is the law, but I have longed to hear white ministers declare: "Follow this decree because integration is morally right and because the Negro is your brother." In the midst of blatant injustices inflicted upon the Negro, I have watched white churchmen stand on the sideline and mouth pious irrelevancies and sanctimonious trivialities. In the midst of a mighty struggle to rid our nation of racial and economic injustice, I have heard many ministers say: "Those are social issues, with which the gospel has no real concern." And I have watched many churches commit themselves to a completely otherworldly religion which makes a strange, unbiblical distinction between body and soul, between the sacred and the secular.

I have traveled the length and breadth of Alabama, Mississippi and all the other southern states. On sweltering summer days and crisp autumn mornings I have looked at the South's beautiful churches with their lofty spires pointing heavenward. I have beheld the impressive outlines of her massive religious-education buildings. Over and over I have found myself asking: "What kind of people worship here? Who is their God? Where were their voices when the lips of Governor Barnett dripped with words of interposition and nullification? Where were they when Governor Wallace gave a clarion call for defiance and hatred? Where were their voices of support when bruised and weary Negro men and women decided to rise from the dark dungeons of complacency to the bright hills of creative protest?"

Yes, these questions are still in my mind. In deep disappointment I have wept over the laxity of the church. But be assured that my tears have been tears of love. There can be no deep disappointment where there is not deep love. Yes, I love the church. How could I do otherwise? I am in the rather unique position of being the son, the grandson and the great-grandson of preachers. Yes, I see the church as the body of Christ. But, oh! How we have blemished and scarred that body through social neglect and through fear of being nonconformists.

There was a time when the church was very powerful—in the time when the early Christians rejoiced at being deemed worthy to suffer for what they believed. In those days the church was not merely a thermometer that recorded the ideas and principles of popular opinion; it was a thermostat that transformed the mores of society. Whenever the early Christians entered a town, the people in power became disturbed and immediately sought to convict the Christians for being "disturbers of the peace" and "outside agitators." But the Christians pressed on, in the conviction that they were "a colony of heaven," called to obey God rather than man. Small in number, they were big in commitment. They were too God-intoxicated to be "astronomically intimidated." By their effort and example they brought an end to such ancient evils as infanticide and gladiatorial contests.

Things are different now. So often the contemporary church is a weak, ineffectual voice with an uncertain sound. So often it is an arch-defender of the status quo. Far from being disturbed by the presence of the church, the power structure of the average community is consoled by the church's silent—and often even vocal—sanction of things as they are.

But the judgment of God is upon the church as never before. If today's church does not recapture the sacrificial spirit of the early church, it will lose its authenticity, forfeit the loyalty of millions, and be dismissed as an irrelevant social club with no meaning for the twentieth century. Every day I meet young people whose disappointment with the church has turned into outright disgust.

Perhaps I have once again been too optimistic. Is organized religion too inextricably bound to the status quo to save our nation and the world? Perhaps I must turn my faith to the inner spiritual church, the church within the church, as the true ekklesia and the hope of the world. But again I am thankful to God that some noble souls from the ranks of organized religion have broken loose from the paralyzing chains of conformity and joined us as active partners in the struggle for freedom. They have left their secure congregations and walked the

40

streets of Albany, Georgia, with us. They have gone down the highways of the South on tortuous rides for freedom. Yes, they have gone to jail with us. Some have been dismissed from their churches, have lost the support of their bishops and fellow ministers. But they have acted in the faith that right defeated is stronger than evil triumphant. Their witness has been the spiritual salt that has preserved the true meaning of the gospel in these troubled times. They have carved a tunnel of hope through the dark mountain of disappointment.

I hope the church as a whole will meet the challenge of this decisive hour. But even if the church does not come to the aid of justice, I have no despair about the future. I have no fear about the outcome of our struggle in Birmingham, even if our motives are at present misunderstood. We will reach the goal of freedom in Birmingham and all over the nation, because the goal of America is freedom. Abused and scorned though we may be, our destiny is tied up with America's destiny. Before the pilgrims landed at Plymouth, we were here. Before the pen of Jefferson etched the majestic words of the Declaration of Independence across the pages of history, we were here. For more than two centuries our forebears labored in this country without wages; they made cotton king; they built the homes of their masters while suffering gross injustice and shameful humiliation—and yet out of a bottomless vitality they continued to thrive and develop. If the inexpressible cruelties of slavery could not stop us, the opposition we now face will surely fail. We will win our freedom because the sacred heritage of our nation and the eternal will of God are embodied in our echoing demands.

45   Before closing I feel impelled to mention one other point in your statement that has troubled me profoundly. You warmly commended the Birmingham police force for keeping "order" and "preventing violence." I doubt that you would have so warmly commended the police force if you had seen its dogs sinking their teeth into unarmed, nonviolent Negroes. I doubt that you would so quickly commend the policemen if you were to observe their ugly and inhumane treatment of Negroes here in the city jail; if you were to watch them push and curse old Negro women and young Negro girls; if you were to see them slap and kick old Negro men and young boys; if you were to observe them, as they did on two occasions, refuse to give us food because we wanted to sing our grace together. I cannot join you in your praise of the Birmingham Police Department.

It is true that the police have exercised a degree of discipline in handling the demonstrators. In this sense they have conducted themselves rather "nonviolently" in public. But for what purpose? To preserve the evil system of segregation. Over the past few years I have consistently preached that nonviolence demands that the means we use must be as pure as the ends we seek. I have tried to make clear that it is wrong to use immoral means to attain moral ends. But now I must affirm that it is just as wrong, or perhaps even more so, to use moral means to preserve immoral ends. Perhaps Mr. Connor and his policemen have been rather nonviolent in public, as was Chief Pritchett in Albany, Georgia, but they have used the moral means of nonviolence to maintain the immoral end of racial injustice. As T. S. Eliot has said: "The last temptation is the greatest treason: To do the right deed for the wrong reason."

I wish you had commended the Negro sit-inners and demonstrators of Birmingham for their sublime courage, their willingness to suffer and their amazing discipline in the midst of great provocation. One day the South will recognize its real heroes. They will be the James Merediths, with the noble sense of purpose that enables them to face jeering and hostile mobs, and with the agonizing loneliness that characterizes the life of the pioneer. They will be old, oppressed, battered Negro women, symbolized in a seventy-two-year-old woman in Montgomery, Alabama, who rose up with a sense of dignity and with her people decided not to ride segregated buses, and who responded with ungrammatical profundity to one who inquired about her weariness: "My feets is tired, but my soul is at rest." They will be the young high school and college students, the young ministers of the gospel and a host of their elders, courageously and nonviolently sitting in at lunch counters and willingly going to jail for conscience sake. One day the South will know that when these disinherited children of God sat down at lunch counters, they were in reality standing up for what is best in the American dream and for the most sacred values in our Judaeo-Christian heritage, thereby bringing our nation back to those great wells of democracy which were dug deep by the founding fathers in their formulation of the Constitution and the Declaration of Independence.

Never before have I written so long a letter. I'm afraid it is much too long to take your precious time. I can assure you that it would have been much shorter if I had been writing from a comfortable desk, but what else can one do when he is alone in a narrow jail cell, other than write long letters, think long thoughts and pray long prayers?

If I have said anything in this letter that overstates the truth and indicates an unreasonable impatience, I beg you to forgive me. If I have said anything that understates the truth and indicates my having a patience that allows me to settle for anything less than brotherhood, I beg God to forgive me.

I hope this letter finds you strong in the faith. I also hope that circumstances 50 will soon make it possible for me to meet each of you, not as an integrationist or a civil-rights leader but as a fellow clergyman and a Christian brother. Let us all hope that the dark clouds of racial prejudice will soon pass away and the deep fog of misunderstanding will be lifted from our fear-drenched communities, and in some not too distant tomorrow the radiant stars of love and brotherhood will shine over our great nation with all their scintillating beauty.

Yours for the cause of Peace and Brotherhood,
Martin Luther King, Jr.

CRITICAL THINKING QUESTIONS

1. How does Martin Luther King, Jr., create an appeal to *pathos*, the emotions of the audience? Cite examples of what you consider the most effective instances of that appeal.

2. What types of evidence does King use in his argument? Cite examples.

3. Are there places in the letter where the argument seems to be more oral than written, places where you can *hear* the words? Provide some examples.

WRITING TOPICS

1. If you were to become an activist, what cause would you support today? Write to a friend inviting that person to join you in your support, citing evidence in the form of reports, personal experience, and authority.

2. **Modeling a Master.** Using King's "Letter from Birmingham Jail" as your model, compose a letter to a target audience that examines a situation that you deem to be unfair and advocates specific action to right the wrong. First, you will need to spend some time studying the master. After reading the "Letter," use the following outline to analyze King's rhetorical strategies; mark passages and make marginal notes to denote each component listed:

   I. **King's Introduction**
       - Presents the issue
       - Explains how this situation came about
       - Establishes common ground with his audience
       - Adopts a tone that is both personal and academic
       - Provides logical analysis of the situation at hand (appeal to *logos*) and invokes value appeals (*pathos*)

   II. **King's Concession**
       - Anticipates and articulates the opposition's case
       - Shows his understanding of the opposition's views (appeal to *ethos*)
       - Addresses the opposition's case; introduces his refutation with a key word, "Wait!"
       - Appeals to *pathos* through the use of personal experience; creates audience empathy, even as he asserts his case against the opposition

   III. **King's Rebuttal—Evidence and Appeals**
        - Uses definition and analysis/appeal to *logos*
        - Uses appeals to authority/*ethos*
        - Uses examples/*logos* and *pathos*
        - Uses a veiled threat, based on a stated assumption/*pathos*
        - Uses comparison/*logos* and *pathos*
        - Uses common-ground value appeals (stated assumptions)/*pathos*

   IV. **King's Closing**
       - Regains audience empathy
       - Strikes common ground by expressing shared needs and values

- States a clear "call to action"
- Creates a final sentence that capitalizes on the use of first-person plural and resonates with "scintillating" imagery

Now it's your turn. Make your case with a specific audience whom you envision to be unsympathetic to your position. Use King's rhetorical tactics and win them over.

Following are some suggested situations:
- The draft has been reinstated, and you are required to sign up. You write a letter to the Selective Service Board (located in your hometown or county) to convince them to give you an exemption.
- You are applying to law school. Recorded on your college transcript is a plagiarism violation. Although you were, indeed, guilty as charged, you write a letter to convince the law school admissions board to give serious consideration to your application.
- Home from college for spring break, you learn that the Oklawahah City Council has approved construction of a Happy-Mart Superstore in a wooded area with a nearby pond. You write a letter to the council to convince its members to rescind their action.
- Create a situation/scenario that places you in the role of writing a letter to a specific audience to defend your act of civil disobedience.

Richard Rodriguez

The Chinese in All of Us (1992)

A Mexican American Explores Multiculturalism

The other day, the phone rang; it was a woman who identified herself as the "talent coordinator" for the "Oprah Winfrey Show." She said Oprah was planning a show on self-hating ethnics. "You know," she confided, "Norwegians who don't want to be Norwegian, Greeks who hate Greek food." Anyway, she said breezily, wouldn't I like to make an appearance?

About 10 years ago I wrote a thin book called Hunger of Memory. It was a book about my education, which is to say, a book about my Americanization. I wrote of losses and triumphs. And, in passing, I wrote about two issues particularly, affirmative action and bilingual education.

I was a nay-sayer. I became, because of my book, a notorious figure among the Ethnic Left in America. Consider me the brown Uncle Tom. I am a traitor, a sellout. The Spanish word is *pocho*. A pocho is someone who forgets his true home. (A shame.) A Richard Rodriguez.

Last year, I was being interviewed by Bill Moyers. "Do you consider your-self American or Hispanic?" he asked.

5   "I think of myself as Chinese," I answered.

A smart-aleck answer, but one that is true enough. I live in San Francisco, a city that has become, in my lifetime, predominantly Asian, predominantly Chinese. I am becoming like them. Do not ask me how, it is too early to tell. But it is inevitable, living side by side, that we should become like each other. So think of me as Chinese.

Oh, my critics say: Look at you Mr. Rod-ree-guess. You have lost your culture.

They mean, I think, that I am not my father, which is true enough. I did not grow up in the state of Jalisco, in the western part of Mexico. I grew up here, in this country, amongst you. I am like you.

My critics mean, when they speak of culture, something solid, something intact. You have lost your culture, they say, as though I lost it at the Greyhound bus station. You have lost your culture, as though culture is a coat I took off one warm afternoon and then forgot.

10   I AM MY CULTURE. Culture is not something opposite us, it is rather something we breathe and sweat and live. My culture? Lucille Ball is my culture. (I love Lucy, after all.) And Michael Jackson. And Benjamin Franklin is my culture. And Elvis Presley and Walter Cronkite. Walt Disney is my culture. The New York Yankees.

My culture is you. You created me; if you don't like it, if I make you uncomfortable now by being too much like you, too bad.

When I was a little boy in Sacramento, California, the son of Mexican immigrant parents, Spanish-speaking mainly, even then, in those years, America came at me. America was everywhere around me. America was in the pace of the traffic lights, the assertion of neon, the slouch of the crowd, the impatience of the fast food counter. America was everywhere.

I recognized America best, in those years, standing outside the culture. I recognized its power, and from the first I knew that it threatened to swallow me up. America did not feel like something to choose or not choose. America felt inevitable.

Truman Capote said somewhere that he never met a true bisexual. He meant, I think, that finally people are one thing or the other.

15   Well, I must tell you that I have never met a truly bicultural person. Oh, I have met people who speak two languages, and all that. But finally, their allegiance belongs more to one side of the border than the other.

And yet, I believe in multiculturalism—my kind of multiculturalism.

I think the adventure of living in a multi-racial, multi-ethnic America leaves one vulnerable to a variety of cultures, a variety of influences. Consider me, for example, Chinese. I am also Irish.

About 10 years ago, I was going to school in England. One weekend, Aer Lingus, the Irish national airline, was offering a reduced fare to Dublin. I thought, "What a lark—it'd be fun to go off to Ireland for the weekend." Strange thing, once I got off the plane, I suddenly felt myself at home. I knew these people. I recognized their faces and their irony and their wit and their sadness.

I'll tell you why. I was educated by Irish Catholic nuns. They were my first, my most important foreign culture, intruding on my Mexican soul, reshaping my soul with their voices.

Sometime after Dublin, I realized something more about myself: All of my best friends from childhood to now, the people I have been closest to, have been Irish-Americans, Irish Catholics.

How is this possible? How is it possible for a Mexican kid from Sacramento, California, to discover himself to be Irish?

In the orthodox American scheme of things, it is nonsense. America is a Protestant country. A low-church Protestant country. America was founded by Puritans who resisted the notion of the group. The most important founding idea of America was the notion of individualism—your freedom from the group, my freedom from you. A most glamorous idea.

Consider this paradox: The belief we share in common as Americans is the belief that we are separate from one another.

There is already with this paradox implied an important tension, one basic to American experience. Our culture, by which I mean our daily experience, is at war with our ideology, by which I mean our Protestant belief in separateness.

Diversity is our strength, we say. There is not an American president who would say anything else: We are a country made stronger by our individuality, by our differences. Which is, in a way, true. But only partly true.

The other truth, I call it my catholic truth about puritan America, is that America exists. America exists as a culture, a sound, an accent, a walk.

Thousands of hotel clerks in thousands of hotels around the world will tell you that America exists. There is a recognizable type. Here they come, the Americans. Bermuda shorts. High-pitched voices. Too easy familiarity. Big tip, insecure tip. A slap on the back.

And when we ourselves are far from home, when we are in the Hilton lobby in Cairo or in Paris, we, too, recognize one another immediately. Across the crowded hotel lobby Americans find one another immediately, either with relief or with slight, acknowledging embarrassment.

It is only when we are home working alongside one another and living next to one another that we wonder whether America exists. We wonder about our individuality. And we talk about our traditional Protestant virtues. We talk about respecting our diversity.

Nativist politicians are saying these days that maybe we should think twice about allowing non-European immigrants into this country. Can America, after all, sustain such diversity?

Liberal American educators end up echoing the point, in a way. They look at faces like mine and they see only what they call "diversity." They wonder, now, if the purpose of education shouldn't be diversity. We should teach our children about their separate cultures—forget the notion of a common culture.

The other day in Las Vegas I was speaking to a group of high school principals. One man, afterward, came up and told me that his school has changed in recent years. In little more than a decade the student body has changed its color, changed its complexion; the school is no longer black and white, but now suddenly Asian and Hispanic.

This principal smiled and said his school has dropped Black History Month in favor of what he calls, "Newcomers Month."

I think this is absurd. I think this is nonsense.

35   There isn't an American whose history is not black history. All of us, by virtue of being Americans, share in the history of black America—the oppression, the endurance, the triumph.

Do not speak to me of your diversity. My cultural forefathers are black slaves and black emancipators. I am an American.

America exists. Nothing more will I tell you, can I tell you.

Let me tell you some stories.

A friend of mine—let's call him Michael—tells me he's confused by America. Mike goes to junior high school in San Francisco. His teacher is always telling him to stand up, look up. "Speak up, Michael, we can't hear you! Look at me, Michael!"

40   Then Michael goes home. His Chinese father is always complaining at home. His Chinese father says that Michael is picking up American ways. "And since when have you started to look your father in the eye?"

America exists, dear Michael.

At the family picnic, the boy listens to his relatives argue and laugh. The spices are as familiar as the jokes. There are arguments about old civil wars and faceless politicians. The family is talking Greek or Chinese or Spanish. The boy grows restless; the boy gets up and wanders away from the family picnic to watch some other boys playing baseball in the distance.

America exists.

My Mexican father looks out at America from the window of his morning newspaper. After all these years in this country, he still doubts that America exists. Look at this place, he says. So many faces. So many colors. So many grandmothers and religions and memories here. This is not a real country. Not a real country like China or Germany or Mexico.

45   It falls to the son to say, America exists, Papa.

There is an unresolved tension between the "I" and the "we." We trust most the "I," though grudgingly we admit the necessity of the "we." The most important communal institution we have is the classroom. We build classrooms, recognize their necessity. But we don't like them.

In the most famous American novel, our greatest book about ourselves, Mark Twain's *Adventures of Huckleberry Finn*, the school marm plays the comic villain. She is always trying to tie down Huck. She tries to make him speak regular. She is always trying to civilize.

We recognize the value of having Huck Finn learn to speak regular, even if we don't like it. And we don't like it. Something in us as Americans forces us to fear the coming of fall, the chill in the woods, the starched shirt, the first day of school.

Let me tell you about my first day of school. I came to the classroom clutching a handful of English. A bilingual child?

The important distinction I want to make here is not between Spanish and 50 English, but between private and public language.

I was the son of working class, immigrant parents. I stress working class. Too often in recent years, we have considered ethnicity and race at the expense of economic standing. Thus, we speak of "minorities" in America and we mean only certain races or so-called "non-white" groups. We use the term minority in a numerical sense. Am I a minority? Well, yes, if we mean that Hispanics generally are "under represented" in American public life. But the term minority is richer as a cultural term. There are certain people in this country who do not imagine themselves to belong to majority society. White. Black. Brown. Most of them are poor. Many of them are uneducated. All of them share a diffidence, a fear, an anxiety about public institutions.

When I walked into the classroom, I was such a minority. I remember the nun wrote my name on the black board: RICHARD RODRIGUEZ. She pronounced it. Then she said, repeat it after me.

It was not that I could not say it. Rather, I would not say it. Why should I? Who was this nun?

She said: Repeat your name after me loud enough so all the boys and girls can understand.

The nun was telling me not just to speak English, but to use language pub- 55 licly. To speak in a voice loud enough to be heard by strangers. (She was calling me to the first and most crucial lesson of grammar school.)

I was a minority child. It wasn't a question of English versus Spanish. It was a question of public language. I didn't want to speak to *you—los gringos*, boys and girls.

I would not. I could not. I refused to speak up, to look up.

Half a year passed. The nuns worried over me. Speak up, Richard. Stand up, Richard. A year passed. A second year began.

Then one Saturday three nuns appeared at our door. They walked into our house and sat on our sagging blue sofa.

Would it be possible, Mrs. Rodriguez, for you and your husband to use 60 English around the house?

Of course, my mother complied. (What would she not do for her children's public success?)

At first, it seemed a kind of game. We practiced English after dinner. But it was still your language.

Until one other Saturday. I remember my mother and father were speaking Spanish to one another in the kitchen. I did not realize they were speaking Spanish until, the moment they saw me, they switched to English.

I felt pushed away. I remember going over to the sink and turning on the water; standing there dumbly, feeling the water on my hand. I wanted to cry. The water was tepid, then warm, then scalding. I wanted to scream. But I didn't. I turned off the faucet and walked out of the room.

65 And now you have forgotten how I used to go after school to your house. I used to watch you. I watched television with you, there on the floor. I used to watch the way you laughed. I used to listen to the way you used words. I wanted to swallow you up, to become you. Five-thirty and your mom said, Well, Rickey, we're going to eat in half an hour. Do you want to stay? And I did. I became you.

Something happens to you in the classroom if you are a very good student. You change.

A friend of mine, who went to Bryn Mawr College in the 1950s—when she was the only black student in her class—remembers coming home to North Carolina. She remembers getting off the Greyhound bus. She remembers walking up the sidewalk on the hot early summer day.

When she got home and walked up the five steps of the front porch, her mother was waiting for her behind the screen door.

"I don't want you talkin' white in here," her mother said.

70 There is a sad story in America about "making it." It is the story of summer vacations. Of no longer being able to speak to one's parents. Of having your Chinese father mock your American ways. ("And since when have you started to look your father in the eye?") It is the story of the girl who learns a different kind of English at school and then is embarrassed to use it at the dinner table.

Bilinguists speak of the necessity of using what they call "family language" in the classroom. If I know anything about education, it is that such a bilingual scheme is bound to fail. Classroom language can never be family language. It is a matter not of different words, but of different contexts.

We don't like to hear such things. We don't like the school marm to change us. We want to believe that August will go on forever and that we can avoid wearing shoes. Huck Finn is America's archetypal bilingual student. He speaks one way—his way, his free way—the school marm wants him to speak another.

As Americans, we must root for Huck.

Americans have lately been searching for a new multi-cultural metaphor for America. We don't like the melting pot. Hispanic Americans particularly have been looking for a new metaphor. Our political coming of age in the late 1960s was accompanied by a stern resistance to the melting pot model of America.

75 America is a stew. (All of us, presumably chunks of beef in a common broth.)

Or America is a mosaic. A Mexican-American bishop recently said that to me. He pointed at a mosaic of the Virgin of Guadalupe. "That is how I think of America," he said. "We are each of us different colors, but united we produce a wonderful, a beautiful effect."

The trouble, I thought to myself, the trouble is that the tiny pieces of glass are static. In our real lives, we are not static.

America is fluid. The best metaphors of America for me are metaphors suggesting fluidity. Our lives melting into one another.

For myself, I like the metaphor of the melting pot. I like it for two reasons.

First, its suggestion of pain—and there is pain. The school teacher can put   80
a sombrero on my head and tell me to feel proud of my heritage, but I know I am becoming a different person than my father. There is pain in the melting pot. Fall in and you are burned.

But there is to the metaphor also a suggestion of alchemy or magic. Fall into the melting pot and you become a new person, changed, like magic, to gold.

Why do we even talk about multiculturalism?

For several reasons, most of them positive. First and foremost is the influence of the great black civil rights movement of the 1950s and 1960s. We are more apt today to recognize the colors of America than perhaps we were several decades ago. On the TV ad, on the football field, in the bank, in a room like this—we have grown used to different shades of America. But that is only to say that we are more apt to be struck by our differences now that we are side by side than in earlier times when segregation legalized separation.

Less positively, the black civil rights movement was undermined by a romantic separatism. Americans were romanced by the moral authority of the outsider, and the benefits of claiming outsider status. White women. Hispanics. Asians. Suddenly, in the 1970s there was a rush to proclaim one's separate status. The benefit was clear: America confronted real social problems. But the decadence also was clear: middle class Americans ended up competing with one another to proclaim themselves society's victims.

The second factor that gives rise to this multicultural preoccupation has   85
recently been the epic migration of non-Europeans into this country.

A friend of mine teaches at a school in Los Angeles where, she says, there are children from 54 language groups. "What possibility is there," she asks, "to teach such a diverse student body anything in common?"

These children do have something in common, however. They may be strangers to Los Angeles, but they are becoming Americans in Los Angeles. That is the beginning.

While I believe in the notion of a common culture, I believe also in the notion of a dynamic culture. Even while America changes the immigrants, the immigrants are changing us. They have always changed us. Assimilation is reciprocal.

Consider American English, for example. It is not British English. The British forced it down our throats, but the language we speak is changed. We speak American here. There are the sighs of German grandmothers and the laughter of Africans in the speech we use. There are in our speech thousands of words imported and brought unregistered through Ellis Island. Swedish words. Yiddish. Italian.

Listen to my voice and you will hear your Lithuanian grandmother. Listen   90
to my American voice and you will hear the echoes of my Chinese neighbors.

Yes, Mr. Bill Moyers, we are all destined to become Chinese.

CRITICAL THINKING QUESTIONS

1. Richard Rodriguez has angered many advocates of bilingual education as well as those arguing for ethnic pride. Identify specific **assertions** that might stir hostility among these groups and discuss why they might incite such a response.

2. How does Rodriguez make use of personal experience, not only as evidence in support of his assertion, but also in establishing an appeal to *ethos*?

WRITING TOPIC

In what specific ways do you think our society is influenced by ethnic diversity? You might look for examples in food, music, fashion, and language. Write an essay in which you offer at least four pieces of evidence to support your claim.

Fred Setterberg

The Usual Story (1992)

I ambled through the Quarter, down Dumaine Street, up Bourbon, along Chartres, heading no place in particular. The narrow streets thronged with drunks and musicians. In Jackson Square, I rested on the cement steps to finish a bottle of beer I had carried out of a dark, noisy joint near Patout's. The moon arched above the statue of General Jackson saddled upon his horse, his hat doffed in one hand to hail the light. A boy with a trumpet stood at the foot of the invader's statue. He bleated and blahed his way through Miles Davis's "All Blues."

I slipped back into the alleyways and zigzagged for another half-hour until I found myself standing in front of Preservation Hall.

I have never been a fan of traditional jazz. Worse, I have always imagined that the traditional jazz featured inside Preservation Hall would be a shuck, like Disneyland Dixieland—an artifice, unfelt, an impersonation for the tourists. The line in front of Preservation Hall was very long, but a good tenor sax player was wandering up and down the street, playing for free, and so I took my place at the end of the line, as much to rest and listen to the sax man as gain entry. When we were finally ushered into the building, I saw that a lack of artifice was Preservation Hall's greatest asset. The hall looked about twice the size of my hotel room, dimly lit like the gloomy altar of some small country church where a few candles sputtered bravely. Six musicians sat upon wooden chairs atop a small stage raised about eighteen inches from the floor. A half-dozen wooden bench pews filed back from the stage; everybody else—maybe seventy-five people—crowded together in the darkness, shoulder to shoulder.

I didn't recognize the band's first tune, but when the trumpet player took the lead, he shaved the melody close, in the style of King Oliver. After the clarinet solo, he stood up once again and sang out to the audience. His woman had left him, giving him the blues; it was the usual story.

Traditional jazz has never seemed risky enough to me. But as the band inside Preservation Hall continued to bang out one number after another, the piano, bass, drums, banjo, clarinet, and trumpet swelling into a sea of collective fakery with sufficient spirit and peculiarity to challenge all the conventional harmonies, I caught for an inspired instant how truly daring the music must have felt at its inception. Even now the friction of creation showed sparks—the painful *hilarity* of squeezing something unheard before from a motley collection of instruments only recently transported to these shores. The band rambled on, and I realized there was nothing at all quaint about this music; it had always been full of risk, unstable, and liable to combust.

"Everyone is familiar with the Negro's modification of the whites' musical instruments," wrote Zora Neale Hurston in a 1911 essay, "Characteristics of Negro Expression," "so that his interpretation has been adopted by the white man himself and then reinterpreted. In so many words, Paul Whiteman is giving an imitation of a Negro orchestra making use of white-invented musical instruments in a Negro way. Thus has arisen a new art in the civilized world, and thus has our so-called civilization come. The exchange and re-exchange of ideas between groups."

The bass player at Preservation Hall seemed determined to prove this point. He launched into a flutter of notes that were both too rapid and dissonant for New Orleans vintage jazz, playing more like Charles Mingus than Pops Foster. He scurried up the instrument's neck from the bridge to the scroll, shattering the tune. The other players grunted encouragement. Together they were demonstrating how music—culture—argues, blends, dissolves, mutates, advances. The odd bird who hears something different plucks his strings too quickly or queerly or flat out plunks the *wrong* note, but he does it over and over until it sounds right. He finds his own groove and fashions new music from the old.

And that's exactly what American music—American culture—has managed to do. As Hurston understood, as the bass player was now showing, our nation's truest anthem contains the funeral dirge of the New Orleans street band combined with the whore-house piano and the last slave's work song and the bickering melodies of two hundred disparate points of origin, from Marseilles to Dakar, from Manaus to Guangzhou, now stretched out over the American plains like the hide of some mythical beast: the confluence of influences that nobody will ever be able to pick apart note-for-note. It has long been a sophisticated complaint to jeer that America has "no culture," but there couldn't be a sillier idea. We have more culture than one people will ever be able to digest. And that helps explain why the melting pot sometimes bubbles up—and when we least expect it, explodes.

CRITICAL THINKING QUESTION

List 3 to 5 musical groups and 3 to 5 songs that you enjoy. What cultures and influences are reflected in the music you listed?

WRITING TOPIC

Read paragraph 88 in Richard Rodriguez's essay "The Chinese in All of Us" (page 165). In what ways does Setterberg's essay support Rodriguez's assumption expressed in that paragraph? Please elaborate on your opinion by providing examples from each literary work.

Jonathan Swift

A Modest Proposal

For Preventing the Children of Poor People in Ireland from Being a Burden to Their Parents or Country, and for Making Them Beneficial to the Public (1729)

It is a melancholy object to those who walk through this great town or travel in the country, when they see the streets, the roads, and cabin doors crowded with beggars of the female sex, followed by three, four, or six children, all in rags and importuning every passenger for an alms. These mothers, instead of being able to work for their honest livelihood, are forced to employ all their time in strolling to beg sustenance for their helpless infants, who, as they grow up, either turn thieves for want of work, or leave their dear native country to fight for the Pretender in Spain, or sell themselves to the Barbadoes.

I think it is agreed by all parties that this prodigious number of children in the arms, or on the backs, or at the heels of their mothers, and frequently of their fathers, is in the present deplorable state of the kingdom a very great additional grievance; and therefore whoever could find out a fair, cheap, and easy method of making these children sound and useful members of the commonwealth would deserve so well of the public as to have his statue set up for a preserver of the nation.

But my intention is very far from being confined to provide only for the children of professed beggars; it is of a much greater extent, and shall take in the whole number of infants at a certain age who are born of parents in effect as little able to support them as those who demand our charity in the streets.

As to my own part, having turned my thoughts for many years upon this important subject, and maturely weighed the several schemes of other projectors, I have always found them grossly mistaken in their computation. It is true a child just dropped from its dam may be supported by her milk for a solar year with little other nourishment, at most not above the value of two shillings, which the mother may certainly get, or the value in scraps, by her lawful occupation of begging; and it is exactly at one year old that I propose to provide for them in such a manner as instead of being a charge upon their parents or the parish, or wanting food and raiment for the rest of their lives, they shall, on the contrary, contribute to the feeding and partly to the clothing of many thousands.

There is likewise another great advantage in my scheme, that it will prevent those voluntary abortions, and that horrid practice of women murdering their bastard children, alas! too frequent among us, sacrificing the poor innocent babes, I doubt, more to avoid the expense than the shame, which would move tears and pity in the most savage and inhuman breast.

The number of souls in this kingdom being usually reckoned one million and a hair, of these I calculate there may be about two hundred thousand couples whose wives are breeders; from which number I subtract thirty thousand couples who are able to maintain their own children, although I apprehend there cannot be so many, under the present distress of the kingdom; but this being granted, there will remain an hundred and seventy thousand breeders. I again subtract fifty thousand for those women who miscarry, or whose children die by accident or disease within the year. There only remain an hundred and twenty thousand children of poor parents annually born. The question therefore is, how this number shall be reared and provided for, which, as I have already said, under the present situation of affairs is utterly impossible by all the methods hitherto proposed. For we can neither employ them in handicraft or agriculture; we neither build houses (I mean in the country) nor cultivate land: they can very seldom pick up a livelihood by stealing till they arrive at six years old, except where they are of towardly parts; although I confess they learn the rudiments much earlier, during which time they can, however, be properly looked upon only as probationers, as I have been informed by a principal gentleman in the county of Cavan, who protested to me that he never knew above one or two instances under the age of six, even in a part of the kingdom so renowned for the quickest proficiency in that art.

I am assured by our merchants that a boy or girl before twelve years old is no salable commodity; and even when they come to this age they will not yield above three pounds or three pounds and half-a-crown at most on the Exchange; which cannot turn to account either to the parents or the kingdom, the charge of nutriment and rags having been at least four times that value.

I shall now therefore humbly propose my own thoughts, which I hope will not be liable to the least objection.

I have been assured by a very knowing American of my acquaintance in London that a young healthy child well nursed is at a year old a most delicious, nourishing, and wholesome food, whether stewed, roasted, baked, or boiled; and I make no doubt that it will equally serve in a fricassee or a ragout.

10   I do therefore humbly offer it to public consideration that of the hundred and twenty thousand children already computed, twenty thousand may be reserved for breed, whereof only one-fourth part to be males, which is more than we allow to sheep, black cattle or swine; and my reason is that these children are seldom the fruits of marriage, a circumstance not much regarded by our savages; therefore one male will be sufficient to serve four females. That the remaining hundred thousand may at a year old be offered in sale to the persons of quality and fortune through the kingdom, always advising the mother to let them suck plentifully in the last month, so as to render them plump and fat for a good table. A child will make two dishes at an entertainment for friends; and when the family dines alone, the fore or hind quarter will make a reasonable dish, and seasoned with a little pepper or salt will be very good boiled on the fourth day, especially in winter.

    I have reckoned upon a medium that a child just born will weigh twelve pounds, and in a solar year if tolerably nursed increaseth to twenty-eight pounds.

    I grant this food will be somewhat dear, and therefore very proper for landlords, who, as they have already devoured most of the parents, seem to have the best title to the children.

    Infants' flesh will be in season throughout the year, but more plentiful in March, and a little before and after; for we are told by a grave author, an eminent French physician, that fish being a prolific diet, there are more children born in Roman Catholic countries about nine months after Lent than at any other season; therefore reckoning a year after Lent, the markets will be more glutted than usual, because the number of popish infants is at least three to one in this kingdom; and therefore it will have one other collateral advantage, by lessening the number of Papists among us.

    I have already computed the charge of nursing a beggar's child (in which list I reckon all cottagers, laborers, and four-fifths of the farmers) to be about two shillings per annum, rags included; and I believe no gentleman would repine to give ten shillings for the carcass of a good fat child, which, as I have said, will make four dishes of excellent nutritive meat, when he hath only some particular friend or his own family to dine with him. Thus the squire will learn to be a good landlord, and grow popular among his tenants; the mother will have eight shillings net profit, and be fit for work till she produces another child.

15   Those who are more thrifty (as I must confess the times require) may flay the carcass; the skin of which artificially dressed will make admirable gloves for ladies, and summer boots for fine gentlemen.

    As to our city of Dublin, shambles may be appointed for this purpose in the most convenient parts of it, and butchers we may be assured will not be wanting; although I rather recommend buying the children alive, and dressing them hot from the knife, as we do roasting pigs.

    A very worthy person, a true lover of his country, and whose virtues I highly esteem, was lately pleased, in discoursing on this matter, to offer a refinement upon my scheme. He said that many gentlemen of this kingdom, having of late destroyed their deer, he conceived that the want of venison might be well supplied by the bodies of young lads and maidens, not exceeding fourteen years of age nor under twelve, so great a number of both sexes in every country being now ready to starve for want of work and service: and these to be disposed of by their parents, if alive, or otherwise by their nearest relations. But with due deference to so excellent a friend and so deserving a patriot, I cannot be altogether in his sentiments. For as to the males, my American acquaintance assured me from frequent experience that their flesh was generally tough and lean, like that of our schoolboys, by continual exercise, and their taste disagreeable; and to fatten them would not answer the charge. Then as to the females, it would, I think, with humble submission, be a loss to the public, because they soon would become breeders themselves: and besides, it is not improbable that some scrupulous people might be apt to censure such a practice (although indeed very unjustly) as a little bordering upon cruelty; which, I confess, hath always been with me the strongest objection against any project, how well soever intended.

But in order to justify my friend, he confessed that this expedient was put into his head by the famous Psalmanazar, a native of the island Formosa, who came from thence to London above twenty years ago, and in conversation told my friend that in his country when any young person happened to be put to death, the executioner sold the carcass to persons of quality as a prime dainty, and that in his time the body of a plump girl of fifteen, who was crucified for an attempt to poison the emperor, was sold to his Imperial Majesty's prime minister of state, and other great mandarins of the court, in joints from the gibbet, at four hundred crowns. Neither indeed can I deny that if the same use were made of several plump young girls in this town, who, without one single groat to their fortunes, cannot stir abroad without a chair, and appear at the playhouse and assemblies in foreign fineries, which they never will pay for, the kingdom would not be the worse.

Some persons of a desponding spirit are in great concern about that vast number of poor people, who are aged, diseased, or maimed, and I have been desired to employ my thoughts what course may be taken to ease the nation of so grievous an encumbrance. But I am not in the least pain upon that matter, because it is very well known that they are every day dying and rotting, by cold and famine, and filth and vermin, as fast as can be reasonably expected. And as to the younger laborers, they are now in almost as hopeful a condition. They cannot get work, and consequently pine away for want of nourishment, to a degree that if at any time they are accidentally hired to common labor, they have not strength to perform it; and thus the country and themselves are happily delivered from the evils to come.

I have too long digressed, and therefore shall return to my subject. I think   20 the advantages by the proposal which I have made are obvious and many, as well as of the highest importance.

For first, as I have already observed, it would greatly lessen the number of Papists, with whom we are yearly overrun, being the principal breeders of the nation as well as our most dangerous enemies; and who stay at home on purpose with a design to deliver the kingdom to the Pretender, hoping to take their advantage by the absence of so many good Protestants, who have chosen rather to leave their country than stay at home and pay tithes against their conscience to an Episcopal curate.

Secondly, the poorer tenants will have something valuable of their own, which by law may be made liable to distress, and help to pay their landlord's rent; their corn and cattle being already seized, and money a thing unknown.

Thirdly, whereas the maintenance of an hundred thousand children, from two years old and upwards, cannot be computed at less than ten shillings apiece per annum, the nation's stock will be thereby increased fifty thousand pounds per annum, besides the profit of a new dish introduced to the tables of all gentlemen of fortune in the kingdom who have any refinement in taste. And the money will circulate among ourselves, the goods being entirely of our own growth and manufacture.

Fourthly, the constant breeders, besides the gain of eight shillings sterling per annum by the sale of their children, will be rid of the charge of maintaining them after the first year.

25 Fifthly, this food would likewise bring great custom to taverns, where the vintners will certainly be so prudent as to procure the best receipts for dressing it to perfection, and consequently have their houses frequented by all the fine gentlemen, who justly value themselves upon their knowledge in good eating; and a skillful cook, who understands how to oblige his guests, will contrive to make it as expensive as they please.

Sixthly, this would be a great inducement to marriage, which all wise nations have either encouraged by rewards or enforced by laws and penalties. It would increase the care and tenderness of mothers toward their children, when they were sure of a settlement for life to the poor babes, provided in some sort by the public, to their annual profit instead of expense. We should see an honest emulation among the married women, which of them could bring the fattest child to the market. Men would become as fond of their wives during the time of their pregnancy as they are now of their mares in foal, their cows in calf, or sows when they are ready to farrow; nor offer to beat or kick them (as is too frequent a practice) for fear of miscarriage.

Many other advantages might be enumerated. For instance, the addition of some thousand carcasses in our exportation of barreled beef, the propagation of swine's flesh, and improvement in the art of making good bacon, so much wanted among us by the great destruction of pigs, too frequent at our tables, and are no way comparable in taste or magnificence to a well-grown, fat yearling child, which roasted whole will make a considerable figure at a lord mayor's feast, or any other public entertainment. But this and many others I omit, being studious of brevity.

Supposing that one thousand families in this city would be constant customers for infants' flesh, besides others who might have it at merry meetings, particularly weddings and christenings, I compute that Dublin would take off annually about twenty thousand carcasses, and the rest of the kingdom (where probably they will be sold somewhat cheaper) the remaining eighty thousand.

I can think of no one objection that will possibly be raised against this proposal, unless it should be urged that the number of people will be thereby much lessened in the kingdom. This I freely own, and it was indeed one principal design in offering it to the world. I desire the reader will observe that I calculate my remedy for this one individual kingdom of Ireland, and for no other that ever was, is, or, I think, ever can be upon earth. Therefore let no man talk to me of other expedients: of taxing our absentees at five shillings a pound; of using neither clothes nor household furniture except what is of our own growth and manufacture; of utterly rejecting the materials and instruments that promote foreign luxury; of curing the expensiveness of pride, vanity, idleness, and gaming in our women; of introducing a vein of parsimony, prudence, and temperance; of learning to love our country, in the want of which we differ even from Laplanders and the inhabitants of Topinamboo; of quitting our animosities and factions, nor act any longer like the Jews, who were murdering one another at the very moment their city was taken; of being a little cautious not to sell our country and consciences for nothing; of teaching landlords to have at least one degree of mercy toward their tenants; lastly, of putting a spirit of honesty, industry, and skill into our shopkeepers, who, if a resolution could now be taken to buy only our native goods, would immediately unite to cheat and exact upon us in the price, the measure, and the goodness, nor could ever yet be brought to make one fair proposal of just dealing, though often and earnestly invited to it.

Therefore I repeat, let no man talk to me of these and the like expedients, 30 till he has at least some glimpse of hope that there will be ever some hearty and sincere attempt to put them in practice.

But as to myself, having been wearied out for many years with offering vain, idle, visionary thoughts, and at length utterly despairing of success, I fortunately fell upon this proposal, which, as it is wholly new, so it has something solid and real, of no expense and little trouble, full in our own power, and whereby we can incur no danger in disobliging England. For this kind of commodity will not bear exportation, the flesh being of too tender a consistence to admit a long continuance in salt, although perhaps I could name a country which would be glad to eat up our whole nation without it.

After all, I am not so violently bent upon my own opinion as to reject any offer proposed by wise men, which shall be found equally innocent, cheap, easy, and effectual. But before something of that kind shall be advanced in contradiction to my scheme, and offering a better, I desire the author or authors will be pleased maturely to consider two points. First, as things now stand, how they will be able to find food and raiment for an hundred thousand useless mouths and backs. And secondly, there being a round million of creatures in human figure throughout this kingdom, whose whole subsistence put into a common stock would leave them in debt two millions of pounds sterling, adding those who are beggars by profession to the bulk of farmers, cottagers, and laborers, with their wives and children, who are beggars in effect; I desire those politicians who dislike my overture, and may perhaps be so bold as to attempt an answer, that they will first ask the parents of these mortals whether they would not at this day think it a great happiness to have been sold for food at a year old in the manner I prescribe, and thereby have avoided such a perpetual scene of misfortunes as they have since gone through by the oppression of landlords, the impossibility of paying rent without money or trade, the want of common sustenance, with neither house nor clothes to cover them from the inclemencies of the weather, and the most inevitable prospect of entailing the like or greater miseries upon their breed for ever.

I profess, in the sincerity of my heart, that I have not the least personal interest in endeavoring to promote this necessary work, having no other motive than the public good of my country, by advancing our trade, providing for infants, relieving the poor, and giving some pleasure to the rich. I have no children by which I can propose to get a single penny; the youngest being nine years old, and my wife past child-bearing.

CRITICAL THINKING QUESTIONS

1. List the incentives Swift suggests will result from his proposal that people begin to eat the babies born to poor Irish mothers.

2. What adjectives would you use to describe the tone of Swift's writing? Why would he employ such a tone? What is the effect on the audience?

WRITING TOPIC

While Swift's proposal was not serious, it did point out very serious problems that needed to be addressed. Select a contemporary issue, such as immigration, and offer an equally outrageous solution that helps point out the importance of the situation.

CHAPTER ACTIVITIES AND TOPICS FOR WRITING ARGUMENTS

1. Write about your concept of the American Dream. As you write, think about specific individuals whom you know who have achieved the dream—or those who have not. What has contributed to their successes or failures? Form a group with several classmates and read each other's writings to compare and contrast your perspectives. Now as a group, read the poems "Burning Dreams on the Sun" (page 127) and "Richard Cory" (page 142). How do these poems extend your group's ideas? Be prepared to share your insights with the class as a whole.

2. Puritans came to these shores seeking freedom, yet, ironically, created one of the more restrictive societies in our country's history. Our ambivalence toward questions of freedom and conformity, therefore, goes back to our very beginnings. Look at the short story "The Foundations of the Earth" (page 107) and the poem "Crazy Courage" (page 148), which might help you gain some perspective on this subject. Where do you observe or personally encounter that ambivalence today? Based on your observations, create a **claim of fact** and list at least three examples of evidence to support your claim.

3. In Washington, Congress regularly considers an amendment to the Constitution making the unconventional use of the flag for social protests or artistic expression illegal. To gain some insight into the concept of just and unjust laws, read the essay "Letter from Birmingham Jail" (page 151) and the poem "In Response to Executive Order 9066" (page 140). Also, read about laws governing the use of the American flag. Write a claim of policy and argue that these laws are just or unjust.

4. What is a hero? How do others define this concept? How do you define it? Think about some of the characters in the selections you have just read; do they fit a definition of "hero"? Think about real people you have encountered in your life; do any of them fit the definition? How does a hero relate to his or her society? Broaden your understanding of a hero by reading the short selection from *Bodega Dreams* (page 120), the poem "Crazy Courage" (page 148), and the essay "The Train from Hate" (page 150). Do some library research in order to extend your understanding of the concept of the hero. Now create your own definition. Support your argument with evidence from your library research, personal experience, and specific examples from your reading in this chapter.

GLOBAL PERSPECTIVES RESEARCH/WRITING TOPICS

1. Individuals and Global Online Communities

Facebook, Instagram, Snapchat, Twitter, and a whole host of other social networking sites bring people together from around the globe who can form online communities based on shared interests. According to pollster John Zogby, young adults, in particular, are active participants in social networking: "Americans between the ages of 18 and 29 are 'the First Globals ... more networked and globally engaged than members of any similar age cohort in American history.'"[2] What in your view does the notion of "First Globals" mean? Do you participate in online social networking, and if so, have you connected with individuals from around the globe? Even if you do not consider yourself to be engaged in global online communities, what are the implications of this global connectivity for individuals? Examine both the positive and negative effects that participating in such communities might have for individuals. Based on your critical analysis of these effects, create an argument that addresses the impact of these online communities on individuals.

2. Nations and Global Connectivity

Traditionally, individuals have defined themselves by nationality; today, however, as online communities form and grow, national boundaries become less pronounced and cultural divisions shrink. Indeed, the term *global citizen* implies that individuals are members of—and have a responsibility to—a global community. The concept of community suggests mutual interests and shared goals, that is, collaboration rather than competition. Addressing climate change and economic issues, for example, has dramatically underscored the vital connectivity among nations; instead of survival of the fittest, it seems that nations must swim together or they will sink together. The twenty-first-century dynamic of interdependent nations represents a shift away from the twentieth-century dynamic of the superpower nation. Some people, however, contend that the superpower nation model has not been discarded but, instead, retooled to reflect the twenty-first century's constellation of influential nations.

Consider an issue that affects the global community, such as nuclear proliferation, climate change, infectious diseases, population control, or energy needs. Imagine that you are attempting to persuade a nation's leader (you can create a fictitious nation/leader) to re-envision his or her nation as a global citizen—a team player—rather than as a superpower nation.

---

[2]qtd. in Anne-Marie Slaughter, "America's Edge," *Foreign Affairs* 1 Feb. 2009: n. pag. *Global NewsBank*, NewsBank Online. Web. 16 Mar. 2015.

COLLABORATION ACTIVITY: CREATING A ROGERIAN
ARGUMENT

For this activity, you will work in small teams to research, write, and present a Rogerian argument on a contemporary issue that has emerged from your exploration of readings in this chapter. The WRITING TOPICS following many of the selections can help you identify an issue. For a discussion of the **Rogerian argument** and a suggested organizational approach to the assignment, please see Chapter 5.

Following are guidelines for this collaboration activity:

- Identify an **issue.**
- Divide the research/writing responsibilities as follows:
  - Student one: introduction section
  - Student two: body section, affirmative position
  - Student three: body section, opposing position
  - Student four: conclusion, summation, and middle-ground position

Following are characteristics of effective collaboration. Each team member should:

- Contribute by collecting information related to the issue.
- Take responsibility by completing assigned work on time.
- Engage with other team members by listening to and considering other viewpoints.

Sample Issue: Immigration Policy

Lines from Emma Lazarus's poem inscribed on the Statue of Liberty say, "Give me your tired, your poor/Your huddled masses yearning to breathe free." Traditionally, the United States has offered immigrants the opportunity to join the community and to add their contributions to the culture and economy. Many Americans continue to value that tradition; however, since the September 11 terrorist attacks and continued threats to internal security, as well as increasing numbers of illegal immigrants, many others have sought to limit immigration. In 2005, to help secure the Mexican border and deter illegal immigration, the U.S. Congress authorized the construction of a 670-mile fence along the border. More recently, states, notably Alabama and Arizona, have passed their own version of "get-tough" immigration laws that authorize aggressive law enforcement procedures. While some strongly support such actions, others are advocating amnesty for illegal immigrants. What immigration policy should be implemented at either a state or federal level?

Literature suggestions: "Mexicans Begin Jogging" and "The Chinese in All of Us" in Chapter 6; "The People in Me" in Chapter 8.

ARGUING THEMES FROM LITERATURE

Each selection in this chapter promoted reflection upon the individual's place in society. To practice your literary argument skills, consider the following questions:

1. In Truman Capote's "Jug of Silver," Hamurabi seems especially sensitive to Appleseed's feelings. Based upon the evidence offered in the story's text, develop an argument as to why the dentist exhibited compassion to this societal outcast. Though difference in age and culture separate the two, what similarities link the two characters?

2. Authors utilize language as a means of foreshadowing upcoming events in short stories. Now that you have read "The Lottery" by Shirley Jackson, revisit the text to examine hints that tragedy looms. In what ways does Jackson use language symbolically to offer clues? Consider, for example, the character's names and other descriptions.

3. People love to idolize celebrities. Often, we erroneously believe that singers, sports stars, or actors have no problems other than spending all the money they make. Many of us have probably daydreamed about trading lives with them. The poem "Richard Cory," by Edwin Arlington Robinson, offers commentary on celebrity status with a biting dose of reality. Do you feel the poem speaks to America's obsession with celebrity culture? Can you identify a modern-day Richard Cory and compare/contrast that celebrity's plight with Cory's struggles?

CHAPTER 7

Crime and Punishment

Crime and punishment themes pervade literary works. Forbidden acts, sins committed in secret, somehow lead to a day of reckoning for those immersed in scandal. If the guilty do not pay, their atonement may prove to be the collateral damage imposed upon their loved ones or those closest to them. The idea that people must pay for their transgressions is a prevalent theme in classic literature and popular media. Whether one of Edgar Allen Poe's jilted characters takes vengeance on a friend who he feels slighted him or a Lanister on HBO's popular series *Game of Thrones* plots the takedown of a political enemy, audiences always seem to have an appetite for watching the guilty receive their just desserts.

Each selection in this chapter provides scenarios where a crime of some sort ultimately brings with it a type of punishment—but those who receive the sentence are not necessarily the offenders. We would like to think that good always triumphs over evil, but certainly some of the stories and characters in the following selections might make us reconsider this expected outcome of justice. As you read the texts in this chapter, consider the characters, their motivations, and the forces that drive their actions in these horrific and confounding tales.

PREWRITING AND DISCUSSION

1. Would you consider crime to be a large personal concern? Do you feel that modern media makes too much of criminal cases, sensationalizing bizarre tales that become high profile and misrepresenting the true extent of criminal activity? Contrarily, do you fully believe that crime is an epidemic? Do you feel perceptions of crime and criminal activity hinder the daily activities of you or someone close to you? If you feel the media incites gross misrepresentations of crime, what fault do we as consumers of the media play in perpetuating the cycle?

2. When it comes to punishment for criminals, how often do you feel that offenders get what they deserve? Do you notice disparities within the criminal justice system that concern you? If so, what specifically do you find bothersome? Additionally, can you think of any laws on the books currently that seem unfair? Can you think of any laws that you would like to see added to current criminal codes?

3. People often say that victims of crimes and their families deserve justice. What does the term *justice* mean to you? Do you feel justice is often rendered or often denied those in need of it? Beyond your personal definitions, what images do you believe justice evokes in the minds of most people? What do people expect in order to feel they have received justice?

FICTION

Ambrose Bierce

An Occurrence at Owl Creek Bridge (1890)

I

A man stood upon a railroad bridge in northern Alabama, looking down into the swift water twenty feet below. The man's hands were behind his back, the wrists bound with a cord. A rope closely encircled his neck. It was attached to a stout cross-timber above his head and the slack fell to the level of his knees. Some loose boards laid upon the sleepers supporting the metals of the railway supplied a footing for him and his executioners—two private soldiers of the Federal army, directed by a sergeant who in civil life may have been a deputy sheriff. At a short remove upon the same temporary platform was an officer in the uniform of his rank, armed. He was a captain. A sentinel[1] at each end of the bridge stood with his rifle in the position known as "support," that is to say, vertical in front of the left shoulder, the hammer resting on the forearm thrown straight across the chest—a formal and unnatural position, enforcing an erect carriage of the body. It did not appear to be the duty of these two men to know what was occurring at the center of the bridge; they merely blockaded the two ends of the foot planking that traversed it.

Beyond one of the sentinels nobody was in sight; the railroad ran straight away into a forest for a hundred yards, then, curving, was lost to view. Doubtless there was an outpost farther along. The other bank of the stream was open ground—a gentle acclivity topped with a stockade of vertical tree trunks, loopholed for rifles, with a single embrasure through which protruded the muzzle of a brass cannon commanding the bridge. Midway of the slope between bridge and fort were the spectators—a single company of infantry in line, at "parade rest," the butts of the rifles on the ground, the barrels inclining slightly backward against the right shoulder, the hands crossed upon the stock. A lieutenant stood

---

[1] **sentinel** armed guard who keeps watch

at the right of the line, the point of his sword upon the ground, his left hand resting upon his right. Excepting the group of four at the center of the bridge, not a man moved. The company faced the bridge, staring stonily, motionless. The sentinels, facing the banks of the stream, might have been statues to adorn the bridge. The captain stood with folded arms, silent, observing the work of his subordinates, but making no sign. Death is a dignitary who when he comes announced is to be received with formal manifestations of respect, even by those most familiar with him. In the code of military etiquette silence and fixity are forms of deference.

The man who was engaged in being hanged was apparently about thirty-five years of age. He was a civilian, if one might judge from his habit, which was that of a planter. His features were good—a straight nose, firm mouth, broad forehead, from which his long, dark hair was combed straight back, falling behind his ears to the collar of his well-fitting frock-coat. He wore a mustache and pointed beard, but no whiskers; his eyes were large and dark gray, and had a kindly expression which one would hardly have expected in one whose neck was in the hemp. Evidently this was no vulgar assassin. The liberal military code makes provision for hanging many kinds of persons, and gentlemen are not excluded.

The preparations being complete, the two private soldiers stepped aside and each drew away the plank upon which he had been standing. The sergeant turned to the captain, saluted and placed himself immediately behind that officer, who in turn moved apart one pace. These movements left the condemned man and the sergeant standing on the two ends of the same plank, which spanned three of the crossties of the bridge. The end upon which the civilian stood almost, but not quite, reached a fourth. This plank had been held in place by the weight of the captain; it was now held by that of the sergeant. At a signal from the former the latter would step aside, the plank would tilt and the condemned man go down between two ties. The arrangement commended itself to his judgment as simple and effective. His face had not been covered nor his eyes bandaged. He looked a moment at his "unsteadfast footing," then let his gaze wander to the swirling water of the stream racing madly beneath his feet. A piece of dancing driftwood caught his attention and his eyes followed it down the current. How slowly it appeared to move! What a sluggish stream!

5   He closed his eyes in order to fix his last thoughts upon his wife and children. The water, touched to gold by the early sun, the brooding mists under the banks at some distance down the stream, the fort, the soldiers, the piece of drift—all had distracted him. And now he became conscious of a new disturbance. Striking through the thought of his dear ones was a sound which he would neither ignore nor understand, a sharp, distinct, metallic percussion like the stroke of a blacksmith's hammer upon the anvil; it had the same ringing quality. He wondered what it was, and whether immeasurably distant or near by—it seemed both. Its recurrence was regular, but as slow as the tolling of a death knell. He awaited each stroke with impatience and—he knew not why—apprehension. The intervals of silence grew progressively longer; the delays became maddening. With

their greater infrequency the sounds increased in strength and sharpness. They hurt his ear like the thrust of a knife; he feared he would shriek. What he heard was the ticking of his watch.

He unclosed his eyes and saw again the water below him. "If I could free my hands," he thought, "I might throw off the noose and spring into the stream. By diving I could evade the bullets and, swimming vigorously, reach the bank, take to the woods and get away home. My home, thank God, is as yet outside their lines; my wife and little ones are still beyond the invader's farthest advance."

As these thoughts, which have here to be set down in words, were flashed into the doomed man's brain rather than evolved from it the captain nodded to the sergeant. The sergeant stepped aside.

II

Peyton Farquhar was a well-to-do planter, of an old and highly respected Alabama family. Being a slave owner and like other slave owners a politician he was naturally an original secessionist and ardently devoted to the Southern cause. Circumstances of an imperious nature, which it is unnecessary to relate here, had prevented him from taking service with the gallant army that had fought the disastrous campaigns ending with the fall of Corinth,[2] and he chafed under the inglorious restraint, longing for the release of his energies, the larger life of the soldier, the opportunity for distinction. That opportunity, he felt, would come, as it comes to all in war time. Meanwhile he did what he could. No service was too humble for him to perform in aid of the South, no adventure too perilous for him to undertake if consistent with the character of a civilian who was at heart a soldier, and who in good faith and without too much qualification assented to at least a part of the frankly villainous dictum that all is fair in love and war.

One evening while Farquhar and his wife were sitting on a rustic bench near the entrance to his grounds, a gray-clad soldier rode up to the gate and asked for a drink of water. Mrs. Farquhar was only too happy to serve him with her own white hands. While she was fetching the water her husband approached the dusty horseman and inquired eagerly for news from the front.

"The Yanks are repairing the railroads," said the man, "and are getting ready   10 for another advance. They have reached the Owl Creek bridge, put it in order and built a stockade on the north bank. The commandant has issued an order, which is posted everywhere, declaring that any civilian caught interfering with the railroad, its bridges, tunnels or trains will be summarily hanged. I saw the order."

"How far is it to the Owl Creek bridge?" Farquhar asked.

"About thirty miles."

"Is there no force on this side the creek?"

---

[2]**Corinth** a town in Mississippi and site of a Confederate army defeat in 1862

"Only a picket post half a mile out, on the railroad, and a single sentinel at this end of the bridge."

15   "Suppose a man—a civilian and student of hanging—should elude the picket post and perhaps get the better of the sentinel," said Farquhar, smiling, "what could he accomplish?"

The soldier reflected. "I was there a month ago," he replied, "I observed that the flood of last winter had lodged a great quantity of driftwood against the wooden pier at this end of the bridge. It is now dry and would burn like tow."

The lady had now brought the water, which the soldier drank. He thanked her ceremoniously, bowed to her husband and rode away. An hour later, after nightfall, he repassed the plantation, going northward in the direction from which he had come. He was a Federal scout.

III

As Peyton Farquhar fell straight downward through the bridge he lost consciousness and was as one already dead. From this state he was awakened—ages later, it seemed to him—by the pain of a sharp pressure upon his throat, followed by a sense of suffocation. Keen, poignant agonies seemed to shoot from his neck downward through every fiber of his body and limbs. These pains appeared to flash along well-defined lines of ramification and to beat with an inconceivably rapid periodicity. They seemed like streams of pulsating fire heating him to an intolerable temperature. As to his head, he was conscious of nothing but a feeling of fullness—of congestion. These sensations were unaccompanied by thought. The intellectual part of his nature was already effaced; he had power only to feel, and feeling was torment. He was conscious of motion. Encompassed in a luminous cloud, of which he was now merely the fiery heart, without material substance, he swung through unthinkable arcs of oscillation, like a vast pendulum. Then all at once, with terrible suddenness, the light about him shot upward with the noise of a loud plash; a frightful roaring was in his ears, and all was cold and dark. The power of thought was restored; he knew that the rope had broken and he had fallen into the stream. There was no additional strangulation; the noose about his neck was already suffocating him and kept the water from his lungs. To die of hanging at the bottom of a river!—the idea seemed to him ludicrous. He opened his eyes in the darkness and saw above him a gleam of light, but how distant, how inaccessible! He was still sinking, for the light became fainter and fainter until it was a mere glimmer. Then it began to grow and brighten, and he knew that he was rising toward the surface—knew it with reluctance, for he was now very comfortable. "To be hanged and drowned," he thought, "that is not so bad; but I do not wish to be shot. No; I will not be shot; that is not fair."

He was not conscious of an effort, but a sharp pain in his wrist apprised him that he was trying to free his hands. He gave the struggle his attention, as an idler might observe the feat of a juggler, without interest in the outcome.

What splendid effort!—what magnificent, what superhuman strength! Ah, that was a fine endeavor! Bravo! The cord fell away; his arms parted and floated upward; the hands dimly seen on each side in the growing light. He watched them with new interest as first one and then the other pounced upon the noose at his neck. They tore it away and thrust it fiercely aside, its undulations resembling those of a water- snake. "Put it back, put it back!" He thought he shouted these words to his hands, for the undoing of the noose had been suc- ceeded by the direst pang that he had yet experienced. His neck ached hor- ribly; his brain was on fire; his heart, which had been fluttering faintly, gave a great leap, trying to force itself out at his mouth. His whole body was racked and wrenched with an insupportable anguish! But his disobedient hands gave no heed to the command. They beat the water vigorously with quick, down- ward strokes, forcing him to the surface. He felt his head emerge; his eyes were blinded by the sunlight; his chest expanded convulsively, and with a supreme and crowning agony his lungs engulfed a great draught of air, which instantly he expelled in a shriek!

He was now in full possession of his physical senses. They were, indeed, 20 preternaturally keen and alert. Something in the awful disturbance of his organ- ic system had so exalted and refined them that they made record of things never before perceived. He felt the ripples upon his face and heard their separate sounds as they struck. He looked at the forest on the bank of the stream, saw the individual trees, the leaves and the veining of each leaf—saw the very insects upon them: the locusts, the brilliant-bodied flies, the gray spiders stretching their webs from twig to twig. He noted the prismatic colors in all the dewdrops upon a million blades of grass. The humming of the gnats that danced above the eddies of the stream, the beating of the dragon-flies' wings, the strokes of water-spider's legs, like oars which had lifted their boat—all these made audible music. A fish slid along beneath his eyes and he heard the rush of its body part- ing the water.

He had come to the surface facing down the stream; in a moment the visible world seemed to wheel slowly round, himself the pivotal point, and he saw the bridge, the fort, the soldiers upon the bridge, the captain, the sergeant, the two privates, his executioners. They were in silhouette against the blue sky. They shouted and gesticulated, pointing at him. The captain had drawn his pistol, but did not fire; the others were unarmed. Their movements were grotesque and horrible, their forms gigantic.

Suddenly he heard a sharp report and something struck the water smartly within a few inches of his head, spattering his face with spray. He heard a sec- ond report, and saw one of the sentinels with his rifle at his shoulder, a light cloud of blue smoke rising from the muzzle. The man in the water saw the eye of the man on the bridge gazing into his own through the sights of the rifle. He observed that it was a gray eye and remembered having read that gray eyes were keenest, and that all famous marksmen had them. Nevertheless, this one had missed.

A counter-swirl had caught Farquhar and turned him half round; he was again looking into the forest on the bank opposite the fort. The sound of a clear, high voice in a monotonous singsong now rang out behind him and came across the water with a distinctness that pierced and subdued all other sounds, even the beating of the ripples in his ears. Although no soldier, he had frequented camps enough to know the dread significance of that deliberate, drawling, aspirated chant; the lieutenant on shore was taking a part in the morning's work. How coldly and pitilessly—with what an even, calm intonation, presaging, and enforcing tranquility in the men—with what accurately measured intervals fell those cruel words:

"Attention, company! ... Shoulder arms! ... Ready! ... Aim! ... Fire!"

25 Farquhar dived—dived as deeply as he could. The water roared in his ears like the voice of Niagara, yet he heard the dulled thunder of the volley and, rising again toward the surface, met shining bits of metal, singularly flattened, oscillating slowly downward. Some of them touched him on the face and hands, then fell away, continuing their descent. One lodged between his collar and neck; it was uncomfortably warm and he snatched it out.

As he rose to the surface, gasping for breath, he saw that he had been a long time under water; he was perceptibly farther down stream—nearer to safety. The soldiers had almost finished reloading; the metal ramrods flashed all at once in the sunshine as they were drawn from the barrels, turned in the air, and thrust into their sockets. The two sentinels fired again, independently and ineffectually.

The hunted man saw all this over his shoulder; he was now swimming vigorously with the current. His brain was as energetic as his arms and legs; he thought with the rapidity of lightning.

"The officer," he reasoned, "will not make that martinet's error a second time. It is as easy to dodge a volley as a single shot. He has probably already given the command to fire at will. God help me, I cannot dodge them all!"

An appalling splash within two yards of him was followed by a loud, rushing sound, *diminuendo*,[3] which seemed to travel back through the air to the fort and died in an explosion which stirred the very river to its deeps! A rising sheet of water curved over him, fell down upon him, blinded him, strangled him! The cannon had taken a hand in the game. As he shook his head free from the commotion of the smitten water he heard the deflected shot humming through the air ahead, and in an instant it was cracking and smashing the branches in the forest beyond.

30 "They will not do that again," he thought; "the next time they will use a charge of grape.[4] I must keep my eye upon the gun; the smoke will apprise me—the report arrives too late; it lags behind the missile. That is a good gun."

---

[3]*diminuendo* lessening in intensity of sound
[4]**grape** refers to a type of ammunition fired from cannons

Suddenly he felt himself whirled round and round—spinning like a top. The water, the banks, the forests, the now distant bridge, fort and men—all were commingled and blurred. Objects were represented by their colors only; circular horizontal streaks of color—that was all he saw. He had been caught in a vortex and was being whirled on with a velocity of advance and gyration that made him giddy and sick. In a few moments he was flung upon the gravel at the foot of the left bank of the stream—the southern bank—and behind a projecting point which concealed him from his enemies. The sudden arrest of his motion, the abrasion of one of his hands on the gravel, restored him, and he wept with delight. He dug his fingers into the sand, threw it over himself in handfuls and audibly blessed it. It looked like diamonds, rubies, emeralds; he could think of nothing beautiful which it did not resemble. The trees upon the bank were giant garden plants; he noted a definite order in their arrangement, inhaled the fragrance of their blooms. A strange, roseate light shone through the spaces among their trunks and the wind made in their branches the music of aeolian harps. He had no wish to perfect his escape—was content to remain in that enchanting spot until retaken.

A whiz and rattle of grapeshot among the branches high above his head roused him from his dream. The baffled cannoneer had fired him a random farewell. He sprang to his feet, rushed up the sloping bank, and plunged into the forest.

All that day he traveled, laying his course by the rounding sun. The forest seemed interminable; nowhere did he discover a break in it, not even a woodman's road. He had not known that he lived in so wild a region. There was something uncanny in the revelation.

By nightfall he was fatigued, footsore, famishing. The thought of his wife and children urged him on. At last he found a road which led him in what he knew to be the right direction. It was as wide and straight as a city street, yet it seemed untraveled. No fields bordered it, no dwelling anywhere. Not so much as the barking of a dog suggested human habitation. The black bodies of the trees formed a straight wall on both sides, terminating on the horizon in a point, like a diagram in a lesson in perspective. Overhead, as he looked up through this rift in the wood, shone great golden stars looking unfamiliar and grouped in strange constellations. He was sure they were arranged in some order which had a secret and malign significance. The wood on either side was full of singular noises, among which—once, twice, and again—he distinctly heard whispers in an unknown tongue.

His neck was in pain and lifting his hand to it he found it horribly swollen.   35
He knew that it had a circle of black where the rope had bruised it. His eyes felt congested; he could no longer close them. His tongue was swollen with thirst; he relieved its fever by thrusting it forward from between his teeth into the cold air. How softly the turf had carpeted the untraveled avenue—he could no longer feel the roadway beneath his feet!

Doubtless, despite his suffering, he had fallen asleep while walking, for now he sees another scene—perhaps he has merely recovered from a delirium. He stands at the gate of his own home. All is as he left it, and all bright and beautiful in the morning sunshine. He must have traveled the entire night. As he pushes open the gate and passes up the wide white walk, he sees a flutter of female garments; his wife, looking fresh and cool and sweet, steps down from the veranda to meet him. At the bottom of the steps she stands waiting, with a smile of ineffable joy, an attitude of matchless grace and dignity. Ah, how beautiful she is! He springs forward with extended arms. As he is about to clasp her he feels a stunning blow upon the back of the neck; a blinding white light blazes all about him with a sound like the shock of a cannon—then all is darkness and silence!

Peyton Farquhar was dead; his body, with a broken neck, swung gently from side to side beneath the timbers of the Owl Creek bridge.

CRITICAL THINKING QUESTIONS

1. What did you think of the ending of this story? Were you shocked, surprised, or let down? Explain your reaction.

2. Examine the text and find any passages you feel may have hinted that Peyton Farquhar really was not successful in his escape from his executioners. Explain fully.

3. What does this story argue about the capacity and complexity of the human mind, particularly during times of extreme emotional and/or physical crises?

WRITING TOPIC

The text explains that the guards at either end of Owl Creek bridge "did not appear ... to know what was occurring at the center of the bridge." In what ways could these guards be metaphorical of many people today when it comes to political and social problems?

Kate Chopin

The Story of an Hour (1894)

Knowing that Mrs. Mallard was afflicted with a heart trouble, great care was taken to break to her as gently as possible the news of her husband's death.

It was her sister Josephine who told her, in broken sentences; veiled hints that revealed in half concealing. Her husband's friend Richards was there, too, near her. It was he who had been in the newspaper office when intelligence of the railroad disaster was received, with Brently Mallard's name leading the list of "killed."[1] He had only taken the time to assure himself of its truth by a second telegram, and had hastened to forestall any less careful, less tender friend in bearing the sad message.

She did not hear the story as many women have heard the same, with a paralyzed inability to accept its significance. She wept at once, with sudden, wild abandonment, in her sister's arms. When the storm of grief had spent itself she went away to her room alone. She would have no one follow her.

There stood, facing the open window, a comfortable, roomy armchair. Into this she sank, pressed down by a physical exhaustion that haunted her body and seemed to reach into her soul.

She could see in the open square before her house the tops of trees that   5
were all aquiver with the new spring life. The delicious breath of rain was in the air. In the street below a peddler was crying his wares. The notes of a distant song which some one was singing reached her faintly, and countless sparrows were twittering in the eaves.

There were patches of blue sky showing here and there through the clouds that had met and piled one above the other in the west facing her window. She sat with her head thrown back upon the cushion of the chair, quite motionless, except when a sob came up into her throat and shook her, as a child who has cried itself to sleep continues to sob in its dreams.

She was young, with a fair, calm face, whose lines bespoke repression and even a certain strength. But now there was a dull stare in her eyes, whose gaze was fixed away off yonder on one of those patches of blue sky. It was not a glance of reflection, but rather indicated a suspension of intelligent thought.

There was something coming to her and she was waiting for it, fearfully. What was it? She did not know; it was too subtle and elusive to name. But she felt it, creeping out of the sky, reaching toward her through the sounds, the scents, the color that filled the air.

Now her bosom rose and fell tumultuously. She was beginning to recognize this thing that was approaching to possess her, and she was striving to beat it back with her will—as powerless as her two white slender hands would have been.

When she abandoned herself a little whispered word escaped her slightly   10
parted lips. She said it over and over under her breath: "free, free, free!" The vacant stare and the look of terror that had followed it went from her eyes. They stayed keen and bright. Her pulses beat fast, and the coursing blood warmed and relaxed every inch of her body.

---

[1]In the nineteenth century, the most expedient communication was via telegram messaging. Newspaper offices were typically the biggest communication centers and the first to receive word of disasters such as train accidents.

She did not stop to ask if it were or were not a monstrous joy that held her. A clear and exalted perception enabled her to dismiss the suggestion as trivial.

She knew that she would weep again when she saw the kind, tender hands folded in death; the face that had never looked save with love upon her, fixed and gray and dead. But she saw beyond that bitter moment a long procession of years to come that would belong to her absolutely. And she opened and spread her arms out to them in welcome.

There would be no one to live for during those coming years; she would live for herself. There would be no powerful will bending hers in that blind persistence with which men and women believe they have a right to impose a private will upon a fellow-creature. A kind intention or a cruel intention made the act seem no less a crime as she looked upon it in that brief moment of illumination.

And yet she had loved him—sometimes. Often she had not. What did it matter! What could love, the unsolved mystery, count for in the face of this possession of self-assertion which she suddenly recognized as the strongest impulse of her being!

15   "Free! Body and soul free!" she kept whispering.

Josephine was kneeling before the closed door with her lips to the keyhole, imploring for admission. "Louise, open the door! I beg; open the door—you will make yourself ill. What are you doing, Louise? For heaven's sake open the door."

"Go away. I am not making myself ill." No; she was drinking in a very elixir of life through that open window.

Her fancy was running riot along those days ahead of her. Spring days, and summer days, and all sorts of days that would be her own. She breathed a quick prayer that life might be long. It was only yesterday she had thought with a shudder that life might be long.

She arose at length and opened the door to her sister's importunities. There was a feverish triumph in her eyes, and she carried herself unwittingly like a goddess of Victory. She clasped her sister's waist, and together they descended the stairs. Richards stood waiting for them at the bottom.

20   Some one was opening the front door with a latchkey. It was Brently Mallard who entered, a little travel-stained, composedly carrying his grip-sack and umbrella. He had been far from the scene of the accident, and did not even know there had been one. He stood amazed at Josephine's piercing cry; at Richards' quick motion to screen him from the view of his wife.

But Richards was too late.

When the doctors came they said she had died of heart disease—of the joy that kills.

CRITICAL THINKING QUESTIONS

1. From Mrs. Mallard's point of view, how would you characterize the Mallard marriage? Did she and Mr. Mallard love each other and seem happy? Upon what do you base your opinions?

2. Why do you think Mrs. Mallard is stricken with a fit of crying at the realization of her husband's death and the implications of what it means for her life? Explain your reasoning.

3. Why do you think Mrs. Mallard dies? What causes her death? Use evidence from the text to explain your answer.

WRITING TOPIC

What is your personal opinion of the character of Louise Mallard? Is she an awful, spiteful lady who got what she deserved? To the contrary, is a she a woman who elicits your sympathy? Use evidence from the text to establish your position.

Kevin Crossley-Holland

The Lay of Thrym (1980)

WHEN THOR AWOKE and reached out to grasp his hammer, it was not there. The Hurler leaped up. He tousled and tangled his red beard; his hair bristled as he searched for Mjollnir[1]. "Listen, Loki!" said Thor. "No god in Asgard has seen my hammer; no man in Midgard has seen my hammer: it has been stolen."

Then Thor and Loki hurried to Folkvang[2], and into Freyja's hall Sessrumnir. They well knew that if the hammer were not found, it would not be long before the giants stormed Asgard's walls and brought the bright halls of the gods crashing to the earth.

"Will you lend me your falcon skin," asked Loki, "so that I can search for Thor's hammer?"

"If it were fashioned of silver," cried Freyja,[3] "you could use it. I would lend it even if it were spun out of gold."   5

Then Loki donned the falcon skin. The feather dress whirred as he climbed into the moving air, and left the world of the gods behind him. He flew until Asgard[4] became no more than a bright haze away to the west; he flew as fast as he could until at last he reached the world of the giants.

---

[1]**Mjollnir** the name of Thor's hammer
[2]**Folkvang** the part of Asgard where Freyja's hall is located
[3]**Freyja** goddess of fertility and love
[4]**Asgard** world of the Norse gods

Thrym, king of the frost giants, felt at ease with the world. He had unteased and combed his horses' manes; he was sitting on a green mound, plaiting gold thread, making collars and leashes for his horrible hounds.

When the Sky Traveller saw Thrym, he swooped down beside him.

"How are things with the gods?" said Thrym. "How are things with the elves? And what brings you to Jotunheim[5] alone?"

"Things are bad for the gods," said Loki. "Things are bad for the elves. Have you stolen Thor's hammer?"

Thrym laughed, and the sound was like the chuckle of broken ice. "I've hidden Thor's hammer eight miles deep in the earth. No one is going to touch it unless he brings Freyja here to be my bride."

Loki grimaced and the sound of Thrym's freezing laughter followed him as he climbed again into the sky. The feather dress whirred. He left the world of the giants behind him and flew as fast as he could until at last he returned to the world of the gods.

Thor was waiting in the courtyard of Bilskirnir[6] and at once asked the Sky Traveller, "What's in your head and what's in your mouth? Real news or mere nuisance?" The Thunder God's eyes blazed and it was clear that he would brook no nonsense. "Stand here and tell me the truth at once. A sitting man forgets his story as often as not, and a man who lies down first lies again afterwards."

"I bring nuisame and I bring news," said the Sly One, the corners of his crooked mouth·curling. "Thrym, king of the frost giants, has your hammer. And no one is going to touch it unless he brings Freyja to be his bride."

Then Thor and Loki hurried to Sessrumnir for a second time and found Freyja there.

"Well, my beautiful!" said Loki, narrowing his eyes. "Put on your bridal veil."

"What?" retorted Freyja.

"We two must hurry," answered Loki, grinning. "You and I are going to Jotunheim. Thrym, king of the frost giants, has taken a fancy to you."

Freyja was so angry that the walls of Sessrumnir shuddered. The gold-studded benches started from the floor. Then Freyja snorted; her face became fiery; her breasts rose and fell; her neck muscles bulged. Then suddenly the marvellous Necklace of the Brisings burst apart—the links snapped and a shower of precious stones rolled around the hall. "How would it look if I went with you to Jotunheim?" demanded Freyja. "Everyone would say the same. A whore! Just a whore!"

Loki raised his eyebrows; Thor sniffed and smirked and shifted from foot to foot and did everything except look Freyja in the eye.

"Go away!" said Freyja. "Both of you."

---

[5]**Jotunheim** realm of the giants
[6]**Bilskirnir** Thor's hall

Then every god headed for Gladsheim, the hall with the silver thatch, to sit in solemn council and discuss how to recover Mjollnir. The goddesses joined them there. The watchman Heimdall had left Himinbjorg[7] and the trembling rainbow bridge. Like the other Vanir, he could read the future. The White God said, "Let us swaddle Thor ..." He paused and looked around "... swaddle Thor in the bridal veil!"

There was a moment of silence and then a howl of laughter from the assembled gods and goddesses.

Heimdall waited until the uproar had died down and then he went on: "Let us repair the Necklace of the Brisings and secure it round his ... his pretty neck."

Once again Gladsheim erupted and Thor looked across at Heimdall with   25
profound distaste. But the White God was unabashed. "He must be decked as befits any bride. A bunch of jingling keys must hang from his waist. And he must wear a becoming dress—as long a dress as possible! We mustn't forget to pin well-wrought brooches on her ... on his breast."

This care for detail delighted the gods and goddesses; and they also saw the force of Heimdall's argument.

"And he'll need a charming cap," concluded Heimdall in a sing-song voice, "a charming cap to crown it all."

Thor scowled. "You'll all mock me and call me unmanly if I put on a bridal veil," he said.

Then Loki, the son of Laufey, called out insolently, "Silence, Thor! There's no argument. Giants will live in Asgard if we don't retrieve your hammer."

So the gods and goddesses swaddled Thor in a bridal veil. They repaired the   30
Necklace of the Brisings and clasped it round his neck. They hung a bunch of jingling keys from his waist, and he wore a becoming dress down to his knees; they pinned well-wrought brooches on his breast, and they crowned it all with a charming cap.

"I'll be your maidservant," warbled Loki. "We two will hurry to Jotunheim."

The Thunderer's goats were rounded up and driven to Bilskirnir. There they were harnessed, and impatiently bucked and wrestled with their halters.

Gaping fissures opened in the fells, flames scorched the earth, and Thor, the son of Odin, galloped with Loki to Jotunheim.

"She will come!" shouted Thrym in a frenzy. "She's coming! Stir your great stumps! Spread straw on the benches! They're bringing Freyja, Njord's daughter from Noatun, to be my bride."

Thrym strode up and down his chilly hall, checking the arrangements. Then   35
he sat on a bench and said to himself: "I've cattle in my stables with horns of gold; I've jet black oxen—beasts to gladden the heart of any man. I've piles of precious stones, and mounds of silver and gold." Thrym's thoughts evaporated in the cold air, and he sighed, "I've had everything I wanted—everything except Freyja."

---

[7]**Himinbjorg** Heimdall's hall

When the travellers from Asgard arrived at Thrym's hall in the early evening, they were welcomed with great ceremony. The same giant servants who had spread straw on the benches now served up a fine supply of good food and drink.

Thrym ushered Thor, in his bridal veil, to the feasting table. With all the courtesy he could command, he pointed out the fine fare drawn from earth, sea and air alike in her honour. Then he led his intended bride to one high seat and himself sat in the other. Loki promptly ensconced himself next to Thor on the other side.

Thor felt hungry. He devoured an entire ox, and followed that with eight salmon. Then he scooped up and scoffed all the delicacies set apart for the women. And to round things off, he downed three horns of mead.[8]

Thrym watched this feat with growing surprise and anticipation. "Who has ever seen a bride with such hunger, such thirst?" he exclaimed. "I've never met a woman who took such huge mouthfuls or who drank so much mead."

40   The subtle bridesmaid sitting at Thor's side took it upon herself to answer Thrym. "Freyja has not eaten for these past eight nights, so wild was her desire for her wedding night."

Thrym leaned forward and peered under the veil; he could not wait to kiss her. The giant king was so startled that he leaped back the whole length of the hall. "Her eyes!" he shouted. "Why are Freyja's eyes so fearsome? They're like burning coals."

The subtle bridesmaid sitting at Thor's side took it upon herself to answer Thrym. "Freyja has not slept for these past eight nights, so wild was her desire for her wedding night."

Now Thrym's luckless sister walked up to the bride and bridesmaid, and she was not half-hearted about asking for a dowry. "If you want my love," she said, "and my loyalty, give me the rings of red gold on your fingers."

"Bring forward the hammer!" called the king of the giants. "Bring forward the hammer to hallow the bride. Put Mjollnir between her knees now so that Var[9] will hear our marriage oath and give us her blessing."

45   The Thunder God's unsparing heart sang and danced when he saw his hammer. As soon as it was placed between his knees, he snatched it up in his mighty grasp, swept off his veil and stood revealed as the god, Thor, the Hurler.

Thrym leapt up from his high seat and his companions leapt up from their benches.

Thor's eyes were as red as his beard. He glared at the company of giants and growled. Then he raised his hammer, took one massive step towards Thrym, and crushed his skull. Thor showed no mercy: he felled all the other giants and giant women at that bridal feast. The hall floor was strewn with a host of bodies. Thrym's luckless sister: had dared ask for gold rings but the iron hammer rang on her skull.

And so Thor, the Son of Odin, won back his hammer.

---

[8]**mead** alcoholic beverage, fermented from honey
[9]**Var** goddess of marriage oaths

CRITICAL THINKING QUESTIONS

1. Why does Freyja react so strongly to Loki's plea for help? Why is Loki more willing to aid Thor?

2. Loki doesn't balk at dressing like a woman; he volunteers to go as a maid-servant. Thor resents it strongly and worries about being mocked. How do these attitudes reveal character traits?

3. We learn a lot about Thor and Loki's deception: how they are dressed, how they explain masculine features, and how they react. Very little of the story describes the resulting violent end. Why is the violence so matter-of-fact?

WRITING TOPIC

Is violence ever an acceptable response to a crime? When might resorting to violence be appropriate? Give specific examples.

―――――――――

Sir Arthur Conan Doyle

The Adventure of the Speckled Band (1892)

On glancing over my notes of the seventy odd cases in which I have during the last eight years studied the methods of my friend Sherlock Holmes, I find many tragic, some comic, a large number merely strange, but none commonplace; for, working as he did rather for the love of his art than for the acquirement of wealth, he refused to associate himself with any investigation which did not tend towards the unusual, and even the fantastic. Of all these varied cases, however, I cannot recall any which presented more singular features than that which was associated with the well-known Surrey family of the Roylotts of Stoke Moran. The events in question occurred in the early days of my association with Holmes, when we were sharing rooms as bachelors in Baker Street. It is possible that I might have placed them upon record before, but a promise of secrecy was made at the time, from which I have only been freed during the last month by the untimely death of the lady to whom the pledge was given. It is perhaps as well that the facts should now come to light, for I have reasons to know that there are widespread rumours as to the death of Dr. Grimesby Roylott which tend to make the matter even more terrible than the truth.

It was early in April in the year' 83[1] that I woke one morning to find Sherlock Holmes standing, fully dressed, by the side of my bed. He was a late riser, as a

―――――――――

[1]1883

rule, and as the clock on the mantelpiece showed me that it was only a quarter-past seven, I blinked up at him in some surprise, and perhaps just a little resentment, for I was myself regular in my habits.

"Very sorry to knock you up, Watson," said he, "but it's the common lot this morning. Mrs. Hudson has been knocked up, she retorted upon me, and I on you."

"What is it, then—a fire?"

5   "No; a client. It seems that a young lady has arrived in a considerable state of excitement, who insists upon seeing me. She is waiting now in the sitting-room. Now, when young ladies wander about the metropolis at this hour of the morning, and knock sleepy people up out of their beds, I presume that it is something very pressing which they have to communicate. Should it prove to be an interesting case, you would, I am sure, wish to follow it from the outset. I thought, at any rate, that I should call you and give you the chance."

"My dear fellow, I would not miss it for anything."

I had no keener pleasure than in following Holmes in his professional investigations, and in admiring the rapid deductions, as swift as intuitions, and yet always founded on a logical basis with which he unravelled the problems which were submitted to him. I rapidly threw on my clothes and was ready in a few minutes to accompany my friend down to the sitting-room. A lady dressed in black and heavily veiled, who had been sitting in the window, rose as we entered.

"Good-morning, madam," said Holmes cheerily. "My name is Sherlock Holmes. This is my intimate friend and associate, Dr. Watson, before whom you can speak as freely as before myself. Ha! I am glad to see that Mrs. Hudson has had the good sense to light the fire. Pray draw up to it, and I shall order you a cup of hot coffee, for I observe that you are shivering."

"It is not cold which makes me shiver," said the woman in a low voice, changing her seat as requested.

10   "What, then?"

"It is fear, Mr. Holmes. It is terror." She raised her veil as she spoke, and we could see that she was indeed in a pitiable state of agitation, her face all drawn and grey, with restless frightened eyes, like those of some hunted animal. Her features and figure were those of a woman of thirty, but her hair was shot with premature grey, and her expression was weary and haggard. Sherlock Holmes ran her over with one of his quick, all-comprehensive glances.

"You must not fear," said he soothingly, bending forward and patting her forearm.

"We shall soon set matters right, I have no doubt. You have come in by train this morning, I see."

"You know me, then?"

"No, but I observe the second half of a return ticket in the palm of your left   15
glove. You must have started early, and yet you had a good drive in a dog-cart,
along heavy roads, before you reached the station."

The lady gave a violent start and stared in bewilderment at my companion.

"There is no mystery, my dear madam," said he, smiling. "The left arm of
your jacket is spattered with mud in no less than seven places. The marks are
perfectly fresh. There is no vehicle save a dog-cart which throws up mud in that
way, and then only when you sit on the left-hand side of the driver."

"Whatever your reasons may be, you are perfectly correct," said she. "I
started from home before six, reached Leatherhead at twenty past, and came in
by the first train to Waterloo. Sir, I can stand this strain no longer; I shall go mad if
it continues. I have no one to turn to—none, save only one, who cares for me, and
he, poor fellow, can be of little aid. I have heard of you, Mr. Holmes; I have heard
of you from Mrs. Farintosh, whom you helped in the hour of her sore need. It was
from her that I had your address. Oh, sir, do you not think that you could help
me, too, and at least throw a little light through the dense darkness which sur-
rounds me? At present it is out of my power to reward you for your services, but
in a month or six weeks I shall be married, with the control of my own income,
and then at least you shall not find me ungrateful."

Holmes turned to his desk and, unlocking it, drew out a small case-book,
which he consulted.

"Farintosh," said he. "Ah yes, I recall the case; it was concerned with an opal   20
tiara. I think it was before your time, Watson. I can only say, madam, that I shall
be happy to devote the same care to your case as I did to that of your friend. As to
reward, my profession is its own reward; but you are at liberty to defray whatever expenses I may be put to, at the time which suits you best. And now I beg that you will
lay before us everything that may help us in forming an opinion upon the matter."

"Alas!" replied our visitor, "the very horror of my situation lies in the fact
that my fears are so vague, and my suspicions depend so entirely upon small
points, which might seem trivial to another, that even he to whom of all others
I have a right to look for help and advice looks upon all that I tell him about it
as the fancies of a nervous woman. He does not say so, but I can read it from his
soothing answers and averted eyes. But I have heard, Mr. Holmes, that you can
see deeply into the manifold wickedness of the human heart. You may advise me
how to walk amid the dangers which encompass me."

"I am all attention, madam."

"My name is Helen Stoner, and I am living with my stepfather, who is the
last survivor of one of the oldest Saxon[2] families in England, the Roylotts of
Stoke Moran, on the western border of Surrey."

Holmes nodded his head. "The name is familiar to me," said he.

---

[2]**Saxon** Germanic tribes that settled in Great Britain in the Middle Ages

25   "The family was at one time among the richest in England, and the estates extended over the borders into Berkshire in the north, and Hampshire in the west. In the last century, however, four successive heirs were of a dissolute and wasteful disposition, and the family ruin was eventually completed by a gambler in the days of the Regency.[3] Nothing was left save a few acres of ground, and the two-hundred-year-old house, which is itself crushed under a heavy mortgage. The last squire dragged out his existence there, living the horrible life of an aristocratic pauper; but his only son, my stepfather, seeing that he must adapt himself to the new conditions, obtained an advance from a relative, which enabled him to take a medical degree and went out to Calcutta,[4] where, by his professional skill and his force of character, he established a large practice. In a fit of anger, however, caused by some robberies which had been perpetrated in the house, he beat his native butler to death and narrowly escaped a capital sentence. As it was, he suffered a long term of imprisonment and afterwards returned to England a morose and disappointed man.

"When Dr. Roylott was in India he married my mother, Mrs. Stoner, the young widow of Major-General Stoner, of the Bengal Artillery. My sister Julia and I were twins, and we were only two years old at the time of my mother's re-marriage. She had a considerable sum of money—not less than 1000 pounds a year—and this she bequeathed to Dr. Roylott entirely while we resided with him, with a provision that a certain annual sum should be allowed to each of us in the event of our marriage. Shortly after our return to England my mother died—she was killed eight years ago in a railway accident near Crewe. Dr. Roylott then abandoned his attempts to establish himself in practice in London and took us to live with him in the old ancestral house at Stoke Moran. The money which my mother had left was enough for all our wants, and there seemed to be no obstacle to our happiness.

"But a terrible change came over our stepfather about this time. Instead of making friends and exchanging visits with our neighbours, who had at first been overjoyed to see a Roylott of Stoke Moran back in the old family seat, he shut himself up in his house and seldom came out save to indulge in ferocious quarrels with whoever might cross his path. Violence of temper approaching to mania has been hereditary in the men of the family, and in my stepfather's case it had, I believe, been intensified by his long residence in the tropics. A series of disgraceful brawls took place, two of which ended in the police-court, until at last he became the terror of the village, and the folks would fly at his approach, for he is a man of immense strength, and absolutely uncontrollable in his anger.

"Last week he hurled the local blacksmith over a parapet into a stream, and it was only by paying over all the money which I could gather together that

---

[3]**Regency** the historical period (1811—1820) when the Prince of Wales ruled for George III due to the latter's mental illness
[4]**Calcutta** a city in India, a colony of Great Britain from the mid-nineteenth century to the mid-twentieth century

I was able to avert another public exposure. He had no friends at all save the wandering gypsies, and he would give these vagabonds leave to encamp upon the few acres of bramble-covered land which represent the family estate, and would accept in return the hospitality of their tents, wandering away with them sometimes for weeks on end. He has a passion also for Indian animals, which are sent over to him by a correspondent, and he has at this moment a cheetah and a baboon, which wander freely over his grounds and are feared by the villagers almost as much as their master.

"You can imagine from what I say that my poor sister Julia and I had no great pleasure in our lives. No servant would stay with us, and for a long time we did all the work of the house. She was but thirty at the time of her death, and yet her hair had already begun to whiten, even as mine has."

"Your sister is dead, then?"

"She died just two years ago, and it is of her death that I wish to speak to you. You can understand that, living the life which I have described, we were little likely to see anyone of our own age and position. We had, however, an aunt, my mother's maiden sister, Miss Honoria Westphail, who lives near Harrow, and we were occasionally allowed to pay short visits at this lady's house. Julia went there at Christmas two years ago, and met there a half-pay major of marines, to whom she became engaged. My stepfather learned of the engagement when my sister returned and offered no objection to the marriage; but within a fortnight of the day which had been fixed for the wedding, the terrible event occurred which has deprived me of my only companion."

Sherlock Holmes had been leaning back in his chair with his eyes closed and his head sunk in a cushion, but he half opened his lids now and glanced across at his visitor.

"Pray be precise as to details," said he.

"It is easy for me to be so, for every event of that dreadful time is seared into my memory. The manor-house is, as I have already said, very old, and only one wing is now inhabited. The bedrooms in this wing are on the ground floor, the sitting-rooms being in the central block of the buildings. Of these bedrooms the first is Dr. Roylott's, the second my sister's, and the third my own. There is no communication between them, but they all open out into the same corridor. Do I make myself plain?"

"Perfectly so."

"The windows of the three rooms open out upon the lawn. That fatal night Dr. Roylott had gone to his room early, though we knew that he had not retired to rest, for my sister was troubled by the smell of the strong Indian cigars which it was his custom to smoke. She left her room, therefore, and came into mine, where she sat for some time, chatting about her approaching wedding. At eleven o'clock she rose to leave me, but she paused at the door and looked back. "'Tell me, Helen,' said she, 'have you ever heard anyone whistle in the dead of the night?' "'Never,' said I.

"'I suppose that you could not possibly whistle, yourself, in your sleep?'

"'Certainly not. But why?'

"'Because during the last few nights I have always, about three in the morning, heard a low, clear whistle. I am a light sleeper, and it has awakened me. I cannot tell where it came from—perhaps from the next room, perhaps from the lawn. I thought that I would just ask you whether you had heard it.'

40 "'No, I have not. It must be those wretched gipsies in the plantation.'

"'Very likely. And yet if it were on the lawn, I wonder that you did not hear it also.'

"'Ah, but I sleep more heavily than you.'

"'Well, it is of no great consequence, at any rate.' She smiled back at me, closed my door, and a few moments later I heard her key turn in the lock."

"Indeed," said Holmes. "Was it your custom always to lock yourselves in at night?"

45 "Always."

"And why?"

"I think that I mentioned to you that the doctor kept a cheetah and a baboon. We had no feeling of security unless our doors were locked."

"I could not sleep that night. A vague feeling of impending misfortune impressed me. My sister and I, you will recollect, were twins, and you know how subtle are the links which bind two souls which are so closely allied. It was a wild night. The wind was howling outside, and the rain was beating and splashing against the windows. Suddenly, amid all the hubbub of the gale, there burst forth the wild scream of a terrified woman. I knew that it was my sister's voice. I sprang from my bed, wrapped a shawl round me, and rushed into the corridor. As I opened my door I seemed to hear a low whistle, such as my sister described, and a few moments later a clanging sound, as if a mass of metal had fallen. As I ran down the passage, my sister's door was unlocked, and revolved slowly upon its hinges. I stared at it horror-stricken, not knowing what was about to issue from it. By the light of the corridor-lamp I saw my sister appear at the opening, her face blanched with terror, her hands groping for help, her whole figure swaying to and fro like that of a drunkard. I ran to her and threw my arms round her, but at that moment her knees seemed to give way and she fell to the ground. She writhed as one who is in terrible pain, and her limbs were dreadfully convulsed. At first I thought that she had not recognised me, but as I bent over her she suddenly shrieked out in a voice which I shall never forget, 'Oh, my God! Helen! It was the band! The speckled band!' There was something else which she would fain have said, and she stabbed with her finger into the air in the direction of the doctor's room, but a fresh convulsion seized her and choked her words. I rushed out, calling loudly for my stepfather, and I met him hastening from his room in his dressing-gown. When he reached my sister's side she was unconscious, and though he poured brandy down her throat and sent for medical aid from the village, all efforts were in vain, for she slowly sank and died without having recovered her consciousness. Such was the dreadful end of my beloved sister."

"One moment," said Holmes, "are you sure about this whistle and metallic sound? Could you swear to it?"

"That was what the county coroner asked me at the inquiry. It is my strong 50 impression that I heard it, and yet, among the crash of the gale and the creaking of an old house, I may possibly have been deceived."

"Was your sister dressed?"

"No, she was in her night-dress. In her right hand was found the charred stump of a match, and in her left a match-box."

"Showing that she had struck a light and looked about her when the alarm took place. That is important. And what conclusions did the coroner come to?"

"He investigated the case with great care, for Dr. Roylott's conduct had long been notorious in the county, but he was unable to find any satisfactory cause of death. My evidence showed that the door had been fastened upon the inner side, and the windows were blocked by old-fashioned shutters with broad iron bars, which were secured every night. The walls were carefully sounded, and were shown to be quite solid all round, and the flooring was also thoroughly examined, with the same result. The chimney is wide, but is barred up by four large staples. It is certain, therefore, that my sister was quite alone when she met her end. Besides, there were no marks of any violence upon her."

"How about poison?"   55

"The doctors examined her for it, but without success."

"What do you think that this unfortunate lady died of, then?"

"It is my belief that she died of pure fear and nervous shock, though what it was that frightened her I cannot imagine."

"Were there gypsies in the plantation at the time?"

"Yes, there are nearly always some there."   60

"Ah, and what did you gather from this allusion to a band—a speckled band?"

"Sometimes I have thought that it was merely the wild talk of delirium, sometimes that it may have referred to some band of people, perhaps to these very gipsies in the plantation. I do not know whether the spotted handkerchiefs which so many of them wear over their heads might have suggested the strange adjective which she used."

Holmes shook his head like a man who is far from being satisfied.

"These are very deep waters," said he; "pray go on with your narrative."

"Two years have passed since then, and my life has been until lately lonelier 65 than ever. A month ago, however, a dear friend, whom I have known for many years, has done me the honour to ask my hand in marriage. His name is Armitage—Percy Armitage—the second son of Mr. Armitage, of Crane Water, near Reading.[5] My stepfather has offered no opposition to the match, and we are to be married in the course of the spring. Two days ago some repairs were started in the west wing of the building, and my bedroom wall has been pierced, so that I

---

[5]**Reading** a town in England

have had to move into the chamber in which my sister died, and to sleep in the very bed in which she slept. Imagine, then, my thrill of terror when last night, as I lay awake, thinking over her terrible fate, I suddenly heard in the silence of the night the low whistle which had been the herald of her own death. I sprang up and lit the lamp, but nothing was to be seen in the room. I was too shaken to go to bed again, however, so I dressed, and as soon as it was daylight I slipped down, got a dog-cart at the Crown Inn, which is opposite, and drove to Leatherhead, from whence I have come on this morning with the one object of seeing you and asking your advice."

"You have done wisely," said my friend. "But have you told me all?"

"Yes, all."

"Miss Roylott, you have not. You are screening your stepfather."

"Why, what do you mean?"

70　　For answer Holmes pushed back the frill of black lace which fringed the hand that lay upon our visitor's knee. Five little livid spots, the marks of four fingers and a thumb, were printed upon the white wrist.

"You have been cruelly used," said Holmes.

The lady coloured deeply and covered over her injured wrist. "He is a hard man," she said, "and perhaps he hardly knows his own strength."

There was a long silence, during which Holmes leaned his chin upon his hands and stared into the crackling fire.

"This is a very deep business," he said at last. "There are a thousand details which I should desire to know before I decide upon our course of action. Yet we have not a moment to lose. If we were to come to Stoke Moran to-day, would it be possible for us to see over these rooms without the knowledge of your stepfather?"

75　　"As it happens, he spoke of coming into town to-day upon some most important business. It is probable that he will be away all day, and that there would be nothing to disturb you. We have a housekeeper now, but she is old and foolish, and I could easily get her out of the way."

"Excellent. You are not averse to this trip, Watson?"

"By no means."

"Then we shall both come. What are you going to do yourself?"

"I have one or two things which I would wish to do now that I am in town. But I shall return by the twelve o'clock train, so as to be there in time for your coming."

80　　"And you may expect us early in the afternoon. I have myself some small business matters to attend to. Will you not wait and breakfast?"

"No, I must go. My heart is lightened already since I have confided my trouble to you. I shall look forward to seeing you again this afternoon." She dropped her thick black veil over her face and glided from the room.

"And what do you think of it all, Watson?" asked Sherlock Holmes, leaning back in his chair. "It seems to me to be a most dark and sinister business."

"Dark enough and sinister enough."

"Yet if the lady is correct in saying that the flooring and walls are sound, and that the door, window, and chimney are impassable, then her sister must have been undoubtedly alone when she met her mysterious end."

"What becomes, then, of these nocturnal whistles, and what of the very   85 peculiar words of the dying woman?"

"I cannot think."

"When you combine the ideas of whistles at night, the presence of a band of gypsies who are on intimate terms with this old doctor, the fact that we have every reason to believe that the doctor has an interest in preventing his step-daughter's marriage, the dying allusion to a band, and, finally, the fact that Miss Helen Stoner heard a metallic clang, which might have been caused by one of those metal bars that secured the shutters falling back into its place, I think that there is good ground to think that the mystery may be cleared along those lines."

"But what, then, did the gypsies do?"

"I cannot imagine."

"I see many objections to any such theory."   90

"And so do I. It is precisely for that reason that we are going to Stoke Moran this day. I want to see whether the objections are fatal, or if they may be explained away. But what in the name of the devil!"

The ejaculation had been drawn from my companion by the fact that our door had been suddenly dashed open, and that a huge man had framed himself in the aperture. His costume was a peculiar mixture of the professional and of the agricultural, having a black top-hat, a long frock-coat, and a pair of high gaiters, with a hunting-crop swinging in his hand. So tall was he that his hat actually brushed the cross bar of the doorway, and his breadth seemed to span it across from side to side. A large face, seared with a thousand wrinkles, burned yellow with the sun, and marked with every evil passion, was turned from one to the other of us, while his deep-set, bile-shot eyes, and his high, thin, fleshless nose, gave him somewhat the resemblance to a fierce old bird of prey.

"Which of you is Holmes?" asked this apparition.

"My name, sir; but you have the advantage of me," said my companion quietly.

"I am Dr. Grimesby Roylott, of Stoke Moran."   95

"Indeed, Doctor," said Holmes blandly. "Pray take a seat."

"I will do nothing of the kind. My stepdaughter has been here. I have traced her. What has she been saying to you?"

"It is a little cold for the time of the year," said Holmes.

"What has she been saying to you?" screamed the old man furiously.

"But I have heard that the crocuses promise well," continued my companion 100 imperturbably. "Ha! You put me off, do you?" said our new visitor, taking a step forward and shaking his hunting-crop. "I know you, you scoundrel! I have heard of you before. You are Holmes, the meddler."

My friend smiled.

"Holmes, the busybody!"

His smile broadened.

"Holmes, the Scotland Yard Jack-in-office!"

105   Holmes chuckled heartily. "Your conversation is most entertaining," said he.

"When you go out close the door, for there is a decided draught."

"I will go when I have said my say. Don't you dare to meddle with my affairs. I know that Miss Stoner has been here. I traced her! I am a dangerous man to fall foul of! See here." He stepped swiftly forward, seized the poker, and bent it into a curve with his huge brown hands.

"See that you keep yourself out of my grip," he snarled, and hurling the twisted poker into the fireplace he strode out of the room.

"He seems a very amiable person," said Holmes, laughing. "I am not quite so bulky, but if he had remained I might have shown him that my grip was not much more feeble than his own." As he spoke he picked up the steel poker and, with a sudden effort, straightened it out again.

110   "Fancy his having the insolence to confound me with the official detective force! This incident gives zest to our investigation, however, and I only trust that our little friend will not suffer from her imprudence in allowing this brute to trace her. And now, Watson, we shall order breakfast, and afterwards I shall walk down to Doctors' Commons, where I hope to get some data which may help us in this matter."

It was nearly one o'clock when Sherlock Holmes returned from his excursion. He held in his hand a sheet of blue paper, scrawled over with notes and figures.

"I have seen the will of the deceased wife," said he. "To determine its exact meaning I have been obliged to work out the present prices of the investments with which it is concerned. The total income, which at the time of the wife's death was little short of 1100 pounds, is now, through the fall in agricultural prices, not more than 750 pounds. Each daughter can claim an income of 250 pounds, in case of marriage. It is evident, therefore, that if both girls had married, this beauty would have had a mere pittance, while even one of them would cripple him to a very serious extent. My morning's work has not been wasted, since it has proved that he has the very strongest motives for standing in the way of anything of the sort. And now, Watson, this is too serious for dawdling, especially as the old man is aware that we are interesting ourselves in his affairs; so if you are ready, we shall call a cab and drive to Waterloo. I should be very much obliged if you would slip your revolver into your pocket. An Eley's No. 2 is an excellent argument with gentlemen who can twist steel pokers into knots. That and a tooth-brush are, I think, all that we need."

At Waterloo[6] we were fortunate in catching a train for Leatherhead, where we hired a trap[7] at the station inn and drove for four or five miles through the

---

[6]**Waterloo** a train station in London, named after the famous battle in Waterloo, Belgium, when the British General, Duke of Wellington, defeated Napoleon of France

[7]**trap** a horse-drawn carriage

lovely Surrey lanes. It was a perfect day, with a bright sun and a few fleecy clouds in the heavens. The trees and wayside hedges were just throwing out their first green shoots, and the air was full of the pleasant smell of the moist earth. To me at least there was a strange contrast between the sweet promise of the spring and this sinister quest upon which we were engaged. My companion sat in the front of the trap, his arms folded, his hat pulled down over his eyes, and his chin sunk upon his breast, buried in the deepest thought. Suddenly, however, he started, tapped me on the shoulder, and pointed over the meadows.

"Look there!" said he.

A heavily timbered park stretched up in a gentle slope, thickening into a 115 grove at the highest point. From amid the branches there jutted out the grey gables and high roof-tree of a very old mansion.

"Stoke Moran?" said he.

"Yes, sir, that be the house of Dr. Grimesby Roylott," remarked the driver.

"There is some building going on there," said Holmes; "that is where we are going." "There's the village," said the driver, pointing to a cluster of roofs some distance to the left; "but if you want to get to the house, you'll find it shorter to get over this stile, and so by the foot- path over the fields. There it is, where the lady is walking."

"And the lady, I fancy, is Miss Stoner," observed Holmes, shading his eyes. "Yes, I think we had better do as you suggest."

We got off, paid our fare, and the trap rattled back on its way to Leatherhead. 120

"I thought it as well," said Holmes as we climbed the stile, "that this fellow should think we had come here as architects, or on some definite business. It may stop his gossip. Good-afternoon, Miss Stoner. You see that we have been as good as our word."

Our client of the morning had hurried forward to meet us with a face which spoke her joy. "I have been waiting so eagerly for you," she cried, shaking hands with us warmly. "All has turned out splendidly. Dr. Roylott has gone to town, and it is unlikely that he will be back before evening."

"We have had the pleasure of making the doctor's acquaintance," said Holmes, and in a few words he sketched out what had occurred. Miss Stoner turned white to the lips as she listened.

"Good heavens!" she cried, "he has followed me, then."

"So it appears."   125

"He is so cunning that I never know when I am safe from him. What will he say when he returns?"

"He must guard himself, for he may find that there is someone more cunning than himself upon his track. You must lock yourself up from him to-night. If he is violent, we shall take you away to your aunt's at Harrow. Now, we must make the best use of our time, so kindly take us at once to the rooms which we are to examine."

The building was of grey, lichen-blotched stone, with a high central portion and two curving wings, like the claws of a crab, thrown out on each side. In one of these wings the windows were broken and blocked with wooden boards, while the roof was partly caved in, a picture of ruin. The central portion was in little better repair, but the right-hand block was comparatively modern, and the blinds in the windows, with the blue smoke curling up from the chimneys, showed that this was where the family resided. Some scaffolding had been erected against the end wall, and the stone-work had been broken into, but there were no signs of any workmen at the moment of our visit. Holmes walked slowly up and down the ill-trimmed lawn and examined with deep attention the outsides of the windows.

"This, I take it, belongs to the room in which you used to sleep, the cen-tre one to your sister's, and the one next to the main building to Dr. Roylott's chamber?"

130 "Exactly so. But I am now sleeping in the middle one."

"Pending the alterations, as I understand. By the way, there does not seem to be any very pressing need for repairs at that end wall."

"There were none. I believe that it was an excuse to move me from my room."

"Ah! That is suggestive. Now, on the other side of this narrow wing runs the corridor from which these three rooms open. There are windows in it, of course?"

"Yes, but very small ones. Too narrow for anyone to pass through."

135 "As you both locked your doors at night, your rooms were unapproachable from that side. Now, would you have the kindness to go into your room and bar your shutters?"

Miss Stoner did so, and Holmes, after a careful examination through the open window, endeavoured in every way to force the shutter open, but without success. There was no slit through which a knife could be passed to raise the bar. Then with his lens he tested the hinges, but they were of solid iron, built firmly into the massive masonry.

"Hum!" said he, scratching his chin in some perplexity, "my theory certainly presents some difficulties. No one could pass these shutters if they were bolted. Well, we shall see if the inside throws any light upon the matter."

A small side door led into the whitewashed corridor from which the three bedrooms opened. Holmes refused to examine the third chamber, so we passed at once to the second, that in which Miss Stoner was now sleeping, and in which her sister had met with her fate. It was a homely little room, with a low ceiling and a gaping fireplace, after the fashion of old country-houses. A brown chest of drawers stood in one corner, a narrow white-counterpaned bed in another, and a dressing-table on the left-hand side of the window. These articles, with two small wicker-work chairs, made up all the furniture in the room save for a square of Wilton carpet in the centre. The boards round and the panelling of the walls were of brown, worm-eaten oak, so old and discoloured that it may have dated from the original building of the house. Holmes drew one of the chairs into a corner and sat silent, while his eyes travelled round and round and up and down, taking in every detail of the apartment.

"Where does that bell communicate with?" he asked at last pointing to a thick bell-rope which hung down beside the bed, the tassel actually lying upon the pillow.

"It goes to the housekeeper's room." 140

"It looks newer than the other things?"

"Yes, it was only put there a couple of years ago."

"Your sister asked for it, I suppose?"

"No, I never heard of her using it. We used always to get what we wanted for ourselves."

"Indeed, it seemed unnecessary to put so nice a bell-pull there. You will 145 excuse me for a few minutes while I satisfy myself as to this floor." He threw himself down upon his face with his lens in his hand and crawled swiftly backward and forward, examining minutely the cracks between the boards. Then he did the same with the wood-work with which the chamber was panelled. Finally he walked over to the bed and spent some time in staring at it and in running his eye up and down the wall. Finally he took the bell-rope in his hand and gave it a brisk tug.

"Why, it's a dummy," said he.

"Won't it ring?"

"No, it is not even attached to a wire. This is very interesting. You can see now that it is fastened to a hook just above where the little opening for the ventilator is."

"How very absurd! I never noticed that before."

"Very strange!" muttered Holmes, pulling at the rope. "There are one or two 150 very singular points about this room. For example, what a fool a builder must be to open a ventilator into another room, when, with the same trouble, he might have communicated with the outside air!"

"That is also quite modern," said the lady.

"Done about the same time as the bell-rope?" remarked Holmes.

"Yes, there were several little changes carried out about that time."

"They seem to have been of a most interesting character—dummy bell-ropes, and ventilators which do not ventilate. With your permission, Miss Stoner, we shall now carry our researches into the inner apartment."

Dr. Grimesby Roylott's chamber was larger than that of his step-daughter, 155 but was as plainly furnished. A camp-bed, a small wooden shelf full of books, mostly of a technical character, an armchair beside the bed, a plain wooden chair against the wall, a round table, and a large iron safe were the principal things which met the eye. Holmes walked slowly round and examined each and all of them with the keenest interest.

"What's in here?" he asked, tapping the safe.

"My stepfather's business papers."

"Oh! You have seen inside, then?"

"Only once, some years ago. I remember that it was full of papers."

"There isn't a cat in it, for example?" 160

"No. What a strange idea!"

"Well, look at this!" He took up a small saucer of milk which stood on the top of it.

"No; we don't keep a cat. But there is a cheetah and a baboon."

"Ah, yes, of course! Well, a cheetah is just a big cat, and yet a saucer of milk does not go very far in satisfying its wants, I daresay. There is one point which I should wish to determine." He squatted down in front of the wooden chair and examined the seat of it with the greatest attention.

165   "Thank you. That is quite settled," said he, rising and putting his lens in his pocket. "Hullo! Here is something interesting!"

The object which had caught his eye was a small dog lash hung on one corner of the bed. The lash, however, was curled upon itself and tied so as to make a loop of whipcord.

"What do you make of that, Watson?"

"It's a common enough lash. But I don't know why it should be tied."

"That is not quite so common, is it? Ah, me! It's a wicked world, and when a clever man turns his brains to crime it is the worst of all. I think that I have seen enough now, Miss Stoner, and with your permission we shall walk out upon the lawn."

170   I had never seen my friend's face so grim or his brow so dark as it was when we turned from the scene of this investigation. We had walked several times up and down the lawn, neither Miss Stoner nor myself liking to break in upon his thoughts before he roused himself from his reverie.

"It is very essential, Miss Stoner," said he, "that you should absolutely follow my advice in every respect."

"I shall most certainly do so."

"The matter is too serious for any hesitation. Your life may depend upon your compliance."

"I assure you that I am in your hands."

175   "In the first place, both my friend and I must spend the night in your room."

Both Miss Stoner and I gazed at him in astonishment.

"Yes, it must be so. Let me explain. I believe that that is the village inn over there?"

"Yes, that is the Crown."

"Very good. Your windows would be visible from there?"

180   "Certainly."

"You must confine yourself to your room, on pretence of a headache, when your stepfather comes back. Then when you hear him retire for the night, you must open the shutters of your window, undo the hasp, put your lamp there as a signal to us, and then withdraw quietly with everything which you are likely to want into the room which you used to occupy. I have no doubt that, in spite of the repairs, you could manage there for one night."

"Oh, yes, easily."

"The rest you will leave in our hands."

"But what will you do?"

"We shall spend the night in your room, and we shall investigate the cause 185
of this noise which has disturbed you."

"I believe, Mr. Holmes, that you have already made up your mind," said
Miss Stoner, laying her hand upon my companion's sleeve. "Perhaps I have."

"Then, for pity's sake, tell me what was the cause of my sister's death."

"I should prefer to have clearer proofs before I speak."

"You can at least tell me whether my own thought is correct, and if she died
from some sudden fright."

"No, I do not think so. I think that there was probably some more tangible 190
cause. And now, Miss Stoner, we must leave you for if Dr. Roylott returned and
saw us our journey would be in vain. Good-bye, and be brave, for if you will do
what I have told you, you may rest assured that we shall soon drive away the
dangers that threaten you."

Sherlock Holmes and I had no difficulty in engaging a bedroom and sitting-room at the Crown Inn. They were on the upper floor, and from our window we could command a view of the avenue gate, and of the inhabited wing
of Stoke Moran Manor House. At dusk we saw Dr. Grimesby Roylott drive
past, his huge form looming up beside the little figure of the lad who drove
him. The boy had some slight difficulty in undoing the heavy iron gates, and
we heard the hoarse roar of the doctor's voice and saw the fury with which he
shook his clinched fists at him. The trap drove on, and a few minutes later we
saw a sudden light spring up among the trees as the lamp was lit in one of the
sitting-rooms.

"Do you know, Watson," said Holmes as we sat together in the gathering
darkness, "I have really some scruples as to taking you to-night. There is a distinct element of danger."

"Can I be of assistance?"

"Your presence might be invaluable."

"Then I shall certainly come."   195

"It is very kind of you."

"You speak of danger. You have evidently seen more in these rooms than was
visible to me."

"No, but I fancy that I may have deduced a little more. I imagine that you
saw all that I did."

"I saw nothing remarkable save the bell-rope, and what purpose that could
answer I confess is more than I can imagine."

"You saw the ventilator, too?"   200

"Yes, but I do not think that it is such a very unusual thing to have a
small opening between two rooms. It was so small that a rat could hardly pass
through."

"I knew that we should find a ventilator before ever we came to Stoke
Moran."

"My dear Holmes!"

"Oh, yes, I did. You remember in her statement she said that her sister could smell Dr. Roylott's cigar. Now, of course that suggested at once that there must be a communication between the two rooms. It could only be a small one, or it would have been remarked upon at the coroner's inquiry. I deduced a ventilator."

205   "But what harm can there be in that?"

"Well, there is at least a curious coincidence of dates. A ventilator is made, a cord is hung, and a lady who sleeps in the bed dies. Does not that strike you?"

"I cannot as yet see any connection."

"Did you observe anything very peculiar about that bed?"

"No."

210   "It was clamped to the floor. Did you ever see a bed fastened like that before?"

"I cannot say that I have."

"The lady could not move her bed. It must always be in the same relative position to the ventilator and to the rope—or so we may call it, since it was clearly never meant for a bell-pull."

"Holmes," I cried, "I seem to see dimly what you are hinting at. We are only just in time to prevent some subtle and horrible crime."

"Subtle enough and horrible enough. When a doctor does go wrong he is the first of criminals. He has nerve and he has knowledge. Palmer and Pritchard were among the heads of their profession. This man strikes even deeper, but I think, Watson, that we shall be able to strike deeper still. But we shall have horrors enough before the night is over; for goodness' sake let us have a quiet pipe and turn our minds for a few hours to something more cheerful."

215   About nine o'clock the light among the trees was extinguished, and all was dark in the direction of the Manor House. Two hours passed slowly away, and then, suddenly, just at the stroke of eleven, a single bright light shone out right in front of us.

"That is our signal," said Holmes, springing to his feet; "it comes from the middle window."

As we passed out he exchanged a few words with the landlord, explaining that we were going on a late visit to an acquaintance, and that it was possible that we might spend the night there. A moment later we were out on the dark road, a chill wind blowing in our faces, and one yellow light twinkling in front of us through the gloom to guide us on our sombre errand.

There was little difficulty in entering the grounds, for unrepaired breaches gaped in the old park wall. Making our way among the trees, we reached the lawn, crossed it, and were about to enter through the window when out from a clump of laurel bushes there darted what seemed to be a hideous and distorted child, who threw itself upon the grass with writhing limbs and then ran swiftly across the lawn into the darkness.

"My God!" I whispered; "did you see it?"

Holmes was for the moment as startled as I. His hand closed like a vice upon 220 my wrist in his agitation. Then he broke into a low laugh and put his lips to my ear.

"It is a nice household," he murmured. "That is the baboon."

I had forgotten the strange pets which the doctor affected. There was a cheetah, too; perhaps we might find it upon our shoulders at any moment. I confess that I felt easier in my mind when, after following Holmes' example and slipping off my shoes, I found myself inside the bedroom. My companion noiselessly closed the shutters, moved the lamp onto the table, and cast his eyes round the room. All was as we had seen it in the daytime. Then creeping up to me and making a trumpet of his hand, he whispered into my ear again so gently that it was all that I could do to distinguish the words:

"The least sound would be fatal to our plans."

I nodded to show that I had heard.

"We must sit without light. He would see it through the ventilator."   225

I nodded again.

"Do not go asleep; your very life may depend upon it. Have your pistol ready in case we should need it. I will sit on the side of the bed, and you in that chair."

I took out my revolver and laid it on the corner of the table.

Holmes had brought up a long thin cane, and this he placed upon the bed beside him. By it he laid the box of matches and the stump of a candle. Then he turned down the lamp, and we were left in darkness.

How shall I ever forget that dreadful vigil? I could not hear a sound, not even 230 the drawing of a breath, and yet I knew that my companion sat open-eyed, within a few feet of me, in the same state of nervous tension in which I was myself. The shutters cut off the least ray of light, and we waited in absolute darkness.

From outside came the occasional cry of a night-bird, and once at our very window a long drawn catlike whine, which told us that the cheetah was indeed at liberty. Far away we could hear the deep tones of the parish clock, which boomed out every quarter of an hour. How long they seemed, those quarters! Twelve struck, and one and two and three, and still we sat waiting silently for whatever might befall.

Suddenly there was the momentary gleam of a light up in the direction of the ventilator, which vanished immediately, but was succeeded by a strong smell of burning oil and heated metal. Someone in the next room had lit a dark-lantern. I heard a gentle sound of movement, and then all was silent once more, though the smell grew stronger. For half an hour I sat with straining ears. Then suddenly another sound became audible—a very gentle, soothing sound, like that of a small jet of steam escaping continually from a kettle. The instant that we heard it, Holmes sprang from the bed, struck a match, and lashed furiously with his cane at the bell-pull.

"You see it, Watson?" he yelled. "You see it?"

But I saw nothing. At the moment when Holmes struck the light I heard a low, clear whistle, but the sudden glare flashing into my weary eyes made it impossible for me to tell what it was at which my friend lashed so savagely. I could, however, see that his face was deadly pale and filled with horror and loathing. He had ceased to strike and was gazing up at the ventilator when suddenly there broke from the silence of the night the most horrible cry to which I have ever listened. It swelled up louder and louder, a hoarse yell of pain and fear and anger all mingled in the one dreadful shriek. They say that away down in the village, and even in the distant parsonage, that cry raised the sleepers from their beds. It struck cold to our hearts, and I stood gazing at Holmes, and he at me, until the last echoes of it had died away into the silence from which it rose.

235   "What can it mean?" I gasped.

"It means that it is all over," Holmes answered. "And perhaps, after all, it is for the best. Take your pistol, and we will enter Dr. Roylott's room."

With a grave face he lit the lamp and led the way down the corridor. Twice he struck at the chamber door without any reply from within. Then he turned the handle and entered, I at his heels, with the cocked pistol in my hand.

It was a singular sight which met our eyes. On the table stood a dark-lantern with the shutter half open, throwing a brilliant beam of light upon the iron safe, the door of which was ajar. Beside this table, on the wooden chair, sat Dr. Grimesby Roylott clad in a long grey dressing-gown, his bare ankles protruding beneath, and his feet thrust into red heelless Turkish slippers. Across his lap lay the short stock with the long lash which we had noticed during the day. His chin was cocked upward and his eyes were fixed in a dreadful, rigid stare at the corner of the ceiling. Round his brow he had a peculiar yellow band, with brownish speckles, which seemed to be bound tightly round his head. As we entered he made neither sound nor motion.

"The band! The speckled band!" whispered Holmes.

240   I took a step forward. In an instant his strange headgear began to move, and there reared itself from among his hair the squat diamond-shaped head and puffed neck of a loathsome serpent.

"It is a swamp adder!" cried Holmes; "the deadliest snake in India. He has died within ten seconds of being bitten. Violence does, in truth, recoil upon the violent, and the schemer falls into the pit which he digs for another. Let us thrust this creature back into its den, and we can then remove Miss Stoner to some place of shelter and let the county police know what has happened."

As he spoke he drew the dog-whip swiftly from the dead man's lap, and throwing the noose round the reptile's neck he drew it from its horrid perch and, carrying it at arm's length, threw it into the iron safe, which he closed upon it.

Such are the true facts of the death of Dr. Grimesby Roylott, of Stoke Moran. It is not necessary that I should prolong a narrative which has already run to too great a length by telling how we broke the sad news to the terrified girl, how we conveyed her by the morning train to the care of her good aunt at Harrow, of how the slow process of official inquiry came to the conclusion that the doctor met his fate while indiscreetly playing with a dangerous pet. The little which I had yet to learn of the case was told me by Sherlock Holmes as we travelled back next day.

"I had," said he, "come to an entirely erroneous conclusion which shows, my dear Watson, how dangerous it always is to reason from insufficient data. The presence of the gypsies, and the use of the word 'band,' which was used by the poor girl, no doubt, to explain the appearance which she had caught a hurried glimpse of by the light of her match, were sufficient to put me upon an entirely wrong scent. I can only claim the merit that I instantly reconsidered my position when, however, it became clear to me that whatever danger threatened an occupant of the room could not come either from the window or the door. My attention was speedily drawn, as I have already remarked to you, to this ventilator, and to the bell-rope which hung down to the bed.

The discovery that this was a dummy, and that the bed was clamped to 245 the floor, instantly gave rise to the suspicion that the rope was there as a bridge for something passing through the hole and coming to the bed. The idea of a snake instantly occurred to me, and when I coupled it with my knowledge that the doctor was furnished with a supply of creatures from India, I felt that I was probably on the right track. The idea of using a form of poison which could not possibly be discovered by any chemical test was just such a one as would occur to a clever and ruthless man who had had an Eastern training. The rapidity with which such a poison would take effect would also, from his point of view, be an advantage. It would be a sharp-eyed coroner, indeed, who could distinguish the two little dark punctures which would show where the poison fangs had done their work. Then I thought of the whistle. Of course he must recall the snake before the morning light revealed it to the victim. He had trained it, probably by the use of the milk which we saw, to return to him when summoned. He would put it through this ventilator at the hour that he thought best, with the certainty that it would crawl down the rope and land on the bed. It might or might not bite the occupant, perhaps she might escape every night for a week, but sooner or later she must fall a victim.

"I had come to these conclusions before ever I had entered his room. An inspection of his chair showed me that he had been in the habit of standing on it, which of course would be necessary in order that he should reach the ventilator. The sight of the safe, the saucer of milk, and the loop of whipcord were enough to finally dispel any doubts which may have remained. The metallic clang heard by Miss Stoner was obviously caused by her stepfather hastily closing the door of his safe upon its terrible occupant. Having once made up my mind, you know the steps which I took in order to put the matter to the proof. I heard the creature hiss as I have no doubt that you did also, and I instantly lit the light and attacked it."

"With the result of driving it through the ventilator."

"And also with the result of causing it to turn upon its master at the other side.

Some of the blows of my cane came home and roused its snakish temper, so that it flew upon the first person it saw. In this way I am no doubt indirectly responsible for Dr. Grimesby Roylott's death, and I cannot say that it is likely to weigh very heavily upon my conscience."

CRITICAL THINKING QUESTIONS

1. What role does Doctor Watson play in this story? What is the effect of the story being told in first person from his **point of view**? Is he a reliable narrator? Why or why not?

2. We associate Sherlock Holmes with intelligence and insight, but he also works hard to solve a crime. Give details from the story to illustrate his method and work ethic.

3. Why does Ms. Stoner seek the help of Sherlock Holmes? What other options might she have had? Why doesn't she just leave home if she feels unsafe? How does her position illustrate the role of women in Victorian England?

WRITING TOPIC

Why does Sherlock Holmes first suspect the gypsies? What does this tell us about their position in that society? How might this story connect to current issues like racial profiling? Give examples to make the connection.

––––––––––––

Nathaniel Hawthorne

Young Goodman Brown (1835)

Young Goodman[1] Brown came forth at sunset, into the street of Salem village, but put his head back, after crossing the threshold, to exchange a parting kiss with his young wife. And Faith, as the wife was aptly named, thrust her own pretty head into the street, letting the wind play with the pink ribbons of her cap, while she called to Goodman Brown.

"Dearest heart," whispered she, softly and rather sadly, when her lips were close to his ear, "pr'y thee,[2] put off your journey until sunrise, and sleep in your

––––––––––––

[1]**Goodman** archaic title for married farmer, typically a rank below a gentleman in terms of societal respectability

[2]**pr'y thee** Old English for *please*

own bed to-night. A lone woman is troubled with such dreams and such thoughts, that she's afeard of herself, sometimes. Pray, tarry with me this night, dear husband, of all nights in the year."

"My love and my Faith," replied young Goodman Brown, "of all nights in the year, this one night must I tarry away from thee. My journey, as thou callest it, forth and back again, must needs be done 'twixt now and sunrise. What, my sweet, pretty wife, dost thou doubt me already, and we but three months married?"

"Then God bless you!" said Faith, with the pink ribbons, "and may you find all well, when you come back."

"Amen!" cried Goodman Brown. "Say thy prayers, dear Faith, and go to bed at dusk, and no harm will come to thee."   5

So they parted; and the young man pursued his way, until, being about to turn the corner by the meeting-house, he looked back and saw the head of Faith still peeping after him, with a melancholy air, in spite of her pink ribbons.

"Poor little Faith!" thought he, for his heart smote him. "What a wretch am I, to leave her on such an errand! She talks of dreams, too. Methought, as she spoke, there was trouble in her face, as if a dream had warned her what work is to be done to-night. But, no, no! 'twould kill her to think it. Well; she's a blessed angel on earth; and after this one night, I'll cling to her skirts and follow her to heaven."

With this excellent resolve for the future, Goodman Brown felt himself justified in making more haste on his present evil purpose. He had taken a dreary road, darkened by all the gloomiest trees of the forest, which barely stood aside to let the narrow path creep through, and closed immediately behind. It was all as lonely as could be; and there is this peculiarity in such a solitude, that the traveller knows not who may be concealed by the innumerable trunks and the thick boughs overhead; so that, with lonely footsteps, he may yet be passing through an unseen multitude.

"There may be a devilish Indian behind every tree," said Goodman Brown to himself; and he glanced fearfully behind him, as he added, "What if the devil himself should be at my very elbow!"

His head being turned back, he passed a crook of the road, and looking for-   10
ward again, beheld the figure of a man, in grave and decent attire, seated at the foot of an old tree. He arose, at Goodman Brown's approach, and walked onward, side by side with him.

"You are late, Goodman Brown," said he. "The clock of the Old South was striking, as I came through Boston; and that is full fifteen minutes agone."

"Faith kept me back awhile," replied the young man, with a tremor in his voice, caused by the sudden appearance of his companion, though not wholly unexpected.

It was now deep dusk in the forest, and deepest in that part of it where these two were journeying. As nearly as could be discerned, the second traveller was about fifty years old, apparently in the same rank of life as Goodman Brown, and bearing a considerable resemblance to him, though perhaps more in expression than features. Still, they might have been taken for father and son. And yet, though the elder person was as simply clad as the younger, and as simple in manner too, he had an indescribable air of one who knew the world, and would not have felt abashed at the governor's dinner-table, or in King William's court, were it possible that his affairs should call him thither. But the only thing about him, that could be fixed upon as remarkable, was his staff, which bore the likeness of a great black snake, so curiously wrought, that it might almost be seen to twist and wriggle itself like a living serpent. This, of course, must have been an ocular deception, assisted by the uncertain light.

"Come, Goodman Brown!" cried his fellow-traveller, "this is a dull pace for the beginning of a journey. Take my staff, if you are so soon weary."

15   "Friend," said the other, exchanging his slow pace for a full stop, "having kept covenant by meeting thee here, it is my purpose now to return whence I came. I have scruples, touching the matter thou wot'st[3] of."

"Sayest thou so?" replied he of the serpent, smiling apart. "Let us walk on, nevertheless, reasoning as we go, and if I convince thee not, thou shalt turn back. We are but a little way in the forest, yet."

"Too far, too far!" exclaimed the goodman, unconsciously resuming his walk. "My father never went into the woods on such an errand, nor his father before him. We have been a race of honest men and good Christians, since the days of the martyrs. And shall I be the first of the name of Brown, that ever took this path and kept—"

"Such company, thou wouldst say," observed the elder person, interrupting his pause. "Well said, Goodman Brown! I have been as well acquainted with your family as with ever a one among the Puritans; and that's no trifle to say. I helped your grandfather, the constable, when he lashed the Quaker woman so smartly through the streets of Salem. And it was I that brought your father a pitch-pine knot, kindled at my own hearth, to set fire to an Indian village, in King Philip's War. They were my good friends, both; and many a pleasant walk have we had along this path, and returned merrily after midnight. I would fain be friends with you, for their sake."

"If it be as thou sayest," replied Goodman Brown, "I marvel they never spoke of these matters. Or, verily, I marvel not, seeing that the least rumor of the sort would have driven them from New England. We are a people of prayer, and good works to boot, and abide no such wickedness."

20   "Wickedness or not," said the traveller with the twisted staff, "I have a very general acquaintance here in New England. The deacons of many a church have drunk the communion wine with me; the selectmen, of divers towns, make me their chairman; and a majority of the Great and General Court are firm supporters of my interest. The governor and I, too—but these are state-secrets."

---

[3]**wot'st** Middle English *know*

"Can this be so?" cried Goodman Brown, with a stare of amazement at his undisturbed companion. "Howbeit, I have nothing to do with the governor and council; they have their own ways, and are no rule for a simple husbandman like me. But, were I to go on with thee, how should I meet the eye of that good old man, our minister, at Salem village? Oh, his voice would make me tremble, both Sabbath day and lecture day."

Thus far, the elder traveller had listened with due gravity, but now burst into a fit of irrepressible mirth, shaking himself so violently that his snake-like staff actually seemed to wriggle in sympathy.

"Ha! ha! ha!" shouted he, again and again; then composing himself, "Well, go on, Goodman Brown, go on; but, prithee, don't kill me with laughing!"

"Well, then, to end the matter at once," said Goodman Brown, considerably nettled, "there is my wife, Faith. It would break her dear little heart; and I'd rather break my own!"

"Nay, if that be the case," answered the other, "e'en go thy ways, Goodman Brown. I would not, for twenty old women like the one hobbling before us, that Faith should come to any harm."   25

As he spoke, he pointed his staff at a female figure on the path, in whom Goodman Brown recognized a very pious and exemplary dame, who had taught him his catechism in youth, and was still his moral and spiritual adviser, jointly with the minister and Deacon Gookin.

"A marvel, truly, that Goody Cloyse should be so far in the wilderness, at night-fall!" said he. "But, with your leave, friend, I shall take a cut through the woods, until we have left this Christian woman behind. Being a stranger to you, she might ask whom I was consorting with, and whither I was going."

"Be it so," said his fellow-traveller. "Betake you to the woods, and let me keep the path."

Accordingly, the young man turned aside, but took care to watch his companion, who advanced softly along the road, until he had come within a staff's length of the old dame. She, meanwhile, was making the best of her way, with singular speed for so aged a woman, and mumbling some indistinct words, a prayer, doubtless, as she went. The traveller put forth his staff, and touched her withered neck with what seemed the serpent's tail.

"The devil!" screamed the pious old lady.   30

"Then Goody Cloyse knows her old friend?" observed the traveller, confronting her, and leaning on his writhing stick.

"Ah, forsooth, and is it your worship, indeed?" cried the good dame. "Yea, truly is it, and in the very image of my old gossip, Goodman Brown, the grandfather of the silly fellow that now is. But—would your worship believe it?—my broomstick hath strangely disappeared, stolen, as I suspect, by that unhanged witch, Goody Cory, and that, too, when I was all anointed with the juice of small-age[4] and cinquefoil and wolf's-bane—"

---

[4]**smallage** herb with strong scent

"Mingled with fine wheat and the fat of a new-born babe," said the shape of old Goodman Brown.

"Ah, your worship knows the recipe," cried the old lady, cackling aloud. "So, as I was saying, being all ready for the meeting, and no horse to ride on, I made up my mind to foot it; for they tell me, there is a nice young man to be taken into communion to-night. But now your good worship will lend me your arm, and we shall be there in a twinkling."

35   "That can hardly be," answered her friend. "I may not spare you my arm, Goody Cloyse, but here is my staff, if you will."

So saying, he threw it down at her feet, where, perhaps, it assumed life, being one of the rods which its owner had formerly lent to Egyptian Magi. Of this fact, however, Goodman Brown could not take cognizance. He had cast up his eyes in astonishment, and looking down again, beheld neither Goody Cloyse nor the serpentine staff, but his fellow-traveller alone, who waited for him as calmly as if nothing had happened.

"That old woman taught me my catechism!" said the young man; and there was a world of meaning in this simple comment.

They continued to walk onward, while the elder traveller exhorted his companion to make good speed and persevere in the path, discoursing so aptly, that his arguments seemed rather to spring up in the bosom of his auditor, than to be suggested by himself. As they went, he plucked a branch of maple, to serve for a walking-stick, and began to strip it of the twigs and little boughs, which were wet with evening dew. The moment his fingers touched them, they became strangely withered and dried up, as with a week's sunshine. Thus the pair proceeded, at a good free pace, until suddenly, in a gloomy hollow of the road, Goodman Brown sat himself down on the stump of a tree, and refused to go any farther.

"Friend," said he, stubbornly, "my mind is made up. Not another step will I budge on this errand. What if a wretched old woman do choose to go to the devil, when I thought she was going to Heaven! Is that any reason why I should quit my dear Faith, and go after her?"

40   "You will think better of this by-and-by," said his acquaintance, composedly. "Sit here and rest yourself awhile; and when you feel like moving again, there is my staff to help you along."

Without more words, he threw his companion the maple stick, and was as speedily out of sight, as if he had vanished into the deepening gloom. The young man sat a few moments by the road-side, applauding himself greatly, and thinking with how clear a conscience he should meet the minister, in his morning-walk, nor shrink from the eye of good old Deacon Gookin. And what calm sleep would be his, that very night, which was to have been spent so wickedly, but purely and sweetly now, in the arms of Faith! Amidst these pleasant and praise-worthy meditations, Goodman Brown heard the tramp of horses along the road, and deemed it advisable to conceal himself within the verge of the forest, conscious of the guilty purpose that had brought him thither, though now so happily turned from it.

On came the hoof tramps and the voices of the riders, two grave old voices, conversing soberly as they drew near. These mingled sounds appeared to pass along the road, within a few yards of the young man's hiding-place; but owing, doubtless, to the depth of the gloom, at that particular spot, neither the travellers nor their steeds were visible. Though their figures brushed the small boughs by the way-side, it could not be seen that they intercepted, even for a moment, the faint gleam from the strip of bright sky, athwart which they must have passed. Goodman Brown alternately crouched and stood on tip-toe, pulling aside the branches, and thrusting forth his head as far as he durst, without discerning so much as a shadow. It vexed him the more, because he could have sworn, were such a thing possible, that he recognized the voices of the minister and Deacon Gookin, jogging along quietly, as they were wont to do, when bound to some ordination or ecclesiastical council. While yet within hearing, one of the riders stopped to pluck a switch.

"Of the two, reverend Sir," said the voice like the deacon's, "I had rather miss an ordination-dinner than tonight's meeting. They tell me that some of our community are to be here from Falmouth and beyond, and others from Connecticut and Rhode-Island; besides several of the Indian powwows, who, after their fashion, know almost as much deviltry as the best of us. Moreover, there is a goodly young woman to be taken into communion."

"Mighty well, Deacon Gookin!" replied the solemn old tones of the minister. "Spur up, or we shall be late. Nothing can be done, you know, until I get on the ground."

The hoofs clattered again, and the voices, talking so strangely in the empty 45 air, passed on through the forest, where no church had ever been gathered, nor solitary Christian prayed. Whither, then, could these holy men be journeying, so deep into the heathen wilderness? Young Goodman Brown caught hold of a tree, for support, being ready to sink down on the ground, faint and overburdened with the heavy sickness of his heart. He looked up to the sky, doubting whether there really was a Heaven above him. Yet, there was the blue arch, and the stars brightening in it.

"With Heaven above, and Faith below, I will yet stand firm against the devil!" cried Goodman Brown.

While he still gazed upward, into the deep arch of the firmament, and had lifted his hands to pray, a cloud, though no wind was stirring, hurried across the zenith, and hid the brightening stars. The blue sky was still visible, except directly overhead, where this black mass of cloud was sweeping swiftly northward. Aloft in the air, as if from the depths of the cloud, came a confused and doubtful sound of voices. Once, the listener fancied that he could distinguish the accent of town's-people of his own, men and women, both pious and ungodly, many of whom he had met at the communion-table, and had seen others rioting at the tavern. The next moment, so indistinct were the sounds, he doubted whether he had heard aught but the murmur of the old forest, whispering without a wind. Then came a stronger swell of those familiar tones, heard daily in the sunshine, at Salem village, but never, until now, from a cloud of night. There was one voice, of a young woman, uttering lamentations, yet with an uncertain sorrow, and entreating for some favor, which, perhaps, it would grieve her to obtain. And all the unseen multitude, both saints and sinners, seemed to encourage her onward.

"Faith!" shouted Goodman Brown, in a voice of agony and desperation; and the echoes of the forest mocked him, crying, "Faith! Faith!" as if bewildered wretches were seeking her, all through the wilderness.

The cry of grief, rage, and terror, was yet piercing the night, when the unhappy husband held his breath for a response. There was a scream, drowned immediately in a louder murmur of voices, fading into far-off laughter, as the dark cloud swept away, leaving the clear and silent sky above Goodman Brown. But something fluttered lightly down through the air, and caught on the branch of a tree. The young man seized it, and beheld a pink ribbon.

50   "My Faith is gone!" cried he, after one stupefied moment. "There is no good on earth; and sin is but a name. Come, devil; for to thee is this world given."

And maddened with despair, so that he laughed loud and long, did Goodman Brown grasp his staff and set forth again, at such a rate, that he seemed to fly along the forest-path, rather than to walk or run. The road grew wilder and drearier, and more faintly traced, and vanished at length, leaving him in the heart of the dark wilderness, still rushing onward, with the instinct that guides mortal man to evil. The whole forest was peopled with frightful sounds—the creaking of the trees, the howling of wild beasts, and the yell of Indians; while, sometimes the wind tolled like a distant church-bell, and sometimes gave a broad roar around the traveller, as if all Nature were laughing him to scorn. But he was himself the chief horror of the scene, and shrank not from its other horrors.

"Ha! ha! ha!" roared Goodman Brown, when the wind laughed at him. "Let us hear which will laugh loudest! Think not to frighten me with your deviltry! Come witch, come wizard, come Indian powwow, come devil himself, and here comes Goodman Brown. You may as well fear him as he fear you."

In truth, all through the haunted forest, there could be nothing more frightful than the figure of Goodman Brown. On he flew, among the black pines, brandishing his staff with frenzied gestures, now giving vent to an inspiration of horrid blasphemy, and now shouting forth such laughter, as set all the echoes of the forest laughing like demons around him. The fiend in his own shape is less hideous, than when he rages in the breast of man. Thus sped the demoniac on his course, until, quivering among the trees, he saw a red light before him, as when the felled trunks and branches of a clearing have been set on fire, and throw up their lurid blaze against the sky, at the hour of midnight. He paused, in a lull of the tempest that had driven him onward, and heard the swell of what seemed a hymn, rolling solemnly from a distance, with the weight of many voices. He knew the tune; it was a familiar one in the choir of the village meeting-house. The verse died heavily away, and was lengthened by a chorus, not of human voices, but of all the sounds of the benighted wilderness, pealing in awful harmony together. Goodman Brown cried out; and his cry was lost to his own ear, by its unison with the cry of the desert.

In the interval of silence, he stole forward, until the light glared full upon his eyes. At one extremity of an open space, hemmed in by the dark wall of the forest, arose a rock, bearing some rude, natural resemblance either to an altar or a pulpit, and surrounded by four blazing pines, their tops aflame, their stems untouched, like candles at an evening meeting. The mass of foliage, that had overgrown the summit of the rock, was all on fire, blazing high into the night, and fitfully illuminating the whole field. Each pendent twig and leafy festoon was in a blaze. As the red light arose and fell, a numerous congregation alternately shone forth, then disappeared in shadow, and again grew, as it were, out of the darkness, peopling the heart of the solitary woods at once.

"A grave and dark-clad company," quoth Goodman Brown.   55

In truth, they were such. Among them, quivering to and fro, between gloom and splendor, appeared faces that would be seen, next day, at the council board of the province, and others which, Sabbath after Sabbath, looked devoutly heavenward, and benignantly over the crowded pews, from the holiest pulpits in the land. Some affirm, that the lady of the governor was there. At least, there were high dames well known to her, and wives of honored husbands, and widows, a great multitude, and ancient maidens, all of excellent repute, and fair young girls, who trembled lest their mothers should espy them. Either the sudden gleams of light, flashing over the obscure field, bedazzled Goodman Brown, or he recognized a score of the church-members of Salem village, famous for their especial sanctity. Good old Deacon Gookin had arrived, and waited at the skirts of that venerable saint, his reverend pastor. But, irreverently consorting with these grave, reputable, and pious people, these elders of the church, these chaste dames and dewy virgins, there were men of dissolute lives and women of spotted fame, wretches given over to all mean and filthy vice, and suspected even of horrid crimes. It was strange to see, that the good shrank not from the wicked, nor were the sinners abashed by the saints. Scattered, also, among their pale-faced enemies, were the Indian priests, or powwows, who had often scared their native forest with more hideous incantations than any known to English witchcraft.

"But, where is Faith?" thought Goodman Brown; and, as hope came into his heart, he trembled.

Another verse of the hymn arose, a slow and mournful strain, such as the pious love, but joined to words which expressed all that our nature can conceive of sin, and darkly hinted at far more. Unfathomable to mere mortals is the lore of fiends. Verse after verse was sung, and still the chorus of the desert swelled between, like the deepest tone of a mighty organ. And, with the final peal of that dreadful anthem, there came a sound, as if the roaring wind, the rushing streams, the howling beasts, and every other voice of the unconverted wilderness, were mingling and according with the voice of guilty man, in homage to the prince of all. The four blazing pines threw up a loftier flame, and obscurely discovered shapes and visages of horror on the smoke-wreaths, above the impious assembly. At the same moment, the fire on the rock shot redly forth, and formed a glowing arch above its base, where now appeared a figure. With reverence be it spoken, the figure bore no slight similitude, both in garb and manner, to some grave divine of the New England churches.

"Bring forth the converts!" cried a voice that echoed through the field and rolled into the forest.

60   At the word, Goodman Brown stepped forth from the shadow of the trees, and approached the congregation, with whom he felt a loathful brotherhood, by the sympathy of all that was wicked in his heart. He could have well-nigh sworn, that the shape of his own dead father beckoned him to advance, looking downward from a smoke-wreath, while a woman, with dim features of despair, threw out her hand to warn him back. Was it his mother? But he had no power to retreat one step, nor to resist, even in thought, when the minister and good old Deacon Gookin seized his arms, and led him to the blazing rock. Thither came also the slender form of a veiled female, led between Goody Cloyse, that pious teacher of the catechism, and Martha Carrier, who had received the devil's promise to be queen of hell. A rampant hag was she! And there stood the proselytes, beneath the canopy of fire.

"Welcome, my children," said the dark figure, "to the communion of your race. Ye have found, thus young, your nature and your destiny. My children, look behind you!"

They turned; and flashing forth, as it were, in a sheet of flame, the fiend-worshippers were seen; the smile of welcome gleamed darkly on every visage.

"There," resumed the sable form, "are all whom ye have reverenced from youth. Ye deemed them holier than yourselves, and shrank from your own sin, contrasting it with their lives of righteousness, and prayerful aspirations heavenward. Yet, here are they all, in my worshipping assembly! This night it shall be granted you to know their secret deeds; how hoary-bearded elders of the church have whispered wanton words to the young maids of their households; how many a woman, eager for widow's weeds, has given her husband a drink at bedtime, and let him sleep his last sleep in her bosom; how beardless youth have made haste to inherit their father's wealth; and how fair damsels—blush not, sweet ones—have dug little graves in the garden, and bidden me, the sole guest, to an infant's funeral. By the sympathy of your human hearts for sin, ye shall scent out all the places—whether in church, bed-chamber, street, field, or forest—where crime has been committed, and shall exult to behold the whole earth one stain of guilt, one mighty blood-spot. Far more than this. It shall be yours to penetrate, in every bosom, the deep mystery of sin, the fountain of all wicked arts, and which inexhaustibly supplies more evil impulses than human power—than my power at its utmost—can make manifest in deeds. And now, my children, look upon each other."

They did so; and, by the blaze of the hell-kindled torches, the wretched man beheld his Faith, and the wife her husband, trembling before that unhallowed altar.

"Lo, there ye stand, my children," said the figure, in a deep and solemn tone, almost sad, with its despairing awfulness, as if his once angelic nature could yet mourn for our miserable race. "Depending upon one another's hearts, ye had still hoped that virtue were not all a dream! Now are ye undeceived! Evil is the nature of mankind. Evil must be your only happiness. Welcome, again, my children, to the communion of your race!"

"Welcome," repeated the fiend-worshippers, in one cry of despair and triumph.

And there they stood, the only pair, as it seemed, who were yet hesitating on the verge of wickedness, in this dark world. A basin was hollowed, naturally, in the rock. Did it contain water, reddened by the lurid light? or was it blood? or, perchance, a liquid flame? Herein did the Shape of Evil dip his hand, and prepare to lay the mark of baptism upon their foreheads, that they might be partakers of the mystery of sin, more conscious of the secret guilt of others, both in deed and thought, than they could now be of their own. The husband cast one look at his pale wife, and Faith at him. What polluted wretches would the next glance show them to each other, shuddering alike at what they disclosed and what they saw!

"Faith! Faith!" cried the husband. "Look up to Heaven, and resist the Wicked One!"

Whether Faith obeyed, he knew not. Hardly had he spoken, when he found himself amid calm night and solitude, listening to a roar of the wind, which died heavily away through the forest. He staggered against the rock, and felt it chill and damp; while a hanging twig, that had been all on fire, besprinkled his cheek with the coldest dew.

The next morning, young Goodman Brown came slowly into the street of Salem village, staring around him like a bewildered man. The good old minister was taking a walk along the graveyard, to get an appetite for breakfast and meditate his sermon, and bestowed a blessing, as he passed, on Goodman Brown. He shrank from the venerable saint, as if to avoid an anathema. Old Deacon Gookin was at domestic worship, and the holy words of his prayer were heard through the open window. "What God doth the wizard pray to?" quoth Goodman Brown. Goody Cloyse, that excellent old Christian, stood in the early sunshine, at her own lattice, catechising[5] a little girl, who had brought her a pint of morning's milk. Goodman Brown snatched away the child, as from the grasp of the fiend himself. Turning the corner by the meeting-house, he spied the head of Faith, with the pink ribbons, gazing anxiously forth, and bursting into such joy at sight

65

70

---

[5]**catechising** teaching religious lessons

of him, that she skipt along the street, and almost kissed her husband before the whole village. But Goodman Brown looked sternly and sadly into her face, and passed on without a greeting.

Had Goodman Brown fallen asleep in the forest, and only dreamed a wild dream of a witch-meeting?

Be it so, if you will. But, alas! it was a dream of evil omen for young Goodman Brown. A stern, a sad, a darkly meditative, a distrustful, if not a desperate man, did he become, from the night of that fearful dream. On the Sabbath-day, when the congregation were singing a holy psalm, he could not listen, because an anthem of sin rushed loudly upon his ear, and drowned all the blessed strain. When the minister spoke from the pulpit, with power and fervid eloquence, and with his hand on the open Bible, of the sacred truths of our religion, and of saint-like lives and triumphant deaths, and of future bliss or misery unutterable, then did Goodman Brown turn pale, dreading lest the roof should thunder down upon the gray blasphemer and his hearers. Often, awaking suddenly at midnight, he shrank from the bosom of Faith, and at morning or eventide, when the family knelt down at prayer, he scowled, and muttered to himself, and gazed sternly at his wife, and turned away. And when he had lived long, and was borne to his grave, a hoary corpse, followed by Faith, an aged woman, and children and grand-children, a goodly procession, besides neighbors, not a few, they carved no hopeful verse upon his tombstone; for his dying hour was gloom.

CRITICAL THINKING QUESTIONS

1. Do you believe Young Goodman Brown forever changed after his journey into the haunted forest? Do you believe it was a literal experience or a dream? Explain.

2. What other notable tragic and historic event occurred in Salem, Massachusetts? How does that fit the theme of this story? Could Hawthorne's story be viewed as a political statement? Explain your reasoning.

3. In what ways do you see this story as a commentary on the institution of religion? Please elaborate fully.

WRITING TOPIC

Do you believe humankind to be naturally good or inherently evil? Are people more inclined to selfishness and greed or sacrifice and kindness when it comes to their fellow man? Offer your response and examples.

Flannery O'Connor

A Good Man Is Hard to Find (1955)

The grandmother didn't want to go to Florida. She wanted to visit some of her connections in east Tennessee and she was seizing at every chance to change Bailey's mind. Bailey was the son she lived with, her only boy. He was sitting on the edge of his chair at the table, bent over the orange sports section of the *Journal.* "Now look here, Bailey," she said, "see here, read this," and she stood with one hand on her thin hip and the other rattling the newspaper at his bald head. "Here this fellow that calls himself The Misfit is aloose from the Federal Pen and headed toward Florida and you read here what it says he did to these people. Just you read it. I wouldn't take my children in any direction with a criminal like that aloose in it. I couldn't answer to my conscience if I did."

Bailey didn't look up from his reading so she wheeled around then and faced the children's mother, a young woman in slacks, whose face was as broad and innocent as a cabbage and was tied around with a green head-kerchief that had two points on the top like rabbit's ears. She was sitting on the sofa, feeding the baby his apricots out of a jar. "The children have been to Florida before," the old lady said. "You all ought to take them somewhere else for a change so they would see different parts of the world and be broad. They never have been to east Tennessee."

The children's mother didn't seem to hear her but the eight-year-old boy, John Wesley, a stocky child with glasses, said, "If you don't want to go to Florida, why dontcha stay at home?" He and the little girl, June Star, were reading the funny papers on the floor.

"She wouldn't stay at home to be queen for a day," June Star said without raising her yellow head.

"Yes and what would you do if this fellow, The Misfit, caught you?" the   5
grandmother asked.

"I'd smack his face," John Wesley said.

"She wouldn't stay at home for a million bucks," June Star said. "Afraid she'd miss something. She has to go everywhere we go."

"All right, Miss," the grandmother said. "Just remember that the next time you want me to curl your hair."

June Star said her hair was naturally curly.

The next morning the grandmother was the first one in the car, ready to go.   10
She had her big black valise that looked like the head of a hippopotamus in one corner, and underneath it she was hiding a basket with Pitty Sing, the cat, in it. She didn't intend for the cat to be left alone in the house for three days because he would miss her too much and she was afraid he might brush against one of her gas burners and accidentally asphyxiate himself. Her son, Bailey, didn't like to arrive at a motel with a cat.

She sat in the middle of the back seat with John Wesley and June Star on either side of her. Bailey and the children's mother and the baby sat in front and they left Atlanta at eight forty-five with the mileage on the car at 55890. The grandmother wrote this down because she thought it would be interesting to say how many miles they had been when they got back. It took them twenty minutes to reach the outskirts of the city.

The old lady settled herself comfortably, removing her white cotton gloves and putting them up with her purse on the shelf in front of the back window. The children's mother still had on slacks and still had her head tied up in a green kerchief, but the grandmother had on a navy blue straw sailor hat with a bunch of white violets on the brim and a navy blue dress with a small white dot in the print. Her collars and cuffs were white organdy trimmed with lace and at her neckline she had pinned a purple spray of cloth violets containing a sachet. In case of an accident, anyone seeing her dead on the highway would know at once that she was a lady.

She said she thought it was going to be a good day for driving, neither too hot nor too cold, and she cautioned Bailey that the speed limit was fifty-five miles an hour and that the patrolmen hid themselves behind billboards and small clumps of trees and sped out after you before you had a chance to slow down. She pointed out interesting details of the scenery: Stone Mountain; the blue granite that in some places came up to both sides of the highway; the brilliant red clay banks slightly streaked with purple; and the various crops that made rows of green lace-work on the ground. The trees were full of silver-white sunlight and the meanest of them sparkled. The children were reading comic magazines and their mother and gone back to sleep.

"Let's go through Georgia fast so we won't have to look at it much," John Wesley said.

15 "If I were a little boy," said the grandmother, "I wouldn't talk about my native state that way. Tennessee has the mountains and Georgia has the hills."

"Tennessee is just a hillbilly dumping ground," John Wesley said, "and Georgia is a lousy state too."

"You said it," June Star said.

"In my time," said the grandmother, folding her thin veined fingers, "children were more respectful of their native states and their parents and everything else. People did right then. Oh look at the cute little pickaninny!" she said and pointed to a Negro child standing in the door of a shack. "Wouldn't that make a picture, now?" she asked and they all turned and looked at the little Negro out of the back window. He waved

"He didn't have any britches on," June Star said.

20 "He probably didn't have any," the grandmother explained. "Little niggers in the country don't have things like we do. If I could paint, I'd paint that picture," she said.

The children exchanged comic books.

The grandmother offered to hold the baby and the children's mother passed him over the front seat to her. She set him on her knee and bounced him and told him about the things they were passing. She rolled her eyes and screwed up her mouth and stuck her leathery thin face into his smooth bland one. Occasionally he gave her a faraway smile. They passed a large cotton field with five or six graves fenced in the middle of it, like a small island. "Look at the graveyard!" the grandmother said, pointing it out. "That was the old family burying ground. That belonged to the plantation."

"Where's the plantation?" John Wesley asked.

"Gone With the Wind" said the grandmother. "Ha. Ha."

When the children finished all the comic books they had brought, they opened the lunch and ate it. The grandmother ate a peanut butter sandwich and an olive and would not let the children throw the box and the paper napkins out the window. When there was nothing else to do they played a game by choosing a cloud and making the other two guess what shape it suggested. John Wesley took one the shape of a cow and June Star guessed a cow and John Wesley said, no, an automobile, and June Star said he didn't play fair, and they began to slap each other over the grandmother.

The grandmother said she would tell them a story if they would keep quiet. When she told a story, she rolled her eyes and waved her head and was very dramatic. She said once when she was a maiden lady she had been courted by a Mr. Edgar Atkins Teagarden from Jasper, Georgia. She said he was a very good-looking man and a gentleman and that he brought her a watermelon every Saturday afternoon with his initials cut in it, E. A. T. Well, one Saturday, she said, Mr. Teagarden brought the watermelon and there was nobody at home and he left it on the front porch and returned in his buggy to Jasper, but she never got the watermelon, she said, because a nigger boy ate it when he saw the initials, E. A. T. ! This story tickled John Wesley's funny bone and he giggled and giggled but June Star didn't think it was any good. She said she wouldn't marry a man that just brought her a watermelon on Saturday. The grandmother said she would have done well to marry Mr. Teagarden because he was a gentleman and had bought Coca-Cola stock when it first came out and that he had died only a few years ago, a very wealthy man.

They stopped at The Tower for barbecued sandwiches. The Tower was a part stucco and part wood filling station and dance hall set in a clearing outside of Timothy. A fat man named Red Sammy Butts ran it and there were signs stuck here and there on the building and for miles up and down the highway saying, TRY RED SAMMY'S FAMOUS BARBECUE. NONE LIKE FAMOUS RED SAMMY'S! RED SAM! THE FAT BOY WITH THE HAPPY LAUGH. A VETERAN! RED SAMMY'S YOUR MAN!

Red Sammy was lying on the bare ground outside The Tower with his head under a truck while a gray monkey about a foot high, chained to a small chinaberry tree, chattered nearby. The monkey sprang back into the tree and got on the highest limb as soon as he saw the children jump out of the car and run toward him.

Inside, The Tower was a long dark room with a counter at one end and tables at the other and dancing space in the middle. They all sat down at a board table next to the nickelodeon and Red Sam's wife, a tall burnt-brown woman with hair and eyes lighter than her skin, came and took their order. The children's mother put a dime in the machine and played "The Tennessee Waltz," and the grandmother said that tune always made her want to dance. She asked Bailey if he would like to dance but he only glared at her. He didn't have a naturally sunny disposition like she did and trips made him nervous. The grandmother's brown eyes were very bright. She swayed her head from side to side and pretended she was dancing in her chair. June Star said play something she could tap to so the children's mother put in another dime and played a fast number and June Star stepped out onto the dance floor and did her tap routine.

30   "Ain't she cute?" Red Sam's wife said, leaning over the counter. "Would you like to come be my little girl?"

"No I certainly wouldn't," June Star said. "I wouldn't live in a broken-down place like this for a million bucks!" and she ran back to the table.

"Ain't she cute?" the woman repeated, stretching her mouth politely.

"Aren't you ashamed?" hissed the grandmother.

Red Sam came in and told his wife to quit lounging on the counter and hurry up with these people's order. His khaki trousers reached just to his hip bones and his stomach hung over them like a sack of meal swaying under his shirt. He came over and sat down at a table nearby and let out a combination sigh and yodel. "You can't win," he said. "You can't win," and he wiped his sweating red face off with a gray handkerchief. "These days you don't know who to trust," he said. "Ain't that the truth?"

35   "People are certainly not nice like they used to be," said the grandmother.

"Two fellers come in here last week," Red Sammy said, "driving a Chrysler. It was a old beat-up car but it was a good one and these boys looked all right to me. Said they worked at the mill and you know I let them fellers charge the gas they bought? Now why did I do that?"

"Because you're a good man!" the grandmother said at once.

"Yes'm, I suppose so," Red Sam said as if he were struck with this answer.

His wife brought the orders, carrying the five plates all at once without a tray, two in each hand and one balanced on her arm. "It isn't a soul in this green world of God's that you can trust," she said. "And I don't count nobody out of that, not nobody," she repeated, looking at Red Sammy.

40   "Did you read about that criminal, The Misfit, that's escaped?" asked the grandmother.

"I wouldn't be a bit surprised if he didn't attack this place right here," said the woman. "If he hears about it being here, I wouldn't be none surprised to see him. If he hears it's two cent in the cash register, I wouldn't be at all surprised if he ..."

"That'll do," Red Sam said. "Go bring these people their Co'-Colas," and the woman went off to get the rest of the order.

"A good man is hard to find," Red Sammy said. "Everything is getting terrible. I remember the day you could go off and leave your screen door unlatched. Not no more."

He and the grandmother discussed better times. The old lady said that in her opinion Europe was entirely to blame for the way things were now. She said the way Europe acted you would think we were made of money and Red Sam said it was no use talking about it, she was exactly right. The children ran outside into the white sunlight and looked at the monkey in the lacy chinaberry tree. He was busy catching fleas on himself and biting each one carefully between his teeth as if it were a delicacy.

They drove off again into the hot afternoon. The grandmother took cat naps   45
and woke up every few minutes with her own snoring. Outside of Toombsboro she woke up and recalled an old plantation that she had visited in this neighborhood once when she was a young lady. She said the house had six white columns across the front and that there was an avenue of oaks leading up to it and two little wooden trellis arbors on either side in front where you sat down with your suitor after a stroll in the garden. She recalled exactly which road to turn off to get to it. She knew that Bailey would not be willing to lose any time looking at an old house, but the more she talked about it, the more she wanted to see it once again and find out if the little twin arbors were still standing. "There was a secret panel in this house," she said craftily, not telling the truth but wishing that she were, "and the story went that all the family silver was hidden in it when Sherman came through but it was never found ..."

"Hey!" John Wesley said. "Let's go see it! We'll find it! We'll poke all the woodwork and find it! Who lives there? Where do you turn off at? Hey Pop, can't we turn off there?"

"We never have seen a house with a secret panel!" June Star shrieked. "Let's go to the house with the secret panel! Hey Pop, can't we go see the house with the secret panel!"

"It's not far from here, I know," the grandmother said. "It wouldn't take over twenty minutes."

Bailey was looking straight ahead. His jaw was as rigid as a horseshoe. "No," he said.

The children began to yell and scream that they wanted to see the house   50
with the secret panel. John Wesley kicked the back of the front seat and June Star hung over her mother's shoulder and whined desperately into her ear that they never had any fun even on their vacation, that they could never do what THEY wanted to do. The baby began to scream and John Wesley kicked the back of the seat so hard that his father could feel the blows in his kidney.

"All right!" he shouted and drew the car to a stop at the side of the road. "Will you all shut up? Will you all just shut up for one second? If you don't shut up, we won't go anywhere."

"It would be very educational for them," the grandmother murmured.

"All right," Bailey said, "but get this: this is the only time we're going to stop for anything like this. This is the one and only time."

"The dirt road that you have to turn down is about a mile back," the grandmother directed. "I marked it when we passed."

55 "A dirt road," Bailey groaned.

After they had turned around and were headed toward the dirt road, the grandmother recalled other points about the house, the beautiful glass over the front doorway and the candle-lamp in the hall. John Wesley said that the secret panel was probably in the fireplace.

"You can't go inside this house," Bailey said. "You don't know who lives there."

"While you all talk to the people in front, I'll run around behind and get in a window," John Wesley suggested.

"We'll all stay in the car," his mother said.

60 They turned onto the dirt road and the car raced roughly along in a swirl of pink dust. The grandmother recalled the times when there were no paved roads and thirty miles was a day's journey. The dirt road was hilly and there were sudden washes in it and sharp curves on dangerous embankments. All at once they would be on a hill, looking down over the blue tops of trees for miles around, then the next minute, they would be in a red depression with the dust-coated trees looking down on them.

"This place had better turn up in a minute," Bailey said, "or I'm going to turn around."

The road looked as if no one had traveled on it in months.

"It's not much farther," the grandmother said and just as she said it, a horrible thought came to her. The thought was so embarrassing that she turned red in the face and her eyes dilated and her feet jumped up, upsetting her valise in the corner. The instant the valise moved, the newspaper top she had over the basket under it rose with a snarl and Pitty Sing, the cat, sprang onto Bailey's shoulder.

The children were thrown to the floor and their mother, clutching the baby, was thrown out the door onto the ground; the old lady was thrown into the front seat. The car turned over once and landed right-side-up in a gulch off the side of the road. Bailey remained in the driver's seat with the cat gray-striped with a broad white face and an orange nose clinging to his neck like a caterpillar.

65 As soon as the children saw they could move their arms and legs, they scrambled out of the car, shouting, "We've had an ACCIDENT!" The grandmother was curled up under the dashboard, hoping she was injured so that Bailey's wrath would not come down on her all at once. The horrible thought she had had before the accident was that the house she had remembered so vividly was not in Georgia but in Tennessee.

Bailey removed the cat from his neck with both hands and flung it out the window against the side of a pine tree. Then he got out of the car and started looking for the children's mother. She was sitting against the side of the red gutted ditch, holding the screaming baby, but she only had a cut down her face and a broken shoulder. "We've had an ACCIDENT!" the children screamed in a frenzy of delight.

"But nobody's killed," June Star said with disappointment as the grandmother limped out of the car, her hat still pinned to her head but the broken front brim standing up at a jaunty angle and the violet spray hanging off the side. They all sat down in the ditch, except the children, to recover from the shock. They were all shaking.

"Maybe a car will come along," said the children's mother hoarsely.

"I believe I have injured an organ," said the grandmother, pressing her side, but no one answered her. Bailey's teeth were clattering. He had on a yellow sport shirt with bright blue parrots designed in it and his face was as yellow as the shirt. The grandmother decided that she would not mention that the house was in Tennessee.

The road was about ten feet above and they could see only the tops of the   70
trees on the other side of it. Behind the ditch they were sitting in there were more woods, tall and dark and deep. In a few minutes they saw a car some distance away on top of a hill, coming slowly as if the occupants were watching them. The grandmother stood up and waved both arms dramatically to attract their attention. The car continued to come on slowly, disappeared around a bend and appeared again, moving even slower, on top of the hill they had gone over. It was a big black battered hearselike automobile. There were three men in it.

It came to a stop just over them and for some minutes, the driver looked down with a steady expressionless gaze to where they were sitting, and didn't speak. Then he turned his head and muttered something to the other two and they got out. One was a fat boy in black trousers and a red sweat shirt with a silver stallion embossed on the front of it. He moved around on the right side of them and stood staring, his mouth partly open in a kind of loose grin. The other had on khaki pants and a blue striped coat and a gray hat pulled down very low, hiding most of his face. He came around slowly on the left side. Neither spoke.

The driver got out of the car and stood by the side of it, looking down at them. He was an older man than the other two. His hair was just beginning to gray and he wore silver-rimmed spectacles that gave him a scholarly look. He had a long creased face and didn't have on any shirt or undershirt. He had on blue jeans that were too tight for him and was holding a black hat and a gun. The two boys also had guns.

"We've had an ACCIDENT!" the children screamed.

The grandmother had the peculiar feeling that the bespectacled man was someone she knew. His face was as familiar to her as if she had known him all her life but she could not recall who he was. He moved away from the car and began to come down the embankment, placing his feet carefully so that he wouldn't slip. He had on tan and white shoes and no socks, and his ankles were red and thin. "Good afternoon," he said. "I see you all had you a little spill."

"We turned over twice!" said the grandmother.   75

"Oncet," he corrected. "We seen it happen. Try their car and see will it run, Hiram," he said quietly to the boy with the gray hat.

"What you got that gun for?" John Wesley asked. "Whatcha gonna do with that gun?"

"Lady," the man said to the children's mother, "would you mind calling them children to sit down by you? Children make me nervous. I want all you all to sit down right together there where you're at."

"What are you telling US what to do for?" June Star asked.

80   Behind them the line of woods gaped like a dark open mouth. "Come here," said their mother.

"Look here now," Bailey began suddenly, "we're in a predicament! We're in ..."

The grandmother shrieked. She scrambled to her feet and stood staring. "You're The Misfit!" she said. "I recognized you at once!"

"Yes'm," the man said, smiling slightly as if he were pleased in spite of himself to be known, "but it would have been better for all of you, lady, if you hadn't of reckernized me."

Bailey turned his head sharply and said something to his mother that shocked even the children. The old lady began to cry and The Misfit reddened.

85   "Lady," he said, "don't you get upset. Sometimes a man says things he don't mean. I don't reckon he meant to talk to you thataway."

"You wouldn't shoot a lady, would you?" the grandmother said and removed a clean handkerchief from her cuff and began to slap at her eyes with it.

The Misfit pointed the toe of his shoe into the ground and made a little hole and then covered it up again. "I would hate to have to," he said.

"Listen," the grandmother almost screamed, "I know you're a good man. You don't look a bit like you have common blood. I know you must come from nice people!"

"Yes ma'm," he said, "finest people in the world." When he smiled he showed a row of strong white teeth. "God never made a finer woman than my mother and my daddy's heart was pure gold," he said. The boy with the red sweat shirt had come around behind them and was standing with his gun at his hip. The Misfit squatted down on the ground. "Watch them children, Bobby Lee," he said. "You know they make me nervous." He looked at the six of them huddled together in front of him and he seemed to be embarrassed as if he couldn't think of anything to say. "Ain't a cloud in the sky," he remarked, looking up at it. "Don't see no sun but don't see no cloud neither."

90   "Yes, it's a beautiful day," said the grandmother. "Listen," she said, "you shouldn't call yourself The Misfit because I know you're a good man at heart. I can just look at you and tell."

"Hush!" Bailey yelled. "Hush! Everybody shut up and let me handle this!" He was squatting in the position of a runner about to sprint forward but he didn't move.

"I pre-chate that, lady," The Misfit said and drew a little circle in the ground with the butt of his gun.

"It'll take a half a hour to fix this here car," Hiram called, looking over the raised hood of it.

"Well, first you and Bobby Lee get him and that little boy to step over yonder with you," The Misfit said, pointing to Bailey and John Wesley. "The boys want to ask you something," he said to Bailey. "Would you mind stepping back in them woods there with them?"

"Listen," Bailey began, "we're in a terrible predicament! Nobody realizes   95 what this is," and his voice cracked. His eyes were as blue and intense as the parrots in his shirt and he remained perfectly still.

The grandmother reached up to adjust her hat brim as if she were going to the woods with him but it came off in her hand. She stood staring at it and after a second she let it fall on the ground. Hiram pulled Bailey up by the arm as if he were assisting an old man. John Wesley caught hold of his father's hand and Bobby Lee followed. They went off toward the woods and just as they reached the dark edge, Bailey turned and supporting himself against a gray naked pine trunk, he shouted, "I'll be back in a minute, Mamma, wait on me!"

"Come back this instant!" his mother shrilled but they all disappeared into the woods.

"Bailey Boy!" the grandmother called in a tragic voice but she found she was looking at The Misfit squatting on the ground in front of her. "I just know you're a good man," she said desperately. "You're not a bit common!"

"Nome, I ain't a good man," The Misfit said after a second as if he had considered her statement carefully, "but I ain't the worst in the world neither. My daddy said I was a different breed of dog from my brothers and sisters. 'You know,' Daddy said, 'it's some that can live their whole life out without asking about it and it's others has to know why it is, and this boy is one of the latters. He's going to be into everything!'" He put on his black hat and looked up suddenly and then away deep into the woods as if he were embarrassed again. "I'm sorry I don't have on a shirt before you ladies," he said, hunching his shoulders slightly. "We buried our clothes that we had on when we escaped and we're just making do until we can get better. We borrowed these from some folks we met," he explained.

"That's perfectly all right," the grandmother said. "Maybe Bailey has an extra   100 shirt in his suitcase."

"I'll look and see terrectly," The Misfit said.

"Where are they taking him?" the children's mother screamed.

"Daddy was a card himself," The Misfit said. "You couldn't put anything over on him. He never got in trouble with the Authorities though. Just had the knack of handling them."

"You could be honest too if you'd only try," said the grandmother. "Think how wonderful it would be to settle down and live a comfortable life and not have to think about somebody chasing you all the time."

The Misfit kept scratching in the ground with the butt of his gun as if he   105 were thinking about it. "Yes'm, somebody is always after you," he murmured.

The grandmother noticed how thin his shoulder blades were just behind his hat because she was standing up looking down on him. "Do you ever pray?" she asked.

He shook his head. All she saw was the black hat wiggle between his shoulder blades. "Nome," he said.

There was a pistol shot from the woods, followed closely by another. Then silence. The old lady's head jerked around. She could hear the wind move through the tree tops like a long satisfied insuck of breath. "Bailey Boy!" she called.

"I was a gospel singer for a while," The Misfit said. "I been most everything. Been in the arm service both land and sea, at home and abroad, been twict married, been an undertaker, been with the railroads, plowed Mother Earth, been in a tornado, seen a man burnt alive oncet," and he looked up at the children's mother and the little girl who were sitting close together, their faces white and their eyes glassy; "I even seen a woman flogged," he said.

110   "Pray, pray," the grandmother began, "pray, pray ..."

"I never was a bad boy that I remember of," The Misfit said in an almost dreamy voice, "but somewheres along the line I done something wrong and got sent to the penitentiary. I was buried alive," and he looked up and held her attention to him by a steady stare.

"That's when you should have started to pray," she said. "What did you do to get sent to the penitentiary that first time?"

"Turn to the right, it was a wall," The Misfit said, looking up again at the cloudless sky. "Turn to the left, it was a wall. Look up it was a ceiling, look down it was a floor. I forget what I done, lady. I set there and set there, trying to remember what it was I done and I ain't recalled it to this day. Oncet in a while, I would think it was coming to me, but it never come."

"Maybe they put you in by mistake," the old lady said vaguely.

115   "Nome," he said. "It wasn't no mistake. They had the papers on me."

"You must have stolen something," she said.

The Misfit sneered slightly. "Nobody had nothing I wanted," he said. "It was a head-doctor at the penitentiary said what I had done was kill my daddy but I known that for a lie. My daddy died in nineteen ought nineteen of the epidemic flu and I never had a thing to do with it. He was buried in the Mount Hopewell Baptist churchyard and you can go there and see for yourself."

"If you would pray," the old lady said, "Jesus would help you."

"That's right," The Misfit said.

120   "Well then, why don't you pray?" she asked trembling with delight suddenly.

"I don't want no hep," he said. "I'm doing all right by myself."

Bobby Lee and Hiram came ambling back from the woods. Bobby Lee was dragging a yellow shirt with bright blue parrots in it.

"Throw me that shirt, Bobby Lee," The Misfit said. The shirt came flying at him and landed on his shoulder and he put it on. The grandmother couldn't name what the shirt reminded her of. "No, lady," The Misfit said while he was buttoning it up, "I found out the crime don't matter. You can do one thing or you can do another, kill a man or take a tire off his car, because sooner or later you're going to forget what it was you done and just be punished for it."

The children's mother had begun to make heaving noises as if she couldn't get her breath. "Lady," he asked, "would you and that little girl like to step off yonder with Bobby Lee and Hiram and join your husband?"

"Yes, thank you," the mother said faintly. Her left arm dangled helplessly   125 and she was holding the baby, who had gone to sleep, in the other. "Hep that lady up, Hiram," The Misfit said as she struggled to climb out of the ditch, "and Bobby Lee, you hold onto that little girl's hand."

"I don't want to hold hands with him," June Star said. "He reminds me of a pig."

The fat boy blushed and laughed and caught her by the arm and pulled her off into the woods after Hiram and her mother.

Alone with The Misfit, the grandmother found that she had lost her voice. There was not a cloud in the sky nor any sun. There was nothing around her but woods. She wanted to tell him that he must pray. She opened and closed her mouth several times before anything came out. Finally she found herself saying, "Jesus. Jesus," meaning, Jesus will help you, but the way she was saying it, it sounded as if she might be cursing.

"Yes'm, The Misfit said as if he agreed. "Jesus thown everything off balance. It was the same case with Him as with me except He hadn't committed any crime and they could prove I had committed one because they had the papers on me. Of course," he said, "they never shown me my papers. That's why I sign myself now. I said long ago, you get you a signature and sign everything you do and keep a copy of it. Then you'll know what you done and you can hold up the crime to the punishment and see do they match and in the end you'll have something to prove you ain't been treated right. I call myself The Misfit," he said, "because I can't make what all I done wrong fit what all I gone through in punishment."

There was a piercing scream from the woods, followed closely by a pistol   130 report. "Does it seem right to you, lady, that one is punished a heap and another ain't punished at all?"

"Jesus!" the old lady cried. "You've got good blood! I know you wouldn't shoot a lady! I know you come from nice people! Pray! Jesus, you ought not to shoot a lady. I'll give you all the money I've got!"

"Lady," The Misfit said, looking beyond her far into the woods, "there never was a body that give the undertaker a tip."

There were two more pistol reports and the grandmother raised her head like a parched old turkey hen crying for water and called, "Bailey Boy, Bailey Boy!" as if her heart would break.

"Jesus was the only One that ever raised the dead," The Misfit continued, "and He shouldn't have done it. He thown everything off balance. If He did what He said, then it's nothing for you to do but throw away everything and follow Him, and if He didn't, then it's nothing for you to do but enjoy the few minutes you got left the best way you can by killing somebody or burning down his house or doing some other meanness to him. No pleasure but meanness," he said and his voice had become almost a snarl.

135   "Maybe He didn't raise the dead," the old lady mumbled, not knowing what she was saying and feeling so dizzy that she sank down in the ditch with her legs twisted under her.

"I wasn't there so I can't say He didn't," The Misfit said. "I wisht I had of been there," he said, hitting the ground with his fist. "It ain't right I wasn't there because if I had of been there I would of known. Listen lady," he said in a high voice, "if I had of been there I would of known and I wouldn't be like I am now." His voice seemed about to crack and the grandmother's head cleared for an instant. She saw the man's face twisted close to her own as if he were going to cry and she murmured, "Why you're one of my babies. You're one of my own children!" She reached out and touched him on the shoulder. The Misfit sprang back as if a snake had bitten him and shot her three times through the chest. Then he put his gun down on the ground and took off his glasses and began to clean them.

Hiram and Bobby Lee returned from the woods and stood over the ditch, looking down at the grandmother who half sat and half lay in a puddle of blood with her legs crossed under her like a child's and her face smiling up at the cloudless sky.

Without his glasses, The Misfit's eyes were red-rimmed and pale and defenseless-looking. "Take her off and thow her where you thown the others," he said, picking up the cat that was rubbing itself against his leg.

"She was a talker, wasn't she?" Bobby Lee said, sliding down the ditch with a yodel.

140   "She would of been a good woman," The Misfit said, "if it had been somebody there to shoot her every minute of her life."

"Some fun!" Bobby Lee said.

"Shut up, Bobby Lee," The Misfit said. "It's no real pleasure in life."

CRITICAL THINKING QUESTIONS

1. Who are the "good" **characters** in this story? How do you define "good"? How do you determine "good"?

2. What does the Misfit mean at the end of the story when he says that the grandmother would have been a good woman if someone could have been there to shoot her every day? What happened between those two characters at the end? Could violence have been beneficial in saving the grandmother? Cite quotations from the story for support.

WRITING TOPIC

The Misfit says that his father died of the flu, but he also states that he was imprisoned for murdering his father. Is it possible that he was wrongfully imprisoned? Could his jail time have turned him into a "misfit"? Reflect on the efficacy of our justice system and recidivism rates (perhaps conduct some research). How likely is it that innocent people are convicted of crimes? How effective is the prison system in rehabilitation? Could a prisoner come away from time served as a better individual? Is it more likely that the offender will commit another crime? What should we change or continue to do to reduce repeat offenders?

Edgar Allen Poe

The Cask[1] of Amontillado[2] (1846)

The thousand injuries of Fortunato I had borne as I best could, but when he ventured upon insult I vowed revenge. You, who so well know the nature of my soul, will not suppose, however, that gave utterance to a threat. At length I would be avenged; this was a point definitely, settled—but the very definitiveness with which it was resolved precluded the idea of risk. I must not only punish but punish with impunity. A wrong is unredressed when retribution overtakes its redresser. It is equally unredressed when the avenger fails to make himself felt as such to him who has done the wrong.

It must be understood that neither by word nor deed had I given Fortunato cause to doubt my good will. I continued, as was my wont, to smile in his face, and he did not perceive that my smile *now* was at the thought of his immolation.

He had a weak point—this Fortunato—although in other regards he was a man to be respected and even feared. He prided himself on his connoisseurship in wine. Few Italians have the true virtuoso spirit. For the most part their enthusiasm is adopted to suit the time and opportunity, to practice imposture upon the British and Austrian *millionaires*. In painting and gemmary, Fortunato, like his countrymen, was a quack, but in the matter of old wines he was sincere. In this respect I did not differ from him materially;—I was skillful in the Italian vintages myself, and bought largely whenever I could.

---

[1]**Cask** an area for storing alcohol
[2]**Amontillado** a type of dry wine—medium Spanish Sherry

It was about dusk, one evening during the supreme madness of the carnival season, that I encountered my friend. He accosted me with excessive warmth, for he had been drinking much. The man wore motley. He had on a tight-fitting parti-striped dress, and his head was surmounted by the conical cap and bells. I was so pleased to see him that I thought I should never have done wringing his hand.

5   I said to him —"My dear Fortunato, you are luckily met. How remarkably well you are looking to-day. But I have received a pipe of what passes for Amontillado, and I have my doubts."

"How?" said he. "Amontillado, A pipe? Impossible! And in the middle of the carnival?"

"I have my doubts," I replied; "and I was silly enough to pay the full Amontillado price without consulting you in the matter. You were not to be found, and I was fearful of losing a bargain."

"Amontillado!"

"I have my doubts."

10   "Amontillado!"

"And I must satisfy them."

"Amontillado!"

"As you are engaged, I am on my way to Luchesi. If any one has a critical turn it is he. He will tell me —"

"Luchesi cannot tell Amontillado from Sherry."

15   "And yet some fools will have it that his taste is a match for your own."

"Come, let us go."

"Whither?"

"To your vaults."

"My friend, no; I will not impose upon your good nature. I perceive you have an engagement. Luchesi—"

20   "I have no engagement; come."

"My friend, no. It is not the engagement, but the severe cold with which I perceive you are afflicted. The vaults are insufferably damp. They are encrusted with nitre."

"Let us go, nevertheless. The cold is merely nothing. Amontillado! You have been imposed upon. And as for Luchesi, he cannot distinguish Sherry from Amontillado."

Thus speaking, Fortunato possessed himself of my arm; and putting on a mask of black silk and drawing a roquelaire[3] closely about my person, I suffered him to hurry me to my palazzo.

There were no attendants at home; they had absconded to make merry in honor of the time. I had told them that I should not return until the morning, and had given them explicit orders not to stir from the house. These orders were

---

[3]**roquelaire** a long coat

sufficient, I well knew, to insure their immediate disappearance, one and all, as soon as my back was turned.

I took from their sconces two flambeaux, and giving one to Fortunato, bowed 25 him through several suites of rooms to the archway that led into the vaults. I passed down a long and winding staircase, requesting him to be cautious as he followed. We came at length to the foot of the descent, and stood together upon the damp ground of the catacombs[4] of the Montresors.

The gait of my friend was unsteady, and the bells upon his cap jingled as he strode.

"The pipe," he said.

"It is farther on," said I; "but observe the white web-work which gleams from these cavern walls."

He turned towards me, and looked into my eyes with two filmy orbs that distilled the rheum[5] of intoxication.

"Nitre?"[6] he asked, at length. 30

"Nitre," I replied. "How long have you had that cough?"

"Ugh! ugh! ugh!—ugh! ugh! ugh!—ugh! ugh! ugh!—ugh! ugh! ugh! — ugh! ugh! ugh!"

My poor friend found it impossible to reply for many minutes.

"It is nothing," he said, at last.

"Come," I said, with decision, "we will go back; your health is precious. You 35 are rich, respected, admired, beloved; you are happy, as once I was. You are a man to be missed. For me it is no matter. We will go back; you will be ill, and I cannot be responsible. Besides, there is Luchesi—"

"Enough," he said; "the cough's a mere nothing; it will not kill me. I shall not die of a cough."

"True—true," I replied; "and, indeed, I had no intention of alarming you unnecessarily—but you should use all proper caution. A draught of this Medoc will defend us from the damps."

Here I knocked off the neck of a bottle which I drew from a long row of its fellows that lay upon the mould.

"Drink," I said, presenting him the wine.

He raised it to his lips with a leer. He paused and nodded to me familiarly, 40 while his bells jingled.

"I drink," he said, "to the buried that repose around us."

"And I to your long life."

He again took my arm, and we proceeded.

"These vaults," he said, "are extensive."

"The Montresors," I replied, "were a great and numerous family." 45

"I forget your arms."

---

[4]**catacombs** underground burial site
[5]**rheum** mucus, indicating presence of a cold
[6]**nitre** a chemical substance likely found inside the cask that could cause Fortunato's cough

"A huge human foot d'or, in a field azure; the foot crushes a serpent rampant whose fangs are imbedded in the heel."

"And the motto?"

"Nemo me impune lacessit."[7]

50   "Good!" he said.

The wine sparkled in his eyes and the bells jingled. My own fancy grew warm with the Medoc. We had passed through long walls of piled skeletons, with casks and puncheons intermingling, into the inmost recesses of the catacombs. I paused again, and this time I made bold to seize Fortunato by an arm above the elbow.

"The nitre!" I said; "see, it increases. It hangs like moss upon the vaults. We are below the river's bed. The drops of moisture trickle among the bones. Come, we will go back ere it is too late. Your cough—"

"It is nothing," he said; "let us go on. But first, another draught of the Medoc."

I broke and reached him a flagon of De Grave. He emptied it at a breath. His eyes flashed with a fierce light. He laughed and threw the bottle upwards with a gesticulation I did not understand.

55   I looked at him in surprise. He repeated the movement—a grotesque one.

"You do not comprehend?" he said.

"Not I," I replied.

"Then you are not of the brotherhood."

"How?"

60   "You are not of the masons."

"Yes, yes," I said; "yes, yes."

"You? Impossible! A mason?"

"A mason," I replied.

"A sign," he said, "a sign."

65   "It is this," I answered, producing from beneath the folds of my roquelaire a trowel.

"You jest," he exclaimed, recoiling a few paces. "But let us proceed to the Amontillado."

"Be it so," I said, replacing the tool beneath the cloak and again offering him my arm. He leaned upon it heavily. We continued our route in search of the Amontillado. We passed through a range of low arches, descended, passed on, and descending again, arrived at a deep crypt, in which the foulness of the air caused our flambeaux rather to glow than flame.

At the most remote end of the crypt there appeared another less spacious. Its walls had been lined with human remains, piled to the vault overhead, in the fashion of the great catacombs of Paris. Three sides of this interior crypt were still ornamented in this manner. From the fourth side the bones had been thrown

---

[7]Translation: "No one attacks me with impunity!"

down, and lay promiscuously upon the earth, forming at one point a mound of some size. Within the wall thus exposed by the displacing of the bones, we perceived a still interior crypt or recess, in depth about four feet, in width three, in height six or seven. It seemed to have been constructed for no especial use within itself, but formed merely the interval between two of the colossal supports of the roof of the catacombs, and was backed by one of their circumscribing walls of solid granite.

It was in vain that Fortunato, uplifting his dull torch, endeavored to pry into the depth of the recess. Its termination the feeble light did not enable us to see.

"Proceed," I said; "herein is the Amontillado. As for Luchesi—" 70

"He is an ignoramus," interrupted my friend, as he stepped unsteadily forward, while I followed immediately at his heels. In an instant he had reached the extremity of the niche, and finding his progress arrested by the rock, stood stupidly bewildered. A moment more and I had fettered him to the granite. In its surface were two iron staples, distant from each other about two feet, horizontally. From one of these depended a short chain, from the other a padlock. Throwing the links about his waist, it was but the work of a few seconds to secure it. He was too much astounded to resist. Withdrawing the key I stepped back from the recess.

"Pass your hand," I said, "over the wall; you cannot help feeling the nitre. Indeed, it is very damp. Once more let me implore you to return. No? Then I must positively leave you. But I must first render you all the little attentions in my power."

"The Amontillado!" ejaculated my friend, not yet recovered from his astonishment.

"True," I replied; "the Amontillado."

As I said these words I busied myself among the pile of bones of which 75 I have before spoken. Throwing them aside, I soon uncovered a quantity of building stone and mortar. With these materials and with the aid of my trowel, I began vigorously to wall up the entrance of the niche.

I had scarcely laid the first tier of the masonry when I discovered that the intoxication of Fortunato had in a great measure worn off. The earliest indication I had of this was a low moaning cry from the depth of the recess. It was not the cry of a drunken man. There was then a long and obstinate silence. I laid the second tier, and the third, and the fourth; and then I heard the furious vibrations of the chain. The noise lasted for several minutes, during which, that I might hearken to it with the more satisfaction, I ceased my labors and sat down upon the bones. When at last the clanking subsided, I resumed the trowel, and finished without interruption the fifth, the sixth, and the seventh tier. The wall was now nearly upon a level with my breast. I again paused, and holding the flambeaux over the mason-work, threw a few feeble rays upon the figure within.

A succession of loud and shrill screams, bursting suddenly from the throat of the chained form, seemed to thrust me violently back. For a brief moment I hesitated, I trembled. Unsheathing my rapier, I began to grope with it about the recess; but the thought of an instant reassured me. I placed my hand upon the solid fabric of the catacombs, and felt satisfied. I reapproached the wall; I replied to the yells of him who clamored. I re-echoed, I aided, I surpassed them in volume and in strength. I did this, and the clamorer grew still.

It was now midnight, and my task was drawing to a close. I had completed the eighth, the ninth and the tenth tier. I had finished a portion of the last and the eleventh; there remained but a single stone to be fitted and plastered in. I struggled with its weight; I placed it partially in its destined position. But now there came from out the niche a low laugh that erected the hairs upon my head. It was succeeded by a sad voice, which I had difficulty in recognizing as that of the noble Fortunato. The voice said—

"Ha! ha! ha!—he! he! he! —a very good joke, indeed—an excellent jest. We will have many a rich laugh about it at the palazzo—he! he! he!—over our wine—he! he! he!"

80   "The Amontillado!" I said.

"He! he! he!—he! he! he!—yes, the Amontillado. But is it not getting late? Will not they be awaiting us at the palazzo, the Lady Fortunato and the rest? Let us be gone."

"Yes," I said, "let us be gone."

"For the love of God, Montresor!"

"Yes," I said, "for the love of God!"

85   But to these words I hearkened in vain for a reply. I grew impatient. I called aloud —

"Fortunato!"

No answer. I called again—

"Fortunato!"

No answer still. I thrust a torch through the remaining aperture and let it fall within. There came forth in return only a jingling of the bells. My heart grew sick; it was the dampness of the catacombs that made it so. I hastened to make an end of my labor. I forced the last stone into its position; I plastered it up. Against the new masonry I re-erected the old rampart of bones. For the half of a century no mortal has disturbed them. *In pace requiescat!*[8]

CRITICAL THINKING QUESTIONS

I. How does Montresor utilize the power of manipulation to execute his plan of revenge against Fortunato?

2. Fortunato is under the influence of alcohol at the time the story commences. What **implied claim** could be argued from this story about the influence of alcohol upon the human mind?

---

[8]**Translation:** "Rest in peace!"

WRITING TOPIC

When you read this story, did you feel that the **narrator** made a literal confession of a commission of a murder, or did you believe the story itself is more figurative in nature? Upon what do you base your belief? Offer your best argument by providing textual evidence from the story.

———————

Edith Wharton

The Choice (1916)

Stilling, that night after dinner, had surpassed himself. He always did, Wrayford reflected, when the small fry from Highfield came to dine. He, Cobham Stilling, who had to find his bearings and keep to his level in the big heedless ironic world of New York, dilated and grew vast in the congenial medium of Highfield. The Red House was the biggest house of the Highfield summer colony, and Cobbam Stilling was its biggest man. No one else within a radius of a hundred miles (on a conservative estimate) had as many horses, as many greenhouses, as many servants, and assuredly no one else had three motors and a motorboat for the lake.

The motorboat was Stilling's latest hobby, and he rode—or steered—it in and out of the conversation all the evening, to the obvious edification of everyone present save his wife and his visitor, Austin Wrayford. The interest of the latter two who, from opposite ends of the drawing room, exchanged a fleeting glance when Stilling again launched his craft on the thin current of the talk—the interest of Mrs. Stilling and Wrayford had already lost its edge by protracted contact with the subject.

But the dinner guests—the Rector, Mr. Swordsley, his wife Mrs. Swordsley, Lucy and Agnes Granger, their brother Addison, and young Jack Emmerton from Harvard—were all, for divers reasons, stirred to the proper pitch of feeling. Mr. Swordsley, no doubt, was saying to himself: "If my good parishioner here can afford to buy a motorboat, in addition to all the other expenditures which an establishment like this must entail, I certainly need not scruple to appeal to him again for a contribution for our Galahad Club." The Granger girls, meanwhile, were evoking visions of lakeside picnics, not unadorned with the presence of young Mr. Emmerton; while that youth himself speculated as to whether his affable host would let him, when he came back on his next vacation, "learn to run the thing himself"; and Mr. Addison Granger, the elderly bachelor brother of the volatile Lucy and Agnes, mentally formulated the precise phrase in which, in his next letter to his cousin Professor Spildyke of the University of East Latmos, he should allude to "our last delightful trip in my old friend Cobham Stilling's ten thousand dollar motor launch"—for East Latmos was still in that primitive stage of culture on which five figures impinge.

Isabel Stilling, sitting beside Mrs. Swordsley, her head slightly bent above the needlework with which on these occasions it was her old-fashioned habit to employ herself—Isabel also had doubtless her reflections to make. As Wrayford leaned back in his corner and looked at her across the wide flower-filled drawing room he noted, first of all—for the how many hundredth time?—the play of her hands above the embroidery frame, the shadow of the thick dark hair on her forehead, the listless droops of the lids over her somewhat full grey eyes. He noted all this with a conscious deliberateness of enjoyment, taking in unconsciously, at the same time, the particular quality in her attitude, in the fall of her dress and the turn of her head, which had set her for him, from the first day, in a separate world; then he said to himself: "She is certainly thinking: 'Where on earth will Cobham get the money to pay for it?'"

5   Stilling, cigar in mouth and thumbs in his waistcoat pockets, was impressively perorating from his usual dominant position on the hearthrug.

"I said: 'If I have the thing at all, I want the best that can be got.' That's my way, you know, Swordsley; I suppose I'm what you'd call fastidious. Always was, about everything, from cigars to wom—" his eye met the apprehensive glance of Mrs. Swordsley, who looked like her husband with his clerical coat cut slightly lower "—so I said: 'If I have the thing at all, I want the best that can be got.' Nothing makeshift for me, no second best. I never cared for the cheap and showy. I always say frankly to a man: 'If you can't give me a first-rate cigar, for the Lord's sake let me smoke my own.'" He paused to do so. "Well, if you have my standards, you can't buy a thing in a minute. You must look round, compare, select. I found there were lots of motorboats on the market, just as there's lots of stuff called champagne. But I said to myself: 'Ten to one there's only one fit to buy, just as there's only one champagne fit for a gentleman to drink.' Argued like a lawyer, eh, Austin?" He tossed this to Wrayford. "Take me for one of your own trade, wouldn't you? Well, I'm not such a fool as I look. I suppose you fellows who are tied to the treadmill—excuse me, Swordsley, but work's work, isn't it?—I suppose you think a man like me has nothing to do but take it easy: loll through life like a woman. By George, sir, I'd like either of you to see the time it takes—I won't say the *brains*—but just the time it takes to pick out a good motorboat. Why, I went—"

Mrs. Stilling set her embroidery frame noiselessly on the table at her side, and turned her head toward Wrayford. "Would you mind ringing for the tray?"

The interruption helped Mrs. Swordsley to waver to her feet. "I'm afraid we ought really to be going; my husband has an early service tomorrow."

Her host intervened with a genial protest. "Going already? Nothing of the sort! Why, the night's still young, as the poet says. Long way from here to the rectory? Nonsense! In our little twenty-horse car we do it in five minutes—don't we, Belle? Ah, you're walking, to be sure—" Stilling's indulgent gesture seemed to concede that, in such a case, allowances must be made, and that he was the last man not to make them. "Well, then, Swordsley—" He held out a thick red hand that seemed to exude beneficence, and the clergyman, pressing it, ventured to murmur a suggestion.

"What, that Galahad Club again? Why, I thought my wife—Isabel, didn't   10
we—No? Well, it must have been my mother, then. Of course, you know, anything my good mother gives is—well—virtually—You haven't asked her? Sure? I could have sworn; I get so many of these appeals. And in these times, you know, we have to go cautiously. I'm sure you recognize that yourself, Swordsley. With my obligations—here now, to show you don't bear malice, have a brandy and soda before you go. Nonsense, man! This brandy isn't liquor, it's liqueur. I picked it up last year in London—last of a famous lot from Lord St. Oswyn's cellar. Laid down here, it stood me at—Eh?" he broke off as his wife moved toward him. "Ah, yes, of course. Miss Lucy, Miss Agnes—a drop of soda water? Look here, Addison, you won't refuse my tipple, I know. Well, take a cigar, at any rate, Swordsley. And, by the way, I'm afraid you'll have to go round the long way by the avenue tonight. Sorry, Mrs. Swordsley, but I forgot to tell them to leave the gate into the lane unlocked. Well, it's a jolly night, and I dare say you won't mind the extra turn along the lake. And, by Jove! If the moon's out, you'll have a glimpse of the motorboat. She's moored just out beyond our boathouse; and it's a privilege to look at her, I can tell you!"

The dispersal of his guests carried Stilling out into the hall, where his pleasantries reverberated under the oak rafters while the Granger girls were being muffled for the drive and the carriages summoned from the stables.

By a common impulse Mrs. Stilling and Wrayford had moved together toward the fireplace, which was hidden by a tall screen from the door into the hall. Wrayford leaned his elbow against the mantelpiece, and Mrs. Stilling stood beside him, her clasped hands hanging down before her.

"Have you anything more to talk over with him?" she asked.

"No. We wound it all up before dinner. He doesn't want to talk about it any more than he can help."

"It's so bad?"   15

"No; but this time he's got to pull up."

She stood silent, with lowered lids. He listened a moment, catching Stilling's farewell shout; then he moved a little nearer, and laid his hand on her arm.

"In an hour?"

She made an imperceptible motion of assent.

"I'll tell you about it then. The key's as usual?"   20

She signed another "Yes" and walked away with her long drifting step as her husband came in from the hall. He went up to the tray and poured himself out a tall glass of brandy and soda.

"The weather is turning queer—black as pitch. I hope the Swordsleys won't walk into the lake—involuntary immersion, eh? He'd come out a Baptist, I suppose. What'd the Bishop do in such a case? There's a problem for a lawyer, my boy!"

He clapped his hand on Wrayford's thin shoulder and then walked over to his wife, who was gathering up her embroidery silks and dropping them into her workbag. Stilling took her by the arms and swung her playfully about so that she faced the lamp-light.

"What's the matter with you tonight?"

25 "The matter?" she echoed, coloring a little, and standing very straight in her desire not to appear eager to shrink from his touch.

"You never opened your lips. Left me the whole job of entertaining those blessed people. Didn't she, Austin?"

Wrayford laughed and lit a cigarette.

"There! You see even Austin noticed it. What's the matter, I say? Aren't they good enough for you? I don't say they're particularly exciting; but, hang it! I like to ask them here—I like to give people pleasure."

"I didn't mean to be dull," said Isabel.

30 "Well, you must learn to make an effort. Don't treat people as if they weren't in the room just because they don't happen to amuse you. Do you know what they'll think? They'll think it's because you've got a bigger house and more money than they have. Shall I tell you something? My mother said she'd noticed the same thing in you lately. She said she sometimes felt you looked down on her for living in a small house. Oh, she was half joking, of course; but you see you do give people that impression. I can't understand treating any one in that way. The more I have myself, the more I want to make other people happy."

Isabel gently freed herself and laid the workbag on her embroidery frame. "I have a headache; perhaps that made me stupid. I'm going to bed." She turned toward Wrayford and held out her hand. "Good night."

"Good night," he answered, opening the door for her.

When he turned back into the room, his host was pouring himself a third glass of brandy and soda.

"Here, have a nip, Austin? Gad, I need it badly, after the shaking up you gave me this afternoon." Stilling laughed and carried his glass to the hearth, where he took up his usual commanding position. "Why the deuce don't you drink something? You look as glum as Isabel. One would think you were the chap that had been hit by this business."

35 Wrayford threw himself into the chair from which Mrs. Stilling had lately risen. It was the one she usually sat in, and to his fancy a faint scent of her clung to it. He leaned back and looked up at Stilling.

"Want a cigar?" the latter continued. "Shall we go into the den and smoke?"

Wrayford hesitated. "If there's anything more you want to ask me about—"

"Gad, no! I had full measure and running over this afternoon. The deuce of it is, I don't see where the money's all gone to. Luckily I've got plenty of nerve; I'm not the kind of man to sit down and snivel because I've been touched in Wall Street."

Wrayford got to his feet again. "Then, if you don't want me, I think I'll go up to my room and put some finishing touches to a brief before I turn in. I must get back to town tomorrow afternoon."

40 "All right, then." Stilling set down his empty glass, and held out his hand with a tinge of alacrity. "Good night, old man."

They shook hands, and Wrayford moved toward the door.

"I say, Austin—stop a minute!" his host called after him. Wrayford turned, and the two men faced each other across the hearthrug. Stilling's eyes shifted uneasily.

"There's one thing more you can do for me before you leave. Tell Isabel about that loan; explain to her that she's got to sign a note for it."

Wrayford, in his turn, flushed slightly. "You want me to tell her?"

"Hang it! I'm softhearted—that's the worst of me." Stilling moved toward 45 the tray, and lifted the brandy decanter. "And she'll take it better from you; she'll *have* to take it from you. She's proud. You can take her out for a row tomorrow morning—look here, take her out in the motor launch if you like. I meant to have a spin in it myself; but if you'll tell her—"

Wrayford hesitated. "All right, I'll tell her."

"Thanks a lot, my dear fellow. And you'll make her see it wasn't my fault, eh? Women are awfully vague about money, and she'll think it's all right if you back me up."

Wrayford nodded. "As you please."

"And, Austin—there's just one more thing. You needn't say anything to Isabel about the other business—I mean about my mother's securities."

"Ah?" said Wrayford, pausing. 50

Stilling shifted from one foot to the other. "I'd rather put that to the old lady myself. I can make it clear to her. She idolizes me, you know—and, hang it! I've got a good record. Up to now, I mean. My mother's been in clover since I married; I may say she's been my first thought. And I don't want her to hear of this beastly business from Isabel. Isabel's a little harsh at times—and of course this isn't going to make her any easier to live with."

"Very well," said Wrayford.

Stilling, with a look of relief, walked toward the window which opened on the terrace. "Gad! what a queer night! Hot as the kitchen range. Shouldn't wonder if we had a squall before morning. I wonder if that infernal skipper took in the launch's awnings before he went home."

Wrayford stopped with his hand on the door. "Yes, I saw him do it. She's shipshape for the night."

"Good! That saves me a run down to the shore." 55

"Good night, then," said Wrayford.

"Good night, old man. You'll tell her?"

"I'll tell her."

"And mum about my mother!" his host called after him.

II

The darkness had thinned a little when Wrayford scrambled down the steep 60 path to the shore. Though the air was heavy the threat of a storm seemed to have vanished, and now and then the moon's edge showed above a torn slope of cloud.

But in the thick shrubbery about the boathouse the darkness was still dense, and Wrayford had to strike a match before he could find the lock and insert his key. He left the door unlatched, and groped his way in. How often he had crept into this warm pine-scented obscurity, guiding himself by the edge of the bench along the wall, and hearing the soft lap of water through the gaps in the flooring! He knew just where one had to duck one's head to avoid the two canoes swung from the rafters, and just where to put his hand on the latch of the farther door that led to the broad balcony above the lake.

The boathouse represented one of Stilling's abandoned whims. He had built it some seven years before, and for a time it had been the scene of incessant nautical exploits. Stilling had rowed, sailed, paddled indefatigably, and all Highfield had been impressed to bear him company, and to admire his versatility. Then motors had come in, and he had forsaken aquatic sports for the flying chariot. The canoes of birch bark and canvas had been hoisted to the roof, the sailboat had rotted at her moorings, and the movable floor of the boathouse, ingeniously contrived to slide back on noiseless runners, had laid undisturbed through several seasons. Even the key of the boathouse had been mislaid—by Isabel's fault, her husband said—and the locksmith had to be called in to make a new one when the purchase of the motorboat made the lake once more the center of Stilling's activity.

As Wrayford entered he noticed that a strange oily odor over-powered the usual scent of dry pine wood; and at the next step his foot struck an object that rolled noisily across the boards. He lighted another match, and found he had overturned a can of grease which the boatman had no doubt been using to oil the runners of the sliding floor.

Wrayford felt his way down the length of the boathouse, and softly opening the balcony door looked out on the lake. A few yards away, he saw the launch lying at anchor in the veiled moonlight; and just below him, on the black water, was the dim outline of the skiff which the boatman kept to paddle out to her. The silence was so intense that Wrayford fancied he heard a faint rustling in the shrubbery on the high bank behind the boathouse, and the crackle of gravel on the path descending to it.

65 He closed the door again and turned back into the darkness; and as he did so the other door, on the land side, swung inward, and he saw a figure in the dim opening. Just enough light entered through the round holes above the respective doors to reveal Mrs. Stilling's cloaked outline, and to guide her to him as he advanced. But before they met she stumbled and gave a little cry.

"What is it?" he exclaimed.

"My foot caught; the floor seemed to give way under me. Ah, of course"—she bent down in the darkness—"I saw the men oiling it this morning."

Wrayford caught her by the arm. "Do take care! It might be dangerous if it slid too easily. The water's deep under here."

"Yes; the water's very deep. I sometimes wish—" She leaned against him without finishing her sentence, and he put both arms about her.

70 "Hush!" he said, his lips to hers.

Suddenly she threw her head back and seemed to listen.

"What's the matter? What do you hear?"

"I don't know." He felt her trembling. "I'm not sure this place is as safe as it used to be—"

Wrayford held her to him reassuringly. "But the boatman sleeps down at the village; and who else should come here at this hour?"

"Cobham might. He thinks of nothing but the launch." 75

"He won't tonight. I told him I'd seen the skipper put her shipshape, and that satisfied him."

"Ah—he did think of coming, then?"

"Only for a minute, when the sky looked so black half an hour ago, and he was afraid of a squall. It's clearing now, and there's no danger."

He drew her down on the bench, and they sat a moment or two in silence, her hands in his. Then she said: "You'd better tell me."

Wrayford gave a faint laugh. "Yes, I suppose I had. In fact, he asked me to." 80

"He asked you to?"

"Yes."

She uttered an exclamation of contempt. "He's afraid!"

Wrayford made no reply, and she went on: "I'm not. Tell me everything, please."

"Well, he's chucked away a pretty big sum again—" 85

"How?"

"He says he doesn't know. He's been speculating, I suppose. The madness of making him your trustee!"

She drew her hands away. "You know why I did it. When we married I didn't want to put him in the false position of the man who contributes nothing and accepts everything; I wanted people to think the money was partly his."

"I don't know what you've made people think; but you've been eminently successful in one respect. *He* thinks it's all his—and he loses it as if it were."

"There are worse things. What was it that he wished you to tell me?" 90

"That you've got to sign another promissory note—for fifty thousand this time."

"Is that all?"

Wrayford hesitated; then he said: "Yes—for the present."

She sat motionless, her head bent, her hand resting passively in his.

He leaned nearer. "What did you mean just now, by worse things?" 95

She hesitated. "Haven't you noticed that he's been drinking a great deal lately?"

"Yes; I've noticed."

They were both silent; then Wrayford broke out, with sudden vehemence: "And yet you won't—"

"Won't?"

"Put an end to it. Good God! Save what's left of your life." 100

She made no answer, and in the stillness the throb of the water underneath them sounded like the beat of a tormented heart.

"Isabel—" Wrayford murmured. He bent over to kiss her. "Isabel! I can't stand it! Listen—"

"No; no. I've thought of everything. There's the boy—the boy's fond of him. He's not a bad father."

"Except in the trifling matter of ruining his son."

105 "And there's his poor old mother. He's a good son, at any rate; he'd never hurt her. And I know her. If I left him, she'd never take a penny of my money. What she has of her own is not enough to live on; and how could he provide for her? If I put him out of doors, I should be putting his mother out too."

"You could arrange that—there are always ways."

"Not for her! She's proud. And then she believes in him. Lots of people believe in him, you know. It would kill her if she ever found out."

Wrayford made an impatient movement. "It will kill you if you stay with him to prevent her finding out."

She laid her other hand on his: "Not while I have you."

110 "Have me? In this way?"

"In any way."

"My poor girl—poor child!"

"Unless you grow tired—unless your patience gives out."

He was silent, and she went on insistently: "Don't you suppose I've thought of that too—foreseen it?"

115 "Well—and then?" he exclaimed.

"I've accepted that too."

He dropped her hands with a despairing gesture. "Then, indeed, I waste my breath!"

She made no answer, and for a time they sat silent again, a little between them. At length he asked: "You're not crying?"

"No."

120 "I can't see your face, it's grown so dark."

"Yes. The storm must be coming." She made a motion as if to rise.

He drew close and put his arm about her. "Don't leave me yet. You know I must go tomorrow." He broke off with a laugh. "I'm to break the news to you tomorrow morning, by the way; I'm to take you out in the motor launch and break it to you." He dropped her hands and stood up. "Good God! How can I go and leave you here with him?"

"You've done it often."

"Yes; but each time it's more damnable. And then I've always had a hope—"

125 She rose also. "Give it up! Give it up!"

"You've none, then, yourself?"

She was silent, drawing the folds of her cloak about her.

"None—none?" he insisted.

He had to bend his head to hear her answer. "Only one!"

130 "What, my dearest? What?"

"Don't touch me! That he may die!"

They drew apart again, hearing each other's quick breathing through the darkness.

"You wish that too?" he said.

"I wish it always—every day, every hour, every moment!" She paused, and then let the words break from her. "You'd better know it; you'd better know the worst of me. I'm not the saint you suppose; the duty I do is poisoned by the thoughts I think. Day by day, hour by hour, I wish him dead. When he goes out I pray for something to happen; when he comes back I say to myself: 'Are you here again?' When I hear of people being killed in accidents, I think: 'Why wasn't he there?' When I read the death notices in he paper I say: 'So-and-so was just his age.' When I see him taking such care of his health and his diet—as he does, you know, except when he gets reckless and begins to drink too much—when I see him exercising and resting, and eating only certain things, and weighing himself, and feeling his muscles, and boasting that he hasn't gained a pound, I think of the men who die from overwork, or who throw their lives away for some great object, and I say to myself: 'What can kill a man who thinks only of himself?' And night after night I keep myself from going to sleep for fear I may dream that he's dead. When I dream that, and wake and find him there it's worse than ever—"

She broke off with a sob, and the loud lapping of the water under the floor 135 was like the beat of a rebellious heart.

"There, you know the truth!" she said.

He answered after a pause: "People do die."

"Do they?" She laughed. "Yes—in happy marriages!"

They were silent again, and Isabel turned, feeling her way toward the door. As she did so, the profound stillness was broken by the sound of a man's voice trolling out unsteadily the refrain of a music-hall song.

The two in the boathouse darted toward each other with a simultaneous 140 movement, clutching hands as they met.

"He's coming!" Isabel said.

Wrayford disengaged his hands.

"He may only be out for a turn before he goes to bed. Wait a minute. I'll see." He felt his way to the bench, scrambled up on it, and stretching his body forward managed to bring his eyes in line with the opening above the door.

"It's as black as pitch. I can't see anything."

The refrain rang out nearer.   145

"Wait! I saw something twinkle. There it is again. It's his cigar. It's coming this way—down the path."

There was a long rattle of thunder through the stillness.

"It's the storm!" Isabel whispered. "He's coming to see about the launch."

Wrayford dropped noiselessly from the bench and she caught him by the arm.

"Isn't there time to get up the path and slip under the shrubbery?"   150

"No, he's in the path now. He'll be here in two minutes. He'll find us."

He felt her hand tighten on his arm.

"You must go in the skiff, then. It's the only way."

"And let him find you? And hear my oars? Listen—there's something I must say."

She flung her arms about him and pressed her face to his.   155

"Isabel, just now I didn't tell you everything. He's ruined his mother—taken everything of hers too. And he's got to tell her; it can't be kept from her."

She uttered an incredulous exclamation and drew back.

"Is this the truth? Why didn't you tell me before?"

"He forbade me. You were not to know."

160 Close above them, in the shrubbery, Stilling warbled:

> "Nita, Juanita,
> Ask thy soul if we must part!"

Wrayford held her by both arms. "Understand this—if he comes in, he'll find us. And if there's a row you'll lose your boy."

She seemed not to hear him. "You—you—you—he'll kill you!" she exclaimed.

Wrayford laughed impatiently and released her, and she stood shrinking against the wall, her hands pressed to her breast. Wrayford straightened himself and she felt that he was listening intently. Then he dropped to his knees and laid his hands against the boards of the sliding floor. It yielded at once, as if with a kind of evil alacrity; and at their feet they saw, under the motionless solid night, another darker night that moved and shimmered. Wrayford threw himself back against the opposite wall, behind the door.

A key rattled in the lock, and after a moment's fumbling the door swung open. Wrayford and Isabel saw a man's black bulk against the obscurity. It moved a step, lurched forward, and vanished out of sight. From the depths beneath them there came a splash and a long cry.

165 "Go! go!" Wrayford cried out, feeling blindly for Isabel in the blackness.

"Oh—" she cried, wrenching herself away from him.

He stood still a moment, as if dazed; then she saw him suddenly plunge from her side, and heard another splash far down, and a tumult in the beaten water.

In the darkness she cowered close to the opening, pressing her face over the edge, and crying out the name of each of the two men in turn. Suddenly she began to see: the obscurity was less opaque, as if a faint moon pallor diluted it. Isabel vaguely discerned the two shapes struggling in the black pit below her; once she saw the gleam of a face. She glanced up desperately for some means of rescue, and caught sight of the oars ranged on brackets against the walls. She snatched the nearest, bent over the opening, and pushed the oar down into the blackness, crying out her husband's name.

The clouds had swallowed the moon again, and she could see nothing below her; but she still heard tumult in the beaten water.

170 "Cobham! Cobham!" she screamed.

As if in answer, she felt a mighty clutch on the oar, a clutch that strained her arms to the breaking point as she tried to brace her knees against the runners on the sliding floor.

"Hold on! Hold on! Hold on!" a voice gasped out from below; and she held on, with racked muscles, with bleeding palms, with eyes straining from their sockets, and a heart that tugged at her as the weight was tugging at the oar.

Suddenly the weight relaxed, and the oar slipped up through her lacerated hands. She felt a wet body scrambling over the edge of the opening, and Stilling's voice, raucous and strange, groaned out, close to her: "God! I thought I was done for."

He staggered to his knees, coughing and sputtering, and the water dripped on her from his streaming clothes.

She flung herself down, again, straining over the pit. Not a sound came up 175 from it.

"Austin! Austin! Quick! Another oar!" she shrieked.

Stilling gave a cry. "My God! Was it Austin? What in hell—Another oar? No, no; untie the skiff, I tell you. But it's no use. Nothing's any use. I felt him lose hold as I came up."

After that she was conscious of nothing till, hours later, as it appeared to her, she became dimly aware of her husband's voice, high, hysterical and important, haranguing a group of scared lantern-struck faces that had sprung up mysteriously about them in the night.

"Poor Austin! Poor Wrayford ... terrible loss to me ... mysterious dispensation. Yes, I do feel gratitude—miraculous escape—but I wish old Austin could have known that I was saved!"

CRITICAL THINKING QUESTIONS

1. When considering the title, do you feel Isabel made a conscious decision as to whose life she saved at the end of the story? Upon what do you base your theory?

2. What significance do you find in the story's title, "The Choice"? To what choice or choices do you think the story's title refers? In formulating an answer, consider fully the motivations of Cobham Stilling, Isabel Stilling, and Austin Wrayford.

3. Over the years, some politicians have suggested that people caught in extramarital affairs should be subject to criminal prosecution. Do you think such a law is a good idea? Why or why not?

WRITING TOPIC

You are tasked with writing an epilogue to "The Choice." Pick up where Wharton's story ends. Offer insight into the ramifications, if any, the Stilling couple will face following the drowning of Austin Wrayford. How will they explain his death? Will they be investigated? Do you think the couple has the clout to hide from the community the true reason the three of them converged on the boathouse on a dark night as a storm moved in to Highfield? Further, knowing what you do of Isabel and Cobham, do you think the Stilling marriage will survive?

POETRY

A.E. Housman

The Use and Abuse of Toads (1919)

As into the garden Elizabeth ran
Pursued by the just indignation of Ann,
She trod on an object that lay in her road,
She trod on an object that looked like a toad.

5   It looked like a toad, and it looked so because
A toad was the actual object it was;
And after supporting Elizabeth's tread
It looked like a toad that was visibly dead.

Elizabeth, leaving her footprint behind,
10 Continued her flight on the wings of the wind,
And Ann in her anger was heard to arrive
At the toad that was not any longer alive.

She was heard to arrive, for the firmament rang
With the sound of a scream and the noise of a bang,
15 As her breath on the breezes she broadly bestowed
And fainted away on Elizabeth's toad.

Elizabeth, saved by the sole of her boot,
Escaped her insensible sister's pursuit;
And if ever hereafter she irritates Ann,
20 She will tread on a toad if she possibly can.

CRITICAL THINKING QUESTIONS

1. What evidence in the poem suggests that Elizabeth has wronged Ann in some way? What might Elizabeth have done to warrant Ann's anger? What is the difference between Ann's and Elizabeth's reactions?

2. Though this poem reads like children's poetry in subject matter, rhythm, and rhyme, what details in the poem are more sophisticated? What is the effect of this juxtaposition?

WRITING TOPIC

One possible theme of this poem is sibling rivalry or, more specifically, the ability of those we know best to provoke us intentionally. Can we protect ourselves from this provocation? How might we do so? Is protecting ourselves from irritation or, worse, emotional pain worth the sacrifice?

Etheridge Knight

Hard Rock Returns to Prison (1986)

from the Hospital for the Criminal Insane

Hard Rock was "known not to take no shit
From nobody," and he had the scars to prove it:
Split purple lips, lumped ears, welts above
His yellow eyes, and one long scar that cut
Across his temple and plowed through a thick   5
Canopy of kinky hair.

The WORD was that Hard Rock wasn't a mean nigger
Anymore, that the doctors had bored a hole in his head,
Cut out part of his brain, and shot electricity
Through the rest. When they brought Hard Rock back,   10
Handcuffed and chained, he was turned loose,
Like a freshly gelded stallion, to try his new status.
And we all waited and watched, like indians at a corral,
To see if the WORD was true.

As we waited we wrapped ourselves in the cloak   15
Of his exploits: "Man, the last time, it took eight
Screws to put him in the Hole." "Yeah, remember when he
Smacked the captain with his dinner tray?" "He set
The record for time in the Hole—67 straight days!"
"Ol Hard Rock! man, that's one crazy nigger."   20
And then the jewel of a myth that Hard Rock had once bit
A screw on the thumb and poisoned him with syphilitic spit.

The testing came, to see if Hard Rock was really tame.
A hillbilly called him a black son of a bitch
And didn't lose his teeth, a screw who knew Hard Rock   25
From before shook him down and barked in his face.
And Hard Rock did *nothing*. Just grinned and looked silly,

His eyes empty like knot holes in a fence.
And even after we discovered that it took Hard Rock
30 Exactly 3 minutes to tell you his first name,
We told ourselves that he had just wised up,
Was being cool; but we could not fool ourselves for long,

And we turned away, our eyes on the ground. Crushed.
He had been our Destroyer, the doer of things
35 We dreamed of doing but could not bring ourselves to do,
The fears of years, like a biting whip,
Had cut grooves too deeply across our backs.

CRITICAL THINKING QUESTIONS

1. How does the poem's speaker use appeal to *pathos*?

2. Describe the speaker and assess his *ethos*.

3. How does this poem affect your attitude toward or feelings about prisoners?

WRITING TOPIC

The hospital procedure that Hard Rock was forced to undergo is no longer allowed; however, solitary time is a form of punishment still used in some prisons for misbehavior. Do some research on high-security prisons and the treatment of individuals for infractions of prison rules, particularly the use of solitary confinement as punishment. Based on your research, write a **claim of policy** argument on the use of solitary confinement (or other punishments) as a correction method for individual prisoners.

Don Marquis

A Communication from Archy the Cockroach (1922)

I was talking to a moth
the other evening
he was trying to break into
an electric light bulb
5 and fry himself on the wires
why do you fellows

pull this stunt I asked him because
it is the conventional
thing for moths or why
if that had been an uncovered   10
candle instead of an electric
light bulb you would
now be a small unsightly cinder
have you no sense
plenty of it he answered   15
but at times we get tired
of using it
we get bored with the routine
and crave beauty
and excitement   20
fire is beautiful
and we know that if we get
too close it will kill us
but what does that matter
it is better to be happy   25
for a moment
and be burned up with beauty
than to live a long time
and be bored all the while
so we wad all our life up   30
into one little roll
and then we shoot the roll
that is what life is for
it is better to be a part of beauty
for one instant and then cease to   35
exist than to exist forever
and never be a part of beauty
our attitude toward life
is come easy go easy
we are like human beings   40
used to be before they became
too civilized to enjoy themselves
and before I could argue him
out of his philosophy
he went and immolated himself   45
on a patent cigar lighter
I do not agree with him
myself I would rather have
half the happiness and twice

50
      the longevity
      but at the same time I wish
      there was something I wanted
      as badly as he wanted to fry himself
      archy

CRITICAL THINKING QUESTIONS

1. The narrator moth says, "we are like humans beings used to be before they became too civilized to enjoy themselves." However, besides the example of his own life and death, he offers no other concrete examples to show how his claim applies to everyday life. Provide several examples to support the moth's claim.

2. Can you think of ways that humans, much like the moth, attempt "to break into an electric light bulb and fry" themselves? What are examples of some life lessons most people have to learn painfully?

WRITING TOPIC

Select another insect or animal and, as Marquis has done with the moth, use its voice to articulate its attitude toward life.

D. H. Lawrence

Snake (1921)

A snake came to my water-trough
On a hot, hot day, and I in pyjamas for the heat,
To drink there.

In the deep, strange-scented shade of the great dark carob tree
5   I came down the steps with my pitcher
And must wait, must stand and wait, for there he was at the trough
            before me.

He reached down from a fissure in the earth-wall in the gloom
And trailed his yellow-brown slackness soft-bellied down, over the
10   edge of the stone trough
And rested his throat upon the stone bottom,
And where the water had dripped from the tap, in a small clearness,
He sipped with his straight mouth,
Softly drank through his straight gums, into his slack long body,
15   Silently.

Someone was before me at my water-trough,
And I, like a second-comer, waiting.

He lifted his head from his drinking, as cattle do,
And looked at me vaguely, as drinking cattle do,
And flickered his two-forked tongue from his lips, and mused a   20
    moment,
And stooped and drank a little more,
Being earth-brown, earth-golden from the burning bowels of the
    earth
On the day of Sicilian July, with Etna smoking.   25

The voice of my education said to me
He must be killed,
For in Sicily the black, black snakes are innocent, the gold are
    venomous.
And voices in me said, If you were a man   30
You would take a stick and break him now, and finish him off.

But must I confess how I liked him,
How glad I was he had come like a guest in quiet, to drink at my
    water-trough
And depart peaceful, pacified, and thankless,   35
Into the burning bowels of this earth?

Was it cowardice, that I dared not kill him?
Was it perversity, that I longed to talk to him?
Was it humility, to feel honoured?
I felt so honoured.   40

And yet those voices:
If you were not afraid you would kill him.

And truly I was afraid, I was most afraid,
But even so, honoured still more   45
That he should seek my hospitality
From out the dark door of the secret earth.

He drank enough
And lifted his head, dreamily, as one who has drunken,
And flickered his tongue like a forked night on the air, so black, 50
Seeming to lick his lips,
And looked around like a god, unseeing into the air,
And slowly turned his head,
And slowly, very slowly, as if thrice adream,
Proceeded to draw his slow length curving round   55
And climb again the broken bank of my wall-face.

And as he put his head into that dreadful hole,
And as he slowly drew up, snake-easing his shoulders, and entered
    further,
60   A sort of horror, a sort of protest against his withdrawing into that
    horrid black hole,
Deliberately going into the blackness, and slowly drawing himself
    after,
Overcame me now his back was turned.

65   I looked round, I put down my pitcher,
I picked up a clumsy log
And threw it at the water-trough with a clatter.

I think it did not hit him,
But suddenly that part of him that was left behind convulsed in
70   undignified haste,
Writhed like lightning, and was gone
Into the black hole, the earth-lipped fissure in the wall-front,
At which, in the intense still noon, I stared with fascination.

And immediately I regretted it.
75   I thought how paltry, how vulgar, what a mean act!
I despised myself and the voices of my accursed human education.

And I thought of the albatross,
And I wished he would come back, my snake.

For he seemed to me again like a king,
80   Like a king in exile, uncrowned in the underworld,
Now due to be crowned again.

And so, I missed my chance with one of the lords
Of life.
And I have something to expiate:
85   A pettiness.

CRITICAL THINKING QUESTIONS

1. Identify the narrator's variety of emotions surrounding the discovery of the snake at the well. Explain your reaction.

2. The narrator makes a comparison of the snake to a cow in how it drinks water. Later in the poem, the narrator draws a parallel between the snake and royalty. What do you think is the purpose of these comparisons?

WRITING TOPIC

Snakes are often viewed as symbols of danger and evil. The narrator struggles against his amazement of the creature verses an urge to try to kill it, or at least to try to be reviled by its presence. As the snake retreats, the narrator throws a stick at the reptile. However, "immediately [he] regretted it" (77). He remarks, "I thought how paltry, how vulgar, what a mean act! I despised myself and the voices of my accursed human education" (78–79). The narrator's reaction seems to be one culturally conditioned and not a genuine act of his own character. Can you think of instances where you have observed other people allowing societal expectations to dictate their reactions to their fellow man in unfair ways? To expand the topic, do you think such cultural conditioning might exert pressure to the way offenders are treated in the criminal justice system? How are convicted felons who have been released after serving prison terms treated by society? Are they really given second chances, or do they often have "sticks" thrown at them? Please explain your views thoroughly.

DRAMA

William Shakespeare

The Tragedy of Macbeth (1623)

SCENE I. [A desert place.]

Thunder and lightning. Enter three Witches

First Witch: When shall we three meet again
       In thunder, lightning, or in rain?
Second Witch: When the hurlyburly's done,
       When the battle's lost and won.
Third Witch: That will be ere the set of sun.   5
First Witch: Where the place?
Second Witch: Upon the heath.
Third Witch: There to meet with Macbeth.
First Witch: I come, Graymalkin!
Second Witch: Paddock calls.   10
Third Witch: Anon.
All: Fair is foul, and foul is fair:
       Hover through the fog and filthy air.

Exeunt

SCENE II. [A camp near Forres.]

Alarum within. Enter Duncan, Malcolm, Donalbain, Lennox, with Attendants, meeting a bleeding Sergeant

Duncan: What bloody man is that? He can report,
      As seemeth by his plight, of the revolt
      The newest state.
Malcolm: This is the sergeant
      Who like a good and hardy soldier fought   5
      'Gainst my captivity. Hail, brave friend!
      Say to the king the knowledge of the broil
      As thou didst leave it.

Sergeant: Doubtful it stood;
As two spent swimmers, that do cling together   10
And choke their art. The merciless Macdonwald—
Worthy to be a rebel, for to that
The multiplying villanies of nature
Do swarm upon him—from the western isles
Of kerns and gallowglasses is supplied;   15
And fortune, on his damned quarrel smiling,
Show'd like a rebel's whore: but all's too weak:
For brave Macbeth—well he deserves that name—
Disdaining fortune, with his brandish'd steel,
Which smoked with bloody execution,   20
Like valour's minion carved out his passage
Till he faced the slave;
Which ne'er shook hands, nor bade farewell to him,
Till he unseam'd him from the nave to the chaps,
And fix'd his head upon our battlements.   25

Duncan: O valiant cousin! worthy gentleman!

Sergeant: As whence the sun 'gins his reflection
Shipwrecking storms and direful thunders break,
So from that spring whence comfort seem'd to come
Discomfort swells. Mark, king of Scotland, mark: 30
No sooner justice had with valour arm'd
Compell'd these skipping kerns to trust their heels,
But the Norweyan lord surveying vantage,
With furbish'd arms and new supplies of men
Began a fresh assault.   35

Duncan: Dismay'd not this
Our captains, Macbeth and Banquo?

Sergeant: Yes;
As sparrows eagles, or the hare the lion.
If I say sooth, I must report they were   40
As cannons overcharged with double cracks, so they
Doubly redoubled strokes upon the foe:
Except they meant to bathe in reeking wounds,
Or memorise another Golgotha,
I cannot tell.   45
But I am faint, my gashes cry for help.

Duncan: So well thy words become thee as thy wounds;
They smack of honour both. Go get him surgeons.

Exit Sergeant, attended

Who comes here?   50

Enter Ross

Malcolm: The worthy thane of Ross.

Lennox: What a haste looks through his eyes! So should he look
        That seems to speak things strange.
Ross: God save the king!   55
Duncan: Whence camest thou, worthy thane?
Ross: From Fife, great king;
        Where the Norweyan banners flout the sky
        And fan our people cold. Norway himself,
        With terrible numbers,   60
        Assisted by that most disloyal traitor
        The thane of Cawdor, began a dismal conflict;
        Till that Bellona's bridegroom, lapp'd in proof,
        Confronted him with self-comparisons,
        Point against point rebellious, arm 'gainst arm.   65
        Curbing his lavish spirit: and, to conclude,
        The victory fell on us.
Duncan: Great happiness!
Ross: That now
        Sweno, the Norways' king, craves composition: 70
        Nor would we deign him burial of his men
        Till he disbursed at Saint Colme's inch
        Ten thousand dollars to our general use.
Duncan: No more that thane of Cawdor shall deceive
        Our bosom interest: go pronounce his present death,   75
        And with his former title greet Macbeth.
Ross: I'll see it done.
Duncan: What he hath lost noble Macbeth hath won.

                                          Exeunt

SCENE III. [A heath near Forres.]

Thunder. Enter the three Witches

First Witch: Where hast thou been, sister?
Second Witch: Killing swine.
Third Witch: Sister, where thou?
First Witch: A sailor's wife had chestnuts in her lap,
        And munch'd, and munch'd, and munch'd:—   5
        'Give me,' quoth I:
        'Aroint thee, witch!' the rump-fed ronyon cries.
        Her husband's to Aleppo gone, master o' the Tiger:
        But in a sieve I'll thither sail,
        And, like a rat without a tail,   10
        I'll do, I'll do, and I'll do.

Second Witch: I'll give thee a wind.

First Witch: Thou'rt kind.

Third Witch: And I another.

First Witch: I myself have all the other, 15
  And the very ports they blow,
  All the quarters that they know
  I' the shipman's card.
  I will drain him dry as hay:
  Sleep shall neither night nor day 20
  Hang upon his pent-house lid;
  He shall live a man forbid:
  Weary se'nnights nine times nine
  Shall he dwindle, peak and pine:
  Though his bark cannot be lost, 25
  Yet it shall be tempest-tost.
  Look what I have.

Second Witch: Show me, show me.

First Witch: Here I have a pilot's thumb,
  Wreck'd as homeward he did come. 30
  Drum within

Third Witch: A drum, a drum!
  Macbeth doth come.

All: The weird sisters, hand in hand,
  Posters of the sea and land, 35
  Thus do go about, about:
  Thrice to thine and thrice to mine
  And thrice again, to make up nine.
  Peace! the charm's wound up.
  Enter Macbeth and Banquo 40

Macbeth: So foul and fair a day I have not seen.

Banquo: How far is't call'd to Forres? What are these
  So wither'd and so wild in their attire,
  That look not like the inhabitants o' the earth,
  And yet are on't? Live you? or are you aught 45
  That man may question? You seem to understand me,
  By each at once her chappy finger laying
  Upon her skinny lips: you should be women,
  And yet your beards forbid me to interpret
  That you are so. 50

Macbeth: Speak, if you can: what are you?

First Witch: All hail, Macbeth! hail to thee, thane of Glamis!

Second Witch: All hail, Macbeth, hail to thee, thane of Cawdor!

Third Witch: All hail, Macbeth, thou shalt be king hereafter!

Banquo: Good sir, why do you start; and seem to fear   55
   Things that do sound so fair? I' the name of truth,
   Are ye fantastical, or that indeed
   Which outwardly ye show? My noble partner
   You greet with present grace and great prediction
   Of noble having and of royal hope,   60
   That he seems rapt withal: to me you speak not.
   If you can look into the seeds of time,
   And say which grain will grow and which will not,
   Speak then to me, who neither beg nor fear
   Your favours nor your hate.   65
First Witch: Hail!
Second Witch: Hail!
Third Witch: Hail!
First Witch: Lesser than Macbeth, and greater.
Second Witch: Not so happy, yet much happier.   70
Third Witch: Thou shalt get kings, though thou be none:
   So all hail, Macbeth and Banquo!
First Witch: Banquo and Macbeth, all hail!
Macbeth: Stay, you imperfect speakers, tell me more:
   By Sinel's death I know I am thane of Glamis;   75
   But how of Cawdor? the thane of Cawdor lives,
   A prosperous gentleman; and to be king
   Stands not within the prospect of belief,
   No more than to be Cawdor. Say from whence
   You owe this strange intelligence? or why   80
   Upon this blasted heath you stop our way
   With such prophetic greeting? Speak, I charge you.
   Witches vanish
Banquo: The earth hath bubbles, as the water has,
   And these are of them. Whither are they vanish'd?   85
Macbeth: Into the air; and what seem'd corporal melted
   As breath into the wind. Would they had stay'd!
Banquo: Were such things here as we do speak about?
   Or have we eaten on the insane root
   That takes the reason prisoner?   90
Macbeth: Your children shall be kings.
Banquo: You shall be king.
Macbeth: And thane of Cawdor too: went it not so?
Banquo: To the selfsame tune and words. Who's here?
   Enter Ross and Angus   95
Ross: The king hath happily received, Macbeth,
   The news of thy success; and when he reads
   Thy personal venture in the rebels' fight,

His wonders and his praises do contend
Which should be thine or his: silenced with that, 100
In viewing o'er the rest o' the selfsame day,
He finds thee in the stout Norweyan ranks,
Nothing afeard of what thyself didst make,
Strange images of death. As thick as hail
Came post with post; and every one did bear 105
Thy praises in his kingdom's great defence,
And pour'd them down before him.

Angus: We are sent
To give thee from our royal master thanks;
Only to herald thee into his sight, 110
Not pay thee.

Ross: And, for an earnest of a greater honour,
He bade me, from him, call thee thane of Cawdor:
In which addition, hail, most worthy thane!
For it is thine. 115

Banquo: What, can the devil speak true?

Macbeth: The thane of Cawdor lives: why do you dress me
In borrow'd robes?

Angus: Who was the thane lives yet;
But under heavy judgment bears that life 120
Which he deserves to lose. Whether he was combined
With those of Norway, or did line the rebel
With hidden help and vantage, or that with both
He labour'd in his country's wreck, I know not;
But treasons capital, confess'd and proved, 125
Have overthrown him.

Macbeth: [Aside] Glamis, and thane of Cawdor!
The greatest is behind.
To Ross and Angus
Thanks for your pains. 130
To Banquo
Do you not hope your children shall be kings,
When those that gave the thane of Cawdor to me
Promised no less to them?

Banquo: That trusted home 135
Might yet enkindle you unto the crown,
Besides the thane of Cawdor. But 'tis strange:
And oftentimes, to win us to our harm,
The instruments of darkness tell us truths,
Win us with honest trifles, to betray's 140
In deepest consequence.
Cousins, a word, I pray you.

Macbeth: [Aside] Two truths are told,
As happy prologues to the swelling act
Of the imperial theme.—I thank you, gentlemen.   145
Aside
Cannot be ill, cannot be good: if ill,
Why hath it given me earnest of success,
Commencing in a truth? I am thane of Cawdor:
If good, why do I yield to that suggestion   150
Whose horrid image doth unfix my hair
And make my seated heart knock at my ribs,
Against the use of nature? Present fears
Are less than horrible imaginings:
My thought, whose murder yet is but fantastical,   155
Shakes so my single state of man that function
Is smother'd in surmise, and nothing is
But what is not.
Banquo: Look, how our partner's rapt.
Macbeth: [Aside] If chance will have me king, why, chance   160
may crown me,
Without my stir.
Banquo: New horrors come upon him,
Like our strange garments, cleave not to their mould
But with the aid of use.
Macbeth: [Aside] Come what come may,   165
Time and the hour runs through the roughest day.
Banquo: Worthy Macbeth, we stay upon your leisure.
Macbeth: Give me your favour: my dull brain was wrought
With things forgotten. Kind gentlemen, your pains
Are register'd where every day I turn   170
The leaf to read them. Let us toward the king.
Think upon what hath chanced, and, at more time,
The interim having weigh'd it, let us speak
Our free hearts each to other.
Banquo: Very gladly.   175
Macbeth: Till then, enough. Come, friends.

Exeunt

SCENE IV. [Forres. The palace.]

Flourish. Enter Duncan, Malcolm, Donalbain, Lennox, and Attendants

Duncan: Is execution done on Cawdor? Are not
Those in commission yet return'd?
Malcolm: My liege,
They are not yet come back. But I have spoke

With one that saw him die: who did report   5
That very frankly he confess'd his treasons,
Implored your highness' pardon and set forth
A deep repentance: nothing in his life
Became him like the leaving it; he died
As one that had been studied in his death   10
To throw away the dearest thing he owed,
As 'twere a careless trifle.

Duncan: There's no art
To find the mind's construction in the face:
He was a gentleman on whom I built   15
An absolute trust.
Enter Macbeth, Banquo, Ross, and Angus
O worthiest cousin!
The sin of my ingratitude even now
Was heavy on me: thou art so far before   20
That swiftest wing of recompense is slow
To overtake thee. Would thou hadst less deserved,
That the proportion both of thanks and payment
Might have been mine! only I have left to say,
More is thy due than more than all can pay.   25

Macbeth: The service and the loyalty I owe,
In doing it, pays itself. Your highness' part
Is to receive our duties; and our duties
Are to your throne and state children and servants,
Which do but what they should, by doing every   30
thing
Safe toward your love and honour.

Duncan: Welcome hither:
I have begun to plant thee, and will labour
To make thee full of growing. Noble Banquo,
That hast no less deserved, nor must be known   35
No less to have done so, let me enfold thee
And hold thee to my heart.

Banquo: There if I grow,
The harvest is your own.

Duncan: My plenteous joys,   40
Wanton in fulness, seek to hide themselves
In drops of sorrow. Sons, kinsmen, thanes,
And you whose places are the nearest, know
We will establish our estate upon
Our eldest, Malcolm, whom we name hereafter   45
The Prince of Cumberland; which honour must
Not unaccompanied invest him only,

But signs of nobleness, like stars, shall shine
On all deservers. From hence to Inverness,
And bind us further to you.   50

Macbeth: The rest is labour, which is not used for you:
I'll be myself the harbinger and make joyful
The hearing of my wife with your approach;
So humbly take my leave.

Duncan: My worthy Cawdor!   55

Macbeth: [Aside] The Prince of Cumberland! that is a step
On which I must fall down, or else o'erleap,
For in my way it lies. Stars, hide your fires;
Let not light see my black and deep desires:
The eye wink at the hand; yet let that be,   60
Which the eye fears, when it is done, to see.

Exit

Duncan: True, worthy Banquo; he is full so valiant,
And in his commendations I am fed;
It is a banquet to me. Let's after him,   65
Whose care is gone before to bid us welcome:
It is a peerless kinsman.

Flourish. Exeunt

SCENE V. [Inverness. Macbeth's castle.]

Enter Lady Macbeth, reading a letter

Lady Macbeth: 'They met me in the day of success: and I have
learned by the perfectest report, they have more in
them than mortal knowledge. When I burned in desire
to question them further, they made themselves air,
into which they vanished. Whiles I stood rapt in   5
the wonder of it, came missives from the king, who
all-hailed me 'Thane of Cawdor;' by which title,
before, these weird sisters saluted me, and referred
me to the coming on of time, with 'Hail, king that
shalt be!' This have I thought good to deliver   10
thee, my dearest partner of greatness, that thou
mightst not lose the dues of rejoicing, by being
ignorant of what greatness is promised thee. Lay it
to thy heart, and farewell.'
Glamis thou art, and Cawdor; and shalt be   15
What thou art promised: yet do I fear thy nature;
It is too full o' the milk of human kindness
To catch the nearest way: thou wouldst be great;

Art not without ambition, but without
The illness should attend it: what thou wouldst highly,   20
That wouldst thou holily; wouldst not play false,
And yet wouldst wrongly win: thou'ldst have,
    great Glamis,
That which cries 'Thus thou must do, if thou have it;
And that which rather thou dost fear to do
Than wishest should be undone.' Hie thee hither,   25
That I may pour my spirits in thine ear;
And chastise with the valour of my tongue
All that impedes thee from the golden round,
Which fate and metaphysical aid doth seem
To have thee crown'd withal.   30
Enter a Messenger
What is your tidings?
Messenger: The king comes here to-night.
Lady Macbeth: Thou'rt mad to say it:
Is not thy master with him? who, were't so,   35
Would have inform'd for preparation.
Messenger: So please you, it is true: our thane is coming:
One of my fellows had the speed of him,
Who, almost dead for breath, had scarcely more
Than would make up his message.   40
Lady Macbeth: Give him tending;
He brings great news.

                                                   Exit Messenger

The raven himself is hoarse
That croaks the fatal entrance of Duncan   45
Under my battlements. Come, you spirits
That tend on mortal thoughts, unsex me here,
And fill me from the crown to the toe top-full
Of direst cruelty! make thick my blood;
Stop up the access and passage to remorse,   50
That no compunctious visitings of nature
Shake my fell purpose, nor keep peace between
The effect and it! Come to my woman's breasts,
And take my milk for gall, you murdering ministers,
Wherever in your sightless substances   55
You wait on nature's mischief! Come, thick night,
And pall thee in the dunnest smoke of hell,
That my keen knife see not the wound it makes,
Nor heaven peep through the blanket of the dark,
To cry 'Hold, hold!'   60
Enter Macbeth

> Great Glamis! worthy Cawdor!
> Greater than both, by the all-hail hereafter!
> Thy letters have transported me beyond
> This ignorant present, and I feel now   65
> The future in the instant.

Macbeth: My dearest love,
> Duncan comes here to-night.

Lady Macbeth: And when goes hence?

Macbeth: To-morrow, as he purposes.   70

Lady Macbeth: O, never
> Shall sun that morrow see!
> Your face, my thane, is as a book where men
> May read strange matters. To beguile the time,
> Look like the time; bear welcome in your eye,   75
> Your hand, your tongue: look like the innocent
>   flower,
> But be the serpent under't. He that's coming
> Must be provided for: and you shall put
> This night's great business into my dispatch;
> Which shall to all our nights and days to come   80
> Give solely sovereign sway and masterdom.

Macbeth: We will speak further.

Lady Macbeth: Only look up clear;
> To alter favour ever is to fear:
> Leave all the rest to me.   85

> *Exeunt*

SCENE VI. [Before Macbeth's castle.]

Hautboys and Torches. Enter Duncan, Malcolm, Donalbain, Banquo, Lennox, Macduff, Ross, Angus, and Attendants

Duncan: This castle hath a pleasant seat; the air
> Nimbly and sweetly recommends itself
> Unto our gentle senses.

Banquo: This guest of summer,
> The temple-haunting martlet, does approve,   5
> By his loved mansionry, that the heaven's breath
> Smells wooingly here: no jutty, frieze,
> Buttress, nor coign of vantage, but this bird
> Hath made his pendent bed and procreant cradle:
> Where they most breed and haunt, I have observed,   10
> The air is delicate.
> *Enter Lady Macbeth*

Duncan: See, see, our honour'd hostess!
          The love that follows us sometime is our trouble,
          Which still we thank as love. Herein I teach you   15
          How you shall bid God 'ild us for your pains,
          And thank us for your trouble.

Lady Macbeth: All our service
          In every point twice done and then done double
          Were poor and single business to contend   20
          Against those honours deep and broad wherewith
          Your majesty loads our house: for those of old,
          And the late dignities heap'd up to them,
          We rest your hermits.

Duncan: Where's the thane of Cawdor?   25
          We coursed him at the heels, and had a purpose
          To be his purveyor: but he rides well;
          And his great love, sharp as his spur, hath holp him
          To his home before us. Fair and noble hostess,
          We are your guest to-night.   30

Lady Macbeth: Your servants ever
          Have theirs, themselves and what is theirs, in compt,
          To make their audit at your highness' pleasure,
          Still to return your own.

Duncan: Give me your hand;   35
          Conduct me to mine host: we love him highly,
          And shall continue our graces towards him.
          By your leave, hostess.

                                        Exeunt

SCENE VII. [Macbeth's castle.]

Hautboys and Torches. Enter a Sewer, and divers Servants with dishes and service, and pass over the stage. Then enter Macbeth

Macbeth: If it were done when 'tis done, then 'twere well
          It were done quickly: if the assassination
          Could trammel up the consequence, and catch
          With his surcease success; that but this blow
          Might be the be-all and the end-all here,   5
          But here, upon this bank and shoal of time,
          We'ld jump the life to come. But in these cases
          We still have judgment here; that we but teach
          Bloody instructions, which, being taught, return
          To plague the inventor: this even-handed justice   10
          Commends the ingredients of our poison'd chalice

To our own lips. He's here in double trust;
First, as I am his kinsman and his subject,
Strong both against the deed; then, as his host,
Who should against his murderer shut the door,   15
Not bear the knife myself. Besides, this Duncan
Hath borne his faculties so meek, hath been
So clear in his great office, that his virtues
Will plead like angels, trumpet-tongued, against
The deep damnation of his taking-off;   20
And pity, like a naked new-born babe,
Striding the blast, or heaven's cherubim, horsed
Upon the sightless couriers of the air,
Shall blow the horrid deed in every eye,
That tears shall drown the wind. I have no spur   25
To prick the sides of my intent, but only
Vaulting ambition, which o'erleaps itself
And falls on the other.
Enter Lady Macbeth
How now! what news?   30

Lady Macbeth: He has almost supp'd: why have
    you left the chamber?

Macbeth: Hath he ask'd for me?

Lady Macbeth: Know you not he has?

Macbeth: We will proceed no further in this business:
    He hath honour'd me of late; and I have bought   35
    Golden opinions from all sorts of people,
    Which would be worn now in their newest gloss,
    Not cast aside so soon.

Lady Macbeth: Was the hope drunk
    Wherein you dress'd yourself? hath it   40
      slept since?
    And wakes it now, to look so green and pale
    At what it did so freely? From this time
    Such I account thy love. Art thou afeard
    To be the same in thine own act and valour
    As thou art in desire? Wouldst thou have that   45
    Which thou esteem'st the ornament of life,
    And live a coward in thine own esteem,
    Letting 'I dare not' wait upon 'I would,'
    Like the poor cat i' the adage?

Macbeth: Prithee, peace: 50
    I dare do all that may become a man;
    Who dares do more is none.

Lady Macbeth: What beast was't, then,
That made you break this enterprise to me?
When you durst do it, then you were a man;   55
And, to be more than what you were, you would
Be so much more the man. Nor time nor place
Did then adhere, and yet you would make both:
They have made themselves, and that their
    fitness now
Does unmake you. I have given suck, and know   60
How tender 'tis to love the babe that milks me:
I would, while it was smiling in my face,
Have pluck'd my nipple from his boneless gums,
And dash'd the brains out, had I so sworn as you
Have done to this.   65
Macbeth: If we should fail?
Lady Macbeth: We fail!
But screw your courage to the sticking-place,
And we'll not fail. When Duncan is asleep—
Whereto the rather shall his day's hard journey   70
Soundly invite him—his two chamberlains
Will I with wine and wassail so convince
That memory, the warder of the brain,
Shall be a fume, and the receipt of reason
A limbeck only: when in swinish sleep   75
Their drenched natures lie as in a death,
What cannot you and I perform upon
The unguarded Duncan? what not put upon
His spongy officers, who shall bear the guilt
Of our great quell?   80
Macbeth: Bring forth men-children only;
For thy undaunted mettle should compose
Nothing but males. Will it not be received,
When we have mark'd with blood those sleepy two
Of his own chamber and used their very daggers,   85
That they have done't?
Lady Macbeth: Who dares receive it other,
As we shall make our griefs and clamour roar
Upon his death?
Macbeth: I am settled, and bend up   90
Each corporal agent to this terrible feat.
Away, and mock the time with fairest show:
False face must hide what the false heart doth know.

                                        Exeunt

ACT II

SCENE I. [Court of Macbeth's castle.]

Enter Banquo, and Fleance bearing a torch before him

Banquo: How goes the night, boy?
Fleance: The moon is down; I have not heard the clock.
Banquo: And she goes down at twelve.
Fleance: I take't, 'tis later, sir.
Banquo: Hold, take my sword. There's husbandry in heaven;   5
         Their candles are all out. Take thee that too.
         A heavy summons lies like lead upon me,
         And yet I would not sleep: merciful powers,
         Restrain in me the cursed thoughts that nature
         Gives way to in repose!   10
         Enter Macbeth, and a Servant with a torch
         Give me my sword.
         Who's there?
Macbeth: A friend.
Banquo: What, sir, not yet at rest? The king's a-bed: 15
         He hath been in unusual pleasure, and
         Sent forth great largess to your offices.
         This diamond he greets your wife withal,
         By the name of most kind hostess; and shut up
         In measureless content.   20
Macbeth: Being unprepared,
         Our will became the servant to defect;
         Which else should free have wrought.
Banquo: All's well.
         I dreamt last night of the three weird sisters: 25
         To you they have show'd some truth.
Macbeth: I think not of them:
         Yet, when we can entreat an hour to serve,
         We would spend it in some words upon that
            business,
         If you would grant the time.   30
Banquo: At your kind'st leisure.
Macbeth: If you shall cleave to my consent, when 'tis,
         It shall make honour for you.
Banquo: So I lose none
         In seeking to augment it, but still keep   35
         My bosom franchised and allegiance clear,
         I shall be counsell'd.
Macbeth: Good repose the while!

Banquo: Thanks, sir: the like to you!

Exeunt Banquo and Fleance 40

Macbeth: Go bid thy mistress, when my drink is ready,
She strike upon the bell. Get thee to bed.

Exit Servant

Is this a dagger which I see before me,
The handle toward my hand? Come, let me   45
    clutch thee.
I have thee not, and yet I see thee still.
Art thou not, fatal vision, sensible
To feeling as to sight? or art thou but
A dagger of the mind, a false creation,
Proceeding from the heat-oppressed brain?   50
I see thee yet, in form as palpable
As this which now I draw.
Thou marshall'st me the way that
    I was going;
And such an instrument I was to use.
Mine eyes are made the fools o' the   55
    other senses,
Or else worth all the rest; I see thee still,
And on thy blade and dudgeon gouts of blood,
Which was not so before. There's no such thing:
It is the bloody business which informs
Thus to mine eyes. Now o'er the one halfworld   60
Nature seems dead, and wicked dreams abuse
The curtain'd sleep; witchcraft celebrates
Pale Hecate's offerings, and wither'd murder,
Alarum'd by his sentinel, the wolf,
Whose howl's his watch, thus with his   65
    stealthy pace.
With Tarquin's ravishing strides, towards
    his design
Moves like a ghost. Thou sure and firm-set earth,
Hear not my steps, which way they walk, for fear
Thy very stones prate of my whereabout,
And take the present horror from the time,   70
Which now suits with it. Whiles I threat, he lives:
Words to the heat of deeds too cold breath gives.
A bell rings
I go, and it is done; the bell invites me.
Hear it not, Duncan; for it is a knell   75
That summons thee to heaven or to hell.

Exit

SCENE II. [The same.]

Enter Lady Macbeth

Lady Macbeth: That which hath made them drunk hath made
        me bold;
    What hath quench'd them hath given me fire.
    Hark! Peace!
    It was the owl that shriek'd, the fatal bellman,
    Which gives the stern'st good-night. He is about it: 5
    The doors are open; and the surfeited grooms
    Do mock their charge with snores: I have drugg'd
        their possets,
    That death and nature do contend about them,
    Whether they live or die.
Macbeth: [Within] Who's there? what, ho!   10
Lady Macbeth: Alack, I am afraid they have awaked,
    And 'tis not done. The attempt and not the deed
    Confounds us. Hark! I laid their daggers ready;
    He could not miss 'em. Had he not resembled
    My father as he slept, I had done't.   15
    Enter Macbeth
    My husband!
Macbeth: I have done the deed. Didst thou not hear a noise?
Lady Macbeth: I heard the owl scream and the crickets cry.
    Did not you speak?   20
Macbeth: When?
Lady Macbeth: Now.
Macbeth: As I descended?
Lady Macbeth: Ay.
Macbeth: Hark!   25
    Who lies i' the second chamber?
Lady Macbeth: Donalbain.
Macbeth: This is a sorry sight.
    Looking on his hands
Lady Macbeth: A foolish thought, to say a sorry sight.   30
Macbeth: There's one did laugh in's sleep, and one cried
    'Murder!'
    That they did wake each other: I stood and
        heard them:
    But they did say their prayers, and address'd them
    Again to sleep.   35
Lady Macbeth: There are two lodged together.

Macbeth: One cried 'God bless us!' and 'Amen' the other;
As they had seen me with these hangman's hands.
Listening their fear, I could not say 'Amen,'
When they did say 'God bless us!'   40
Lady Macbeth: Consider it not so deeply.
Macbeth: But wherefore could not I pronounce 'Amen'?
I had most need of blessing, and 'Amen'
Stuck in my throat.
Lady Macbeth: These deeds must not be thought   45
After these ways; so, it will make us mad.
Macbeth: Methought I heard a voice cry 'Sleep no more!
Macbeth does murder sleep', the innocent sleep,
Sleep that knits up the ravell'd sleeve of care,
The death of each day's life, sore labour's bath,   50
Balm of hurt minds, great nature's second course,
Chief nourisher in life's feast,—
Lady Macbeth: What do you mean?
Macbeth: Still it cried 'Sleep no more!' to all the house:
'Glamis hath murder'd sleep, and therefore Cawdor   55
Shall sleep no more; Macbeth shall sleep no more.'
Lady Macbeth: Who was it that thus cried? Why, worthy thane,
You do unbend your noble strength, to think
So brainsickly of things. Go get some water,
And wash this filthy witness from your hand.   60
Why did you bring these daggers from the place?
They must lie there: go carry them; and smear
The sleepy grooms with blood.
Macbeth: I'll go no more:
I am afraid to think what I have done;   65
Look on't again I dare not.
Lady Macbeth: Infirm of purpose!
Give me the daggers: the sleeping and the dead
Are but as pictures: 'tis the eye of childhood
That fears a painted devil. If he do bleed,   70
I'll gild the faces of the grooms withal;
For it must seem their guilt.

Exit. Knocking within

Macbeth: Whence is that knocking?
How is't with me, when every noise appals me?   75
What hands are here? ha! they pluck out mine
     eyes.
Will all great Neptune's ocean wash this blood

Clean from my hand? No, this my hand will rather
The multitudinous seas in incarnadine,
Making the green one red.   80
Re-enter Lady Macbeth
Lady Macbeth: My hands are of your colour; but I shame
To wear a heart so white.
Knocking within
I hear a knocking   85
At the south entry: retire we to our chamber;
A little water clears us of this deed:
How easy is it, then! Your constancy
Hath left you unattended.
Knocking within   90
Hark! more knocking.
Get on your nightgown, lest occasion call us,
And show us to be watchers. Be not lost
So poorly in your thoughts.

Macbeth: To know my deed, 'twere best not know myself.   95
Knocking within
Wake Duncan with thy knocking! I would thou couldst!
                                                   Exeunt

SCENE III. [The same.]

Knocking within. Enter a Porter

Porter: Here's a knocking indeed! If a
man were porter of hell-gate, he should have
old turning the key.
Knocking within
Knock,   5
knock, knock! Who's there, i' the name of
Beelzebub? Here's a farmer, that hanged
himself on the expectation of plenty: come in
time; have napkins enow about you; here
you'll sweat for't.   10
Knocking within
Knock,
knock! Who's there, in the other devil's
name? Faith, here's an equivocator, that could
swear in both the scales against either scale;   15
who committed treason enough for God's sake,
yet could not equivocate to heaven: O, come
in, equivocator.

Knocking within
Knock,   20
knock, knock! Who's there? Faith, here's an
English tailor come hither, for stealing out of
a French hose: come in, tailor; here you may
roast your goose.
Knocking within   25
Knock,
knock; never at quiet! What are you? But
this place is too cold for hell. I'll devil-porter
it no further: I had thought to have let in
some of all professions that go the primrose   30
way to the everlasting bonfire.
Knocking within
Anon, anon! I pray you, remember the porter.
Opens the gate
Enter Macduff and Lennox   35

Macduff: Was it so late, friend, ere you went to bed,
    That you do lie so late?
Porter: 'Faith sir, we were carousing till the
      second cock: and drink, sir, is a great
      provoker of three things.   40
Macduff: What three things does drink especially provoke?
Porter: Marry, sir, nose-painting, sleep, and
      urine. Lechery, sir, it provokes, and unprovokes;
      it provokes the desire, but it takes
      away the performance: therefore, much drink   45
      may be said to be an equivocator with lechery:
      it makes him, and it mars him; it sets
      him on, and it takes him off; it persuades him,
      and disheartens him; makes him stand to, and
      not stand to; in conclusion, equivocates him   50
      in a sleep, and, giving him the lie, leaves him.
Macduff: I believe drink gave thee the lie last night.
Porter: That it did, sir, i' the very throat on
      me: but I requited him for his lie; and, I
      think, being too strong for him, though he took   55
      up my legs sometime, yet I made a shift to cast
      him.
Macduff: Is thy master stirring?
    Enter Macbeth
    Our knocking has awaked him; here he comes.
Lennox: Good morrow, noble sir.   60

Macbeth: Good morrow, both.

Macduff: Is the king stirring, worthy thane?

Macbeth: Not yet.

Macduff: He did command me to call timely on him:
I have almost slipp'd the hour. 65

Macbeth: I'll bring you to him.

Macduff: I know this is a joyful trouble to you;
But yet 'tis one.

Macbeth: The labour we delight in physics pain.
This is the door. 70

Macduff: I'll make so bold to call,
For 'tis my limited service.

Exit

Lennox: Goes the king hence to-day?

Macbeth: He does: he did appoint so. 75

Lennox: The night has been unruly: where we lay,
Our chimneys were blown down; and, as they say,
Lamentings heard i' the air; strange screams of
death,
And prophesying with accents terrible
Of dire combustion and confused events 80
New hatch'd to the woeful time: the obscure bird
Clamour'd the livelong night: some say, the earth
Was feverous and did shake.

Macbeth: 'Twas a rough night.

Lennox: My young remembrance cannot parallel 85
A fellow to it.
Re-enter Macduff

Macduff: O horror, horror, horror! Tongue nor heart
Cannot conceive nor name thee!

Macbeth Lennox: What's the matter. 90

Macduff: Confusion now hath made his masterpiece!
Most sacrilegious murder hath broke ope
The Lord's anointed temple, and stole thence
The life o' the building!

Macbeth: What is 't you say? the life? 95

Lennox: Mean you his majesty?

Macduff: Approach the chamber, and destroy your sight
With a new Gorgon: do not bid me speak;
See, and then speak yourselves.
Exeunt Macbeth and Lennox 100

Awake, awake!
Ring the alarum-bell. Murder and treason!
Banquo and Donalbain! Malcolm! awake!

Shake off this downy sleep, death's counterfeit,
And look on death itself! up, up, and see   105
The great doom's image! Malcolm! Banquo!
As from your graves rise up, and walk like sprites,
To countenance this horror! Ring the bell.
Bell rings
Enter Lady Macbeth   110

Lady Macbeth: What's the business,
That such a hideous trumpet calls to parley
The sleepers of the house? speak, speak!

Macduff: O gentle lady,
'Tis not for you to hear what I can speak: 115
The repetition, in a woman's ear,
Would murder as it fell.
Enter Banquo
O Banquo, Banquo,
Our royal master 's murder'd!   120

Lady Macbeth: Woe, alas!
What, in our house?

Banquo: Too cruel any where.
Dear Duff, I prithee, contradict thyself,
And say it is not so.   125
Re-enter Macbeth and Lennox, with Ross

Macbeth: Had I but died an hour before this chance,
I had lived a blessed time; for, from this instant,
There 's nothing serious in mortality:
All is but toys: renown and grace is dead;   130
The wine of life is drawn, and the mere lees
Is left this vault to brag of.
Enter Malcolm and Donalbain

Donalbain: What is amiss?

Macbeth: You are, and do not know't: 135
The spring, the head, the fountain of your blood
Is stopp'd; the very source of it is stopp'd.

Macduff: Your royal father 's murder'd.

Malcolm: O, by whom?

Lennox: Those of his chamber, as it seem'd, had done 't: 140
Their hands and faces were an badged with blood;
So were their daggers, which unwiped we found
Upon their pillows:
They stared, and were distracted; no man's life
Was to be trusted with them.   145

Macbeth: O, yet I do repent me of my fury,
That I did kill them.

Macduff: Wherefore did you so?

Macbeth: Who can be wise, amazed, temperate and furious,
Loyal and neutral, in a moment? No man: 150
The expedition my violent love
Outrun the pauser, reason. Here lay Duncan,
His silver skin laced with his golden blood;
And his gash'd stabs look'd like a breach in nature
For ruin's wasteful entrance: there, the murderers,   155
Steep'd in the colours of their trade, their daggers
Unmannerly breech'd with gore: who could refrain,
That had a heart to love, and in that heart
Courage to make's love known?

Lady Macbeth: Help me hence, ho!   160

Macduff: Look to the lady.

Malcolm: [Aside to Donalbain] Why do we hold our tongues,
That most may claim this argument for ours?

Donalbain: [Aside to Malcolm] What should be spoken here,
where our fate,   165
Hid in an auger-hole, may rush, and seize us?
Let 's away;
Our tears are not yet brew'd.

Malcolm: [Aside to Donalbain] Nor our strong sorrow
Upon the foot of motion.   170

Banquo: Look to the lady:
Lady Macbeth is carried out
And when we have our naked frailties hid,
That suffer in exposure, let us meet,
And question this most bloody piece of work,   175
To know it further. Fears and scruples shake us:
In the great hand of God I stand; and thence
Against the undivulged pretence I fight
Of treasonous malice.

Macduff: And so do I.   180

All: So all.

Macbeth: Let's briefly put on manly readiness,
And meet i' the hall together.

All: Well contented.
        Exeunt all but Malcolm and Donalbain. 185

Malcolm: What will you do? Let's not consort with them:
To show an unfelt sorrow is an office
Which the false man does easy. I'll to England.

Donalbain: To Ireland, I; our separated fortune
Shall keep us both the safer: where we are,   190

There's daggers in men's smiles: the near in blood,
The nearer bloody.

Malcolm: This murderous shaft that's shot
Hath not yet lighted, and our safest way
Is to avoid the aim. Therefore, to horse; 195
And let us not be dainty of leave-taking,
But shift away: there's warrant in that theft
Which steals itself, when there's no mercy left.

Exeunt

SCENE IV. [Outside Macbeth's castle.]

Enter Ross and an old Man

Old Man: Threescore and ten I can remember well:
Within the volume of which time I have seen
Hours dreadful and things strange; but this sore
night
Hath trifled former knowings.

Ross: Ah, good father, 5
Thou seest, the heavens, as troubled with man's act,
Threaten his bloody stage: by the clock, 'tis day,
And yet dark night strangles the travelling lamp:
Is't night's predominance, or the day's shame,
That darkness does the face of earth entomb, 10
When living light should kiss it?

Old Man: 'Tis unnatural,
Even like the deed that's done. On Tuesday last,
A falcon, towering in her pride of place,
Was by a mousing owl hawk'd at and kill'd. 15

Ross: And Duncan's horses—a thing most strange
and certain—
Beauteous and swift, the minions of their race,
Turn'd wild in nature, broke their stalls, flung out,
Contending 'gainst obedience, as they would make
War with mankind. 20

Old Man: 'Tis said they eat each other.

Ross: They did so, to the amazement of mine eyes
That look'd upon't. Here comes
the good Macduff.
Enter Macduff
How goes the world, sir, now? 25

Macduff: Why, see you not?

Ross: Is't known who did this more than bloody deed?

Macduff: Those that Macbeth hath slain.

Ross: Alas, the day!
        What good could they pretend?   30
Macduff: They were suborn'd:
        Malcolm and Donalbain, the king's two sons,
        Are stol'n away and fled; which puts upon them
        Suspicion of the deed.
Ross: 'Gainst nature still!   35
        Thriftless ambition, that wilt ravin up
        Thine own life's means! Then 'tis most like
        The sovereignty will fall upon Macbeth.
Macduff: He is already named, and gone to Scone
        To be invested.   40
Ross: Where is Duncan's body?
Macduff: Carried to Colmekill,
        The sacred storehouse of his predecessors,
        And guardian of their bones.
Ross: Will you to Scone?   45
Macduff: No, cousin, I'll to Fife.
Ross: Well, I will thither.
Macduff: Well, may you see things well done there: adieu!
        Lest our old robes sit easier than our new!
Ross: Farewell, father.   50
Old Man: God's benison go with you; and with those
        That would make good of bad, and friends of foes!

                                     Exeunt

ACT III

SCENE I. [Forres. The palace.]

Enter Banquo

Banquo: Thou hast it now: king, Cawdor, Glamis, all,
        As the weird women promised, and, I fear,
        Thou play'dst most foully for't: yet it was said
        It should not stand in thy posterity,
        But that myself should be the root and father   5
        Of many kings. If there come truth
             from them—
        As upon thee, Macbeth, their
             speeches shine—
        Why, by the verities on thee made good,
        May they not be my oracles as well,
        And set me up in hope? But hush! no more.   10
        Sennet sounded. Enter Macbeth, as king, Lady Macbeth, as queen,
        Lennox, Ross, Lords, Ladies, and Attendants

Macbeth: Here's our chief guest.

Lady Macbeth: If he had been forgotten,
      It had been as a gap in our great feast, 15
      And all-thing unbecoming.

Macbeth: To-night we hold a solemn supper sir,
      And I'll request your presence.

Banquo: Let your highness
      Command upon me; to the which my duties 20
      Are with a most indissoluble tie
      For ever knit.

Macbeth: Ride you this afternoon?

Banquo: Ay, my good lord.

Macbeth: We should have else desired your good advice, 25
      Which still hath been both grave and prosperous,
      In this day's council; but we'll take to-morrow.
      Is't far you ride?

Banquo: As far, my lord, as will fill up the time
      'Twixt this and supper: go not my horse the better, 30
      I must become a borrower of the night
      For a dark hour or twain.

Macbeth: Fail not our feast.

Banquo: My lord, I will not.

Macbeth: We hear, our bloody cousins are bestow'd 35
      In England and in Ireland, not confessing
      Their cruel parricide, filling their hearers
      With strange invention: but of that to-morrow,
      When therewithal we shall have cause of state
      Craving us jointly. Hie you to horse: adieu, 40
      Till you return at night. Goes Fleance with you?

Banquo: Ay, my good lord: our time does call upon 's.

Macbeth: I wish your horses swift and sure of foot;
      And so I do commend you to their backs. Farewell.

                                    Exit Banquo 45

      Let every man be master of his time
      Till seven at night: to make society
      The sweeter welcome, we will keep ourself
      Till supper-time alone: while then, God be with you!

            Exeunt all but Macbeth, and an attendant 50

      Sirrah, a word with you: attend those men
      Our pleasure?

Attendant: They are, my lord, without the palace gate.

Macbeth: Bring them before us.

                                 Exit Attendant 55

To be thus is nothing;
But to be safely thus.—Our fears in Banquo
Stick deep; and in his royalty of nature
Reigns that which would be fear'd: 'tis much
      he dares;
And, to that dauntless temper of his mind,   60
He hath a wisdom that doth guide his valour
To act in safety. There is none but he
Whose being I do fear: and, under him,
My Genius is rebuked; as, it is said,
Mark Antony's was by Caesar. He chid the sisters   65
When first they put the name of king upon me,
And bade them speak to him: then prophet-like
They hail'd him father to a line of kings:
Upon my head they placed a fruitless crown,
And put a barren sceptre in my gripe,   70
Thence to be wrench'd with an unlineal hand,
No son of mine succeeding. If 't be so,
For Banquo's issue have I filed my mind;
For them the gracious Duncan have I murder'd;
Put rancours in the vessel of my peace   75
Only for them; and mine eternal jewel
Given to the common enemy of man,
To make them kings, the seed of Banquo kings!
Rather than so, come fate into the list.
And champion me to the utterance! Who's there!   80
Re-enter Attendant, with two Murderers
Now go to the door, and stay there till we call.

                               Exit Attendant

Was it not yesterday we spoke together?
First Murderer: It was, so please your highness.   85
Macbeth: Well then, now
Have you consider'd of my speeches? Know
That it was he in the times past which held you
So under fortune, which you thought had been
Our innocent self: this I made good to you   90
In our last conference, pass'd in probation with you,
How you were borne in hand, how cross'd,
      the instruments,
Who wrought with them, and all things else
      that might
To half a soul and to a notion crazed
Say 'Thus did Banquo.'   95

First Murderer: You made it known to us.

Macbeth: I did so, and went further, which is now
    Our point of second meeting. Do you find
    Your patience so predominant in your nature
    That you can let this go? Are you so gospell'd   100
    To pray for this good man and for his issue,
    Whose heavy hand hath bow'd you to the grave
    And beggar'd yours for ever?

First Murderer: We are men, my liege.

Macbeth: Ay, in the catalogue ye go for men;   105
    As hounds and greyhounds, mongrels, spaniels, curs,
    Shoughs, water-rugs and demi-wolves, are clept
    All by the name of dogs: the valued file
    Distinguishes the swift, the slow, the subtle,
    The housekeeper, the hunter, every one   110
    According to the gift which bounteous nature
    Hath in him closed; whereby he does receive
    Particular addition. from the bill
    That writes them all alike: and so of men.
    Now, if you have a station in the file,   115
    Not i' the worst rank of manhood, say 't;
    And I will put that business in your bosoms,
    Whose execution takes your enemy off,
    Grapples you to the heart and love of us,
    Who wear our health but sickly in his life,   120
    Which in his death were perfect.

Second Murderer: I am one, my liege,
    Whom the vile blows and buffets of the world
    Have so incensed that I am reckless what
    I do to spite the world.   125

First Murderer: And I another
    So weary with disasters, tugg'd with fortune,
    That I would set my lie on any chance,
    To mend it, or be rid on't.

Macbeth: Both of you   130
    Know Banquo was your enemy.

Both Murderers: True, my lord.

Macbeth: So is he mine; and in such bloody distance,
    That every minute of his being thrusts
    Against my near'st of life: and though I could   135
    With barefaced power sweep him from my sight
    And bid my will avouch it, yet I must not,
    For certain friends that are both his and mine,

> Whose loves I may not drop, but wail his fall
> Who I myself struck down; and thence it is,   140
> That I to your assistance do make love,
> Masking the business from the common eye
> For sundry weighty reasons.
> **Second Murderer:** We shall, my lord,
>   Perform what you command us.   145
> **First Murderer:** Though our lives—
> **Macbeth:** Your spirits shine through you. Within this hour at most
>   I will advise you where to plant yourselves;
>   Acquaint you with the perfect spy o' the time,
>   The moment on't; for't must be done to-night,   150
>   And something from the palace; always thought
>   That I require a clearness: and with him—
>   To leave no rubs nor botches in the work—
>   Fleance his son, that keeps him company,
>   Whose absence is no less material to me   155
>   Than is his father's, must embrace the fate
>   Of that dark hour. Resolve yourselves apart:
>   I'll come to you anon.
> **Both Murderers:** We are resolved, my lord.
> **Macbeth:** I'll call upon you straight: abide within.   160

Exeunt Murderers

> It is concluded. Banquo, thy soul's flight,
> If it find heaven, must find it out to-night.

Exit

SCENE II. [The palace.]

Enter Lady Macbeth and a Servant

Lady Macbeth: Is Banquo gone from court?
Servant: Ay, madam, but returns again to-night.
Lady Macbeth: Say to the king, I would attend his leisure
       For a few words.
Servant: Madam, I will.   5

Exit

Lady Macbeth: Nought's had, all's spent,
       Where our desire is got without content:
       'Tis safer to be that which we destroy
       Than by destruction dwell in doubtful joy.   10
       Enter Macbeth
       How now, my lord! why do you keep alone,

Of sorriest fancies your companions making,
Using those thoughts which should indeed
   have died
With them they think on? Things without all   15
   remedy
Should be without regard: what's done is done.
Macbeth: We have scotch'd the snake, not kill'd it:
She'll close and be herself, whilst our poor malice
Remains in danger of her former tooth.
But let the frame of things disjoint, both the   20
   worlds suffer,
Ere we will eat our meal in fear and sleep
In the affliction of these terrible dreams
That shake us nightly: better be with the dead,
Whom we, to gain our peace, have sent to peace,
Than on the torture of the mind to lie   25
In restless ecstasy. Duncan is in his grave;
After life's fitful fever he sleeps well;
Treason has done his worst: nor steel, nor poison,
Malice domestic, foreign levy, nothing,
Can touch him further.   30
Lady Macbeth: Come on;
Gentle my lord, sleek o'er your rugged looks;
Be bright and jovial among your guests to-night.
Macbeth: So shall I, love; and so, I pray, be you:
Let your remembrance apply to Banquo;   35
Present him eminence, both with eye and tongue:
Unsafe the while, that we
Must lave our honours in these flattering streams,
And make our faces vizards to our hearts,
Disguising what they are.   40
Lady Macbeth: You must leave this.
Macbeth: O, full of scorpions is my mind, dear wife!
Thou know'st that Banquo, and his Fleance,
   lives.
Lady Macbeth: But in them nature's copy's not eterne.
Macbeth: There's comfort yet; they are assailable;   45
Then be thou jocund: ere the bat hath flown
His cloister'd flight, ere to black Hecate's summons
The shard-borne beetle with his drowsy hums
Hath rung night's yawning peal, there shall be done
A deed of dreadful note.   50
Lady Macbeth: What's to be done?

Macbeth: Be innocent of the knowledge, dearest chuck,
　　　　　　Till thou applaud the deed. Come, seeling night,
　　　　　　Scarf up the tender eye of pitiful day;
　　　　　　And with thy bloody and invisible hand　　　　　　　55
　　　　　　Cancel and tear to pieces that great bond
　　　　　　Which keeps me pale! Light thickens; and the crow
　　　　　　Makes wing to the rooky wood:
　　　　　　Good things of day begin to droop and drowse;
　　　　　　While night's black agents to their preys do rouse.　　　60
　　　　　　Thou marvell'st at my words: but hold thee still;
　　　　　　Things bad begun make strong themselves by ill.
　　　　　　So, prithee, go with me.

　　　　　　　　　　　　　　　　　　　　　　　　　Exeunt

SCENE III. [A park near the palace.]

Enter three Murderers

First Murderer: But who did bid thee join with us?
Third Murderer: Macbeth.
Second Murderer: He needs not our mistrust, since he delivers
　　　　　　Our offices and what we have to do
　　　　　　To the direction just.　　　　　　　　　　　　　　5
First Murderer: Then stand with us.
　　　　　　The west yet glimmers with some streaks of day:
　　　　　　Now spurs the lated traveller apace
　　　　　　To gain the timely inn; and near approaches
　　　　　　The subject of our watch.　　　　　　　　　　　　10
Third Murderer: Hark! I hear horses.
Banquo: [Within] Give us a light there, ho!
Second Murderer: Then 'tis he: the rest
　　　　　　That are within the note of expectation
　　　　　　Already are i' the court.　　　　　　　　　　　　15
First Murderer: His horses go about.
Third Murderer: Almost a mile: but he does usually,
　　　　　　So all men do, from hence to the palace gate
　　　　　　Make it their walk.
Second Murderer: A light, a light!　　　　　　　　　　20
　　　　　　Enter Banquo, and Fleance with a torch
Third Murderer: 'Tis he.
First Murderer: Stand to't.
Banquo: It will be rain to-night.
First Murderer: Let it come down.　　　　　　　　　　25
　　　　　　They set upon Banquo

Banquo: O, treachery! Fly, good Fleance, fly, fly, fly!
   Thou mayst revenge. O slave!
   Dies. Fleance escapes
Third Murderer: Who did strike out the light?   30
First Murderer: Wast not the way?
Third Murderer: There's but one down; the son is fled.
Second Murderer: We have lost
   Best half of our affair.
First Murderer: Well, let's away, and say how much is done.   35

                Exeunt

SCENE IV. [The same. Hall in the palace.]

A banquet prepared. Enter Macbeth, Lady Macbeth, Ross, Lennox, Lords, and Attendants

Macbeth: You know your own degrees; sit down: at first
   And last the hearty welcome.
Lords: Thanks to your majesty.
Macbeth: Ourself will mingle with society,
   And play the humble host.   5
   Our hostess keeps her state, but in best time
   We will require her welcome.
Lady Macbeth: Pronounce it for me, sir, to all our friends;
   For my heart speaks they are welcome.
   First Murderer appears at the door   10
Macbeth: See, they encounter thee with their hearts' thanks.
   Both sides are even: here I'll sit i' the midst:
   Be large in mirth; anon we'll drink a measure
   The table round.
   Approaching the door   15
   There's blood on thy face.
First Murderer: 'Tis Banquo's then.
Macbeth: 'Tis better thee without than he within.
   Is he dispatch'd?
First Murderer: My lord, his throat is cut; that I did for him.   20
Macbeth: Thou art the best o' the cut-throats: yet he's good
   That did the like for Fleance: if thou didst it,
   Thou art the nonpareil.
First Murderer: Most royal sir,
   Fleance is 'scaped.   25
Macbeth: Then comes my fit again: I had else been perfect,
   Whole as the marble, founded as the rock,
   As broad and general as the casing air:
   But now I am cabin'd, cribb'd, confined, bound in

        To saucy doubts and fears. But Banquo's safe?   30
First Murderer: Ay, my good lord: safe in a ditch he bides,
        With twenty trenched gashes on his head;
        The least a death to nature.
Macbeth: Thanks for that:
        There the grown serpent lies; the worm that's fled   35
        Hath nature that in time will venom breed,
        No teeth for the present. Get thee gone: to-morrow
        We'll hear, ourselves, again.

                                       Exit Murderer

Lady Macbeth: My royal lord,   40
        You do not give the cheer: the feast is sold
        That is not often vouch'd, while 'tis a-making,
        'Tis given with welcome: to feed were best at home;
        From thence the sauce to meat is ceremony;
        Meeting were bare without it.   45
Macbeth: Sweet remembrancer!
        Now, good digestion wait on appetite,
        And health on both!
Lennox: May't please your highness sit.
        The Ghost of Banquo enters, and sits in   50
        Macbeth's place
Macbeth: Here had we now our country's honour roof'd,
        Were the graced person of our Banquo present;
        Who may I rather challenge for unkindness
        Than pity for mischance!   55
Ross: His absence, sir,
        Lays blame upon his promise. Please't your
           highness
        To grace us with your royal company.
Macbeth: The table's full.
Lennox: Here is a place reserved, sir.   60
Macbeth: Where?
Lennox: Here, my good lord. What is't that moves
          your highness?
Macbeth: Which of you have done this?
Lords: What, my good lord?
Macbeth: Thou canst not say I did it: never shake   65
        Thy gory locks at me.
Ross: Gentlemen, rise: his highness is not well.
Lady Macbeth: Sit, worthy friends: my lord is often thus,
        And hath been from his youth: pray you, keep seat;
        The fit is momentary; upon a thought   70
        He will again be well: if much you note him,

You shall offend him and extend his passion:
Feed, and regard him not. Are you a man?

Macbeth: Ay, and a bold one, that dare look on that
Which might appal the devil. 75

Lady Macbeth: O proper stuff!
This is the very painting of your fear:
This is the air-drawn dagger which, you said,
Led you to Duncan. O, these flaws and starts,
Impostors to true fear, would well become 80
A woman's story at a winter's fire,
Authorized by her grandam. Shame itself!
Why do you make such faces? When all's done,
You look but on a stool.

Macbeth: Prithee, see there! behold! look! lo! 85
how say you?
Why, what care I? If thou canst nod, speak too.
If charnel-houses and our graves must send
Those that we bury back, our monuments
Shall be the maws of kites. 90

Ghost of Banquo vanishes

Lady Macbeth: What, quite unmann'd in folly?

Macbeth: If I stand here, I saw him.

Lady Macbeth: Fie, for shame!

Macbeth: Blood hath been shed ere now, i' the olden time, 95
Ere human statute purged the gentle weal;
Ay, and since too, murders have been perform'd
Too terrible for the ear: the times have been,
That, when the brains were out, the man would die,
And there an end; but now they rise again, 100
With twenty mortal murders on their crowns,
And push us from our stools: this is more strange
Than such a murder is.

Lady Macbeth: My worthy lord,
Your noble friends do lack you. 105

Macbeth: I do forget.
Do not muse at me, my most worthy friends,
I have a strange infirmity, which is nothing
To those that know me. Come, love and health to all;
Then I'll sit down. Give me some wine; fill full. 110
I drink to the general joy o' the whole table,
And to our dear friend Banquo, whom we miss;
Would he were here! to all, and him, we thirst,
And all to all.

Lords: Our duties, and the pledge. 115
        Re-enter Ghost of Banquo
Macbeth: Avaunt! and quit my sight! let the earth hide thee!
        Thy bones are marrowless, thy blood is cold;
        Thou hast no speculation in those eyes
        Which thou dost glare with! 120
Lady Macbeth: Think of this, good peers,
        But as a thing of custom: 'tis no other;
        Only it spoils the pleasure of the time.
Macbeth: What man dare, I dare:
        Approach thou like the rugged Russian bear, 125
        The arm'd rhinoceros, or the Hyrcan tiger;
        Take any shape but that, and my firm nerves
        Shall never tremble: or be alive again,
        And dare me to the desert with thy sword;
        If trembling I inhabit then, protest me 130
        The baby of a girl. Hence, horrible shadow!
        Unreal mockery, hence!
        Ghost of Banquo vanishes
        Why, so: being gone,
        I am a man again. Pray you, sit still. 135
Lady Macbeth: You have displaced the mirth, broke
                the good meeting,
        With most admired disorder.
Macbeth: Can such things be,
        And overcome us like a summer's cloud,
        Without our special wonder? You make me strange 140
        Even to the disposition that I owe,
        When now I think you can behold such sights,
        And keep the natural ruby of your cheeks,
        When mine is blanched with fear.
Ross: What sights, my lord? 145
Lady Macbeth: I pray you, speak not; he grows worse and worse;
        Question enrages him. At once, good night:
        Stand not upon the order of your going,
        But go at once.
Lennox: Good night; and better health 150
        Attend his majesty!
Lady Macbeth: A kind good night to all!
                Exeunt all but Macbeth and Lady Macbeth
Macbeth: It will have blood; they say, blood will have blood:
        Stones have been known to move and trees 155
            to speak;

  Augurs and understood relations have
  By magot-pies and choughs and rooks brought forth
  The secret'st man of blood. What is the night?
Lady Macbeth: Almost at odds with morning, which is which.
Macbeth: How say'st thou, that Macduff denies his person 160
  At our great bidding?
Lady Macbeth: Did you send to him, sir?
Macbeth: I hear it by the way; but I will send:
  There's not a one of them but in his house
  I keep a servant fee'd. I will to-morrow, 165
  And betimes I will, to the weird sisters:
  More shall they speak; for now I am bent to know,
  By the worst means, the worst. For mine own good,
  All causes shall give way: I am in blood
  Stepp'd in so far that, should I wade no more, 170
  Returning were as tedious as go o'er:
  Strange things I have in head, that will to hand;
  Which must be acted ere they may be scann'd.
Lady Macbeth: You lack the season of all natures, sleep.
Macbeth: Come, we'll to sleep. My strange and self-abuse 175
  Is the initiate fear that wants hard use:
  We are yet but young in deed.

                 Exeunt

SCENE V. [A Heath.]

Thunder. Enter the three Witches meeting Hecate

First Witch: Why, how now, Hecate! you look angerly.
Hecate: Have I not reason, beldams as you are,
  Saucy and overbold? How did you dare
  To trade and traffic with Macbeth
  In riddles and affairs of death; 5
  And I, the mistress of your charms,
  The close contriver of all harms,
  Was never call'd to bear my part,
  Or show the glory of our art?
  And, which is worse, all you have done 10
  Hath been but for a wayward son,
  Spiteful and wrathful, who, as others do,
  Loves for his own ends, not for you.
  But make amends now: get you gone,
  And at the pit of Acheron 15
  Meet me i' the morning: thither he

Will come to know his destiny:
Your vessels and your spells provide,
Your charms and every thing beside.
I am for the air; this night I'll spend   20
Unto a dismal and a fatal end:
Great business must be wrought ere noon:
Upon the corner of the moon
There hangs a vaporous drop profound;
I'll catch it ere it come to ground: 25
And that distill'd by magic sleights
Shall raise such artificial sprites
As by the strength of their illusion
Shall draw him on to his confusion:
He shall spurn fate, scorn death, and bear   30
He hopes 'bove wisdom, grace and fear:
And you all know, security
Is mortals' chiefest enemy.
Music and a song within: 'Come away, come away,' & c
Hark! I am call'd; my little spirit, see,   35
Sits in a foggy cloud, and stays for me.

Exit

First Witch: Come, let's make haste; she'll soon be back again.

Exeunt

SCENE VI. [Forres. The palace.]

Enter Lennox and another Lord

Lennox: My former speeches have but hit your thoughts,
Which can interpret further: only, I say,
Things have been strangely borne. The
    gracious Duncan
Was pitied of Macbeth: marry, he was dead:
And the right-valiant Banquo walk'd too late;   5
Whom, you may say, if't please you, Fleance kill'd,
For Fleance fled: men must not walk too late.
Who cannot want the thought how monstrous
It was for Malcolm and for Donalbain
To kill their gracious father? damned fact!   10
How it did grieve Macbeth! did he not straight
In pious rage the two delinquents tear,
That were the slaves of drink and thralls of sleep?
Was not that nobly done? Ay, and wisely too;
For 'twould have anger'd any heart alive   15
To hear the men deny't. So that, I say,

He has borne all things well: and I do think
That had he Duncan's sons under his key—
As, an't please heaven, he shall not—they
    should find
What 'twere to kill a father; so should Fleance.   20
But, peace! for from broad words and 'cause he
    fail'd
His presence at the tyrant's feast, I hear
Macduff lives in disgrace: sir, can you tell
Where he bestows himself?

Lord: The son of Duncan,   25
From whom this tyrant holds the due of birth
Lives in the English court, and is received
Of the most pious Edward with such grace
That the malevolence of fortune nothing
Takes from his high respect: thither Macduff   30
Is gone to pray the holy king, upon his aid
To wake Northumberland and warlike Siward:
That, by the help of these—with Him above
To ratify the work—we may again
Give to our tables meat, sleep to our nights,   35
Free from our feasts and banquets
    bloody knives,
Do faithful homage and receive free honours:
All which we pine for now: and this report
Hath so exasperate the king that he
Prepares for some attempt of war.   40

Lennox: Sent he to Macduff?

Lord: He did: and with an absolute 'Sir, not I,'
The cloudy messenger turns me his back,
And hums, as who should say 'You'll rue
    the time
That clogs me with this answer.'   45

Lennox: And that well might
Advise him to a caution, to hold
    what distance
His wisdom can provide. Some holy angel
Fly to the court of England and unfold
His message ere he come, that a swift blessing   50
May soon return to this our suffering country
Under a hand accursed!

Lord: I'll send my prayers with him.

                                   Exeunt

ACT IV

SCENE I. [A cavern. In the middle, a boiling cauldron.]

Thunder. Enter the three Witches

First Witch: Thrice the brinded cat hath mew'd.
Second Witch: Thrice and once the hedge-pig whined.
Third Witch: Harpier cries 'Tis time, 'tis time.
First Witch: Round about the cauldron go;
      In the poison'd entrails throw.   5
      Toad, that under cold stone
      Days and nights has thirty-one
      Swelter'd venom sleeping got,
      Boil thou first i' the charmed pot.
All: Double, double toil and trouble;   10
      Fire burn, and cauldron bubble.
Second Witch: Fillet of a fenny snake,
      In the cauldron boil and bake;
      Eye of newt and toe of frog,
      Wool of bat and tongue of dog,   15
      Adder's fork and blind-worm's sting,
      Lizard's leg and owlet's wing,
      For a charm of powerful trouble,
      Like a hell-broth boil and bubble.
All: Double, double toil and trouble;   20
      Fire burn and cauldron bubble.
Third Witch: Scale of dragon, tooth of wolf,
      Witches' mummy, maw and gulf
      Of the ravin'd salt-sea shark,
      Root of hemlock digg'd i' the dark,   25
      Liver of blaspheming Jew,
      Gall of goat, and slips of yew
      Silver'd in the moon's eclipse,
      Nose of Turk and Tartar's lips,
      Finger of birth-strangled babe   30
      Ditch-deliver'd by a drab,
      Make the gruel thick and slab:
      Add thereto a tiger's chaudron,
      For the ingredients of our cauldron.
All: Double, double toil and trouble;   35
      Fire burn and cauldron bubble.
Second Witch: Cool it with a baboon's blood,
      Then the charm is firm and good.
      Enter Hecate to the other three Witches

Hecate: O well done! I commend your pains;   40
    And every one shall share i' the gains;
    And now about the cauldron sing,
    Live elves and fairies in a ring,
    Enchanting all that you put in.
    Music and a song: 'Black spirits,' & c 45
    Hecate retires
Second Witch: By the pricking of my thumbs,
    Something wicked this way comes.
    Open, locks,
    Whoever knocks!   50
    Enter Macbeth
Macbeth: How now, you secret, black, and midnight hags!
    What is't you do?
All: A deed without a name.
Macbeth: I conjure you, by that which you profess, 55
    Howe'er you come to know it, answer me:
    Though you untie the winds and let them fight
    Against the churches; though the yesty waves
    Confound and swallow navigation up;
    Though bladed corn be lodged and trees blown 60
     down;
    Though castles topple on their warders' heads;
    Though palaces and pyramids do slope
    Their heads to their foundations; though the
     treasure
    Of nature's germens tumble all together,
    Even till destruction sicken; answer me 65
    To what I ask you.
First Witch: Speak.
Second Witch: Demand.
Third Witch: We'll answer.
First Witch: Say, if thou'dst rather hear it from our mouths, 70
    Or from our masters?
Macbeth: Call 'em; let me see 'em.
First Witch: Pour in sow's blood, that hath eaten
    Her nine farrow; grease that's sweaten
    From the murderer's gibbet throw 75
    Into the flame.
All: Come, high or low;
    Thyself and office deftly show!
    Thunder. First Apparition: an armed Head
Macbeth: Tell me, thou unknown power,— 80

First Witch: He knows thy thought:
      Hear his speech, but say thou nought.
First Apparition: Macbeth! Macbeth! Macbeth! beware Macduff;
      Beware the thane of Fife. Dismiss me. Enough.
      Descends   85
Macbeth: Whate'er thou art, for thy good caution, thanks;
      Thou hast harp'd my fear aright: but one
      word more,—
First Witch: He will not be commanded: here's another,
      More potent than the first.   90
      Thunder. Second Apparition: A bloody Child
Second Apparition: Macbeth! Macbeth! Macbeth!
Macbeth: Had I three ears, I'ld hear thee.
Second Apparition: Be bloody, bold, and resolute; laugh to scorn
      The power of man, for none of woman born   95
      Shall harm Macbeth.
      Descends
Macbeth: Then live, Macduff: what need I fear of thee?
      But yet I'll make assurance double sure,
      And take a bond of fate: thou shalt not live;   100
      That I may tell pale-hearted fear it lies,
      And sleep in spite of thunder.
      Thunder. Third Apparition: a Child crowned, with a tree in his hand
      What is this
      That rises like the issue of a king,   105
      And wears upon his baby-brow the round
      And top of sovereignty?
All: Listen, but speak not to't.
Third Apparition: Be lion-mettled, proud; and take no care
      Who chafes, who frets, or where conspirers are: 110
      Macbeth shall never vanquish'd be until
      Great Birnam wood to high Dunsinane hill
      Shall come against him.
      Descends
Macbeth: That will never be   115
      Who can impress the forest, bid the tree
      Unfix his earth-bound root? Sweet bodements! good!
      Rebellion's head, rise never till the wood
      Of Birnam rise, and our high-placed Macbeth
      Shall live the lease of nature, pay his breath   120
      To time and mortal custom. Yet my heart
      Throbs to know one thing: tell me, if your art
      Can tell so much: shall Banquo's issue ever
      Reign in this kingdom?

All: Seek to know no more.   125
Macbeth: I will be satisfied: deny me this,
               And an eternal curse fall on you! Let me know.
               Why sinks that cauldron? and what noise is this?
               Hautboys
First Witch: Show!   130
Second Witch: Show!
Third Witch: Show!
All: Show his eyes, and grieve his heart;
          Come like shadows, so depart!
          A show of Eight Kings, the last with a glass in his hand; Ghost of Banquo 135
               following
Macbeth: Thou art too like the spirit of Banquo: down!
               Thy crown does sear mine eye-balls. And thy hair,
               Thou other gold-bound brow, is like the first.
               A third is like the former. Filthy hags!
               Why do you show me this? A fourth! Start, eyes!   140
               What, will the line stretch out to the crack of
                  doom?
               Another yet! A seventh! I'll see no more:
               And yet the eighth appears, who bears a glass
               Which shows me many more; and some I see
               That two-fold balls and treble scepters carry: 145
               Horrible sight! Now, I see, 'tis true;
               For the blood-bolter'd Banquo smiles upon me,
               And points at them for his.
               Apparitions vanish
               What, is this so?   150
First Witch: Ay, sir, all this is so: but why
               Stands Macbeth thus amazedly?
               Come, sisters, cheer we up his sprites,
               And show the best of our delights:
               I'll charm the air to give a sound,   155
               While you perform your antic round:
               That this great king may kindly say,
               Our duties did his welcome pay.
               Music. The witches dance and then vanish, with
                  Hecate
Macbeth: Where are they? Gone? Let this pernicious hour   160
               Stand aye accursed in the calendar!
               Come in, without there!
                                                              Enter Lennox

Lennox: What's your grace's will?
Macbeth: Saw you the weird sisters?   165

Lennox: No, my lord.

Macbeth: Came they not by you?

Lennox: No, indeed, my lord.

Macbeth: Infected be the air whereon they ride;

And damn'd all those that trust them! I did hear 170

The galloping of horse: who was't came by?

Lennox: 'Tis two or three, my lord, that bring you word

Macduff is fled to England.

Macbeth: Fled to England!

Lennox: Ay, my good lord. 175

Macbeth: Time, thou anticipatest my dread exploits:

The flighty purpose never is o'ertook

Unless the deed go with it; from this moment

The very firstlings of my heart shall be

The firstlings of my hand. And even now, 180

To crown my thoughts with acts, be it thought

and done:

The castle of Macduff I will surprise;

Seize upon Fife; give to the edge o' the sword

His wife, his babes, and all unfortunate souls

That trace him in his line. No boasting like a fool; 185

This deed I'll do before this purpose cool.

But no more sights!—Where are these gentlemen?

Come, bring me where they are.

Exeunt

SCENE II. [Fife. Macduff's castle.]

Enter Lady Macduff, her Son, and Ross

Lady Macduff: What had he done, to make him fly the land?

Ross: You must have patience, madam.

Lady Macduff: He had none:

His flight was madness: when our actions do not,

Our fears do make us traitors. 5

Ross: You know not

Whether it was his wisdom or his fear.

Lady Macduff: Wisdom! to leave his wife, to leave his babes,

His mansion and his titles in a place

From whence himself does fly? He loves us not; 10

He wants the natural touch: for the poor wren,

The most diminutive of birds, will fight,

Her young ones in her nest, against the owl.

All is the fear and nothing is the love;

As little is the wisdom, where the flight   15
So runs against all reason.
Ross: My dearest coz,
    I pray you, school yourself: but for your husband,
    He is noble, wise, judicious, and best knows
    The fits o' the season. I dare not speak   20
        much further;
    But cruel are the times, when we are traitors
    And do not know ourselves, when we hold rumour
    From what we fear, yet know not what we fear,
    But float upon a wild and violent sea
    Each way and move. I take my leave of you: 25
    Shall not be long but I'll be here again:
    Things at the worst will cease, or else climb upward
    To what they were before. My pretty cousin,
    Blessing upon you!
Lady Macduff: Father'd he is, and yet he's fatherless.   30
Ross: I am so much a fool, should I stay longer,
    It would be my disgrace and your discomfort:
    I take my leave at once.

                                         Exit

Lady Macduff: Sirrah, your father's dead;
    And what will you do now? How will you live?   35
Son: As birds do, mother.
Lady Macduff: What, with worms and flies?
Son: With what I get, I mean; and so do they.
Lady Macduff: Poor bird! thou'ldst never fear the net nor lime,
    The pitfall nor the gin.   40
Son: Why should I, mother? Poor birds they are not set for.
    My father is not dead, for all your saying.
Lady Macduff: Yes, he is dead; how wilt thou do for a father?
Son: Nay, how will you do for a husband?
Lady Macduff: Why, I can buy me twenty at any market.   45
Son: Then you'll buy 'em to sell again.
Lady Macduff: Thou speak'st with all thy wit: and yet, i' faith,
    With wit enough for thee.
Son: Was my father a traitor, mother?
Lady Macduff: Ay, that he was.   50
Son: What is a traitor?
Lady Macduff: Why, one that swears and lies.
Son: And be all traitors that do so?
Lady Macduff: Every one that does so is a traitor, and must be hanged.
Son: And must they all be hanged that swear and lie?   55
Lady Macduff: Every one.

Son: Who must hang them?
Lady Macduff: Why, the honest men.
Son: Then the liars and swearers are fools,
   for there are liars and swearers enow to beat
   the honest men and hang up them.
Lady Macduff: Now, God help thee, poor monkey!   60
   But how wilt thou do for a father?
Son: If he were dead, you'ld weep for
   him: if you would not, it were a good sign
   that I should quickly have a new father.
Lady Macduff: Poor prattler, how thou talk'st!
   Enter a Messenger
Messenger: Bless you, fair dame! I am not to you known,   65
   Though in your state of honour I am perfect.
   I doubt some danger does approach you nearly:
   If you will take a homely man's advice,
   Be not found here; hence, with your little ones.
   To fright you thus, methinks, I am too savage;   70
   To do worse to you were fell cruelty,
   Which is too nigh your person. Heaven preserve you!
   I dare abide no longer.

                      Exit

Lady Macduff: Whither should I fly?   75
   I have done no harm. But I remember now
   I am in this earthly world; where to do harm
   Is often laudable, to do good sometime
   Accounted dangerous folly: why then, alas,
   Do I put up that womanly defence,   80
   To say I have done no harm?
   Enter Murderers
   What are these faces?
First Murderer: Where is your husband?
Lady Macduff: I hope, in no place so unsanctified   85
   Where such as thou mayst find him.
First Murderer: He's a traitor.
Son: Thou liest, thou shag-hair'd villain!
First Murderer: What, you egg!
   Stabbing him   90
   Young fry of treachery!
Son: He has kill'd me, mother:
   Run away, I pray you!
   Dies
   Exit Lady Macduff, crying 'Murder!' Exeunt Murderers, following her   95

SCENE III. [England. Before the King's palace.]

Enter Malcolm and Macduff

Malcolm: Let us seek out some desolate shade, and there
    Weep our sad bosoms empty.
Macduff: Let us rather
    Hold fast the mortal sword, and like good men
    Bestride our down-fall'n birthdom: each new morn   5
    New widows howl, new orphans cry, new sorrows
    Strike heaven on the face, that it resounds
    As if it felt with Scotland and yell'd out
    Like syllable of dolour.
Malcolm: What I believe I'll wail,   10
    What know believe, and what I can redress,
    As I shall find the time to friend, I will.
    What you have spoke, it may be so perchance.
    This tyrant, whose sole name blisters our tongues,
    Was once thought honest: you have loved him well.   15
    He hath not touch'd you yet. I am young;
        but something
    You may deserve of him through me, and wisdom
    To offer up a weak poor innocent lamb
    To appease an angry god.
Macduff: I am not treacherous.   20
Malcolm: But Macbeth is.
    A good and virtuous nature may recoil
    In an imperial charge. But I shall crave
        your pardon;
    That which you are my thoughts cannot transpose:
    Angels are bright still, though the brightest fell;   25
    Though all things foul would wear the brows of grace,
    Yet grace must still look so.
Macduff: I have lost my hopes.
Malcolm: Perchance even there where I did find my doubts.
    Why in that rawness left you wife and child,   30
    Those precious motives, those strong knots of love,
    Without leave-taking? I pray you,
    Let not my jealousies be your dishonours,
    But mine own safeties. You may be rightly just,
    Whatever I shall think.   35
Macduff: Bleed, bleed, poor country!
    Great tyranny! lay thou thy basis sure,
    For goodness dare not cheque thee: wear thou
        thy wrongs;

           The title is affeer'd! Fare thee well, lord:

           I would not be the villain that thou think'st   40

           For the whole space that's in the tyrant's grasp,

           And the rich East to boot.

Malcolm: Be not offended:

           I speak not as in absolute fear of you.

           I think our country sinks beneath the yoke;   45

           It weeps, it bleeds; and each new day a gash

           Is added to her wounds: I think withal

           There would be hands uplifted in my right;

           And here from gracious England have

               I offer

           Of goodly thousands: but, for all this,   50

           When I shall tread upon the tyrant's head,

           Or wear it on my sword, yet my poor country

           Shall have more vices than it had before,

           More suffer and more sundry ways than ever,

           By him that shall succeed.   55

Macduff: What should he be?

Malcolm: It is myself I mean: in whom I know

           All the particulars of vice so grafted

           That, when they shall be open'd, black Macbeth

           Will seem as pure as snow, and the poor state   60

           Esteem him as a lamb, being compared

           With my confineless harms.

Macduff: Not in the legions

           Of horrid hell can come a devil more damn'd

           In evils to top Macbeth.   65

Malcolm: I grant him bloody,

           Luxurious, avaricious, false, deceitful,

           Sudden, malicious, smacking of every sin

           That has a name: but there's no bottom, none,

           In my voluptuousness: your wives, your daughters,   70

           Your matrons and your maids, could not fill up

           The cistern of my lust, and my desire

           All continent impediments would o'erbear

           That did oppose my will: better Macbeth

           Than such an one to reign.   75

Macduff: Boundless intemperance

           In nature is a tyranny; it hath been

           The untimely emptying of the happy throne

           And fall of many kings. But fear not yet

           To take upon you what is yours: you may   80

           Convey your pleasures in a spacious plenty,

And yet seem cold, the time you may so hoodwink.
We have willing dames enough: there cannot be
That vulture in you, to devour so many
As will to greatness dedicate themselves,   85
Finding it so inclined.

Malcolm: With this there grows
In my most ill-composed affection such
A stanchless avarice that, were I king,
I should cut off the nobles for their lands,   90
Desire his jewels and this other's house:
And my more-having would be as a sauce
To make me hunger more; that I should forge
Quarrels unjust against the good and loyal,
Destroying them for wealth.   95

Macduff: This avarice
Sticks deeper, grows with more pernicious root
Than summer-seeming lust, and it hath been
The sword of our slain kings: yet do not fear;
Scotland hath foisons to fill up your will.   100
Of your mere own: all these are portable,
With other graces weigh'd.

Malcolm: But I have none: the king-becoming graces,
As justice, verity, temperance, stableness,
Bounty, perseverance, mercy, lowliness,   105
Devotion, patience, courage, fortitude,
I have no relish of them, but abound
In the division of each several crime,
Acting it many ways. Nay, had I power, I should
Pour the sweet milk of concord into hell,   110
Uproar the universal peace, confound
All unity on earth.

Macduff: O Scotland, Scotland!

Malcolm: If such a one be fit to govern, speak:
I am as I have spoken.   115

Macduff: Fit to govern!
No, not to live. O nation miserable,
With an untitled tyrant bloody-scepter'd,
When shalt thou see thy wholesome days again,
Since that the truest issue of thy throne   120
By his own interdiction stands accursed,
And does blaspheme his breed? Thy royal father
Was a most sainted king: the queen that bore thee,
Oftener upon her knees than on her feet,
Died every day she lived. Fare thee well!   125
These evils thou repeat'st upon thyself

Have banish'd me from Scotland. O my breast,
Thy hope ends here!

Malcolm: Macduff, this noble passion,
Child of integrity, hath from my soul   130
Wiped the black scruples, reconciled my thoughts
To thy good truth and honour. Devilish Macbeth
By many of these trains hath sought to win me
Into his power, and modest wisdom plucks me
From over-credulous haste: but God above   135
Deal between thee and me! for even now
I put myself to thy direction, and
Unspeak mine own detraction, here abjure
The taints and blames I laid upon myself,
For strangers to my nature. I am yet   140
Unknown to woman, never was forsworn,
Scarcely have coveted what was mine own,
At no time broke my faith, would not betray
The devil to his fellow and delight
No less in truth than life: my first false speaking   145
Was this upon myself: what I am truly,
Is thine and my poor country's to command:
Whither indeed, before thy here-approach,
Old Siward, with ten thousand warlike men,
Already at a point, was setting forth.   150
Now we'll together; and the chance of goodness
Be like our warranted quarrel! Why are you silent?

Macduff: Such welcome and unwelcome things at once
        'Tis hard to reconcile.

Enter a Doctor   155

Malcolm: Well; more anon.—Comes the king forth, I pray you?

Doctor: Ay, sir; there are a crew of wretched souls
That stay his cure: their malady convinces
The great assay of art; but at his touch—
Such sanctity hath heaven given his hand—   160
They presently amend.

Malcolm: I thank you, doctor.

Exit Doctor

Macduff: What's the disease he means?

Malcolm: 'Tis call'd the evil: 165
A most miraculous work in this good king;
Which often, since my here-remain in England,
I have seen him do. How he solicits heaven,
Himself best knows: but strangely-visited people,
All swoln and ulcerous, pitiful to the eye,   170

The mere despair of surgery, he cures,
Hanging a golden stamp about their necks,
Put on with holy prayers: and 'tis spoken,
To the succeeding royalty he leaves
The healing benediction. With this strange virtue,   175
He hath a heavenly gift of prophecy,
And sundry blessings hang about his throne,
That speak him full of grace.
    Enter Ross
Macduff: See, who comes here?   180
Malcolm: My countryman; but yet I know him not.
Macduff: My ever-gentle cousin, welcome hither.
Malcolm: I know him now. Good God, betimes remove
      The means that makes us strangers!
Ross: Sir, amen.   185
Macduff: Stands Scotland where it did?
Ross: Alas, poor country!
      Almost afraid to know itself. It cannot
      Be call'd our mother, but our grave; where nothing,
      But who knows nothing, is once seen to smile;   190
      Where sighs and groans and shrieks that rend the air
      Are made, not mark'd; where violent sorrow seems
      A modern ecstasy; the dead man's knell
      Is there scarce ask'd for who; and good men's lives
      Expire before the flowers in their caps,   195
      Dying or ere they sicken.
Macduff: O, relation
      Too nice, and yet too true!
Malcolm: What's the newest grief?
Ross: That of an hour's age doth hiss the speaker: 200
      Each minute teems a new one.
Macduff: How does my wife?
Ross: Why, well.
Macduff: And all my children?
Ross: Well too.   205
Macduff: The tyrant has not batter'd at their peace?
Ross: No; they were well at peace when I did
      leave 'em.
Macduff: But not a niggard of your speech: how goes't?
Ross: When I came hither to transport the tidings,
      Which I have heavily borne, there ran   210
        a rumour
      Of many worthy fellows that were out;
      Which was to my belief witness'd the rather,

For that I saw the tyrant's power a-foot:
Now is the time of help; your eye in Scotland
Would create soldiers, make our women fight,   215
To doff their dire distresses.

Malcolm: Be't their comfort
We are coming thither: gracious England hath
Lent us good Siward and ten thousand men;
An older and a better soldier none   220
That Christendom gives out.

Ross: Would I could answer
This comfort with the like! But I have words
That would be howl'd out in the desert air,
Where hearing should not latch them.   225

Macduff: What concern they?
The general cause? or is it a fee-grief
Due to some single breast?

Ross: No mind that's honest
But in it shares some woe; though the main part   230
Pertains to you alone.

Macduff: If it be mine,
Keep it not from me, quickly let me have it.

Ross: Let not your ears despise my tongue for ever,
Which shall possess them with the
heaviest sound   235
That ever yet they heard.

Macduff: Hum! I guess at it.

Ross: Your castle is surprised; your wife and babes
Savagely slaughter'd: to relate the manner,
Were, on the quarry of these murder'd deer,   240
To add the death of you.

Malcolm: Merciful heaven!
What, man! ne'er pull your hat upon your brows;
Give sorrow words: the grief that does not speak
Whispers the o'er-fraught heart and bids it break.   245

Macduff: My children too?

Ross: Wife, children, servants, all
That could be found.

Macduff: And I must be from thence!
My wife kill'd too?   250

Ross: I have said.

Malcolm: Be comforted:
Let's make us medicines of our great revenge,
To cure this deadly grief.

Macduff: He has no children. All my pretty ones?   255
   Did you say all? O hell-kite! All?
   What, all my pretty chickens and their dam
   At one fell swoop?
Malcolm: Dispute it like a man.
Macduff: I shall do so;   260
   But I must also feel it as a man:
   I cannot but remember such things were,
   That were most precious to me. Did heaven look on,
   And would not take their part? Sinful Macduff,
   They were all struck for thee! naught that I am,   265
   Not for their own demerits, but for mine,
   Fell slaughter on their souls. Heaven rest them now!
Malcolm: Be this the whetstone of your sword: let grief
   Convert to anger; blunt not the heart, enrage it.
Macduff: O, I could play the woman with mine eyes   270
   And braggart with my tongue! But, gentle heavens,
   Cut short all intermission; front to front
   Bring thou this fiend of Scotland and myself;
   Within my sword's length set him; if he 'scape,
   Heaven forgive him too!   275
Malcolm: This tune goes manly.
   Come, go we to the king; our power is ready;
   Our lack is nothing but our leave; Macbeth
   Is ripe for shaking, and the powers above
   Put on their instruments. Receive what cheer   280
    you may:
   The night is long that never finds the day.

                Exeunt

ACT V

SCENE I. [Dunsinane. Ante-room in the castle.]

Enter a Doctor of Physic and a Waiting-Gentlewoman

Doctor: I have two nights watched with you, but can perceive
   no truth in your report. When was it she last walked?
Gentlewoman: Since his majesty went into the field, I have seen
   her rise from her bed, throw her night-gown upon
   her, unlock her closet, take forth paper, fold it,   5
   write upon't, read it, afterwards seal it, and again
   return to bed; yet all this while in a most fast sleep.
Doctor: A great perturbation in nature, to receive at once
   the benefit of sleep, and do the effects of

watching! In this slumbery agitation, besides her   10
walking and other actual performances, what, at any
time, have you heard her say?

Gentlewoman: That, sir, which I will not report after her.

Doctor: You may to me: and 'tis most meet you should.

Gentlewoman: Neither to you nor any one; having no witness to   15
confirm my speech.

Enter Lady Macbeth, with a taper

Lo you, here she comes! This is her very guise;
and, upon my life, fast asleep. Observe her;
stand close.

Doctor: How came she by that light?

Gentlewoman: Why, it stood by her: she has light by her   20
continually; 'tis her command.

Doctor: You see, her eyes are open.

Gentlewoman: Ay, but their sense is shut.

Doctor: What is it she does now? Look, how she rubs
her hands.

Gentlewoman: It is an accustomed action with her, to seem thus   25
washing her hands: I have known her continue in
this a quarter of an hour.

Lady Macbeth: Yet here's a spot.

Doctor: Hark! she speaks: I will set down what comes from
her, to satisfy my remembrance the more strongly.   30

Lady Macbeth: Out, damned spot! out, I say!—One: two: why,
then, 'tis time to do't.—Hell is murky!—Fie, my
lord, fie! a soldier, and afeard? What need we
fear who knows it, when none can call our power to
account?—Yet who would have thought the old man   35
to have had so much blood in him.

Doctor: Do you mark that?

Lady Macbeth: The thane of Fife had a wife: where is she now?—
What, will these hands ne'er be clean?—No more o'
that, my lord, no more o' that: you mar all with   40
this starting.

Doctor: Go to, go to; you have known what you should not.

Gentlewoman: She has spoke what she should not, I am sure of
that: heaven knows what she has known.

Lady Macbeth: Here's the smell of the blood still: all the   45
perfumes of Arabia will not sweeten this little
hand. Oh, oh, oh!

Doctor: What a sigh is there! The heart is sorely charged.

Gentlewoman: I would not have such a heart in my bosom for the
dignity of the whole body.   50

Doctor: Well, well, well,—

Gentlewoman: Pray God it be, sir.

Doctor: This disease is beyond my practise: yet I have known
   those which have walked in their sleep who
    have died
   holily in their beds.   55

Lady Macbeth: Wash your hands, put on your nightgown; look not so
   pale.—I tell you yet again, Banquo's buried; he
   cannot come out on's grave.

Doctor: Even so?

Lady Macbeth: To bed, to bed! there's knocking at the gate: 60
   come, come, come, come, give me your hand. What's
   done cannot be undone.—To bed, to bed, to bed!

                     Exit

Doctor: Will she go now to bed?

Gentlewoman: Directly.   65

Doctor: Foul whisperings are abroad: unnatural deeds
   Do breed unnatural troubles: infected minds
   To their deaf pillows will discharge their secrets:
   More needs she the divine than the physician.
   God, God forgive us all! Look after her;   70
   Remove from her the means of all annoyance,
   And still keep eyes upon her. So, good night:
   My mind she has mated, and amazed my sight.
   I think, but dare not speak.

Gentlewoman: Good night, good doctor.   75

                  Exeunt

SCENE II. [The country near Dunsinane.]

Drum and Colours. Enter Menteith, Caithness, Angus, Lennox, and Soldiers

Menteith: The English power is near, led on by Malcolm,
   His uncle Siward and the good Macduff:
   Revenges burn in them; for their dear causes
   Would to the bleeding and the grim alarm
   Excite the mortified man.   5

Angus: Near Birnam wood
   Shall we well meet them; that way are they coming.

Caithness: Who knows if Donalbain be with his brother?

Lennox: For certain, sir, he is not: I have a file
   Of all the gentry: there is Siward's son,   10
   And many unrough youths that even now
   Protest their first of manhood.

Menteith: What does the tyrant?
Caithness: Great Dunsinane he strongly fortifies:
          Some say he's mad; others that lesser hate him   15
          Do call it valiant fury: but, for certain,
          He cannot buckle his distemper'd cause
          Within the belt of rule.
Angus: Now does he feel
          His secret murders sticking on his hands;   20
          Now minutely revolts upbraid his faith-breach;
          Those he commands move only in command,
          Nothing in love: now does he feel his title
          Hang loose about him, like a giant's robe
          Upon a dwarfish thief.   25
Menteith: Who then shall blame
          His pester'd senses to recoil and start,
          When all that is within him does condemn
          Itself for being there?
Caithness: Well, march we on,   30
          To give obedience where 'tis truly owed:
          Meet we the medicine of the sickly weal,
          And with him pour we in our country's purge
          Each drop of us.
Lennox: Or so much as it needs,   35
          To dew the sovereign flower and drown the weeds.
          Make we our march towards Birnam.

                                       Exeunt, marching

SCENE III. [Dunsinane. A room in the castle.]

Enter Macbeth, Doctor, and Attendants

Macbeth: Bring me no more reports; let them fly all:
          Till Birnam wood remove to Dunsinane,
          I cannot taint with fear. What's the boy Malcolm?
          Was he not born of woman? The spirits that know
          All mortal consequences have pronounced me thus: 5
          'Fear not, Macbeth; no man that's born of woman
          Shall e'er have power upon thee.' Then fly,
             false thanes,
          And mingle with the English epicures:
          The mind I sway by and the heart I bear
          Shall never sag with doubt nor shake with fear.   10
          Enter a Servant
          The devil damn thee black, thou cream-faced loon!
          Where got'st thou that goose look?

Servant: There is ten thousand—

Macbeth: Geese, villain! 15

Servant: Soldiers, sir.

Macbeth: Go prick thy face, and over-red thy fear,
    Thou lily-liver'd boy. What soldiers, patch?
    Death of thy soul! those linen cheeks of thine
    Are counsellors to fear. What soldiers, whey-face? 20

Servant: The English force, so please you.

Macbeth: Take thy face hence.

                    Exit Servant

    Seyton!—I am sick at heart,
    When I behold—Seyton, I say!—This push 25
    Will cheer me ever, or disseat me now.
    I have lived long enough: my way of life
    Is fall'n into the sear, the yellow leaf;
    And that which should accompany old age,
    As honour, love, obedience, troops of friends, 30
    I must not look to have; but, in their stead,
    Curses, not loud but deep, mouth-honour, breath,
    Which the poor heart would fain deny, and dare
        not. Seyton!
    Enter Seyton

Seyton: What is your gracious pleasure? 35

Macbeth: What news more?

Seyton: All is confirm'd, my lord, which was reported.

Macbeth: I'll fight till from my bones my flesh be hack'd.
    Give me my armour.

Seyton: 'Tis not needed yet. 40

Macbeth: I'll put it on.
    Send out more horses; skirr the country round;
    Hang those that talk of fear. Give me mine armour.
    How does your patient, doctor?

Doctor: Not so sick, my lord, 45
    As she is troubled with thick coming fancies,
    That keep her from her rest.

Macbeth: Cure her of that.
    Canst thou not minister to a mind diseased,
    Pluck from the memory a rooted sorrow, 50
    Raze out the written troubles of the brain
    And with some sweet oblivious antidote
    Cleanse the stuff'd bosom of that perilous stuff
    Which weighs upon the heart?

Doctor: Therein the patient 55
    Must minister to himself.

Macbeth: Throw physic to the dogs; I'll none of it.
Come, put mine armour on; give me my staff.
Seyton, send out. Doctor, the thanes fly from me.
Come, sir, dispatch. If thou couldst, doctor, cast   60
The water of my land, find her disease,
And purge it to a sound and pristine health,
I would applaud thee to the very echo,
That should applaud again.—Pull't off, I say.—
What rhubarb, cyme, or what purgative drug,   65
Would scour these English hence? Hear'st thou
   of them?
Doctor: Ay, my good lord; your royal preparation
Makes us hear something.
Macbeth: Bring it after me.   70
I will not be afraid of death and bane,
Till Birnam forest come to Dunsinane.
Doctor: [Aside] Were I from Dunsinane away and clear,
Profit again should hardly draw me here.

Exeunt   75

SCENE IV. [Country near Birnam wood.]

Drum and Colours. Enter Malcolm, Siward and Young Siward, Macduff, Mente-
ith, Caithness, Angus, Lennox, Ross, and Soldiers, marching

Malcolm: Cousins, I hope the days are near at hand
That chambers will be safe.
Menteith: We doubt it nothing.
Siward: What wood is this before us?
Menteith: The wood of Birnam.   5
Malcolm: Let every soldier hew him down a bough
And bear't before him: thereby shall we shadow
The numbers of our host and make discovery
Err in report of us.
Soldiers: It shall be done.   10
Siward: We learn no other but the confident tyrant
Keeps still in Dunsinane, and will endure
Our setting down before 't.
Malcolm: 'Tis his main hope:
For where there is advantage to be given,   15
Both more and less have given him the revolt,
And none serve with him but constrained things
Whose hearts are absent too.
Macduff: Let our just censures
Attend the true event, and put we on   20
Industrious soldiership.

Siward: The time approaches
That will with due decision make us know
What we shall say we have and what we owe.
Thoughts speculative their unsure hopes relate,   25
But certain issue strokes must arbitrate:
Towards which advance the war.

Exeunt, marching

SCENE V. [Dunsinane. Within the castle.]

Enter Macbeth, Seyton, and Soldiers, with Drum and Colours

Macbeth: Hang out our banners on the outward walls;
The cry is still 'They come:' our castle's strength
Will laugh a siege to scorn: here let them lie
Till famine and the ague eat them up:
Were they not forced with those that should be ours,   5
We might have met them dareful, beard to beard,
And beat them backward home.
A cry of women within
What is that noise?
Seyton: It is the cry of women, my good lord.   10

Exit

Macbeth: I have almost forgot the taste of fears;
The time has been, my senses would have cool'd
To hear a night-shriek; and my fell of hair
Would at a dismal treatise rouse and stir   15
As life were in't: I have supp'd full with horrors;
Direness, familiar to my slaughterous thoughts
Cannot once start me.
Re-enter Seyton
Wherefore was that cry?   20
Seyton: The queen, my lord, is dead.
Macbeth: She should have died hereafter;
There would have been a time for such a word.
To-morrow, and to-morrow, and to-morrow,
Creeps in this petty pace from day to day   25
To the last syllable of recorded time,
And all our yesterdays have lighted fools
The way to dusty death. Out, out, brief candle!
Life's but a walking shadow, a poor player
That struts and frets his hour upon the stage   30
And then is heard no more: it is a tale
Told by an idiot, full of sound and fury,

            Signifying nothing.
            Enter a Messenger
            Thou comest to use thy tongue; thy story quickly.   35

Messenger: Gracious my lord,
            I should report that which I say I saw,
            But know not how to do it.

Macbeth: Well, say, sir.

Messenger: As I did stand my watch upon the hill,   40
            I look'd toward Birnam, and anon, methought,
            The wood began to move.

Macbeth: Liar and slave!

Messenger: Let me endure your wrath, if't be not so:
            Within this three mile may you see it coming;   45
            I say, a moving grove.

Macbeth: If thou speak'st false,
            Upon the next tree shalt thou hang alive,
            Till famine cling thee: if thy speech be sooth,
            I care not if thou dost for me as much.   50
            I pull in resolution, and begin
            To doubt the equivocation of the fiend
            That lies like truth: 'Fear not, till Birnam wood
            Do come to Dunsinane:' and now a wood
            Comes toward Dunsinane. Arm, arm, and out!   55
            If this which he avouches does appear,
            There is nor flying hence nor tarrying here.
            I gin to be aweary of the sun,
             And wish the estate o' the world were now undone.
            Ring the alarum-bell! Blow, wind! come, wrack!   60
            At least we'll die with harness on our back.

                                                    Exeunt

SCENE VI. [Dunsinane. Before the castle.]

Drum and colours. Enter Malcolm, Siward, Macduff, and their Army, with boughs

Malcolm: Now near enough: your leafy screens throw down.
            And show like those you are. You, worthy uncle,
            Shall, with my cousin, your right-noble son,
            Lead our first battle: worthy Macduff and we
            Shall take upon 's what else remains to do,   5
            According to our order.

Siward: Fare you well.
            Do we but find the tyrant's power to-night,
            Let us be beaten, if we cannot fight.

Macduff: Make all our trumpets speak; give them all breath,   10
Those clamorous harbingers of blood and death.

                          Exeunt

SCENE VII. [Another part of the field.]

Alarums. Enter Macbeth

Macbeth: They have tied me to a stake; I cannot fly,
      But, bear-like, I must fight the course. What's he
      That was not born of woman? Such a one
      Am I to fear, or none.
      Enter Young Siward   5
Young Siward: What is thy name?
Macbeth: Thou'lt be afraid to hear it.
Young Siward: No; though thou call'st thyself a hotter name
      Than any is in hell.
Macbeth: My name's Macbeth.   10
Young Siward: The devil himself could not pronounce a title
      More hateful to mine ear.
Macbeth: No, nor more fearful.
Young Siward: Thou liest, abhorred tyrant; with my sword
      I'll prove the lie thou speak'st.   15
      They fight and Young Siward is slain
Macbeth: Thou wast born of woman
      But swords I smile at, weapons laugh to scorn,
      Brandish'd by man that's of a woman born.

                     Exit 20
      Alarums. Enter Macduff
Macduff: That way the noise is. Tyrant, show thy face!
      If thou be'st slain and with no stroke of mine,
      My wife and children's ghosts will haunt me still.
      I cannot strike at wretched kerns, whose arms   25
      Are hired to bear their staves: either thou, Macbeth,
      Or else my sword with an unbatter'd edge
      I sheathe again undeeded. There thou shouldst be;
      By this great clatter, one of greatest note
      Seems bruited. Let me find him, fortune!   30
      And more I beg not.

                   Exit. Alarums

      Enter Malcolm and Siward
Siward: This way, my lord; the castle's gently render'd:
      The tyrant's people on both sides do fight;   35
      The noble thanes do bravely in the war;

> The day almost itself professes yours,
> And little is to do.

Malcolm: We have met with foes
> That strike beside us.   40

Siward: Enter, sir, the castle.

> *Exeunt. Alarums*

SCENE VIII. [Another part of the field.]

Enter Macbeth

Macbeth: Why should I play the Roman fool, and die
> On mine own sword? whiles I see lives, the gashes
> Do better upon them.
> *Enter Macduff*

Macduff: Turn, hell-hound, turn!   5

Macbeth: Of all men else I have avoided thee:
> But get thee back; my soul is too much charged
> With blood of thine already.

Macduff: I have no words:
> My voice is in my sword: thou bloodier villain   10
> Than terms can give thee out!
> *They fight*

Macbeth: Thou losest labour:
> As easy mayst thou the intrenchant air
> With thy keen sword impress as make me bleed: 15
> Let fall thy blade on vulnerable crests;
> I bear a charmed life, which must not yield,
> To one of woman born.

Macduff: Despair thy charm;
> And let the angel whom thou still hast served   20
> Tell thee, Macduff was from his mother's womb
> Untimely ripp'd.

Macbeth: Accursed be that tongue that tells me so,
> For it hath cow'd my better part of man!
> And be these juggling fiends no more believed,   25
> That palter with us in a double sense;
> That keep the word of promise to our ear,
> And break it to our hope. I'll not fight with thee.

Macduff: Then yield thee, coward,
> And live to be the show and gaze o' the time: 30
> We'll have thee, as our rarer monsters are,
> Painted on a pole, and underwrit,
> 'Here may you see the tyrant.'

Macbeth: I will not yield,
> To kiss the ground before young Malcolm's feet,   35
> And to be baited with the rabble's curse.
> Though Birnam wood be come to Dunsinane,
> And thou opposed, being of no woman born,
> Yet I will try the last. Before my body
> I throw my warlike shield. Lay on, Macduff,   40
> And damn'd be him that first cries, 'Hold, enough!'
>> *Exeunt, fighting. Alarums*
> *Retreat. Flourish. Enter, with drum and colours, Malcolm, Siward,*
> *Ross, the other Thanes, and Soldiers*

Malcolm: I would the friends we miss were safe arrived.

Siward: Some must go off: and yet, by these I see,   45
> So great a day as this is cheaply bought.

Malcolm: Macduff is missing, and your noble son.

Ross: Your son, my lord, has paid a soldier's debt:
> He only lived but till he was a man;
> The which no sooner had his prowess confirm'd   50
> In the unshrinking station where he fought,
> But like a man he died.

Siward: Then he is dead?

Ross: Ay, and brought off the field: your cause of sorrow
> Must not be measured by his worth, for then   55
> It hath no end.

Siward: Had he his hurts before?

Ross: Ay, on the front.

Siward: Why then, God's soldier be he!
> Had I as many sons as I have hairs,   60
> I would not wish them to a fairer death:
> And so, his knell is knoll'd.

Malcolm: He's worth more sorrow,
> And that I'll spend for him.

Siward: He's worth no more   65
> They say he parted well, and paid his score:
> And so, God be with him! Here comes newer
>> comfort.
> *Re-enter Macduff, with Macbeth's head*

Macduff: Hail, king! for so thou art: behold, where stands
> The usurper's cursed head: the time is free: 70
> I see thee compass'd with thy kingdom's pearl,
> That speak my salutation in their minds;
> Whose voices I desire aloud with mine:
> Hail, King of Scotland!

All: Hail, King of Scotland!   75
          Flourish
Malcolm: We shall not spend a large expense of time
              Before we reckon with your several loves,
              And make us even with you. My thanes and kinsmen,
              Henceforth be earls, the first that ever Scotland   80
              In such an honour named. What's more to do,
              Which would be planted newly with the time,
              As calling home our exiled friends abroad
              That fled the snares of watchful tyranny;
              Producing forth the cruel ministers   85
              Of this dead butcher and his fiend-like queen,
              Who, as 'tis thought, by self and violent hands
              Took off her life; this, and what needful else
              That calls upon us, by the grace of Grace,
              We will perform in measure, time and place: 90
              So, thanks to all at once and to each one,
              Whom we invite to see us crown'd at Scone.

Flourish. Exeunt

CRITICAL THINKING QUESTIONS

1. When Macbeth murders Duncan, he murders his king, his kinsman, and his guest. What is Macbeth's motive for the murder of Duncan? Do you know anyone who has made unethical decisions to get ahead? How common is this practice (maybe not murder, but other crimes)? What are the consequences?

2. One powerful scene in this **tragedy** is Macduff's reaction to his family's murder. We meet Lady Macduff and one of her sons in the previous scene, and then we witness Macduff's grief when learning that he lost "all [his] pretty chickens and their dam/At one fell swoop." Malcolm advises him to "dispute it like a man," but Macduff must first "feel it like a man." These passages about masculinity make an interesting contrast to Lady Macbeth's soliloquy when she asks that spirits "unsex" her to prepare her to commit murder. How does the play define masculinity and femininity?

3. What crime does Lady Macbeth commit? What is her punishment; how does she suffer? Does she deserve her fate? Why or why not? What is the implied claim about the effects of guilt on our consciousness? Give evidence from the play for support.

WRITING TOPIC

Macbeth begins the play as a military hero and nobleman, a favorite of the king. He ends up corrupted by his ambition. Is ambition ever a positive trait? How does ambition motivate successful people? How does it corrupt them? Can you think of current leaders or prominent figures who might have been corrupted by ambition or used it to drive them to succeed?

NONFICTION

George Orwell

A Hanging (1931)

It was in Burma, a sodden morning of the rains. A sickly light, like yellow tinfoil, was slanting over the high walls into the jail yard. We were waiting outside the condemned cells, a row of sheds fronted with double bars, like small animal cages. Each cell measured about ten feet by ten and was quite bare within except for a plank bed and a pot for drinking water. In some of them brown, silent men were squatting at the inner bars, with their blankets draped round them. These were the condemned men, due to be hanged within the next week or two.

One prisoner had been brought out of his cell. He was a Hindu, a puny wisp of a man, with a shaven head and vague liquid eyes. He had a thick, sprouting mustache, absurdly too big for his body, rather like the mustache of a comic man on the films. Six tall Indian warders were guarding him and getting him ready for the gallows. Two of them stood by with rifles and fixed bayonets, while the others handcuffed him, passed a chain through his handcuffs and fixed it to their belts, and lashed his arms tight to his sides. They crowded very close about him, with their hands always on him in a careful, caressing grip, as though all the while feeling him to make sure he was there. It was like men handling a fish which is still alive and may jump back into the water. But he stood quite unresisting, yielding his arms limply to the ropes, as though he hardly noticed what was happening.

Eight o'clock struck and a bugle call, desolately thin in the wet air, floated from the distant barracks. The superintendent of the jail, who was standing apart from the rest of us, moodily prodding the gravel with his stick, raised his head at the sound. He was an army doctor, with a gray toothbrush mustache and a gruff voice. "For God's sake, hurry up, Francis," he said irritably. "The man ought to have been dead by this time. Aren't you ready yet?"

Francis, the head jailer, a fat Dravidian in a white drill suit and gold spectacles, waved his black hand. "Yes sir, yes sir," he bubbled. "All iss satisfactorily prepared. The hangman iss waiting. We shall proceed."

"Well, quick march, then. The prisoners can't get their breakfast till this job's over." 5

We set out for the gallows. Two warders marched on either side of the prisoner, with their rifles at the slope; two others marched close against him, gripping him by arm and shoulder, as though at once pushing and supporting him. The rest of us, magistrates and the like, followed behind. Suddenly, when we had gone ten yards, the procession stopped short without any order or warning. A dreadful thing had happened—a dog, come goodness knows whence, had appeared in the yard. It came bounding among us with a loud volley of barks and leapt round up wagging its whole body, wild with glee at finding so many human beings together. It was a large woolly dog, half Airedale, half pariah. For a moment it pranced around us, and then, before anyone could stop it, it had made a dash for the prisoner, and jumping up tried to lick his face. Everybody stood aghast, too taken aback even to grab the dog.

"Who let that bloody brute in here?" said the superintendent angrily. "Catch it, someone!"

A warder detached from the escort charged clumsily after the dog, but it danced and gamboled just out of his reach, taking everything as part of the game. A young Eurasian jailer picked up a handful of gravel and tried to stone the dog away, but it dodged the stones and came after us again. Its yaps echoed from the jail walls. The prisoner, in the grasp of the two warders, looked on incuriously, as though this was another formality of the hanging. It was several minutes before someone managed to catch the dog. Then we put my handkerchief through its collar and moved off once more, with the dog still straining and whimpering.

It was about forty yards to the gallows. I watched the bare brown back of the prisoner marching in front of me. He walked clumsily with his bound arms, but quite steadily, with that bobbing gait of the Indian who never straightens his knees. At each step his muscles slid neatly into place, the lock of hair on his scalp danced up and down, his feet printed themselves on the wet gravel. And once, in spite of the men who gripped him by each shoulder, he stepped lightly aside to avoid a puddle on the path.

It is curious; but till that moment I had never realized what it means to destroy a healthy, conscious man. When I saw the prisoner step aside to avoid the puddle, I saw the mystery, the unspeakable wrongness, of cutting a life short when it is in full tide. This man was not dying, he was alive just as we are alive. All the organs of his body were working—bowels digesting food, skin renewing itself, nails growing, tissues forming—all toiling away in solemn foolery. His nails would still be growing when he stood on the drop, when he was falling through the air with a tenth-of-a-second to live. His eyes saw the yellow gravel and the gray walls, and his brain still remembered, foresaw, reasoned—even about puddles. He and we were a party of men walking together, seeing, hearing, feeling, understanding the same world; and in two minutes, with a sudden snap, one of us would be gone—one mind less, one world less. 10

The gallows stood in a small yard, separate from the main grounds of the prison, and overgrown with tall prickly weeds. It was a brick erection like three sides of a shed, with planking on top, and above that two beams and a crossbar with the rope dangling. The hangman, a gray-haired convict in the white uniform of the prison, was waiting beside his machine. He greeted us with a servile crouch as we entered. At a word from Francis the two warders, gripping the prisoner more closely than ever, half led, half pushed him to the gallows and helped him clumsily up the ladder. Then the hangman climbed up and fixed the rope round the prisoner's neck.

We stood waiting, five yards away. The warders had formed in a rough circle round the gallows. And then, when the noose was fixed, the prisoner began crying out to his god. It was a high, reiterated cry of "Ram! Ram! Ram! Ram!" not urgent and fearful like a prayer or cry for help, but steady, rhythmical, almost like the tolling of a bell. The dog answered the sound with a whine. The hangman, still standing on the gallows, produced a small cotton bag like a flour bag and drew it down over the prisoner's face. But the sound, muffled by the cloth, still persisted, over and over again: "Ram! Ram! Ram! Ram! Ram!"

The hangman climbed down and stood ready, holding the lever. Minutes seemed to pass. The steady, muffled crying from the prisoner went on and on, "Ram! Ram! Ram!" never faltering for an instant. The superintendent, his head on his chest, was slowly poking the ground with his stick; perhaps he was counting the cries, allowing the prisoner a fixed number—fifty, perhaps, or a hundred. Everyone had changed color. The Indians had gone gray like bad coffee, and one or two of the bayonets were wavering. We looked at the lashed, hooded man on the drop, and listened to his cries—each cry another second of life; the same thought was in all our minds; oh, kill him quickly, get it over, stop that abominable noise!

Suddenly the superintendent made up his mind. Throwing up his head he made a swift motion with his stick. "Chalo!" he shouted almost fiercely.

15   There was a clanking noise, and then dead silence. The prisoner had vanished, and the rope was twisting on itself. I let go of the dog, and it galloped immediately to the back of the gallows; but when it got there it stopped short, barked, and then retreated into a corner of the yard, where it stood among the weeds, looking timorously out at us. We went round the gallows to inspect the prisoner's body. He was dangling with his toes pointed straight downwards, very slowly revolving, as dead as a stone.

The superintendent reached out with his stick and poked the bare brown body; it oscillated slightly. "*He's* all right," said the superintendent. He backed out from under the gallows, and blew out a deep breath. The moody look had gone out of his face quite suddenly. He glanced at his wristwatch. "Eight minutes past eight. Well, that's all for this morning, thank God."

The warders unfixed bayonets and marched away. The dog, sobered and conscious of having misbehaved itself, slipped after them. We walked out of the gallows yard, past the condemned cells with their waiting prisoners, into the big central yard of the prison. The convicts, under the command of warders armed with lathis,[1] were already receiving their breakfast. They squatted in long rows, each man holding a tin pannikin,[2] while two warders with buckets marched around ladling out rice; it seemed quite a homely, jolly scene, after the hanging. An enormous relief had come upon us now that the job was done. One felt an impulse to sing, to break into a run, to snigger. All at once everyone began chattering gaily.

The Eurasian boy walking beside me nodded towards the way we had come, with a knowing smile: "Do you know sir, our friend (he meant the dead man) when he heard his appeal had been dismissed, he pissed on the floor of his cell. From fright. Kindly take one of my cigarettes, sir. Do you not admire my new silver case, sir? From the boxwallah,[3] two rupees eight annas. Classy European style."

Several people laughed—at what, nobody seemed certain.

Francis was walking by the superintendent, talking garrulously: "Well, sir, all 20
has passed off with the utmost satisfactoriness. It was all finished—flick! Like that. It iss not always so—oah, no! I have known cases where the doctor wass obliged to go beneath the gallows and pull the prisoner's legs to ensure decease. Most disagreeable!"

"Wriggling about, eh? That's bad," said the superintendent.

"Ach, sir, it iss worse when they become refractory! One man, I recall, clung to the bars of hiss cage when we went to take him out. You will scarcely credit, sir, that it took six warders to dislodge him, three pulling at each leg. We reasoned with him, 'My dear fellow,' we said, 'think of all the pain and trouble you are causing to us!' But no, he would not listen! Ach, he wass very troublesome!"

I found that I was laughing quite loudly. Everyone was laughing. Even the superintendent grinned in a tolerant way. "You'd better all come out and have a drink," he said quite genially. "I've got a bottle of whiskey in the car. We could do with it."

We went through the big double gates of the prison into the road. "Pulling at his legs!" exclaimed a Burmese magistrate suddenly, and burst into a loud chuckling. We all began laughing again. At that moment Francis' anecdote seemed extraordinarily funny. We all had a drink together, native and European alike, quite amicably. The dead man was a hundred yards away.

CRITICAL THINKING QUESTIONS

1. The powers of peace and order have structured this execution perfectly, and all the details seem so right, so correct. What small event allows Orwell to see past all the trappings of justice being carried out?

2. Why does everyone laugh at the end? Surely an execution cannot be humorous.

---

[1]**lathis** police club
[2]**pannikin** metal container
[3]**boxwallah** vendors who sold from boxes on the streets of India

WRITING TOPIC

Orwell cannot disconnect himself from the shared humanity between the condemned and himself: "It is curious; but till that moment I had never realized what it means to destroy a healthy, conscious man. When I saw the prisoner step aside to avoid the puddle, I saw the mystery, the unspeakable wrongness, of cutting a life short when it is in full tide. This man was not dying, he was alive just as we are alive." In your opinion, how are people able to separate themselves from their job duties when work duties clash with their own personal value systems? Have you ever been in a circumstance on a job that made you uncomfortable? If so, how did you handle the situation?

Edward Abbey

Eco-Defense (1985)

If a stranger batters your door down with an axe, threatens your family and yourself with deadly weapons, and proceeds to loot your home of whatever he wants, he is committing what is universally recognized—by law and in common morality—as a crime. In such a situation the householder has both the right and the obligation to defend himself, his family, and his property by whatever means are necessary. This right and this obligation is universally recognized, justified, and praised by all civilized human communities. Self-defense against attack is one of the basic laws not only of human society but of life itself, not only of human life but of all life.

The American wilderness, what little remains, is now undergoing exactly such an assault. With bulldozer, earth mover, chainsaw, and dynamite the international timber, mining, and beef industries are invading our public lands—property of all Americans—bashing their way into our forests, mountains, and rangelands and looting them for everything they can get away with. This for the sake of short-term profits in the corporate sector and multimillion-dollar annual salaries for the three-piece-suited gangsters (MBA—Harvard, Yale, University of Tokyo, et alia) who control and manage these bandit enterprises. Cheered on, naturally, by *Time, Newsweek*, and *The Wall Street Journal*, actively encouraged, inevitably, by those jellyfish government agencies that are supposed to *protect* the public lands, and as always aided and abetted in every way possible by the compliant politicians of our Western states, such as Babbitt, DeConcini, Goldwater, McCain, Hatch, Garn, Simms, Hansen, Andrus, Wallop, Domenici and Co. Inc.—who would sell the graves of their mothers if there's a quick buck in the deal, over or under the table, what do they care.

Representative government in the United States has broken down. Our legislators do not represent the public, the voters, or even those who voted for them but rather the commercial industrial interests that finance their political campaigns and control the organs of communication—the TV, the newspapers, the billboards, the radio. Politics is a game for the rich only. Representative government in the USA represents money, not people, and therefore has forfeited our allegiance and moral support. We owe it nothing but the taxation it extorts from us under threats of seizure of property, imprisonment, or in some cases already, when resisted, a violent death by gunfire.

Such is the nature and structure of the industrial megamachine (in Lewis Mumford's term) which is now attacking the American wilderness. That wilderness is our ancestral home, the primordial homeland of all living creatures including the human, and the present final dwelling place of such noble beings as the grizzly bear, the mountain lion, the eagle and the condor, the moose and the elk and the pronghorn antelope, the redwood tree, the yellow pine, the bristlecone pine, and yes, why not say it?—the streams, waterfalls, rivers, the very bedrock itself of our hills, canyons, deserts, mountains. For many of us, perhaps for most of us, the wilderness is more our home than the little stucco boxes, wallboard apartments, plywood trailer-houses, and cinderblock condominiums in which the majority are now confined by the poverty of an overcrowded industrial culture.

And if the wilderness is our true home, and if it is threatened with invasion, 5 pillage, and destruction—as it certainly is—then we have the right to defend that home, as we would our private quarters, by whatever means are necessary. (An Englishman's home is his castle; the American's home is his favorite forest, river, fishing stream, her favorite mountain or desert canyon, his favorite swamp or woods or lake.) We have the right to resist and we have the obligation; not to defend that which we love would be dishonorable. The majority of the American people have demonstrated on every possible occasion that they support the ideal of wilderness preservation; even our politicians are forced by popular opinion to *pretend* to support the idea; as they have learned, a vote against wilderness is a vote against their own reelection. We are justified then in defending our homes—our private home and our public home—not only by common law and common morality but also by common belief. We are the majority; they—the powerful—are in the minority.

How best defend our homes? Well, that is a matter of the strategy, tactics, and technique which eco-defense is all about.

What is eco-defense? Eco-defense means fighting back. Eco-defense means sabotage. Eco-defense is risky but sporting; unauthorized but fun; illegal but ethically imperative. Next time you enter a public forest scheduled for chainsaw massacre by some timber corporation and its flunkies in the US Forest Service, carry a hammer and a few pounds of 60-penny nails in your creel, saddlebag, game bag, backpack, or picnic basket. Spike those trees; you won't hurt them;

they'll be grateful for the protection; and you may save the forest. Loggers hate nails. My Aunt Emma back in West Virginia has been enjoying this pleasant exercise for years. She swears by it. It's good for the trees, it's good for the woods, and it's good for the human soul. Spread the word.

CRITICAL THINKING QUESTIONS

1. Abbey sets up an enemy who threatens the environment: "three-piece-suited gangsters," he calls them. Compare his use of this enemy with the enemy Montresor creates in his **dramatic monologue**, "The Cask of Amontillado," on page 243.

2. Abbey closes his essay with the example of "My Aunt Emma." What do you think is his purpose in closing with this personal example, and how does it affect your overall viewpoint on Abbey's argument?

WRITING TOPIC

Abbey openly calls for spiking trees, a practice that can lead to serious bodily injury among loggers and is illegal. He asks you, the reader, to willfully violate the law in an act of civil disobedience. Similarly, a number of environmental organizations today practice and sometimes advocate civil disobedience. For example, Greenpeace boats illegally disrupt whaling and fishing activities, PETA members block hunters, Sea Shepherd followers sometimes intervene in the legal capture of dolphins, and the Animal Liberation Front has burned veterinary labs. Is there an environmental cause for which you would consider breaking the law? Argue with evidence that this particular cause would or would not justify civil disobedience.

Francis Bacon

Of Revenge (1597)

Revenge is a kind of wild justice, which the more man's nature runs to, the more ought law to weed it out. For as for the first wrong, it doth but offend the law, but the revenge of that wrong putteth the law out of office. Certainly in taking revenge, a man is but even with his enemy, but in passing it over, he is superior, for it is a prince's part to pardon. And Solomon, I am sure, saith, "It is the glory of a man to pass by an offense." That which is past is gone and irrevocable, and wise men have enough to do with things present and to come; therefore they do but trifle with themselves that labor in past matters. There is no man doth a wrong for the wrong's sake, but thereby to purchase himself profit, or pleasure, or honor, or the like. Therefore why should I be angry with a man for loving himself better than me? And if any man should do wrong merely out of ill nature, why, yet it is but like the thorn or briar, which prick and scratch because they can do no other. The most tolerable sort of revenge is for those wrongs which there is no law to remedy, but then let a man take heed the revenge be such as there is no law to punish; else a man's enemy is still beforehand, and it is two for one. Some, when they take revenge, are desirous the party should know whence it cometh. This the more generous. For the delight seemeth to not be so much in doing the hurt as in making the party repent. But base and crafty cowards are like the arrow that flieth in the dark. Cosmus, duke of Florence, had a desperate saying against perfidious or neglecting friends, as if those wrongs were unpardonable: "You shall read," saith he, "that we are commanded to forgive our enemies; but you never read that we are commanded to forgive our friends." But yet the spirit of Job was in better tune: "Shall we," saith he, "take good at God's hands, and not be content to take evil also?" And so of friends in a proportion. This is certain, that a man that studieth revenge keeps his own wounds green, which otherwise would heal and do well. Public revenges are for the most part fortunate, as that for the death of Caesar, for the death of Pertinax, for the death of Henry the Third of France, and many more. But in private revenges it is not so. Nay rather, vindictive persons live the life of witches, who, as they are mischievous, so end they unfortunate.

CRITICAL THINKING QUESTIONS

1. What does Bacon believe of the character of the person who does not seek revenge?

2. Bacon says someone who does seek revenge is nobler if he or she lets his or her identity be known to the person against whom they have taken vengeance. Would you agree with him? Why?

WRITING TOPIC

Bacon tells us, "Vindictive persons live the life of witches, who, as they are mischievous, so end they unfortunate." Furthermore, he claims, "This is certain, that a man that studieth revenge keeps his own wounds green, which otherwise would heal and do well." Bacon counsels us, "That which is past is gone and irrevocable, and wise men have enough to do with things present and to come; therefore they do but trifle with themselves that labor in past matters." No doubt Bacon takes the high ground when it comes to vengeance on his fellow man. Why do you think that so many people probably agree in theory with Bacon's ideals, but yet in reality do not practice them? What is it about human nature that drives people to desire to "get even"? In what ways does our culture encourage the revenge mentality?

Rhett Morgan

Scene of the Crime: House's History Stuns New Owner (2009)

A Navy veteran who recently had served three years in Europe, Valinda Martinez was thrilled to be putting down roots for herself and her two small children.

Closing on a home two weeks ago, she began moving in during a rare spring snowstorm.

"The yard is huge, and the house is big," she said. "It just looked like the perfect house."

Until a few days later, when a technician dropped a bomb.

5   "The cable guy walks in and he's like, 'Wow I'm not trying to freak you out, but this is that house where those murders were.'"

Horrified, Martinez did some Internet research, which confirmed the unfathomable. The home she had just purchased in the El Rio Vista addition of the city was the same residence in which three people, including a 10-year-old girl, were shot to death in August 2005. The last of the three men convicted of the murders was sentenced a year ago.

Neither the sellers, Joe and Tonya Morgan, nor their real estate agent, Marilyn Hardacre of Collinsville, had disclosed this information to Martinez or her representative, she said.

"This is the first house I've ever bought on my own," said Martinez, 27, who spent about eight years in the Navy. "I'm a single woman, just out of the military. I'm trying to make something. I feel so upset that I got so wronged."

Although Martinez was home on leave when the triple homicide occurred, she was soon shipped back to Spain, where she was a hospital corpsman from October 2004 to December 2007. Her mother called her about a week later to tell her police arrested three men in connection with the crime.

10   Martinez was too busy with her service abroad to give much thought to happenings on the mainland. When she began searching for a house, she did earnest homework, Googling the area for sex predators, she said.

But Martinez never envisioned it would turn out like this.

"It's very sad when you can't feel comfortable in something," she said. "It took a long time for me to be able to do this."

The law sides with the sellers.

The state's Residential Property Condition Disclosure Act requires sellers to answer questions about a dwelling's history. That includes environmental inquiries, such as whether the property has been exposed to lead-based paint, asbestos or the manufacture of methamphetamine.

Martinez's purchase falls under "psychologically impacted" real estate. Accord-   15
ing to the Oklahoma Real Estate License Code and Rules, real estate that was or is suspected to have been the site of a "suicide, homicide or other felony is not a material fact that must be disclosed in a real estate action."

A home buyer has some relief—to a point.

In the process of making a "bona fide" offer, the purchaser can request such history from the owner, statutes indicate. But the owner isn't legally obligated to provide those details, nor is the agent able to volunteer that information without the owner's consent.

Hardacre referred questions about the sale to Terrie Foster, team leader/ general manager of Keller Williams Realty in Owasso.

"I totally understand the question you are asking because you're saying, 'Don't we ever feel?'" Foster said, cutting off the thought. "Well, of course we do. But by law, if we did, then we're held liable by our seller if they didn't want it disclosed.

"If the buyer asks and the seller chooses not to (answer), then the buyer's   20
remedy is to say, 'OK, fine. I don't feel comfortable with that. I'm out of here.' And they get their money back."

Anne Woody is executive director of the Oklahoma Real Estate Commission.

"If a licensee was to call us for guidance, we would say they would have to comply with the law as is written," she said. Woody said that if a seller refuses to disclose requested information, "then the purchaser could assume that there's something there."

None of this is any consolation to Martinez, who said she has spent only one night in the house. For the time being, she is sleeping on the couch at her parents'.

"Right now I'm just trying to look at options," said Martinez, adding that she is unsure whether to stay put or rent out the property. "I'm grasping at straws."

The Morgans in 2006 purchased the home that Martinez bought, Tulsa   25
County land records show. Efforts to reach them by phone were unsuccessful.

"I did not want to live in this house," said Martinez, a medical assistant at a local treatment center. "It would be different if they would have disclosed that to us. We could have said, 'You know what? We're going to overcome this—or not.' But she stole that right from us to make that educated decision."

Martinez said her church has offered to bless the house when and if she desires. For now, however, she simply wants to raise awareness about nondisclosure laws she calls "ludicrous."

"They've taken something that should have been the best thing I've ever done on my own, and they've made it something that I can hardly stand," she said. "They followed the law just as underhandedly as they could have. And that was the problem."

CRITICAL THINKING QUESTIONS

1. Do you believe Valinda Martinez would have ever wanted to leave her new home had she never found out about the murders that occurred there? Upon what do you base your opinion? Does your answer influence your feelings about Martinez's claims of being treated unfairly by the sellers of the former crime scene?

2. Should the law be changed nationally to require sellers of homes and dwellings reported to be the sites of murders, suicides, deaths, and rumored hauntings to disclose the information to potential buyers? Why do you feel the way you do on this topic?

WRITING TOPIC

Homes where murders, suicides, criminal operations, and even alleged paranormal activities reportedly occurred are often known in real estate circles as "stigmatized" or "psychologically impacted" properties. As we learned from Rhett Morgan's article, laws vary from state to state as to whether sellers must inform potential buyers of a property's past. Suppose you found a beautiful mansion for sale in a gorgeous neighborhood—and within your budget. Your real estate agent takes you for a tour of the home, and you fall in love. There's no structural damage. The real estate agent will only inform you the seller is "motivated" to get rid of the property because you live in a state where disclosure of criminal activity on a property is not required. Upon doing your own research on the Internet, you find that the home you love is the scene of a multiple homicide three years earlier. Would you be able to take advantage of this unbelievable deal, or would you have a problem buying the house knowing its history?

Courts Today

The 2% Death Penalty: How a Minority of Counties Produce Most Death Cases at Enormous Costs to All (2014)

Contrary to the assumption that the death penalty is widely practiced across the country, it is actually the domain of a small percentage of U.S. counties in a handful of states. The burdens created by this narrow but aggressive use, however, are shifted to the majority of counties that almost never use it.

The disparate and highly clustered use of the death penalty raises serious questions of unequal and arbitrary application of the law. It also forces the jurisdictions that have resisted the death penalty for decades to pay for a costly legal process that is often marred with injustice.

Only 2% of the counties in the U.S. have been responsible for the majority of cases leading to executions since 1976. Likewise, only 2% of the counties are responsible for the majority of today's death row population and recent death sentences. To put it another way, all of the state executions since the death penalty was reinstated stem from cases in just 15% of the counties in the U.S. All of the 3,125 inmates on death row as of January 1, 2013 came from just 20% of the counties.

Each decision to seek the death penalty is made by a single county district attorney, who is answerable only to the voters of that county. Nevertheless, all state taxpayers will have to bear the substantial financial costs of each death penalty case, and some of the costs will even be borne on a national level.

The counties that use the death penalty the most have some of the highest reversal rates and many have been responsible for errors of egregious injustice. As their cases are reversed, more money will be spent on retrials and further appeals. For example:

Maricopa County in Arizona had four times the number of pending death penalty cases as Los Angeles or Houston on a per capita basis. The District Attorney responsible for this aggressive use was recently disbarred for misconduct.

Philadelphia County, with the third largest number of inmates on death row in the country, ranked lowest in the state in paying attorneys representing those inmates.

During the tenure of one district attorney in New Orleans, four death row inmates were exonerated and freed because of prosecutorial misconduct, bringing a stinging rebuke from four Justices of the U.S. Supreme Court.

Some states have recently chosen to opt out of this process altogether, greatly limiting their obligations for its high costs and disrepute. As the death penalty is seen more as the insistent campaign of a few at tremendous cost to the many, more states may follow that course.

CRITICAL THINKING QUESTIONS

1. What is the writer's primary argument concerning the death penalty? What evidence is offered to persuade readers to embrace the writer's point of view?

2. Does the author indicate a stance as to what states should do regarding the death penalty? What does the author indicate would be the appropriate action on the part of state governments?

WRITING TOPIC

The death penalty remains a highly divisive topic. Proponents say that it can deter violent crimes and offer a greater sense of justice to the families of murder victims. Opponents say that one death never justifies another and that the death penalty seems barbaric in a highly evolved society. What do you believe? If you had the power to make a final decision, would you keep the death penalty as an alternative to punish people convicted of capital crimes, or do you believe that all life should be protected, even that of violent criminals who have killed others? Offer some outside research to support your ruling on this controversial topic.

George G. Vest

Eulogy of the Dog[1]

September 23, 1870 (Warrensburg, Missouri)

Gentlemen of the jury. The best friend a man has in the world may turn against him and become his enemy. His son or daughter whom he has reared with loving care may prove ungrateful. Those who are nearest and dearest to us, those whom we trust with our happiness and our good name, may become traitors to their faith. The money that a man has he may lose. It flies away from him perhaps when he needs it most. A man's reputation may be sacrificed in a moment of ill-considered action. The people who are prone to fall on their knees to do us honor when success is with us may be the first to throw the stone of malice when failure settles its cloud upon our heads. The one absolutely unselfish friend that a man can have in this selfish world, the one that never deserts him, the one that never proves ungrateful or treacherous, is the dog.

Gentlemen of the jury, a man's dog stands by him in prosperity and in poverty, in health and in sickness. He will sleep on the cold ground when the wintry winds blow and the snow drives fiercely, if only he can be near his master's side.

---

[1] U.S., Congress, Senate, *Congressional Record*, 101st Cong., 2d sess., pp. S4823–24 (daily edition).

He will kiss the hand that has no food to offer, he will lick the wounds and sores that come in encounter with the roughness of the world. He guards the sleep of his pauper master as if he were a prince.

When all other friends desert, he remains. When riches take wings and reputation falls to pieces, he is as constant in his love as the sun in its journey through the heavens. If fortune drives the master forth an outcast into the world, friendless and homeless, the faithful dog asks no higher privilege than that of accompanying him, to guard him against danger, to fight against his enemies. And when the last scene of all comes, and death takes his master in its embrace and his body is laid in the cold ground, no matter if all other friends pursue their way, there by his graveside will the noble dog be found, his head between his paws and his eyes sad but open, in alert watchfulness, faithful and true, even unto death.

CRITICAL THINKING QUESTIONS

1. Which rhetorical appeal or appeals (*logos*, *ethos*, *pathos*) do you feel are most prevalent in Vest's speech? Offer examples.

2. Vest clearly implies the loyalty of canine companionship far surpasses the loyalty of fellow human beings. Do you agree with his claim? Why or why not?

WRITING TOPIC

Vest's speech is actually the closing argument he presented as an attorney in a famous Missouri court case. Research the details of the case and outcome of the civil suit. Do you feel the jury reached a fair verdict? Was justice served? How would you have voted if you had been on the jury? Why?

CHAPTER ACTIVITIES AND TOPICS FOR WRITING ARGUMENTS

1. People often make assumptions that the guilty pay in some way for their misdeeds. Consider "The Story of an Hour" (page 194) and "The Cask of Amontillado" (page 243). In each story, we are given a brief glimpse into a quick moment of the characters' lives. Do you think the demises of Louise Ballard and Fortunato have to do with past misdeeds on their parts? Did they, in some way, get what they deserved, or were they innocent victims of circumstance? Discuss your ideas within a small group, and look for textual evidence to argue these characters might be facing a judgment day of their own making. To the contrary, explain if you are more comfortable casting Louise and Fortunato in victim roles. Please share your answers with your group and the class.

2. Judging others is human nature. Some of us may practice fighting the urge to be judgmental more than others, but it is a very active battle. What lessons can you argue the characters from "A Good Man Is Hard to Find" (page 231) and "Young Goodman Brown" (page 220) teach readers regarding the dangers of being judgmental?

3. "A Hanging" (page 332) and "An Occurrence at Owl Creek Bridge" (page 187) are two different genres of literature. Orwell's "A Hanging" is a nonfiction essay, whereas Bierce's "An Occurrence at Owl Creek Bridge" is a fictitious short story. However, the two pieces of writing have similar storylines. Besides the methods of execution, what similarities and differences do these pieces of literature share? For example, do you see similarities between the reactions and emotions of the condemned men and the executioners in each story?

GLOBAL PERSPECTIVES RESEARCH/WRITING TOPICS

1. Gun Control Laws

The world over, gun control laws remain a hotly debated topic. While some countries have strict firearms legislation, others take a more lenient stance where guns are concerned. Proponents of gun rights argue that tighter gun restrictions make purchasing guns harder for law-abiding citizens and do little to reduce violent shooting deaths. A recent study indicates that tightened laws by Canadian authorities in 1995 have done little to curb gun violence against women.[1] Research gun laws in several countries including the Unit-

---

[1] McPhedran, Samara, PhD., and Gary Mauser PhD. "Lethal Firearm-Related Violence Against Canadian Women: Did Tightening Gun Laws have an Impact on Women's Health and Safety?" *Violence and victims* 28.5 (2013): 875-83. *ProQuest*. Web. 12 May 2015.

ed States. Which country do you believe has the most practical firearms policies and laws? Why?

2. Capital Punishment

According to Amnesty International, "today, over two-thirds of the world's nations have ended capital punishment in law or practice."[2] However, capital punishment remains a part of the American criminal justice system. A recent survey among law officers in North Carolina found the majority of law enforcement supports the death penalty, while simultaneously acknowledging a flawed system that has convicted and executed innocent people in some cases.[3] Given the slightest possibility of executing an innocent person, do you think America should follow the lead of other countries that are completely abolishing capital punishment? Offer some research statistics to solidify your argument.

COLLABORATION ACTIVITY: CREATING A ROGERIAN ARGUMENT

For this activity, you will work in small teams to research, write, and present a **Rogerian argument** on a contemporary issue that has emerged from your exploration of readings in this chapter. The WRITING TOPICS following many of the selections can help you identify an issue. For a discussion of the Rogerian argument and a suggested organizational approach to the assignment, please see Chapter 5.

Following are guidelines for this collaboration activity:

- Identify an **issue**.
- Divide the research/writing responsibilities as follows:
  - Student one: introduction section
  - Student two: body section, affirmative position
  - Student three: body section, opposing position
  - Student four: conclusion, summation, and middle-ground position

Following are characteristics of effective collaboration. Each team member should:

- Contribute by collecting information related to the issue.
- Take responsibility by completing assigned work on time.
- Engage with other team members by listening to and considering other viewpoints.

---

[2]"International Death Penalty." *Amnesty International USA.* Web. 12 May 2015
[3]Hughes, Cyndy Caravelis, and Matthew Robinson. "Perceptions of Law Enforcement Officers on Capital Punishment in the United States." *International Journal of Criminal Justice Sciences* 8.2 (2013): 153–65. *ProQuest.* Web. 12 May 2015

SAMPLE ISSUE: MANDATORY SENTENCING FOR DISTRACTED DRIVERS

As the world embraces technology, distracted drivers grow on America's streets, highways, freeways, and interstates. Some states have made texting and driving illegal and allow law enforcement officers to pull over drivers for that violation alone. Other states allow traffic officers to cite drivers for being distracted, but the law does not allow for officers to stop a driver who is texting as a primary offense—meaning the driver must be breaking another law in order for an officer to be legally justified in making a stop.

Tragically, the cost of distracted driving is more than annoyed motorists who have to honk at the green light to get the driver ahead of them to quit texting and proceed. In some cases, the results of distracted driving are deadly. A 19-year-old California woman struck four teenage pedestrians in April 2014, injuring three of them and killing a 14-year-old boy. When the judge sentenced the woman in April 2015, she received probation and a 30-day jail sentence that would be satisfied with completion of a work program and many hours of community service. She would not have to spend an actual night in jail. The judge cited the young offender's expression of remorse and lack of a criminal record in rendering his decision. Some were relieved by the ruling, while others were outraged she did not receive time in prison.

As distracted driving becomes an ever-growing deadly epidemic, should the courts establish a mandatory prison sentence for those who seriously injure and/or kill others when they are driving while distracted? What are the advantages and disadvantages of such mandatory sentences? Is it a deterrent that could save lives?

ARGUING THEMES FROM LITERATURE

1. In Nathaniel Hawthorne's "Young Goodman Brown," identify a few of the author's many uses of **symbolism**. What ideals or institutions do you feel Hawthorne calls to task? Please explain fully.

2. In "The Choice" by Edith Wharton, are you able to look back in the text and identify language in that passage that **foreshadows** tragedy? Please select several examples you feel hint at an unhappy ending. Analyze the symbolic nature of the language that hints that tragedy looms before the evening ends.

3. Do you feel Kate Chopin's "The Story of an Hour" is a commentary on feminism for the time period in which it was written? Considering Louise's strong reaction to being "free," what do you think this says about the expected gender norms of the time period? Research gender roles of the mid-to-late 1800s. When examining the story, can you make an argument that Louise might have been a victim of society and the time period in which she lived? If so, why would Chopin have killed her in the story? Please fully explore your thoughts.

CHAPTER 8

Family and Identity

The American family dynamic of the twenty-first century is fluid and evolving. Hollywood and traditional values offer us a typical love story that develops between a man and woman, followed by marriage, children, economic success, and a happily-ever-after type of ending. Of course, the well-documented reality is that many couples neither live happily together nor ever after. In fact, couples are choosing cohabitation without marriage and, increasingly, without children. Meanwhile, a parent may be pushing the baby in the stroller without a partner or, perhaps, with a partner of the same sex. Some applaud these variations on the family; after all, they argue, a loving family is a healthy one, and neither laws nor social custom should attempt to dictate the bonds of love. Equally passionate are those who decry these variations. They claim that the collapse of the traditional (heterosexual, two-parent) family structure has eroded "family values" and instigated a contagion of social illnesses that threaten the moral fiber of the country. Clearly, no single definition of the family can be agreed upon; even so, most of us do agree upon the primary importance of family in our individual lives and, as adults, aspire to create a family of our own—however different that family may be.

As you read the literature selections in this chapter, some pieces undoubtedly will reinforce your assumptions and ideas about family and identity, while others may provoke you to question assumptions.

When you look to the past and to the future, how do you assess the "state" of the family? And how do your experiences with family shape your identity as an individual? As you read the selections in this chapter, you may ask yourself what story you have to tell and how it "connects [you] to a history" that shapes your identity.

PREWRITING AND DISCUSSION

1. Write about your concept of *family*. Describe specific experiences, observations, or ideas that inform your definition.

2. Describe your role as a member of a family. How is your *identity* defined by your experiences with your family? What personal values do you attribute directly to these experiences?

FICTION

Kate Chopin

The Storm (written 1898, first published 1969)

I

The leaves were so still that even Bibi thought it was going to rain. Bobinôt, who was accustomed to converse on terms of perfect equality with his little son, called the child's attention to certain sombre clouds that were rolling with sinister intention from the west, accompanied by a sullen, threatening roar. They were at Friedheimer's store and decided to remain there till the storm had passed. They sat within the door on two empty kegs. Bibi was four years old and looked very wise.

"Mama'll be' fraid, yes," he suggested with blinking eyes.

"She'll shut the house. Maybe she got Sylvie helpin' her this evening," Bobinôt responded reassuringly.

"No; she ent got Sylvie. Sylvie was helpin' her yistiday," piped Bibi.

5   Bobinôt arose and going across to the counter purchased a can of shrimps, of which Calixta was very fond. Then he returned to his perch on the keg and sat stolidly holding the can of shrimps while the storm burst. It shook the wooden store and seemed to be ripping great furrows in the distant field. Bibi laid his little hand on his father's knee and was not afraid.

II

Calixta, at home, felt no uneasiness for their safety. She sat at a side window sewing furiously on a sewing machine. She was greatly occupied and did not notice the approaching storm. But she felt very warm and often stopped to mop her face on which the perspiration gathered in beads. She unfastened her white sacque at the throat. It began to grow dark, and suddenly realizing the situation she got up hurriedly and went about closing windows and doors.

Out on the small front gallery she had hung Bobinôt's Sunday clothes to air and she hastened out to gather them before the rain fell. As she stepped outside, Alcée Laballière rode in at the gate. She had not seen him very often since her marriage, and never alone. She stood there with Bobinôt's coat in her hands, and the big rain drops began to fall. Alcée rode his horse under the shelter of a side projection where the chickens had huddled and there were plows and a harrow piled up in the corner.

"May I come and wait on your gallery till the storm is over, Calixta?" he asked.

"Come 'long in, M'sieur Alcée."

His voice and her own startled her as if from a trance, and she seized   10 Bobinôt's vest. Alcée, mounting to the porch, grabbed the trousers and snatched Bibi's braided jacket that was about to be carried away by a sudden gust of wind. He expressed an intention to remain outside, but it was soon apparent that he might as well have been out in the open: the water beat in upon the boards in driving sheets, and he went inside, closing the door after him. It was even necessary to put something beneath the door to keep the water out.

"My! what a rain! It's good two years since it rain' like that," exclaimed Calixta as she rolled up a piece of bagging and Alcée helped her to thrust it beneath the crack.

She was a little fuller of figure than five years before when she married; but she had lost nothing of her vivacity. Her blue eyes still retained their melting quality; and her yellow hair, dishevelled by the wind and rain, kinked more stubbornly than ever about her ears and temples.

The rain beat upon the low, shingled roof with a force and clatter that threatened to break an entrance and deluge them there. They were in the dining room—the sitting room—the general utility room. Adjoining was her bed room, with Bibi's couch along side her own. The door stood open, and the room with its white, monumental bed, its closed shutters, looked dim and mysterious.

Alcée flung himself into a rocker and Calixta nervously began to gather up from the floor the lengths of a cotton sheet which she had been sewing.

"If this keeps up, *Dieu sait* if the levees goin' to stan' it!" she exclaimed.   15

"What have you got to do with the levees?"

"I got enough to do! An' there's Bobinôt with Bibi out in that storm—if he only didn' left Friedheimer's!"

"Let us hope, Calixta, that Bobinôt's got sense enough to come in out of a cyclone."

She went and stood at the window with a greatly disturbed look on her face. She wiped the frame that was clouded with moisture. It was stiflingly hot. Alcée got up and joined her at the window, looking over her shoulder. The rain was coming down in sheets obscuring the view of far-off cabins and enveloping the distant wood in a gray mist. The playing of the lighting was incessant. A bolt struck a tall chinaberry tree at the edge of the field. It filled all visible space with a blinding glare and the crash seemed to invade the very boards they stood upon.

Calixta put her hands to her eyes, and with a cry, staggered backward. Alcée's   20 arm encircled her, and for an instant he drew her close and spasmodically to him.

"*Bonté!*" she cried, releasing herself from his encircling arm and retreating from the window, "the house'll go next! If I only knew w'ere Bibi was!" She would not compose herself; she would not be seated. Alcée clasped her shoulders and looked into her face. The contact of her warm, palpitating body when he had unthinkingly drawn her into his arms, had aroused all the old-time infatuation and desire for her flesh.

"Calixta," he said, "don't be frightened. Nothing can happen. The house is too low to be struck, with so many tall trees standing about. There! aren't you going to be quiet? say, aren't you?" He pushed her hair back from her face that was warm and steaming. Her lips were as red and moist as pomegranate seed. Her white neck and a glimpse of her full, firm bosom disturbed him powerfully. As she glanced up at him the fear in her liquid blue eyes had given place to a drowsy gleam that unconsciously betrayed a sensuous desire. He looked down into her eyes and there was nothing for him to do but to gather her lips in a kiss. It reminded him of Assumption.

"Do you remember—in Assumption, Calixta?" he asked in a low voice broken by passion. Oh! she remembered; for in Assumption he had kissed her and kissed and kissed her; until his senses would well nigh fail, and to save her he would resort to a desperate flight. If she was not an immaculate dove in those days, she was still inviolate; a passionate creature whose very defenselessness had made her defense, against which his honor forbade him to prevail. Now— well, now—her lips seemed in a manner free to be tasted, as well as her round, white throat and her whiter breasts.

They did not heed the crashing torrents, and the roar of the elements made her laugh as she lay in his arms. She was a revelation in that dim, mysterious chamber; as white as the couch she lay upon. Her firm, elastic flesh that was knowing for the first time its birthright, was like a creamy lily that the sun invites to contribute its breath and perfume to the undying life of the world.

25   The generous abundance of her passion, without guile or trickery, was like a white flame which penetrated and found response in depths of his own sensuous nature that had never yet been reached.

When he touched her breasts they gave themselves up in quivering ecstasy, inviting his lips. Her mouth was a fountain of delight. And when he possessed her, they seemed to swoon together at the very borderland of life's mystery.

He stayed cushioned upon her, breathless, dazed, enervated, with his heart beating like a hammer upon her. With one hand she clasped his head, her lips lightly touching his forehead. The other hand stroked with a soothing rhythm his muscular shoulders.

The growl of the thunder was distant and passing away. The rain beat softly upon the shingles, inviting them to drowsiness and sleep. But they dared not yield.

The rain was over; and the sun was turning the glistening green world into a palace of gems. Calixta, on the gallery, watched Alcée ride away. He turned and smiled at her with a beaming face; and she lifted her pretty chin in the air and laughed aloud.

III

Bobinôt and Bibi, trudging home, stopped without at the cistern to make them- 30
selves presentable.

"My! Bibi, w'at will yo' mama say! You ought to be ashame'. You oughtn'
put on those good pants. Look at' em! An' that mud on yo' collar! How you got
that mud on yo' collar, Bibi? I never saw such a boy!" Bibi was the picture of
pathetic resignation. Bobinôt was the embodiment of serious solicitude as he
strove to remove from his own person and his son's the signs of their tramp over
heavy roads and through wet fields. He scraped the mud off Bibi's bare legs and
feet with a stick and carefully removed all traces from his heavy brogans. Then,
prepared for the worst—the meeting with an over-scrupulous housewife, they
entered cautiously at the back door.

Calixta was preparing supper. She had set the table and was dripping coffee
at the hearth. She sprang up as they came in.

"Oh! Bobinôt! You back! My! but I was uneasy. W'ere you been during the
rain? An' Bibi? he ain't wet? he ain't hurt?" She had clasped Bibi and was kissing
him effusively. Bobinôt's explanations and apologies which he had been composing all along the way, died on his lips as Calixta felt him to see if he were dry, and
seemed to express nothing but satisfaction at their safe return.

"I brought you some shrimps, Calixta," offered Bobinôt, hauling the can
from his ample side pocket and laying it on the table.

"Shrimps! Oh, Bobinôt! you too good fo' anything!" and she gave him a 35
smacking kiss on the cheek that resounded. "*J'vous réponds*, we'll have a feas' to
night! umph-umph!"

Bobinôt and Bibi began to relax and enjoy themselves, and when the three
seated themselves at table they laughed much and so loud that anyone might
have heard them as far away as Laballière's.

IV

Alcée Laballière wrote to his wife, Clarisse, that night. It was a loving letter, full
of tender solicitude. He told her not to hurry back, but if she and the babies
liked it at Biloxi, to stay a month longer. He was getting on nicely; and though he
missed them, he was willing to bear the separation a while longer—realizing that
their health and pleasure were the first things to be considered.

V

As for Clarisse, she was charmed upon receiving her husband's letter. She and
the babies were doing well. The society was agreeable; many of her old friends
and acquaintances were at the bay. And the first free breath since her marriage
seemed to restore the pleasant liberty of her maiden days. Devoted as she was
to her husband, their intimate conjugal life was something which she was more
than willing to forego for a while.

So the storm passed and everyone was happy.

CRITICAL THINKING QUESTIONS

1. How does Bobinôt's role as a husband shape his self-identity? How does Calixta's role as a wife inform hers?

2. What **claim** about marriage does "The Storm" imply? Point to specific evidence in the story that supports this claim. Are you convinced? Why or why not?

WRITING TOPIC

The closing line asserts, "So the storm passed and everyone was happy." Is this a "happy" ending? What **assumptions** about happiness underlie the narrator's assertion? Do you accept or reject those assumptions? Why?

Lydia Davis

Break It Down (1986)

He's sitting there staring at a piece of paper in front of him. He's trying to break it down. He says:

I'm breaking it all down. The ticket was $600 and then after that there was more for the hotel and food and so on, for just ten days. Say $80 a day, no, more like $100 a day. And we made love, say, once a day on the average. That's $100 a shot. And each time it lasted maybe two or three hours so that would be anywhere from $33 to $50 an hour, which is expensive.

Though of course that wasn't all that went on, because we were together almost all day long. She would keep looking at me and every time she looked at me it was worth something, and she smiled at me and didn't stop talking and singing, something I said, she would sail into it, a snatch, for me, she would be gone from me a little ways but smiling too, and tell me jokes, and I loved it but didn't exactly know what to do about it and just smiled back at her and felt slow next to her, just not quick enough. So she talked and touched me on the shoulder and the arm, she kept touching and stayed close to me. You're with each other all day long and it keeps happening, the touches and smiles, and it adds up, it builds up, and you know where you'll be that night, you're talking and every now and then you think about it, no, you don't think, you just feel it as a kind of destination, what's coming up after you leave wherever you are all evening, and you're happy about it and you're planning it all, not in your head, really, somewhere inside your body, or all through your body, it's all mounting up and coming together so that when you get in bed you can't help it, it's a real performance, it all pours out, but slowly, you go easy until you can't anymore, or you hold back the whole time, you hold back and touch the edges of everything, you edge around until you have to plunge in and finish it off, and when you're finished, you're too weak to stand but after a while you have to go to the bathroom and you stand, your legs are trembling, you hold on to the door frames, there's a little light coming in through the window, you can see your way in and out, but you can't really see the bed.

So it's not really $100 a shot because it goes on all day, from the start when you wake up and feel her body next to you, and you don't miss a thing, not a thing of what's next to you, her arm, her leg, her shoulder, her face, that good skin, I have felt other good skin, but this skin is just the edge of something else, and you're going to start going, and no matter how much you crawl all over each other it won't be enough, and when your hunger dies down a little then you think how much you love her and that starts you off again, and her face, you look over at her face and can't believe how you got there and how lucky and it's still all a surprise and it never stops, even after it's over, it never stops being a surprise.

It's more like you have a good sixteen or eighteen hours a day of this going on, even when you're not with her it's going on, it's good to be away because it's going to be so good to go back to her, so it's still here, and you can't go off and look at some old street or some old painting without still feeling it in your body and a few things that happened the day before that don't mean much by themselves or wouldn't mean much if you weren't having this thing together, but you can't forget and it's all inside you all the time, so that's more like, say, sixteen into a hundred would be $6 an hour, which isn't too much.

And then it really keeps going on while you're asleep, though you're probably dreaming about something else, a building, maybe, I kept dreaming, every night, almost, about this building, because I would spend a lot of every morning in this old stone building and when I closed my eyes I would see these cool spaces and have this peace inside me, I would see the bricks of the floor and the stone arches and the space, the emptiness between, like a kind of dark frame around what I could see beyond, a garden, and this space was like stone too because of the coolness of it and the gray shadow, that kind of luminous shade, that was glowing with the light of the sun falling beyond the arches, and there was also the great height of the ceiling, all this was in my mind all the time though I didn't know it until I closed my eyes, I'm asleep and I'm not dreaming about her but she's lying next to me and I wake up enough times in the night to remember she's there, and notice, say, once she was lying on her back but now she's curled around me, I look at her closed eyes, I want to kiss her eyelids, I want to feel that soft skin under my lips, but I don't want to disturb her, I don't want to see her frown as though in her sleep she has forgotten who I am and feels just that something is bothering her and so I just look at her and hold on to it all, these times when I'm watching over her sleep and she's next to me and isn't away from me the way she will be later, I want to stay awake all night just to go

5

on feeling that, but I can't, I fall asleep again, though I'm sleeping lightly, still trying to hold on to it.

But it isn't over when it ends, it goes on after it's all over, she's still inside you like a sweet liquor, you are filled with her, everything about her has kind of bled into you, her smell, her voice, the way her body moves, it's all inside you, at least for a while after, then you begin to lose it, and I'm beginning to lose it, you're afraid of how weak you are, that you can't get her all back into you again and now the whole thing is going out of your body and it's more in your mind than your body, the pictures come to you one by one and you look at them, some of them last longer than others, you were together in a very white clean place, a coffeehouse, having breakfast together, and the place is so white that against it you can see her clearly, her blue eyes, her smile, the colors of her clothes, even the print of the newspaper she's reading when she's not looking up at you, the light brown and red and gold of her hair when she's got her head down reading, the brown coffee, the brown rolls, all against that white table and those white plates and silver urns and silver knives and spoons, and against that quiet of the sleepy people in that room sitting alone at their tables with just some chinking and clattering of spoons and cups in saucers and some hushed voices her voice now and then rising and falling. The pictures come to you and you have to hope they won't lose their life too fast and dry up though you know they will and that you'll also forget some of what happened, because already you're turning up little things that you nearly forgot.

We were in bed and she asked me, Do I seem fat to you? and I was surprised because she didn't seem to worry about herself at all in that way and I guess I was reading into it that she did worry about herself so I answered what I was thinking and said stupidly that she had a very beautiful body, that her body was perfect, and I really meant it as an answer, but she said kind of sharply, That's not what I asked, and so I had to try to answer her again, exactly what she had asked.

And once she lay over against me late in the night and she started talking, her breath in my ear, and she just went on and on, and talked faster and faster, she couldn't stop, and I loved it, I just felt that all that life in her was running into me too, I had so little life in me, her life, her fire, was coming into me, in that hot breath in my ear, and I just wanted her to go on talking forever right there next to me, and I would go on living, like that, I would be able to go on living, but without her I don't know.

10   Then you forget some of it all, maybe most of it all, almost all of it, in the end, and you work hard at remembering everything now so you won't ever forget, but you can kill it too even by thinking about it too much, though you can't help thinking about it nearly all the time.

And then when the pictures start to go you start asking some questions, just little questions, that sit in your mind without any answers, like why did she have the light on when you came in to bed one night, but it was off the next, but she had it on the night after that and she had it off the last night, why, and other questions, little questions that nag at you like that.

And finally the pictures go and these dry little questions just sit there without any answers and you're left with this large heavy pain in you that you try to numb by reading, or you try to ease it by getting out into public places where there will be people around you, but no matter how good you are at pushing that pain away, just when you think you're going to be all right for a while, that you're safe, you're kind of holding it off with all your strength and you're staying in some little bare numb spot of ground, then suddenly it will all come back, you'll hear a noise, maybe it's a cat crying or a baby, or something else like her cry, you hear it and make that connection in a part of you you have no control over and the pain comes back so hard that you're afraid, afraid of how you're falling back into it again and you wonder, no, you're terrified to ask how you're ever going to climb out of it.

And so it's not only every hour of the day while it's happening, but it's really for hours and hours every day after that, for weeks, though less and less, so that you could work out the ratio if you wanted, maybe after six weeks you're only thinking about it an hour or so in the day altogether, a few minutes here and there spread over, or a few minutes here and there and half an hour before you go to sleep, or sometimes it all comes back and you stay awake with it half the night.

So when you add up all that, you've only spent maybe $3 an hour on it.

If you have to figure in the bad times too, I don't know. There weren't any 15 bad times with her, though maybe there was one bad time, when I told her I loved her. I couldn't help it, this was the first time this had happened with her, now I was half falling in love with her or maybe completely if she had let me but she couldn't or I couldn't completely because it was all going to be so short and other things too, and so I told her, and didn't know of any way to tell her first that she didn't have to feel this was a burden, the fact that I loved her, or that she didn't have to feel the same about me, or say the same back, that it was just that I had to tell her, that's all, because it was bursting inside me, and saying it wouldn't even begin to take care of what I was feeling, really I couldn't say anything of what I was feeling because there was so much, words couldn't handle it, and making love only made it worse because then I wanted words badly but they were no good, no good at all, but I told her anyway, I was lying on top of her and her hands were up by her head and my hands were on hers and our fingers were locked and there was a little light on her face from the window but I couldn't really see her and I was afraid to say it but I had to say it because I wanted her to know, it was the last night, I had to tell her then or I'd never have another chance, I just said, Before you go to sleep, I have to tell you before you go to sleep that I love you, and immediately, right away after, she said, I love you too, and it sounded to me as if she didn't mean it, a little flat, but then it usually sounds a little flat when someone says, I love you too, because they're just saying it back even if they do mean it, and the problem is that I'll never know if she meant it, or maybe someday she'll tell me whether she meant it or not, but there's no way to know now, and I'm sorry I did that, it was a trap I didn't mean to put her in, I can see it was a trap, because if she hadn't said anything at all I know that would have hurt too, as though she were taking something from me and just accepting it and not giving anything back, so she really had to, even just to be kind to me, she had to say it, and I don't really know now if she meant it.

Another bad time, or it wasn't exactly bad, but it wasn't easy either, was when I had to leave, the time was coming, and I was beginning to tremble and feel empty, nothing in the middle of me, nothing inside, and nothing to hold me up on my legs, and then it came, everything was ready, and I had to go, and so it was just a kiss, a quick one, as though we were afraid of what might happen after a kiss, and she was almost wild then, she reached up to a hook by the door and took an old shirt, a green and blue shirt from the hook, and put it in my arms, for me to take away, the soft cloth was full of her smell, and then we stood there close together looking at a piece of paper she had in her hand and I didn't lose any of it, I was holding it tight, that last minute or two, because this was it, we'd come to the end of it, things always change, so this was really it, over.

Maybe it works out all right, maybe you haven't lost for doing it, I don't know, no, really, sometimes when you think of it you feel like a prince really, you feel just like a king, and then other times you're afraid, you're afraid, not all the time but now and then, of what it's going to do to you, and it's hard to know what to do with it now.

Walking away I looked back once and the door was still open, I could see her standing far back in the dark of the room, I could only really see her white face still looking out at me, and her white arms.

I guess you get to a point where you look at that pain as if it were there in front of you three feet away lying in a box, an open box, in a window somewhere. It's hard and cold, like a bar of metal. You just look at it there and say, All right, I'll take it, I'll buy it. That's what it is. Because you know all about it before you even go into this thing. You know the pain is part of the whole thing. And it isn't that you can say afterwards the pleasure was greater than the pain and that's why you would do it again. That has nothing to do with it. You can't measure it, because the pain comes after and it lasts longer. So the question really is, Why doesn't that pain make you say, I won't do it again? When the pain is so bad that you have to say that, but you don't.

20   So I'm just thinking about it, how you can go in with $600, more like $1,000, and how you can come out with an old shirt.

CRITICAL THINKING QUESTIONS

1. By examining the writing style, you will see that the author breaks all the rules for sentence construction, sometimes creating long run-on or fused sentences. How does this style contribute to the author's purpose? *Hint:* First identify what you believe to be the author's purpose.

2. Identify the claim the narrator is making about romantic relationships. Why do you think he uses money as a means of attempting to measure his investment in romance?

3. "Break It Down" is an example of a story told only from the narrator's perspective. Is that perspective accurate? How would the story differ if it were told from the woman's point of view?

WRITING TOPIC

Many young adults have muted the wedding bells. While some would say American culture is becoming more open-minded to couples living together, others decry the trend as a moral decay in society. Is cohabitation a selfish, if not an immoral, choice, a way to enjoy sexual intimacy without the legal constraints and social refinements of marriage? Or is it a reasonable alternative or perhaps prelude to marriage, a way to share domesticity and build the foundations of a lifelong relationship? To examine diverse perspectives, do some firsthand research by interviewing friends and relatives.

Ernest Hemingway

Hills Like White Elephants (1927)

The hills across the valley of the Ebro were long and white. On this side there was no shade and no trees and the station was between two lines of rails in the sun. Close against the side of the station there was the warm shadow of the building and a curtain, made of strings of bamboo beads, hung across the open door into the bar, to keep out flies. The American and the girl with him sat at a table in the shade, outside the building. It was very hot and the express from Barcelona would come in forty minutes. It stopped at this junction for two minutes and went on to Madrid.

"What should we drink?" the girl asked. She had taken off her hat and put it on the table.

"It's pretty hot," the man said.

"Let's drink beer."

"Dos cervezas," the man said into the curtain. 5

"Big ones?" a woman asked from the doorway.

"Yes. Two big ones."

The woman brought two glasses of beer and two felt pads. She put the felt pads and the beer glasses on the table and looked at the man and the girl. The girl was looking off at the line of hills. They were white in the sun and the country was brown and dry.

"They look like white elephants," she said.

"I've never seen one," the man drank his beer.

"No, you wouldn't have."

"I might have," the man said. "Just because you say I wouldn't have doesn't prove anything."

The girl looked at the bead curtain. "They've painted something on it," she said. "What does it say?"

"Anis del Toro. It's a drink."

"Could we try it?"

The man called "Listen" through the curtain. The woman came out from the bar.

"Four reales."

"We want two Anis del Toro."

"With water?"

"Do you want it with water?"

"I don't know," the girl said. "Is it good with water?"

"It's all right."

"You want them with water?" asked the woman.

"Yes, with water."

"It tastes like licorice," the girl said and put the glass down.

"That's the way with everything."

"Yes," said the girl. "Everything tastes of licorice. Especially all the things you've waited so long for, like absinthe."

"Oh, cut it out."

"You started it," the girl said. "I was being amused. I was having a fine time."

"Well, let's try and have a fine time."

"All right. I was trying. I said the mountains looked like white elephants. Wasn't that bright?"

"That was bright."

"I wanted to try this new drink. That's all we do, isn't it—look at things and try new drinks?"

"I guess so."

The girl looked across at the hills.

"They're lovely hills," she said. "They don't really look like white elephants. I just meant the coloring of their skin through the trees."

"Should we have another drink?"

"All right."

The warm wind blew the bead curtain against the table.

"The beer's nice and cool," the man said.

"It's lovely," the girl said.

"It's really an awfully simple operation, Jig," the man said. "It's not really an operation at all."

The girl looked at the ground the table legs rested on.

"I know you wouldn't mind it, Jig. It's really not anything. It's just to let the air in."

The girl did not say anything.   45

"I'll go with you and I'll stay with you all the time. They just let the air in and then it's all perfectly natural."

"Then what will we do afterward?"

"We'll be fine afterward. Just like we were before."

"What makes you think so?"

"That's the only thing that bothers us. It's the only thing that's made us   50
unhappy."

The girl looked at the bead curtain, put her hand out and took hold of two of the strings of beads.

"And you think then we'll be all right and be happy."

"I know we will. You don't have to be afraid. I've known lots of people that have done it."

"So have I," said the girl. "And afterward they were all so happy."

"Well," the man said, "if you don't want to you don't have to. I wouldn't have you do it if you didn't want to. But I know it's perfectly simple."   55

"And you really want to?"

"I think it's the best thing to do. But I don't want you to do it if you don't really want to."

"And if I do it you'll be happy and things will be like they were and you'll love me?"

"I love you now. You know I love you."

"I know. But if I do it, then it will be nice again if I say things are like white elephants, and you'll like it?"   60

"I'll love it. I love it now but I just can't think about it. You know how I get when I worry."

"If I do it you won't ever worry?"

"I won't worry about that because it's perfectly simple."

"Then I'll do it. Because I don't care about me."

"What do you mean?"   65

"I don't care about me."

"Well, I care about you."

"Oh, yes. But I don't care about me. And I'll do it and then everything will be fine."

"I don't want you to do it if you feel that way."

The girl stood up and walked to the end of the station. Across, on the other side, were fields of grain and trees along the banks of the Ebro. Far away, beyond the river, were mountains. The shadow of a cloud moved across the field of grain and she saw the river through the trees.   70

"And we could have all this," she said. "And we could have everything and every day we make it more impossible."

"What did you say?"

"I said we could have everything."

"We can have everything."

75   "No, we can't."

"We can have the whole world."

"No, we can't."

"We can go everywhere."

"No, we can't. It isn't ours any more."

80   "It's ours."

"No, it isn't. And once they take it away, you never get it back."

"But they haven't taken it away."

"We'll wait and see."

"Come on back in the shade," he said. "You mustn't feel that way."

85   "I don't feel any way," the girl said. "I just know things."

"I don't want you to do anything that you don't want to do—"

"Nor that isn't good for me," she said. "I know. Could we have another beer?"

"All right. But you've got to realize—"

"I realize," the girl said. "Can't we maybe stop talking?"

90   They sat down at the table and the girl looked across at the hills on the dry side of the valley and the man looked at her and at the table.

"You've got to realize," he said, "that I don't want you to do it if you don't want to. I'm perfectly willing to go through with it if it means anything to you."

"Doesn't it mean anything to you? We could get along."

"Of course it does. But I don't want anybody but you. I don't want anyone else. And I know it's perfectly simple."

"Yes, you know it's perfectly simple."

95   "It's all right for you to say that, but I do know it."

"Would you do something for me now?"

"I'd do anything for you."

"Would you please please please please please please please stop talking?"

He did not say anything but looked at the bags against the wall of the station. There were labels on them from all the hotels where they had spent nights.

100   "But I don't want you to," he said. "I don't care anything about it."

"I'll scream," the girl said.

The woman came out through the curtains with two glasses of beer and put them down on the damp felt pads. "The train comes in five minutes," she said.

"What did she say?" asked the girl.

"That the train is coming in five minutes."

105   The girl smiled brightly at the woman, to thank her.

"I'd better take the bags over to the other side of the station," the man said. She smiled at him.

"All right. Then come back and we'll finish the beer."

He picked up the two heavy bags and carried them around the station to the other tracks. He looked up the tracks but could not see the train. Coming back, he walked through the barroom, where people waiting for the train were drinking. He drank an Anis at the bar and looked at the people. They were all waiting reasonably for the train. He went out through the bead curtain. She was sitting at the table and smiled at him.

"Do you feel better?" he asked.

"I feel fine," she said. "There's nothing wrong with me. I feel fine." 110

CRITICAL THINKING QUESTIONS

1. Do the "man" and "girl" mean what they say? Does he really want what is best for her as he proclaims? Does she really believe she is just "fine"? Point to specific passages to support your judgment.

2. The man is persistent in his effort to persuade his partner to go through with "it." Write out his reasons. In paragraph 60, the girl says, "But if I do it, then it will be nice again if I say things are like white elephants, and you'll like it?" All in all, do you think the man has convinced her to go through with it?

3. Both the man and the girl regularly use the pronoun "it," for example, as noted in Question 2. For another instance of their use of this pronoun, reread their exchange in paragraphs 70–94. List both characters' uses of "it," and write out the noun or noun phrases to which you think the pronoun refers. Based on this analysis, make an **inference** about the source of the tension in the couple's relationship.

4. At the end of the story, who has control of the situation—the man or the girl? Why? Point to textual evidence to support your conclusion.

WRITING TOPIC

Read Anne Sexton's poem "Cinderella," found later in this chapter. How does the couple in Hemingway's story illustrate, in Sexton's words, "That story"?

O. HENRY

The Gift of the Magi (1905)

One dollar and eighty-seven cents. That was all. And sixty cents of it was in pennies. Pennies saved one and two at a time by bulldozing the grocer and the vegetable man and the butcher until one's cheeks burned with the silent imputation of parsimony that such close dealing implied. Three times Della counted it. One dollar and eighty-seven cents. And the next day would be Christmas.

There was clearly nothing to do but flop down on the shabby little couch and howl. So Della did it. Which instigates the moral reflection that life is made up of sobs, sniffles, and smiles, with sniffles predominating.

While the mistress of the home is gradually subsiding from the first stage to the second, take a look at the home. A furnished flat at $8 per week. It did not exactly beggar description, but it certainly had that word on the lookout for the mendicancy squad.

In the vestibule below was a letter-box into which no letter would go, and an electric button from which no mortal finger could coax a ring. Also appertaining thereunto was a card bearing the name "Mr. James Dillingham Young."

5   The "Dillingham" had been flung to the breeze during a former period of prosperity when its possessor was being paid $30 per week. Now, when the income was shrunk to $20, the letters of "Dillingham" looked blurred, as though they were thinking seriously of contracting to a modest and unassuming D. But whenever Mr. James Dillingham Young came home and reached his flat above he was called "Jim" and greatly hugged by Mrs. James Dillingham Young, already introduced to you as Della. Which is all very good.

Della finished her cry and attended to her cheeks with the powder rag. She stood by the window and looked out dully at a gray cat walking a gray fence in a gray backyard. Tomorrow would be Christmas Day, and she had only $1.87 with which to buy Jim a present. She had been saving every penny she could for months, with this result. Twenty dollars a week doesn't go far. Expenses had been greater than she had calculated. They always are. Only $1.87 to buy a present for Jim. Her Jim. Many a happy hour she had spent planning for something nice for him. Something fine and rare and sterling—something just a little bit near to being worthy of the honor of being owned by Jim.

There was a pier-glass between the windows of the room. Perhaps you have seen a pier-glass in an $8 flat. A very thin and very agile person may, by observing his reflection in a rapid sequence of longitudinal strips, obtain a fairly accurate conception of his looks. Della, being slender, had mastered the art.

Suddenly she whirled from the window and stood before the glass. Her eyes were shining brilliantly, but her face had lost its color within twenty seconds. Rapidly she pulled down her hair and let it fall to its full length.

Now, there were two possessions of the James Dillingham Youngs in which they both took a mighty pride. One was Jim's gold watch that had been his father's and his grandfather's. The other was Della's hair. Had the Queen of Sheba lived in the flat across the airshaft, Della would have let her hair hang out the window some day to dry just to depreciate Her Majesty's jewels and gifts. Had King Solomon been the janitor, with all his treasures piled up in the basement, Jim would have pulled out his watch every time he passed, just to see him pluck at his beard from envy.

So now Della's beautiful hair fell about her rippling and shining like a cascade   10
of brown waters. It reached below her knee and made itself almost a garment for her. And then she did it up again nervously and quickly. Once she faltered for a minute and stood still while a tear or two splashed on the worn red carpet.

On went her old brown jacket; on went her old brown hat. With a whirl of skirts and with the brilliant sparkle still in her eyes, she fluttered out the door and down the stairs to the street.

Where she stopped the sign read: "Mme. Sofronie. Hair Goods of All Kinds." One flight up Della ran, and collected herself, panting. Madame, large, too white, chilly, hardly looked the "Sofronie."

"Will you buy my hair?" asked Della.

"I buy hair," said Madame. "Take yer hat off and let's have a sight at the looks of it."

Down rippled the brown cascade.   15

"Twenty dollars," said Madame, lifting the mass with a practised hand.

"Give it to me quick," said Della.

Oh, and the next two hours tripped by on rosy wings. Forget the hashed metaphor. She was ransacking the stores for Jim's present.

She found it at last. It surely had been made for Jim and no one else. There was no other like it in any of the stores, and she had turned all of them inside out. It was a platinum fob chain simple and chaste in design, properly proclaiming its value by substance alone and not by meretricious ornamentation—as all good things should do. It was even worthy of The Watch. As soon as she saw it she knew that it must be Jim's. It was like him. Quietness and value—the description applied to both. Twenty-one dollars they took from her for it, and she hurried home with the 87 cents. With that chain on his watch Jim might be properly anxious about the time in any company. Grand as the watch was, he sometimes looked at it on the sly on account of the old leather strap that he used in place of a chain.

When Della reached home her intoxication gave way a little to prudence   20
and reason. She got out her curling irons and lighted the gas and went to work repairing the ravages made by generosity added to love. Which is always a tremendous task, dear friends—a mammoth task.

Within forty minutes her head was covered with tiny, close-lying curls that made her look wonderfully like a truant schoolboy. She looked at her reflection in the mirror long, carefully, and critically.

"If Jim doesn't kill me," she said to herself, "before he takes a second look at me, he'll say I look like a Coney Island chorus girl. But what could I do—oh! what could I do with a dollar and eighty-seven cents?"

At 7 o'clock the coffee was made and the frying-pan was on the back of the stove hot and ready to cook the chops.

Jim was never late. Della doubled the fob chain in her hand and sat on the corner of the table near the door that he always entered. Then she heard his step on the stair away down on the first flight, and she turned white for just a moment. She had a habit of saying little silent prayers about the simplest everyday things, and now she whispered: "Please God, make him think I am still pretty."

25 The door opened and Jim stepped in and closed it. He looked thin and very serious. Poor fellow, he was only twenty-two—and to be burdened with a family! He needed a new overcoat and he was without gloves.

Jim stopped inside the door, as immovable as a setter at the scent of quail. His eyes were fixed upon Della, and there was an expression in them that she could not read, and it terrified her. It was not anger, nor surprise, nor disapproval, nor horror, nor any of the sentiments that she had been prepared for. He simply stared at her fixedly with that peculiar expression on his face.

Della wriggled off the table and went for him.

"Jim, darling," she cried, "don't look at me that way. I had my hair cut off and sold it because I couldn't have lived through Christmas without giving you a present. It'll grow out again—you won't mind, will you? I just had to do it. My hair grows awfully fast. Say 'Merry Christmas!' Jim, and let's be happy. You don't know what a nice—what a beautiful, nice gift I've got for you."

"You've cut off your hair?" asked Jim, laboriously, as if he had not arrived at that patent fact yet even after the hardest mental labor.

30 "Cut it off and sold it," said Della. "Don't you like me just as well, anyhow? I'm me without my hair, ain't I?"

Jim looked about the room curiously.

"You say your hair is gone?" he said, with an air almost of idiocy.

"You needn't look for it," said Della. "It's sold, I tell you—sold and gone, too. It's Christmas Eve, boy. Be good to me, for it went for you. Maybe the hairs of my head were numbered," she went on with a sudden serious sweetness, "but nobody could ever count my love for you. Shall I put the chops on, Jim?"

Out of his trance Jim seemed quickly to wake. He enfolded his Della. For ten seconds let us regard with discreet scrutiny some inconsequential object in the other direction. Eight dollars a week or a million a year—what is the difference? A mathematician or a wit would give you the wrong answer. The magi brought valuable gifts, but that was not among them. This dark assertion will be illuminated later on.

35 Jim drew a package from his overcoat pocket and threw it upon the table.

"Don't make any mistake, Dell," he said, "about me. I don't think there's anything in the way of a haircut or a shave or a shampoo that could make me like my girl any less. But if you'll unwrap that package you may see why you had me going a while at first."

White fingers and nimble tore at the string and paper. And then an ecstatic scream of joy; and then, alas! a quick feminine change to hysterical tears and wails, necessitating the immediate employment of all the comforting powers of the lord of the flat.

For there lay The Combs—the set of combs, side and back, that Della had worshipped for long in a Broadway window. Beautiful combs, pure tortoise shell, with jewelled rims—just the shade to wear in the beautiful vanished hair. They were expensive combs, she knew, and her heart had simply craved and yearned over them without the least hope of possession. And now, they were hers, but the tresses that should have adorned the coveted adornments were gone.

But she hugged them to her bosom, and at length she was able to look up with dim eyes and a smile and say: "My hair grows so fast, Jim!"

And then Della leaped up like a little singed cat and cried, "Oh, oh!"   40

Jim had not yet seen his beautiful present. She held it out to him eagerly upon her open palm. The dull precious metal seemed to flash with a reflection of her bright and ardent spirit.

"Isn't it a dandy, Jim? I hunted all over town to find it. You'll have to look at the time a hundred times a day now. Give me your watch. I want to see how it looks on it."

Instead of obeying, Jim tumbled down on the couch and put his hands under the back of his head and smiled.

"Dell," said he, "let's put our Christmas presents away and keep' em a while. They're too nice to use just at present. I sold the watch to get the money to buy your combs. And now suppose you put the chops on."

The magi, as you know, were wise men—wonderfully wise men—who   45 brought gifts to the Babe in the manger. They invented the art of giving Christmas presents. Being wise, their gifts were no doubt wise ones, possibly bearing the privilege of exchange in case of duplication. And here I have lamely related to you the uneventful chronicle of two foolish children in a flat who most unwisely sacrificed for each other the greatest treasures of their house. But in a last word to the wise of these days let it be said that of all who give gifts these two were the wisest. Of all who give and receive gifts, such as they are wisest. Everywhere they are wisest. They are the magi.

CRITICAL THINKING QUESTIONS

I. In the final paragraph, the narrator tells us of Della and Jim "that of all who give gifts these two were the wisest." How do you interpret this? Based on your reading, what type of claim is being argued (fact, policy, or value)? Give reasons for your choice.

2. Though Jim and Della no longer have the items that would make their gifts to each other complete, what do you think each has learned of the other as a result of this experience?

3. Do you believe the couple enjoyed this particular Christmas or felt a sense of loss? Explain.

WRITING TOPIC

Each year, American consumers spend billions on gifts for loved ones, friends, and others close to them. To get good deals, some people camp outside of stores on Thanksgiving to prepare for Black Friday shopping marathons. Some stores, to meet consumer demand and maximize profits, have even shortened their employees' Thanksgiving holiday in order to open earlier. Many of these holiday bargains are charged to credit accounts. Research how much consumer debt accrued over recent Christmas shopping seasons. What are the implications for the American economy, both for businesses and consumers? Why do people feel the pressure much like Della and Jim to purchase gifts to express their feelings toward others? Do you feel our culture values items more so than sentiments?

———————————

Katherine Mansfield

The Garden Party

And after all the weather was ideal. They could not have had a more perfect day for a garden-party if they had ordered it. Windless, warm, the sky without a cloud. Only the blue was veiled with a haze of light gold, as it is sometimes in early summer. The gardener had been up since dawn, mowing the lawns and sweeping them, until the grass and the dark flat rosettes where the daisy plants had been seemed to shine. As for the roses, you could not help feeling they understood that roses are the only flowers that impress people at garden-parties; the only flowers that everybody is certain of knowing. Hundreds, yes, literally hundreds, had come out in a single night; the green bushes bowed down as though they had been visited by archangels.

Breakfast was not yet over before the men came to put up the marquee.

"Where do you want the marquee put, mother?"

"My dear child, it's no use asking me. I'm determined to leave everything to you children this year. Forget I am your mother. Treat me as an honoured guest."

5   But Meg could not possibly go and supervise the men. She had washed her hair before breakfast, and she sat drinking her coffee in a green turban, with a

dark wet curl stamped on each cheek. Jose, the butterfly, always came down in a silk petticoat and a kimono jacket.

"You'll have to go, Laura; you're the artistic one."

Away Laura flew, still holding her piece of bread-and-butter. It's so delicious to have an excuse for eating out of doors, and besides, she loved having to arrange things; she always felt she could do it so much better than anybody else.

Four men in their shirt-sleeves stood grouped together on the garden path. They carried staves covered with rolls of canvas, and they had big tool-bags slung on their backs. They looked impressive. Laura wished now that she had not got the bread-and-butter, but there was nowhere to put it, and she couldn't possibly throw it away. She blushed and tried to look severe and even a little bit short-sighted as she came up to them.

"Good morning," she said, copying her mother's voice. But that sounded so fearfully affected that she was ashamed, and stammered like a little girl, "Oh—er—have you come—is it about the marquee?"

"That's right, miss," said the tallest of the men, a lanky, freckled fellow,   10
and he shifted his tool-bag, knocked back his straw hat and smiled down at her. "That's about it."

His smile was so easy, so friendly that Laura recovered. What nice eyes he had, small, but such a dark blue! And now she looked at the others, they were smiling too. "Cheer up, we won't bite," their smile seemed to say. How very nice workmen were! And what a beautiful morning! She mustn't mention the morning; she must be business-like. The marquee.

"Well, what about the lily-lawn? Would that do?"

And she pointed to the lily-lawn with the hand that didn't hold the bread-and-butter. They turned, they stared in the direction. A little fat chap thrust out his under-lip, and the tall fellow frowned.

"I don't fancy it," said he. "Not conspicuous enough. You see, with a thing like a marquee," and he turned to Laura in his easy way, "you want to put it somewhere where it'll give you a bang slap in the eye, if you follow me."

Laura's upbringing made her wonder for a moment whether it was quite   15
respectful of a workman to talk to her of bangs slap in the eye. But she did quite follow him.

"A corner of the tennis-court," she suggested. "But the band's going to be in one corner."

"H'm, going to have a band, are you?" said another of the workmen. He was pale. He had a haggard look as his dark eyes scanned the tennis-court. What was he thinking?

"Only a very small band," said Laura gently. Perhaps he wouldn't mind so much if the band was quite small. But the tall fellow interrupted.

"Look here, miss, that's the place. Against those trees. Over there. That'll do fine."

Against the karakas. Then the karaka-trees would be hidden. And they were   20
so lovely, with their broad, gleaming leaves, and their clusters of yellow fruit.

They were like trees you imagined growing on a desert island, proud, solitary, lifting their leaves and fruits to the sun in a kind of silent splendour. Must they be hidden by a marquee?

They must. Already the men had shouldered their staves and were making for the place. Only the tall fellow was left. He bent down, pinched a sprig of lavender, put his thumb and forefinger to his nose and snuffed up the smell. When Laura saw that gesture she forgot all about the karakas in her wonder at him caring for things like that—caring for the smell of lavender. How many men that she knew would have done such a thing? Oh, how extraordinarily nice workmen were, she thought. Why couldn't she have workmen for her friends rather than the silly boys she danced with and who came to Sunday night supper? She would get on much better with men like these.

It's all the fault, she decided, as the tall fellow drew something on the back of an envelope, something that was to be looped up or left to hang, of these absurd class distinctions. Well, for her part, she didn't feel them. Not a bit, not an atom… And now there came the chock-chock of wooden hammers. Some one whistled, some one sang out, "Are you right there, matey?" "Matey!" The friendliness of it, the—the—Just to prove how happy she was, just to show the tall fellow how at home she felt, and how she despised stupid conventions, Laura took a big bite of her bread-and-butter as she stared at the little drawing. She felt just like a work-girl.

"Laura, Laura, where are you? Telephone, Laura!" a voice cried from the house.

"Coming!" Away she skimmed, over the lawn, up the path, up the steps, across the veranda, and into the porch. In the hall her father and Laurie were brushing their hats ready to go to the office.

25   "I say, Laura," said Laurie very fast, "you might just give a squiz at my coat before this afternoon. See if it wants pressing."

"I will," said she. Suddenly she couldn't stop herself. She ran at Laurie and gave him a small, quick squeeze. "Oh, I do love parties, don't you?" gasped Laura.

"Ra-ther," said Laurie's warm, boyish voice, and he squeezed his sister too, and gave her a gentle push. "Dash off to the telephone, old girl."

The telephone. "Yes, yes; oh yes. Kitty? Good morning, dear. Come to lunch? Do, dear. Delighted of course. It will only be a very scratch meal—just the sandwich crusts and broken meringue-shells and what's left over. Yes, isn't it a perfect morning? Your white? Oh, I certainly should. One moment—hold the line. Mother's calling." And Laura sat back. "What, mother? Can't hear."

Mrs. Sheridan's voice floated down the stairs. "Tell her to wear that sweet hat she had on last Sunday."

30   "Mother says you're to wear that sweet hat you had on last Sunday. Good. One o'clock. Bye-bye."

Laura put back the receiver, flung her arms over her head, took a deep breath, stretched and let them fall. "Huh," she sighed, and the moment after the sigh she sat up quickly. She was still, listening. All the doors in the house seemed to be open. The house was alive with soft, quick steps and running voices. The green baize door that led to the kitchen regions swung open and shut with a muffled thud. And now there came a long, chuckling absurd sound. It was the heavy piano being moved on its stiff castors. But the air! If you stopped to notice, was the air always like this? Little faint winds were playing chase, in at the tops of the windows, out at the doors. And there were two tiny spots of sun, one on the inkpot, one on a silver photograph frame, playing too. Darling little spots. Especially the one on the inkpot lid. It was quite warm. A warm little silver star. She could have kissed it.

The front door bell pealed, and there sounded the rustle of Sadie's print skirt on the stairs. A man's voice murmured; Sadie answered, careless, "I'm sure I don't know. Wait. I'll ask Mrs Sheridan."

"What is it, Sadie?" Laura came into the hall.

"It's the florist, Miss Laura."

It was, indeed. There, just inside the door, stood a wide, shallow tray full   35
of pots of pink lilies. No other kind. Nothing but lilies—canna lilies, big pink flowers, wide open, radiant, almost frighteningly alive on bright crimson stems.

"O-oh, Sadie!" said Laura, and the sound was like a little moan. She crouched down as if to warm herself at that blaze of lilies; she felt they were in her fingers, on her lips, growing in her breast.

"It's some mistake," she said faintly. "Nobody ever ordered so many. Sadie, go and find mother."

But at that moment Mrs. Sheridan joined them.

"It's quite right," she said calmly. "Yes, I ordered them. Aren't they lovely?" She pressed Laura's arm. "I was passing the shop yesterday, and I saw them in the window. And I suddenly thought for once in my life I shall have enough canna lilies. The garden-party will be a good excuse."

"But I thought you said you didn't mean to interfere," said Laura. Sadie had   40
gone. The florist's man was still outside at his van. She put her arm round her mother's neck and gently, very gently, she bit her mother's ear.

"My darling child, you wouldn't like a logical mother, would you? Don't do that. Here's the man."

He carried more lilies still, another whole tray.

"Bank them up, just inside the door, on both sides of the porch, please," said Mrs. Sheridan. "Don't you agree, Laura?"

"Oh, I do, mother."

In the drawing-room Meg, Jose and good little Hans had at last succeeded   45
in moving the piano.

"Now, if we put this chesterfield against the wall and move everything out of the room except the chairs, don't you think?"

"Quite."

"Hans, move these tables into the smoking-room, and bring a sweeper to take these marks off the carpet and—one moment, Hans—" Jose loved giving orders to the servants, and they loved obeying her. She always made them feel they were taking part in some drama. "Tell mother and Miss Laura to come here at once."

"Very good, Miss Jose."

She turned to Meg. "I want to hear what the piano sounds like, just in case   50
I'm asked to sing this afternoon. Let's try over 'This life is Weary.'"

Pom! Ta-ta-ta Tee-ta! The piano burst out so passionately that Jose's face changed. She clasped her hands. She looked mournfully and enigmatically at her mother and Laura as they came in.

> *"This Life is Wee-ary,*
> *A Tear—a Sigh.*
> *A Love that Chan-ges,*
>
> *This Life is Wee-ary,*
> *A Tear—a Sigh.*
> *A Love that Chan-ges,*
> *And then... Good-bye!"*

55

But at the word "Good-bye," and although the piano sounded more desperate than ever, her face broke into a brilliant, dreadfully unsympathetic smile.

60   "Aren't I in good voice, mummy?" she beamed.

> *"This Life is Wee-ary,*
> *Hope comes to Die.*
> *A Dream—a Wa-kening."*

But now Sadie interrupted them. "What is it, Sadie?"

65   "If you please, m'm, Cook says have you got the flags for the sandwiches?"

"The flags for the sandwiches, Sadie?" echoed Mrs. Sheridan dreamily. And the children knew by her face that she hadn't got them. "Let me see." And she said to Sadie firmly, "Tell Cook I'll let her have them in ten minutes."

Sadie went.

"Now, Laura," said her mother quickly, "come with me into the smoking-room. I've got the names somewhere on the back of an envelope. You'll have to write them out for me. Meg, go upstairs this minute and take that wet thing off your head. Jose, run and finish dressing this instant. Do you hear me, children, or shall I have to tell your father when he comes home to-night? And—and, Jose, pacify Cook if you do go into the kitchen, will you? I'm terrified of her this morning."

The envelope was found at last behind the dining-room clock, though how it had got there Mrs. Sheridan could not imagine.

70   "One of you children must have stolen it out of my bag, because I remember vividly—cream cheese and lemon-curd. Have you done that?"

"Yes."

"Egg and—" Mrs. Sheridan held the envelope away from her. "It looks like mince. It can't be mince, can it?"

"Olive, pet," said Laura, looking over her shoulder.

"Yes, of course, olive. What a horrible combination it sounds. Egg and olive."

75   They were finished at last, and Laura took them off to the kitchen. She found Jose there pacifying the Cook, who did not look at all terrifying.

"I have never seen such exquisite sandwiches," said Jose's rapturous voice. "How many kinds did you say there were, Cook? Fifteen?"

"Fifteen, Miss Jose."

"Well, Cook, I congratulate you."

Cook swept up crusts with the long sandwich knife, and smiled broadly.

"Godber's has come," announced Sadie, issuing out of the pantry. She had   80
seen the man pass the window.

That meant the cream puffs had come. Godber's were famous for their
cream puffs. Nobody ever thought of making them at home.

"Bring them in and put them on the table, my girl," ordered Cook.

Sadie brought them in and went back to the door. Of course Laura and Jose
were far too grown-up to really care about such things. All the same, they couldn't
help agreeing that the puffs looked very attractive. Very. Cook began arranging
them, shaking off the extra icing sugar.

"Don't they carry one back to all one's parties?" said Laura.

"I suppose they do," said practical Jose, who never liked to be carried back.   85
"They look beautifully light and feathery, I must say."

"Have one each, my dears," said Cook in her comfortable voice. "Yer ma
won't know."

Oh, impossible. Fancy cream puffs so soon after breakfast. The very idea
made one shudder. All the same, two minutes later Jose and Laura were licking
their fingers with that absorbed inward look that only comes from whipped cream.

"Let's go into the garden, out by the back way," suggested Laura. "I want to
see how the men are getting on with the marquee. They're such awfully nice men."

But the back door was blocked by Cook, Sadie, Godber's man and Hans.

Something had happened.   90

"Tuk-tuk-tuk," clucked Cook like an agitated hen. Sadie had her hand
clapped to her cheek as though she had toothache. Hans's face was screwed up
in the effort to understand. Only Godber's man seemed to be enjoying himself;
it was his story.

"What's the matter? What's happened?"

"There's been a horrible accident," said Cook. "A man killed."

"A man killed! Where? How? When?"

But Godber's man wasn't going to have his story snatched from under his   95
very nose.

"Know those little cottages just below here, miss?" Know them? Of course,
she knew them. "Well, there's a young chap living there, name of Scott, a carter.
His horse shied at a traction-engine, corner of Hawke Street this morning, and
he was thrown out on the back of his head. Killed."

"Dead!" Laura stared at Godber's man.

"Dead when they picked him up," said Godber's man with relish. "They
were taking the body home as I come up here." And he said to the Cook, "He's
left a wife and five little ones."

"Jose, come here." Laura caught hold of her sister's sleeve and dragged her
through the kitchen to the other side of the green baize door. There she paused
and leaned against it. "Jose!" she said, horrified, "however are we going to stop
everything?"

"Stop everything, Laura!" cried Jose in astonishment. "What do you mean?"   100

"Stop the garden-party, of course." Why did Jose pretend?

But Jose was still more amazed. "Stop the garden-party? My dear Laura, don't be so absurd. Of course we can't do anything of the kind. Nobody expects us to. Don't be so extravagant."

"But we can't possibly have a garden-party with a man dead just outside the front gate."

That really was extravagant, for the little cottages were in a lane to themselves at the very bottom of a steep rise that led up to the house. A broad road ran between. True, they were far too near. They were the greatest possible eyesore, and they had no right to be in that neighbourhood at all. They were little mean dwellings painted a chocolate brown. In the garden patches there was nothing but cabbage stalks, sick hens and tomato cans. The very smoke coming out of their chimneys was poverty-stricken. Little rags and shreds of smoke, so unlike the great silvery plumes that un-curled from the Sheridans' chimneys. Washerwomen lived in the lane and sweeps and a cobbler, and a man whose house-front was studded all over with minute bird-cages. Children swarmed. When the Sheridans were little they were forbidden to set foot there because of the revolting language and of what they might catch. But since they were grown up, Laura and Laurie on their prowls sometimes walked through. It was disgusting and sordid. They came out with a shudder. But still one must go everywhere; one must see everything. So through they went.

105   "And just think of what the band would sound like to that poor woman," said Laura.

"Oh, Laura!" Jose began to be seriously annoyed. "If you're going to stop a band playing every time some one has an accident, you'll lead a very strenuous life. I'm every bit as sorry about it as you. I feel just as sympathetic." Her eyes hardened. She looked at her sister just as she used to when they were little and fighting together. "You won't bring a drunken workman back to life by being sentimental," she said softly.

"Drunk! Who said he was drunk?" Laura turned furiously on Jose. She said, just as they had used to say on those occasions, "I'm going straight up to tell mother."

"Do, dear," cooed Jose.

"Mother, can I come into your room?" Laura turned the big glass door-knob.

110   "Of course, child. Why, what's the matter? What's given you such a colour?" And Mrs. Sheridan turned round from her dressing-table. She was trying on a new hat.

"Mother, a man's been killed," began Laura.

"Not in the garden?" interrupted her mother.

"No, no!"

"Oh, what a fright you gave me!" Mrs. Sheridan sighed with relief, and took off the big hat and held it on her knees.

115   "But listen, mother," said Laura. Breathless, half-choking, she told the dreadful story. "Of course, we can't have our party, can we?" she pleaded. "The band and everybody arriving. They'd hear us, mother; they're nearly neighbours!"

To Laura's astonishment her mother behaved just like Jose; it was harder to bear because she seemed amused. She refused to take Laura seriously.

"But, my dear child, use your common sense. It's only by accident we've heard of it. If some one had died there normally—and I can't understand how they keep alive in those poky little holes—we should still be having our party, shouldn't we?"

Laura had to say "yes" to that, but she felt it was all wrong. She sat down on her mother's sofa and pinched the cushion frill.

"Mother, isn't it terribly heartless of us?" she asked.

"Darling!" Mrs. Sheridan got up and came over to her, carrying the hat. Be- 120 fore Laura could stop her she had popped it on. "My child!" said her mother, "the hat is yours. It's made for you. It's much too young for me. I have never seen you look such a picture. Look at yourself!" And she held up her hand-mirror.

"But, mother," Laura began again. She couldn't look at herself; she turned aside.

This time Mrs. Sheridan lost patience just as Jose had done.

"You are being very absurd, Laura," she said coldly. "People like that don't expect sacrifices from us. And it's not very sympathetic to spoil everybody's enjoyment as you're doing now."

"I don't understand," said Laura, and she walked quickly out of the room into her own bedroom. There, quite by chance, the first thing she saw was this charming girl in the mirror, in her black hat trimmed with gold daisies, and a long black velvet ribbon. Never had she imagined she could look like that. Is mother right? she thought. And now she hoped her mother was right. Am I being extravagant? Perhaps it was extravagant. Just for a moment she had another glimpse of that poor woman and those little children, and the body being carried into the house. But it all seemed blurred, unreal, like a picture in the newspaper. I'll remember it again after the party's over, she decided. And somehow that seemed quite the best plan…

Lunch was over by half-past one. By half-past two they were all ready for 125 the fray. The green-coated band had arrived and was established in a corner of the tennis-court.

"My dear!" trilled Kitty Maitland, "aren't they too like frogs for words? You ought to have arranged them round the pond with the conductor in the middle on a leaf."

Laurie arrived and hailed them on his way to dress. At the sight of him Laura remembered the accident again. She wanted to tell him. If Laurie agreed with the others, then it was bound to be all right. And she followed him into the hall.

"Laurie!"

"Hallo!" He was half-way upstairs, but when he turned round and saw Laura he suddenly puffed out his cheeks and goggled his eyes at her. "My word, Laura! You do look stunning," said Laurie. "What an absolutely topping hat!"

Laura said faintly "Is it?" and smiled up at Laurie, and didn't tell him 130 after all.

Soon after that people began coming in streams. The band struck up; the hired waiters ran from the house to the marquee. Wherever you looked there were couples strolling, bending to the flowers, greeting, moving on over the lawn. They were like bright birds that had alighted in the Sheridans' garden for this one afternoon, on their way to—where? Ah, what happiness it is to be with people who all are happy, to press hands, press cheeks, smile into eyes.

"Darling Laura, how you look!"

"What a becoming hat, child!"

"Laura, you look quite Spanish. I've never seen you look so striking."

135 And Laura, glowing, answered softly, "Have you had tea? Won't you have an ice? The passion-fruit ices really are rather special." She ran to her father and begged him. "Daddy darling, can't the band have something to drink?"

And the perfect afternoon slowly ripened, slowly faded, slowly its petals closed.

"Never a more delightful garden-party… " "The greatest success… " "Quite the most… "

Laura helped her mother with the good-byes. They stood side by side in the porch till it was all over.

"All over, all over, thank heaven," said Mrs. Sheridan. "Round up the others, Laura. Let's go and have some fresh coffee. I'm exhausted. Yes, it's been very successful. But oh, these parties, these parties! Why will you children insist on giving parties!" And they all of them sat down in the deserted marquee.

140 "Have a sandwich, daddy dear. I wrote the flag."

"Thanks." Mr. Sheridan took a bite and the sandwich was gone. He took another. "I suppose you didn't hear of a beastly accident that happened to-day?" he said.

"My dear," said Mrs. Sheridan, holding up her hand, "we did. It nearly ruined the party. Laura insisted we should put it off."

"Oh, mother!" Laura didn't want to be teased about it.

"It was a horrible affair all the same," said Mr. Sheridan. "The chap was married too. Lived just below in the lane, and leaves a wife and half a dozen kiddies, so they say."

145 An awkward little silence fell. Mrs. Sheridan fidgeted with her cup. Really, it was very tactless of father…

Suddenly she looked up. There on the table were all those sandwiches, cakes, puffs, all uneaten, all going to be wasted. She had one of her brilliant ideas.

"I know," she said. "Let's make up a basket. Let's send that poor creature some of this perfectly good food. At any rate, it will be the greatest treat for the children. Don't you agree? And she's sure to have neighbours calling in and so on. What a point to have it all ready prepared. Laura!" She jumped up. "Get me the big basket out of the stairs cupboard."

"But, mother, do you really think it's a good idea?" said Laura.

Again, how curious, she seemed to be different from them all. To take scraps from their party. Would the poor woman really like that?

150 "Of course! What's the matter with you to-day? An hour or two ago you were insisting on us being sympathetic, and now—"

Oh well! Laura ran for the basket. It was filled, it was heaped by her mother.

"Take it yourself, darling," said she. "Run down just as you are. No, wait, take the arum lilies too. People of that class are so impressed by arum lilies."

"The stems will ruin her lace frock," said practical Jose.

So they would. Just in time. "Only the basket, then. And, Laura!"—her mother followed her out of the marquee—"don't on any account—"

"What mother?"   155

No, better not put such ideas into the child's head! "Nothing! Run along."

It was just growing dusky as Laura shut their garden gates. A big dog ran by like a shadow. The road gleamed white, and down below in the hollow the little cottages were in deep shade. How quiet it seemed after the afternoon. Here she was going down the hill to somewhere where a man lay dead, and she couldn't realize it. Why couldn't she? She stopped a minute. And it seemed to her that kisses, voices, tinkling spoons, laughter, the smell of crushed grass were somehow inside her. She had no room for anything else. How strange! She looked up at the pale sky, and all she thought was, "Yes, it was the most successful party."

Now the broad road was crossed. The lane began, smoky and dark. Women in shawls and men's tweed caps hurried by. Men hung over the palings; the children played in the doorways. A low hum came from the mean little cottages. In some of them there was a flicker of light, and a shadow, crab-like, moved across the window. Laura bent her head and hurried on. She wished now she had put on a coat. How her frock shone! And the big hat with the velvet streamer—if only it was another hat! Were the people looking at her? They must be. It was a mistake to have come; she knew all along it was a mistake. Should she go back even now?

No, too late. This was the house. It must be. A dark knot of people stood outside. Beside the gate an old, old woman with a crutch sat in a chair, watching. She had her feet on a newspaper. The voices stopped as Laura drew near. The group parted. It was as though she was expected, as though they had known she was coming here.

Laura was terribly nervous. Tossing the velvet ribbon over her shoulder, she 160 said to a woman standing by, "Is this Mrs. Scott's house?" and the woman, smiling queerly, said, "It is, my lass."

Oh, to be away from this! She actually said, "Help me, God," as she walked up the tiny path and knocked. To be away from those staring eyes, or to be covered up in anything, one of those women's shawls even. I'll just leave the basket and go, she decided. I shan't even wait for it to be emptied.

Then the door opened. A little woman in black showed in the gloom.

Laura said, "Are you Mrs. Scott?" But to her horror the woman answered, "Walk in please, miss," and she was shut in the passage.

"No," said Laura, "I don't want to come in. I only want to leave this basket. Mother sent—"

The little woman in the gloomy passage seemed not to have heard her. 165 "Step this way, please, miss," she said in an oily voice, and Laura followed her.

She found herself in a wretched little low kitchen, lighted by a smoky lamp. There was a woman sitting before the fire.

"Em," said the little creature who had let her in. "Em! It's a young lady." She turned to Laura. She said meaningly, "I'm 'er sister, miss. You'll excuse 'er, won't you?"

"Oh, but of course!" said Laura. "Please, please don't disturb her. I—I only want to leave—"

But at that moment the woman at the fire turned round. Her face, puffed up, red, with swollen eyes and swollen lips, looked terrible. She seemed as though she couldn't understand why Laura was there. What did it mean? Why was this stranger standing in the kitchen with a basket? What was it all about? And the poor face puckered up again.

170   "All right, my dear," said the other. "I'll thenk the young lady."

And again she began, "You'll excuse her, miss, I'm sure," and her face, swollen too, tried an oily smile.

Laura only wanted to get out, to get away. She was back in the passage. The door opened. She walked straight through into the bedroom, where the dead man was lying.

"You'd like a look at 'im, wouldn't you?" said Em's sister, and she brushed past Laura over to the bed. "Don't be afraid, my lass,"—and now her voice sounded fond and sly, and fondly she drew down the sheet—"'e looks a picture. There's nothing to show. Come along, my dear."

Laura came.

175   There lay a young man, fast asleep—sleeping so soundly, so deeply, that he was far, far away from them both. Oh, so remote, so peaceful. He was dreaming. Never wake him up again. His head was sunk in the pillow, his eyes were closed; they were blind under the closed eyelids. He was given up to his dream. What did garden-parties and baskets and lace frocks matter to him? He was far from all those things. He was wonderful, beautiful. While they were laughing and while the band was playing, this marvel had come to the lane. Happy... happy... All is well, said that sleeping face. This is just as it should be. I am content.

But all the same you had to cry, and she couldn't go out of the room without saying something to him. Laura gave a loud childish sob.

"Forgive my hat," she said.

And this time she didn't wait for Em's sister. She found her way out of the door, down the path, past all those dark people. At the corner of the lane she met Laurie.

He stepped out of the shadow. "Is that you, Laura?"

180   "Yes."

"Mother was getting anxious. Was it all right?"

"Yes, quite. Oh, Laurie!" She took his arm, she pressed up against him.

"I say, you're not crying, are you?" asked her brother.

Laura shook her head. She was.

185   Laurie put his arm round her shoulder. "Don't cry," he said in his warm, loving voice. "Was it awful?"

"No," sobbed Laura. "It was simply marvellous. But Laurie—" She stopped, she looked at her brother. "Isn't life," she stammered, "isn't life—" But what life was she couldn't explain. No matter. He quite understood.

"Isn't it, darling?" said Laurie.

CRITICAL THINKING QUESTIONS

1. When Laura suggests to her mother that the garden party be canceled due to the tragedy involving their neighbor, Mrs. Sheridan responds icily, "People like that don't expect sacrifices from us. And it's not very sympathetic to spoil everybody's enjoyment as you're doing now" (par. 121). Would you agree with Mrs. Sheridan that her poverty-stricken neighbors would not expect any show of sympathy, compassion, or respect from their wealthy, upper-class neighbors? Imagine yourself in Mrs. Sheridan's position and a neighbor you did not know personally died in an accident close to your home on the day you had an extravagant party planned. Would you postpone your event? Explain your reasoning.

2. Do you find it significant that the workmen and Cook are not given names in the story? Why might Mansfield have avoided naming these characters? What point might the author be making?

3. Do you think that Mrs. Sheridan sent Laura over to the neighbors' house with the food basket with benevolent intentions, or do you think she wanted to teach her daughter a lesson of a different kind about intermingling with another class? What lesson do you feel Laura took away from the experience?

WRITING TOPIC

What do you believe drives the need for people to separate themselves into classes? In "The Garden Party," the Sheridan family has clearly remained divided socially from the poor families who live in the cottages down the hill from their estate. Though we would like to believe we have evolved into a society that treats each other equally regardless of socioeconomic class, today such divides are still quite prevalent. Do you think as time progresses, this division will lessen, or do you feel there will always be class divides based on how much wealth families amass? Why do people care so much about the perceptions of wealth, and how does ascribing socioeconomic roles limit relationships?

Alice Walker

Everyday Use (1973)

for your grandmama

I will wait for her in the yard that Maggie and I made so clean and wavy yesterday afternoon. A yard like this is more comfortable than most people know. It is not just a yard. It is like an extended living room. When the hard clay is swept clean as a floor and the fine sand around the edges lined with tiny, irregular grooves, anyone can come and sit and look up into the elm tree and wait for the breezes that never come inside the house.

Maggie will be nervous until after her sister goes: she will stand hopelessly in corners, homely and ashamed of the burn scars down her arms and legs, eyeing her sister with a mixture of envy and awe. She thinks her sister has held life always in the palm of one hand, that "no" is a word the world never learned to say to her.

You've no doubt seen those TV shows where the child who has "made it" is confronted, as a surprise, by her own mother and father, tottering in weakly from backstage. (A pleasant surprise, of course: What would they do if parent and child came on the show only to curse out and insult each other?) On TV mother and child embrace and smile into each other's faces. Sometimes the mother and father weep, the child wraps them in her arms and leans across the table to tell how she would not have made it without their help. I have seen these programs.

Sometimes I dream a dream in which Dee and I are suddenly brought together on a TV program of this sort. Out of a dark and soft-seated limousine I am ushered into a bright room filled with many people. There I meet a smiling, gray, sporty man like Johnny Carson who shakes my hand and tells me what a fine girl I have. Then we are on the stage and Dee is embracing me with tears in her eyes. She pins on my dress a large orchid, even though she has told me once that she thinks orchids are tacky flowers.

5   In real life I am a large, big-boned woman with rough, man-working hands. In the winter I wear flannel nightgowns to bed and overalls during the day. I can kill and clean a hog as mercilessly as a man. My fat keeps me hot in zero weather. I can work outside all day, breaking ice to get water for washing; I can eat pork liver cooked over the open fire minutes after it comes steaming from the hog. One winter I knocked a bull calf straight in the brain between the eyes with a sledge hammer and had the meat hung up to chill before nightfall. But of course all this does not show on television. I am the way my daughter would want me to be: a hundred pounds lighter, my skin like an uncooked barley pancake. My hair glistens in the hot bright lights. Johnny Carson has much to do to keep up with my quick and witty tongue.

But that is a mistake. I know even before I wake up. Who ever knew a Johnson with a quick tongue? Who can even imagine me looking a strange white man in the eye? It seems to me I have talked to them always with one foot raised in flight, with my head turned in whichever way is farthest from them. Dee, though. She would always look anyone in the eye. Hesitation was no part of her nature.

"How do I look, Mama?" Maggie says, showing just enough of her thin body enveloped in pink skirt and red blouse for me to know she's there, almost hidden by the door.

"Come out into the yard," I say.

Have you ever seen a lame animal, perhaps a dog run over by some careless person rich enough to own a car, sidle up to someone who is ignorant enough to be kind to him? That is the way my Maggie walks. She has been like this, chin on chest, eyes on ground, feet in shuffle, ever since the fire that burned the other house to the ground.

10   Dee is lighter than Maggie, with nicer hair and a fuller figure. She's a woman now, though sometimes I forget. How long ago was it that the other house burned?

Ten, twelve years? Sometimes I can still hear the flames and feel Maggie's arms sticking to me, her hair smoking and her dress falling off her in little black papery flakes. Her eyes seemed stretched open, blazed open by the flames reflected in them. And Dee. I see her standing off under the sweet gum tree she used to dig gum out of; a look of concentration on her face as she watched the last dingy gray board of the house fall in toward the red-hot brick chimney. Why don't you do a dance around the ashes? I'd wanted to ask her. She had hated the house that much.

I used to think she hated Maggie, too. But that was before we raised the money, the church and me, to send her to Augusta to school. She used to read to us without pity; forcing words, lies, other folks' habits, whole lives upon us two, sitting trapped and ignorant underneath her voice. She washed us in a river of make-believe, burned us with a lot of knowledge we didn't necessarily need to know. Pressed us to her with the serious way she read, to shove us away at just the moment, like dimwits, we seemed about to understand.

Dee wanted nice things. A yellow organdy dress to wear to her graduation from high school; black pumps to match a green suit she'd made from an old suit somebody gave me. She was determined to stare down any disaster in her efforts. Her eyelids would not flicker for minutes at a time. Often I fought off the temptation to shake her. At sixteen she had a style of her own: and knew what style was.

I never had an education myself. After second grade the school was closed down. Don't ask me why: in 1927 colored asked fewer questions than they do now. Sometimes Maggie reads to me. She stumbles along good-naturedly but can't see well. She knows she is not bright. Like good looks and money, quickness passed her by. She will marry John Thomas (who has mossy teeth in an earnest face) and then I'll be free to sit here and I guess just sing church songs to myself. Although I never was a good singer. Never could carry a tune. I was always better at a man's job. I used to love to milk till I was hooked in the side in' 49. Cows are soothing and slow and don't bother you, unless you try to milk them the wrong way.

I have deliberately turned my back on the house. It is three rooms, just like the one that burned, except the roof is tin; they don't make shingle roofs any more. There are no real windows, just some holes cut in the sides, like the portholes in a ship, but not round and not square, with rawhide holding the shutters up on the outside. This house is in a pasture, too, like the other one. No doubt when Dee sees it she will want to tear it down. She wrote me once that no matter where we "choose" to live, she will manage to come see us. But she will never bring her friends. Maggie and I thought about this and Maggie asked me, "Mama, when did Dee ever *have* any friends?"

She had a few. Furtive boys in pink shirts hanging about on washday after 15 school. Nervous girls who never laughed. Impressed with her they worshiped the well-turned phrase, the cute shape, the scalding humor that erupted like bubbles in lye. She read to them.

When she was courting Jimmy T she didn't have much time to pay to us, but turned all her fault finding power on him. He *flew* to marry a cheap city girl from a family of ignorant flashy people. She hardly had time to recompose herself.

When she comes I will meet—but there they are!

Maggie attempts to make a dash for the house; in her shuffling way, but I stay her with my hand. "Come back here," I say. And she stops and tries to dig a well in the sand with her toe.

It is hard to see them clearly through the strong sun. But even the first glimpse of leg out of the car tells me it is Dee. Her feet were always neat-looking, as if God himself had shaped them with a certain style. From the other side of the car comes a short, stocky man. Hair is all over his head a foot long and hanging from his chin like a kinky mule tail. I hear Maggie suck in her breath. "Uhnnnh," is what it sounds like. Like when you see the wriggling end of a snake just in front of your foot on the road. "Uhnnnh."

20 Dee next. A dress down to the ground, in this hot weather. A dress so loud it hurts my eyes. There are yellows and oranges enough to throw back the light of the sun. I feel my whole face warming from the heat waves it throws out. Earrings gold, too, and hanging down to her shoulders. Bracelets dangling and making noises when she moves her arm up to shake the folds of the dress out of her armpits. The dress is loose and flows, and as she walks closer, I like it. I hear Maggie go "Uhnnnh" again. It is her sister's hair. It stands straight up like the wool on a sheep. It is black as night and around the edges are two long pigtails that rope about like small lizards disappearing behind her ears.

"Wa-su-zo-Tean-o!" she says, coming on in that gilding way the dress makes her move. The short stocky fellow with the hair to his navel is all grinning and he follows up with "Asalamalakim, my mother and sister!" He moves to hug Maggie but she falls back, right up against the back of my chair. I feel her trembling there and when I look up I see the perspiration falling off her chin.

"Don't get up," says Dee. Since I am stout it takes something of a push. You can see me trying to move a second or two before I make it. She turns, showing white heels through her sandals, and goes back to the car. Out she peeks next with a Polaroid. She stoops down quickly and lines up picture after picture of me sitting there in front of the house with Maggie cowering behind me. She never takes a shot without making sure the house is included. When a cow comes nibbling around the edge of the yard she snaps it and me and Maggie *and* the house. Then she puts the Polaroid in the back seat of the car, and comes up and kisses me on the forehead.

Meanwhile Asalamalakim is going through motions with Maggie's hand. Maggie's hand is as limp as a fish, and probably as cold, despite the sweat, and she keeps trying to pull it back. It looks like Asalamalakim wants to shake hands but wants to do it fancy. Or maybe he don't know how people shake hands. Anyhow, he soon gives up on Maggie.

"Well," I say. "Dee."

25 "No, Mama," she says. "Not 'Dee,' Wangero Leewanika Kemanjo!"

"What happened to 'Dee'?" I wanted to know.

"She's dead," Wangero said. "I couldn't bear it any longer, being named after the people who oppress me."

"You know as well as me you was named after your aunt Dicie," I said. Dicie is my sister. She named Dee. We called her "Big Dee" after Dee was born.

"But who was *she* named after?" asked Wangero.

"I guess after Grandma Dee," I said.   30

"And who was she named after?" asked Wangero.

"Her mother," I said, and saw Wangero was getting tired. "That's about as far back as I can trace it," I said. Though, in fact, I probably could have carried it back beyond the Civil War through the branches.

"Well," said Asalamalakim, "there you are."

"Uhnnnh," I heard Maggie say.

"There I was not," I said, "before 'Dicie' cropped up in our family, so why   35
should I try to trace it that far back?"

He just stood there grinning, looking down on me like somebody inspecting a Model A car. Every once in a while he and Wangero sent eye signals over my head.

"How do you pronounce this name?" I asked.

"You don't have to call me by it if you don't want to," said Wangero.

"Why shouldn't I?" I asked. "If that's what you want us to call you, we'll call you."

"I know it might sound awkward at first," said Wangero.   40

"I'll get used to it," I said. "Ream it out again."

Well, soon we got the name out of the way. Asalamalakim had a name twice as long and three times as hard. After I tripped over it two or three times he told me to just call him Hakim-a-barber. I wanted to ask him was he a barber, but I didn't really think he was, so I didn't ask.

"You must belong to those beef-cattle peoples down the road," I said. They said "Asalamalakim" when they met you, too, but they didn't shake hands. Always too busy: feeding the cattle, fixing the fences, putting up salt-lick shelters, throwing down hay. When the white folks poisoned some of the herd the men stayed up all night with rifles in their hands. I walked a mile and a half just to see the sight.

Hakim-a-barber said, "I accept some of their doctrines, but farming and raising cattle is not my style." (They didn't tell me, and I didn't ask, whether Wangero (Dee) had really gone and married him.)

We sat down to eat and right away he said he didn't eat collards and pork   45
was unclean. Wangero, though, went on through the chitlins and corn bread, the greens and everything else. She talked a blue streak over the sweet potatoes. Everything delighted her. Even the fact that we still used the benches her daddy made for the table when we couldn't afford to buy chairs.

"Oh, Mama!" she cried. Then turned to Hakim-a-barber. "I never knew how lovely these benches are. You can feel the rump prints," she said, running her hands underneath her and along the bench. Then she gave a sigh and her hand closed over Grandma Dee's butter dish. "That's it!" she said. "I knew there was something I wanted to ask you if I could have." She jumped up from the table and went over in the corner where the churn stood, the milk in it clabber by now. She looked at the churn and looked at it.

"This churn top is what I need," she said. "Didn't Uncle Buddy whittle it out of a tree you all used to have?"

50   "Yes," I said.

"Uh huh," she said happily. "And I want the dasher, too."

"Uncle Buddy whittle that, too?" asked the barber.

Dee (Wangero) looked up at me.

"Aunt Dee's first husband whittled the dash," said Maggie so low you almost couldn't hear her. "His name was Henry, but they called him Stash."

55   "Maggie's brain is like an elephant's," Wangero said, laughing. "I can use the churn top as a centerpiece for the alcove table," she said, sliding a plate over the churn, "and I'll think of something artistic to do with the dasher."

When she finished wrapping the dasher the handle stuck out. I took it for a moment in my hands. You didn't even have to look close to see where hands pushing the dasher up and down to make butter had left a kind of sink in the wood. In fact, there were a lot of small sinks; you could see where thumbs and fingers had sunk into the wood. It was beautiful light yellow wood, from a tree that grew in the yard where Big Dee and Stash had lived.

After dinner Dee (Wangero) went to the trunk at the foot of my bed and started rifling through it. Maggie hung back in the kitchen over the dishpan. Out came Wangero with two quilts. They had been pieced by Grandma Dee and then Big Dee and me had hung them on the quilt frames on the front porch and quilted them. One was in the Lone Star pattern. The other was Walk Around the Mountain. In both of them were scraps of dresses Grandma Dee had worn fifty and more years ago. Bits and pieces of Grandpa Jarrell's Paisley shirts. And one teeny faded blue piece, about the size of a penny matchbox, that was from Great Grandpa Ezra's uniform that he wore in the Civil War.

"Mama," Wangero said sweet as a bird. "Can I have these old quilts?"

I heard something fall in the kitchen, and a minute later the kitchen door slammed.

60   "Why don't you take one or two of the others?" I asked. "These old things was just done by me and Big Dee from some tops your grandma pieced before she died."

"No," said Wangero. "I don't want those. They are stitched around the borders by machine."

"That'll make them last better," I said.

"That's not the point," said Wangero. "These are all pieces of dresses Grandma used to wear. She did all this stitching by hand. Imagine!" She held the quilts securely in her arms, stroking them.

"Some of the pieces, like those lavender ones, come from old clothes her mother handed down to her," I said, moving up to touch the quilts. Dee (Wangero) moved back just enough so that I couldn't reach the quilts. They already belonged to her.

"Imagine!" she breathed again, clutching them closely to her bosom.   65

"The truth is," I said, "I promised to give them quilts to Maggie, for when she marries John Thomas."

She gasped like a bee had stung her.

"Maggie can't appreciate these quilts!" she said. "She'd probably be backward enough to put them to everyday use."

"I reckon she would," I said. "God knows I been saving' em for long enough with nobody using' em. I hope she will!" I didn't want to bring up how I had offered Dee (Wangero) a quilt when she went away to college. Then she had told me they were old-fashioned, out of style.

"But they're *priceless!*" she was saying now, furiously; for she has a temper.   70
"Maggie would put them on the bed and in five years they'd be in rags. Less than that!"

"She can always make some more," I said. "Maggie knows how to quilt."

Dee (Wangero) looked at me with hatred. "You just will not understand. The point is these quilts, *these* quilts!"

"Well," I said, stumped. "What would *you* do with them?"

"Hang them," she said. As if that was the only thing you *could* do with quilts.

Maggie by now was standing in the door. I could almost hear the sound her   75
feet made as they scraped over each other.

"She can have them, Mama," she said, like somebody used to never winning anything, or having anything reserved for her. "I can' member Grandma Dee without the quilts."

I looked at her hard. She had filled her bottom lip with checkerberry snuff and it gave her face a kind of dopey, hangdog look. It was Grandma Dee and Big Dee who taught her how to quilt herself. She stood there with her scarred hands hidden in the folds of her skirt. She looked at her sister with something like fear but she wasn't mad at her. This was Maggie's portion. This was the way she knew God to work.

When I looked at her like that something hit me in the top of my head and ran down to the soles of my feet. Just like when I'm in church and the spirit of God touches me and I get happy and shout. I did something I never had done before: hugged Maggie to me, then dragged her on into the room, snatched the quilts out of Miss Wangero's hands and dumped them into Maggie's lap. Maggie just sat there on my bed with her mouth open.

"Take one or two of the others," I said to Dee.

But she turned without a word and went out to Hakim-a-barber.   80

"You just don't understand," she said, as Maggie and I came out to the car.

"What don't I understand?" I wanted to know.

"Your heritage," she said. And then she turned to Maggie, kissed her, and said, "You ought to try to make something of yourself, too, Maggie. It's really a new day for us. But from the way you and Mama still live you'd never know it."

She put on some sunglasses that hid everything above the tip of her nose and her chin.

Maggie smiled; maybe at the sunglasses. But a real smile, not scared. After we watched the car dust settle I asked Maggie to bring me a dip of snuff. And then the two of us sat there just enjoying, until it was time to go in the house and go to bed.

CRITICAL THINKING QUESTIONS

1. What is Walker's implied **claim of value** about family heritage? What evidence in the story supports this claim? Do you agree or disagree with this claim?

2. When the mother refuses Dee's demand for the quilts and hands them over to Maggie, how did you react? What values informed your reaction?

3. In the closing scene, how is the author using appeal to *pathos*?

WRITING TOPIC

In a classic rock song, the Rolling Stones sing, "You can't always get what you want, but if you try sometimes, you just might find you get what you need." Relating this quote to Walker's "Everyday Use" and your personal experiences/observations, develop your own claim about getting what you want…trying, and finding what you need. Using evidence from the story and your experience, write an essay supporting your claim.

POETRY

Anne Bradstreet

To My Dear and Loving Husband (1641)

If ever two were one, then surely we.
If ever man were loved by wife, then thee;
If ever wife was happy in a man,
Compare with me, ye women, if you can.
I prize thy love more than whole mines of gold   5
Or all the riches that the East doth hold.
Nor ought but love from thee, give recompense.
My love is such that rivers cannot quench,
Thy love is such I can no way repay,
The heavens reward thee manifold, I pray.   10
Then while we live, in love let's so persevere
That when we live no more, we may live ever.

CRITICAL THINKING QUESTION

What point do you think is made by the narrator in the last line of the poem? In examining the line, what claim is made regarding love?

WRITING TOPIC

You might be tempted to jump to the conclusion that the poet had been married only recently and, thus, is still in the "honeymoon" frame of mind. Read about Anne Bradstreet in the "Authors' Biographical Notes" at the back of the book. Based on these facts, you can reasonably assume that Bradstreet's married life was one of daily, arduous, physical toil and constant danger—hardly a recipe for a "happy" marriage. Yet her poem is an eloquent tribute to marital love. To what degree does the poem reflect love in today's marriages? Does the poem describe marital love as it is—or as it *should* be?

Relate specific personal observations and examples to support your viewpoint. For a different perspective on marital love, read Kate Chopin's story "The Storm" (page 350).

Gwendolyn Brooks

The Mother (1991)

Abortions will not let you forget.
You remember the children you got that you did not get,
The damp small pulps with a little or with no hair,
The singers and workers that never handled the air.
5   You will never neglect or beat
Them, or silence or buy with a sweet.
You will never wind up the sucking-thumb
Or scuttle off ghosts that come.
You will never leave them, controlling your luscious sigh,
10   Return for a snack of them, with gobbling mother-eye.

I have heard in the voices of the wind the voices of my dim
    killed children.
I have contracted. I have eased
My dim dears at the breasts they could never suck.
I have said, Sweets, if I sinned, if I seized
15   Your luck
And your lives from your unfinished reach,
If I stole your births and your names,
Your straight baby tears and your games,
Your stilted or lovely loves, your tumults, your marriages, aches,
    and your deaths,
20   If I poisoned the beginnings of your breaths,
Believe that even in my deliberateness I was not deliberate.
Though why should I whine,
Whine that the crime was other than mine?—
Since anyhow you are dead.
25   Or rather, or instead,
You were never made.

But that too, I am afraid,
Is faulty: oh, what shall I say, how is the truth to be said?

You were born, you had body, you died.
It is just that you never giggled or planned or cried.   30
Believe me, I loved you all.
Believe me, I knew you, though faintly, and I loved, I loved you
All.

CRITICAL THINKING QUESTIONS

1. Beginning with line 21, when the speaker says, "Believe...," she seems to be sorting through her conscience in trying to articulate "the truth." How do you interpret lines 21 through 30? How do you think she is judging herself as "the mother"? Working with three or four classmates, read and compare your interpretations and then collaborate on a statement for your group to present to the rest of the class. Be prepared to point to specific evidence from the poem to support your interpretation.

2. What is the effect of repetition in the poem's closing stanza? Whom is the speaker, the mother, trying to convince?

3. Examining this poem as an **argument**, what is its **implied claim**? What **evidence** in the poem supports your statement of the claim?

4. Assess the speaker's *ethos.*

WRITING TOPIC

For five seasons, MTV's reality show *16 and Pregnant* pulled in huge audiences. The show chronicled the lives of teenaged moms. As you might imagine, the show brought with it considerable controversy. Some scolded producers for glamorizing teen pregnancy, while others complimented the series for showing young people the real-world consequences of becoming young parents. According to statistics released by the U.S. Department of Health and Human Services, teen birth rates in the United States have steadily declined over the past 20 years.[1] While people generally have become more accepting—and more supportive—of teenage moms, the health risks for mother and child and the costs for taxpayers remain high. Do some research on the comparative rates of teenage pregnancies and births among developed countries. Select one or two countries to compare and contrast to the United States. After further research, draw some conclu-

---

[1] "Overview: Teen Pregnancy and Childbearing." *Office of Adolescent Health.* United States Department of Health and Human Services. 16 Mar 2015. Web. 28 March 2015.

sions about the cultural factors that may contribute to the disparate rates. Based on your conclusions, develop a claim of policy argument that outlines strategies for bringing the United States' teen birth rate more in line with other developing countries.

Michael Cleary

Boss's Son (2005)

The first weeks were the worst.
They were all full-timers
half a generation older at least,
and me headed for college, pegged for sure
5 among beer drinking, beer trucking men.
And they let me know it,
their muscle cars and pick-ups more real
than jock glory and SAT's.

Whatever I'd done, they stuck
10 a big fat "but" on its skinny ass:
I was football captain, but I was quarterback—
just another name for bossing guys around.
I was strong enough, *but* I liked books.
I had a pretty girl, *but* I was pussywhipped.
15 My pride unraveled like a baseball's snarled insides.
So I did twice my share, blisters
torn til calluses covered my hands like shells.

Gradually, they taught me their secrets:
let your legs do the lifting and save your back.
20 Load last things first so pints, quarts, cans, kegs
come undone top to bottom, back to front,
first stop to last and handle everything just once.
Snugging the load, making it stay that way all day
so corners and dumbshit drivers don't tumble it away
25 in explosions of foam soaking up half a day's pay.
After work we hung around and drank for free.
I salvaged bottles from the cooler's breakage bin,
hosing off scum and bits of glass.
I guzzled, smoked, swore with the best of them.
30 Playing the boy at night, I played the man

next morning, showed up early
and tried not to puke on company time.

Paydays we went to sour-smelling hangouts
of touchy pride and easy violence. Once
I saw a logger bite off a chunk   35
of a guy's cheek like an apple, then promise
to wait til he got back from the emergency room.
We waited, too, and they went at it again
for what seemed a good half hour.
Blood splattered all over the alley.   40

Those summers I changed
into that life easy as T-shirts and steel-toed boots,
doing the grunt work and putting down salesmen
like my father with their soft hands and ties,
gloried in sweat and sore muscles and hangovers   45
like nobody's goddamn boss's son.
After four years I was out of college
and out of there forever. Three months later,
the artery that burst inside my father's head
dropped him to the warehouse floor and he was gone.   50

What did he wonder about me living so hard,
trying to prove myself to everyone but him?
It was one more thing between us
I couldn't explain and he wouldn't understand.
I wanted the world to love me, I suppose,   55
on its own rough terms,
but I wanted him to love me, too,
for whatever man I was or was trying to be,
for the first time not in the name of the father
but some pilgrim who could be any man's son.   55

CRITICAL THINKING QUESTIONS

1. Write about what you see as the **connotations** of the word "pride" in line 15 and then again about its connotations in line 34.

2. How does pride help this young adult establish his independence and identity?

3. Read back over the poem's closing four lines, beginning with, "but I wanted him to love me, too...." Exercise your creative thinking and offer your interpretation of those final lines. As you speculate, consider the phrase, "in the name of the father," juxtaposed with the image of "some pilgrim."

WRITING TOPIC

Read Scott Russell Sanders's essay on page 421. Both Sanders's essay and Cleary's poem address issues of class differences. While we like to think of the United States as an egalitarian society, both Sanders's essay and Cleary's poem suggest otherwise. In what ways do they challenge the notion of egalitarianism? Do you agree or disagree with the writers? Use evidence to support your opinion.

———————

Gregory Corso

Marriage (1988)

Should I get married? Should I be good?
Astound the girl next door with my velvet suit and faustus hood?
Don't take her to movies but to cemeteries
tell all about werewolf bathtubs and forked clarinets
then desire her and kiss her and all the preliminaries
and she going just so far and I understanding why
not getting angry saying You must feel! It's beautiful to feel!
Instead take her in my arms lean against an old crooked tombstone
and woo her the entire night the constellations in the sky—

When she introduces me to her parents
back straightened, hair finally combed, strangled by a tie,
should I sit knees together on their 3rd degree sofa
and not ask Where's the bathroom?
How else to feel other than I am,
often thinking Flash Gordon soap—
O how terrible it must be for a young man
seated before a family and the family thinking
We never saw him before! He wants our Mary Lou!
After tea and homemade cookies they ask What do you do for a living?

Should I tell them? Would they like me then?
Say All right get married, we're losing a daughter
but we're gaining a son—
And should I then ask Where's the bathroom?

5

10

15

20

O God, and the wedding! All her family and her friends
and only a handful of mine all scroungy and bearded   25
just wait to get at the drinks and food—
And the priest! he looking at me as if I masturbated
asking me Do you take this woman for your lawful wedded
    wife?
And I trembling what to say say Pie Glue!
I kiss the bride all those corny men slapping me on the back   30
She's all yours, boy! Ha-ha-ha!
And in their eyes you could see some obscene honeymoon
    going on—
Then all that absurd rice and clanky cans and shoes
Niagara Falls! Hordes of us! Husbands! Wives! Flowers!
    Chocolates!
All streaming into cozy hotels   35
All going to do the same thing tonight

The indifferent clerk he knowing what was going to happen
The lobby zombies they knowing what
The whistling elevator man he knowing
The winking bellboy knowing   40
Everybody knowing! I'd be almost inclined not to do anything!
Stay up all night! Stare that hotel clerk in the eye!
Screaming: I deny honeymoon! I deny honeymoon!
running rampant into those almost climactic suites
yelling Radio belly! Cat shovel!   45
O I'd live in Niagara forever! in a dark cave beneath the Falls
I'd sit there the Mad Honeymooner
devising ways to break marriages, a scourge of bigamy
a saint of divorce—

But I should get married I should be good   50
How nice it'd be to come home to her
and sit by the fireplace and she in the kitchen
aproned young and lovely wanting my baby
      55
and so happy about me she burns the roast beef
and comes crying to me and I get up from my big papa chair
saying Christmas teeth! Radiant brains! Apple deaf!
God what a husband I'd make! Yes, I should get married!
So much to do! like sneaking into Mr Jones' house late at night
and cover his golf clubs with 1920 Norwegian books

Like hanging a picture of Rimbaud on the lawnmower   60
like pasting Tannu Tuva postage stamps all over the picket
    fence

like when Mrs Kindhead comes to collect for the Community
   Chest
grab her and tell her There are unfavorable omens in the sky!
And when the mayor comes to get my vote tell him
65   When are you going to stop people killing whales!
And when the milkman comes leave him a note in the bottle
Penguin dust, bring me penguin dust, I want penguin dust—

Yet if I should get married and it's Connecticut and snow
and she gives birth to a child and I am sleepless, worn,
70   up for nights, head bowed against a quiet window, the past
   behind me,
finding myself in the most common of situations a trembling man
knowledged with responsibility not twig-smear nor Roman
   coin soup—
O what would that be like!
Surely I'd give it for a nipple a rubber Tacitus
75   For a rattle a bag of broken Bach records
Tack Della Francesca all over its crib
Sew the Greek alphabet on its bib
And build for its playpen a roofless Parthenon

No, I doubt I'd be that kind of father
80   Not rural not snow no quiet window
but hot smelly tight New York City
seven flights up, roaches and rats in the walls
a fat Reichian wife screeching over potatoes Get a job!
And five nose running brats in love with Batman
85   And the neighbors all toothless and dry haired
like those hag masses of the 18th century
all wanting to come in and watch TV

The landlord wants his rent
Grocery store Blue Cross Gas & Electric Knights of Columbus
90   Impossible to lie back and dream Telephone snow, ghost
   parking—
No! I should not get married I should never get married!
But—imagine if I were married to a beautiful sophisticated
   woman
tall and pale wearing an elegant black dress and long black
   gloves
holding a cigarette holder in one hand and a highball in the
   other
95   and we lived high up in a penthouse with a huge window

from which we could see all of New York and ever farther on
  clearer days
No, can't imagine myself married to that pleasant prison
  dream—

O but what about love? I forget love
not that I am incapable of love
it's just that I see love as odd as wearing shoes—   100
I never wanted to marry a girl who was like my mother
And Ingrid Bergman was always impossible
And there's maybe a girl now but she's already married
And I don't like men and—
but there's got to be somebody!   105
Because what if I'm 60 years old and not married,
all alone in a furnished room with pee stains on my underwear
and everybody else is married! All the universe married but me!

Ah, yet well I know that were a woman possible as I am possible
then marriage would be possible—   110
Like SHE in her lonely alien gaud waiting her Egyptian lover
so I wait—bereft of 2,000 years and the bath of life.

CRITICAL THINKING QUESTIONS

1. The poet poses the question, "Should I get married?" List the evidence he provides for both sides of the argument under the headings "Marry"…"Don't Marry."

2. From your own perspective, make a list of evidence under the headings "Marry"…"Don't Marry" and compare and contrast your second list with your first.

WRITING TOPIC

What do you believe to be the primary motivation for marriage? Do most people enter the commitment for the correct reasons? Do you think the majority of couples wed because they truly believe they are in love with each other, or do you think the fear of being alone prompts many people to pursue matrimony? Upon what do you base your feelings? Can you relate to any of the concerns the narrator expresses in this poem?

Nikki Giovanni

Mothers (1968)

the last time i was home
to see my mother we kissed
exchanged pleasantries
and unpleasantries pulled a warm
5   comforting silence around
us and read separate books

i remember the first time
i consciously saw her
we were living in a three room
10   apartment on burns avenue
mommy always sat in the dark
i don't know how i knew that but she did

that night i stumbled into the kitchen
maybe because i've always been
15   a night person or perhaps because i had wet the bed
she was sitting on a chair
the room was bathed in moonlight diffused through
those thousands of panes landlords who rented
to people with children were prone to put in windows
20   she may have been smoking but maybe not
her hair was three-quarters her height
which made me a strong believer in the samson myth
and very black

i'm sure i just hung there by the door
25   i remember thinking: what a beautiful lady

she was very deliberately waiting
perhaps for my father to come home
from his night job or maybe for a dream
that had promised to come by
30   "come here" she said "i'll teach you
a poem:
        i see the moon
        the moon sees me
        god bless the moon
        and god bless me"
i taught it to my son
who recited it for her

just to say we must learn
to bear the pleasures　　　　　　　　　　　　　　　　35
as we have borne the pains

CRITICAL THINKING QUESTIONS

1. Examine the details of the speaker's depiction of her childhood memory, and draw some inferences about the mother's life at this time.

2. In teaching the poem, what message is the mother imparting to her daughter?

3. The speaker also has taught the poem to her son, and it is he who now recites it for his grandmother. In light of the poem's title, how is this detail significant?

WRITING TOPIC

Some social critics argue that the failure of parents (and, some add, schools) to teach values to children is a primary cause for the increasing problems among youth—from rude behavior and bullying to drug use and violence. What is the poet's implied claim about the teaching of values? Reflecting on your childhood, can you recall a moment when you learned a lesson about values? How do you think children should be taught values?

———————————

Thomas Hardy

The Ruined Maid (written 1866; first published in 1903)

"O 'Melia, my dear, this does everything crown!
Who could have supposed I should meet you in Town?
And whence such fair garments, such prosperi-ty?"
"O didn't you know I'd been ruined?" said she.

"You left us in tatters, without shoes or socks,　　　　　　5
Tired of digging potatoes, and spudding up docks;
And now you've gay bracelets and bright feathers three!"
"Yes: that's how we dress when we're ruined," said she.

"At home in the barton you said 'thee' and 'thou,'
And 'thik oon,' and 'theäs oon,' and 't'other'; but now　　　10

Your talking quite fits' ee for high compa-ny!"
"Some polish is gained with one's ruin," said she.

"Your hands were like paws then, your face blue and bleak
But now I'm bewitched by your delicate cheek,
And your little gloves fit as on any la-dy!"
"We never do work when we're ruined," said she.

15

"You used to call home-life a hag-ridden dream,
And you'd sigh, and you'd sock; but at present you seem
To know not of megrims or melancho-ly!"
"True. One's pretty lively when ruined," said she.

20

"I wish I had feathers, a fine sweeping gown,
And a delicate face, and could strut about Town!"
"My dear—a raw country girl, such as you be,
Cannot quite expect that. You ain't ruined," said she.

CRITICAL THINKING QUESTIONS

1. By leaving her home life on the farm, what has 'Melia left behind? What has she gained by her new life in Town?

2. Compare and contrast the values associated with her previous lifestyle to those associated with her present one.

3. Her former acquaintance, who still lives in the country, seems to think that 'Melia has found prosperity and happiness in Town. How does this inference represent flawed reasoning?

WRITING TOPIC

Manners—the word itself has a quaint ring to it, suggesting a bygone era of rigid social customs, class codes, and, above all, leisure time (for example, to set a formal table for a family dinner). For parents today, however, many of whom must work full time to maintain their households, little time is left for formalities as they race to the rhythm of fast-paced and demanding schedules. Some would assert that, as a result, many parents do not teach their children proper politeness. Are manners a class code that perpetuates snobbery and the stratification of society, or are they a malleable set of social skills that help individuals to bridge economic and cultural gaps? What manners should be taught and how? Should this age-old parental job be shared among the larger culture, and if so, how?

Seamus Heney

Mid-term Break (1966)

I sat all morning in the college sick bay
Counting bells knelling classes to a close.
At two o'clock our neighbours drove me home.

In the porch I met my father crying—
He had always taken funerals in his stride—   5
And Big Jim Evans saying it was a hard blow.

The baby cooed and laughed and rocked the pram
When I came in, and I was embarrassed
By old men standing up to shake my hand

And tell me they were 'sorry for my trouble'.   10
Whispers informed strangers I was the eldest,
Away at school, as my mother held my hand

In hers and coughed out angry tearless sighs.
At ten o'clock the ambulance arrived
With the corpse, stanched and bandaged by the nurses.   15

Next morning I went up into the room. Snowdrops
And candles soothed the bedside; I saw him
For the first time in six weeks. Paler now,

Wearing a poppy bruise on his left temple,
He lay in the four-foot box as in his cot.   20
No gaudy scars, the bumper knocked him clear.

A four-foot box, a foot for every year.

CRITICAL THINKING QUESTIONS

1. What common assumptions regarding the role of the eldest child in the family dynamic are addressed and/or implied in this poem?

2. What are we able to infer prompted the narrator to take a break from school? What details are we able to discern?

3. Do your feelings regarding the title of the poem change once you have read the poem? If so, how? What ways does this title challenge assumptions we make when we hear of someone taking a "break" from school or work?

WRITING TOPIC

Reflecting on your own experiences and observations, what role do you think family heritage plays in shaping an individual's identity and outlook? As you answer, consider your own family dynamics. What role do you feel you have been expected to fulfill in your family? What pressures or challenges have you faced as a result of these expectations?

Peter Meinke

Advice to My Son (1981)

—FOR TIM

The trick is, to live your days
as if each one may be your last
(for they go fast, and young men lose their lives
in strange and unimaginable ways)
but at the same time, plan long range
(for they go slow: if you survive
the shattered windshield and the bursting shell
you will arrive
at our approximation here below
of heaven or hell).
To be specific, between the peony and the rose
plant squash and spinach, turnips and tomatoes;
beauty is nectar
and nectar, in a desert, saves—
but the stomach craves stronger sustenance
than the honied vine.
Therefore, marry a pretty girl
after seeing her mother;
speak truth to one man,
work with another;

5

10

15

20

and always serve bread with your wine.
But, son,
always serve wine.

CRITICAL THINKING QUESTION

In lines 17 and 18, the speaker makes the claim, "Therefore, marry a pretty girl," with the qualifying phrase "after seeing her mother." What **value assumptions** underlie that statement? Are they valid? Why or why not?

WRITING TOPIC

Meinke is giving advice to his son, "—FOR TIM." Working with several other students (preferably in mixed-gender groups), create a female version of Meinke's poem "Advice to My Daughter." Be prepared to present your poem to the rest of the class.

———————————————

Sharon Olds

I Go Back to May, 1937 (1987)

I see them standing at the formal gates of their colleges,
I see my father strolling out
under the ochre sandstone arch, the
red tiles glinting like bent
plates of blood behind his head, I   15
see my mother with a few light books at her hip
standing at the pillar made of tiny bricks with the
wrought-iron gate still open behind her, its
sword-tips black in the May air,
they are about to graduate, they are about to get married,   10
they are kids, they are dumb, all they know is they are
innocent, they would never hurt anybody.
I want to go up to them and say Stop,
don't do it—she's the wrong woman,
he's the wrong man, you are going to do things   15
you cannot imagine you would ever do,
you are going to do bad things to children,
you are going to suffer in ways you never heard of,

you are going to want to die. I want to go
20   up to them there in the late May sunlight and say it,
her hungry pretty blank face turning to me,
her pitiful beautiful untouched body,
his arrogant handsome blind face turning to me,
his pitiful beautiful untouched body,
25   but I don't do it. I want to live. I
take them up like the male and female
paper dolls and bang them together
at the hips like chips of flint as if to
strike sparks from them, I say
30   Do what you are going to do, and I will tell about it.

CRITICAL THINKING QUESTIONS

1. Olds's poem addresses the following **issue**: Should the daughter try to stop her parents from marrying each other? Why or why not?

2. List the evidence the speaker provides in examining the issue. Why does she decide not to stop her parents from marrying?

WRITING TOPIC

Consider Olds's poem from a broad perspective: What if we could see into the future, see how our lives will play out? Would this be a good thing? You can expand your thinking on this topic by researching biotechnology (the Human Genome Project), which may open the door—or, many critics say, Pandora's box—for us to program our genes and, thus, "predict" and presumably improve our lives. To what degree, if any, is experimenting with human DNA acceptable?

Mary Oliver

The Black Walnut Tree (1972)

My mother and I debate:
we could sell
the black walnut tree
to the lumberman,

and pay off the mortgage.   5
Likely some storm anyway
will churn down its dark boughs,
smashing the house. We talk
slowly, two women trying
in a difficult time to be wise.   10
Roots in the cellar drains,
I say, and she replies
that the leaves are getting heavier
every year, and the fruit
harder to gather away.   15
But something brighter than money
moves in our blood—an edge
sharp and quick as a trowel
that wants us to dig and sow.
So we talk, but we don't do   20
anything. That night I dream
of my fathers out of Bohemia
filling the blue fields
of fresh and generous Ohio
with leaves and vines and orchards.   25
What my mother and I both know
is that we'd crawl with shame
in the emptiness we'd made
in our own and our fathers' backyard.
So the black walnut tree   30
swings through another year
of sun and leaping winds,
of leaves and bounding fruit,
and, month after month, the whip-
crack of the mortgage.   35

CRITICAL THINKING QUESTIONS

1. In debating the sale of the black walnut tree, how does the speaker appeal
to *pathos*?

2. How does the speaker appeal to **logos?**

3. What assumption supports the women's decision to preserve the tree? Is it
valid? Can you think of issues you have debated in which this assumption
entered into the argument?

WRITING TOPIC

Do you think the mother's and daughter's fathers would agree or disagree with the women's decision? Why?

Dudley Randall

Ballad of Birmingham (1968)

(On the Bombing of a Church in Birmingham, Alabama, 1963)

"Mother dear, may I go downtown
Instead of out to play,
And march the streets of Birmingham
In a Freedom March today?"

5   "No, baby, no, you may not go,
For the dogs are fierce and wild,
And clubs and hoses, guns and jails
Aren't good for a little child."

"But, mother, I won't be alone.
10   Other children will go with me,
And march the streets of Birmingham
To make our country free."

"No, baby, no, you may not go,
For I fear those guns will fire.
15   But you may go to church instead
And sing in the children's choir."

She has combed and brushed her night-dark hair.
And bathed rose petal sweet.
And drawn white gloves on her small brown hands,
20   And white shoes on her feet.
The mother smiled to know her child
Was in the sacred place,
But that smile was the last smile
To come upon her face.

25   For when she heard the explosion,
Her eyes grew wet and wild.
She raced through the streets of Birmingham
Calling for her child.

She clawed through bits of glass and brick.
Then lifted out a shoe.   30
"Oh, here's the shoe my baby wore,
But, baby, where are you?"

CRITICAL THINKING QUESTIONS

1. Working in small groups, write out at least two implied claims for this poem. List evidence for each claim.

2. In committing an act of terrorism, what value assumption does the terrorist use to justify his or her act?

3. How does Randall's poem refute the terrorist's assumption?

WRITING TOPIC

Both Randall's poem and Giovanni's poem "Mothers" (page 396) feature the depth and power of maternal love. Compare and contrast the perspectives that each piece of literature presents. Based on your study, develop a **Rogerian argument** about the conflicting powers of maternal love.

Adrienne Rich

Aunt Jennifer's Tigers (1951)

Aunt Jennifer's tigers prance across a screen,
Bright topaz denizens of a world of green.
They do not fear the men beneath the tree;
They pace in sleek chivalric certainty.

Aunt Jennifer's fingers fluttering through her wool   5
Find even the ivory needle hard to pull.
The massive weight of Uncle's wedding band
Sits heavily upon Aunt Jennifer's hand.

When Aunt is dead, her terrified hands will lie
Still ringed with ordeals she was mastered by.
The tigers in the panel that she made   10
Will go on prancing, proud and unafraid.

CRITICAL THINKING QUESTION

What implied claims are made by this poem regarding Aunt Jennifer's marriage and her own identity? Identify clues from the poem that support your answer.

WRITING TOPIC

Have you observed ways in which a person's identity seems to change when he or she marries? Consider a friend or family member, or even a character from a movie, television show, or book. In what ways did the individual's identity change for the better and/or worse after marrying? Does marrying mean the members of the couple are expected to change and/or sacrifice their own identities? Please explain your insights.

———————

Adrienne Rich

Delta (1989)

> If you have taken this rubble for my past
> raking through it for fragments you could sell
> know that I long ago moved on
> deeper into the heart of the matter
>
> 5 If you think you can grasp me, think again:
> my story flows in more than one direction
> a delta springing from the riverbed
> with its five fingers spread

CRITICAL THINKING QUESTION

How is the author of the poem using the image of a delta as a **metaphor**? Upon what do you base your answer? Do you agree the use of the **imagery** is appropriate for her point?

WRITING TOPIC

Recall a time in your life when you overcame a difficult circumstance. In what ways did it change you and your outlook on life? What lessons did you take away from the experience? Would you say that the moment defines who you are today or that it is only one element of the person you have become? Please explain fully.

———————

Anne Sexton

Cinderella (1971)

You always read about it:
the plumber with twelve children
who wins the Irish Sweepstakes.
From toilets to riches.
That story.   5

Or the nursemaid,
some luscious sweet from Denmark
who captures the oldest son's heart.
From diapers to Dior.
That story.   10

Or a milkman who serves the wealthy,
eggs, cream, butter, yogurt, milk,
the white truck like an ambulance
who goes into real estate
and makes a pile.   15
From homogenized to martinis at lunch.

Or the charwoman
who is on the bus when it cracks up
and collects enough from the insurance.
From mops to Bonwit Teller.   20
That story.

Once
the wife of a rich man was on her deathbed
and she said to her daughter Cinderella:
Be devout. Be good. Then I will smile   25
down from heaven in the seam of a cloud.
The man took another wife who had
two daughters, pretty enough
but with hearts like blackjacks.
Cinderella was their maid.   30
She slept on the sooty hearth each night
and walked around looking like Al Jolson.
Her father brought presents home from town,
jewels and gowns for the other women
but the twig of a tree for Cinderella.   35
She planted that twig on her mother's grave
and it grew to a tree where a white dove sat.
Whenever she wished for anything the dove

would drop it like an egg upon the ground.
40   The bird is important, my dears, so heed him.

Next came the ball, as you all know.
It was a marriage market.
The prince was looking for a wife.
All but Cinderella were preparing
45   and gussying up for the big event.
Cinderella begged to go too.
Her stepmother threw a dish of lentils
into the cinders and said: Pick them
up in an hour and you shall go.
50   The white dove brought all his friends;
all the warm wings of the fatherland came,
and picked up the lentils in a jiffy.

No, Cinderella, said the stepmother,
you have no clothes and cannot dance.
55   That's the way with stepmothers.
Cinderella went to the tree at the grave
and cried forth like a gospel singer:
Mama! Mama! My turtledove,
send me to the prince's ball!
60   The bird dropped down a golden dress
and delicate little gold slippers.
Rather a large package for a simple bird.
So she went. Which is no surprise.
Her stepmother and sisters didn't
65   recognize her without her cinder face
and the prince took her hand on the spot
and danced with no other the whole day.

As nightfall came she thought she'd better
get home. The prince walked her home
70   and she disappeared into the pigeon house
and although the prince took an axe and broke
it open she was gone. Back to her cinders.
These events repeated themselves for three days.
However on the third day the prince
75   covered the palace steps with cobbler's wax
and Cinderella's gold shoe stuck upon it.
Now he would find whom the shoe fit
and find his strange dancing girl for keeps.
He went to their house and the two sisters
80   were delighted because they had lovely feet.
The eldest went into a room to try the slipper on

but her big toe got in the way so she simply
sliced it off and put on the slipper.
The prince rode away with her until the white dove
told him to look at the blood pouring forth.   85
That is the way with amputations.
They don't just heal up like a wish.
The other sister cut off her heel
but the blood told as blood will.
The prince was getting tired.   90
He began to feel like a shoe salesman.
But he gave it one last try.
This time Cinderella fit into the shoe
like a love letter into its envelope.
At the wedding ceremony   95
the two sisters came to curry favor
and the white dove pecked their eyes out.
Two hollow spots were left
like soup spoons.
Cinderella and the prince   100
lived, they say, happily ever after,
like two dolls in a museum case
never bothered by diapers or dust,
never arguing over the timing of an egg,
never telling the same story twice,   105
never getting a middle-aged spread,
their darling smiles pasted on for eternity
Regular Bobbsey Twins.
That story.

CRITICAL THINKING QUESTIONS

1. Sexton's poem mocks the fantasy of happiness forever. Besides fairy tales, which by definition are fantasies, how do popular culture and the media feed our fantasies of the "happily-ever-after" life? Provide several specific examples to show how popular media fuel this myth of everlasting happiness.

2. Related to the myth of the happily-ever-after life is the quest for eternal youth and beauty. The themes are present in children's stories such as *Cinderella* and *Sleeping Beauty*. What value assumption is reinforced by the physical perfection of characters in fairy tales? Do you think the target audience of such fiction is affected in any way by this emphasis on beauty?

WRITING TOPIC

Defend the place of the myth of happily-ever-after in our culture. In what ways might the fantasy of everlasting happiness be a positive force? Provide specific examples to make your case in support of the myth.

———————————

Gary Snyder

Not Leaving the House (1970)

When Kai is born
I quit going out

Hang around the kitchen—make cornbread
Let nobody in.
5   Mail is flat.
Masa lies on her side, Kai sighs,
Non washes and sweeps
We sit and watch
Masa nurse, and drink green tea.

10   Navajo turquoise beads over the bed
A peacock tail feather at the head
A badger pelt from Nagano-ken
For a mattress; under the sheet;
A pot of yogurt setting
15   Under the blankets, at his feet.

Masa, Kai,
And Non, our friend
In the green garden light reflected in
Not leaving the house.
20   From dawn til late at night
making a new world of ourselves
around this life.

CRITICAL THINKING QUESTION

What view of a father does this poem present? Point to specific lines and images that develop this view.

WRITING TOPIC

Some career women are choosing single motherhood by using sperm donors to conceive a child. Implicit in this choice is an assumption or value assumption about the father's role and the family. What is this assumption? How does Snyder's poem implicitly refute this assumption? Using this poem and other literature selections in this chapter, as well as your own primary evidence (personal experience and observations), write and defend a claim of value about the father's role in a family.

Mark Strand

The Continuous Life (1990)

What of the neighborhood homes awash
In a silver light, of children hunched in the bushes,
Watching the grownups for signs of surrender,
Signs the irregular pleasures of moving
From day to day, of being adrift on the swell of duty   5
Have run their course? O parents, confess
To your little ones the night is a long way off
And your taste for the mundane grows; tell them
Your worship of household chores has barely begun;
Describe the beauty of shovels and rakes, brooms and mops;   10
Say there will always be cooking and cleaning to do,
That one thing leads to another, which leads to another;
Explain that you live between two great darks, the first
With an ending, the second without one, that the luckiest
Thing is having been born, that you live in a blur   15
Of hours and days, months and years, and believe
It has meaning, despite the occasional fear
You are slipping away with nothing completed, nothing
To prove you existed. Tell the children to come inside,
That your search goes on for something you lost: a name,   20
A book of the family that fell from its own small matter
Into another, a piece of the dark that might have been yours—
You don't really know. Say that each of you tries
To keep busy, learning to lean down close and hear
The careless breathing of earth and feel its available   25

> Languor come over you, wave after wave, sending
> Small tremors of love through your brief,
> Undeniable selves, into your days, and beyond.

CRITICAL THINKING QUESTIONS

1. Analyze this poem as a Rogerian argument:
   a. State the issue that is implied in the poem's first six lines.
   b. Examine the evidence in lines 6 through 22. Describe the speaker's tone as he postulates responses to the issue question. What words or phrases contribute to a Rogerian tone?
   c. Reading the last six lines (23 through 28) as the conclusion to the speaker's argument, write out a Rogerian argument claim statement in response to the issue.

2. Reflecting on your experiences and observations of the lives of parents, defend or refute the claim you articulated in Question 1c.

WRITING TOPIC

Do you believe parents should always be honest with their children, or are there times when lying to a child is justified? When we are younger, we often expect our parents to have all of life's answers, but as we grow older, we learn they are experiencing many of the same feelings we are on life's journey. Is a parent justified in telling a child everything is okay, even if the parent is sure things are not? Does a parent's role as protector demand making the child feel better in all circumstances or come with an implied duty to be completely honest? Recall your childhood and explain your thoughts.

———————————

Margaret Walker

Lineage (1989)

> My grandmothers were strong.
> They followed plows and bent to toil.
> They moved through fields sowing seed.
> They touched earth and grain grew.
> They were full of sturdiness and singing.

5

My grandmothers were strong.
My grandmothers are full of memories.
Smelling of soap and onions and wet clay
With veins rolling roughly over quick hands
They have many clean words to say.   10
My grandmothers were strong.
Why am I not as they?

CRITICAL THINKING QUESTIONS

1. What qualities does the speaker imply she has lost that her grandmothers possessed?

2. How does this poem define "strong"? List specific words and phrases that create this definition.

3. What value assumptions does the speaker make about the rewards of physical toil? Do you accept them? Why or why not?

WRITING TOPIC

Many of us admire someone in our family from generations preceding our own. Consider your family history. Can you identify one relative for whom you have a particular admiration? If not, can you identify a historical figure who inspires you? Tell the story of your chosen relative/historical figure, and explain why you admire the individual so much. In what ways does he or she make you proud? Compare yourself and the qualities you possess to those of your chosen relative/historical figure. In what ways are you the same and/or different? For what qualities do you hope to be remembered by generations to come?

Richard Wilbur

The Writer (1971)

In her room at the prow of the house
Where light breaks, and the windows are tossed with linden,
My daughter is writing a story.

I pause in the stairwell, hearing
From her shut door a commotion of typewriter-keys   5
Like a chain hauled over a gunwale.

Young as she is, the stuff
Of her life is a great cargo, and some of it heavy:
I wish her a lucky passage.

But now it is she who pauses,
As if to reject my thought and its easy figure.
A stillness greatens, in which

The whole house seems to be thinking,
And then she is at it again with a bunched clamor
Of strokes, and again is silent.

I remember the dazed starling
Which was trapped in that very room, two years ago,
How we stole in, lifted a sash

And retreated, not to affright it;
And how for a helpless hour, through the crack of the door,
We watched the sleek, wild, dark

And iridescent creature
Batter against the brilliance, drop like a glove
To the hard floor, or the desk-top,

And wait then, humped and bloody,
For the wits to try it again; and how our spirits
Rose when, suddenly sure,

It lifted off from a chair-back,
Beating a smooth course for the right window
And clearing the sill of the world.

It is always a matter, my darling,
Of life or death, as I had forgotten. I wish
What I wished you before, but harder.

(line numbers in left margin: 10, 15, 20, 25, 30)

CRITICAL THINKING QUESTIONS

1. Who is the teacher, and who is the learner, in this poem? Explain your reasoning.

2. What claim does this poem imply about the process of learning?

3. Compare and contrast this poem and Meinke's "Advice to My Son" (page 400). How do the two fathers illustrate different styles of parental counseling?

WRITING TOPIC

Do you think a child's gender influences a father's parenting style and techniques? What specific experiences and observations inform your conclusion?

NONFICTION

Major Sullivan Ballou's Last Letter to His Wife (first published 1986)

A week before the Civil War Battle of Bull Run, Sullivan Ballou, a Major in the Second Rhode Island Volunteers, wrote home to his wife in Smithfield.

July 14, 1861
Sara Ballou
Washington, D.C.

Dear Sara,

The indications are very strong that we shall move in a few days, perhaps tomorrow. Less I shall not be able to write you again, I feel compelled to write a few lines that may fall under your eye when I am no more.

Our movement may be one of a few days duration and full of pleasure—and it may be one of severe conflict and death to me. Not my will, but thine O God, be done. If it is necessary that I should fall on the battlefield for my country, I am ready. I have no misgivings about or lack of confidence in the cause in which I am engaged, and my courage does not halt or falter. I know how American civilization now leans upon the triumph of the government and how great a debt we owe to those who went before us through the blood and suffering of the revolution. I am willing, perfectly willing, to lay down all my joys in this life to help maintain this government and to pay that debt.

But, my dear wife, when I know that with my own joys I lay down nearly all of yours, and replace them in this life with cares and sorrows—when, after having eaten for long years the bitter fruit of orphanage myself, I must offer it as their only sustenance to my dear little children—is it weak or dishonorable, while the banner of my purpose floats calmly and proudly in the breeze, that my unbounded love for you, my darling wife and children, should struggle in fierce, though useless, contest with my love of country?

I cannot describe to you my feelings on this calm summer night, when two thousand men are sleeping around me, many of them enjoying the last, perhaps, before that of death—and I, suspicious that Death is creeping behind me with his fatal dart, am communing with God, my country, and thee.

I have sought most closely and diligently, and often in my breast, for a wrong motive in thus hazarding the happiness of those I loved and I could not find one.

A pure love of my country and of the principles have often advocated before the people and "the name of honor that I love more than I fear death" have called upon me, and I have obeyed.

5

Sara, my love for you is depthless. It seems to bind me with mighty cables that nothing but omnipotence can break. Yet my love of country comes over me like a strong wind and bears me irresistibly with all those chains to the battlefield. The memory of all the blissful moments I have enjoyed with you come crowding over me. I feel most deeply grateful to God and you that I have enjoyed them for so long. How hard it is for me to give them up and burn to ashes our hopes and future years when, God willing, we might still have lived and loved together and seen our boys grown up to honorable manhood around us. I have, I know, but few and small claims upon Divine Providence, but something whispers to me— perhaps it is the wafted prayer of my little Edgar—that I shall return to my loved ones unharmed. If I do not, my dear Sara, never forget how much I love you, and when my last breath escapes me on the battlefield, it will whisper your name.

Forgive my many faults and the many pains I have caused you. How thoughtless, how foolish I have sometimes been. How gladly would I wash out with my tears every little spot upon your happiness, and struggle with all the misfortune of this world, to shield you and my children from harm. But I cannot. I must watch you from the spirit land and hover near you, while you buffet the storms with your precious little freight, and wait with sad patience till we meet to part no more. But, oh Sara, if the dead can come back to this earth and fly unseen around those they love, I shall always be with you on the brightest day and the darkest night. Always. Always. When the soft breeze fans your cheek, it shall be my breath. When the cool air caresses your throbbing temple, it shall be my spirit passing by. Sara, do not mourn me dead. Think I am gone and wait for me. We shall meet again.

As for my little boys, they will grow as I have done, and never know a father's love and care. Little Willie is too young to remember me long, and my blue-eyed Edgar will keep my frolics with him among the dimmest memories of his childhood. Sara, I have unlimited confidence in your maternal care and your development of their characters. Tell my two mothers his and hers I call God's blessing upon them. O Sara,

I wait for you there! Come to me, and lead thither my children.

Your loving husband,

Sullivan Ballou

A week after writing this letter, Major Ballou was killed at the first Battle of Bull Run.

CRITICAL THINKING QUESTIONS

1. Major Ballou's letter is not only a poignant expression of his love for his family—his wife Sara and his two young sons—but also an articulate description of his conflict centered on his love of family and his love of country. Write out the passages that depict this conflict. Examine the **figurative language**. In what specific ways does this language reveal this husband/father/soldier's conflict? How has he resolved his conflict?

2. Analyze this letter as a Rogerian argument centered on the personal conflict the war creates for Major Ballou. What is Ballou's compromise or middle-ground position? You may want to refer to "Rogerian Argument" in Chapter 5.

3. Imagine that Major Ballou's letter was actually written by a suicide bomber to the family he or she was leaving behind. Imagine also that the letter is addressed to the individual's husband or wife, for example, "Dear Alexander," and signed, "Your loving wife, Mary," and it can only be discerned from the details within the letter that the writer is planning to detonate explosives on herself in a crowded shopping area the following day. How might this change in authorship affect your response to the letter?

WRITING TOPIC

Examine paragraph 7 for its rhetorical strategies—for example, sentence rhythm, patterns, and lengths; use of figurative language; repetition. Try modeling the paragraph. Cast yourself in the role of one who is writing a letter to an intimate friend to explain to him or her your feelings about a difficult choice—for example, you must leave your hometown to go away to college, or you must leave the country in order to avoid military service for a war you believe is immoral.

Robin D. G. Kelley

The People in Me (2003)

"So, what are you?" I don't know how many times people have asked me that. "Are you Puerto Rican? Dominican? Indian or something? You must be mixed." My stock answer has rarely changed: "My mom is from Jamaica but grew up in New York, and my father was from North Carolina but grew up in Boston. Both black."

My family has lived with "the question" for as long as I can remember. We're "exotics," all cursed with "good hair" and strange accents—we don't sound like we from da Souf or the Norwth, and don't have that West Coast-by-way-of-Texas Calabama thang going on. The only one with the real West Indian singsong vibe is my grandmother, who looks even more East Indian than my sisters. Whatever Jamaican patois my mom possessed was pummeled out of her by cruel preteens who never had sensitivity seminars in diversity. The result for us was a nondescript way of talking, walking, and being that made us not black enough, not white enough—just a bunch of not-quite-nappy-headed enigmas.

My mother never fit the "black momma" media image. A beautiful, demure, light brown woman, she didn't drink, smoke, curse, or say things like "Lawd Jesus" or "hallelujah," nor did she Cook chitlins or gumbo. A vegetarian, she played the harmonium (a foot-pumped miniature organ), spoke softly with textbook diction, meditated, followed the teachings of Paramahansa Yogananda, and had wild hair like Chaka Khan. She burned incense in our tiny Harlem apartment, sometimes walked the streets barefoot, and, when she could afford it, cooked foods from the East.

To this day, my big sister gets misidentified for Pakistani or Bengali or Ethiopian. (Of course, changing her name from Sheral Anne Kelley to Makani Themba has not helped.) Not long ago, an Oakland cab driver, apparently a Sikh who had immigrated from India, treated my sister like dirt until he discovered that she was not a "scoundrel from Sri Lanka," but a common black American. Talk about ironic. How often are black women spared indignities *because* they are African American?

"What are you?" dogged my little brother more than any of us. He came out looking just like his father, who was white. In the black communities of Los Angeles and Pasadena, my baby bro' had to fight his way into blackness, usually winning only when he invited his friends to the house. When he got tired of this, he became what people thought he was—a cool white boy. Today he lives in Tokyo, speaks fluent Japanese, and is happily married to a Japanese woman (who is actually Korean passing as Japanese!) He stands as the perfect example of our mulattoness: a black boy trapped in a white body who speaks English with a slight Japanese accent and has a son who will spend his life confronting "the question."

Although folk had trouble naming us, we were never blanks or aliens in a "black world." We were and are "polycultural," and I'm talking about all peoples in the Western world. It is not skin, hair, walk, or talk that renders black people so diverse. Rather, it is the fact that most of them are products of different "cultures"—living cultures, not dead ones. These cultures live in and through us every day, with almost no self-consciousness about hierarchy or meaning. "Polycultural" works better than "multicultural," which implies that cultures are fixed, discrete entities that exist side by side—a kind of zoological approach to culture. Such a view obscures power relations, but often reifies race and gender differences.

Black people were polycultural from the get-go. Most of our ancestors came to these shores not as Africans, but as Ibo, Yoruba, Hausa, Kongo, Bambara, Mende, Mandingo, and so on. Some of our ancestors came as Spanish, Portuguese, French, Dutch, Irish, English, Italian. And more than a few of us, in

North America as well as in the Caribbean and Latin America, have Asian and Native American roots.

Our lines of biological descent are about as pure as O. J.'s blood sample, and our cultural lines of descent are about as mixed up as a pot of gumbo. What we know as "black culture" has always been fluid and hybrid. In Harlem in the late 1960s and 1970s, Nehru suits were as popular—and as "black"—as dashikis, and martial arts films placed Bruce Lee among a pantheon of black heroes that included Walt Frazier of the New York Knicks and Richard Rountree, who played John Shaft in blaxploitation cinema. How do we understand the zoot suit—or the conk—without the pachuco culture of Mexican American youth, or low riders in black communities without Chicanos? How can we discuss black visual artists in the interwar years without reference to the Mexican muralists, or the radical graphics tradition dating back to the late 19th century, or the Latin American artists influenced by surrealism?

Vague notions of "Eastern" religion and philosophy, as well as a variety of Orientalist assumptions, were far more important to the formation of the Lost-Found Nation of Islam than anything coming out of Africa. And Rastafarians drew many of their ideas from South Asians, from vegetarianism to marijuana, which was introduced into Jamaica by Indians. Major black movements like Garveyism and the African Blood Brotherhood are also the products of global developments. We won't understand these movements until we see them as part of a dialogue with Irish nationalists from the Easter Rebellion, Russian and Jewish émigrés from the 1905 and 1917 revolutions, and Asian socialists like India's M. N. Roy and Japan's Sen Katayama.

10 Indeed, I'm not sure we can even limit ourselves to Earth. How do we make sense of musicians Sun Ra, George Clinton, and Lee "Scratch" Perry or, for that matter, the Nation of Islam, when we consider the fact that space travel and notions of intergalactic exchange constitute a key source of their ideas?

So-called "mixed race" children are not the only ones with a claim to multiple heritages. All of us are inheritors of European, African, Native American, and Asian pasts, even if we can't exactly trace our bloodlines to these continents.

To some people that's a dangerous concept. Too many Europeans don't want to acknowledge that Africans helped create so-called Western civilization, that they are both indebted to and descendants of those they enslaved. They don't want to see the world as One—a tiny little globe where people and cultures are always on the move, where nothing stays still no matter how many times we name it. To acknowledge our polycultural heritage and cultural dynamism is not to give up our black identity. It does mean expanding our definition of blackness, taking our history more seriously, and looking at the rich diversity within us with new eyes.

So next time you see me, don't ask where I'm from or what I am, unless you're ready to sit through a long-ass lecture. As singer/songwriter Abbey Lincoln once put it, "I've got some people in me."

CRITICAL THINKING QUESTIONS

1. What polycultural enigmas have you faced? Do you have trouble *naming* people you encounter? Do people have difficulty *naming* you?

2. The writer claims, "All of us are inheritors of European, African, Native American, and Asian pasts…" (par. 11). Who might find this idea threatening, and why? On the other hand, who might argue that polyculturalism is advantageous, and why?

WRITING TOPIC

"Say it out loud. I'm hybrid and I'm proud," poet Andreu Cordesci proclaimed on National Public Radio's *All Things Considered.* Can you think of families you know, personally or otherwise, whom you would describe as polycultural? Do you share Kelley's and Cordesci's enthusiasm for this expanded definition of family and heritage? Why or why not?

Scott Russell Sanders

The Men We Carry in Our Minds (1984)

This must be a hard time for women," I say to my friend Anneke. "They have so many paths to choose from, and so many voices calling them."

"I think it's a lot harder for men," she replies.

"How do you figure that?"

"The women I know feel excited, innocent, like crusaders in a just cause. The men I know are eaten up with guilt."

We are sitting at the kitchen table drinking sassafras tea, our hands wrapped   5 around the mugs because this April morning is cool and drizzly. "Like a Dutch morning," Anneke told me earlier. She is Dutch herself, a writer and midwife and peacemaker, with the round face and sad eyes of a woman in a Vermeer painting who might be waiting for the rain to stop, for a door to open. She leans over to sniff a sprig of lilac, pale lavender, that rises from a vase of cobalt blue.

"Women feel such pressure to be everything, do everything," I say. "Career kids, art, politics. Have their babies and get back to the office a week later. It's as if they're trying to overcome a million years' worth of evolution in one lifetime."

"But we help one another. We don't try to lumber on alone, like so many wounded grizzly bears, the way men do." Anneke sips her tea. I gave her the mug with owls on it, for wisdom. "And we have this deep-down sense that we're in the *right*—we've been held back, passed over, used—while men feel they're in the wrong. Men are the ones who've been discredited, who have to search their souls."

I search my soul. I discover guilty feelings aplenty—toward the poor, the Vietnamese, Native Americans, the whales, an endless list of debts—a guilt in each case that is as bright and unambiguous as a neon sign. But toward women I feel something more confused, a snarl of shame, envy, wary tenderness, and amazement. This muddle troubles me. To hide my unease I say, "You're right, it's tough being a man these days."

"Don't laugh." Anneke frowns at me, mournful-eyed, through the sassafras steam. "I wouldn't be a man for anything. It's much easier being the victim. All the victim has to do is break free. The persecutor has to live with his past."

10   How deep is that past? I find myself wondering after Anneke has left. How much of an inheritance do I have to throw off? Is it just the beliefs I breathed in as a child? Do I have to scour memory back through father and grandfather? Through St. Paul? Beyond Stonehenge and into the twilit caves? I'm convinced the past we must contend with is deeper even than speech. When I think back on my childhood, on how I learned to see men and women, I have a sense of ancient, dizzying depths. The back roads of Tennessee and Ohio where I grew up were probably closer, in their sexual patterns, to the campsites of Stone Age hunters than to the genderless cities of the future into which we are rushing.

The first men, besides my father, I remember seeing were black convicts and white guards, in the cottonfield across the road from our farm on the outskirts of Memphis. I must have been three or four. The prisoners wore dingy gray-and-black zebra suits, heavy as canvas, sodden with sweat. Hatless, stooped, they chopped weeds in the fierce heat, row after row, breathing the acrid dust of boll-weevil poison. The overseers wore dazzling white shirts and broad shadowy hats. The oiled barrels of their shotguns flashed in the sunlight. Their faces in memory are utterly blank. Of course those men, white and black, have become for me an emblem of racial hatred. But they have also come to stand for the twin poles of my early vision of manhood—the brute toiling animal and the boss.

When I was a boy, the men I knew labored with their bodies. They were marginal farmers, just scraping by, or welders, steelworkers, carpenters; they swept floors, dug ditches, mined coal, or drove trucks, their forearms ropy with muscle; they trained horses, stoked furnaces, built tires, stood on assembly lines wrestling parts onto cars and refrigerators. They got up before light, worked all day long whatever the weather, and when they came home at night they looked as though somebody had been whipping them. In the evenings and on weekends they worked on their own places, tilling gardens that were lumpy with clay, fixing broken-down cars, hammering on houses that were always too drafty, too leaky, too small.

The bodies of the men I knew were twisted and maimed in ways visible and invisible. The nails of their hands were black and split, the hands tattooed with scars. Some had lost fingers. Heavy lifting had given many of them finicky backs and guts weak from hernias. Racing against conveyor belts had given them ulcers. Their ankles and knees ached from years of standing on concrete. Anyone who had worked for long around machines was hard of hearing. They squinted, and the skin of their faces was creased like the leather of old work gloves. There were times, studying them, when I dreaded growing up. Most of them coughed, from dust or cigarettes, and most of them drank cheap wine or whiskey, so their eyes looked bloodshot and bruised. The fathers of my friends always seemed older than the mothers. Men wore out sooner. Only women lived into old age.

As a boy I also knew another sort of men, who did not sweat and break down like mules. They were soldiers, and so far as I could tell they scarcely worked at all. During my early school years we lived on a military base, an arsenal in Ohio, and every day I saw GIs in the guardshacks, on the stoops of barracks, at the wheels of olive drab Chevrolets. The chief fact of their lives was boredom. Long after I left the Arsenal I came to recognize the sour smell the soldiers gave off as that of souls in limbo. They were all waiting—for wars, for transfers, for leaves, for promotions, for the end of their hitch—like so many braves waiting for the hunt to begin. Unlike the warriors of older tribes, however, they would have no say about when the battle would start or how it would be waged. Their waiting was broken only when they practiced for war. They fired guns at targets, drove tanks across the churned-up fields of the military reservation, set off bombs in the wrecks of old fighter planes. I knew this was all play. But I also felt certain that when the hour for killing arrived, they would kill. When the real shooting started, many of them would die. This was what soldiers were *for*, just as a hammer was for driving nails.

Warriors and toilers: those seemed, in my boyhood vision, to be the chief destinies for men. They weren't the only destinies, as I learned from having a few male teachers, from reading books, and from watching television. But the men on television—the politicians, the astronauts, the generals, the savvy lawyers, the philosophical doctors, the bosses who gave orders to both soldiers and laborers—seemed as remote and unreal to me as the figures in tapestries. I could no more imagine growing up to become one of these cool, potent creatures than I could imagine becoming a prince.

A nearer and more hopeful example was that of my father, who had escaped from a red-dirt farm to a tire factory, and from the assembly line to the front office. Eventually he dressed in a white shirt and tie. He carried himself as if he had been born to work with his mind. But his body, remembering the earlier years of slogging work, began to give out on him in his fifties, and it quit on him entirely before he turned sixty-five. Even such a partial escape from man's fate as he had accomplished did not seem possible for most of the boys I knew. They joined the Army, stood in line for jobs in the smoky plants, helped build highways. They were bound to work as their fathers had worked, killing themselves or preparing to kill others.

A scholarship enabled me not only to attend college, a rare enough feat in my circle, but even to study in a university meant for the children of the rich.

Here I met for the first time young men who had assumed from birth that they would lead lives of comfort and power. And for the first time I met women who told me that men were guilty of having kept all the joys and privileges of the earth for themselves. I was baffled. What privileges? What joys? I thought about the maimed, dismal lives of most of the men back home. What had they stolen from their wives and daughters? The right to go five days a week, twelve months a year, for thirty or forty years to a steel mill or a coal mine? The right to drop bombs and die in war? The right to feel every leak in the roof, every gap in the fence, every cough in the engine, as a wound they must mend? The right to feel, when the lay-off comes or the plant shuts down, not only afraid but ashamed?

I was slow to understand the deep grievances of women. This was because, as a boy, I had envied them. Before college, the only people I had ever known who were interested in art or music or literature, the only ones who read books, the only ones who ever seemed to enjoy a sense of ease and grace were the mothers and daughters. Like the menfolk, they fretted about money, they scrimped and made-do. But, when the pay stopped coming in, they were not the ones who had failed. Nor did they have to go to war, and that seemed to me a blessed fact. By comparison with the narrow, ironclad days of fathers, there was an expansiveness, I thought, in the days of mothers. They went to see neighbors, to shop in town, to run errands at school, at the library, at church. No doubt, had I looked harder at their lives, I would have envied them less. It was not my fate to become a woman, so it was easier for me to see the graces. Few of them held jobs outside the home, and those who did filled thankless roles as clerks and waitresses. I didn't see, then, what a prison a house could be, since houses seemed to me brighter, handsomer places than any factory. I did not realize—because such things were never spoken of—how often women suffered from men's bullying. I did learn about the wretchedness of abandoned wives, single mothers, widows; but I also learned about the wretchedness of lone men. Even then I could see how exhausting it was for a mother to cater all day to the needs of young children. But if I had been asked, as a boy, to choose between tending a baby and tending a machine, I think I would have chosen the baby. (Having now tended both, I know I would choose the baby.)

So I was baffled when the women at college accused me and my sex of having cornered the world's pleasures. I think something like my bafflement has been felt by other boys (and by girls as well) who grew up in dirt-poor farm country, in mining country, in black ghettos, in Hispanic barrios, in the shadows of factories, in Third World nations—any place where the fate of men is as grim and bleak as the fate of women. Toilers and warriors. I realize now how ancient these identities are, how deep the tug they exert on men, the undertow of a thousand generations. The miseries I saw, as a boy, in the lives of nearly all men I continue to see in the lives of many—the body-breaking toil, the tedium, the call to be tough, the humiliating powerlessness, the battle for a living and for territory.

20   When the women I met at college thought about the joys and privileges of men, they did not carry in their minds the sort of men I had known in my

childhood. They thought of their fathers, who were bankers, physicians, architects, stockbrokers, the big wheels of the big cities. These fathers rode the train to work or drove cars that cost more than any of my childhood houses. They were attended from morning to night by female helpers, wives and nurses and secretaries. They were never laid off, never short of cash at month's end, never lined up for welfare. These fathers made decisions that mattered. They ran the world.

The daughters of such men wanted to share in this power, this glory. So did I. They yearned for a say over their future, for jobs worthy of their abilities, for the right to live at peace, unmolested, whole. Yes, I thought, yes yes. The difference between me and these daughters was that they saw me, because of my sex, as destined from birth to become like their fathers, and therefore as an enemy to their desires. But I knew better. I wasn't an enemy, in fact or in feeling. I was an ally. If I had known, then, how to tell them so, would they have believed me? Would they now?

CRITICAL THINKING QUESTIONS

1. Rewrite Sanders's first paragraph (the essay's first two sentences) as a claim statement followed by *because: Women must have . . . because they. . . .*

2. What **assumption** links the support clause (*because...*) to the claim? Do you accept the assumption, and why or why not?

WRITING TOPIC

Sanders concludes that the women he met at college should have regarded him as an ally rather than as an enemy. How does Sanders's closing **assertion** reframe the initial issue raised in the essay: Who has it better, men or women? Write out the question that frames the argument for Sanders's closing assertion. Based on the images of men and women that you carry in your mind, which issue question has more relevance and validity today? Write an essay defending your claim.

Amy Schalet

The Sleepover Question (2011)

NOT under my roof. That's the attitude most American parents have toward teenagers and their sex lives. Squeamishness and concern describe most parents' approach to their offspring's carnality. We don't want them doing it—whatever "it" is!—in our homes. Not surprisingly, teenage sex is a source of conflict in many American families.

Would Americans increase peace in family life and strengthen family bonds if they adopted more accepting attitudes about sex and what's allowable under the family roof? I've interviewed 130 people, all white, middle class and not particularly religious, as part of a study of teenage sex and family life here and in the Netherlands. My look into cultural differences suggests family life might be much improved, for all, if Americans had more open ideas about teenage sex. The question of who sleeps where when a teenager brings a boyfriend or girlfriend home for the night fits within the larger world of culturally divergent ideas about teenage sex, lust and capacity for love.

Kimberly and Natalie dramatize the cultural differences in the way young women experience their sexuality. (I have changed their names to protect confidentiality.) Kimberly, a 16-year-old American, never received sex education at home. "God, no! No, no! That's not going to happen," she told me. She'd like to tell her parents that she and her boyfriend are having sex, but she believes it is easier for her parents not to know because the truth would "shatter" their image of her as their "little princess."

Natalie, who is also 16 but Dutch, didn't tell her parents immediately when she first had intercourse with her boyfriend of three months. But, soon after, she says, she was so happy, she wanted to share the good news. Initially her father was upset and worried about his daughter and his honor. "Talk to him," his wife advised Natalie; after she did, her father made peace with the change. Essentially Natalie and her family negotiated a life change together and figured out, as a family, how to adjust to changed circumstance.

5   Respecting what she understood as her family's "don't ask, don't tell" policy, Kimberly only slept with her boyfriend at his house, when no one was home. She enjoyed being close to her boyfriend but did not like having to keep an important part of her life secret from her parents. In contrast, Natalie and her boyfriend enjoyed time and a new closeness with her family; the fact that her parents knew and approved of her boyfriend seemed a source of pleasure.

The difference in their experiences stems from divergent cultural ideas about sex and what responsible parents ought to do about it. Here, we see teenagers as helpless victims beset by raging hormones and believe parents should protect them from urges they cannot control. Matters aren't helped by the stereotype that all boys want the same thing, and all girls want love and cuddling. This compounds the burden on parents to steer teenage children away from relationships that will do more harm than good.

The Dutch parents I interviewed regard teenagers, girls and boys, as capable of falling in love, and of reasonably assessing their own readiness for sex. Dutch parents like Natalie's talk to their children about sex and its unintended consequences and urge them to use contraceptives and practice safe sex.

Cultural differences about teenage sex are more complicated than clichéd images of puritanical Americans and permissive Europeans. Normalizing ideas about teenage sex in fact allows the Dutch to exert *more* control over their children. Most of the parents I interviewed actively discouraged promiscuous behavior. And Dutch teenagers often reinforced what we see as 1950s-style mores: eager to win approval, they bring up their partners in conversation, introduce them to their parents and help them make favorable impressions.

Some Dutch teenagers went so far as to express their ideas about sex and love in self-consciously traditional terms; one Dutch boy said the advantage of spending the night with a partner was that it was "Like Mom and Dad, like when you're married, you also wake up next to the person you love."

Normalizing teenage sex under the family roof opens the way for more   10 responsible sex education. In a national survey, 7 of 10 Dutch girls reported that by the time they were 16, their parents had talked to them about pregnancy and contraception. It seems these conversations helped teenagers prepare, responsibly, for active sex lives: 6 of 10 Dutch girls said they were on the pill when they first had intercourse. Widespread use of oral contraceptives contributes to low teenage pregnancy rates—more than 4 times lower in the Netherlands than in the United States.

Obviously sleepovers aren't a direct route to family happiness. But even the most traditional parents can appreciate the virtue of having their children be comfortable bringing a girlfriend or boyfriend home, rather than have them sneak around.

Unlike the American teenagers I interviewed, who said they felt they had to split their burgeoning sexual selves from their family roles, the Dutch teens had a chance to integrate different parts of themselves into their family life. When children feel safe enough to tell parents what they are doing and feeling, presumably it's that much easier for them to ask for help. This allows parents to have more influence, to control through connection.

Sexual maturation is awkward and difficult. The Dutch experience suggests that it is possible for families to stay connected when teenagers start having sex, and that if they do, the transition into adulthood need not be so painful for parents or children.

CRITICAL THINKING QUESTIONS

1. When beginning to analyze an argument, first turn to the authority of your own experience. As a teenager, did you feel you had to separate your "burgeoning sexual" self from the self perceived by your family? Does your experience prompt you to question or to support the validity of this argument?

2. The writer uses an inductive pattern of organization for her argument: she delays her claim until the end of her article. Throughout the previous paragraphs, she provides evidence that leads to her claim.
   a. What is the effect of Schalet's organizational strategy on the reader? How does the organization contribute to or detract from the effectiveness of the argument?
   b. What is the impact of Schalet's use of the word *suggests* in her claim?

3. In the second paragraph, the writer poses a **rhetorical question**: "Would Americans increase peace in family life and strengthen family bonds if they adopted more accepting attitudes about sex and what's allowable under the family roof?" How does this question help determine the structure of the essay? In what sense does Schalet expect the reader to answer this question?

WRITING TOPIC

Write your response to the rhetorical question in paragraph two (see Question 3).

George Will

The Tangled Web of Conflicting Rights (2012)

Elaine Huguenin, who with her husband operates Elane Photography in New Mexico, asks only to be let alone. But instead of being allowed a reasonable zone of sovereignty in which to live her life in accordance with her beliefs, she is being bullied by people wielding government power.

In 2006, Vanessa Willock, who was in a same-sex relationship, emailed Elane Photography about photographing a "commitment ceremony" that she and her partner were planning. Willock said this would be a "same-gender ceremony." Elane Photography responded that it photographed "traditional weddings." The Huguenins are Christians who, for religious reasons, disapprove of same-sex unions. Willock sent a second email asking whether this meant that the company "does not offer photography services to same-sex couples." Elane Photography responded "you are correct."

Willock could then have said regarding Elane Photography what many same-sex couples have long hoped a tolerant society would say regarding them—"live and let live." Willock could have hired a photographer with no objections to such events. Instead, Willock and her partner set out to break the Huguenins to the state's saddle.

Willock's partner, without disclosing her relationship with Willock, emailed Elane Photography. She said she was getting married—actually, she and Willock were having a "commitment ceremony," because New Mexico does not recognize same-sex marriages—and asked if the company would travel to photograph it. The company said yes. Willock's partner never responded.

Instead, Willock, spoiling for a fight, filed a discrimination claim with the   5
New Mexico Human Rights Commission, charging that Elane Photography is a "public accommodation," akin to a hotel or restaurant, that denied her its services because of her sexual orientation. The NMHRC found against Elane Photography and ordered it to pay $6,600 in attorney fees.

But what a tangled web we weave when we undertake to regulate more and more behaviors under overlapping codifications of conflicting rights.

Elaine Huguenin says she is being denied her right to the "free exercise" of religion guaranteed by the U.S. Constitution's First Amendment and a similar provision in the New Mexico constitution.

Furthermore, New Mexico's Religious Freedom Restoration Act defines "free exercise" as "an act or a refusal to act that is substantially motivated by religious belief," and forbids government from abridging that right except to "further a compelling government interest."

So New Mexico, whose marriage laws discriminate against same-sex unions, has a "compelling interest" in compelling Huguenin to provide a service she finds repugnant and others would provide? Strange.

Eugene Volokh of the UCLA School of Law thinks Huguenin can also make   10
a "compelled speech argument": She cannot be coerced into creating expressive works, such as photographs, which express something she is uncomfortable expressing.

A New Mexico court, however, has held that Elane Photography is merely "a conduit for another's expression."

New Mexico's Supreme Court is going to sort all this out, which has been thoroughly reported and discussed by the invaluable blog *The Volokh Conspiracy*, where you can ponder this: In jurisdictions such as the District of Columbia and Seattle, which ban discrimination on the basis of political affiliation or ideology, would a photographer, even a Jewish photographer, be compelled to record a Nazi Party ceremony?

The Huguenin case demonstrates how advocates of tolerance become tyrannical.

First, a disputed behavior, such as sexual activities between people of the same sex, is declared so personal and intimate that government should have no jurisdiction over it.

Then, having won recognition of what Louis Brandeis, a pioneer of the pri-   15
vacy right, called "the right to be let alone," some who have benefited from this achievement assert a right not to let other people alone.

It is the right to coerce anyone who disapproves of the now-protected behavior into acting as though they approve it or at least into not acting on their disapproval.

So, in the name of tolerance, government declares intolerable individuals such as the Huguenins, who disapprove of a certain behavior but ask only to be let alone in their quiet disapproval. Perhaps advocates of gay rights should begin to restrain the bullies in their ranks.

CRITICAL THINKING QUESTIONS

1. Identify the author's feelings on the issue addressed in the article. What textual clues do you find useful in understanding the writer's views?

2. Suppose you were the deciding Supreme Court justice in the case argued in Will's editorial. How would you rule? Why?

3. Will claims that there are "bullies" among those fighting for gay rights. How would you respond to this assertion?

WRITING TOPIC

Do you feel a business owner's religious views should be allowed to dictate the way a privately owned business is run? If owners operate their businesses based on religious beliefs, do you feel this can promote discrimination? Contrarily, do you believe not allowing business owners to run their own businesses according to their personal values violates the right to freedom of religion/speech? Explain your reasoning and provide specific examples.

CHAPTER ACTIVITIES AND TOPICS FOR WRITING ARGUMENTS

1. What is "marital bliss"? Should you expect to experience self-development and equality within a marriage? What does it mean to choose a marriage partner in the twenty-first century? Should engaged couples create and sign a prenuptial contract? Do some background research on prenuptial contracts. Then conduct primary research on the state of marriage in the twenty-first century: Interview peers, friends, and family members and ask them their views on the above questions. (For a representative sample, be sure to talk with persons representing different age groups and to include an even gender mix in your sample.) Based on your research findings and several chapter readings, write an argument that advocates or disputes prenuptial contracts. Or write a Rogerian argument that advocates a rethinking of the conventional concept of marriage (literature suggestions: Chopin's "The Storm" [page 350]; Bradstreet's "To My Dear and Loving Husband" [page 387]; Corso's "Marriage" [page 392].

2. The nineteenth-century Russian writer Leo Tolstoy opens Chapter 1 of his novel *Anna Karenina* with this two-part assertion: "All happy families are like one another; each unhappy family is unhappy in its own way."[1] What assumptions are implied in his assertion about "happy families"? What assumptions are implied about "unhappy families"? Extend your thinking beyond Tolstoy's assertions to your own experience, observations, and several readings in this chapter. Write an essay that defends, refutes, and/or qualifies Tolstoy's assertions about happy and unhappy families (literature suggestions: Chopin's "The Storm" [page 350]; Snyder's "Not Leaving the House" [page 410]).

3. What is the role of a father? Is a father's participation in a child's growing up more significant in a son's or in a daughter's long-term well being? If a parent's personal income is sufficient, can a single parent (Mom or Dad) be "good enough" for child rearing? How important is it for a child to have regular, daily contact with both his or her mom and dad? Conduct research to find out what family therapists and sociologists are saying about these parenting issues; also, ask friends for their viewpoints. Based on your research findings and several literature selections, argue a position on an aspect of parenting (literature suggestions: Meinke's "Advice to My Son" [page 400]; Cleary's "Boss's Son" [page 390]; Wilbur's "The Writer" [page 413]).

4. How do family traditions and cultural legacies contribute to and/or inhibit an individual's self-identity? What do you know about your family history? How is this history shared, and how is it valued among individual family members? Beyond its literal meaning, what are the broader implications of the cliché "keeping the family name alive"? Or has this cliché outlived its validity? A number of readings in this chapter address an aspect of family tradition/cultural heritage and individual identity and fulfillment—for example, Walker's "Everyday Use" (page 379); Rich's "Delta" (page 406); Kelley's "The People in Me" (page 418). Drawing on evidence from several

---

[1]Leo Tolstoy, *Anna Karenina* (New York: Signet Classics, 1961), 17.

readings and your own experience and observations, write a claim of value argument about an aspect of family heritage and individual identity.

5. Why get married? As noted in the chapter introduction, couples increasingly are choosing to form intimate relationships and cohabitate without getting married. As such, these couples side-step the legal constraints—and benefits—of the marriage bond. Moreover, social attitudes seem to be softening. This lifestyle option, once wholly rejected, is now tolerated by many and applauded by some. Write an argument in response to the question, Why get married? (literature suggestions: Davis's "Break It Down" [page 354]; Hemingway's "Hills Like White Elephants" [page 359]; Corso's "Marriage" [page 392]; Hardy's "The Ruined Maid" [page 397]).

GLOBAL PERSPECTIVES RESEARCH/WRITING TOPICS

1. Family Planning Options

Family planning is a controversial topic around the globe. The perspectives vary by region and religious views. President Obama repealed rules instituted by former President Bush that had restricted federal money from going to any international organization that "performs or actively promotes abortion as a method of family planning in foreign countries…including providing advice, counseling or information regarding abortion." In doing so, Obama said that the Bush policy had "undermined efforts to promote safe and effective voluntary family planning in developing countries."[2] Obama's order met with equally vociferous approval and condemnation. After researching this topic to learn more about the effects of both Bush's and Obama's policies on family planning in developing countries, create an argument either supporting Obama's order or calling for its repeal.

2. International Adoption

International adoption has been considered one possible way to improve the lives of at least some children who are living in impoverished conditions. And on the surface, it would seem to be a beneficial approach to addressing child poverty: A child is given an opportunity to grow up in a home where parents can provide for him or her, and a couple is granted the child for whom they have longed. However, child-trafficking scandals have been exposed that suggest that the process is fraught with exploitation. Also, because an international adoption usually means that a child will grow up in a family of a different culture or ethnicity, some people question whether such an adoption, overall, serves the child's best interests. Meanwhile, poverty continues to fester in the child's country of origin.

---

[2]Peter Baker, "Obama Reverses Rule on U.S. Abortion Aid." *New York Times*, January 24, 2009.

While condemning fraudulent and unethical adoptions, proponents of international adoption also believe that cases of corruption can be addressed without stopping the adoptions altogether. The Hague Convention on Intercountry Adoption, a treaty involving more than seventy countries including the United States, represents an international effort to do just that: "It [the Hague Convention] mandates safeguards to protect the interests of children, birth parents, and adoptive parents."[3] Moreover, the mother of an internationally adopted child from South Korea asserts, "International adoptive families are pretty much the same as other families out there. I don't think the majority of parents who adopt foreign children are thinking about solving child poverty. Most are looking to adoption as a way to create a family." After researching different perspectives on international adoption, develop an argument that supports or opposes international adoption.

COLLABORATION ACTIVITY: CREATING A ROGERIAN ARGUMENT

For this activity, you will work in small teams to research, write, and present a Rogerian argument on a contemporary issue that has emerged from your exploration of readings in this chapter. The WRITING TOPICS following many of the selections can help you identify an issue. For a discussion of the Rogerian argument and a suggested organizational approach to the assignment, please see Chapter 5.

Following are guidelines for this collaboration activity:

- Identify an **issue**.
- Divide the research/writing responsibilities as follows:
  - Student one: introduction section
  - Student two: body section, affirmative position
  - Student three: body section, opposing position
  - Student four: conclusion, summation, and middle-ground position

Following are characteristics of effective collaboration. Each team member should:

- Contribute by collecting information related to the issue.
- Take responsibility by completing assigned work on time.
- Engage with other team members by listening to and considering other viewpoints.

SAMPLE ISSUE: SAME-SEX MARRIAGE

In June 2015, the U.S. Supreme Court legalized gay marriage in a 5–4 ruling. Previously, thirty-seven states, including the District of Columbia, had either voted in favor of legalized same-sex marriages or rendered court

---

[3]"Hague Convention on Intercountry Adoption Enters into Full Force." *Embassy of the United States.* Montevideo, Uruguay: 1 Apr. 2008. Web. 17 Mar. 2015.

rulings that demanded states legally recognize gay marriage. The historical Supreme Court ruling appears to reflect America's growing acceptance of gay rights. A May 2014 Gallup poll found support for gay marriage at an all-time high, with 55 percent of Americans supporting same-sex marriage. In 2012, President Obama endorsed the right of same-sex couples to marry, thereby becoming the first U.S. president to support same-sex marriage. However, even given the final word from the Supreme Court, the controversy is far from finished. Some state officials have vowed to continue to fight against same-sex marriage. While opponents argue that sanctioning marriage between same-sex couples undermines the institution of marriage, advocates claim that no couple, regardless of gender, should be denied the civil rights associated with marriage. Do you agree with the Supreme Court's ruling on same-sex marriage?

ARGUING THEMES FROM LITERATURE

Each selection in this chapter promoted reflection upon family and identity. To practice your literary argument skills, consider the following questions:

1. In Alice Walker's "Everyday Use" (page 379), a major **conflict** arises when Dee says she wants the handmade quilts Mama has promised Maggie. Consider the dynamic of the **characters** in relation to their expected family roles. In what ways do the characters not follow traditional family hierarchy? Support your views with textual evidence.

2. Kate Chopin's "The Storm" (page 350) explores the complexity of marital relationships by giving readers a glimpse into the lives of characters within a very short period of time. Based upon your interpretation of the reading, what exactly do you think happened between Calixta and Alcée during the storm? Also what do you make of Alcée writing Clarisse and telling her and the children to extend their stay in Biloxi? Do you believe that Bobinôt and Clarissa have any hint as to what could be developing and/or going on between their spouses? In what ways does the symbolism of a storm hint at what could be about to happen in the lives of the two couples?

3. Consider Katherine Mansfield's "The Garden Party" (page 368). Based upon your reading, do you think that Laura will grow up to accept or reject her family's values and class position? Use the text to defend your viewpoint.

CHAPTER 9

Power and Responsibility

Do you recall a playground bully from your childhood, that child whose strength and physical power made him intimidating? What was frightening was not merely his strength, but how he chose to use that strength. He was threatening because sometimes he did not act responsibly and, thus, could hurt you. On the other hand, not all threatening children were physically powerful; some gained control through manipulation. They, too, could exert a power over you, potentially harming you by irresponsibly starting rumors and exploiting gossip to achieve their goals.

As adults, we continue to witness the abuse of power by individuals who seek to influence and control others for their own gain. In our eyes, such individuals act irresponsibly when they buy votes in our government, create insider stock deals on Wall Street, or merely forget to consider the feelings of others as they pursue their goals. The hard truth is that with power comes responsibility, for we are all answerable, eventually accountable, for our actions.

PREWRITING AND DISCUSSION

1. What do people mean when they talk about *power*? Focus on a particular context, such as state government, the family, the schools, or the community. Who has power and who does not—and why? Is power related to money? To respect?

2. Consider the saying "Power corrupts, and absolute power corrupts absolutely." Can you think of examples where that phrase has proven to be true? Can you think of examples of powerful people who are above corruption, people who forego personal benefits in order to work for the good of others?

3. Write for a few minutes about *responsibility*. What responsibility do we as individuals have to our families, communities, or nation? In small groups, discuss your ideas of power and responsibility.

FICTION

Raymond Carver

Cathedral (1983)

This blind man, an old friend of my wife's, he was on his way to spend the night. His wife had died. So he was visiting the dead wife's relatives in Connecticut. He called my wife from his in-laws'. Arrangements were made. He would come by train, a five-hour trip, and my wife would meet him at the station. She hadn't seen him since she worked for him one summer in Seattle ten years ago. But she and the blind man had kept in touch. They made tapes and mailed them back and forth. I wasn't enthusiastic about his visit. He was no one I knew. And his being blind bothered me. My idea of blindness came from the movies. In the movies, the blind moved slowly and never laughed. Sometimes they were led by seeing-eye dogs. A blind man in my house was not something I looked forward to.

That summer in Seattle she had needed a job. She didn't have any money. The man she was going to marry at the end of the summer was in officers' training school. He didn't have any money, either. But she was in love with the guy, and he was in love with her, etc. She'd seen something in the paper: HELP WANTED—*Reading to Blind Man*, and a telephone number. She phoned and went over, was hired on the spot. She'd worked with this blind man all summer. She read stuff to him, case studies, reports, that sort of thing. She helped him organize his little office in the county social-service department. They'd become good friends, my wife and the blind man. How do I know these things? She told me. And she told me something else. On her last day in the office, the blind man asked if he could touch her face. She agreed to this. She told me he touched his fingers to every part of her face, her nose—even her neck! She never forgot it. She even tried to write a poem about it. She was always trying to write a poem. She wrote a poem or two every year, usually after something really important had happened to her.

When we first started going out together, she showed me the poem. In the poem, she recalled his fingers and the way they had moved around over her face. In the poem, she talked about what she had felt at the time, about what went through her mind when the blind man touched her nose and lips. I can remember

I didn't think much of the poem. Of course, I didn't tell her that. Maybe I just don't understand poetry. I admit it's not the first thing I reach for when I pick up something to read.

Anyway, this man who'd first enjoyed her favors, the officer-to-be, he'd been her childhood sweetheart. So okay. I'm saying that at the end of the summer she let the blind man run his hands over her face, said goodbye to him, married her childhood etc., who was now a commissioned officer, and she moved away from Seattle. But they'd kept in touch, she and the blind man. She made the first contact after a year or so. She called him up one night from an Air Force base in Alabama. She wanted to talk. They talked. He asked her to send him a tape and tell him about her life. She did this. She sent the tape. On the tape, she told the blind man about her husband and about their life together in the military. She told the blind man she loved her husband but she didn't like it where they lived and she didn't like it that he was a part of the military-industrial thing. She told the blind man she'd written a poem and he was in it. She told him that she was writing a poem about what it was like to be an Air Force officer's wife. The poem wasn't finished yet. She was still writing it. The blind man made a tape. He sent her the tape. She made a tape. This went on for years. My wife's officer was posted to one base and then another. She sent tapes from Moody AFB, McGuire, McConnell, and finally Travis, near Sacramento, where one night she got to feeling lonely and cut off from people she kept losing in that moving-around life. She got to feeling she couldn't go it another step. She went in and swallowed all the pills and capsules in the medicine chest and washed them down with a bottle of gin. Then she got into a hot bath and passed out.

But instead of dying, she got sick. She threw up. Her officer—why should he   5 have a name? he was the childhood sweetheart, and what more does he want?— came home from somewhere, found her, and called the ambulance. In time, she put it all on a tape and sent the tape to the blind man. Over the years, she put all kinds of stuff on tapes and sent the tapes off lickety-split. Next to writing a poem every year, I think it was her chief means of recreation. On one tape, she told the blind man she'd decided to live away from her officer for a time. On another tape, she told him about her divorce. She and I began going out, and of course she told her blind man about it. She told him everything, or so it seemed to me. Once she asked me if I'd like to hear the latest tape from the blind man. This was a year ago. I was on the tape, she said. So I said okay, I'd listen to it. I got us drinks and we settled down in the living room. We made ready to listen. First she inserted the tape into the player and adjusted a couple of dials. Then she pushed a lever. The tape squeaked and someone began to talk in this loud voice. She lowered the volume. After a few minutes of harmless chitchat, I heard my own name in the mouth of this stranger, this blind man I didn't even know! And then this: "From all you've said about him, I can only conclude—" But we were interrupted, a knock at the door, something, and we didn't ever get back to the tape. Maybe it was just as well. I'd heard all I wanted to.

Now this same blind man was coming to sleep in my house.

"Maybe I could take him bowling," I said to my wife. She was at the draining board doing scalloped potatoes. She put down the knife she was using and turned around.

"If you love me," she said, "you can do this for me. If you don't love me, okay. But if you had a friend, any friend, and the friend came to visit, I'd make him feel comfortable." She wiped her hands with the dish towel.

"I don't have any blind friends," I said.

10   "You don't have *any* friends," she said. "Period. Besides," she said, "goddamn it, his wife's just died! Don't you understand that? The man's lost his wife!"

I didn't answer. She'd told me a little about the blind man's wife. Her name was Beulah. Beulah! That's a name for a colored woman.

"Was his wife a Negro?" I asked.

"Are you crazy?" my wife said. "Have you just flipped or something?" She picked up a potato. I saw it hit the floor, then roll under the stove. "What's wrong with you?" she said. "Are you drunk?"

"I'm just asking," I said.

15   Right then my wife filled me in with more detail than I cared to know. I made a drink and sat at the kitchen table to listen. Pieces of the story began to fall into place.

Beulah had gone to work for the blind man the summer after my wife had stopped working for him. Pretty soon Beulah and the blind man had themselves a church wedding. It was a little wedding—who'd want to go to such a wedding in the first place?—just the two of them, plus the minister and the minister's wife. But it was a church wedding just the same. It was what Beulah had wanted, he'd said. But even then Beulah must have been carrying the cancer in her glands. After they had been inseparable for eight years—my wife's word, *inseparable*—Beulah's health went into a rapid decline. She died in a Seattle hospital room, the blind man sitting beside the bed and holding on to her hand. They'd married, lived and worked together, slept together—had sex, sure—and then the blind man had to bury her. All this without his having ever seen what the goddamned woman looked like. It was beyond my understanding. Hearing this, I felt sorry for the blind man for a little bit. And then I found myself thinking what a pitiful life this woman must have led. Imagine a woman who could never see herself as she was seen in the eyes of her loved one. A woman who could go on day after day and never receive the smallest compliment from her beloved. A woman whose husband could never read the expression on her face, be it misery or something better. Someone who could wear makeup or not—what difference to him? She could, if she wanted, wear green eyeshadow around one eye, a straight pin in her nostril, yellow slacks and purple shoes, no matter. And then to slip off into death, the blind man's hand on her hand, his blind eyes streaming tears—I'm imagining now—her last thought maybe this: that he never even knew what she looked like, and she on an express to the grave. Robert was left with a small insurance policy and half of a twenty-peso Mexican coin. The other half of the coin went into the box with her. Pathetic.

So when the time rolled around, my wife went to the depot to pick him up. With nothing to do but wait—sure, I blamed him for that—I was having a drink and watching the TV when I heard the car pull into the drive. I got up from the sofa with my drink and went to the window to have a look.

I saw my wife laughing as she parked the car. I saw her get out of the car and shut the door. She was still wearing a smile. Just amazing. She went around to the other side of the car to where the blind man was already starting to get out. This blind man, feature this, he was wearing a full beard! A beard on a blind man! Too much, I say. The blind man reached into the back seat and dragged out a suitcase. My wife took his arm, shut the car door, and, talking all the way, moved him down the drive and then up the steps to the front porch. I turned off the TV. I finished my drink, rinsed the glass, dried my hands. Then I went to the door.

My wife said, "I want you meet Robert. Robert, this is my husband. I've told you all about him." She was beaming. She had this blind man by his coat sleeve.

The blind man let go of his suitcase and up came his hand. I took it. He 20 squeezed hard, held my hand, and then he let it go.

"I feel like we've already met," he boomed.

"Likewise," I said. I didn't know what else to say. Then I said, "Welcome. I've heard a lot about you." We began to move then, a little group, from the porch into the living room, my wife guiding him by the arm. The blind man was carrying his suitcase in his other hand. My wife said things like, "To your left here, Robert. That's right. Now watch it, there's a chair. That's it. Sit down right here. This is the sofa. We just bought this sofa two weeks ago."

I started to say something about the old sofa. I'd like that old sofa. But I didn't say anything. Then I wanted to say something else, small-talk, about the scenic ride along the Hudson. How going *to* New York, you should sit on the right-hand side of the train, and coming *from* New York, the left-hand side.

"Did you have a good train ride?" I said, "Which side of the train did you sit on, by the way?"

"What a question, which side!" my wife said. "What's it matter which side?" 25 she said.

"I just asked," I said.

"Right side," the blind man said. "I hadn't been on a train in nearly forty years. Not since I was a kid. With my folks. That's been a long time. I'd nearly forgotten the sensation. I have winter in my beard now," he said. "So I've been told, anyway. Do I look distinguished, my dear?" the blind man said to my wife.

"You look distinguished, Robert," she said. "Robert," she said. "Robert, it's just so good to see you."

My wife finally took her eyes off the blind man and looked at me. I had the feeling she didn't like what she saw. I shrugged.

I've never met, or personally known, anyone who was blind. This blind man 30 was late forties, a heavy-set, balding man with stooped shoulders, as if he carried a great weight there. He wore brown slacks, brown shoes, a light-brown shirt, a tie, a sports coat. Spiffy. He also had this full beard. But he didn't use a cane and he didn't wear dark glasses. I'd always thought dark glasses were a must for the blind. Fact was, I wished he had a pair. At first glance, his eyes looked like anyone else's eyes. But if you looked close, there was something different about them. Too much white in the iris, for one thing, and the pupils seemed to move round in the sockets without his knowing it or being able to stop it. Creepy. As I stared at his face, I saw the left pupil turn in toward his nose while the other made an effort to keep in one place. But it was only an effort, for that eye was on the roam without knowing it or wanting it to be.

I said, "Let me get you a drink. What's your pleasure? We have a little of everything. It's one of our pastimes."

"Bub, I'm a Scotch man myself," he said fast enough in this big voice.

"Right," I said. Bub! "Sure you are. I knew it."

He let his fingers touch his suitcase, which was sitting alongside the sofa. He was taking his bearings. I didn't blame him for that.

35   "I'll move that up to your room," my wife said.

"No, that's fine," the blind man said loudly. "It can go up when I go up."

"A little water with the Scotch?" I said.

"Very little," he said.

"I knew it," I said.

40   He said, "Just a tad. The Irish actor, Barry Fitzgerald? I'm like that fellow. When I drink water, Fitzgerald said, I drink water. When I drink whiskey, I drink whiskey." My wife laughed. The blind man brought his hand up under his beard. He lifted his beard slowly and let it drop.

I did the drinks, three big glasses of Scotch with a splash of water in each. Then we made ourselves comfortable and talked about Robert's travels. First the long flight from the West Coast to Connecticut, we covered that. Then from Connecticut up here by train. We had another drink concerning that leg of the trip.

I remembered having read somewhere that the blind didn't smoke because, as speculation had it, they couldn't see the smoke they exhaled. I thought I knew that much and that much only about blind people. But this blind man smoked his cigarette down to the nubbin and then lit another one. This blind man filled his ashtray and my wife emptied it.

When we sat down at the table for dinner, we had another drink. My wife heaped Robert's plate with cube steak, scalloped potatoes, green beans. I buttered him up two slices of bread. I said, "Here's bread and butter for you." I swallowed some of my drink. "Now let us pray," I said, and the blind man lowered his head. My wife looked at me, her mouth agape. "Pray the phone won't ring and the food doesn't get cold," I said.

We dug in. We ate everything there was to eat on the table. We ate like there was no tomorrow. We didn't talk. We ate. We scarfed. We grazed that table. We were into serious eating. The blind man had right away located his foods, he knew just where everything was on his plate. I watched with admiration as he used his knife and fork on the meat. He'd cut two pieces of meat, fork the meat into his mouth, and then go all out for the scalloped potatoes, the beans next, and then he'd tear off a hunk of buttered bread and eat that. He'd follow this up with a big drink of milk. It didn't seem to bother him to use his fingers once in a while, either.

We finished everything, including half a strawberry pie. For a few moments, 45 we sat as if stunned. Sweat beaded on our faces. Finally, we got up from the table and left the dirty plates. We didn't look back. We took ourselves into the living room and sank into our places again. Robert and my wife sat on the sofa. I took the big chair. We had us two or three more drinks while they talked about the major things that had come to pass for them in the past ten years. For the most part, I just listened.

Now and then I joined in. I didn't want him to think I'd left the room, and I didn't want her to think I was feeling left out. They talked of things that had happened to them—to them!—these past ten years. I waited in vain to hear my name on my wife's sweet lips: "And then my dear husband came into my life"— something like that. But I heard nothing of the sort. More talk of Robert. Robert had done a little of everything, it seemed, a regular blind jack-of-all trades. But most recently he and his wife had had an Amway distributorship, from which, I gathered, they'd earned their living, such as it was. The blind man was also a ham radio operator. He talked in his loud voice about conversations he'd had with fellow operators in Guam, in the Philippines, in Alaska, and even in Tahiti. He said he'd have a lot of friends there if he ever wanted to go visit those places. From time to time, he'd turn his blind face toward me, put his hand under his beard, ask me something. How long had I been in my present position? (Three years.) Did I like my work? (I didn't.) Was I going to stay with it? (What were the options?) Finally, when I thought he was beginning to run down, I got up and turned on the TV.

My wife looked at me with irritation. She was heading toward a boil. Then she looked at the blind man and sad, "Robert, do you have a TV?"

The blind man said, "My dear, I have two TVs. I have a color set and a black-and-white thing, an old relic. It's funny, but if I turn the TV on, and I'm always turning it on, I turn on the color set. It's funny, don't you think?"

I didn't know what to say to that. I had absolutely nothing to say to that. No opinion. So I watched the news program and tried to listen to what the announcer was saying.

"This is a color TV," the blind man said. "Don't ask me how, but I can tell." 50

"We traded up a while ago," I said.

The blind man had another taste of his drink. He lifted his beard, sniffed it, and let it fall. He leaned forward on the sofa. He positioned his ashtray on the coffee table, then put the lighter to his cigarette. He leaned back on the sofa and crossed his legs at the ankles.

My wife covered her mouth, and then she yawned. She stretched. She said, "I think I'll go upstairs and put on my robe. I think I'll change into something else. Robert, you make yourself comfortable," she said.

"I'm comfortable," the blind man said.

55   "I want you to feel comfortable in this house," she said.

"I am comfortable," the blind man said.

After she'd left the room, he and I listened to the weather report and then to the sports roundup. By that time, she'd been gone so long I didn't know if she was going to come back. I thought she might have gone to bed. I wished she'd come back downstairs. I didn't want to be left alone with a blind man. I asked him if he wanted another drink, and he said sure. Then I asked if he wanted to smoke some dope with me. I said I'd just rolled a number. I hadn't, but I planned to do so in about two shakes.

"I'll try some with you," he said.

"Damn right," I said. "That's the stuff."

60   I got our drinks and sat down on the sofa with him. Then I rolled us two fat numbers. I lit one and passed it. I brought it to his fingers. He took it and inhaled.

"Hold it as long as you can," I said. I could tell he didn't know the first thing.

My wife came back downstairs wearing her pink robe and her pink slippers.

"What do I smell?" she said.

"We thought we'd have us some cannabis," I said.

65   My wife gave me a savage look. Then she looked at the blind man and said, "Robert, I didn't know you smoked."

He said, "I do now, my dear. There's a first time for everything. But I don't feel anything yet."

"This stuff is pretty mellow," I said. "This stuff is mild. It's dope you can reason with," I said. "It doesn't mess you up."

"Not much it doesn't, bub," he said, and laughed.

My wife sat on the sofa between the blind man and me. I passed her the number. She took it and toked and then passed it back to me. "Which way is this going?" she said. Then she said, "I shouldn't be smoking this. I can hardly keep my eyes open as it is. That dinner did me in. I shouldn't have eaten so much."

70   "It was the strawberry pie," the blind man said. "That's what did it," he said, and he laughed his big laugh. Then he shook his head.

"There's more strawberry pie," I said.

"Do you want some more, Robert?" my wife said.

"Maybe in a little while," he said.

We gave out attention to the TV. My wife yawned again. She said, "Your bed is made up when you feel like going to bed, Robert. I know you must have had a long day. When you're ready to go to bed, say so." She pulled his arm. "Robert?"

75   He came to and said, "I've had a real nice time. This beats tapes, doesn't it?"

I said, "Coming at you," and I put the number between his fingers. He inHaled, held the smoke, and then let it go. It was like he'd been doing it since he was nine years old.

"Thanks, bub," he said. "But I think this is all for me. I think I'm beginning to feel it," he said. He held the burning roach out for my wife.

"Same here," she said. "Ditto. Me, too." She took the roach and passed it to me. "I may just sit here for a while between you two guys with my eyes closed. But don't let me bother you, okay? Either one of you. If it bothers you, say so. Otherwise, I may just sit here with my eyes closed until you're ready to go to bed," she said. "Your bed's made up, Robert, when you're ready. It's right next to our room at the top of the stairs. We'll show you up when you're ready. You wake me up now, you guys, if I fall asleep." She said that and then she closed her eyes and went to sleep.

The news program ended. I got up and changed the channel. I sat back down on the sofa. I wished my wife hadn't pooped out. Her head lay across the back of the sofa, her mouth open. She'd turned so that her robe had slipped away from her legs, exposing a juicy thigh. I reached to draw her robe back over her, and it was then that I glanced at the blind man. What the hell! I flipped the robe open again.

"You say when you want some strawberry pie," I said.　　80

"I will," he said.

I said, "Are you tired? Do you want me to take you up to your bed? Are you ready to hit the hay?"

"Not yet," he said. "No, I'll stay up with you, bub. If that's all right. I'll stay up until you're ready to turn in. We haven't had a chance to talk. Know what I mean? I feel like me and her monopolized the evening." He lifted his beard and he let it fall. He picked up his cigarettes and his lighter.

"That's all right," I said. Then I said, "I'm glad for the company."

And I guess I was. Every night I smoked dope and stayed up as long as I　　85 could before I fell asleep. My wife and I hardly ever went to bed at the same time. When I did go to sleep, I had these dreams. Sometimes I'd wake up from one of them, my heart going crazy.

Something about the church and the Middle Ages was on the TV. Not your run-of-the-mill TV fare. I wanted to watch something else. I turned to the other channels. But there was nothing on them, either. So I turned back to the first channel and apologized.

"Bub, it's all right," the blind man said. "It's fine with me. Whatever you want to watch is okay. I'm always learning something. Learning never ends. It won't hurt me to learn something tonight. I got ears," he said.

We didn't say anything for a time. He was leaning forward with his head turned at me, his right ear aimed in the direction of the set. Very disconcerting. Now and then his eyelids drooped and then they snapped open again. Now and then he put his fingers into his beard and tugged, like he was thinking about something he was hearing on the television.

On the screen, a group of men wearing cowls was being set upon and tormented by men dressed in skeleton costumes and men dressed as devils. The men dressed as devils wore devil masks, horns, and long tails. This pageant was part of a procession. The Englishman who was narrating the thing said it took place in Spain once a year. I tried to explain to the blind man what was happening.

90   "Skeletons," he said. "I know about skeletons," he said, and he nodded.

The TV showed this one cathedral. Then there was a long, slow look at another one. Finally, the picture switched to the famous one in Paris, with its flying buttresses and its spires reaching up to the clouds. The camera pulled away to show the whole of the cathedral rising above the skyline.

There were times when the Englishman who was telling the thing would shut up, would simply let the camera move around over the cathedrals. Or else the camera would tour the countryside, men in fields walking behind oxen. I waited as long as I could. Then I felt I had to say something. I said, "They're showing the outside of this cathedral now. Gargoyles. Little statues carved to look like monsters. Now I guess they're in Italy. Yeah, they're in Italy. There's paintings on the walls of this one church."

"Are those fresco paintings, bub?" he asked, and he sipped from his drink.

I reached for my glass. But it was empty. I tried to remember what I could remember. "You're asking me are those frescoes?" I said. "That's a good question. I don't know."

95   The camera moved to a cathedral outside Lisbon. The differences in the Portuguese cathedral compared with the French and Italian were not that great. But they were there. Mostly the interior stuff. Then something occurred to me, and I said, "Something has occurred to me. Do you have any idea what a cathedral is? What they look like, that is? Do you follow me? If somebody says cathedral to you, do you have any notion what they're talking about? Do you know the difference between that and a Baptist church, say?"

He let the smoke dribble from his mouth. "I know they took hundreds of workers fifty or a hundred years to build," he said. "I just heard the man say that, of course. I know generations of the same families worked on a cathedral. I heard him say that, too. The men who began their life's work on them, they never lived to see the completion of their work. In that wise, bub, they're no different from the rest of us, right?" He laughed. Then his eyelids drooped again. His head nodded. He seemed to be snoozing. Maybe he was imagining himself in Portugal. The TV was showing another cathedral now. This one was in Germany. The Englishman's voice droned on. "Cathedrals," the blind man said. He sat up and rolled his head back and forth. "If you want the truth, bub, that's about all I know. What I just said. What I heard him say. But maybe you could describe one to me? I wish you'd do it. I'd like that. If you want to know, I really don't have a good idea."

I stared hard at the shot of the cathedral on the TV. How could I even begin to describe it? But say my life depended on it. Say my life was being threatened by an insane guy who said I had to do it or else.

I stared some more at the cathedral before the picture flipped off into the countryside. There was no use. I turned to the blind man and said, "To begin with, they're very tall." I was looking around the room for clues. "They reach way up. Up and up. Toward the sky. They're so big, some of them, they have to have these supports. To help hold them up, so to speak. These supports are called buttresses. They remind me of viaducts, for some reason. But maybe you don't know viaducts, either? Sometimes the cathedrals have devils and such carved into the front. Sometimes lords and ladies. Don't ask me why this is," I said.

He was nodding. The whole upper part of his body seemed to be moving back and forth.

"I'm not doing so good, am I?" I said.　　　　　　　　　　　　　100

He stopped nodding and leaned forward on the edge of the sofa. As he listened to me, he was running his fingers through his beard. I wasn't getting through to him, I could see that. But he waited for me to go on just the same. He nodded, like he was trying to encourage me. I tried to think what else to say. "They're really big," I said. "They're massive. They're built of stone. Marble, too, sometimes. In those olden days, when they built cathedrals, men wanted to be close to God. In those olden days, God was an important part of everyone's life. You could tell this from their cathedral-building. I'm sorry," I said, "but it looks like that's the best I can do for you. I'm just no good at it."

"That's all right, bub," the blind man said. "Hey, listen. I hope you don't mind my asking you. Can I ask you something? Let me ask you a simple question, yes or no. I'm just curious and there's no offense. You're my host. But let me ask if you are in any way religious? You don't mind my asking?"

I shook my head. He couldn't see that, though. A wink is the same as a nod to a blind man. "I guess I don't believe in it. In anything. Sometimes it's hard. You know what I'm saying?"

"Sure, I do," he said.

"Right," I said.　　　　　　　　　　　　　　　　　　　　105

The Englishman was still holding forth. My wife sighed in her sleep. She drew a long breath and went on with her sleeping.

"You'll have to forgive me," I said. "But I can't tell you what a cathedral looks like. It just isn't in me to do it. I can't do any more than I've done."

The blind man sat very still, his head down, as he listened to me.

I said, "The truth is, cathedrals don't mean anything special to me. Nothing. Cathedrals. They're something to look at on late-night TV. That's all they are."

It was then that the blind man cleared his throat. He brought something 110 up. He took a handkerchief from his back pocket. Then he said. "I get it, bub. It's okay. It happens. Don't worry about it," he said. "Hey, listen to me. Will you do me a favor? I got an idea. Why don't you find us some heavy paper? And a pen. We'll do something. We'll draw one together. Get us a pen and some heavy paper. Go on, bub, get the stuff," he said.

So I went upstairs. My legs felt like they didn't have any strength in them. They felt like they did after I'd done some running. In my wife's room, I looked around. I found some ballpoints in a little basket on her table. And then I tried to think where to look for the kind of paper he was talking about.

Downstairs, in the kitchen, I found a shopping bag with onion skins in the bottom of the bag. I emptied the bag and shook it. I brought it into the living room and sat down with it near his legs. I moved some things, smoothed the wrinkles from the bag, spread it out on the coffee table.

The blind man got down from the sofa and sat next to me on the carpet.

He ran his fingers over the paper. He went up and down the sides of the paper. The edges, even the edges. He fingered the corners.

115 "All right," he said. "All right, let's do her."

He found my hand, the hand with the pen. He closed his hand over my hand. "Go ahead, bub, draw," he said. "Draw. You'll see. I'll follow along with you. It'll be okay. Just begin now like I'm telling you. You'll see. Draw," the blind man said.

So I began. First I drew a box that looked like a house. It could have been the house I lived in. Then I put a roof on it. At either end of the roof, I drew spires. Crazy.

"Swell," he said. "Terrific. You're doing fine," he said. "Never thought anything like this could happen in your lifetime, did you, bub? Well, it's a strange life, we all know that. Go on now. Keep it up."

I put in windows with arches. I drew flying buttresses. I hung great doors. I couldn't stop. The TV station went off the air. I put down the pen and closed and opened my fingers. The blind man felt around over the paper. He moved the tips of his fingers over the paper, all over what I had drawn, and he nodded.

120 "Doing fine," the blind man said.

I took up the pen again, and he found my hand. I kept at it. I'm no artist. But I kept drawing just the same.

My wife opened up her eyes and gazed at us. She sat up on the sofa, her robe hanging open. She said, "What are you doing? Tell me, I want to know."

I didn't answer her.

The blind man said, "We're drawing a cathedral. Me and him are working on it. Press hard," he said to me. "That's right. That's good," he said. "Sure. You got it, bub. I can tell. You didn't think you could. But you can, can't you? You're cooking with gas now. You know what I'm saying? We're going to really have us something here in a minute. How's the old arm?" he said. "Put some people in there now. What's a cathedral without people?"

125 My wife said, "What's going on? Robert, what are you doing? What's going on?"

"It's all right," he said to her. "Close your eyes now," the blind man said to me.

I did it. I closed them just like he said.

"Are they closed?" he said. "Don't fudge."

"They're closed," I said.

130 "Keep them that way," he said. He said, "Don't stop now. Draw."

So we kept on with it. His fingers rode my fingers as my hand went over the paper. It was like nothing else in my life up to now.

Then he said, "I think that's it. I think you got it," he said. "Take a look. What do you think?"

But I had my eyes closed. I thought I'd keep them that way for a little longer. I thought it was something I ought to do.

"Well?" he said. "Are you looking?"

My eyes were still closed. I was in my house. I knew that. But I didn't feel 135 like I was inside anything.

"It's really something," I said.

CRITICAL THINKING QUESTIONS

1. Collaborating with several classmates, list characteristics—personality and character traits—to describe both the narrator and Robert. Based on your lists, what conclusions can you draw about each individual?

2. Early on, the narrator reveals that he is not looking forward to his wife's friend's visit. Why not? Can you think of reasons—besides those which the narrator expresses—for his attitude toward Robert? As the night progresses, does his attitude change, and if so, when and why?

3. At the end of the story, the narrator and Robert sit together and draw a cathedral on a shopping bag. The narrator seems to undergo some sort of transformation: "It's really something," he says. What does he mean? Do you think the narrator will be a changed man when he wakes up the next morning? Can people actually gain insight in an instant, or is such a change more likely to occur only in fiction?

WRITING TOPIC

Write a brief personal experience essay about a time in your life when you gained insight into something. What had your attitude been previously? What triggered the insight? How did your attitude change?

Nathaniel Hawthorne

The Birth-Mark (1844)

In the latter part of the last century there lived a man of science, an eminent proficient in every branch of natural philosophy, who not long before our story opens had made experience of a spiritual affinity more attractive than any chemical one. He had left his laboratory to the care of an assistant, cleared his fine countenance from the furnace smoke, washed the stain of acids from his fingers, and persuaded a beautiful woman to become his wife. In those days when the comparatively recent discovery of electricity and other kindred mysteries of Nature seemed to open paths into the region of miracle, it was not unusual for the love of science to rival the love of woman in its depth and absorbing energy. The higher intellect, the imagination, the spirit, and even the heart might all find their congenial aliment in pursuits which, as some of their ardent votaries believed, would ascend from one step of powerful intelligence to another, until the philosopher should lay his hand on the secret of creative force and perhaps make new worlds for himself. We know not whether Aylmer possessed this degree of faith in man's ultimate control over Nature. He had devoted himself, however, too unreservedly to scientific studies ever to be weaned from them by any second passion. His love for his young wife might prove the stronger of the two; but it could only be by intertwining itself with his love of science, and uniting the strength of the latter to his own.

Such a union accordingly took place, and was attended with truly remarkable consequences and a deeply impressive moral. One day, very soon after their marriage, Aylmer sat gazing at his wife with a trouble in his countenance that grew stronger until he spoke.

"Georgiana," said he, "has it never occurred to you that the mark upon your cheek might be removed?"

"No, indeed," said she, smiling; but perceiving the seriousness of his manner, she blushed deeply. "To tell you the truth it has been so often called a charm that I was simple enough to imagine it might be so."

5   "Ah, upon another face perhaps it might," replied her husband; "but never on yours. No, dearest Georgiana, you came so nearly perfect from the hand of Nature that this slightest possible defect, which we hesitate whether to term a defect or a beauty, shocks me, as being the visible mark of earthly imperfection."

"Shocks you, my husband!" cried Georgiana, deeply hurt; at first reddening with momentary anger, but then bursting into tears. "Then why did you take me from my mother's side? You cannot love what shocks you!"

To explain this conversation it must be mentioned that in the centre of Georgiana's left cheek there was a singular mark, deeply interwoven, as it were, with the texture and substance of her face. In the usual state of her complexion—a healthy though delicate bloom—the mark wore a tint of deeper crimson, which imperfectly defined its shape amid the surrounding rosiness. When she blushed it gradually became more indistinct, and finally vanished amid the triumphant rush of blood that bathed the whole cheek with its brilliant glow. But if any shifting motion caused her to turn pale there was the mark again, a crimson stain upon the snow, in which Aylmer sometimes deemed an almost fearful distinctness. Its shape bore not a little similarity to the human hand, though of the smallest pygmy size. Georgiana's loves were wont to say that some fairy at her birth hour had laid her tiny hand upon the infant's cheek, and left this impress there in token of the magic endowments that were to give her such sway over all hearts. Many a desperate swain would have risked life for the privilege of pressing his lips to the mysterious hand. It must not be concealed, however, that the impression wrought by this fairy sign manual varied exceedingly, according to the difference of temperament in the beholders.

Some fastidious persons—but they were exclusively of her own sex—affirmed that the bloody hand, as they chose to call it, quite destroyed the effect of Georgiana's beauty, and rendered her countenance even hideous. But it would be as reasonable to say that one of those small blue stains which sometimes occur in the purest statuary marble would convert the Eve of Powers to a monster. Masculine observers, if the birth-mark did not heighten their admiration, contented themselves with wishing it away, that the world might possess one living specimen of ideal loveliness without the semblance of a flaw. After his marriage—for he thought little or nothing of the matter before—Aylmer discovered that this was the case with himself.

Had she been less beautiful—if Envy's self could have found aught else to sneer at—he might have felt his affection heightened by the prettiness of this mimic hand, now vaguely portrayed, now lost, now stealing forth again and glimmering to and fro with every pulse of emotion that throbbed within her heart; but seeing her otherwise so perfect, he found this one defect grow more and more intolerable with every moment of their united lives. It was the fatal flaw of humanity which Nature, in one shape or another, stamps ineffaceably on all her productions, either to imply that they are temporary and finite, or that their perfection must be wrought by toil and pain. The crimson hand expressed the ineludible gripe in which mortality clutches the highest and purest of earthly mould, degrading them into kindred with the lowest, and even with the very brutes, like whom their visible frames return to the dust. In this manner, selecting it as the symbol of his wife's liability to sin, sorrow, decay, and death, Aylmer's sombre imagination was not long in rendering the birth-mark a frightful object, causing him more trouble and horror than ever Georgiana's beauty, whether of soul or sense, had given him delight.

At all the seasons which should have been their happiest, he invariably and without intending it, nay, in spite of a purpose to the contrary, reverted to this one disastrous topic. Trifling as it at first appeared, it so connected itself with innumerable trains of thought and modes of feeling that it became the central point of all. With the morning twilight Aylmer opened his eyes upon his wife's face and recognized the symbol of imperfection; and when they sat together at the evening hearth his eyes wandered stealthily to her cheek, and beheld, flickering with the blaze of the wood fire, the spectral hand that wrote mortality where he would fain have worshipped. Georgiana soon learned to shudder at his gaze. It needed but a glance with the peculiar expression that his face often wore to change the roses of her cheek into a deathlike paleness, amid which the crimson hand was brought strongly out, like bas-relief of ruby on the whitest marble.

Late one night when the lights were growing dim, so as hardly to betray the 10 stain on the poor wife's cheek, she herself, for the first time, voluntarily took up the subject.

"Do you remember, my dear Aylmer," said she, with a feeble attempt at a smile, "have you any recollection of a dream last night about this odious hand?"

"None! none whatever!" replied Aylmer, starting; but then he added, in a dry, cold tone, affected for the sake of concealing the real depth of his emotion, "I might well dream of it; for before I fell asleep it had taken a pretty firm hold of my fancy."

"And you did dream of it?" continued Georgiana, hastily; for she dreaded lest a gush of tears should interrupt what she had to say. "A terrible dream! I wonder that you can forget it. Is it possible to forget this one expression?—'It is in her heart now; we must have it out!' Reflect, my husband; for by all means I would have you recall that dream."

The mind is in a sad state when Sleep, the all-involving, cannot confine her spectres within the dim region of her sway, but suffers them to break forth, affrighting this actual life with secrets that perchance belong to a deeper one. Aylmer now remembered his dream. He had fancied himself with his servant Aminadab, attempting an operation for the removal of the birth-mark; but the deeper went the knife, the deeper sank the hand, until at length its tiny grasp appeared to have caught hold of Georgiana's heart; whence, however, her husband was inexorably resolved to cut or wrench it away.

15   When the dream had shaped itself perfectly in his memory, Aylmer sat in his wife's presence with a guilty feeling. Truth often finds its way to the mind close muffled in robes of sleep, and then speaks with uncompromising directness of matters in regard to which we practise an unconscious self-deception during our waking moments. Until now he had not been aware of the tyrannizing influence acquired by one idea over his mind, and of the lengths which he might find in his heart to go for the sake of giving himself peace.

"Aylmer," resumed Georgiana, solemnly, "I know not what may be the cost to both of us to rid me of this fatal birth-mark. Perhaps its removal may cause cureless deformity; or it may be the stain goes as deep as life itself. Again: do we know that there is a possibility, on any terms, of unclasping the firm gripe of this little hand which was laid upon me before I came into the world?"

"Dearest Georgiana, I have spent much thought upon the subject," hastily interrupted Aylmer. "I am convinced of the perfect practicability of its removal."

"If there be the remotest possibility of it," continued Georgiana, "let the attempt be made at whatever risk. Danger is nothing to me; for life, while this hateful mark makes me the object of your horror and disgust—life is a burden which I would fling down with joy. Either remove this dreadful hand, or take my wretched life! You have deep science. All the world bears witness of it. You have achieved great wonders. Cannot you remove this little, little mark, which I cover with the tips of two small fingers? Is this beyond your power, for the sake of your own peace, and to save your poor wife from madness?"

"Noblest, dearest, tenderest wife," cried Aylmer, rapturously, "doubt not my power. I have already given this matter the deepest thought—thought which might almost have enlightened me to create a being less perfect than yourself. Georgiana, you have led deeper than ever into the heart of science. I feel myself fully competent to render this dear cheek as faultless as its fellow; and then, most beloved, what will be my triumph when I shall have corrected what Nature left imperfect in her fairest work! Even Pygmalion, when his sculptured woman assumed life, felt not greater ecstasy than mine will be."

"It is resolved, then," said Georgiana, faintly smiling. "And, Aylmer, spare   20 me not, though you should find the birth-mark take refuge in my heart at last."

Her husband tenderly kissed her cheek—her right cheek—not that which bore the impress of the crimson hand.

The next day Aylmer apprised his wife of a plan that he had formed whereby he might have opportunity for the intense thought and constant watchfulness which the proposed operation would require; while Georgiana, likewise, would enjoy the perfect repose essential to its success. They were to seclude themselves in the extensive apartments occupied by Aylmer as a laboratory, and where, during his toilsome youth, he had made discoveries in the elemental powers of Nature that had roused the admiration of all the learned societies in Europe. Seated calmly in this laboratory, the pale philosopher had investigated the secrets of the highest cloud region and of the profoundest mines; he had satisfied himself of the causes that kindled and kept alive the fires of the volcano; and had explained the mystery of the fountains, and how it is that they gush forth, some so bright and pure, and others with such rich medicinal virtues, from the dark bosom of the earth. Here, too, at an earlier period, he had studied the wonders of the human frame, and attempted to fathom the very process by which Nature assimilates all her precious influences from earth and air, and from the spiritual world, to create and foster man, her masterpiece. The latter pursuit, however, Aylmer had long laid aside in unwilling recognition of the truth—against which all seekers sooner or later stumble—that our great creative Mother, while she amuses us with apparently working in the broadest sunshine, is yet severely careful to keep her own secrets, and, in spite of her pretended openness, shows us nothing but results. She permits us, indeed, to mar, but seldom to mend, and, like a jealous patentee, on no account to make. Now, however, Aylmer resumed these half-forgotten investigations; not, of course, with such hopes or wishes as first suggested them; but because they involved much physiological truth and lay in the path of his proposed scheme for the treatment of Georgiana.

As he led her over the threshold of the laboratory, Georgiana was cold tremulous. Aylmer looked cheerfully into her face, with intent to reassure her, but was so startled with the intense glow of the birth-mark upon the whiteness of her cheek that he could not restrain a strong convulsive shudder. His wife fainted.

"Aminadab! Aminadab!" shouted Aylmer, stamping violently on the floor.

Forthwith there issued from an inner apartment a man of low stature, but   25 bulky frame, with shaggy hair hanging about his visage, which was grimed with the vapors of the furnace. This personage had been Aylmer's underworker during his whole scientific career, and was admirably fitted for that office by his great mechanical readiness, and the skill with which, while incapable of comprehending a single principle, he executed all the details of his master's experiments.

With his vast strength, his shaggy hair, his smoky aspect, and the indescribable earthiness that incrusted him, he seemed to represent man's physical nature; while Aylmer's slender figure, and pale, intellectual face, were no less apt a type of the spiritual element.

"Throw open the door of the boudoir, Aminadab," said Aylmer, "and burn a pastil."

"Yes, master," answered Aminadab, looking intently at the lifeless form of Georgiana; and then he muttered to himself, "If she were my wife, I'd never part with that birth-mark."

When Georgiana recovered consciousness she found herself breathing an atmosphere of penetrating fragrance, the gentle potency of which had recalled her from her deathlike faintness. The scene around her looked like enchantment. Aylmer had converted those smoky, dingy, sombre rooms, where he had spent his brightest years in recondite pursuits, into a series of beautiful apartments not unfit to be the secluded abode of a lovely woman. The walls were hung with gorgeous curtains, which imparted the combination of grandeur and grace that no other species of adornment can achieve; and as they fell from the ceiling to the floor, their rich and ponderous folds, concealing all angles and straight lines, appeared to shut in the scene from infinite space. For aught Georgiana knew, it might be a pavilion among the clouds. And Aylmer, excluding the sunshine, which would have interfered with his chemical processes, had supplied its place with perfumed lamps, emitting flames of various hue, but all uniting in a soft, impurpled radiance. He now knelt by his wife's side, watching her earnestly, but without alarm; for he was confident in his science, and felt that he could draw a magic circle round her within which no evil might intrude.

"Where am I? Ah, I remember," said Georgiana, faintly; and she placed her hand over her cheek to hide the terrible mark from her husband's eyes.

30   "Fear not, dearest!" exclaimed he. "Do not shrink from me! Believe me, Georgiana, I even rejoice in this single imperfection, since it will be such a rapture to remove it."

"Oh, spare me!" sadly replied his wife. "Pray do not look at it again. I never can forget that convulsive shudder."

In order to soothe Georgiana, and, as it were, to release her mind from the burden of actual things, Aylmer now put in practice some of the light and playful secrets which science had taught him among its profounder lore. Airy figures, absolutely bodiless ideas, and forms of unsubstantial beauty came and danced before her, imprinting their momentary footsteps on beams of light. Though she had some indistinct idea of the method of these optical phenomena, still the illusion was almost perfect enough to assumption the belief that her husband possessed sway over the spiritual world. Then again, when she felt a wish to look forth from her seclusion, immediately, as if her thoughts were answered, the procession of external existence flitted across a screen. The scenery and the figures of actual life were perfectly represented, but with that bewitching, yet indescribable difference which always makes a picture, an image, or a shadow so much more attractive than the original. When wearied of this Aylmer bade her cast her eyes upon a vessel containing a quantity of earth. She did so, with little interest at first; but was soon startled to perceive the germ of a plant shooting upward from the soil. Then came the slender stalk; the leaves gradually unfolded themselves; and amid them was a perfect and lovely flower.

"It is magical!" cried Georgiana. "I dare not touch it."

"Nay, pluck it," answered Aylmer—"pluck it, and inHale its brief perfume while you may. The flower will wither in a few moments and leave nothing save its brown seed vessels; but thence may be perpetuated a race as ephemeral as itself."

But Georgiana had no sooner touched the flower than the whole plant suf- 35
fered a blight, its leaves turning coal-black as if by the agency of fire.

"There was too powerful a stimulus," said Aylmer, thoughtfully.

To make up for this abortive experiment, he proposed to take her portrait by a scientific process of his own invention. It was to be effected by rays of light striking upon a polished plate of metal. Georgiana assented; but, on looking at the result, was affrighted to find the features of the portrait blurred and indefinable; while the minute figure of a hand appeared where the cheek should have been. Aylmer snatched the metallic plate and threw it into a jar of corrosive acid.

Soon, however, he forgot these mortifying failures. In the intervals of study and chemical experiment he came to her flushed and exhausted, but seemed invigorated by her presence, and spoke in glowing language of the resources of his art. He gave a history of the long dynasty of the alchemists, who spent so many ages in quest of the universal solvent by which the golden principle might be elicited from all things vile and base. Aylmer appeared to believe that, by the plainest scientific logic, it was altogether within the limits of possibility to discover this long-sought medium; "but," he added, "a philosopher who should go deep enough to acquire the power would attain too lofty a wisdom to stoop to the exercise of it." Not less singular were his opinions in regard to the elixir vitae. He more than intimated that it was at his option to concoct a liquid that should prolong life for years, perhaps interminably; but that it would produce a discord in Nature which all the world, and chiefly the quaffer of the immortal nostrum, would find cause to curse.

"Aylmer, are you in earnest?" asked Georgiana, looking at him with amazement and fear. "It is terrible to possess such power, or even to dream of possessing it."

"Oh, do not tremble, my love," said her husband. "I would not wrong either 40
you or myself by working such inharmonious effects upon our lives; but I would have you consider how trifling, in comparison, is the skill requisite to remove this little hand."

At the mention of the birth-mark, Georgiana, as usual, shrank as if a redhot iron had touched her cheek.

Again Aylmer applied himself to his labors. She could hear his voice in the distant furnace room giving directions to Aminadab, whose harsh, uncouth, mishapen tones were audible in response, more like the grunt or growl of a brute than human speech. After hours of absence, Aylmer reappeared and proposed that she should now examine his cabinet of chemical products and natural treasures of the earth. Among the former he showed her a small vial, in which, he remarked, was contained a gentle yet most powerful fragrance, capable of impregnating all the breezes that blow across a kingdom. They were of inestimable value, the contents of that little vial; and, as he said so, he threw some of the perfume into the air and filled the room with piercing and invigorating delight.

"And what is this?" asked Georgiana, pointing to a small crystal globe containing a gold-colored liquid. "It is so beautiful to the eye that I could imagine it the elixir of life."

"In one sense it is," replied Aylmer; "or, rather, the elixir of immortality. It is the most precious poison that ever was concocted in this world. By its aid I could apportion the lifetime of any mortal at whom you might point your finger. The strength of the dose would determine whether he were to linger out years, or drop dead in the midst of a breath. No king on his guarded throne could keep his life if I, in my private station, should deem that the welfare of millions justified me in depriving him of it."

45   "Why do you keep such a terrific drug?" inquired Georgiana in horror.

"Do not mistrust me, dearest," said her husband, smiling; "its virtuous potency is yet greater than its harmful one. But see! here is a powerful cosmetic. With a few drops of this in a vase of water, freckles may be washed away as easily as the hands are cleansed. A stronger infusion would take the blood out of the cheek, and leave the rosiest beauty a pale ghost."

"Is it with this lotion that you intend to bathe my cheek?" asked Georgiana anxiously.

"Oh, no," hastily replied her husband; "this is merely superficial. Your case demands a remedy that shall go deeper."

In his interviews with Georgiana, Aylmer generally made minute inquiries as to her sensations and whether the confinement of the rooms and the temperature of the atmosphere agreed with her. These questions had such a particular drift that Georgiana began to conjecture that she was already subjected to certain physical influences, either breathed in with the fragrant air or taken with her food. She fancied likewise, but it might be altogether fancy, that there was a stirring up of her system—a strange, indefinite sensation creeping through her veins, and tingling, half painfully, half pleasurably, at her heart. Still, whenever she dared to look into the mirror, there she beheld herself pale as a white rose and with the crimson birth-mark stamped upon her cheek. Not even Aylmer now hated it so much as she.

50   To dispel the tedium of the hours which her husband found it necessary to devote to the processes of combination and analysis, Georgiana turned over the volumes of his scientific library. In many dark old tomes she met with chapters full of romance and poetry. They were the works of philosophers of the middle ages, such as Albertus Magnus, Cornelius Agrippa, Paracelsus, and the famous

friar who created the prophetic Brazen Head. All these antique naturalists stood in advance of their centuries, yet were imbued with some of their credulity, and therefore were believed, and perhaps imagined themselves to have acquired from the investigation of Nature a power above Nature, and from physics a sway over the spiritual world. Hardly less curious and imaginative were the early volumes of the Transactions of the Royal Society, in which the members, knowing little of the limits of natural possibility, were continually recording wonders or proposing methods whereby wonders might be wrought.

But to Georgiana the most engrossing volume was a large folio from her husband's own hand, in which he had recorded every experiment of his scientific career, its original aim, the methods adopted for its development, and its final success or failure, with the circumstances to which either event was attributable. The book, in truth, was both the history and emblem of his ardent, ambitious, imaginative, yet practical and laborious life. He handled physical details as if there were nothing beyond them; yet spiritualized them all, and redeemed himself from materialism by his strong and eager aspiration towards the infinite. In his grasp the veriest clod of earth assumed a soul. Georgiana, as she read, reverenced Aylmer and loved him more profoundly than ever, but with a less entire dependence on his judgment than heretofore. Much as he had accomplished, she could not but observe that his most splendid successes were almost invariably failures, if compared with the ideal at which he aimed. His brightest diamonds were the merest pebbles, and felt to be so by himself, in comparison with the inestimable gems which lay hidden beyond his reach. The volume, rich with achievements that had won renown for its author, was yet as melancholy a record as ever mortal hand had penned. It was the sad confession and continual exemplification of the shortcomings of the composite man, the spirit burdened with clay and working in matter, and of the despair that assails the higher nature at finding itself so miserably thwarted by the earthly part. Perhaps every man of genius in whatever sphere might recognize the image of his own experience in Aylmer's journal.

So deeply did these reflections affect Georgiana that she laid her face upon the open volume and burst into tears. In this situation she was found by her husband.

"It is dangerous to read in a sorcerer's books," said he with a smile, though his countenance was uneasy and displeased. "Georgiana, there are pages in that volume which I can scarcely glance over and keep my senses. Take heed lest it prove as detrimental to you."

"It has made me worship you more than ever," said she.

"Ah, wait for this one success," rejoined he, "then worship me if you will. 55 I shall deem myself hardly unworthy of it. But come, I have sought you for the luxury of your voice. Sing to me, dearest."

So she poured out the liquid music of her voice to quench the thirst of his spirit. He then took his leave with a boyish exuberance of gayety, assuring her that her seclusion would endure but a little longer, and that the result was already certain. Scarcely had he departed when Georgiana felt irresistibly impelled to follow him. She had forgotten to inform Aylmer of a symptom which for two or three hours past had begun to excite her attention. It was a sensation in the fatal birth-mark, not painful, but which induced a restlessness throughout her system. Hastening after her husband, she intruded for the first time into the laboratory.

The first thing that struck her eye was the furnace, that hot and feverish worker, with the intense glow of its fire, which by the quantities of soot clustered above it seemed to have been burning for ages. There was a distilling apparatus in full operation. Around the room were retorts, tubes, cylinders, crucibles, and other apparatus of chemical research. An electrical machine stood ready for immediate use. The atmosphere felt oppressively close, and was tainted with gaseous odors which had been tormented forth by the processes of science. The severe and homely simplicity of the apartment, with its naked walls and brick pavement, looked strange, accustomed as Georgiana had become to the fantastic elegance of her boudoir. But what chiefly, indeed almost solely, drew her attention, was the aspect of Aylmer himself.

He was pale as death, anxious and absorbed, and hung over the furnace as if it depended upon his utmost watchfulness whether the liquid which it was distilling should be the draught of immortal happiness or misery. How different from the sanguine and joyous mien that he had assumed for Georgiana's encouragement!

"Carefully now, Aminadab; carefully, thou human machine; carefully, thou man of clay!" muttered Aylmer, more to himself than his assistant. "Now if there be a thought too much or too little, it is all over."

60   "Ho! ho!" mumbled Aminadab. "Look, master! look!"

Aylmer raised his eyes hastily, and at first reddened, then grew paler than ever, on beholding Georgiana. He rushed towards her and seized her arm with a grip that left the print of his fingers upon it.

"Why do you come hither? Have you no trust in your husband?" cried he, impetuously, "Would you throw the blight of that fatal birth-mark over my labors? It is not well done. Go, prying woman, go!"

"Nay, Aylmer," said Georgiana with the firmness of which she possessed no stinted endowment, "it is not you that have a right to complain. You mistrust your wife; you have concealed the anxiety with which you watch the development of this experiment. Think not so unworthily of me, my husband. Tell me all the risk we run, and fear not that I shall shrink; for my share in it is less than your own."

"No, no, Georgiana!" said Aylmer, impatiently; "it must not be."

65   "I submit," replied she calmly. "And, Aylmer, I shall quaff whatever draught you bring me; but it will be on the same principle that would induce me to take a dose of poison if offered by your hand."

"My noble wife," said Aylmer, deeply moved, "I knew not the height and depth of your nature until now. Nothing shall be concealed. Know, then, that this crimson hand, superficial as it seems, has clutched its grasp into your being with a strength of which I had no previous conception. I have already administered agents powerful enough to do aught except to change your entire physical system. Only one thing remains to be tried. If that fails us we are ruined."

"Why did you hesitate to tell me this?" asked she.

"Because, Georgiana," said Aylmer, in a low voice, "there is danger."

"Danger? There is but one danger—that this horrible stigma shall be left upon my cheek!" cried Georgiana. "Remove it, remove it, whatever be the cost, or we shall both go mad!"

"Heaven knows your words are too true," said Aylmer, sadly. "And now, dearest, return to your boudoir. In a little while all will be tested." 70

He conducted her back and took leave of her with a solemn tenderness which spoke far more than his words how much was now at stake. After his departure, Georgiana became rapt in musings. She considered the character of Aylmer, and did it completer justice than at any previous moment. Her heart exulted, while it trembled, at his honorable love—so pure and lofty that it would accept nothing less than perfection nor miserably make itself contented with an earthlier nature than he had dreamed of. She felt how much more precious was such a sentiment than that meaner kind which would have borne with the imperfection for her sake, and have been guilty of treason to holy love by degrading its perfect idea to the level of the actual; and with her whole spirit she prayed that, for a single moment, she might satisfy his highest and deepest conception. Longer than one moment she well knew it could not be; for his spirit was ever on the march, ever ascending, and each instant required something that was beyond the scope of the instant before.

The sound of her husband's footsteps aroused her. He bore a crystal goblet containing a liquor colorless as water, but bright enough to be the draught of immortality. Aylmer was pale; but it seemed rather the consequence of a highly wrought state of mind and tension of spirit than of fear or doubt.

"The concoction of the draught has been perfect," said he, in answer to Georgiana's look. "Unless all my science have deceived me, it cannot fail."

"Save on your account, my dearest Aylmer," observed his wife, "I might wish to put off this birth-mark of mortality by relinquishing mortality itself in preference to any other mode. Life is but a sad possession to those who have attained precisely the degree of moral advancement at which I stand. Were I weaker and blinder it might be happiness. Were I stronger, it might be endured hopefully. But being what I find myself, methinks I am of all mortals the most fit to die."

"You are fit for heaven without tasting death!" replied her husband. "But 75 why do we speak of dying? The draught cannot fail. Behold its effect upon this plant."

On the window seat there stood a geranium diseased with yellow blotches, which had overspread all its leaves. Aylmer poured a small quantity of the liquid upon the soil in which it grew. In a little time, when the roots of the plant had taken up the moisture, the unsightly blotches began to be extinguished in a living verdure.

"There needed no proof," said Georgiana, quietly. "Give me the goblet. I joyfully stake all upon your word."

"Drink, then, thou lofty creature!" exclaimed Aylmer, with fervid admiration. "There is no taint of imperfection on thy spirit. Thy sensible frame, too, shall soon be all perfect."

She quaffed the liquid and returned the goblet to his hand.

80   "It is grateful," said she with a placid smile. "Methinks it is like water from a heavenly fountain; for it contains I know not what of unobtrusive fragrance and deliciousness. It allays a feverish thirst that had parched me for many days. Now, dearest, let me sleep. My earthly senses are closing over my spirit like the leaves around the heart of a rose at sunset."

She spoke the last words with a gentle reluctance, as if it required almost more energy than she could command to pronounce the faint and lingering syllables. Scarcely had they loitered through her lips ere she was lost in slumber. Aylmer sat by her side, watching her aspect with the emotions proper to a man the whole value of whose existence was involved in the process now to be tested. Mingled with this mood, however, was the philosophic investigation characteristic of the man of science. Not the minutest symptom escaped him. A heightened flush of the cheek, a slight irregularity of breath, a quiver of the eyelid, a hardly perceptible tremor through the frame—such were the details which, as the moments passed, he wrote down in his folio volume. Intense thought had set its stamp upon every previous page of that volume, but the thoughts of years were all concentrated upon the last.

While thus employed, he failed not to gaze often at the fatal hand, and not without a shudder. Yet once, by a strange and unaccountable impulse, he pressed it with his lips. His spirit recoiled, however, in the very act; and Georgiana, out of the midst of her deep sleep, moved uneasily and murmured as if in remonstrance. Again Aylmer resumed his watch. Nor was it without avail. The crimson hand, which at first had been strongly visible upon the marble paleness of Georgiana's cheek, now grew more faintly outlined. She remained not less pale than ever; but the birth-mark, with every breath that came and went, lost somewhat of its former distinctness. Its presence had been awful; its departure was more awful still. Watch the stain of the rainbow fading out the sky, and you will know how the mysterious symbol passed away.

"By Heaven! it is well-nigh gone!" said Aylmer to himself, in almost irrepressible ecstasy. "I can scarcely trace it now. Success! success! And now it is like the faintest rose color. The lightest flush of blood across her cheek would overcome it. But she is so pale!"

He drew aside the window curtain and suffered the light of natural day to fall into the room and rest upon her cheek. At the same time he heard a gross, hoarse chuckle, which he had long known as his servant Aminadab's expression of delight.

85   "Ah, clod! ah, earthly mass!" cried Aylmer, laughing in a sort of frenzy,

"you have served me well! Matter and spirit—earth and heaven—have both done their part in this! Laugh, thing of the senses! You have earned the right to laugh."

These exclamations broke Georgiana's sleep. She slowly unclosed her eyes and gazed into the mirror which her husband had arranged for that purpose. A faint smile flitted over her lips when she recognized how barely perceptible was now that crimson hand which had once blazed forth with such disastrous brilliancy as to scare away all their happiness. But then her eyes sought Aylmer's face with a trouble and anxiety that he could by no means account for.

"My poor Aylmer!" murmured she.

"Poor? Nay, richest, happiest, and most favored!" exclaimed he. "My peerless bride, it is successful! You are perfect!"

"My poor Aylmer," she repeated, with a more than human tenderness, "you have aimed loftily; you have done nobly. Do not repent that with so high and pure a feeling, you have rejected the best the earth could offer. Aylmer, dearest Aylmer, I am dying!"

Alas! it was too true! the fatal hand had grappled with the mystery of life, and 90 was the bond by which an angelic spirit kept itself in union with a mortal frame. As the last crimson tint of the birth-mark—that sole token of human imperfection—faded from her cheek, the parting breath of the now perfect woman passed into the atmosphere, and her soul, lingering a moment near her husband, took its heavenward flight. Then a hoarse, chuckling laugh was heard again! Thus ever does the gross fatality of earth exult in its invariable triumph over the immortal essence which, in this dim sphere of half development, demands the completeness of a higher state. Yet, had Aylmer reached a profounder wisdom, he need not thus have flung away the happiness which would have woven his mortal life of the selfsame texture with the celestial. The momentary circumstance was too strong for him; he failed to look beyond the shadowy scope of time, and, living once for all in eternity, to find the perfect future in the present.

CRITICAL THINKING QUESTIONS

1. What claim about the power of the scientist does the **character** of Aylmer suggest? How does the story's narrator view Aylmer's belief in himself as a scientist?

2. As a critical thinker, one should consider an opposing perspective to the story's critique of Aylmer's perspective on his role as a scientist. For example, the human impulse to decipher the "mystery of life," to experiment, has led to significant scientific advances. What is the role of the scientist? In responding to this question, consider textual evidence from Hawthorne's story as well as evidence from your own direct observations and firsthand knowledge.

3. In the story's closing sentence, the narrator tells us, "…he [Aylmer] failed to look beyond the shadowy scope of time, and, living once for all in eternity, to find the perfect future in the present." In what ways do people today fail to find the perfect future in the present? On the other hand, how do certain individuals succeed in doing so?

4. Hawthorne's story also implies **claims** related to gender, as revealed by the dynamics between Aylmer and Georgiana. Create a claim related to gender and support it with textual evidence as well as your own firsthand information and experiences.

WRITING TOPIC

In 1998, researchers isolated and derived stem cells from human embryos. Since then, the issue of the ethics of stem cell research has been vigorously debated among scientists, policymakers, and private citizens. Because stem cells have the capacity to develop into any type of cell or body system, proponents of this research hail its promise for treating debilitating conditions such as Alzheimer's, diabetes, and heart disease and for rejuvenating paralyzed limbs. However, the technology for deriving the stem cells requires the use of human embryonic tissues, a procedure that presents ethical and moral concerns for many people. Not surprisingly, some opponents of stem cell research have made allusions to Hawthorne's "The Birth-Mark," suggesting that it is human hubris to presume to solve "the mystery of life" (par. 90). On the other hand, advocates of the research question the moral qualms over the use of this tissue, when a viable human being's quality and longevity of life hang in the balance. As is often the case, reasonable and compassionate persons disagree on this issue. After researching this topic, develop your own argument on the issue of the ethics of stem cell research.

Washington Irving

The Legend of Sleepy Hollow (1820)

Found among the papers of the late Diedrich Knickerbocker

> A pleasing land of drowsy head it was,
> Of dreams that wave before the half-shut eye;
> And of gay castles in the clouds that pass,
> Forever flushing round a summer sky.
> Castle of Indolence

In the bosom of one of those spacious coves which indent the eastern shore of the Hudson, at that broad expansion of the river denominated by the ancient Dutch navigators the Tappan Zee, and where they always prudently shortened sail and implored the protection of St. Nicholas when they crossed, there lies a small market town or rural port, which by some is called Greensburgh, but which is more generally and properly known by the name of Tarry Town. This name was given, we are told, in former days, by the good housewives of the adjacent country, from the inveterate propensity of their husbands to linger about the village tavern on market days. Be that as it may, I do not vouch for the fact, but merely advert to it, for the sake of being precise and authentic. Not far from this village, perhaps about two miles, there is a little valley or rather lap of land among high hills, which is one of the quietest places in the whole world. A small brook glides through it, with just murmur enough to lull one to repose; and the occasional whistle of a quail or tapping of a woodpecker is almost the only sound that ever breaks in upon the uniform tranquillity.

I recollect that, when a stripling, my first exploit in squirrel-shooting was in a grove of tall walnut-trees that shades one side of the valley. I had wandered into it at noontime, when all nature is peculiarly quiet, and was startled by the roar of my own gun, as it broke the Sabbath stillness around and was prolonged and reverberated by the angry echoes. If ever I should wish for a retreat whither I might steal from the world and its distractions, and dream quietly away the remnant of a troubled life, I know of none more promising than this little valley.

From the listless repose of the place, and the peculiar character of its inhabitants, who are descendants from the original Dutch settlers, this sequestered glen has long been known by the name of SLEEPY HOLLOW, and its rustic lads are called the Sleepy Hollow Boys throughout all the neighboring country. A drowsy, dreamy influence seems to hang over the land, and to pervade the very atmosphere. Some say that the place was bewitched by a High German doctor, during the early days of the settlement; others, that an old Indian chief, the prophet or wizard of his tribe, held his powwows there before the country was discovered by Master Hendrick Hudson. Certain it is, the place still continues under the sway of some witching power, that holds a spell over the minds of the good people, causing them to walk in a continual reverie. They are given to all kinds of marvellous beliefs, are subject to trances and visions, and frequently see strange sights, and hear music and voices in the air. The whole neighborhood abounds with local tales, haunted spots, and twilight superstitions; stars shoot and meteors glare oftener across the valley than in any other part of the country, and the nightmare, with her whole ninefold, seems to make it the favorite scene of her gambols.

The dominant spirit, however, that haunts this enchanted region, and seems to be commander-in-chief of all the powers of the air, is the apparition of a figure on horseback, without a head. It is said by some to be the ghost of a Hessian trooper, whose head had been carried away by a cannon-ball, in some nameless battle during the Revolutionary War, and who is ever and anon seen by the country folk hurrying along in the gloom of night, as if on the wings of the wind. His haunts are not confined to the valley, but extend at times to the adjacent roads, and especially to the vicinity of a church at no great distance. Indeed, certain of the most authentic historians of those parts, who have been careful in collecting and collating the floating facts concerning this spectre, allege that the body of the trooper having been buried in the churchyard, the ghost rides forth to the scene of battle in nightly quest of his head, and that the rushing speed with which he sometimes passes along the Hollow, like a midnight blast, is owing to his being belated, and in a hurry to get back to the churchyard before daybreak.

5 　　Such is the general purport of this legendary superstition, which has furnished materials for many a wild story in that region of shadows; and the spectre is known at all the country firesides, by the name of the Headless Horseman of Sleepy Hollow.

It is remarkable that the visionary propensity I have mentioned is not confined to the native inhabitants of the valley, but is unconsciously imbibed by every one who resides there for a time. However wide awake they may have been before they entered that sleepy region, they are sure, in a little time, to inhale the witching influence of the air, and begin to grow imaginative, to dream dreams, and see apparitions.

I mention this peaceful spot with all possible laud, for it is in such little retired Dutch valleys, found here and there embosomed in the great State of New York, that population, manners, and customs remain fixed, while the great torrent of migration and improvement, which is making such incessant changes in other parts of this restless country, sweeps by them unobserved. They are like those little nooks of still water, which border a rapid stream, where we may see the straw and bubble riding quietly at anchor, or slowly revolving in their mimic harbor, undisturbed by the rush of the passing current. Though many years have elapsed since I trod the drowsy shades of Sleepy Hollow, yet I question whether I should not still find the same trees and the same families vegetating in its sheltered bosom.

In this by-place of nature there abode, in a remote period of American history, that is to say, some thirty years since, a worthy wight of the name of Ichabod Crane, who sojourned, or, as he expressed it, "tarried," in Sleepy Hollow, for the purpose of instructing the children of the vicinity. He was a native of Connecticut, a State which supplies the Union with pioneers for the mind as well as for the forest, and sends forth yearly its legions of frontier woodmen and country schoolmasters. The cognomen of Crane was not inapplicable to his person. He was tall, but exceedingly lank, with narrow shoulders, long arms and legs, hands that dangled a mile out of his sleeves, feet that might have served for shovels, and his whole frame most loosely hung together. His head was small, and flat at top, with huge ears, large green glassy eyes, and a long snipe nose, so that it looked like a weather-cock perched upon his spindle neck to tell which way the wind blew. To see him striding along the profile of a hill on a windy day, with his clothes bagging and fluttering about him, one might have mistaken him for the genius of famine descending upon the earth, or some scarecrow eloped from a cornfield.

His schoolhouse was a low building of one large room, rudely constructed of logs; the windows partly glazed, and partly patched with leaves of old copybooks. It was most ingeniously secured at vacant hours, by a withe twisted in the handle of the door, and stakes set against the window shutters; so that though a thief might get in with perfect ease, he would find some embarrassment in getting out,—an idea most probably borrowed by the architect, Yost Van Houten, from the mystery of an eelpot. The schoolhouse stood in a rather lonely but pleasant situation, just at the foot of a woody hill, with a brook running close by, and a formidable birch-tree growing at one end of it. From hence the low murmur of his pupils' voices, conning over their lessons, might be heard in a drowsy summer's day, like the hum of a beehive; interrupted now and then by the authoritative voice of the master, in the tone of menace or command, or, peradventure, by the appalling sound of the birch, as he urged some tardy loiterer along the flowery path of knowledge. Truth to say, he was a conscientious man, and ever bore in mind the golden maxim, "Spare the rod and spoil the child." Ichabod Crane's scholars certainly were not spoiled.

I would not have it imagined, however, that he was one of those cruel poten-   10
tates of the school who joy in the smart of their subjects; on the contrary, he administered justice with discrimination rather than severity; taking the burden off the backs of the weak, and laying it on those of the strong. Your mere puny stripling, that winced at the least flourish of the rod, was passed by with indulgence; but the claims of justice were satisfied by inflicting a double portion on some little tough wrong-headed, broad-skirted Dutch urchin, who sulked and swelled and grew dogged and sullen beneath the birch. All this he called "doing his duty by their parents;" and he never inflicted a chastisement without following it by the assurance, so consolatory to the smarting urchin, that "he would remember it and thank him for it the longest day he had to live."

When school hours were over, he was even the companion and playmate of the larger boys; and on holiday afternoons would convoy some of the smaller ones home, who happened to have pretty sisters, or good housewives for mothers, noted for the comforts of the cupboard. Indeed, it behooved him to keep on good terms with his pupils. The revenue arising from his school was small, and would have been scarcely sufficient to furnish him with daily bread, for he was a huge feeder, and, though lank, had the dilating powers of an anaconda; but to help out his maintenance, he was, according to country custom in those parts, boarded and lodged at the houses of the farmers whose children he instructed. With these he lived successively a week at a time, thus going the rounds of the neighborhood, with all his worldly effects tied up in a cotton handkerchief.

That all this might not be too onerous on the purses of his rustic patrons, who are apt to consider the costs of schooling a grievous burden, and schoolmasters as mere drones, he had various ways of rendering himself both useful and agreeable. He assisted the farmers occasionally in the lighter labors of their farms, helped to make hay, mended the fences, took the horses to water, drove the cows from pasture, and cut wood for the winter fire. He laid aside, too, all the dominant dignity and absolute sway with which he lorded it in his little empire, the school, and became wonderfully gentle and ingratiating. He found favor in the eyes of the mothers by petting the children, particularly the youngest; and like the lion bold, which whilom so magnanimously the lamb did hold, he would sit with a child on one knee, and rock a cradle with his foot for whole hours together.

In addition to his other vocations, he was the singing-master of the neighborhood, and picked up many bright shillings by instructing the young folks in psalmody. It was a matter of no little vanity to him on Sundays, to take his station in front of the church gallery, with a band of chosen singers; where, in his own mind, he completely carried away the palm from the parson. Certain it is, his voice resounded far above all the rest of the congregation; and there are peculiar quavers still to be heard in that church, and which may even be heard half a mile off, quite to the opposite side of the millpond, on a still Sunday morning, which are said to be legitimately descended from the nose of Ichabod Crane. Thus, by divers little makeshifts, in that ingenious way which is commonly denominated "by hook and by crook," the worthy pedagogue got on tolerably enough, and was thought, by all who understood nothing of the labor of headwork, to have a wonderfully easy life of it.

The schoolmaster is generally a man of some importance in the female circle of a rural neighborhood; being considered a kind of idle, gentlemanlike personage, of vastly superior taste and accomplishments to the rough country swains, and, indeed, inferior in learning only to the parson. His appearance, therefore, is apt to occasion some little stir at the tea-table of a farmhouse, and the addition of a supernumerary dish of cakes or sweetmeats, or, peradventure, the parade of a silver teapot. Our man of letters, therefore, was peculiarly happy in the smiles of all the country damsels. How he would figure among them in the churchyard, between services on Sundays; gathering grapes for them from the wild vines that overran the surrounding trees; reciting for their amusement all the epitaphs on the tombstones; or sauntering, with a whole bevy of them, along the banks of the adjacent millpond; while the more bashful country bumpkins hung sheepishly back, envying his superior elegance and address.

15   From his half-itinerant life, also, he was a kind of travelling gazette, carrying the whole budget of local gossip from house to house, so that his appearance was always greeted with satisfaction. He was, moreover, esteemed by the women as a man of great erudition, for he had read several books quite through, and was a perfect master of Cotton Mather's "History of New England Witchcraft," in which, by the way, he most firmly and potently believed.

He was, in fact, an odd mixture of small shrewdness and simple credulity. His appetite for the marvellous, and his powers of digesting it, were equally extraordinary; and both had been increased by his residence in this spell-bound region. No tale was too gross or monstrous for his capacious swallow. It was often his delight, after his school was dismissed in the afternoon, to stretch himself on the rich bed of clover bordering the little brook that whimpered by his schoolhouse, and there con over old Mather's direful tales, until the gathering dusk of evening made the printed page a mere mist before his eyes. Then, as he wended his way by swamp and stream and awful woodland, to the farmhouse where he happened to be quartered, every sound of nature, at that witching hour, fluttered his excited imagination,—the moan of the whip-poor-will from the hillside, the boding cry of the tree toad, that harbinger of storm, the dreary hooting of the screech owl, or the sudden rustling in the thicket of birds frightened from their roost. The fireflies, too, which sparkled most vividly in the darkest places, now and then startled him, as one of uncommon brightness would stream across his path; and if, by chance, a huge blockhead of a beetle came winging his blundering flight against him, the poor varlet was ready to give up the ghost, with the idea that he was struck with a witch's token. His only resource on such occasions, either to drown thought or drive away evil spirits, was to sing psalm tunes and the good people of Sleepy Hollow, as they sat by their doors of an evening, were often filled with awe at hearing his nasal melody, "in linked sweetness long drawn out," floating from the distant hill, or along the dusky road.

Another of his sources of fearful pleasure was to pass long winter evenings with the old Dutch wives, as they sat spinning by the fire, with a row of apples roasting and spluttering along the hearth, and listen to their marvellous tales of ghosts and goblins, and haunted fields, and haunted brooks, and haunted bridges, and haunted houses, and particularly of the headless horseman, or Galloping Hessian of the Hollow, as they sometimes called him. He would delight them equally by his anecdotes of witchcraft, and of the direful omens and portentous sights and sounds in the air, which prevailed in the earlier times of Connecticut; and would frighten them woefully with speculations upon comets and shooting stars; and with the alarming fact that the world did absolutely turn round, and that they were half the time topsy-turvy!

But if there was a pleasure in all this, while snugly cuddling in the chimney corner of a chamber that was all of a ruddy glow from the crackling wood fire, and where, of course, no spectre dared to show its face, it was dearly purchased by the terrors of his subsequent walk homewards. What fearful shapes and shadows beset his path, amidst the dim and ghastly glare of a snowy night! With what wistful look did he eye every trembling ray of light streaming across the waste fields from some distant window! How often was he appalled by some shrub covered with snow, which, like a sheeted spectre, beset his very path! How often did he shrink with curdling awe at the sound of his own steps on the frosty crust beneath his feet; and dread to look over his shoulder, lest he should behold some uncouth being tramping close behind him! And how often was he thrown into complete dismay by some rushing blast, howling among the trees, in the idea that it was the Galloping Hessian on one of his nightly scourings!

All these, however, were mere terrors of the night, phantoms of the mind that walk in darkness; and though he had seen many spectres in his time, and been more than once beset by Satan in divers shapes, in his lonely perambulations, yet daylight put an end to all these evils; and he would have passed a pleasant life of it, in despite of the Devil and all his works, if his path had not been crossed by a being that causes more perplexity to mortal man than ghosts, goblins, and the whole race of witches put together, and that was—a woman.

20   Among the musical disciples who assembled, one evening in each week, to receive his instructions in psalmody, was Katrina Van Tassel, the daughter and only child of a substantial Dutch farmer. She was a blooming lass of fresh eighteen; plump as a partridge; ripe and melting and rosy-cheeked as one of her father's peaches, and universally famed, not merely for her beauty, but her vast expectations. She was withal a little of a coquette, as might be perceived even in her dress, which was a mixture of ancient and modern fashions, as most suited to set off her charms. She wore the ornaments of pure yellow gold, which her great-great-grandmother had brought over from Saardam; the tempting stomacher of the olden time, and withal a provokingly short petticoat, to display the prettiest foot and ankle in the country round.

Ichabod Crane had a soft and foolish heart towards the sex; and it is not to be wondered at that so tempting a morsel soon found favor in his eyes, more especially after he had visited her in her paternal mansion. Old Baltus Van Tassel was a perfect picture of a thriving, contented, liberal-hearted farmer. He seldom, it is true, sent either his eyes or his thoughts beyond the boundaries of his own farm; but within those everything was snug, happy and well-conditioned. He was satisfied with his wealth, but not proud of it; and piqued himself upon the hearty abundance, rather than the style in which he lived. His stronghold was situated on the banks of the Hudson, in one of those green, sheltered, fertile nooks in which the Dutch farmers are so fond of nestling. A great elm tree spread its broad branches over it, at the foot of which bubbled up a spring of the softest and sweetest water, in a little well formed of a barrel; and then stole sparkling away through the grass, to a neighboring brook, that babbled along among alders and dwarf willows. Hard by the farmhouse was a vast barn, that might have served for a church; every window and crevice of which seemed bursting forth with the treasures of the farm; the flail was busily resounding within it from morning to night; swallows and martins skimmed twittering about the eaves; and rows of pigeons, some with one eye turned up, as if watching the weather, some with their heads under their wings or buried in their bosoms, and others swelling, and cooing, and bowing about their dames, were enjoying the sunshine on the roof. Sleek unwieldy porkers were grunting in the repose and abundance of their pens, from whence sallied forth, now and then, troops of sucking pigs, as if to snuff the air. A stately squadron of snowy geese were riding in an adjoining pond, convoying whole fleets of ducks; regiments of turkeys were gobbling through the farmyard, and Guinea fowls fretting about it, like ill-tempered housewives, with their peevish, discontented cry. Before the barn door strutted the gallant cock, that pattern of a husband, a warrior and a fine gentleman, clapping his burnished wings and crowing in the pride and gladness of his heart,—sometimes tearing up the earth with his feet, and then generously calling his ever-hungry family of wives and children to enjoy the rich morsel which he had discovered.

The pedagogue's mouth watered as he looked upon this sumptuous promise of luxurious winter fare. In his devouring mind's eye, he pictured to himself every roasting-pig running about with a pudding in his belly, and an apple in his mouth; the pigeons were snugly put to bed in a comfortable pie, and tucked in with a coverlet of crust; the geese were swimming in their own gravy; and the ducks pairing cosily in dishes, like snug married couples, with a decent competency of onion sauce. In the porkers he saw carved out the future sleek side of bacon, and juicy relishing ham; not a turkey but he beheld daintily trussed up, with its gizzard under its wing, and, peradventure, a necklace of savory sausages; and even bright chanticleer himself lay sprawling on his back, in a side dish, with uplifted claws, as if craving that quarter which his chivalrous spirit disdained to ask while living.

As the enraptured Ichabod fancied all this, and as he rolled his great green eyes over the fat meadow lands, the rich fields of wheat, of rye, of buckwheat, and Indian corn, and the orchards burdened with ruddy fruit, which surrounded the warm tenement of Van Tassel, his heart yearned after the damsel who was to inherit these domains, and his imagination expanded with the idea, how they might be readily turned into cash, and the money invested in immense tracts of wild land, and shingle palaces in the wilderness. Nay, his busy fancy already realized his hopes, and presented to him the blooming Katrina, with a whole family of children, mounted on the top of a wagon loaded with household trumpery, with pots and kettles dangling beneath; and he beheld himself bestriding a pacing mare, with a colt at her heels, setting out for Kentucky, Tennessee,—or the Lord knows where!

When he entered the house, the conquest of his heart was complete. It was one of those spacious farmhouses, with high-ridged but lowly sloping roofs, built in the style handed down from the first Dutch settlers; the low projecting eaves forming a piazza along the front, capable of being closed up in bad weather. Under this were hung flails, harness, various utensils of husbandry, and nets for fishing in the neighboring river. Benches were built along the sides for summer use; and a great spinning-wheel at one end, and a churn at the other, showed the various uses to which this important porch might be devoted. From this piazza the wondering Ichabod entered the hall, which formed the centre of the mansion, and the place of usual residence. Here rows of resplendent pewter, ranged on a long dresser, dazzled his eyes. In one corner stood a huge bag of wool, ready to be spun; in another, a quantity of linsey-woolsey just from the loom; ears of Indian corn, and strings of dried apples and peaches, hung in gay festoons along the walls, mingled with the gaud of red peppers; and a door left ajar gave him a peep into the best parlor, where the claw-footed chairs and dark mahogany tables shone like mirrors; andirons, with their accompanying shovel and tongs, glistened from their covert of asparagus tops; mock-oranges and conch-shells decorated the mantelpiece; strings of various-colored birds eggs were suspended above it; a great ostrich egg was hung from the centre of the room, and a corner cupboard, knowingly left open, displayed immense treasures of old silver and well-mended china.

25   From the moment Ichabod laid his eyes upon these regions of delight, the peace of his mind was at an end, and his only study was how to gain the affections of the peerless daughter of Van Tassel. In this enterprise, however, he had more real difficulties than generally fell to the lot of a knight-errant of yore, who seldom had anything but giants, enchanters, fiery dragons, and such like easily conquered adversaries, to contend with and had to make his way merely through gates of iron and brass, and walls of adamant to the castle keep, where the lady of his heart was confined; all which he achieved as easily as a man would carve his way to the centre of a Christmas pie; and then the lady gave him her hand as a matter of course. Ichabod, on the contrary, had to win his way to the heart of a country coquette, beset with a labyrinth of whims and caprices, which were forever presenting new difficulties and impediments; and he had to encounter a host of fearful adversaries of real flesh and blood, the numerous rustic admirers, who beset every portal to her heart, keeping a watchful and angry eye upon each other, but ready to fly out in the common cause against any new competitor.

    Among these, the most formidable was a burly, roaring, roystering blade, of the name of Abraham, or, according to the Dutch abbreviation, Brom Van Brunt, the hero of the country round, which rang with his feats of strength and hardihood. He was broad-shouldered and double-jointed, with short curly black hair, and a bluff but not unpleasant countenance, having a mingled air of fun and arrogance. From his Herculean frame and great powers of limb he had received the nickname of BROM BONES, by which he was universally known. He was famed for great knowledge and skill in horsemanship, being as dexterous on horseback as a Tartar. He was foremost at all races and cock fights; and, with the ascendancy which bodily strength always acquires in rustic life, was the umpire in all disputes, setting his hat on one side, and giving his decisions with an air and tone that admitted of no gainsay or appeal. He was always ready for either a fight or a frolic; but had more mischief than ill-will in his composition; and with all his overbearing roughness, there was a strong dash of waggish good humor at bottom. He had three or four boon companions, who regarded him as their model, and at the head of whom he scoured the country, attending every scene of feud or merriment for miles round. In cold weather he was distinguished by a fur cap, surmounted with a flaunting fox's tail; and when the folks at a country gathering descried this well-known crest at a distance, whisking about among a squad of hard riders, they always stood by for a squall. Sometimes his crew would be heard dashing along past the farmhouses at midnight, with whoop and halloo, like a troop of Don Cossacks; and the old dames, startled out of their sleep, would listen for a moment till the hurry-scurry had clattered by, and then exclaim, "Ay, there goes Brom Bones and his gang!" The neighbors looked upon him with a mixture of awe, admiration, and good-will; and, when any madcap prank or rustic brawl occurred in the vicinity, always shook their heads, and warranted Brom Bones was at the bottom of it.

This rantipole hero had for some time singled out the blooming Katrina for the object of his uncouth gallantries, and though his amorous toyings were something like the gentle caresses and endearments of a bear, yet it was whispered that she did not altogether discourage his hopes. Certain it is, his advances were signals for rival candidates to retire, who felt no inclination to cross a lion in his amours; insomuch, that when his horse was seen tied to Van Tassel's paling, on a Sunday night, a sure sign that his master was courting, or, as it is termed, "sparking," within, all other suitors passed by in despair, and carried the war into other quarters.

Such was the formidable rival with whom Ichabod Crane had to contend, and, considering all things, a stouter man than he would have shrunk from the competition, and a wiser man would have despaired. He had, however, a happy mixture of pliability and perseverance in his nature; he was in form and spirit like a supple-jack—yielding, but tough; though he bent, he never broke; and though he bowed beneath the slightest pressure, yet, the moment it was away—jerk!—he was as erect, and carried his head as high as ever.

To have taken the field openly against his rival would have been madness; for he was not a man to be thwarted in his amours, any more than that stormy lover, Achilles. Ichabod, therefore, made his advances in a quiet and gently insinuating manner. Under cover of his character of singing-master, he made frequent visits at the farmhouse; not that he had anything to apprehend from the meddlesome interference of parents, which is so often a stumbling-block in the path of lovers. Balt Van Tassel was an easy indulgent soul; he loved his daughter better even than his pipe, and, like a reasonable man and an excellent father, let her have her way in everything. His notable little wife, too, had enough to do to attend to her housekeeping and manage her poultry; for, as she sagely observed, ducks and geese are foolish things, and must be looked after, but girls can take care of themselves. Thus, while the busy dame bustled about the house, or plied her spinning-wheel at one end of the piazza, honest Balt would sit smoking his evening pipe at the other, watching the achievements of a little wooden warrior, who, armed with a sword in each hand, was most valiantly fighting the wind on the pinnacle of the barn. In the mean time, Ichabod would carry on his suit with the daughter by the side of the spring under the great elm, or sauntering along in the twilight, that hour so favorable to the lover's eloquence.

I profess not to know how women's hearts are wooed and won. To me they 30 have always been matters of riddle and admiration. Some seem to have but one vulnerable point, or door of access; while others have a thousand avenues, and may be captured in a thousand different ways. It is a great triumph of skill to gain the former, but a still greater proof of generalship to maintain possession of the latter, for man must battle for his fortress at every door and window. He who wins a thousand common hearts is therefore entitled to some renown; but he who keeps undisputed sway over the heart of a coquette is indeed a hero. Certain it is, this was not the case with the redoubtable Brom Bones; and from the moment Ichabod Crane made his advances, the interests of the former evidently declined: his horse was no longer seen tied to the palings on Sunday nights, and a deadly feud gradually arose between him and the preceptor of Sleepy Hollow.

Brom, who had a degree of rough chivalry in his nature, would fain have carried matters to open warfare and have settled their pretensions to the lady, according to the mode of those most concise and simple reasoners, the knights-errant of yore,—by single combat; but Ichabod was too conscious of the superior might of his adversary to enter the lists against him; he had overheard a boast of Bones, that he would "double the schoolmaster up, and lay him on a shelf of his own schoolhouse;" and he was too wary to give him an opportunity. There was something extremely provoking in this obstinately pacific system; it left Brom no alternative but to draw upon the funds of rustic waggery in his disposition, and to play off boorish practical jokes upon his rival. Ichabod became the object of whimsical persecution to Bones and his gang of rough riders. They harried his hitherto peaceful domains; smoked out his singing school by stopping up the chimney; broke into the schoolhouse at night, in spite of its formidable fastenings of withe and window stakes, and turned everything topsy-turvy, so that the poor schoolmaster began to think all the witches in the country held their meetings there. But what was still more annoying, Brom took all opportunities of turning him into ridicule in presence of his mistress, and had a scoundrel dog whom he taught to whine in the most ludicrous manner, and introduced as a rival of Ichabod's, to instruct her in psalmody.

In this way matters went on for some time, without producing any material effect on the relative situations of the contending powers. On a fine autumnal afternoon, Ichabod, in pensive mood, sat enthroned on the lofty stool from whence he usually watched all the concerns of his little literary realm. In his hand he swayed a ferule, that sceptre of despotic power; the birch of justice reposed on three nails behind the throne, a constant terror to evil doers, while on the desk before him might be seen sundry contraband articles and prohibited weapons, detected upon the persons of idle urchins, such as half-munched apples, popguns, whirligigs, fly-cages, and whole legions of rampant little paper gamecocks. Apparently there had been some appalling act of justice recently inflicted, for his scholars were all busily intent upon their books, or slyly whispering behind them with one eye kept upon the master; and a kind of buzzing stillness reigned throughout the schoolroom. It was suddenly interrupted by the appearance of a negro in tow-cloth jacket and trowsers, a round-crowned fragment of a hat, like the cap of Mercury, and mounted on the back of a ragged, wild, half-broken colt, which he managed with a rope by way of halter. He came clattering up to the school door with an invitation to Ichabod to attend a merry-making or "quilting frolic," to be held that evening at Mynheer Van Tassel's; and having delivered his message with that air of importance, and effort at fine language, which a negro is apt to display on petty embassies of the kind, he dashed over the brook, and was seen scampering away up the hollow, full of the importance and hurry of his mission.

All was now bustle and hubbub in the late quiet schoolroom. The scholars were hurried through their lessons without stopping at trifles; those who were nimble skipped over half with impunity, and those who were tardy had a smart application now and then in the rear, to quicken their speed or help them over a tall word. Books were flung aside without being put away on the shelves, inkstands were overturned, benches thrown down, and the whole school was turned loose an hour before the usual time, bursting forth like a legion of young imps, yelping and racketing about the green in joy at their early emancipation.

The gallant Ichabod now spent at least an extra half hour at his toilet, brushing and furbishing up his best, and indeed only suit of rusty black, and arranging his locks by a bit of broken looking-glass that hung up in the schoolhouse. That he might make his appearance before his mistress in the true style of a cavalier, he borrowed a horse from the farmer with whom he was domiciliated, a choleric old Dutchman of the name of Hans Van Ripper, and, thus gallantly mounted, issued forth like a knight-errant in quest of adventures. But it is meet I should, in the true spirit of romantic story, give some account of the looks and equipments of my hero and his steed. The animal he bestrode was a broken-down plow-horse, that had outlived almost everything but its viciousness. He was gaunt and shagged, with a ewe neck, and a head like a hammer; his rusty mane and tail were tangled and knotted with burs; one eye had lost its pupil, and was glaring and spectral, but the other had the gleam of a genuine devil in it. Still he must have had fire and mettle in his day, if we may judge from the name he bore of Gunpowder. He had, in fact, been a favorite steed of his master's, the choleric Van Ripper, who was a furious rider, and had infused, very probably, some of his own spirit into the animal; for, old and broken-down as he looked, there was more of the lurking devil in him than in any young filly in the country.

Ichabod was a suitable figure for such a steed. He rode with short stirrups, which brought his knees nearly up to the pommel of the saddle; his sharp elbows stuck out like grasshoppers'; he carried his whip perpendicularly in his hand, like a sceptre, and as his horse jogged on, the motion of his arms was not unlike the flapping of a pair of wings. A small wool hat rested on the top of his nose, for so his scanty strip of forehead might be called, and the skirts of his black coat fluttered out almost to the horses tail. Such was the appearance of Ichabod and his steed as they shambled out of the gate of Hans Van Ripper, and it was altogether such an apparition as is seldom to be met with in broad daylight.

It was, as I have said, a fine autumnal day; the sky was clear and serene, and nature wore that rich and golden livery which we always associate with the idea of abundance. The forests had put on their sober brown and yellow, while some trees of the tenderer kind had been nipped by the frosts into brilliant dyes of orange, purple, and scarlet. Streaming files of wild ducks began to make their appearance high in the air; the bark of the squirrel might be heard from the groves of beech and hickory-nuts, and the pensive whistle of the quail at intervals from the neighboring stubble field.

The small birds were taking their farewell banquets. In the fullness of their revelry, they fluttered, chirping and frolicking from bush to bush, and tree to tree, capricious from the very profusion and variety around them. There was the honest cock robin, the favorite game of stripling sportsmen, with its loud querulous note; and the twittering blackbirds flying in sable clouds; and the golden-winged woodpecker with his crimson crest, his broad black gorget, and splendid plumage; and the cedar bird, with its red-tipt wings and yellow-tipt tail and its little monteiro cap of feathers; and the blue jay, that noisy coxcomb, in his gay light blue coat and white underclothes, screaming and chattering, nodding and bobbing and bowing, and pretending to be on good terms with every songster of the grove.

As Ichabod jogged slowly on his way, his eye, ever open to every symptom of culinary abundance, ranged with delight over the treasures of jolly autumn. On all sides he beheld vast store of apples; some hanging in oppressive opulence on the trees; some gathered into baskets and barrels for the market; others heaped up in rich piles for the cider-press. Farther on he beheld great fields of Indian corn, with its golden ears peeping from their leafy coverts, and holding out the promise of cakes and hasty-pudding; and the yellow pumpkins lying beneath them, turning up their fair round bellies to the sun, and giving ample prospects of the most luxurious of pies; and anon he passed the fragrant buckwheat fields breathing the odor of the beehive, and as he beheld them, soft anticipations stole over his mind of dainty slapjacks, well buttered, and garnished with honey or treacle, by the delicate little dimpled hand of Katrina Van Tassel.

Thus feeding his mind with many sweet thoughts and "sugared suppositions," he journeyed along the sides of a range of hills which look out upon some of the goodliest scenes of the mighty Hudson. The sun gradually wheeled his broad disk down in the west. The wide bosom of the Tappan Zee lay motionless and glassy, excepting that here and there a gentle undulation waved and prolonged the blue shadow of the distant mountain. A few amber clouds floated in the sky, without a breath of air to move them. The horizon was of a fine golden tint, changing gradually into a pure apple green, and from that into the deep blue of the mid-heaven. A slanting ray lingered on the woody crests of the precipices that overhung some parts of the river, giving greater depth to the dark gray and purple of their rocky sides. A sloop was loitering in the distance, dropping slowly down with the tide, her sail hanging uselessly against the mast; and as the reflection of the sky gleamed along the still water, it seemed as if the vessel was suspended in the air.

40   It was toward evening that Ichabod arrived at the castle of the Heer Van Tassel, which he found thronged with the pride and flower of the adjacent country. Old farmers, a spare leathern-faced race, in homespun coats and breeches, blue stockings, huge shoes, and magnificent pewter buckles. Their brisk, withered little dames, in close-crimped caps, long-waisted short gowns, homespun petticoats, with scissors and pincushions, and gay calico pockets hanging on the

outside. Buxom lasses, almost as antiquated as their mothers, excepting where a straw hat, a fine ribbon, or perhaps a white frock, gave symptoms of city innovation. The sons, in short square-skirted coats, with rows of stupendous brass buttons, and their hair generally queued in the fashion of the times, especially if they could procure an eel-skin for the purpose, it being esteemed throughout the country as a potent nourisher and strengthener of the hair.

Brom Bones, however, was the hero of the scene, having come to the gathering on his favorite steed Daredevil, a creature, like himself, full of mettle and mischief, and which no one but himself could manage. He was, in fact, noted for preferring vicious animals, given to all kinds of tricks which kept the rider in constant risk of his neck, for he held a tractable, well-broken horse as unworthy of a lad of spirit.

Fain would I pause to dwell upon the world of charms that burst upon the enraptured gaze of my hero, as he entered the state parlor of Van Tassel's mansion. Not those of the bevy of buxom lasses, with their luxurious display of red and white; but the ample charms of a genuine Dutch country tea-table, in the sumptuous time of autumn. Such heaped up platters of cakes of various and almost indescribable kinds, known only to experienced Dutch housewives! There was the doughty doughnut, the tender oly koek, and the crisp and crumbling cruller; sweet cakes and short cakes, ginger cakes and honey cakes, and the whole family of cakes. And then there were apple pies, and peach pies, and pumpkin pies; besides slices of ham and smoked beef; and moreover delectable dishes of preserved plums, and peaches, and pears, and quinces; not to mention broiled shad and roasted chickens; together with bowls of milk and cream, all mingled higgledy-piggledy, pretty much as I have enumerated them, with the motherly teapot sending up its clouds of vapor from the midst—Heaven bless the mark! I want breath and time to discuss this banquet as it deserves, and am too eager to get on with my story. Happily, Ichabod Crane was not in so great a hurry as his historian, but did ample justice to every dainty.

He was a kind and thankful creature, whose heart dilated in proportion as his skin was filled with good cheer, and whose spirits rose with eating, as some men's do with drink. He could not help, too, rolling his large eyes round him as he ate, and chuckling with the possibility that he might one day be lord of all this scene of almost unimaginable luxury and splendor. Then, he thought, how soon he'd turn his back upon the old schoolhouse; snap his fingers in the face of Hans Van Ripper, and every other niggardly patron, and kick any itinerant pedagogue out of doors that should dare to call him comrade!

Old Baltus Van Tassel moved about among his guests with a face dilated with content and good humor, round and jolly as the harvest moon. His hospitable attentions were brief, but expressive, being confined to a shake of the hand, a slap on the shoulder, a loud laugh, and a pressing invitation to "fall to, and help themselves."

And now the sound of the music from the common room, or hall, summoned 45
to the dance. The musician was an old gray-headed negro, who had been the

itinerant orchestra of the neighborhood for more than half a century. His instrument was as old and battered as himself. The greater part of the time he scraped on two or three strings, accompanying every movement of the bow with a motion of the head; bowing almost to the ground, and stamping with his foot whenever a fresh couple were to start.

Ichabod prided himself upon his dancing as much as upon his vocal powers. Not a limb, not a fibre about him was idle; and to have seen his loosely hung frame in full motion, and clattering about the room, you would have thought St. Vitus himself, that blessed patron of the dance, was figuring before you in person. He was the admiration of all the negroes; who, having gathered, of all ages and sizes, from the farm and the neighborhood, stood forming a pyramid of shining black faces at every door and window, gazing with delight at the scene, rolling their white eyeballs, and showing grinning rows of ivory from ear to ear. How could the flogger of urchins be otherwise than animated and joyous? The lady of his heart was his partner in the dance, and smiling graciously in reply to all his amorous oglings; while Brom Bones, sorely smitten with love and jealousy, sat brooding by himself in one corner.

When the dance was at an end, Ichabod was attracted to a knot of the sager folks, who, with Old Van Tassel, sat smoking at one end of the piazza, gossiping over former times, and drawing out long stories about the war.

This neighborhood, at the time of which I am speaking, was one of those highly favored places which abound with chronicle and great men. The British and American line had run near it during the war; it had, therefore, been the scene of marauding and infested with refugees, cowboys, and all kinds of border chivalry. Just sufficient time had elapsed to enable each storyteller to dress up his tale with a little becoming fiction, and, in the indistinctness of his recollection, to make himself the hero of every exploit.

There was the story of Doffue Martling, a large blue-bearded Dutchman, who had nearly taken a British frigate with an old iron nine-pounder from a mud breastwork, only that his gun burst at the sixth discharge. And there was an old gentleman who shall be nameless, being too rich a mynheer to be lightly mentioned, who, in the battle of White Plains, being an excellent master of defence, parried a musket-ball with a small sword, insomuch that he absolutely felt it whiz round the blade, and glance off at the hilt; in proof of which he was ready at any time to show the sword, with the hilt a little bent. There were several more that had been equally great in the field, not one of whom but was persuaded that he had a considerable hand in bringing the war to a happy termination.

50 But all these were nothing to the tales of ghosts and apparitions that succeeded. The neighborhood is rich in legendary treasures of the kind. Local tales and superstitions thrive best in these sheltered, long-settled retreats; but are trampled under foot by the shifting throng that forms the population of most of our country places. Besides, there is no encouragement for ghosts in most of our villages, for they have scarcely had time to finish their first nap and turn themselves in their graves, before their surviving friends have travelled away

from the neighborhood; so that when they turn out at night to walk their rounds, they have no acquaintance left to call upon. This is perhaps the reason why we so seldom hear of ghosts except in our long-established Dutch communities.

The immediate cause, however, of the prevalence of supernatural stories in these parts, was doubtless owing to the vicinity of Sleepy Hollow. There was a contagion in the very air that blew from that haunted region; it breathed forth an atmosphere of dreams and fancies infecting all the land. Several of the Sleepy Hollow people were present at Van Tassel's, and, as usual, were doling out their wild and wonderful legends. Many dismal tales were told about funeral trains, and mourning cries and wailings heard and seen about the great tree where the unfortunate Major André was taken, and which stood in the neighborhood. Some mention was made also of the woman in white, that haunted the dark glen at Raven Rock, and was often heard to shriek on winter nights before a storm, having perished there in the snow. The chief part of the stories, however, turned upon the favorite spectre of Sleepy Hollow, the Headless Horseman, who had been heard several times of late, patrolling the country; and, it was said, tethered his horse nightly among the graves in the churchyard.

The sequestered situation of this church seems always to have made it a favorite haunt of troubled spirits. It stands on a knoll, surrounded by locust-trees and lofty elms, from among which its decent, whitewashed walls shine modestly forth, like Christian purity beaming through the shades of retirement. A gentle slope descends from it to a silver sheet of water, bordered by high trees, between which, peeps may be caught at the blue hills of the Hudson. To look upon its grass-grown yard, where the sunbeams seem to sleep so quietly, one would think that there at least the dead might rest in peace. On one side of the church extends a wide woody dell, along which raves a large brook among broken rocks and trunks of fallen trees. Over a deep black part of the stream, not far from the church, was formerly thrown a wooden bridge; the road that led to it, and the bridge itself, were thickly shaded by overhanging trees, which cast a gloom about it, even in the daytime; but occasioned a fearful darkness at night. Such was one of the favorite haunts of the Headless Horseman, and the place where he was most frequently encountered. The tale was told of old Brouwer, a most heretical disbeliever in ghosts, how he met the Horseman returning from his foray into Sleepy Hollow, and was obliged to get up behind him; how they galloped over bush and brake, over hill and swamp, until they reached the bridge; when the Horseman suddenly turned into a skeleton, threw old Brouwer into the brook, and sprang away over the tree-tops with a clap of thunder.

This story was immediately matched by a thrice marvellous adventure of Brom Bones, who made light of the Galloping Hessian as an arrant jockey. He affirmed that on returning one night from the neighboring village of Sing Sing, he had been overtaken by this midnight trooper; that he had offered to race with him for a bowl of punch, and should have won it too, for Daredevil beat the goblin horse all hollow, but just as they came to the church bridge, the Hessian bolted, and vanished in a flash of fire.

All these tales, told in that drowsy undertone with which men talk in the dark, the countenances of the listeners only now and then receiving a casual gleam from the glare of a pipe, sank deep in the mind of Ichabod. He repaid them in kind with large extracts from his invaluable author, Cotton Mather, and added many marvellous events that had taken place in his native State of Connecticut, and fearful sights which he had seen in his nightly walks about Sleepy Hollow.

55   The revel now gradually broke up. The old farmers gathered together their families in their wagons, and were heard for some time rattling along the hollow roads, and over the distant hills. Some of the damsels mounted on pillions behind their favorite swains, and their light-hearted laughter, mingling with the clatter of hoofs, echoed along the silent woodlands, sounding fainter and fainter, until they gradually died away,—and the late scene of noise and frolic was all silent and deserted. Ichabod only lingered behind, according to the custom of country lovers, to have a tête-à-tête with the heiress; fully convinced that he was now on the high road to success. What passed at this interview I will not pretend to say, for in fact I do not know. Something, however, I fear me, must have gone wrong, for he certainly sallied forth, after no very great interval, with an air quite desolate and chapfallen. Oh, these women! these women! Could that girl have been playing off any of her coquettish tricks? Was her encouragement of the poor pedagogue all a mere sham to secure her conquest of his rival? Heaven only knows, not I! Let it suffice to say, Ichabod stole forth with the air of one who had been sacking a henroost, rather than a fair lady's heart. Without looking to the right or left to notice the scene of rural wealth, on which he had so often gloated, he went straight to the stable, and with several hearty cuffs and kicks roused his steed most uncourteously from the comfortable quarters in which he was soundly sleeping, dreaming of mountains of corn and oats, and whole valleys of timothy and clover.

It was the very witching time of night that Ichabod, heavy-hearted and crestfallen, pursued his travels homewards, along the sides of the lofty hills which rise above Tarry Town, and which he had traversed so cheerily in the afternoon. The hour was as dismal as himself. Far below him the Tappan Zee spread its dusky and indistinct waste of waters, with here and there the tall mast of a sloop, riding quietly at anchor under the land. In the dead hush of midnight, he could even hear the barking of the watchdog from the opposite shore of the Hudson; but it was so vague and faint as only to give an idea of his distance from this faithful companion of man. Now and then, too, the long-drawn crowing of a cock, accidentally awakened, would sound far, far off, from some farmhouse away among the hills—but it was like a dreaming sound in his ear. No signs of life occurred near him, but occasionally the melancholy chirp of a cricket, or perhaps the guttural twang of a bullfrog from a neighboring marsh, as if sleeping uncomfortably and turning suddenly in his bed.

All the stories of ghosts and goblins that he had heard in the afternoon now came crowding upon his recollection. The night grew darker and darker; the stars seemed to sink deeper in the sky, and driving clouds occasionally hid them from his sight. He had never felt so lonely and dismal. He was, moreover, approaching the very place where many of the scenes of the ghost stories had been laid. In the centre of the road stood an enormous tulip-tree, which towered like a giant above all the other trees of the neighborhood, and formed a kind of landmark. Its limbs were gnarled and fantastic, large enough to form trunks for ordinary trees, twisting down almost to the earth, and rising again into the air. It was connected with the tragical story of the unfortunate André, who had been taken prisoner hard by; and was universally known by the name of Major André's tree. The common people regarded it with a mixture of respect and superstition, partly out of sympathy for the fate of its ill-starred namesake, and partly from the tales of strange sights, and doleful lamentations, told concerning it.

As Ichabod approached this fearful tree, he began to whistle; he thought his whistle was answered; it was but a blast sweeping sharply through the dry branches. As he approached a little nearer, he thought he saw something white, hanging in the midst of the tree: he paused and ceased whistling but, on looking more narrowly, perceived that it was a place where the tree had been scathed by lightning, and the white wood laid bare. Suddenly he heard a groan—his teeth chattered, and his knees smote against the saddle: it was but the rubbing of one huge bough upon another, as they were swayed about by the breeze. He passed the tree in safety, but new perils lay before him.

About two hundred yards from the tree, a small brook crossed the road, and ran into a marshy and thickly-wooded glen, known by the name of Wiley's Swamp. A few rough logs, laid side by side, served for a bridge over this stream. On that side of the road where the brook entered the wood, a group of oaks and chestnuts, matted thick with wild grape-vines, threw a cavernous gloom over it. To pass this bridge was the severest trial. It was at this identical spot that the unfortunate André was captured, and under the covert of those chestnuts and vines were the sturdy yeomen concealed who surprised him. This has ever since been considered a haunted stream, and fearful are the feelings of the schoolboy who has to pass it alone after dark.

As he approached the stream, his heart began to thump; he summoned up, 60 however, all his resolution, gave his horse half a score of kicks in the ribs, and attempted to dash briskly across the bridge; but instead of starting forward, the perverse old animal made a lateral movement, and ran broadside against the fence. Ichabod, whose fears increased with the delay, jerked the reins on the other side, and kicked lustily with the contrary foot: it was all in vain; his steed started, it is true, but it was only to plunge to the opposite side of the road into a thicket of brambles and alder bushes. The schoolmaster now bestowed both whip and heel upon the starveling ribs of old Gunpowder, who dashed forward, snuffling and snorting, but came to a stand just by the bridge, with a suddenness that had nearly sent his rider sprawling over his head. Just at this moment a plashy tramp by the side of the bridge caught the sensitive ear of Ichabod. In the dark shadow of the grove, on the margin of the brook, he beheld something huge, misshapen and towering. It stirred not, but seemed gathered up in the gloom, like some gigantic monster ready to spring upon the traveller.

The hair of the affrighted pedagogue rose upon his head with terror. What was to be done? To turn and fly was now too late; and besides, what chance was there of escaping ghost or goblin, if such it was, which could ride upon the wings of the wind? Summoning up, therefore, a show of courage, he demanded in stammering accents, "Who are you?" He received no reply. He repeated his demand in a still more agitated voice. Still there was no answer. Once more he cudgelled the sides of the inflexible Gunpowder, and, shutting his eyes, broke forth with involuntary fervor into a psalm tune. Just then the shadowy object of alarm put itself in motion, and with a scramble and a bound stood at once in the middle of the road. Though the night was dark and dismal, yet the form of the unknown might now in some degree be ascertained. He appeared to be a horseman of large dimensions, and mounted on a black horse of powerful frame. He made no offer of molestation or sociability, but kept aloof on one side of the road, jogging along on the blind side of old Gunpowder, who had now got over his fright and waywardness.

Ichabod, who had no relish for this strange midnight companion, and bethought himself of the adventure of Brom Bones with the Galloping Hessian, now quickened his steed in hopes of leaving him behind. The stranger, however, quickened his horse to an equal pace. Ichabod pulled up, and fell into a walk, thinking to lag behind,—the other did the same. His heart began to sink within him; he endeavored to resume his psalm tune, but his parched tongue clove to the roof of his mouth, and he could not utter a stave. There was something in the moody and dogged silence of this pertinacious companion that was mysterious and appalling. It was soon fearfully accounted for. On mounting a rising ground, which brought the figure of his fellow-traveller in relief against the sky, gigantic in height, and muffled in a cloak, Ichabod was horror-struck on perceiving that he was headless!—but his horror was still more increased on observing that the head, which should have rested on his shoulders, was carried before him on the pommel of his saddle! His terror rose to desperation; he rained a shower of kicks and blows upon Gunpowder, hoping by a sudden movement to give his companion the slip; but the spectre started full jump with him. Away, then, they dashed through thick and thin; stones flying and sparks flashing at every bound. Ichabod's flimsy garments fluttered in the air, as he stretched his long lank body away over his horse's head, in the eagerness of his flight.

They had now reached the road which turns off to Sleepy Hollow; but Gunpowder, who seemed possessed with a demon, instead of keeping up it, made an opposite turn, and plunged headlong downhill to the left. This road leads through a sandy hollow shaded by trees for about a quarter of a mile, where it crosses the bridge famous in goblin story; and just beyond swells the green knoll on which stands the whitewashed church.

As yet the panic of the steed had given his unskilful rider an apparent advantage in the chase, but just as he had got half way through the hollow, the girths of the saddle gave way, and he felt it slipping from under him. He seized it by the pommel, and endeavored to hold it firm, but in vain; and had just time to save himself by clasping old Gunpowder round the neck, when the saddle fell to the earth, and he heard it trampled under foot by his pursuer. For a moment the terror of Hans Van Ripper's wrath passed across his mind,—for it was his Sunday saddle; but this was no time for petty fears; the goblin was hard on his haunches; and (unskilful rider that he was!) he had much ado to maintain his seat; sometimes slipping on one side, sometimes on another, and sometimes jolted on the high ridge of his horse's backbone, with a violence that he verily feared would cleave him asunder.

An opening in the trees now cheered him with the hopes that the church bridge was at hand. The wavering reflection of a silver star in the bosom of the brook told him that he was not mistaken. He saw the walls of the church dimly glaring under the trees beyond. He recollected the place where Brom Bones's ghostly competitor had disappeared. "If I can but reach that bridge," thought Ichabod, "I am safe." Just then he heard the black steed panting and blowing close behind him; he even fancied that he felt his hot breath. Another convulsive kick in the ribs, and old Gunpowder sprang upon the bridge; he thundered over the resounding planks; he gained the opposite side; and now Ichabod cast a look behind to see if his pursuer should vanish, according to rule, in a flash of fire and brimstone. Just then he saw the goblin rising in his stirrups, and in the very act of hurling his head at him. Ichabod endeavored to dodge the horrible missile, but too late. It encountered his cranium with a tremendous crash,—he was tumbled headlong into the dust, and Gunpowder, the black steed, and the goblin rider, passed by like a whirlwind. 65

The next morning the old horse was found without his saddle, and with the bridle under his feet, soberly cropping the grass at his master's gate. Ichabod did not make his appearance at breakfast; dinner-hour came, but no Ichabod. The boys assembled at the schoolhouse, and strolled idly about the banks of the brook; but no schoolmaster. Hans Van Ripper now began to feel some uneasiness about the fate of poor Ichabod, and his saddle. An inquiry was set on foot, and after diligent investigation they came upon his traces. In one part of the road leading to the church was found the saddle trampled in the dirt; the tracks of horses' hoofs deeply dented in the road, and evidently at furious speed, were traced to the bridge, beyond which, on the bank of a broad part of the brook, where the water ran deep and black, was found the hat of the unfortunate Ichabod, and close beside it a shattered pumpkin.

The brook was searched, but the body of the schoolmaster was not to be discovered. Hans Van Ripper as executor of his estate, examined the bundle which contained all his worldly effects. They consisted of two shirts and a half; two stocks for the neck; a pair or two of worsted stockings; an old pair of corduroy small-clothes; a rusty razor; a book of psalm tunes full of dog's-ears; and a broken pitch-pipe. As to the books and furniture of the schoolhouse, they belonged to the community, excepting Cotton Mather's "History of Witchcraft," a "New England Almanac," and a book of dreams and fortune-telling; in which last was a sheet of foolscap much scribbled and blotted in several fruitless attempts to make a copy of verses in honor of the heiress of Van Tassel. These magic books and the poetic scrawl were forthwith consigned to the flames by Hans Van Ripper; who, from that time forward, determined to send his children no more to school, observing that he never knew any good come of this same reading and writing. Whatever money the schoolmaster possessed, and he had received his quarter's pay but a day or two before, he must have had about his person at the time of his disappearance.

The mysterious event caused much speculation at the church on the following Sunday. Knots of gazers and gossips were collected in the churchyard, at the bridge, and at the spot where the hat and pumpkin had been found. The stories of Brouwer, of Bones, and a whole budget of others were called to mind; and when they had diligently considered them all, and compared them with the symptoms of the present case, they shook their heads, and came to the conclusion that Ichabod had been carried off by the Galloping Hessian. As he was a bachelor, and in nobody's debt, nobody troubled his head any more about him; the school was removed to a different quarter of the hollow, and another pedagogue reigned in his stead.

It is true, an old farmer, who had been down to New York on a visit several years after, and from whom this account of the ghostly adventure was received, brought home the intelligence that Ichabod Crane was still alive; that he had left the neighborhood partly through fear of the goblin and Hans Van Ripper, and partly in mortification at having been suddenly dismissed by the heiress; that he had changed his quarters to a distant part of the country; had kept school and studied law at the same time; had been admitted to the bar; turned politician; electioneered; written for the newspapers; and finally had been made a justice of the Ten Pound Court. Brom Bones, too, who, shortly after his rival's disappearance conducted the blooming Katrina in triumph to the altar, was observed to look exceedingly knowing whenever the story of Ichabod was related, and always burst into a hearty laugh at the mention of the pumpkin; which led some to suspect that he knew more about the matter than he chose to tell.

70   The old country wives, however, who are the best judges of these matters, maintain to this day that Ichabod was spirited away by supernatural means; and it is a favorite story often told about the neighborhood round the winter evening fire. The bridge became more than ever an object of superstitious awe; and that may be the reason why the road has been altered of late years, so as to approach the church by the border of the millpond. The schoolhouse being deserted soon fell to decay, and was reported to be haunted by the ghost of the unfortunate pedagogue and the plowboy, loitering homeward of a still summer evening, has often fancied his voice at a distance, chanting a melancholy psalm tune among the tranquil solitudes of Sleepy Hollow.

POSTSCRIPT.
FOUND IN THE HANDWRITING OF MR. KNICKERBOCKER.

The preceding tale is given almost in the precise words in which I heard it related at a Corporation meeting at the ancient city of Manhattoes, at which were present many of its sagest and most illustrious burghers. The narrator was a pleasant, shabby, gentlemanly old fellow, in pepper-and-salt clothes, with a sadly humourous face, and one whom I strongly suspected of being poor–he made such efforts to be entertaining. When his story was concluded, there was much laughter and approbation, particularly from two or three deputy aldermen, who had been asleep the greater part of the time. There was, however, one tall, dry-looking old gentleman, with beetling eyebrows, who maintained a grave and rather severe face throughout, now and then folding his arms, inclining his head, and looking down upon the floor, as if turning a doubt over in his mind. He was one of your wary men, who never laugh but upon good grounds–when they have reason and law on their side. When the mirth of the rest of the company had subsided, and silence was restored, he leaned one arm on the elbow of his chair, and sticking the other akimbo, demanded, with a slight, but exceedingly sage motion of the head, and contraction of the brow, what was the moral of the story, and what it went to prove?

The story-teller, who was just putting a glass of wine to his lips, as a refreshment after his toils, paused for a moment, looked at his inquirer with an air of infinite deference, and, lowering the glass slowly to the table, observed that the story was intended most logically to prove–

"That there is no situation in life but has its advantages and pleasures–provided we will but take a joke as we find it:

"That, therefore, he that runs races with goblin troopers is likely to have rough riding of it.

"Ergo, for a country schoolmaster to be refused the hand of a Dutch heiress   75
is a certain step to high preferment in the state."

The cautious old gentleman knit his brows tenfold closer after this explanation, being sorely puzzled by the ratiocination of the syllogism, while, methought, the one in pepper-and-salt eyed him with something of a triumphant leer. At length he observed that all this was very well, but still he thought the story a little on the extravagant–there were one or two points on which he had his doubts.

"Faith, sir," replied the story-teller, "as to that matter, I don't believe one-half of it myself." D. K.

THE END.

CRITICAL THINKING QUESTIONS:

I. Reflecting upon Ichabod Crane's interest in Katrina Van Tassel, is he motivated primarily by lust of love or lust of power? Point to textual evidence to defend your position.

2. "Ichabod Crane greatly contributed to his own demise." Though the ending of the story is ambiguous, to what extent do you agree or disagree with the preceding statement? What clues are offered in the story?

3. Brom Bones is depicted as a powerful character in terms of strength and physical ability, whereas Ichabod Crane is painted as mostly intellectual. In what ways do these characterizations promote or inhibit these characters' senses of power?

WRITING TOPIC

Whether it was tales of witches or the Headless Horseman, the Sleepy Hollow community believed and perpetuated its supernatural tales. In what ways has superstition influenced historical figures? In what ways does superstition still play a part in the lives of the twenty-first-century American? Why do superstitions hold such power upon us?

Tim O'Brien

The Things They Carried (1990)

First Lieutenant Jimmy Cross carried letters from a girl named Martha, a junior at Mount Sebastian College in New Jersey. They were not love letters, but Lieutenant Cross was hoping, so he kept them folded in plastic at the bottom of his rucksack. In the late afternoon, after a day's march, he would dig his foxhole, wash his hands under a canteen, unwrap the letters, hold them with the tips of his fingers, and spend the last hour of light pretending. He would imagine romantic camping trips into the White Mountains in New Hampshire. He would sometimes taste the envelope flaps, knowing her tongue had been there. More than anything, he wanted Martha to love him as he loved her, but the letters were mostly chatty, elusive on the matter of love. She was a virgin, he was almost sure. She was an English major at Mount Sebastian, and she wrote beautifully about her professors and roommates and midterm exams, about her respect for Chaucer and her great affection for Virginia Woolf. She often quoted lines of poetry; she never mentioned the war, except to say, Jimmy, take care of yourself. The letters weighed 10 ounces. They were signed Love, Martha, but Lieutenant Cross understood that Love was only a way of signing and did not mean what he sometimes pretended it meant. At dusk, he would carefully return the letters to his rucksack. Slowly, a bit distracted, he would get up and move among his men, checking the perimeter, then at full dark he would return to his hole and watch the night and wonder if Martha was a virgin.

The things they carried were largely determined by necessity. Among the necessities or near-necessities were P-38 can openers, pocket knives, heat tabs, wrist-watches, dog tags, mosquito repellent, chewing gum, candy, cigarettes, salt tablets, packets of Kool-Aid, lighters, matches, sewing kits, Military Payment Certificates, C rations, and two or three canteens of water. Together, these items weighed between 15 and 20 pounds, depending upon a man's habits or rate of metabolism. Henry Dobbins, who was a big man, carried extra rations; he was especially fond of canned peaches in heavy syrup over pound cake. Dave Jensen, who practiced field hygiene, carried a toothbrush, dental floss, and several hotel-sized bars of soap he'd stolen on R&R in Sydney, Australia. Ted Lavender, who was scared, carried tranquilizers until he was shot in the head outside the village of Than Khe in mid-April. By necessity, and because it was SOP, they all carried steel helmets that weighed 5 pounds including the liner and camouflage cover. They carried the standard fatigue jackets and trousers. Very few carried underwear. On their feet they carried jungle boots—2.1 pounds—and Dave Jensen carried three pairs of socks and a can of Dr. Scholl's foot powder as a precaution against trench foot. Until he was shot, Ted Lavender carried six or seven ounces of premium dope, which for him was a necessity. Mitchell Sanders, the RTO, carried condoms. Norman Bowker carried a diary. Rat Kiley carried comic books. Kiowa, a devout Baptist, carried an illustrated New Testament that had been presented to him by his father, who taught Sunday school in Oklahoma City, Oklahoma. As a hedge against bad times, however, Kiowa also carried his grandmother's distrust of the white man, his grandfather's old hunting hatchet. Necessity dictated. Because the land was mined and booby-trapped, it was SOP for each man to carry a steelcentered, nylon-covered flak jacket, which weighed 6.7 pounds, but which on hot days seemed much heavier. Because you could die so quickly, each man carried at least one large compress bandage, usually in the helmet band for easy access. Because the nights were cold, and because the monsoons were wet, each carried a green plastic poncho that could be used as a raincoat or groundsheet or makeshift tent. With its quilted liner, the poncho weighed almost two pounds, but it was worth every ounce. In April, for instance, when Ted Lavender was shot, they used his poncho to wrap him up, then to carry him across the paddy, then to lift him into the chopper that took him away.

They were called legs or grunts.

To carry something was to hump it, as when Lieutenant Jimmy Cross humped his love for Martha up the hills and through the swamps. In its intransitive form, to hump meant to walk, or to march, but it implied burdens far beyond the intransitive.

Almost everyone humped photographs. In his wallet, Lieutenant Cross carried two photographs of Martha. The first was a Kodacolor snapshot signed Love, though he knew better. She stood against a brick wall. Her eyes were gray and neutral, her lips slightly open as she stared straight-on at the camera. At night, sometimes, Lieutenant Cross wondered who had taken the picture, because he knew she had boyfriends, because he loved her so much, and because he could

5

see the shadow of the picture-taker spreading out against the brick wall. The second photograph had been clipped from the 1968 Mount Sebastian yearbook. It was an action shot—women's volleyball—and Martha was bent horizontal to the floor, reaching, the palms of her hands in sharp focus, the tongue taut, the expression frank and competitive. There was no visible sweat. She wore white gym shorts. Her legs, he thought, were almost certainly the legs of a virgin, dry and without hair, the left knee cocked and carrying her entire weight, which was just over one hundred pounds. Lieutenant Cross remembered touching that left knee. A dark theater, he remembered, and the movie was *Bonnie and Clyde,* and Martha wore a tweed skirt, and during the final scene, when he touched her knee, she turned and looked at him in a sad, sober way that made him pull his hand back, but he would always remember the feel of the tweed skirt and the knee beneath it and the sound of the gunfire that killed Bonnie and Clyde, how embarrassing it was, how slow and oppressive. He remembered kissing her good night at the dorm door. Right then, he thought, he should've done something brave. He should've carried her up the stairs to her room and tied her to the bed and touched that left knee all night long. He should've risked it. Whenever he looked at the photographs, he thought of new things he should've done.

What they carried was partly a function of rank, partly of field specialty.

As a first lieutenant and platoon leader, Jimmy Cross carried a compass, maps, code books, binoculars, and a .45-caliber pistol that weighed 2.9 pounds fully loaded. He carried a strobe light and the responsibility for the lives of his men.

As an RTO, Mitchell Sanders carried the PRC-25 radio, a killer, 26 pounds with its battery.

As a medic, Rat Kiley carried a canvas satchel filled with morphine and plasma and malaria tablets and surgical tape and comic books and all the things a medic must carry, including M&M's for especially bad wounds, for a total weight of nearly 20 pounds.

10   As a big man, therefore a machine gunner, Henry Dobbins carried the M-60 which weighed 23 pounds unloaded, but which was almost always loaded. In addition, Dobbins carried between 10 and 15 pounds of ammunition draped in belts across his chest and shoulders.

As PFCs or Spec 4s, most of them were common grunts and carried the standard M-16 gas-operated assault rifle. The weapon weighed 7.5 pounds unloaded, 8.2 pounds with its full 20-round magazine. Depending on numerous factors, such as topography and psychology, the riflemen carried anywhere from 12 to 20 magazines, usually in cloth bandoliers, adding on another 8.4 pounds at minimum, 14 pounds at maximum. When it was available, they also carried M-16 maintenance gear—rods and steel brushes and swabs and tubes of LSA oil—all of which weighed about a pound. Among the grunts, some carried the M-79 grenade launcher, 5.9 pounds unloaded, a reasonably light weapon except for the ammunition, which was heavy. A single round weighed 10 ounces. The typical load was 25 rounds. But Ted Lavender, who was scared, carried 34 rounds when he was shot and killed outside Than Khe, and he went down under an exceptional burden, more than 20 pounds of ammunition, plus the flak jacket and helmet and rations and water and toilet paper and tranquilizers and all the rest, plus the unweighed fear. He was dead weight. There was no twitching or flopping. Kiowa, who saw it happen, said it was like watching a rock fall, or a big sandbag or something—just boom, then down—not like the movies where the dead guy rolls around and does fancy spins and goes ass over teakettle—not like that, Kiowa said, the poor bastard just flat-fuck fell. Boom. Down. Nothing else. It was a bright morning in mid-April. Lieutenant Cross felt the pain. He blamed himself. They stripped off Lavender's canteens and ammo, all the heavy things, and Rat Kiley said the obvious, the guy's dead, and Mitchell Sanders used his radio to report one U.S. KIA and to request a chopper. Then they wrapped Lavender in his poncho. They carried him out to a dry paddy, established security, and sat smoking the dead man's dope until the chopper came. Lieutenant Cross kept to himself. He pictured Martha's smooth young face, thinking he loved her more than anything, more than his men, and now Ted Lavender was dead because he loved her so much and could not stop thinking about her. When the dustoff arrived, they carried Lavender aboard. Afterward they burned Than Khe. They marched until dusk, then dug their holes, and that night Kiowa kept explaining how you had to be there, how fast it was, how the poor guy just dropped like so much concrete. Boom-down, he said. Like cement.

In addition to the three standard weapons—the M-60, M-16, and M-79—they carried whatever presented itself, or whatever seemed appropriate as a means of killing or staying alive. They carried catch-as-catch-can. At various times, in various situations, they carried M-14s and CAR-15s and Swedish Ks and grease guns and captured AK-47s and Chi-Coms and RPGs and Simonov carbines and black market Uzis and .38-caliber Smith & Wesson handguns and 66 mm LAWs and shotguns and silencers and blackjacks and boyonets and C-4 plastic explosives. Lee Strunk carried a slingshot; a weapon of last resort, he called it. Mitchell Sanders carried brass knuckles. Kiowa carried his grandfather's feathered hatchet. Every third or fourth man carried a Claymore antipersonnel mine—3.5 pounds with its firing device. They all carried fragmentation grenades—14 ounces each. They all carried at least one M-18 colored smoke grenade—24 ounces. Some carried CS or tear gas grenades. Some carried white phosphorus grenades. They carried all they could bear, and then some, including a silent awe for the terrible power of the things they carried.

In the first week of April, before Lavender died, Lieutenant Jimmy Cross received a good-luck charm from Martha. It was a simple pebble, an ounce at most. Smooth to the touch, it was a milky white color with flecks of orange and violet, oval-shaped, like a miniature egg. In the accompanying letter, Martha wrote that she had found the pebble on the Jersey shoreline, precisely where the land touched water at high tide, where things came together but also separated.

It was this separate-but-together quality, she wrote, that had inspired her to pick up the pebble and to carry it in her breast pocket for several days, where it seemed weightless, and then to send it through the mail, by air, as a token of her truest feelings for him. Lieutenant Cross found this romantic. But he wondered what her truest feelings were, exactly, and what she meant by separate-but-together. He wondered how the tides and waves had come into play on that afternoon along the Jersey shoreline when Martha saw the pebble and bent down to rescue it from geology. He imagined bare feet. Martha was a poet, with the poet's sensibilities, and her feet would be brown and bare, the toenails unpainted, the eyes chilly and somber like the ocean in March, and though it was painful, he wondered who had been with her that afternoon. He imagined a pair of shadows moving along the strip of sand where things came together but also separated. It was phantom jealousy, he knew, but he couldn't help himself. He loved her so much. On the march, through the hot days of early April, he carried the pebble in his mouth, turning it with his tongue, tasting sea salt and moisture. His mind wandered. He had difficulty keeping his attention on the war. On occasion he would yell at his men to spread out the column, to keep their eyes open, but then he would slip away into daydreams, just pretending, walking barefoot along the Jersey shore, with Martha, carrying nothing. He would feel himself rising. Sun and waves and gentle winds, all love and lightness.

What they carried varied by mission.

15   When a mission took them to the mountains, they carried mosquito netting, machetes, canvas tarps, and extra bug juice.

If a mission seemed especially hazardous, or if it involved a place they knew to be bad, they carried everything they could. In certain heavily mined AOs, where the land was dense with Toe Poppers and Bouncing Betties, they took turns humping a 28-pound mine detector. With its headphones and big sensing plate, the equipment was a stress on the lower back and shoulders, awkward to handle, often useless because of the shrapnel in the earth, but they carried it anyway, partly for safety, partly for the illusion of safety.

On ambush, or other night missions, they carried peculiar little odds and ends. Kiowa always took along his New Testament and a pair of moccasins for silence. Dave Jensen carried night-sight vitamins high in carotene. Lee Strunk carried his slingshot; ammo, he claimed, would never be a problem. Rat Kiley carried brandy and M&M's candy. Until he was shot, Ted Lavender carried the starlight scope, which weighed 6.3 pounds with its aluminum carrying case. Henry Dobbins carried his girlfriend's pantyhose wrapped around his neck as a comforter. They all carried ghosts. When dark came, they would move out single file across the meadows and paddies to their ambush coordinates, where they would quietly set up the Claymores and lie down and spend the night waiting.

Other missions were more complicated and required special equipment. In mid-April, it was their mission to search out and destroy the elaborate tunnel complexes in the Than Khe area south of Chu Lai. To blow the tunnels, they carried one-pound blocks of pentrite high explosives, four blocks to a man, 68 pounds in all. They carried wiring, detonators, and battery-powered clackers. Dave Jensen carried earplugs. Most often, before blowing the tunnels, they were ordered by higher command to search them, which was considered bad news, but by and large they just shrugged and carried out orders. Because he was a big man, Henry Dobbins was excused from tunnel duty. The others would draw numbers. Before Lavender died there were 17 men in the platoon, and whoever drew the number 17 would strip off his gear and crawl in headfirst with a flashlight and Lieutenant Cross's .45-caliber pistol. The rest of them would fan out as security. They would sit down or kneel, not facing the hole, listening to the ground beneath them, imagining cobwebs and ghosts, whatever was down there—the tunnel walls squeezing in—how the flashlight seemed impossibly heavy in the hand and how it was tunnel vision in the very strictest sense, compression in all ways, even time, and how you had to wiggle in—ass and elbows— a swallowed-up feeling—and how you found yourself worrying about odd things: Will your flashlight go dead? Do rats carry rabies? If you screamed, how far would the sound carry? Would your buddies hear it? Would they have the courage to drag you out? In some respects, though not many, the waiting was worse than the tunnel itself. Imagination was a killer.

On April 16, when Lee Strunk drew the number 17, he laughed and muttered something and went down quickly. The morning was hot and very still. Not good, Kiowa said. He looked at the tunnel opening, then out across a dry paddy toward the village of Than Khe. Nothing moved. No clouds or birds or people. As they waited, the men smoked and drank Kool-Aid, not talking much, feeling sympathy for Lee Strunk but also feeling the luck of the draw. You win some, you lose some, said Mitchell Sanders, and sometimes you settle for a rain check. It was a tired line and no one laughed.

Henry Dobbins ate a tropical chocolate bar. Ted Lavender popped a tranquilizer and went off to pee.   20

After five minutes, Lieutenant Jimmy Cross moved to the tunnel, leaned down, and examined the darkness. Trouble, he thought—a cave-in maybe. And then suddenly, without willing it, he was thinking about Martha. The stresses and fractures, the quick collapse, the two of them buried alive under all that weight. Dense, crushing love. Kneeling, watching the hole, he tried to concentrate on Lee Strunk and the war, all the dangers, but his love was too much for him, he felt paralyzed, he wanted to sleep inside her lungs and breathe her blood and be smothered. He wanted her to be a virgin and not a virgin, all at once. He wanted to know her. Intimate secrets: Why poetry? Why so sad? Why that grayness in her eyes? Why so alone? Not lonely, just alone—riding her bike across campus or sitting off by herself in the cafeteria—even dancing, she danced alone—and it was the aloneness that filled him with love. He remembered telling her that one evening. How she nodded and looked away. And how, later, when he kissed her, she received the kiss without returning it, her eyes wide open, not afraid, not a virgin's eyes, just flat and uninvolved.

Lieutenant Cross gazed at the tunnel. But he was not there. He was buried with Martha under the white sand at the Jersey shore. They were pressed together, and the pebble in his mouth was her tongue. He was smiling. Vaguely, he was aware of how quiet the day was, the sullen paddies, yet he could not bring himself to worry about matters of security. He was beyond that. He was just a kid at war, in love. He was twenty-four years old. He couldn't help it.

A few moments later Lee Strunk crawled out of the tunnel. He came up grinning, filthy but alive. Lieutenant Cross nodded and closed his eyes while the others clapped Strunk on the back and made jokes about rising from the dead.

Worms, Rat Kiley said. Right out of the grave. Fuckin' zombie.

25   The men laughed. They all felt great relief.

Spook city, said Mitchell Sanders.

Lee Strunk made a funny ghost sound, a kind of moaning, yet very happy, and right then, when Strunk made that high happy moaning sound, when we went *Ahhooooo*, right then Ted Lavender was shot in the head on his way back from peeing. He lay with his mouth open. The teeth were broken. There was a swollen black bruise under his left eye. The cheekbone was gone. Oh shit, Rat Kiley said, the guy's dead. The guy's dead, he kept saying, which seemed profound—the guy's dead. I mean really.

The things they carried were determined to some extent by superstition. Lieutenant Cross carried his good-luck pebble. Dave Jensen carried a rabbit's foot. Norman Bowker, otherwise a very gentle person, carried a thumb that had been presented to him as a gift by Mitchell Sanders. The thumb was dark brown, rubbery to the touch, and weighed four ounces at most. It had been cut from a VC corpse, a boy of fifteen or sixteen. They'd found him at the bottom of an irrigation ditch, badly burned, flies in his mouth and eyes. The boy wore black shorts and sandals. At the time of his death he had been carrying a pouch of rice, a rifle and three magazines of ammunition.

You want my opinion, Mitchell Sanders said, there's a definite moral here.

30   He put his hand on the dead boy's wrist. He was quiet for a time, as if counting a pulse, then he patted the stomach, almost affectionately, and used Kiowa's hunting hatchet to remove the thumb.

Henry Dobbins asked what the moral was.

Moral?

You know. *Moral.*

Sanders wrapped the thumb in toilet paper and handed it across to Norman Bowker. There was no blood. Smiling, he kicked the boy's head, watched the flies scatter, and said, It's like with that old TV show—Paladin. Have gun, will travel.

35   Henry Dobbins thought about it.

Yeah, well, he finally said. I don't see no moral.

There it *is*, man.

Fuck off.

They carried USO stationery and pencils and pens. They carried Sterno, safety pins, trip flares, signal flares, spools of wire, razor blades, chewing tobacco, liberated joss sticks and statuettes of the smiling Buddha, candles, grease pencils, *The Stars and Stripes*, fingernail clippers, Psy Ops leaflets, bush hats, bolos, and much more. Twice a week, when the resupply choppers came in, they carried hot chow in green mermite cans and large canvas bags filled with iced beer and soda pop. They carried plastic water containers, each with a two-gallon capacity. Mitchell Sanders carried a set of starched tiger fatigues for special occasions. Henry Dobbins carried Black Flag insecticide. Dave Jensen carried empty sandbags that could be filled at night for added protection. Lee Strunk carried tanning lotion. Some things they carried in common. Taking turns, they carried the big PRC-77 scrambler radio, which weighed 30 pounds with its battery. They shared the weight of memory. They took up what others could no longer bear. Often, they carried each other, the wounded or weak. They carried infections. They carried chess sets, basketballs, Vietnamese-English dictionaries, insignia of rank, Bronze Stars and Purple Hearts, plastic cards imprinted with the Code of Conduct. They carried diseases, among them malaria and dysentery. They carried lice and ringworm and leeches and paddy algae and various rots and molds. They carried the land itself—Vietnam, the place, the soil—a powdery orange-red dust that covered their boots and fatigues and faces. They carried the sky. The whole atmosphere, they carried it, the humidity, the monsoons, the stink of fungus and decay, all of it, they carried gravity. They moved like mules. By daylight they took sniper fire, at night they were mortared, but it was not battle, it was just the endless march, village to village, without purpose, nothing won or lost. They marched for the sake of the march. They plodded along slowly, dumbly, leaning forward against the heat, unthinking, all blood and bone, simple grunts, soldiering with their legs, toiling up the hills and down into the paddies and across the rivers and up again and down, just humping, one step and then the next and then another, but no volition, no will, because it was automatic, it was anatomy, and the war was entirely a matter of posture and carriage, the hump was everything, a kind of inertia, a kind of emptiness, a dullness of desire and intellect and conscience and hope and human sensibility. Their principles were in their feet. Their calculations were biological. They had no sense of strategy or mission. They searched the villages without knowing what to look for, not caring, kicking over jars of rice, frisking children and old men, blowing tunnels, sometimes setting fires and sometimes not, then forming up and moving on to the next village, then other villages, where it would always be the same. They carried their own lives. The pressures were enormous. In the heat of early afternoon, they would remove their helmets and flak jackets, walking bare, which was dangerous but which helped ease the strain. They would often discard things along the route of march. Purely for comfort, they would throw away rations, blow their Claymores and grenades, no matter, because by nightfall the resupply choppers would arrive with more of the same, then a day or two later still more, fresh watermelons and crates of ammunition and sunglasses and woolen sweaters—the resources were stunning—sparklers for the Fourth of July, colored eggs for Easter—it was the great American war chest—the fruits of science, the smokestacks, the canneries, the arsenals at Hartford, the Minnesota forests, the machine shops, the vast fields of corn and wheat—they carried like freight trains; they carried it on their backs and shoulders—and for all the ambiguities of Vietnam, all the mysteries and unknowns, there was at least the single abiding certainty that they would never be at a loss for things to carry.

40   After the chopper took Lavender away, Lieutenant Jimmy Cross led his men into the village of Than Khe. They burned everything. They shot chickens and dogs, they trashed the village well, they called in artillery and watched the wreckage, then they marched for several hours through the hot afternoon, and then at dusk, while Kiowa explained how Lavender died, Lieutenant Cross found himself trembling.

He tried not to cry. With his entrenching tool, which weighed five pounds, he began digging a hole in the earth.

He felt shame. He hated himself. He had loved Martha more than his men, and as a consequence Lavender was now dead, and this was something he would have to carry like a stone in his stomach for the rest of the war.

All he could do was dig. He used his entrenching tool like an ax, slashing, feeling both love and hate, and then later, when it was full dark, he sat at the bottom of his foxhole and wept. It went on for a long while. In part, he was grieving for Ted Lavender, but mostly it was for Martha, and for himself, because she belonged to another world, which was not quite real, and because she was a junior at Mount Sebastian College in New Jersey, a poet and a virgin and uninvolved, and because he realized she did not love him and never would.

Like cement, Kiowa whispered in the dark. I swear to God—boom, down. Not a word.

45   I've heard this, said Norman Bowker.

A pisser, you know? Still zipping himself up. Zapped while zipping.

All right, fine. That's enough.

Yeah, but you had to see it, the guy just—

I *heard*, man. Cement. So why not shut the fuck *up?*

50   Kiowa shook his head sadly and glanced over at the hole where Lieutenant Jimmy Cross sat watching the night. The air was thick and wet. A warm dense fog had settled over the paddies and there was the stillness that precedes rain.

After a time Kiowa sighed.

One thing for sure, he said. The lieutenant's in some deep hurt. I mean that crying jag—the way he was carrying on—it wasn't fake or anything, it was real heavy-duty hurt. The man cares.

Sure, Norman Bowker said.

Say what you want, the man does care.

55   We all got problems.

Not Lavender.

No, I guess not, Bowker said. Do me a favor, though.

Shut up?

That's a smart Indian. Shut up.

Shrugging, Kiowa pulled off his boots. He wanted to say more, just to   60
lighten up his sleep, but instead he opened his New Testament and arranged it
beneath his head as a pillow. The fog made things seem hollow and unattached.
He tried not to think about Ted Lavender, but then he was thinking how fast
it was, no drama, down and dead, and how it was hard to feel anything except
surprise. It seemed unchristian. He wished he could find some great sadness,
or even anger, but the emotion wasn't there and he couldn't make it happen.
Mostly he felt pleased to be alive. He liked the smell of the New Testament
under his cheek, the leather and ink and paper and glue, whatever the chemi-
cals were. He liked hearing the sounds of night. Even his fatigue, it felt fine,
the stiff muscles and the prickly awareness of his own body, a floating feeling.
He enjoyed not being dead. Lying there, Kiowa admired Lieutenant Jimmy
Cross's capacity for grief. He wanted to share the man's pain, he wanted to care
as Jimmy Cross cared. And yet when he closed his eyes, all he could think was
Boom-down, and all he could feel was the pleasure of having his boots off and
the fog curling in around him and the damp soil and the Bible smells and the
plush comfort of night.

After a moment Norman Bowker sat up in the dark.

What the hell, he said. You want to talk, *talk*. Tell it to me.

Forget it.

No, man, go on. One thing I hate, it's a silent Indian.

For the most part they carried themselves with poise, a kind of dignity. Now   65
and then, however, there were times of panic, when they squealed or wanted
to squeal but couldn't, when they twitched and made moaning sounds and
covered their heads and said Dear Jesus and flopped around on the earth and
fired their weapons blindly and cringed and sobbed and begged for the noise
to stop and went wild and made stupid promises to themselves and to God and
to their mothers and fathers, hoping not to die. In different ways, it happened
to all of them. Afterward, when the firing ended, they would blink and peek
up. They would touch their bodies, feeling shame, then quickly hiding it. They
would force themselves to stand. As if in slow motion, frame by frame, the world
would take on the old logic—absolute silence, then the wind, then sunlight, then
voices. It was the burden of being alive. Awkwardly, the men would reassemble
themselves, first in private, then in groups, becoming soldiers again. They would
repair the leaks in their eyes. They would check for casualties, call in dust-offs,
light cigarettes, try to smile, clear their throats and spit and begin cleaning their
weapons. After a time someone would shake his head and say. No lie, I almost
shit my pants, and someone else would laugh, which meant it was bad, yes,
but the guy had obviously not shit his pants, it wasn't that bad, and in any case

nobody would ever do such a thing and then go ahead and talk about it. They would squint into the dense, oppressive sunlight. For a few moments, perhaps, they would fall silent, lighting a joint and tracking its passage from man to man, inhaling, holding in the humiliation. Scary stuff, one of them might say. But then someone else would grin or flick his eyebrows and say, Roger-dodger, almost cut me a new asshole, *almost*.

There were numerous such poses. Some carried themselves with a sort of wistful resignation, others with pride or stiff soldierly discipline or good humor or macho zeal. They were afraid of dying but they were even more afraid to show it.

They found jokes to tell.

They used a hard vocabulary to contain the terrible softness. *Greased* they'd say. *Offed, lit up, zapped while zipping.* It wasn't cruelty, just stage presence. They were actors. When someone died, it wasn't quite dying, because in a curious way it seemed scripted, and because they had their lines mostly memorized, irony mixed with tragedy, and because they called it by other names, as if to encyst and destroy the reality of death itself. They kicked corpses. They cut off thumbs. They talked grunt lingo. They told stories about Ted Lavender's supply of tranquilizers, how the poor guy didn't feel a thing, how incredibly tranquil he was.

There's a moral here, said Mitchell Sanders.

70   They were waiting for Lavender's chopper, smoking the dead man's dope.

The moral's pretty obvious, Sanders said, and winked. Stay away from drugs. No joke, they'll ruin your day every time.

Cute, said Henry Dobbins.

Mind blower, get it? Talk about wiggy. Nothing left, just blood and brains.

They made themselves laugh.

75   There it is, they'd say. Over and over—there it is, my friend, there it is—as if the repetition itself were an act of poise, a balance between crazy and almost crazy, knowing without going, there it is, which meant be cool, let it ride, because Oh yeah man, you can't change what can't be changed, there it is, there it absolutely and positively and fucking well *is*.

They were tough.

They carried all the emotional baggage of men who might die. Grief, terror, love, longing—these were intangibles, but the intangibles had their own mass and specific gravity, they had tangible weight. They carried shameful memories. They carried the common secret of cowardice barely restrained, the instinct to run or freeze or hide, and in many respects this was the heaviest burden of all, for it could never be put down, it required perfect balance and perfect posture. They carried their reputations. They carried the soldier's greatest fear, which was the fear of blushing. Men killed, and died, because they were embarrassed not to. It was what had brought them to the war in the first place, nothing positive, no dream of glory or honor, just to avoid the blush of dishonor. They died so as not to die of embarrassment. They crawled into tunnels and walked point and advanced under fire. Each morning, despite the unknowns, they made their legs move. They endured. They kept humping. They did not submit to the obvious alternative, which was simply to close the eyes and fall. So easy, really. Go limp and tumble to the ground and let the muscles unwind and not speak and not bulge until your buddies picked you up and lifted you into the chopper that would roar and dip its nose and carry you off to the world. A mere matter of falling, yet no one ever fell. It was not courage, exactly; the object was not valor. Rather, they were too frightened to be cowards.

By and large they carried these things inside, maintaining the masks of composure. They sneered at sick call. They spoke bitterly about guys who had found release by shooting off their own toes or fingers. Pussies, they'd say. Candy-asses. It was fierce, mocking talk, with only a trace of envy or awe, but even so the image played itself out behind their eyes.

They imagined the muzzle against flesh. So easy: squeeze the trigger and blow away a toe. They imagined it. They imagined the quick, sweet pain, then the evacuation to Japan, then a hospital with warm beds and cute geisha nurses.

And they dreamed of freedom birds.

At night, on guard, staring into the dark, they were carried away by jumbo jets. They felt the rush of takeoff. *Gone!* they yelled. And then velocity—wings and engines—a smiling stewardess—but it was more than a plane, it was a real bird, a big sleek silver bird with feathers and talons and high screeching. They were flying. The weights fell off; there was nothing to bear. They laughed and held on tight, feeling the cold slap of wind and altitude, soaring, thinking *It's over, I'm gone!*—they were naked, they were light and free—it was all lightness, bright and fast and buoyant, light as light, a helium buzz in the brain, a giddy bubbling in the lungs as they were taken up over the clouds and the war, beyond duty, beyond gravity and mortification and global entanglements—*Sin loi!* they yelled. *I'm sorry, motherfuckers, but I'm out of it, I'm goofed, I'm on a space cruise, I'm gone!*—and it was a restful, unencumbered sensation, just riding the light waves, sailing that big silver freedom bird over the mountains and oceans, over America, over the farms and great sleeping cities and cemeteries and highways and the golden arches of McDonald's, it was flight, a kind of fleeing, a kind of falling, falling higher and higher, spinning off the edge of the earth and beyond the sun and through the vast, silent vacuum where there were no burdens and where everything weighed exactly nothing—*Gone!* they screamed. *I'm sorry but I'm gone!*—and so at night, not quite dreaming, they gave themselves over to lightness, they were carried, they were purely borne.

On the morning after Ted Lavender died, First Lieutenant Jimmy Cross crouched at the bottom of his foxhole and burned Martha's letters. Then he burned the two photographs. There was a steady rain falling, which made it difficult, but he used heat tabs and Sterno to build a small fire, screening it with his body, holding the photographs over the tight blue flame with the tips of his fingers.

80

He realized it was only a gesture. Stupid, he thought. Sentimental, too, but mostly just stupid.

Lavender was dead. You couldn't burn the blame.

85   Besides, the letters were in his head. And even now, without photographs, Lieutenant Cross could see Martha playing volleyball in her white gym shorts and yellow T-shirt. He could see her moving in the rain.

When the fire died out, Lieutenant Cross pulled his poncho over his shoulders and ate breakfast from a can.

There was no great mystery, he decided.

In those burned letters Martha had never mentioned the war, except to say, Jimmy, take care of yourself. She wasn't involved. She signed the letters Love, but it wasn't love, and all the fine lines and technicalities did not matter. Virginity was no longer an issue. He hated her. Yes, he did. He hated her. Love, too, but it was a hard, hating kind of love.

The morning came up wet and blurry. Everything seemed part of everything else, the fog and Martha and the deepening rain.

90   He was a soldier, after all.

Half smiling, Lieutenant Jimmy Cross took out his maps. He shook his head hard, as if to clear it, then bent forward and began planning the day's march. In ten minutes, or maybe twenty, he would rouse the men and they would pack up and head west, where the maps showed the country to be green and inviting. They would do what they had always done. The rain might add some weight, but otherwise it would be one more day layered upon all the other days.

He was realistic about it. There was that new hardness in his stomach. He loved her but he hated her.

No more fantasies, he told himself.

Henceforth, when he thought about Martha, it would be only to think that she belonged elsewhere. He would shut down the daydreams. This was not Mount Sebastian, it was another world, where there were no pretty poems or midterm exams, a place where men died because of carelessness and gross stupidity. Kiowa was right. Boomdown, and you were dead, never partly dead.

95   Briefly, in the rain, Lieutenant Cross saw Martha's gray eyes gazing back at him.

He understood.

It was very sad, he thought. The things men carried inside. The things men did or felt they had to do.

He almost nodded at her, but didn't.

Instead he went back to his maps. He was now determined to perform his duties firmly and without negligence. It wouldn't help Lavender, he knew that, but from this point on he would comport himself as an officer. He would dispose of his good-luck pebble. Swallow it, maybe, or use Lee Strunk's slingshot, or just drop it along the trail. On the march he would impose strict field discipline. He would be careful to send out flank security, to prevent straggling or bunching up, to keep his troops moving at the proper pace and at the proper interval. He would insist on clean weapons. He would confiscate the remainder of Lavender's dope. Later in the day, perhaps, he would call the men together and speak to them plainly. He would accept the blame for what had happened to Ted Lavender. He would be a man about it. He would look them in the eyes, keeping his chin level, and he would issue the new SOPs in a calm, impersonal tone of voice, a lieutenant's voice, leaving no room for argument or discussion. Commencing immediately, he'd tell them, they would no longer abandon equipment along the route of march. They would police up their acts. They would get their shit together, and keep it together, and maintain it neatly and in good working order.

He would not tolerate laxity. He would show strength, distancing himself.   100

Among the men there would be grumbling, of course, and maybe worse, because their days would seem longer and their loads heavier, but Lieutenant Jimmy Cross reminded himself that his obligation was not to be loved but to lead. He would dispense with love; it was not now a factor. And if anyone quarreled or complained, he would simply tighten his lips and arrange his shoulders in the correct command posture. He might give a curt little nod. Or he might not. He might just shrug and say, Carry on, then they would saddle up and form into a column and move out toward the villages west of Than Khe.

CRITICAL THINKING QUESTIONS

1. The story's title is a steady refrain throughout the story: "The things they carried were largely determined by necessity" (par. 2); "They carried all they could bear, and then some, including a silent awe for the terrible power of the things they carried" (par. 11); "they all carried ghosts" (par. 16). List the various "things" the men carry. How do these things affect your response to the men, in particular, when juxtaposed with some of the unsavory and brutish actions of the men?

2. As the leader of his platoon, young Lieutenant Cross bears the heavy burden of power and responsibility. He blames himself for Ted Lavender's death. To what degree do you believe Cross is responsible?

3. Despite its terrible consequences, war is sometimes remembered as a time of bonding and friendship like no other. What is there in such a horrible situation that could make soldiers later miss it?

4. Sometimes the Vietnam War is portrayed to young people as the only war that fostered demonstrations and civil disobedience. Were there protests against our involvement in World War I or II, or is the Hollywood image of happy, singing Army volunteers generally accurate?

WRITING TOPIC

Read Wilfred Owen's poem *"Dulce Et Decorum Est"* in Chapter 3 (page 43). In O'Brien's story, find **imagery** that supports Owen's claim. For a creative activity, working with several classmates, use Owen's poem as a model and turn the imagery you identified from O'Brien's story into a poem.

Virgil Suarez

Bombardment (2014)

When I close my eyes, I see the ropes.

Ropes hanging from the paneled ceiling. Ropes and their round metal necks to signify to the climber this is the limit, as far as you can go. This is a gym in Henry T Gage Junior High School in Los Angeles, California. This is circa 1974.

When I close my eyes I see the braided mesh wire between the glass panes high up on the gym windows where ash and sepia-colored pigeons flock to roost.

When I close my eyes I see the crow, there to steal another pigeon's egg, breaking it open between its own claws, tasting the yolk, looking down at us.

5   It squawks twice, then takes off with the broken egg in clenched claws.

When I close my eyes I see each letter in the word *bombardment* fall from the rafters down to the bleachers. A bee's buzz around the basketball score-keeper. The 'o' of our mouths when Mr. Stupen barks at us to pick teams, knowing how it is going to go.

Lil' Ruben and Ratboy Marcos choose their own team of homeboys—they, of course, are to be shirts, though they sometimes wanted to be skins to show off their Virgin of Guadalupe tattoos on their pectorals, shoulders or arms.

When I close my eyes I hear the 'm' stutter of Benny who always plays on our team, the skins, *los carneritos*, as they call us for *carne*, and he goes down first. Last time he went to the clinic with a bruised rib that hurt like a motherfucker. He believes that once a rib breaks you have less luck in life. Maybe so, Benny. Maybe so.

One time, Chempo, the meanest of them all, got his nose broken. B is for ball. Bad ball. For its heavy, dark weight that bruises the skin where the ball makes contact with our bodies.

10   A is for the assholes who gang up against us, allow to do so by the lack of supervision by the fucked-up gym teachers. Mr. Stupen, bless his masochist heart, never once looked in on us after be blew his whistle to signal the beginning of the 50-minute bout.

'May the last man standing win,' he'd say, turn around, and leave for a smoke or a nap, or, rumor had it, spy on the girls in the locker room through a peep hole in his office.

When I close my eyes I see the 'R' of his striped referee shirt.

Stinky Watson, the only white kid on the team, likes to spit loogies into our faces. He spits them like bullets. After each spit, he works the mouth and tongue, saving up some more saliva.

'M' is for *mierda*, for what I always said when I found two or three of Watson's spits in my hair. Though I never liked to shower at school, I would have to. I hated it the sound Watson made as be hocked up another one.

When I close my eyes I see the entanglements of flesh, how one boy falls   15
on the ground and then there'd be a pile-up. Who didn't believe in the story of Humpty Dumpty, the little egg that fell off the fence and fell apart? You could almost hear the extinction of breath from the victim.

All of us moved back at the start of the game. If there were rules, they were not followed as the homeboys ganged up against us, one by one, drawing us away from the walls to the center of the court where they could take better aim with the bombardment ball and nail us on our backs.

'T' is for the hollow *thuck-thuck* of that ball hitting our flesh.

'*Pinches cabrones*,' Ramirez, the Mexican, would say. He was made crazy at school by bombardment.

When he and his family crossed the Rio Grande, bombardment wasn't the school activity he had in mind. He said he'd much rather work in the factories, and he did. A year after they broke his arm, he left school. We never heard from or saw Ramirez again. We need you now, Ramirez. Where are you?

There are three Cubans on the skins team and we bonded. We fight back. I   20
stop fighting after they take me down day and tie me up with the climbing ropes. I believe they will hang me. And if they hang me, I will not ever have to do this again. And they hang me all right, but all they do is line up and throw the ball at my body as hard as they can.

I hang there and they taunt me. A couple miss, and most of the blows come down below the waist. I cover my groin and my head as I try to guess which way the ball is coming at me.

Fifty minutes lasts an eternity. I can hear the sound of my own heart beating between my burning ears. If there is blood coursing through my veins, it is like the Almendares River of my childhood in Cuba gushing after a downpour.

When that bell rings, Mr. Stupen never even bothers to come back and blow the whistle, so the gangsters run at us, stampede us with their kicks, wild-thrown punches. They snap their moist-with-sweat, stinky shirts at us.

They claw and tear through our shirts, ripping them off our waists, taking the good ones and keeping them.

Thank God we didn't share lockers with any of them. Us, the recent arrivals   25
from Cuba, Mexico (Tijuana), Salvador, Nicaragua... we're all wetbacks. Nobody wants us for locker partncrs. Shit, that's what they call us. The skin shits.

'Wetback skins,' someone shouts and then there are the whistles to signify the bomb-ball's drop.

This is warfare. A ball rains down from the I-beam rafters. The *thuds* of the ball hitting our bodies echoes ad infinitum, loud enough to see the pigeons, sparrows, crows aflutter. They are our only audience. Our only witnesses. I say they are the choir in some Greek drama.

When I close my eyes I see the heavy ball falling from the sky.

'WacHale!' someone shouts. 'Take cover!'

30   In my nightmares there's more than one ball. They rain down upon us, knocking us to the ground, breaking our bones.

Nobody ever speaks about this.

We hide our bruised limbs as best as we could. From our families. From our parents. 'What's that?' my father will say looking at a bruise on my arm peeking through my t-shirt sleeve. 'Nothing,' I say.

Most of us are twelve, thirteen, fourteen—we don't have to show our bodies to anyone. 'Why are you limping?' my mother wants to know. 'Shoes,' I tell her. 'A little tight.'

The bruises bloom and darken our skins, spilled ink in water, a flowering right underneath our epidermis where the hurt sends shockwaves to our brain, our hearts.

35   When we close our eyes we see our broken souls.

When we close our eyes we see the scoreboard and how much we are behind, how much we are losing, how much harder we have to try to keep from going down for good.

When we close our eyes we see nothing but the purple and yellow of our cowardice. How, though we keep getting up and dusting our hands off, we keep getting pushed down, ground by a stranger's heel, our cheeks to the hard earth, our ears tuned to the muted sound of some poor sap somewhere moaning about a nosebleed, a broken finger, a fistful of hair missing.

Thuck-thud, thuck-thud, when we close our eyes we can still hear the most frightening of sounds: a bombardment ball rolling across an empty gymnasium court floor, coming to a final rest under put-away bleachers.

We hear ourselves crying, 'Stay close, stay together, stay…'

40   What is the sound of such a big ball whizzing by you, thrown with deliberate speed, with deliberate maliciousness?

What is the sound of that ball, that ball, hitting your rib cage, knocking the wind out of you? Or hitting the back of your head and knocking you down and out, teeth ground into the wood of the floor?

How does your blood taste as you tilt your head up to keep it from trickling down your mouth and chin? It's blood-in-the-water mentality—one drop and they see your weakness. They'll set upon you and beat you to a pulp.

You don't want to let them know your hurt, your pains and aches, the throbbing between your ears. It's a matter of time, you think. It's only a matter of time before something happens and all this fades away.

Nowhere to run, or hide. Stand up straight. Find out your next move.

Move!

Now keep your eyes closed to pretend this heavy, scuffed ball is never going 45
to find you.

CRITICAL THINKING QUESTIONS

1. Though "Bombardment" is set in 1974, in what ways do the experiences mentioned by the **narrator** parallel those of current middle and high school students? Further, how do they extend today to students in ethnic minorities?

2. What do you make of the following line from the passage: "He [Benny] believes that once a rib breaks you have less luck in life. Maybe so, Benny. Maybe so." What **inferences** might you make about Benny's life experiences and how they correlate with this statement? What about the narrator's own reflection on the matter?

3. The narrator never tells his parents the truth about the bruises and other marks on his body. Why do you believe he does so? In what way does he see keeping the truth as guarding his masculinity?

WRITING TOPIC

Do you recall being bullied in middle or high school or witnessing acts of bullying on classmates? Relay your experiences. In doing so, reflect upon why you believe that bullying persists as a problem among people in an educated and highly evolved society. What does the perpetuation of bullying reveal about human nature? How can we empower and embrace bullying victims in this age of cyberbullying?

Ed Vega

Spanish Roulette (1991)

Sixto Andrade snapped the gun open and shut several times and then spun the cylinder, intrigued by the kaleidoscopic pattern made by the empty chambers. He was fascinated by the blue-black color of the metal, but more so by the almost toy-like quality of the small weapon. As the last rays of sunlight began their retreat from the four-room tenement flat, Sixto once again snapped the cylinder open and began loading the gun. It pleased him that each brass and lead projectile fit easily into each one of the chambers and yet would not fall out. When he had finished inserting the last of the bullets, he again closed the cylinder and, enjoying the increased weight of the gun, pointed it at the ceiling and pulled back the hammer.

"What's the piece for, man?"

Sixto had become so absorbed in the gun that he did not hear Willie Collazo, with whom he shared the apartment, come in. His friend's question came at him suddenly, the words intruding into the world he had created since the previous weekend.

"Nothing," he said, lowering the weapon.

5   "What do you mean, 'nothing'?" said Willie. "You looked like you were ready to play Russian roulette when I came in, bro."

"No way, man," said Sixto, and as he had been shown by Tommy Ramos, he let the hammer fall back gently into place. "It's called Spanish roulette," he added, philosophically.

Willie's dark face broke into a wide grin and his eyes, just as if he were playing his congas, laughed before he did. "No kidding, man," he said. "You taking up a new line of work? I know things are rough but sticking up people and writing poetry don't go together."

Sixto put the gun on the table, tried to smile but couldn't, and recalled the last time he had read at the cafe on Sixth Street. Willie had played behind him, his hands making the drums sing a background to his words. "I gotta take care of some business, Willie," he said, solemnly, and, turning back to his friend, walked across the worn linoleum to the open window of the front room.

"Not like that, *panita*," Willie said as he followed him.

10   "Family stuff, bro."

"Who?"

"My sister," Sixto said without turning.

"Mandy?"

Sixto nodded, his small body taut with the anger he had felt when Mandy had finished telling him of the attack. He looked out over the street four flights below and fought an urge to jump. It was one solution but not *the* solution. Despairingly, he shook his head at the misery below: burned out buildings, torched by landlords because it was cheaper than fixing them; empty lots, overgrown with weeds and showing the ravages of life in the neighborhood. On the sidewalk, the discarded refrigerator still remained as a faceless sentinel standing guard over the lot, its door removed too late to save the little boy from Avenue B. He had been locked in it half the day while his mother, going crazy with worry, searched the streets so that by the time she saw the blue-faced child, she was too far gone to understand what it all meant.

15   He tried to cheer himself up by focusing his attention on the children playing in front of the open fire hydrant, but could not. The twilight rainbow within the stream of water, which they intermittently shot up in the air to make it cascade in a bright arc of white against the asphalt, was an illusion, *un engaño*, a poetic image of his childhood created solely to contrast his despair. He thought again of the crushed innocence on his sister's face and his blood felt like sand as it ran in his veins.

"You want to talk about it?" asked Willie.

"No, man," Sixto replied. "I don't."

Up the street, in front of the *bodega*, the old men were already playing dominoes and drinking beer. Sixto imagined them joking about each other's weaknesses, always, he thought ironically, with respect. They had no worries. Having lived a life of service to that which now beckoned him, they could afford to be light-hearted. It was as if he had been programmed early on for the task now facing him. He turned slowly, wiped an imaginary tear from his eyes and recalled his father's admonition about crying: "*Usted es un machito y los machos no lloran,* machos don't cry." How old had he been? Five or six, no more. He had fallen in the playground and cut his lip. His father's friends had laughed at the remark, but he couldn't stop crying and his father had shaken him. "*Le dije que usted no es una chancleta. ¡Apréndalo bien!*" "You are not a girl, understand that once and for all!"

Concerned with Sixto's mood, once again Willie tried drawing him out. "*Coño,* bro, she's only fifteen," he said. "*¿Qué pasó?*"

The gentleness and calm which Sixto so much admired had faded from Willie's face and now mirrored his own anguish. It was wrong to involve his friend but perhaps that was part of it. Willie was there to test his resolve. He had been placed there by fate to make sure the crime did not go unpunished. In the end, when it came to act, he'd have only his wits and manhood.   20

"It's nothing, bro," Sixto replied, walking back into the kitchen. "I told you, family business. Don't worry about it."

"Man, don't be like that."

There was no injury in Willie's voice and as if someone had suddenly punched him in the stomach to obtain a confession, the words burst out of Sixto.

"*Un tipo la mangó en el rufo,* man. Some dude grabbed her. You happy now?"

"Where?" Willie asked, knowing that uttering the words was meaningless.   25 "In the projects?"

"Yeah, last week. She got let out of school early and he grabbed her in the elevator and brought her up to the roof."

"And you kept it all in since you came back from your Mom's Sunday night?"

"What was I supposed to do, man? Go around broadcasting that my sister got took off?"

"I'm sorry, Sixto. You know I don't mean it like that."

"I know, man. I know."   30

"Did she know the guy? *Un cocolo,* right? A black dude. They're the ones that go for that stuff."

"No, man. It wasn't no *cocolo.*"

"But she knew him."

"Yeah, you know. From seeing him around the block. *Un bonitillo,* man. Pretty dude that deals coke and has a couple of women hustling for him. A dude named Lino."

"*¿Bien blanco?* Pale dude with Indian hair like yours?"   35

"Yeah, that's the guy."

"Drives around in a gold Camaro, right?"

"Yeah, I think so." Willie nodded several times and then shook his head.

"He's Shorty Pardo's cousin, right?" Sixto knew about the family connection but hadn't wanted to admit it until now.

40   "So?" he said, defiantly.

"Those people are crazy, bro," said Willie.

"I know."

"They've been dealing *tecata* up there in El Barrio since forever, man. Even the Italians stay clear of them, they're so crazy."

"That doesn't mean nothing to me," said Sixto, feeling his street manhood, the bravado which everyone develops growing up in the street, surfacing. Bad talk was the antidote to fear and he wasn't immune to it. "I know how crazy they are, but I'm gonna tell you something. I don't care who the dude is. I'm gonna burn him. Gonna set his heart on fire with that piece."

45   "Hey, go easy, *panita*," said Willie. "Be cool, bro. I know how you feel but that ain't gonna solve nothing. You're an artist, man. You know that? A poet. And a playwright. You're gonna light up Broadway one of these days." Willie was suddenly silent as he reflected on his words. He sat down on one of the kitchen chairs and lowered his head. After a few moments he looked up and said: "Forget what I said, man. I don't know what I'm talking about. I wouldn't know what to do if that happened to one of the women in my family. I probably would've done the dude in by now. I'm sorry I said anything. I just don't wanna see you messed up. And I'm not gonna tell you to go to the cops, either."

Sixto did not answer Willie. They both knew going to the police would serve no purpose. As soon as the old man found out, he'd beat her for not protecting herself. It would become a personal matter, as if it had been he who had submitted. He'd rant and rave about short skirts and lipstick and music and then compare everything to the way things were on the island and his precious hometown, his beloved Cacimar, like it was the center of the universe and the place where all the laws governing the human race had been created. But Sixto had nothing to worry about. He was different from his father. He was getting an education, had been enlightened to truth and beauty and knew about equality and justice. Hell, he was a new man, forged out of steel and concrete, not old banana leaves and coconuts. And yet, he wanted to strike back and was sick to his stomach because he wanted Lino Quintana in front of him, on his knees, begging for mercy. He'd smoke a couple of joints and float back uptown to the Pardo's turf and then blast away at all of them like he was the Lone Ranger.

He laughed sarcastically at himself and thought that in the end he'd probably back down, allow the matter to work itself out and let Mandy live with the scar for the rest of her life. And he'd tell himself that rape was a common thing, even in families, and that people went on living and working and making babies like a bunch of zombies, like somebody's puppets without ever realizing who was pulling the strings. It was all crazy. You were born and tagged with a name: Rodríguez, Mercado, Torres, Cartagena, Pantoja, Maldonado, Sandoval, Ballester, Nieves, Carmona. All of them, funny-ass Spanish names. And then you were told to speak English and be cool because it was important to try and get over by imitating the Anglo-Saxon crap, since that's where all the money and success were to be found. Nobody actually came out and said it, but it was written clearly in everything you saw, printed boldly between the lines of books, television, movies, advertising. And at the place where you got your love, your mother's milk, your rice and beans, you were told to speak Spanish and be respectful and defend your honor and that of the women around you.

"I'm gonna burn him, Willie," Sixto repeated. "Gonna burn him right in his *güevos*. Burn him right there in his balls so he can feel the pain before I blow him away and let God deal with him. He'll understand, man, because I don't." Sixto felt the dizzying anger blind him for a moment. "*Coño*, man, she was just fifteen," he pleaded, as if Willie could absolve him of his sin before it had been committed. "I have to do it, man. She was just a kid. *Una nena*, man. A little innocent girl who dug Latin music and danced only with her girlfriends at home and believed all the nonsense about purity and virginity, man. And now this son of a bitch went and did it to her. *Le hizo el daño.*"

That's what women called it. That damage. And it was true. Damaged goods. He didn't want to believe it but that's how he felt. In all his educated, enlightened splendor, that's how he felt. Like she had been rendered untouchable, her femaleness soiled and smeared forever. Like no man would want to love her, knowing what had happened. The whole thing was so devastating that he couldn't imagine what it was like to be a woman. If they felt even a little of what he was experiencing, it was too much. And he, her own brother, already talking as if she were dead. That's how bad it was. Like she was a memory.

"I'm gonna kill him, Willie," said Sixto once more, pounding on the wall. 50 "*¿Lo mato, coño! Lo mato, lo mato,*" he repeated the death threat over and over in a frenzy. Willie stood up and reached for his arm but Sixto pulled roughly away. "It's cool, man," he said, and put his opened hands in front of him. "I'm all right. Everything's cool."

"Slow down," Willie pleaded. "Slow down."

"You're right, man. I gotta slow down." Sixto sat down but before long was up again. "Man, I couldn't sleep the last couple of nights. I kept seeing myself wearing the shame the rest of my life. I gave myself every excuse in the book. I even prayed, Willie. Me, a spic from the streets of the Big Apple, hip and slick, writing my *jíbaro* poetry; *saliéndome las palabras de las entrañas; inventando foquin mundos* like a god; like *foquin* Juracán pitching lightning bolts at the people to wake them from their stupor, man. Wake them up from their lethargy and their four-hundred-year-old sleep of self-induced tyranny, you know?"

"I understand, man."

"Willie, man, I wanted my words to thunder, to shake the earth *pa' que la gente le pida a Yuquiyú que los salve.*"

"And it's gonna be that way, bro. You're the poet, man. The voice." 55

"And me praying. Praying, man. And not to Yuquiyú but to some distorted European idea. I'm messed up, bro. Really messed up. Writing all this jive poetry that's supposed to incite the people to take up arms against the oppressor and all the while my heart is dripping with feelings of love and brotherhood and peace like some programmed puppet, Willie."

"I hear you."

"I mean, I bought all that stuff, man. All that liberal American jive. I bought it. I marched against the war in Vietnam, against colonialism and capitalism, and for the Chicano brothers cracking their backs in the fields, marched till my feet were raw, and every time I saw lettuce or grapes, I saw poison. And man, it felt right, Willie."

"It was a righteous cause, man."

60   "And I marched for the independence of the island, of Puerto Rico, Willie: *de Portorro, de Borinquen, la buena, la sagrada, el terruño, madre de todos nosotros; bendita seas entre todas las mujeres y bendito sea el fruto de tu vientre pelú.* I marched for the land of our people and it felt right."

"It is right, man."

"You know, once and for all I had overcome all the anger of being a colonized person without a country and my culture being swallowed up, digested and thrown back up so you can't even recognize what it's all about. I had overcome all the craziness and could stand above it; I could look down on the brothers and sisters who took up arms in '50 and '54 when I wasn't even a fantasy in my pop's mind, man. I could stand above all of them, even the ones with their bombs now. I could pay tribute to them with words but still judge them crazy. And it was okay. It felt right to wear two faces, to go back and forth from poetic fury to social condescension or whatever you wanna call it. I thought I had it beat with the education and the poetry and opening up my heart like some long-haired, brown-skinned hippy. And now this. I'm a hypocrite, man."

Like the water from the open fire hydrant, the words had rushed out of him. And yet he couldn't say exactly what it was that troubled him about the attack on his sister, couldn't pinpoint what it was that made his face hot and his blood race angrily in his veins. Willie, silenced by his own impotence, sat looking at him. He knew he could neither urge him on nor discourage him and inevitably he would have to stand aside and let whatever was to happen run its course. His voice almost a whisper, he said, "It's okay, Sixto. I know how it feels. Just let the pain come out, man. Just let it out. Cry if you have to."

But the pain would never leave him. Spics weren't Greeks and the word katharsis had no meaning in private tragedy. Sixto's mind raced back into time, searching for an answer, knowing, even as it fled like a wounded animal seeking refuge from its tormentors, that it was an aimless search. It was like running a maze. Like the rats in the psychology films and the puzzles in the children's section of weekend newspapers. One followed a path with a pencil until he came to a dead end, then retraced his steps. Thousands of years passed before him in a matter of minutes.

65   The Tainos: a peaceful people, some history books said. No way, he thought. They fought the Spaniards, drowned them to test their immortality. And their

caciques were as fierce and as brave as Crazy Horse or Geronimo. Proud chiefs they were. Jumacao, Daguao, Yaureibo, Caguax, Agueybaná, Mabodamaca, Aymamón, Urayoán, Orocobix, Guarionex all fought the Spaniards with all they had...*guasábara*...*guasábara*...*guas ábara*...their battle cry echoing through the hills like an eerie phantom; they fought their horses and dogs; they fought their swords and guns and when there was no other recourse, rather than submitting, they climbed sheer cliffs and, holding their children to their breasts, leapt into the sea.

And the blacks: *los negros*, whose blood and heritage he carried. They didn't submit to slavery but escaped and returned to conduct raids against the oppressors, so that the whole *negrito lindo* business, so readily accepted as a term of endearment, was a joke, an appeasement on the part of the Spaniards. The *bombas* and *bembas* and *ginganbó* and their all night dances and *oraciones* to Changó: warrior men of the Jelofe, Mandingo, Mende, Yoruba, Dahomey, Ashanti, Ibo, Fante, Baule and Congro tribes, choosing battle over slavery.

And the Spaniards: certainly not a peaceful people. For centuries they fought each other and then branched out to cross the sea and slaughter hundreds of thousands of Indians, leaving an indelible mark on entire civilizations, raping and pillaging and gutting the earth of its riches, so that when it was all done and they laid in a drunken stupor four hundred years later, their pockets empty, they rose again to fight themselves in civil war.

And way back, way back before El Cid Campeador began to wage war: The Moors. *Los moros*...*alhambra, alcázar, alcohol, almohada, alcade, alboroto*...NOISE... CRIES OF WAR...A thousand years the maze traveled and it led to a dead end with dark men atop fleet Arabian stallions, dark men, both in visage and intent, raising their scimitars against those dishonoring their house...they had invented algebra and Arabic numbers and it all added up to war...there was no other way...

"I gotta kill him, bro," Sixto heard himself say. "I gotta. Otherwise I'm as good as dead." One had to live with himself and that was the worst part of it; he had to live with the knowledge and that particular brand of cowardice that eroded the mind and destroyed one's soul. And it wasn't so much that his sister had been wronged. He'd seen that. The injury came from not retaliating. He was back at the beginning. Banana leaves and coconuts and machete duels at sundown. Just like his father and his *jíbaro* values. For even if the aggressor never talked, even if he never mentioned his act to another soul for whatever reason, there was still another person, another member of the tribe, who could single him out in a crowd and say to himself: "That one belongs to me and so does his sister."

Sixto tried to recall other times when his manhood had been challenged, but 70 it seemed as if everything had happened long ago and hadn't been important: kid fights over mention of his mother, rights of ownership of an object, a place in the hierarchy of the block, a word said of his person, a lie, a bump by a stranger on a crowded subway train—nothing ever going beyond words or at worst, a sudden shoving match quickly broken up by friends.

But this was different. His brain was not functioning properly, he thought. He tried watching himself, tried to become an observer, the impartial judge of his actions. Through a small opening in his consciousness, he watched the raging battle. His heart called for the blood of the enemy and his brain urged him to use caution. There was no thought of danger, for in that region of struggle, survival meant not so much escaping with his life, but conquering fear and regaining his honor.

Sixto picked up the gun and studied it once more. He pushed the safety to make sure it was locked and placed the gun between the waistband of his pants and the flesh of his stomach. The cold metal sent slivers of ice running down his legs. It was a pleasant sensation, much as if a woman he had desired for some time had suddenly let him know, in an unguarded moment, that intimacy was possible between them. Avoiding Willie's eyes, he walked around the kitchen, pulled out his shirt and let it hang out over his pants. It was important that he learn to walk naturally and reduce his self-consciousness about the weapon. But it was his mind working tricks again. Nobody would notice. The idea was to act calmly. That's what everyone said: the thieves, the cheap stickup men who mugged old people and taxi drivers; the burglars who, like vultures, watched the movement of a family until certain that they were gone, swooped down and cleaned out the apartment, even in the middle of the day; the check specialists, who studied mailboxes as if they were bank vaults so they could break them open and steal welfare checks or fat letters from the island on the chance they might contain money orders or cash. They all said it. Even the young gang kids said it. Don't act suspiciously. Act as if you were going about your business.

Going to shoot someone was like going to work. That was it. He'd carry his books and nobody would suspect that he was carrying death. He laughed inwardly at the immense joke. He'd once seen a film in which Robert Mitchum, posing as a preacher, had pulled a derringer out of a Bible in the final scene. Why not. He'd hollow out his Western Civilization text and place the gun in it. It was his duty. The act was a way of surviving, of earning what was truly his. Whether a pay check or an education, it meant nothing without self-respect.

But the pieces of the puzzle did not fit and Sixto sat down dejectedly. He let his head fall into his hands and for a moment thought he would cry. Willie said nothing and Sixto waited, listening, the void of silence becoming larger and larger, expanding so that the sounds of the street, a passing car, the excitement of a child, the rushing water from the open hydrant, a mother's window warning retreated, became fainter and seemed to trim the outer edges of the nothingness within the silence. He could hear his own breathing and the beating of his heart and still he waited.

75   And then slowly, as if waking from a refreshing sleep, Sixto felt himself grow calmer and a pleasant coldness entered his body as heart and mind finally merged and became tuned to his mission. He smiled at the feeling and knew he had gone through the barrier of doubt and fear which had been erected to protect him from himself, to make sure he did not panic at the last moment. War had to be similar. He had heard the older men, the ones who had survived Viet-

nam, talk about it. Sonny Maldonado with his plastic foot, limping everywhere he went, quiet and unassuming, talked about going through a doorway and into a quiet room where one died a little and then came out again, one's mind alive but the rest of the body already dead to the upcoming pain.

It had finally happened, he thought. There was no anger or regret, no rationalizations concerning future actions. No more justifications or talk about honor and dignity. Instead, Sixto perceived the single objective coldly. There was neither danger nor urgency in carrying out the sentence and avenging the wrong. It seemed almost too simple. If it took years he knew the task would be accomplished. He would study the habits of his quarry, chart his every movement, and one day he'd strike. He would wait in a deserted hallway some late night, calmly walk out of the shadows, only his right index finger and his brain connected and say: "How you doing, Lino?" and his voice alone would convey the terrible message. Sixto smiled to himself and saw, as in a slow motion cinematic shot, his mind's ghost delicately squeeze the trigger repeatedly, the small animal muzzle of the gun following Lino Quintana's body as it fell slowly and hit the floor, the muscles of his victim's face twitching and life ebbing away forever. It happened all the time and no one was ever discovered.

Sixto laughed, almost too loudly. He took the gun out from under his shirt and placed it resolutely on the table. "I gotta think some more, man," he said. "That's crazy rushing into the thing. You wanna beer, Willie?"

Willie was not convinced of his friend's newly found calm. Reluctantly, he accepted the beer. He watched Sixto and tried to measure the depth of his eyes. They had become strangely flat, the glint of trust in them absent. It was as if a thin, opaque veil had been sewn over the eyes to mask Sixto's emotions. He felt helpless but said nothing. He opened the beer and began mourning the loss. Sixto was right, he thought. It was Spanish roulette. Spics were born and the cylinder spun. When it stopped one was handed the gun and, without looking, had to bring it to one's head, squeeze the trigger and take his chances.

The belief was pumped into the bloodstream, carved into the flesh through generations of strife, so that being was the enactment of a ritual rather than the beginning of a new life. One never knew his own reactions until faced with Sixto's dilemma. And yet the loss would be too great, the upcoming grief too profound and the ensuing suffering eternal. The violence would be passed on to another generation to be displayed as an invisible coat of arms, much as Sixto's answer had come to him as a relic. His friend would never again look at the world with wonder, and poetry would cease to spring from his heart. If he did write, the words would be guarded, careful, full of excuses and apologies for living. Willie started to raise the beer in a toast but thought better of it and set the can on the table.

"Whatever you do, bro," he said, "be careful."

"Don't worry, man," Sixto replied. "I got the thing under control." He laughed once again and suddenly his eyes were ablaze were hatred. He picked up the gun, stuck it back into his pants and stood up. "No good, man," he said,

80

seemingly to himself, and rushed out, slamming the door of the apartment behind him.

Beyond the sound of the door, Willie could hear the whirring cylinder as it began to slow down, each minute click measuring the time before his friend had to raise the weapon to his head and kill part of himself.

CRITICAL THINKING QUESTIONS

1. There is a clear **conflict** in this story between the forces of learning and the forces of violence. Should Willie intervene? Which is the good side? Explain your reasoning.

2. How do the main characters define the concept of justice?

WRITING TOPIC

Assuming Willie would argue for the poetic/learning side while Sixto would argue for the necessity for revenge, write a dialogue between the two men in which each states his side of the argument. Further, imagine yourself as a third-party mediator. Consider how you might construct a **Rogerian argument** resolution (conclusion) to the conflict in this story.

POETRY

Gwendolyn Brooks

The Boy Died in My Alley (1975)

Without my having known.
Policeman said, next morning,
"Apparently died Alone."
"You heard a shot?" Policeman said.
Shots I hear and Shots I hear.   5
I never see the dead.

The Shot that killed him yes I heard
as I heard the Thousand shots before;
careening tinnily down the nights
across my years and arteries.   10

Policeman pounded on my door.
"Who is it?" "police!" Policeman yelled.
"A boy was dying in your alley.
A boy is dead, and in your alley.
And have you known this Boy before?"   15

I have known this Boy before.
I have known this Boy before, who
ornaments my alley.
I never saw his face at all.
I never saw his futurefall.   20
But I have known this Boy.

I have always heard him deal with death.
I have always heard the shout, the volley.
I have closed my heart-ears late and early.
And I have killed him ever.   25

I joined the Wild and killed him
with knowledgeable unknowing.

I saw where he was going.
I saw him Crossed. And seeing.
30   I did not take him down.

He cried not only "Father!"
but "Mother!
Sister!
Brother!"
35   The cry climbed up the alley.
It went up to the wind.
It hung upon the heaven
for a long
stretch-strain of Moment.

40   The red floor of my alley
is a special speech to me.

CRITICAL THINKING QUESTION

The speaker expresses special concern for this dead boy whom she does not
know. Why is she concerned?

WRITING TOPIC

Reread the last two lines of the poem. What does the narrator mean when
she tells us, "The red floor of my alley/is a special speech to me"? Write
your version of this "special speech."

Martín Espada

Bully (1990)

Boston, *Massachusetts, 1987*

In the school auditorium,
the Theodore Roosevelt statue
is nostalgic
for the Spanish-American War,
5   each fist lonely for a saber
or the reins of anguish-eyed horses,
or a podium to clatter with speeches
glorying in the malaria of conquest.

But now the Roosevelt school
is pronounced *Hernández*.   10
Puerto Rico has invaded Roosevelt
with its army of Spanish-singing children
in the hallways,
brown children devouring
the stockpiles of the cafeteria,   15
children painting *Taíno* ancestors
that leap naked across murals.

Roosevelt is surrounded
by all the faces
he ever shoved in eugenic spite   20
and cursed as mongrels, skin of one race,
hair and cheekbones of another.

Once Marines tramped
from the newsreel of his imagination;
now children plot to spray graffiti   25
in parrot-brilliant colors
across the Victorian mustache
and monocle.

CRITICAL THINKING QUESTIONS

1. What is the poet's **claim of value** about Theodore Roosevelt?

2. On which rhetorical appeal (**ethos, logos, pathos**) does he base his argument?

3. Find examples of **connotation** (see Glossary). Do these word usages contribute to or detract from the poet's argument? Explain your response.

WRITING TOPIC

Assume a role as Theodore Roosevelt's defender. Do some research and write a rebuttal to this poem's argument.

Carolyn Forché

The Colonel (1981)

What you have heard is true. I was in his house. His wife carried a tray of coffee and sugar. His daughter filed her nails, his son went out for the night. There were daily papers, pet dogs, a pistol on the cushion beside him. The moon swung bare on its black cord over the house. On the television was a cop show. It was in English. Broken bottles were embedded in the walls around the house to scoop the kneecaps from a man's legs or cut his hands to lace. On the windows there were gratings like those in liquor stores. We had dinner, rack of lamb, good wine, a gold bell was on the table for calling the maid. The maid brought green mangoes, salt, a type of bread. I was asked how I enjoyed the country. There was a brief commercial in Spanish. His wife took everything away. There was some talk then of how difficult it had become to govern. The parrot said hello on the terrace. The colonel told it to shut up, and pushed himself from the table. My friend said to me with his eyes: say nothing. The colonel returned with a sack used to bring groceries home. He spilled many human ears on the table. They were like dried peach halves. There is no other way to say this. He took one of them in his hands, shook it in our faces, dropped it into a water glass. It came alive there. I am tired of fooling around he said. As for the rights of anyone, tell your people they can go fuck themselves. He swept the ears to the floor with his arm and held the last of his wine in the air. Something for your poetry, no? he said. Some of the ears on the floor caught this scrap of his voice. Some of the ears on the floor were pressed to the ground.

CRITICAL THINKING QUESTIONS

1. In terms of persuasion, the colonel is not subtle. What is the by-product of his approach to persuasion? Think about what usually happens to dictators in the end.

2. Is there no way to argue with such a man as the colonel except through violence? If so, how could such an argument be executed in a nonviolent manner?

WRITING TOPIC

The colonel does not care about the rights of anyone, and in his situation he seems to be able to get away with this approach to governing and controlling people. Threatening people with physical violence creates an effective short-term argument; however, the by-product is anger and hostility, which, in the long run, often are counterproductive. Using examples, argue that the carrot is more powerful than the stick.

Robert Frost

Mending Wall (1914)

Something there is that doesn't love a wall,
That sends the frozen-ground-swell under it,
And spills the upper boulders in the sun;
And makes gaps even two can pass abreast.
The work of hunters is another thing: 5
I have come after them and made repair
Where they have left not one stone on a stone,
But they would have the rabbit out of hiding,
To please the yelping dogs. The gaps I mean,
No one has seen them made or heard them made,   10
But at spring mending-time we find them there.
I let my neighbor know beyond the hill;
And on a day we meet to walk the line
And set the wall between us once again.
We keep the wall between us as we go.   15
To each the boulders that have fallen to each.
And some are loaves and some so nearly balls
We have to use a spell to make them balance:
"Stay where you are until our backs are turned!"
We wear our fingers rough with handling them.   20
Oh, just another kind of outdoor game,
One on a side. It comes to little more:
There where it is we do not need the wall:
He is all pine and I am apple orchard.
My apple trees will never get across   25
And eat the cones under his pines, I tell him.
He only says, "Good fences make good neighbors."
Spring is the mischief in me, and I wonder
If I could put a notion in his head:
"*Why* do they make good neighbors? Isn't it   30
Where there are cows? But here there are no cows.
Before I built a wall I'd ask to know

What I was walling in or walling out,
And to whom I was like to give offense.
35   Something there is that doesn't love a wall,
That wants it down." I could say "Elves" to him,
But it's not elves exactly, and I'd rather
He said it for himself. I see him there
Bringing a stone grasped firmly by the top
40   In each hand, like an old-stone savage armed.
He moves in darkness as it seems to me,
Not of woods only and the shade of trees.
He will not go behind his father's saying,
And he likes having thought of it so well
45   He says again, "Good fences make good neighbors."

CRITICAL THINKING QUESTIONS

1. How does the speaker appeal to *logos* to argue against the fence between him and his neighbor?

2. In lines 32 and 33, the speaker says, "Before I built a wall I'd ask to know/What I was walling in or walling out." What might fences wall in, and what might they wall out?

3. Whose viewpoint do you support, the speaker's, "Something there is that doesn't love a wall," or the neighbor's, "Good fences make good neighbors"?

WRITING TOPIC

Seeking security within a homogenous community, homeowners are increasingly choosing to live in gated communities. While many champion this lifestyle choice as a way to revive the virtues and values of small towns—where you can go next door to borrow a cup of sugar, where your children can ride their bikes without your direct supervision—others claim that these communities are widening the chasm between the haves and the have-nots, as well as creating barriers that segregate rather than integrate society. Is this a case of "good fences make good neighbors"? Or is there something in the urban environment that "doesn't love a wall"? Write an argument to support or refute the concept of the gated community.

Langston Hughes

Democracy (1949)

Democracy will not come
Today, this year
Nor ever
Through compromise and fear.

I have as much right   5
As the other fellow has
To stand
On my two feet
And own the land.

I tire so of hearing people say,   10
Let things take their course.
Tomorrow is another day.
I do not need my freedom when I'm dead.
I cannot live on tomorrow's bread.

Freedom   15
Is a strong seed
Planted
In a great need.
I live here, too.
I want freedom   20
Just as you.

CRITICAL THINKING QUESTION

When you see the word *democracy*, what thoughts come to your mind? What does *democracy* mean to you? Would you say that democratic ideals are fully realized and demonstrated in twenty-first-century American society? Please explain.

WRITING TOPIC

Write out the first four lines of the poem "Democracy" as a **prose** statement. In the context of contemporary America, does the concept democracy remain "unrealized"? Argue that compared to sixty years ago, when Hughes wrote the poem, the country has made great strides toward democracy, *or* argue that compared to sixty years ago, while some aspects have changed, others remain much as they were. Use specific examples to support your claim and avoid merely making generalizations.

Langston Hughes

Theme for English B (1949)

The instructor said,
Go home and write
a page tonight.
And let that page come out of you—
5 *Then, it will be true.*

I wonder if it's that simple?
I am twenty-two, colored, born in Winston-Salem.
I went to school there, then Durham, then here
to this college on the hill above Harlem.
10 I am the only colored student in my class.
The steps from the hill lead down into Harlem,
through a park, then I cross St. Nicholas,
Eighth Avenue, Seventh, and I come to the Y,
the Harlem Branch Y, where I take the elevator
15 up to my room, sit down, and write this page:

It's not easy to know what is true for you or me
at twenty-two, my age. But I guess I'm what
I feel and see and hear, Harlem, I hear you:
hear you, hear me—we two—you, me, talk on this page.
20 (I hear New York, too.) Me—who?

Well, I like to eat, sleep, drink, and be in love.
I like to work, read, learn, and understand life.
I like a pipe for a Christmas present,
or records—Bessie, bop, or Bach.
25 I guess being colored doesn't make me *not* like
the same things other folks like who are other races.
So will my page be colored that I write?
Being me, it will not be white.
But it will be
a part of you, instructor.
30 You are white—

yet a part of me, as I am a part of you.
That's American.
Sometimes perhaps you don't want to be a part of me.
35 Nor do I often want to be a part of you.
But we are, that's true!
As I learn from you,

I guess you learn from me—
although you're older—and white—   40
and somewhat more free.

This is my page for English B.

CRITICAL THINKING QUESTIONS

1. What power issues is the poem's speaker addressing?

2. In resolving his power issues, what Rogerian position does the speaker articulate? What is your opinion of this position?

WRITING TOPIC

Read several articles about *multiculturalism* so that you understand the term and some of the controversy surrounding it. Many colleges' and universities' curricula include multicultural course requirements; argue for or against a multicultural requirement on your campus.

Claude McKay

America (1919)

Although she feeds me bread of bitterness,
And sinks into my throat her tiger's tooth,
Stealing my breath of life, I will confess
I love this cultured hell that tests my youth!
Her vigor flows like tides into my blood,   5
Giving me strength erect against her hate.
Her bigness sweeps my being like a flood.
Yet as a rebel fronts a king in state,
I stand within her walls with not a shred
Of terror, malice, not a word of jeer.   10
Darkly I gaze into the days ahead,
And see her might and granite wonders there,
Beneath the touch of Time's unerring hand,
Like priceless treasures sinking in the sand.

CRITICAL THINKING QUESTIONS

1. In line 4, the speaker proclaims, "I love this cultured hell that tests my youth!"

   a. List details from the poem that depict this love.

   b. Look up **ambiguity** in the Glossary. Which details create ambiguity regarding this love?

2. Write out a **claim of value** about America that the speaker implies. To what degree do you agree or disagree with this claim?

WRITING TOPIC

As you consider the current political and social climates of America, do you find yourself feeling more optimistic or pessimistic when it comes the future of the United States? What are your biggest social, political, and/or personal concerns about the state of the nation? If you could facilitate one change in our country, what would it be and why?

James Merrill

Casual Wear (1992)

Your average tourist: Fifty. 2.3
Times married. Dressed, this year, in Ferdi Plinthbower
Originals. Odds 1 to 9
Against her strolling past the Embassy

5   Today at noon. Your average terrorist:
Twenty-five. Celibate. No use for trends,
At least in clothing. Mark, though, where it ends.
People have come forth made of colored mist

Unsmiling on one hundred million screens
To tell of his prompt phone call to the station,
10   "Claiming responsibility"—devastation
Signed with a flourish, like the dead wife's jeans.

CRITICAL THINKING QUESTION

This poem especially resonates with readers as the war on terror continues across the globe. In what ways have global terrorists attacks, including the September 11, 2001, attacks on America, changed the ways we view the world? What about how we look at each other? On a personal note, does the threat of terrorist attacks make you hesitant when it comes to traveling, especially abroad?

WRITING TOPIC

Read about a particular terrorist activity somewhere in the world. Then read further to gain some understanding of the group's motivation. First, attempt to explain how and why this group justifies its activities; then write a rebuttal of the leader's argument.

Edna St. Vincent Millay

Apostrophe to Man (1934)

(On reflecting that the world is ready to go to war again)

Detestable race, continue to expunge yourself, die out.
Breed faster, crowd, encroach, sing hymns, build bombing airplanes;
Make speeches, unveil statues, issue bonds, parade;
Convert again into explosives the bewildered ammonia and the
    distracted cellulose;
Convert again into putrescent matter drawing flies   5
The hopeful bodies of the young; exhort,
Pray, pull long faces, be earnest, be all but overcome, be
    photographed;
Confer, perfect your formulae, commercialize
Bacteria harmful to human tissue,
Put death on the market;   10
Breed, crowd, encroach, expand, expunge yourself, die out,
Homo called *sapiens*

CRITICAL THINKING QUESTIONS

1. Much of this poem is a list, an enumeration of specifics. How is this strategy an effective organizational approach for Millay's subject?

2. Explain why the last line of the poem is an example of **irony** (see Glossary). You will need to look up *homo* and *sapiens* in a dictionary if you are not absolutely certain you know what each means.

3. Judging by this poem, we might well describe the poet as *cynical.* Look up the meaning of *cynic.* Who were the cynics in Ancient Greece? Why do you believe Millay would or would not have fit in well with this group of philosophers?

WRITING TOPIC

Model the structure of this poem by creating your own version; however, begin your version with the words "Admirable race" and continue by creating a list of positive attributes.

John Milton

When I Consider How My Light Is Spent (1673)

When I consider how my light is spent,
 Ere half my days in this dark world and wide,
 And that one talent which is death to hide
Lodged with me useless, though my soul more bent
5 To serve therewith my Maker, and present
 My true account, lest He returning chide;
 "Doth God exact day-labor, light denied?"
I fondly ask. But Patience, to prevent
That murmur, soon replies, "God doth not need
10 Either man's work or His own gifts. Who best
Bear His mild yoke, they serve Him best. His state
Is kingly: thousands at His bidding speed,
And post o'er land and ocean without rest;
They also serve who only stand and wait."

CRITICAL THINKING QUESTION

According to Milton, in deciding how to use one's individual talents, what **assumption** about the purpose of one's life underlies that choice? Do you accept this assumption, and why or why not?

WRITING TOPIC

In your opinion, what values should inform one's choice of a career or profession? Why are these values important?

———————————

Naomi Shihab Nye

Famous (1995)

The river is famous to the fish.
The loud voice is famous to silence,
which knew it would inherit the earth
before anybody said so.
The cat sleeping on the fence is famous to the birds   5
watching him from the birdhouse.

The tear is famous, briefly, to the cheek.
The idea you carry close to your bosom
is famous to your bosom.

The boot is famous to the earth,   10
more famous than the dress shoe,
which is famous only to floors.

The bent photograph is famous to the one who carries it
and not at all famous to the one who is pictured.

I want to be famous to shuffling men   15
who smile while crossing streets,
sticky children in grocery lines,
famous as the one who smiled back.

I want to be famous in the way a pulley is famous,
or a buttonhole, not because it did anything spectacular,   20
but because it never forgot what it could do.

CRITICAL THINKING QUESTIONS

1. What is Nye's **implied claim** for evaluating the concept of famous?

2. In a culture that glorifies celebrity, what images are attached to fame? What definition of "famous" do these images suggest?

WRITING TOPIC

Compare and contrast Nye's viewpoint on famous and the viewpoint projected by popular culture. What values do you think should be associated with famous? Based on your consideration of these perspectives, write your own argument for defining famous.

Sharon Olds

The Promise (1990)

With the second drink, at the restaurant,
holding hands on the bare table
we are at it again, renewing our promise
to kill each other. You are drinking gin,
5   night-blue juniper berry
dissolving in your body, I am drinking Fumé,
chewing its fragrant dirt and smoke, we are
taking on earth, we are part soil already,
and always, wherever we are, we are also in our
10   bed, fitted naked closely
along each other, half passed out
after love, drifting back and
forth across the border of consciousness, our
bodies buoyant, clasped. Your hand
15   tightens on the table. You're a little afraid
I'll chicken out. What you do not want
is to lie in a hospital bed for a year
after a stroke, without being able to
think or die, you do not want
20   to be tied to a chair like my prim grandmother,
cursing. The room is dim around us,
ivory globes, pink curtains
bound at the waist, and outside
a weightless bright lifted-up
25   summer twilight. I tell you you don't
know me if you think I will not
kill you. Think how we have floated together
eye to eye, nipple to nipple,
sex to sex, the halves of a single creature
30   drifting up to the lip of matter

and over it—you know me from the bright, blood-flecked
delivery room, if a beast
had you in its jaws I would attack it, if the ropes
binding your soul are your own wrists I will cut them.

CRITICAL THINKING QUESTIONS

1. What is this poem's implied claim on the issue of active euthanasia or "mercy killing"?

2. What evidence does the speaker provide in making her case for keeping "our promise/to kill each other"? On which rhetorical appeal (*ethos, logos, pathos*) does she rely?

3. Has the speaker succeeded in persuading you that she must keep the promise? Why or why not?

WRITING TOPIC

The poet's image of "[lying] in a hospital bed for a year/after a stroke, without being able to/think or die" brings to mind difficult end-of-life issues for not only the stroke victim but also for his or her family, friends, and doctors. When does life cease to have meaning? Certainly, this is a moral and ethical question with which individuals wrestle. But to what degree should laws intervene—either to allow or not to allow terminally ill individuals to choose to end their lives? As of spring 2015, only four states—Oregon, Washington, Vermont, and Montana—have laws legalizing doctor-assisted suicide. In Montana, doctor-assisted suicide is legal only after a mentally competent, terminally ill patient requests permission through the courts. Research this issue, specifically the consequences of Oregon's, Washington's, Vermont's, and Montana's laws. Should other states follow their lead?

Linda Pastan

Ethics (1981)

In ethics class so many years ago
our teacher asked this question every fall:
if there were a fire in a museum
which would you save, a Rembrandt painting

5   or an old woman who hadn't many
years left anyhow? Restless on hard chairs
caring little for pictures or old age
we'd opt one year for life, the next for art
and always half-heartedly. Sometimes
10   the woman borrowed my grandmother's face
leaving her usual kitchen to wander
some drafty, half-imagined museum.
One year, feeling clever, I replied
why not let the woman decide herself?
15   Linda, the teacher would report, eschews
the burdens of responsibility.
This fall in a real museum I stand
before a real Rembrandt, old woman,
or nearly so, myself. The colors
20   within this frame are darker than autumn,
darker even than winter—the browns of earth,
though earth's most radiant elements burn
through the canvas. I know now that woman
and painting and season are almost one
25   and all beyond saving by children.

CRITICAL THINKING QUESTION

What is your visceral reaction to this poem? Is the dilemma presented in this work a fair one? Why would the author pose the question of saving an old woman versus a Rembrandt painting?

WRITING TOPIC

Pastan argues that we cannot expect children to make the kind of ethical decision her teacher posed. In contrast, however, many people argue that today, schools often fail to teach values. Write a description of instances during your childhood, in school or out of school, when you received instruction in morals and values.

———————————

DRAMA

Susan Glaspell

Trifles (1916)

George Henderson (County Attorney)
Henry Peters (Sheriff)
Lewis Hale, A Neighboring Farmer
Mrs. Peters
Mrs. Hale

Scene: *The kitchen is the now abandoned farmhouse of* John Wright, *a gloomy kitchen, and left without having been put in order—unwashed pans under the sink, a loaf of bread outside the bread-box, a dish-towel on the table—other signs of incompleted work. At the rear the outer door opens and the* Sheriff *comes in followed by the* County Attorney *and* Hale. *The* Sheriff *and* Hale *are men in middle life, the* County Attorney *is a young man; all are much bundled up and go at once to the stove. They are followed by the two women—the* Sheriff's *wife first; she is a slight wiry woman, a thin nervous face.* Mrs. Hale *is larger and would ordinarily be called more comfortable looking, but she is disturbed now and looks fearfully about as she enters. The women have come in slowly, and stand close together near the door.*

County Attorney: (*rubbing his hands*) This feels good. Come up to the fire, ladies.
Mrs. Peters: (*after taking a step forward*) I'm not—cold.
Sheriff: (*unbuttoning his overcoat and stepping away from the stove as if to mark the beginning of official business*) Now, Mr. Hale, before we move things about, you explain to Mr. Henderson just what you saw when you came here yesterday morning.
County Attorney: By the way, has anything been moved? Are things just as you left them yesterday?
Sheriff: (*looking about*) It's just the same. When it dropped below zero last night I thought I'd better send Frank out this morning to make a fire for us—no use getting pneumonia with a big case on, but I told him not to touch anything except the stove—and you know Frank.
County Attorney: Somebody should have been left here yesterday.

Sheriff: Oh—yesterday. When I had to send Frank to Morris Center for that man who went crazy—I want you to know I had my hands full yesterday. I knew you could get back from Omaha by today and as long as I went over everything here myself—

County Attorney: Well, Mr. Hale, tell just what happened when you came here yesterday morning.

Hale: Harry and I had started to town with a load of potatoes. We came along the road from my place and as I got here I said, "I'm going to see if I can't get John Wright to go in with me on a party telephone." I spoke to Wright about it once before and he put me off, saying folks talked too much anyway, and all he asked was peace and quiet—I guess you know about how much he talked himself; but I thought maybe if I went to the house and talked about it before his wife, though I said to Harry that I didn't know as what his wife wanted made much difference to John—

County Attorney: Let's talk about that later, Mr. Hale. I do want to talk about that, but tell now just what happened when you got to the house.

Hale: I didn't hear or see anything; I knocked at the door, and still it was all quiet inside. I knew they must be up, it was past eight o'clock. So I knocked again, and I thought I heard somebody say, 'Come in.' I wasn't sure, I'm not sure yet, but I opened the door—this door (*indicating the door by which the two women are still standing*) and there in that rocker—(*pointing to it*) sat Mrs. Wright.
(*They all look at the rocker.*)

County Attorney: What—was she doing?

Hale: She was rockin' back and forth. She had her apron in her hand and was kind of—pleating it.

County Attorney: And how did she—look?

Hale: Well, she looked queer.

County Attorney: How do you mean—queer?

Hale: Well, as if she didn't know what she was going to do next. And kind of done up.

County Attorney: How did she seem to feel about your coming?

Hale: Why, I don't think she minded—one way or other. She didn't pay much attention. I said, 'How do, Mrs. Wright it's cold, ain't it?' And she said, 'Is it?'—and went on kind of pleating at her apron. Well, I was surprised; she didn't ask me to come up to the stove, or to set down, but just sat there, not even looking at me, so I said, 'I want to see John.' And then she—laughed. I guess you would call it a laugh. I thought of Harry and the team outside, so I said a little sharp: 'Can't I see John?' 'No', she says, kind o' dull like. 'Ain't he home?' says I. 'Yes', says she, 'he's home'. 'Then why can't I see him?' I asked her, out of patience. "Cause he's dead', says she. '*Dead?*' says I. She just nodded her head, not getting a bit excited, but rockin' back and forth. 'Why—where is he?' says I, not knowing what to say. She just pointed upstairs—like that (*himself pointing* *to the room above*) I got up, with the idea of going up there. I walked from there to here—then I says, 'Why, what did he die of?' 'He died of a rope round his neck', says she, and just went on pleatin' at her apron. Well, I went out and called Harry. I thought I might—need help. We went upstairs and there he was lyin'—

County Attorney: I think I'd rather have you go into that upstairs, where you can point it all out. Just go on now with the rest of the story.

Hale: Well, my first thought was to get that rope off. It looked … (*stops, his face twitches*) … but Harry, he went up to him, and he said, 'No, he's dead all right, and we'd better not touch anything.' So we went back down stairs. She was still sitting that same way. 'Has anybody been notified?' I asked. 'No', says she unconcerned. 'Who did this, Mrs. Wright?' said Harry. He said it business-like—and she stopped pleatin' of her apron. 'I don't know', she says. 'You don't *know*?' says Harry. 'No', says she. 'Weren't you sleepin' in the bed with him?' says Harry. 'Yes', says she, 'but I was on the inside'. 'Somebody slipped a rope round his neck and strangled him and you didn't wake up?' says Harry. 'I didn't wake up', she said after him. We must 'a looked as if we didn't see how that could be, for after a minute she said, 'I sleep sound'. Harry was going to ask her more questions but I said maybe we ought to let her tell her story first to the coroner, or the Sheriff, so Harry went fast as he could to Rivers' place, where there's a telephone.

County Attorney: And what did Mrs. Wright do when she knew that you had gone for the coroner?

Hale: She moved from that chair to this one over here (*pointing to a small chair in the corner*) and just sat there with her hands held together and looking down. I got a feeling that I ought to make some conversation, so I said I had come in to see if John wanted to put in a telephone, and at that she started to laugh, and then she stopped and looked at me—scared, (*the* County Attorney, *who has had his notebook out, makes a note*) I dunno, maybe it wasn't scared. I wouldn't like to say it was. Soon Harry got back, and then Dr. Lloyd came, and you, Mr. Peters, and so I guess that's all I know that you don't.

County Attorney: (*looking around*) I guess we'll go upstairs first—and then out to the barn and around there, (*to the* Sheriff) You're convinced that there was nothing important here—nothing that would point to any motive.

Sheriff: Nothing here but kitchen things. (*The* County Attorney, *after again looking around the kitchen, opens the door of a cupboard closet. He gets up on a chair and looks on a shelf. Pulls his hand away, sticky.*)

County Attorney: Here's a nice mess. (*The women draw nearer.*)

Mrs. Peters: (*to the other woman*) Oh, her fruit; it did freeze, (*to the* LAWYER) She worried about that when it turned so cold. She said the fire'd go out and her jars would break.

Sheriff: Well, can you beat the women! Held for murder and worryin' about her preserves.

County Attorney: I guess before we're through she may have something more serious than preserves to worry about.

Hale: Well, women are used to worrying over trifles. (*The two women move a little closer together.*)

County Attorney: (*with the gallantry of a young politician*) And yet, for all their worries, what would we do without the ladies? (*the women do not unbend. He goes to the sink, takes a dipperful of water from the pail and pouring it into a basin, washes his hands. Starts to wipe them on the roller-towel, turns it for a cleaner place*) Dirty towels! (*kicks his foot against the pans under the sink*) Not much of a housekeeper, would you say, ladies?

Mrs Hale: (*stiffly*) There's a great deal of work to be done on a farm.

County Attorney: To be sure. And yet (*with a little bow to her*) I know there are some Dickson county farmhouses which do not have such roller towels. (*He gives it a pull to expose its length again.*)

Mrs Hale: Those towels get dirty awful quick. Men's hands aren't always as clean as they might be.

County Attorney: Ah, loyal to your sex, I see. But you and Mrs. Wright were neighbors. I suppose you were friends, too.

Mrs Hale: (*shaking her head*) I've not seen much of her of late years. I've not been in this house—it's more than a year.

County Attorney: And why was that? You didn't like her?

Mrs Hale: I liked her all well enough. Farmers' wives have their hands full, Mr. Henderson. And then—

County Attorney: Yes—?

Mrs Hale: (*looking about*) It never seemed a very cheerful place.

County Attorney: No—it's not cheerful. I shouldn't say she had the homemaking instinct.

Mrs Hale: Well, I don't know as Wright had, either.

County Attorney: You mean that they didn't get on very well?

Mrs Hale: No, I don't mean anything. But I don't think a place'd be any cheerfuller for John Wright's being in it.

County Attorney: I'd like to talk more of that a little later. I want to get the lay of things upstairs now. (*He goes to the left, where three steps lead to a stair door.*)

Sheriff: I suppose anything Mrs. Peters does'll be all right. She was to take in some clothes for her, you know, and a few little things. We left in such a hurry yesterday.

County Attorney: Yes, but I would like to see what you take, Mrs. Peters, and keep an eye out for anything that might be of use to us.

Mrs. Peters: Yes, Mr. Henderson.

(*The women listen to the men's steps on the stairs, then look about the kitchen.*)

Mrs Hale: I'd hate to have men coming into my kitchen, snooping around and criticizing. (*She arranges the pans under sink which the* Lawyer *had shoved out of place.*)

Mrs. Peters: Of course it's no more than their duty.

Mrs Hale: Duty's all right, but I guess that deputy Sheriff that came out to make the fire might have got a little of this on. (*gives the roller towel a pull*) Wish I'd thought of that sooner. Seems mean to talk about her for not having things slicked up when she had to come away in such a hurry.

Mrs. Peters: (*who has gone to a small table in the left rear corner of the room, and lifted one end of a towel that covers a pan*) She had bread set. (*Stands still.*)

Mrs Hale: (*eyes fixed on a loaf of bread beside the bread-box, which is on a low shelf at the other side of the room. Moves slowly toward it*) She was going to put this in there, (*picks up loaf, then abruptly drops it. In a manner of returning to familiar things*) It's a shame about her fruit. I wonder if it's all gone. (*gets up on the chair and looks*) I think there's some here that's all right, Mrs. Peters. Yes—here; (*holding it toward the window*) this is cherries, too. (*looking again*) I declare I believe that's the only one. (*gets down, bottle in her hand. Goes to the sink and wipes it off on the outside*) She'll feel awful bad after all her hard work in the hot weather. I remember the afternoon I put up my cherries last summer.

(*She puts the bottle on the big kitchen table, center of the room. With a sigh, is about to sit down in the rocking-chair. Before she is seated realizes what chair it is; with a slow look at it, steps back. The chair which she has touched rocks back and forth.*)

Mrs. Peters: Well, I must get those things from the front room closet, (*she goes to the door at the right, but after looking into the other room, steps back*) You coming with me, Mrs. Hale? You could help me carry them. (*They go in the other room; reappear,* Mrs. Peters *carrying a dress and skirt,* Mrs. Hale *following with a pair of shoes.*)

Mrs. Peters: My, it's cold in there. (*She puts the clothes on the big table, and hurries to the stove.*)

Mrs Hale: (*examining the skirt*) Wright was close. I think maybe that's why she kept so much to herself. She didn't even belong to the Ladies Aid. I suppose she felt she couldn't do her part, and then you don't enjoy things when you feel shabby. She used to wear pretty clothes and be lively, when she was Minnie Foster, one of the town girls singing in the choir. But that—oh, that was thirty years ago. This all you was to take in?

Mrs. Peters: She said she wanted an apron. Funny thing to want, for there isn't much to get you dirty in jail, goodness knows. But I suppose just to make her feel more natural. She said they was in the top drawer in this cupboard. Yes, here. And then her little shawl that always hung behind the door. (*opens stair door and looks*) Yes, here it is. (*Quickly shuts door leading upstairs.*)

Mrs Hale: (*abruptly moving toward her*) Mrs. Peters?

Mrs. Peters: Yes, Mrs. Hale?

Mrs Hale: Do you think she did it?

Mrs. Peters: (*in a frightened voice*) Oh, I don't know.

Mrs Hale: Well, I don't think she did. Asking for an apron and her little shawl. Worrying about her fruit.

Mrs. Peters: (*starts to speak, glances up, where footsteps are heard in the room above. In a low voice*) Mr. Peters says it looks bad for her. Mr. Henderson is awful sarcastic in a speech and he'll make fun of her sayin' she didn't wake up.

Mrs Hale: Well, I guess John Wright didn't wake when they was slipping that rope under his neck.

Mrs. Peters: No, it's strange. It must have been done awful crafty and still. They say it was such a—funny way to kill a man, rigging it all up like that.

Mrs Hale: That's just what Mr. Hale said. There was a gun in the house. He says that's what he can't understand.

Mrs. Peters: Mr. Henderson said coming out that what was needed for the case was a motive; something to show anger, or—sudden feeling.

Mrs Hale: (*who is standing by the table*) Well, I don't see any signs of anger around here, (*she puts her hand on the dish towel which lies on the table, stands looking down at table, one half of which is clean, the other half messy*) It's wiped to here, (*makes a move as if to finish work, then turns and looks at loaf of bread outside the breadbox. Drops towel. In that voice of coming back to familiar things.*) Wonder how they are finding things upstairs. I hope she had it a little more red-up up there. You know, it seems kind of sneaking. Locking her up in town and then coming out here and trying to get her own house to turn against her!

Mrs. Peters: But Mrs. Hale, the law is the law.

Mrs Hale: I s'pose 'tis, (*unbuttoning her coat*) Better loosen up your things, Mrs. Peters. You won't feel them when you go out.

(Mrs. Peters *takes off her fur tippet, goes to hang it on hook at back of room, stands looking at the under part of the small corner table.*)

Mrs. Peters: She was piecing a quilt. (*She brings the large sewing basket and they look at the bright pieces.*)

Mrs Hale: It's log cabin pattern. Pretty, isn't it? I wonder if she was goin' to quilt it or just knot it?

(*Footsteps have been heard coming down the stairs.* The Sheriff enters followed by Hale and the County Attorney.)

Sheriff: They wonder if she was going to quilt it or just knot it! (*The men laugh, the women look abashed.*)

County Attorney: (*rubbing his hands over the stove*) Frank's fire didn't do much up there, did it? Well, let's go out to the barn and get that cleared up. (*The men go outside.*)

Mrs Hale: (*resentfully*) I don't know as there's anything so strange, our takin' up our time with little things while we're waiting for them to get the evidence.

(*she sits down at the big table smoothing out a block with decision*) I don't see as it's anything to laugh about.

Mrs. Peters: (*apologetically*) Of course they've got awful important things on their minds. (*Pulls up a chair and joins Mrs. Hale at the table.*)

Mrs Hale: (*examining another block*) Mrs. Peters, look at this one. Here, this is the one she was working on, and look at the sewing! All the rest of it has been so nice and even. And look at this! It's all over the place! Why, it looks as if she didn't know what she was about! (*After she has said this they look at each other, then start to glance back at the door. After an instant* Mrs. Hale *has pulled at a knot and ripped the sewing.*)

Mrs. Peters: Oh, what are you doing, Mrs. Hale?

Mrs Hale: (*mildly*) Just pulling out a stitch or two that's not sewed very good. (*threading a needle*) Bad sewing always made me fidgety.

Mrs. Peters: (nervously) I don't think we ought to touch things.

Mrs Hale: I'll just finish up this end. (*suddenly stopping and leaning forward*) Mrs.Peters?

Mrs. Peters: Yes, Mrs. Hale?

Mrs Hale: What do you suppose she was so nervous about?

Mrs. Peters: Oh—I don't know. I don't know as she was nervous. I sometimes sew awful queer when I'm just tired. (Mrs. Hale *starts to say something, looks at* Mrs. Peters, *then goes on sewing*) Well I must get these things wrapped up. They may be through sooner than we think, (*putting apron and other things together*) I wonder where I can find a piece of paper, and string.

Mrs Hale: In that cupboard, maybe.

Mrs. Peters: (*looking in cupboard*) Why, here's a bird-cage, (*holds it up*) Did she have a bird, Mrs. Hale?

Mrs Hale: Why, I don't know whether she did or not—I've not been here for so long. There was a man around last year selling canaries cheap, but I don't know as she took one; maybe she did. She used to sing real pretty herself.

Mrs. Peters: (*glancing around*) Seems funny to think of a bird here. But she must have had one, or why would she have a cage? I wonder what happened to it.

Mrs Hale: I s'pose maybe the cat got it.

Mrs. Peters: No, she didn't have a cat. She's got that feeling some people have about cats—being afraid of them. My cat got in her room and she was real upset and asked me to take it out.

Mrs Hale: My sister Bessie was like that. Queer, ain't it?

Mrs. Peters: (*examining the cage*) Why, look at this door. It's broke. One hinge is pulled apart.

Mrs Hale: (*looking too*) Looks as if someone must have been rough with it.

Mrs. Peters: Why, yes. (*She brings the cage forward and puts it on the table.*)

Mrs Hale: I wish if they're going to find any evidence they'd be about it. I don't like this place.

Mrs. Peters: But I'm awful glad you came with me, Mrs. Hale. It would be lonesome for me sitting here alone.

Mrs Hale: It would, wouldn't it? (*dropping her sewing*) But I tell you what I do wish, Mrs. Peters. I wish I had come over sometimes when *she* was here. I—(*looking around the room*)—wish I had.

Mrs. Peters: But of course you were awful busy, Mrs. Hale—your house and your children.

Mrs Hale: I could've come. I stayed away because it weren't cheerful—and that's why I ought to have come. I—I've never liked this place. Maybe because it's down in a hollow and you don't see the road. I dunno what it is, but it's a lonesome place and always was. I wish I had come over to see Minnie Foster sometimes. I can see now—(*shakes her head*)

Mrs. Peters: Well, you mustn't reproach yourself, Mrs. Hale. Somehow we just don't see how it is with other folks until—something comes up.

Mrs Hale: Not having children makes less work—but it makes a quiet house, and Wright out to work all day, and no company when he did come in. Did you know John Wright, Mrs. Peters?

Mrs. Peters: Not to know him; I've seen him in town. They say he was a good man.

Mrs Hale: Yes—good; he didn't drink, and kept his word as well as most, I guess, and paid his debts. But he was a hard man, Mrs. Peters. Just to pass the time of day with him—(*shivers*) Like a raw wind that gets to the bone, (*pauses, her eye falling on the cage*) I should think she would 'a wanted a bird. But what do you suppose went with it?

Mrs. Peters: I don't know, unless it got sick and died. (*She reaches over and swings the broken door, swings it again, both women watch it.*)

Mrs Hale: You weren't raised round here, were you? (*Mrs. Peters shakes her head*) You didn't know—her?

Mrs. Peters: Not till they brought her yesterday.

Mrs Hale: She—come to think of it, she was kind of like a bird herself—real sweet and pretty, but kind of timid and—fluttery. How—she—did—change. (*silence; then as if struck by a happy thought and relieved to get back to everyday things*) Tell you what, Mrs. Peters, why don't you take the quilt in with you? It might take up her mind.

Mrs. Peters: Why, I think that's a real nice idea, Mrs. Hale. There couldn't possibly be any objection to it, could there? Now, just what would I take? I wonder if her patches are in here—and her things. (*They look in the sewing basket.*)

Mrs Hale: Here's some red. I expect this has got sewing things in it. (*brings out a fancy box*) What a pretty box. Looks like something somebody would give you. Maybe her scissors are in here. (*Opens box. Suddenly puts her hand to her nose*) Why—(Mrs. Peters *bends nearer, then turns her face away*) There's something wrapped up in this piece of silk.

Mrs. Peters: Why, this isn't her scissors.

Mrs Hale: (*lifting the silk*) Oh, Mrs. Peters—it's—(Mrs. Peters *bends closer.*)

Mrs. Peters: It's the bird.

Mrs Hale: (*jumping up*) But, Mrs. Peters—look at it! It's neck! Look at its neck! It's all—other side *to.*

Mrs. Peters: Somebody—wrung—its—neck.

(*Their eyes meet. A look of growing comprehension, of horror. Steps are heard outside.* Mrs. Hale *slips box under quilt pieces, and sinks into her chair. Enter* Sheriff *and* County Attorney. Mrs. Peters *rises.*)

County Attorney: (*as one turning from serious things to little pleasantries*) Well ladies, have you decided whether she was going to quilt it or knot it?

Mrs. Peters: We think she was going to—knot it.

County Attorney: Well, that's interesting, I'm sure. (*seeing the birdcage*) Has the bird flown?

Mrs Hale: (*putting more quilt pieces over the box*) We think the—cat got it.

County Attorney: (*preoccupied*) Is there a cat?

(Mrs. Hale *glances in a quick covert way at* Mrs. Peters.)

Mrs. Peters: Well, not now. They're superstitious, you know. They leave.

County Attorney: (*to* Sheriff Peters, *continuing an interrupted conversation*) No sign at all of anyone having come from the outside. Their own rope. Now let's go up again and go over it piece by piece. (*they start upstairs*) It would have to have been someone who knew just the—(Mrs. Peters *sits down. The two women sit there not looking at one another, but as if peering into something and at the same time holding back. When they talk now it is in the manner of feeling their way over strange ground, as if afraid of what they are saying, but as if they cannot help saying it.*)

Mrs Hale: She liked the bird. She was going to bury it in that pretty box.

Mrs. Peters: (*in a whisper*) When I was a girl—my kitten—there was a boy took a hatchet, and before my eyes—and before I could get there—(*covers her face an instant*) If they hadn't held me back I would have—(*catches herself, looks upstairs where steps are heard, falters weakly*)—hurt him.

Mrs Hale: (*with a slow look around her*) I wonder how it would seem never to have had any children around, (*pause*) No, Wright wouldn't like the bird—a thing that sang. She used to sing. He killed that, too.

Mrs. Peters: (*moving uneasily*) We don't know who killed the bird.

Mrs Hale: I knew John Wright.

Mrs. Peters: It was an awful thing was done in this house that night, Mrs. Hale. Killing a man while he slept, slipping a rope around his neck that choked the life out of him.

Mrs Hale: His neck. Choked the life out of him.

(*Her hand goes out and rests on the bird-cage.*)

Mrs. Peters: (*with rising voice*) We don't know who killed him. We don't *know*.

Mrs Hale: (*her own feeling not interrupted*) If there'd been years and years of nothing, then a bird to sing to you, it would be awful—still, after the bird was still.

Mrs. Peters: (*something within her speaking*) I know what stillness is. When we homesteaded in Dakota, and my first baby died—after he was two years old, and me with no other then—

Mrs Hale: (*moving*) How soon do you suppose they'll be through, looking for the evidence?

Mrs. Peters: I know what stillness is. (*pulling herself back*) The law has got to punish crime, Mrs. Hale.

Mrs Hale: (*not as if answering that*) I wish you'd seen Minnie Foster when she wore a white dress with blue ribbons and stood up there in the choir and sang. (*a look around the room*) Oh, I *wish* I'd come over here once in a while! That was a crime! That was a crime! Who's going to punish that?

Mrs. Peters: (*looking upstairs*) We mustn't—take on.

Mrs Hale: I might have known she needed help! I know how things can be—for women. I tell you, it's queer, Mrs. Peters. We live close together and we live far apart. We all go through the same things—it's all just a different kind of the same thing, (*brushes her eyes, noticing the bottle of fruit, reaches out for it*) If I was you, I wouldn't tell her her fruit was gone. Tell her it *ain't*. Tell her it's all right. Take this in to prove it to her. She—she may never know whether it was broke or not.

Mrs. Peters: (*takes the bottle, looks about for something to wrap it in; takes petticoat from the clothes brought from the other room, very nervously begins winding this around the bottle. In a false voice*) My, it's a good thing the men couldn't hear us. Wouldn't they just laugh! Getting all stirred up over a little thing like a—dead canary. As if that could have anything to do with—with—wouldn't they *laugh*!

(*The men are heard coming down stairs.*)

Mrs Hale: (*under her breath*) Maybe they would—maybe they wouldn't.

County Attorney: No, Peters, it's all perfectly clear except a reason for doing it. But you know juries when it comes to women. If there was some definite thing. Something to show—something to make a story about—a thing that would connect up with this strange way of doing it—

(*The women's eyes meet for an instant. Enter Hale from outer door.*)

Hale: Well, I've got the team around. Pretty cold out there.

County Attorney: I'm going to stay here a while by myself, (*to the* Sheriff) You can send Frank out for me, can't you? I want to go over everything. I'm not satisfied that we can't do better.

Sheriff: Do you want to see what Mrs. Peters is going to take in?

(*The* LAWYER *goes to the table, picks up the apron, laughs.*)

County Attorney: Oh, I guess they're not very dangerous things the ladies have picked out. (*Moves a few things about, disturbing the quilt pieces which cover the box. Steps back*) No, Mrs. Peters doesn't need supervising. For that matter, a Sheriff's wife is married to the law. Ever think of it that way, Mrs. Peters?

Mrs. Peters: Not—just that way.

Sheriff: (*chuckling*) Married to the law. (*moves toward the other room*) I just want you to come in here a minute, George. We ought to take a look at these windows.

County Attorney: (*scoffingly*) Oh, windows!

Sheriff: We'll be right out, Mr. Hale.

(Hale *goes outside. The* Sheriff *follows the* County Attorney *into the other room. Then* Mrs. Hale *rises, hands tight together, looking intensely at* Mrs. Peters, *whose eyes make a slow turn, finally meeting* Mrs. Hale's. *A moment* Mrs. Hale *holds her, then her own eyes point the way to where the box is concealed. Suddenly* Mrs. Peters *throws back quilt pieces and tries to put the box in the bag she is wearing. It is too big. She opens box, starts to take bird out, cannot touch it, goes to pieces, stands there helpless. Sound of a knob turning in the other room.* Mrs. Hale *snatches the box and puts it in the pocket of her big coat. Enter* County Attorney *and* Sheriff.)

County Attorney: (*facetiously*) Well, Henry, at least we found out that she was not going to quilt it. She was going to—what is it you call it, ladies?

Mrs Hale: (*her hand against her pocket*) We call it—knot it, Mr. Henderson.

(CURTAIN)

CRITICAL THINKING QUESTIONS

1. Explain the attitude of the men towards Minnie Wright. Connect this attitude to the title of the play.

2. Mrs. Peters, the Sheriff's wife, is "married to the law." At the beginning of the play, she is supportive of her husband. What events in the play and what memories cause her to sympathize with Minnie Wright?

3. Minnie Wright's character never appears in the play. We only hear about her situation through the accounts of the other characters. What is the effect of Mrs. Hale's description of Minnie Wright?

WRITING TOPIC

Mrs. Hale and Mrs. Peters conceal evidence from the authorities. Do you believe that they have a greater responsibility to protect Minnie or to obey the law? Choose a position and craft an argument supporting your choice.

———————————

NONFICTION

Chief Joseph

I Will Fight No More Forever (1877)

At his surrender in the Bear Paw Mountains, 1877

Tell General Howard that I know his heart. What he told me before I have in my heart. I am tired of fighting. Our Chiefs are killed. Looking Glass is dead, Tu-hul-hul-sote is dead. The old men are all dead. It is the young men who now say yes or no. He who led the young men [Joseph's brother Alikut] is dead. It is cold and we have no blankets. The little children are freezing to death. My people, some of them, have run away to the hills and have no blankets and no food. No one knows where they are—perhaps freezing to death. I want to have time to look for my children and see how many of them I can find. Maybe I shall find them among the dead. Hear me, my Chiefs, my heart is sick and sad. From where the sun now stands I will fight no more forever.

CRITICAL THINKING QUESTIONS

1. What **rhetorical appeal** would you say is most dominant in Chief Joseph's speech (*logos*, *ethos*, or *pathos*)? Offer examples.

2. When Chief Joseph says, "I will fight no more against the white man," is this an admission that he now agrees with the white man? Upon what do you base this belief?

WRITING TOPIC

Can you recall a time in your life when you or someone close to you suffered an injustice but decided to give up the fight instead of pursue all avenues of recourse? Why was this decision made? Describe the circumstances and the considerations that led to the decision. What emotions developed as a result of the decision?

Allan Gurganus

Captive Audience (2003)

From 1966 to 1970, I disappeared from snapshots. I hid, even from my parents' camera. See, I was ashamed, of the uniform. I'd tried for "conscientious objector" in my Carolina county and was laughed out of the office. So, avoiding six years in a federal pen, I spent four in bell-bottoms, floating just off Southeast Asia. Buddies wore their caps cocked, making this assigned life feel more personal. I wore my uniform as a prisoner wears his. Why am I finally "coming out" about all this? I never ever speak of it. The new war drives me. My "service" years I freeze-dried. Till last week, I kept them stashed in the dark rear corner of a lead-lined meat locker. Now they're thawing—fact is, "My name is Allan and I am secretly...B-32-37-38." Name, hometown and serial number, that's what Iraqi captors ask of our latest P.O.W.s. These kids' faces are banged up, squinty. Eyes shocked and awed at gunpoint, they recall me to myself. Such dulled innocence drives me to confess.

If you live long enough, you can become your own parent. I am now that to me, even a granddad. Against the Defense Department, I so long to defend my former grandson self and all these other kids. A graying 55-year-old homeowner can see just how young 18 really is! I served in another such Children's Crusade. I'm qualified to call it a disaster. Even the generals who were in charge back then admit that now. The same guys are helping plan this new one. I was a kid enlisted, against his will, to do the heavy lifting for a nation launched on a mission botched from the start. The entrance imperative: all macho force. The exit strategy? None whatever. Only very young kids would be fool enough to go that far and do as told. Some claim they didn't even mind. I myself remember. And, for me, and for this new crop, I mind. I'm watching.

I know these trapped boys from the inside. Perfect physical specimens, they are cocksure about absolutely everything because they know next to nothing. From a commander's perspective, of course, that's very good. These kids signed up mostly to get some education. Their parents couldn't swing the loans. No college otherwise. All they know of war is from Dolby-deafening action movies. Mainly these kids rage in the fist of the hormonal, the impulsive, the puppy-playful. Girl-crazy, full of stock-car lore and vague dreams of executive glory—great soldier material.

It's spring here, and my jonquils have never been more plentiful and lush, but I walk around as if hooked by black extension cord to CNN, memories de-icing. It comes from my feelings for them. For those idiotic gung-ho kids who really believe they are making up the rules, who consider they are rugged individualists (and therefore take orders beautifully). Many probably never had a plane ride before (it sure was long!), only to sleep all night under a tarp in a sandstorm sitting up against some truck (nobody my age could walk for a week after doing that). And already they write home: "Don't worry about me, Mom.

We'll straighten out this mess fast. Just keep my Camaro washed good." I also sent such letters. It is reassuring to reassure. Love becomes a kind of sedative for whatever killing chores you're forced to do tomorrow.

I want to tell you, I have never known a loneliness like it. It's Dante's 11th 5
circle, to be dressed in ugly clothes exactly like 4,000 others, to be called by a number, to be stuck among men who will brag and scrap and fight but never admit to any terror, any need. To sleep in bunks stacked five high, to defecate in booths without doors, you sitting with knees almost meeting the knees of a hunched stranger. To know that you are so much smarter than the jobs assigned, to guess that you are serving in a struggle you can neither approve nor ever understand because the old guys in charge—guys whose sons are safe, golfing at home—they don't speak the local language, either.

During the soldiers' first week, except for blowing sand, it might all seem a lark. Decisions are made by others who give you enough trigger-finger wiggle room so that you can feel a bit expressive, as baby-faced as terrifying. Such volunteers are as intentionally cut off from the effects of their killing as any placated 8-year-old glazed over the lethal thumb work of his Game boy. These G.I.'s imagine glory, girlfriends waiting at home. The geopolitical picture is as far beyond their reach as the notion that learning a Kurdish dialect just might save their lives.

After my own tour of duty ended, I slouched home and simply sat there for six days, scared to leave my parents' house, too tired to drive a car. "So…what are your plans?"—my father saw my state yet chose to treat me with all the tender care of a corporate job interviewer. But Mom must have noticed that the family album featured no photos of me since the draft. So she gathered up my medals, awards for nothing more than my offering my body as another vote against the Cong. Mom assembled these little trophies I was meant to care about. A pretty red-and-yellow ribbon and its bronze coin called the Vietnam Expeditionary. Mom bought a craft-shop shadow box, a nice one too, real wood, and lined with red velvet-like plush for displaying family heirlooms. She arranged my citations under glass, protecting them. But I'd won too few to make a really pleasing pattern. So Mom dipped into my old Boy Scout badges, fleshing out my history with the brass of "God and Country." Then she added my childhood Sunday School pin for perfect attendance. "You see? Impressive." She handed it over. I thanked her and sat staring down at it. Whenever my folks visited, I would get it out and prop it up somewhere until they left. It usually stayed in the attic, where it dwells, I guess, today. In some cardboard box stacked with letters I've really been meaning to answer since '79 or so. But thanks anyway, Mom. Not your fault. Not mine. But whose then?

The latest captured Americans from a downed helicopter squat here on camera, and you see their inexperience in how they're big-eyed scared as kids at their first horror flick. Boys hang their heads with a shame almost sexual. They're blaming themselves for crashing, guilty at how sand can spoil the rotor blades of our most costly chopper. These kids mainly "volunteered," to get ahead. And now, this learning curve. They are prisoners because to start at Burger King, even for a go-getter like Larry here, would get him to only assistant manager in, say, three or four years, and you can't do too darn much on 12 grand a year, can you? These are the ambitious kids, the "good kids," the ones who wanted to make something useful and shapely of their lives.

Now they know that Mom will see them, captured, on "Alive at Five." They know she'll cover her mouth while screaming: "Al, come quick. It's Larry! They got our Larry!"

10   My parents believed in honor, duty and rendering up firstborns to Uncle Sam. For them Sam was at least as real as Santa. Avuncular, if some-what over-dressed in stripes and gambler's goatee, he tended to look stern and to point right out at you. So when he knocked at our door and said he wanted me, my folks grinned: "He's hiding in the back bedroom, writing essays for the draft board all about peace and Quaker stuff. Though, fact is, he grew up Presbyterian. We'll go get him. Won't take a sec. You comfortable there?"

This week's young captives might just be released. Some will come home, back to their folks' ghetto stoops or trailers or tract houses strung with computer–generated welcomes, personalized, too. Their college years are still ahead of them. So look on the bright side. Bones that young knit fast. And, after a while, even after all the pain and not knowing why they did it, they will get to call this "their" war. And, of course, the medals will be splendid.

CRITICAL THINKING QUESTIONS

1. Gurganus describes the situation as he returns from the Vietnam War. Why does the returning soldier not want to leave his parents' home?

2. As you may recall from the discussion of **evidence** in Chapter 3, citing personal experience in an argument can bring forth a highly emotional response. Of course, the degree to which personal experience is able to elicit such a response depends completely upon audience. Since "Captive Audience" appeared in *The New York Times*, we can assume that a wide variety of people read the piece. Explain how two readers might react quite differently to the author's description of his experience when his mother made a box for his medals.

3. Sometimes **tone** can be difficult to interpret in a piece of writing. If someone says, "That sure was a great party," we can tell by her tone of voice that she actually thought the party was about as dull as any party could be. However, without the clues in vocal inflections, we might come away asking, "So, did she really like the party or did she hate it?" Reread the last sentence in "Captive Audience," and explain the tone you believe the author intended these words to carry. What clues has the author already given readers throughout the essay?

WRITING TOPIC

Gurganus does not offer the reader an **explicit claim** in his writing, yet he seems to be making a statement about war and its effects on young soldiers. In a single sentence, compose a claim that you believe might be appropriate for this selection, citing specific words, phrases, images, and sentences from the essay as evidence.

John F. Kennedy

Inaugural Address, January 20, 1961 (1961)

My Fellow Citizens:

We observe today not a victory of party but a celebration of freedom—symbolizing an end as well as a beginning—signifying renewal as well as change. For I have sworn before you and Almighty God the same solemn oath our forebears prescribed nearly a century and three quarters ago.

The world is very different now. For man holds in his mortal hands the power to abolish all form of human poverty and to abolish all form of human life. And yet the same revolutionary beliefs for which our forebears fought are still at issue around the globe—the belief that the rights of man come not from the generosity of the state but from the hand of God.

We dare not forget today that we are the heirs of that first revolution. Let the word go forth from this time and place, to friend and foe alike, that the torch has been passed to a new generation of Americans—born in this century, tempered by war, disciplined by a cold and bitter peace, proud of our ancient heritage—and unwilling to witness or permit the slow undoing of those human rights to which this nation has always been committed, and to which we are committed today.

Let every nation know, whether it wish us well or ill, that we shall pay any price, bear any burden, meet any hardship, support any friend or oppose any foe in order to assure the survival and success of liberty.

This much we pledge—and more.   5

To those old allies whose cultural and spiritual origins we share, we pledge the loyalty of faithful friends. United, there is little we cannot do in a host of new cooperative ventures. Divided, there is little we can do—for we dare not meet a powerful challenge at odds and split asunder.

To those new states whom we now welcome to the ranks of the free, we pledge our word that one form of colonial control shall not have passed merely to be replaced by a far more iron tyranny. We shall not always expect to find them supporting our every view. But we shall always hope to find them strongly supporting their own freedom—and to remember that, in the past, those who foolishly sought to find power by riding on the tiger's back inevitably ended up inside.

To those people in the huts and villages of half the globe struggling to break the bonds of mass misery, we pledge our best efforts to help them help themselves, for whatever period is required—not because the communists are doing it, not because we seek their votes, but because it is right. If the free society cannot help the many who are poor, it can never save the few who are rich.

To our sister republics south of our border, we offer a special pledge—to convert our good words into good deeds—in a new alliance for progress—to assist free men and free governments in casting off the chains of poverty. But this peaceful revolution of hope cannot become the prey of hostile powers. Let all our neighbors know that we shall join with them to oppose aggression or subversion anywhere in the Americas. And let every other power know that this Hemisphere intends to remain the master of its own house.

10   To that world assembly of sovereign states, the United Nations, our last best hope in an age where the instruments of war have far outpaced the instruments of peace, we renew our pledge of support—to prevent its becoming merely a forum for invective—to strengthen its shield of the new and the weak—and to enlarge the area to which its writ may run.

Finally, to those nations who would make themselves our adversary, we offer not a pledge but a request: that both sides begin anew the quest for peace, before the dark powers of destruction unleashed by science engulf all humanity in planned or accidental self-destruction.

We dare not tempt them with weakness. For only when our arms are sufficient beyond doubt can we be certain beyond doubt that they will never be employed.

But neither can two great and powerful groups of nations take comfort from their present course—both sides overburdened by the cost of modern weapons, both rightly alarmed by the steady spread of the deadly atom, yet both racing to alter that uncertain balance of terror that stays the hand of mankind's final war.

So let us begin anew—remembering on both sides that civility is not a sign of weakness, and sincerity is always subject to proof. Let us never negotiate out of fear. But let us never fear to negotiate.

15   Let both sides explore what problems unite us instead of belaboring the problems that divide us.

Let both sides, for the first time, formulate serious and precise proposals for the inspection and control of arms—and bring the absolute power to destroy other nations under the absolute control of all nations.

Let both sides join to invoke the wonders of science instead of its terrors. Together let us explore the stars, conquer the deserts, eradicate disease, tap the ocean depths and encourage the arts and commerce.

Let both sides unite to heed in all corners of the earth the command of Isaiah—to "undo the heavy burdens...(and) let the oppressed go free."

And if a beach-head of cooperation can be made in the jungles of suspicion, let both sides join in the next task: creating, not a new balance of power, but a new world of law, where the strong are just and the weak secure and the peace preserved forever.

All this will not be finished in the first one hundred days. Nor will it be   20
finished in the first one thousand days, nor in the life of this Administration, nor even perhaps in our lifetime on this planet. But let us begin.

In your hands, my fellow citizens, more than in mine, will rest the final success or failure of our course. Since this country was founded, each generation has been summoned to give testimony to its national loyalty. The graves of young Americans who answered that call encircle the globe.

Now the trumpet summons us again—not as a call to bear arms, though arms we need—not as a call to battle, though embattled we are—but a call to bear the burden of a long twilight struggle, year in and year out, "rejoicing in hope, patient in tribulation"—a struggle against the common enemies of man: tyranny, poverty, disease and war itself.

Can we forge against these enemies a grand and global alliance, North and South, East and West, that can assure a more fruitful life for all mankind? Will you join in that historic effort?

In the long history of the world, only a few generations have been granted the role of defending freedom in its hour of maximum danger. I do not shrink from this responsibility—I welcome it. I do not believe that any of us would exchange places with any other people or any other generation. The energy, the faith and the devotion which we bring to this endeavor will light our country and all who serve it—and the glow from that fire can truly light the world.

And so, my fellow Americans: ask not what your country will do for you—ask   25
what you can do for your country.

My fellow citizens of the world: ask not what America will do for you, but what together we can do for the freedom of man.

Finally, whether you are citizens of America or of the world, ask of us the same high standards of strength and sacrifice that we shall ask of you. With a good conscience our only sure reward, with history the final judge of our deeds, let us go forth to lead the land we love, asking His blessing and His help, but knowing that here on earth God's work must truly be our own.

CRITICAL THINKING QUESTIONS

1. Notice how short the paragraphs are in this address. What effect does this structure have on the listener or reader?

2. What **rhetorical devices** do you see Kennedy using in this address? Make a list of pairs of words Kennedy uses, such as *united/divided* or *not because/but because.*

3. In what sense does this address argue for power, and in what sense does it argue for responsibility?

WRITING TOPIC

Read one other inaugural address by a recent U.S. president (search "Inaugural Addresses of the Presidents of the United States"). Summarize and compare the arguments offered by Kennedy and the president you selected.

Martin Luther King, Jr.

I Have a Dream (1963)

I am happy to join with you today in what will go down in history as the greatest demonstration for freedom in the history of our nation.

Five score years ago, a great American, in whose symbolic shadow we stand today, signed the Emancipation Proclamation. This momentous decree came as a great beacon light of hope to millions of Negro slaves who had been seared in the flames of withering injustice. It came as a joyous daybreak to end the long night of their captivity.

But one hundred years later, the Negro still is not free. One hundred years later, the life of the Negro is still sadly crippled by the manacles of segregation and the chains of discrimination. One hundred years later, the Negro lives on a lonely island of poverty in the midst of a vast ocean of material prosperity. One hundred years later, the Negro is still languishing in the corners of American society and finds himself an exile in his own land. So we have come here today to dramatize a shameful condition.

In a sense we have come to our nation's capital to cash a check. When the architects of our republic wrote the magnificent words of the Constitution and the Declaration of Independence, they were signing a promissory note to which every American was to fall heir. This note was a promise that all men, yes, black men as well as white men, would be guaranteed the unalienable rights of life, liberty, and the pursuit of happiness.

5   It is obvious today that America has defaulted on this promissory note insofar as her citizens of color are concerned. Instead of honoring this sacred obligation, America has given the Negro people a bad check, a check which has come

back marked "insufficient funds." But we refuse to believe that the bank of justice is bankrupt. We refuse to believe that there are insufficient funds in the great vaults of opportunity of this nation. So we have come to cash this check—a check that will give us upon demand the riches of freedom and the security of justice. We have also come to this hallowed spot to remind America of the fierce urgency of now. This is no time to engage in the luxury of cooling off or to take the tranquilizing drug of gradualism. Now is the time to make real the promises of democracy. Now is the time to rise from the dark and desolate valley of segregation to the sunlit path of racial justice. Now is the time to lift our nation from the quick sands of racial injustice to the solid rock of brotherhood. Now is the time to make justice a reality for all of God's children.

It would be fatal for the nation to overlook the urgency of the moment. This sweltering summer of the Negro's legitimate discontent will not pass until there is an invigorating autumn of freedom and equality. Nineteen sixty-three is not an end, but a beginning. Those who hope that the Negro needed to blow off steam and will now be content will have a rude awakening if the nation returns to business as usual. There will be neither rest nor tranquility in America until the Negro is granted his citizenship rights. The whirlwinds of revolt will continue to shake the foundations of our nation until the bright day of justice emerges.

But there is something that I must say to my people who stand on the warm threshold which leads into the palace of justice. In the process of gaining our rightful place we must not be guilty of wrongful deeds. Let us not seek to satisfy our thirst for freedom by drinking from the cup of bitterness and hatred.

We must forever conduct our struggle on the high plane of dignity and discipline. We must not allow our creative protest to degenerate into physical violence. Again and again we must rise to the majestic heights of meeting physical force with soul force. The marvelous new militancy which has engulfed the Negro community must not lead us to a distrust of all white people, for many of our white brothers, as evidenced by their presence here today, have come to realize that their destiny is tied up with our destiny. They have come to realize that their freedom is inextricably bound to our freedom. We cannot walk alone.

As we walk, we must make the pledge that we shall always march ahead. We cannot turn back. There are those who are asking the devotees of civil rights, "When will you be satisfied?" We can never be satisfied as long as the Negro is the victim of the unspeakable horrors of police brutality. We can never be satisfied, as long as our bodies, heavy with the fatigue of travel, cannot gain lodging in the motels of the highways and the hotels of the cities. We cannot be satisfied as long as the Negro's basic mobility is from a smaller ghetto to a larger one. We can never be satisfied as long as our children are stripped of their selfhood and robbed of their dignity by signs stating "For Whites Only." We cannot be satisfied as long as a Negro in Mississippi cannot vote and a Negro in New York believes he has nothing for which to vote. No, no, we are not satisfied, and we will not be satisfied until justice rolls down like waters and righteousness like a mighty stream.

10   I am not unmindful that some of you have come here out of great trials and tribulations. Some of you have come fresh from narrow jail cells. Some of you have come from areas where your quest for freedom left you battered by the storms of persecution and staggered by the winds of police brutality. You have been the veterans of creative suffering. Continue to work with the faith that unearned suffering is redemptive.

Go back to Mississippi, go back to Alabama, go back to South Carolina, go back to Georgia, go back to Louisiana, go back to the slums and ghettos of our northern cities, knowing that somehow this situation can and will be changed. Let us not wallow in the valley of despair.

I say to you today, my friends, so even though we face the difficulties of today and tomorrow, I still have a dream. It is a dream deeply rooted in the American dream.

I have a dream that one day this nation will rise up and live out the true meaning of its creed: "We hold these truths to be self-evident: that all men are created equal."

I have a dream that one day on the red hills of Georgia the sons of former slaves and the sons of former slave owners will be able to sit down together at the table of brotherhood.

15   I have a dream that one day even the state of Mississippi, a state sweltering with the heat of injustice, sweltering with the heat of oppression, will be transformed into an oasis of freedom and justice.

I have a dream that my four little children will one day live in a nation where they will not be judged by the color of their skin but by the content of their character.

I have a dream today.

I have a dream that one day, down in Alabama, with its vicious racists, with its governor having his lips dripping with the words of interposition and nullification; one day right there in Alabama, little black boys and black girls will be able to join hands with little white boys and white girls as sisters and brothers.

I have a dream today.

20   I have a dream that one day every valley shall be exalted, every hill and mountain shall be made low, the rough places will be made plain, and the crooked places will be made straight, and the glory of the Lord shall be revealed, and all flesh shall see it together.

This is our hope. This is the faith that I go back to the South with. With this faith we will be able to hew out of the mountain of despair a stone of hope. With this faith we will be able to transform the jangling discords of our nation into a beautiful symphony of brotherhood. With this faith we will be able to work together, to pray together, to struggle together, to go to jail together, to stand up for freedom together, knowing that we will be free one day.

This will be the day when all of God's children will be able to sing with a new meaning, "My country, 'tis of thee, sweet land of liberty, of thee I sing. Land where my fathers died, land of the pilgrim's pride, from every mountainside, let freedom ring."

And if America is to be a great nation this must become true. So let freedom ring from the prodigious hilltops of New Hampshire. Let freedom ring from the mighty mountains of New York. Let freedom ring from the heightening Alleghenies of Pennsylvania!

Let freedom ring from the snowcapped Rockies of Colorado!

Let freedom ring from the curvaceous slopes of California!   25

But not only that; let freedom ring from Stone Mountain of Georgia!

Let freedom ring from Lookout Mountain of Tennessee!

Let freedom ring from every hill and molehill of Mississippi. From every mountainside, let freedom ring.

And when this happens, when we allow freedom to ring, when we let it ring from every village and every hamlet, from every state and every city, we will be able to speed up that day when all of God's children, black men and white men, Jews and Gentiles, Protestants and Catholics, will be able to join hands and sing in the words of the old Negro spiritual, "Free at last! free at last! thank God Almighty, we are free at last!"

CRITICAL THINKING QUESTIONS

1. Dr. King uses the **metaphor** of an uncashed check to call attention to the current state of race relations at the time he made this speech in 1963. Do you find this comparison effective? Why or why not?

2. How does Dr. King seek to inspire his audience despite the dire circumstances of the social climate in 1963? How does he try to demonstrate to his listeners the fight for equality involves every race of people? Can you identify passages in his speech that encourage his listeners to remain optimistic that positive changes are on the horizon?

WRITING TOPIC

Dr. King is recognized as a writer with an ability to connect with audiences through his powerful and artful use of language. His speeches and writings were designed to include everyone in the quest for equality. Re-examine his "I Have a Dream" speech. Identify areas in which he uses all three rhetorical appeals (*logos*, *ethos*, and *pathos*) and critique the effectiveness of his words.

Abraham Lincoln

Second Inaugural Address, March 4, 1865 (1865)

At this second appearing to take the oath of the presidential office, there is less occasion for an extended address than there was at the first. Then a statement, somewhat in detail, of a course to be pursued, seemed fitting and proper. Now, at the expiration of four years, during which public declarations have been constantly called forth on every point and phase of the great contest which still absorbs the attention, and engrosses the energies of the nation, little that is new could be presented. The progress of our arms, upon which all else chiefly depends, is as well known to the public as to myself; and it is, I trust, reasonably satisfactory and encouraging to all. With high hope for the future, no prediction in regard to it is ventured.

On the occasion corresponding to this four years ago, all thoughts were anxiously directed to an impending civil war. All dreaded it—all sought to avert it. While the inaugural address was being delivered from this place, devoted altogether to *saving* the Union without war, insurgent agents were in the city seeking to *destroy* it without war—seeking to dissol[v]e the Union, and divide effects, by negotiation. Both parties deprecated war; but one of them would *make* war rather than let the nation survive; and the other would *accept* war rather than let it perish. And the war came.

One eighth of the whole population were colored slaves, not distributed generally over the Union, but localized in the Southern part of it. These slaves constituted a peculiar and powerful interest. All knew that this interest was, somehow, the cause of the war. To strengthen, perpetuate, and extend this interest was the object for which the insurgents would rend the Union, even by war; while the government claimed no right to do more than to restrict the territorial enlargement of it. Neither party expected for the war, the magnitude, or the duration, which it has already attained. Neither anticipated that the *cause* of the conflict might cease with, or even before, the conflict itself should cease. Each looked for an easier triumph, and a result less fundamental and astounding. Both read the same Bible, and pray to the same God; and each invokes His aid against the other. It may seem strange that any men should dare to ask a just God's assistance in wringing their bread from the sweat of other men's faces; but let us judge not that we be not judged. The prayers of both could not be answered; that of neither has been answered fully. The Almighty has his own purposes. "Woe unto the world because of offences! for it must needs be that offences come; but woe to that man by whom the offence cometh!" If we shall suppose that American Slavery is one of those offences which, in the providence of God, must needs come, but which, having continued through His appointed time, He now wills to remove, and that He gives to both North and South, this terrible war, as the woe due to those by whom the offence came, shall we discern therein any departure from those divine attributes which the believers in a Living God always ascribe to Him? Fondly do we hope—fervently do we pray—that this mighty scourge of war may speedily pass away. Yet, if God wills that it continue, until all the wealth piled by the bond-man's two hundred and fifty years of unrequited toil shall be sunk, and until every drop of blood drawn with the lash, shall be paid by another drawn with the sword, as was said three thousand years ago, so still it must be said "the judgments of the Lord, are true and righteous altogether."

With malice toward none; with charity for all; with firmness in the right, as God gives us to see the right, let us strive on to finish the work we are in; to bind up the nation's wounds; to care for him who shall have borne the battle, and for his widow, and his orphan—to do all which may achieve and cherish a just and lasting peace, among ourselves, and with all nations.

CRITICAL THINKING QUESTIONS

1. What do you see as Lincoln's primary purpose in this address?

2. Identify passages that illustrate each of the rhetorical appeals—*pathos, logos, ethos.*

3. a. List several **value assumptions** about leadership that Lincoln's address illustrates.

  b. Can you think of individuals who represent the leadership values you listed in part a? Try to think of persons living now or from recent history.

WRITING TOPIC

Based on your responses to Question 3, write a paragraph in which you define leadership; include specific examples and descriptions to elaborate. Besides showing what leadership is, you can use comparison and contrast—that is, also provide examples of what leadership is *not*—to develop your definition. (See also Tim O'Brien's story "The Things They Carried," page 482.)

Katherine Anne Porter

To Dr. William Ross (1951)

March 4, 1951

Dear Dr. Ross,

I cannot possibly sign the oath of allegiance you sent me, and I'm sorry I was not told in your first letter that this would be required of me, for a good deal of time and trouble would have been spared both of us.

This is the first time I've encountered this dangerous nonsense, but I have known from the beginning what my answer must be. My memory goes back easily thirty years to the time this law was passed in Colorado, in a time of war, fright and public hysteria being whipped up by the same kind of people who are doing this work now. Only now we're worse for thirty years of world disaster.

I believed then, and still do believe, that this requirement of an oath of allegiance was more of a device for embarrassing and humiliating honest persons than an effective trap for traitors and subversive people. We, all of us, do quite a lot of ceremonial oath-taking on many important occasions of life as an act of faith, a public testimony of honorable intention, and it is the mere truth that an oath binds only those persons who meant to keep their promises anyway, with or without an oath. The others cannot be touched or controlled in any such way. We all know this so why assist at such a cynical fraud.

I'm entirely hostile to the principle of Communism and to every form of totalitarian society, whether it calls itself Communism, Fascism, or whatever. I feel indeed that Communism and Fascism are two names for the same thing, that the present struggle is really a civil war between two factions of totalitarianism. But Fascism is older, more insidious, harder to identify, easier to disguise. No one can be a Communist without knowing what he is doing. A man may be a most poisonous Fascist without even in the least recognizing his malady.

5   It is not the oath itself that troubles me. There is nothing in it I do not naturally and instinctively observe as I have and will. My people are the old stock. They helped to found colonies, to break new trails, and to survey wildernesses. They set up little log cabin academies, all the way from Virginia and Pennsylvania to Kentucky and clear into Texas. They have fought in all the wars, they have been governors of states, and military attachés, and at least one ambassador among us. We're not suspect, nor liable to the questionings of the kind of people we would never have invited to our tables.

You can see what the root of my resentment is. My many family branches helped to make this country. My feeling about my country and its history is as tender and intimate as about my own parents, and I really suffer to have them violated by the irresponsible acts of cheap politicians who prey on public fears in times of trouble and force their betters into undignified positions.

Our duty, Dr. Ross, is to circumvent them. To see through them and stop them in their tracks in time and not to be hoodwinked or terrorized by them, not to rationalize and excuse that weakness in us which leads us to criminal collusion with them for the sake of our jobs or the hope of being left in peace. That is not the road to any kind of safety. Nothing really effective is being done here against either Communism or Fascism, at least not by the politicians because they do not want anything settled. Their occupation and careers would be gone. We're going to be made sorry very soon for our refusal to reject unconditionally the kind of evil that disguises itself as patriotism, as love of virtue, as religious faith, as the crusador against the internal enemy. These people are themselves the enemy.

I do not propose to sit down quietly and be told by them what my duty is to my country and my government. My feelings and beliefs are nothing they could understand. I do not like being told that I must take an oath of allegiance to my government and flag under the threat of losing my employment if I do not. This is blackmail, and I have never been blackmailed successfully yet and do not intend to begin now.

So please destroy the contract we have made, as it is no longer valid. I know I run some little risk of nasty publicity in this matter. I hope not. I am not in the least a martyr. I have no time for heroics and indeed distrust them deeply. I am an artist who wishes to be left in peace to do my work. I hope that work will speak in the long run very clearly for me and all my kind, will be in some sort my testimony and my share of the battle against the elements of corruption and dissolution that come upon us so insidiously from all sides we hardly know where to begin to oppose them.

You may say this is a great how-do-you-do about a small matter. I can only   10 say it is not a small matter when added to all other small matters of the kind that finally make an army of locusts.

Dr. Ross, I thank you for your courteous letter and hope you will take my word that this letter has nothing personal in it. That towards you I intend nothing but human respect in the assurance that I believe I understand your situation which must be extremely difficult.

What has this kind of meanness and cheapness to do with education? What is wrong that undesirable applicants for the faculty are not quietly discovered and refused before they are appointed? Why must a person like me be asked to do a stupid, meaningless thing because one person with a bad political record got into your college once? No, I can't have it, and neither can you. The amusing side of all this brou-ha-ha is I really did not expect to have any occasion to mention the flag or the laws of Colorado or the Communist Alger Hiss or even the Fascist Senator McCarthy. I meant to talk about literature, life understood and loved in terms of the human heart in the personal experience. The life of the imagination and the search for the true meaning of our fate in this world, of the soul as a pilgrim on a stony path and of faithfulness to an ideal good and tenacity in the love of truth. Whether or not we ever find it, we still must look for it to the very end.

Any real study of great literature must take in human life at every possible level and search out every dark corner. And its natural territory is the whole human experience, no less. It does not astonish me that young people love to hear about these things, love to talk about them, and think about them. It is sometimes surprising to me how gay my classes can be, as if we had found some spring of joy in the tragic state to which all of us are born. This is the service the arts do, and the totalitarian's first idea is to destroy exactly this. They can do great harm but not for long. I am not in the least afraid of them.

With my sincere good wishes, and apologies for this overlong letter,

Yours,

Katherine Anne Porter

CRITICAL THINKING QUESTIONS

1. Why does the writer make a loose distinction between communism and fascism? Does she imply by this definition that Dr. Ross may be a fascist?

2. When she describes her role as a teacher, how does that affect her appeal to *ethos*? What part of her description do you find most effective? Contrarily, if you had written this letter, would you have explored a different approach? Explain.

WRITING TOPIC

The fallacy of **ad populum** substitutes content with a "just plain folks" appeal, which sometimes "disguises itself as patriotism." With that idea in mind, what does Katherine Anne Porter see as her duty?

Frank Schaeffer and John Schaeffer

My Son the Marine? (2002)

When two Marine recruiters showed up at our Salisbury, Mass., home in dress blues, they bedazzled my younger son, John. He had talked to recruiters from the Army, Navy and Air Force too, but his eyes lit up while the Marines spoke. I watched, inwardly alarmed. John seemed to relate to these stern, clean men with their insanely flawless uniforms in some basic way that I could barely comprehend. My wife, Genie, looking concerned and a bit drawn, turned to one of the men and asked, "But when he's done with the Marines, I mean—what will he have?"

The recruiter said, "Have, ma'am? I don't understand."

"I meant, what will he get out of it?"

The man's cheeks flushed. "He'll be a United States Marine, ma'am!"

5   There were no promises of college funds, "signing bonuses" or great "civilian opportunities" later on in life. Instead, the Marines promised that if John joined the Corps, he would find standards that had not been lowered. A young man wanting to measure himself against the tradition of maximum endurance would not be disappointed. "Boot camp's still tough as hell," one of the recruiters told us.

When the men left, John said to me, "I'm not sure I want to go into the military, Dad. But if I do, it'll be the Marines. Otherwise, what's the point?"

I was born in Switzerland to American missionaries, the youngest of four children. Perhaps because they were overprotective of me after I contracted polio—I wore a leg brace—my parents home-schooled me, and then sent me to private schools in England and Wales.

Genie and I married in 1970 and moved to America ten years later. In September 1980, our son John was born. From the moment he entered our lives to his last high school poetry reading, I doted on him. He made the meaning of life clear to me.

So when he finally decided to join the Marines, I had no picture of how things would go. I felt ignorant. I vaguely imagined my son leaving for boot camp, and then after he graduated, being sent off to the ends of the earth. Why the hell was John going into the Marines?

It had been hard enough sending my two older children off to college. The normal separations were just about unbearable. Our daughter, Jessica, went to New York University, and our other son, Francis, to Georgetown. Couldn't John have gone on to college first? No other parent in our affluent town on the North Shore of Boston had a son or daughter who was going into the military, let alone as an enlisted recruit.

When I told another parent of John's decision to join the Marines, the man was incredulous. "He's so bright and talented and could do anything!" the man said. "What a waste!"

The day John left for boot camp at Parris Island in South Carolina, I woke very early. I had to get him to the local recruiting office by 4:30. At our front door, John and his mother hugged and she cried steady, silent tears. John told his mother he loved her.

At the recruiting office, I looked at my son as he shook the staff sergeant's hand and thought, *What is he trying to prove?* More than once during the last few months, I had asked him, "Why do you want to do this?" Sometimes he'd say, "I want self-discipline." The best answer he gave was, "I just do." We parted with a hug and a handshake. "I'll miss you, boy," I said. "I'll write every day."

"Okay."

"I love you, John."

"I love you, Dad."

Driving home, I lost my way twice on a road I'd driven a thousand times. I'd never experienced pride and fear as one emotion before. *Oh, Lord, please protect my boy and bring him home safe!* was all I could think as I peered forlornly into the gloom while trying to remember my way home.

After a brief call letting us know he'd arrived—plus two form letters sent by the Marines—John was not allowed to contact us. I bought a book by Thomas E. Ricks called *Making the Corps*, which, with its day-by-day account of boot-camp training, quickly became my bible. I followed John's activities: drill marching; classes in subjects like Tactical Weapons of Opportunity (i.e., using things like rocks and sticks to smash the enemy with when a rifle wasn't handy); and physical training—miles of running, thousands of repetitions of exercises, pugil stick fighting, and endless humps (marches in full combat gear and pack).

Writing to John was a poignant experience. There was something so unequal about writing to him from the lap of luxury when he had essentially died and gone to hell.

20   For the first time in both our lives, my son was beyond my help. Did he have it in him to become a Marine? I knew that John's idea of a good time was to curl up in front of the fireplace and reread his favorite bits of *The Hobbit*. When he caught fish, he let them go. How could my son become a Marine? What sort of a person would he be when the Corps was done with him? Would John be absolutely devastated if he failed? I felt sick.

But he did not fail. Three months after John had left us, Genie and I went down to Parris Island for his graduation. We stood in the stands for the ceremony and watched our son parade in, third man from the front, a tall Marine—my son.

I wiped my eyes and looked around. It occurred to me that this was the first time I'd been in an integrated crowd of this size dedicated to one purpose and of one mind. We were dark-skinned, weather-beaten, Spanish-speaking grandfathers; black kids wearing head rags; Southern-accented mothers with big hair and tight sweat suits; and some people who looked like us.

The platitudes my educated friends mouthed about "racial harmony" and "economic and gender diversity" were nothing compared to the spirit shared among the people gathered in the stands that day to honor our Marines. Our children would room together as they had in boot camp, drink together, work together, united by a high purpose: the defense of our country and loyalty to the Corps.

Nearly two years later, I was packing my bags to fly down to Florida to visit John at his new base, where he was a squad leader and had been nominated by his platoon to represent it as "Marine of the Quarter," the best performer of his unit for that time period. My biggest worry was whether I would have trouble checking the cooler full of food I was bringing to John. It was September 10, 2001.

25   The next day, all flights were canceled, and civil air traffic over the United States was shut down for the first time in history. The cooler of food was forgotten. I was so scared for John. I longed to hold on to my son for dear life.

I finally spoke to him the next day, on September 12. He sounded calm and confident.

"Hey, Dad, this is worse for you than for me," he said.

"How's that?"

"All you have to do with yourself is worry, but we have a job to do." He paused. "Dad? I love you."

30   After I hung up the phone, I stared at the television. There were fire-fighters, cops and military personnel struggling to find survivors and thousands of dead. I felt deeply frustrated at being able to do nothing. At least I knew that I could look the men and women in uniform in the eye. My son, after all, was one of them.

CRITICAL THINKING QUESTIONS

1. In analyzing an argument, we look at the choices the author made: Why did the writer choose to begin the piece in this way? Why did he place the evidence in this order? Why did he use this particular metaphor or this descriptive phrase? In "My Son the Marine?", why did the writers choose to mention the son's "last high school poetry reading"? How do the writers use similar information later in the piece? How does this information relate to the title?

2. Although we cannot point to an explicit claim in "My Son the Marine?", we can articulate an implied claim. What might the authors want their readers to believe after reading this piece?

3. Compare and contrast the authors' use of rhetorical appeals (*ethos, logos, pathos*) in this essay to Alan Gurganus's use of appeals in "Captive Audience" (page 538). Based on your critical analyses of the two arguments, which one is more persuasive?

WRITING TOPIC

Think of a personal experience that was meaningful to you. If you were to relate this experience to other people, write out a sentence in which you succinctly state what you would like them to conclude (your explicit claim). Now write out a description of your personal experience so that readers will understand your claim without seeing it stated in a specific sentence (your implied claim). As a simplistic example, your description of an automobile accident might imply that drinking and driving is not a good thing to do.

Richard Wright

from *Black Boy* (1937)

One morning I arrived early at work and went into the bank lobby where the Negro porter was mopping. I stood at a counter and picked up the Memphis *Commercial Appeal* and began my free reading of the press. I came finally to the editorial page and saw an article dealing with one H. L. Mencken. I knew by hearsay that he was the editor of the *American Mercury*, but aside from that I knew nothing about him. The article was a furious denunciation of Mencken, concluding with one, hot, short sentence: Mencken is a fool.

I wondered what on earth this Mencken had done to call down upon him the scorn of the South. The only people I had ever heard denounced in the South were Negroes, and this man was not a Negro. Then what ideas did Mencken hold that made a newspaper like the *Commercial Appeal* castigate him publicly? Undoubtedly he must be advocating ideas that the South did not like. Were there, then, people other than Negroes who criticized the South? I knew that during the Civil War the South had hated northern whites, but I had not encountered such hate during my life. Knowing no more of Mencken than I did at that moment, I felt a vague sympathy for him. Had not the South, which had assigned me the role of a non-man, cast at him its hardest words?

Now, how could I find out about this Mencken? There was a huge library near the riverfront, but I knew that Negroes were not allowed to patronize its shelves any more than they were the parks and playgrounds of the city. I had gone into the library several times to get books for the white men on the job. Which of them would now help me to get books? And how could I read them without causing concern to the white men with whom I worked? I had so far been successful in hiding my thoughts and feelings from them, but I knew that I would create hostility if I went about this business of reading in a clumsy way.

I weighed the personalities of the men on the job. There was Don, a Jew; but I distrusted him. His position was not much better than mine and I knew that he was uneasy and insecure; he had always treated me in an offhand, bantering way that barely concealed his contempt. I was afraid to ask him to help me to get books; his frantic desire to demonstrate a racial solidarity with the whites against Negroes might make him betray me.

5   Then how about the boss? No, he was a Baptist and I had the suspicion that he would not be quite able to comprehend why a black boy would want to read Mencken. There were other white men on the job whose attitudes showed clearly that they were Kluxers or sympathizers, and they were out of the question.

There remained only one man whose attitude did not fit into an anti-Negro category, for I had heard the white men refer to him as a "Pope lover." He was an Irish Catholic and was hated by the white Southerners. I knew that he read books, because I had got him volumes from the library several times. Since he, too, was an object of hatred, I felt that he might refuse me but would hardly betray me. I hesitated, weighing and balancing the imponderable realities.

One morning I paused before the Catholic fellow's desk.

"I want to ask you a favor," I whispered to him.

"What is it?"

10   "I want to read. I can't get books from the library. I wonder if you'd let me use your card?"

He looked at me suspiciously.

"My card is full most of the time," he said.

"I see," I said and waited, posing my question silently.

"You're not trying to get me into trouble, are you, boy?" he asked, staring at me.

"Oh, no, sir."   15

"What book do you want?"

"A book by H. L. Mencken."

"Which one?"

"I don't know. Has he written more than one?"

"He has written several."   20

"I didn't know that."

"What makes you want to read Mencken?"

"Oh, I just saw his name in the newspaper," I said.

"It's good of you to want to read," he said. "But you ought to read the right things."

I said nothing. Would he want to supervise my reading?   25

"Let me think," he said. "I'll figure out something."

I turned from him and he called me back. He stared at me quizzically.

"Richard, don't mention this to the other white men," he said.

"I understand," I said. "I won't say a word."

A few days later he called me to him.   30

"I've got a card in my wife's name," he said. "Here's mine."

"Thank you, sir."

"Do you think you can manage it?"

"I'll manage fine," I said.

"If they suspect you, you'll get in trouble," he said.   35

"I'll write the same kind of notes to the library that you wrote when you sent me for books," I told him. "I'll sign your name."

He laughed.

"Go ahead. Let me see what you get," he said.

That afternoon I addressed myself to forging a note. Now, what were the names of books written by H. L. Mencken? I did not know any of them. I finally wrote what I thought would be a foolproof note: *Dear Madam: Will you please let this nigger boy*—I used the word "nigger" to make the librarian feel that I could not possibly be the author of the note—*have some books by H. L. Mencken?* I forged the white man's name.

I entered the library as I had always done when on errands for whites, but   40
I felt that I would somehow slip up and betray myself. I doffed my hat, stood a respectful distance from the desk, looked as unbookish as possible, and waited for the white patrons to be taken care of. When the desk was clear of people, I still waited. The white librarian looked at me.

"What do you want, boy?"

As though I did not possess the power of speech, I stepped forward and simply handed her the forged note, not parting my lips.

"What books by Mencken does he want?" she asked.

"I don't know, ma'am," I said, avoiding her eyes.

45 "Who gave you this card?"

"Mr. Falk," I said.

"Where is he?"

"He's at work, at the M—— Optical Company," I said. "I've been in here for him before."

"I remember," the woman said. "But he never wrote notes like this."

50 Oh, God, she's suspicious. Perhaps she would not let me have the books? If she had turned her back at that moment, I would have ducked out the door and never gone back. Then I thought of a bold idea.

"You can call him up, ma'am," I said, my heart pounding.

"You're not using these books, are you?" she asked pointedly.

"Oh, no, ma'am. I can't read."

"I don't know what he wants by Mencken," she said under her breath.

55 I knew now that I had won; she was thinking of other things and the race question had gone out of her mind. She went to the shelves. Once or twice she looked over her shoulder at me, as though she was still doubtful. Finally she came forward with two books in her hand.

"I'm sending him two books," she said. "But tell Mr. Falk to come in next time, or send me the names of the books he wants. I don't know what he wants to read."

I said nothing. She stamped the card and handed me the books. Not daring to glance at them, I went out of the library, fearing that the woman would call me back for further questioning. A block away from the library I opened one of the books and read a title: *A Book of Prefaces.* I was nearing my nineteenth birthday and I did not know how to pronounce the word "preface." I thumbed the pages and saw strange words and strange names. I shook my head, disappointed. I look at the other book; it was called *Prejudices.* I knew what that word meant; I had heard it all my life. And right off I was on guard against Mencken's books. Why would a man want to call a book *Prejudices?* The word was so stained with all my memories of racial hate that I could not conceive of anybody using it for a title. Perhaps I had made a mistake about Mencken? A man who had prejudices must be wrong.

When I showed the books to Mr. Falk, he looked at me and frowned.

"That librarian might telephone you," I warned him.

60 "That's all right," he said. "But when you're through reading those books, I want you to tell me what you get out of them."

That night in my rented room, while letting the hot water run over my can of pork and beans in the sink, I opened *A Book of Prefaces* and began to read. I was jarred and shocked by the style, the clear, clean, sweeping sentences. Why did he write like that? And how did one write like that? I pictured the man as a raging demon, slashing with his pen, consumed with hate, denouncing everything American, extolling everything European or German, laughing at the weaknesses of people, mocking God, authority. What was this? I stood up, trying to realize what reality lay behind the meaning of the words…Yes, this man was fighting, fighting with words. He was using words as a weapon, using them as one would use a club. Could words be weapons? Well, yes, for here they were. Then, maybe, perhaps, I could use them as a weapon? No. It frightened me. I read on and what amazed me was not what he said, but how on earth anybody had the courage to say it.

Occasionally I glanced up to reassure myself that I was alone in the room. Who were these men about whom Mencken was talking so passionately? Who was Anatole France? Joseph Conrad? Sinclair Lewis, Sherwood Anderson, Dostoevski, George Moore, Gustave Flaubert, Maupassant, Tolstoy, Frank Harris, Mark Twain, Thomas Hardy, Arnold Bennett, Stephen Crane, Zola, Norris, Gorky, Bergson, Ibsen, Balzac, Bernard Shaw, Dumas, Poe, Thomas Mann, O. Henry, Dreiser, H. G. Wells, Gogol, T. S. Eliot, Gide, Baudelaire, Edgar Lee Masters, Stendhal, Turgenev, Huneker, Nietzsche, and scores of others? Were these men real? Did they exist or had they existed? And how did one pronounce their names?

I ran across many words whose meanings I did not know, and I either looked them up in a dictionary or, before I had a chance to do that, encountered the word in a context that made its meaning clear. But what strange world was this? I concluded the book with the conviction that I had somehow overlooked something terribly important in life. I had once tried to write, had once reveled in feeling, had let my crude imagination roam, but the impulse to dream had been slowly beaten out of me by experience. Now it surged up again and I hungered for books, new ways of looking and seeing. It was not a matter of believing or disbelieving what I read, but of feeling something new, of being affected by something that made the look of the world different.

As dawn broke I ate my pork and beans, feeling dopey, sleepy. I went to work, but the mood of the book would not die; it lingered, coloring everything I saw, heard, did. I now felt that I knew what the white men were feeling. Merely because I had read a book that had spoken of how they lived and thought, I identified myself with that book. I felt vaguely guilty. Would I, filled with bookish notions, act in a manner that would make the whites dislike me?

I forged more notes and my trips to the library became frequent. Reading   65
grew into a passion. My first serious novel was Sinclair Lewis's *Main Street*. It made me see my boss, Mr. Gerlad, and identify him as an American type. I would smile when I saw him lugging his golf bags into the office. I had always felt a vast distance separating me from the boss, and now I felt closer to him, though still distant. I felt now that I knew him, that I could feel the very limits of his narrow life. And this had happened because I had read a novel about a mythical man called George F. Babbitt.

The plots and stories in the novels did not interest me so much as the point of view revealed. I gave myself over to each novel without reserve, without trying to criticize it; it was enough for me to see and feel something different. And for me, everything was something different. Reading was like a drug, a dope. The novels created moods in which I lived for days. But I could not conquer my sense of guilt, my feeling that the white men around me knew that I was changing, that I had begun to regard them differently.

Whenever I brought a book to the job, I wrapped it in newspaper—a habit that was to persist for years in other cities and under other circumstances. But some of the white men pried into my packages when I was absent and they questioned me.

"Boy, what are you reading those books for?"

"Oh, I don't know, sir."

70

"That's deep stuff you're reading, boy."

"I'm just killing time, sir."

"You'll addle your brains if you don't watch out."

I read Dreiser's *Jennie Gerhardt* and *Sister Carrie* and they revived in me a vivid sense of my mother's suffering; I was overwhelmed. I grew silent, wondering about the life around me. It would have been impossible for me to have told anyone what I derived from these novels, for it was nothing less than a sense of life itself. All my life had shaped me for the realism, the naturalism of the modern novel, and I could not read enough of them.

Steeped in new moods and ideas, I bought a ream of paper and tried to write; but nothing would come, or what did come was flat beyond telling. I discovered that more than desire and feeling were necessary to write and I dropped the idea. Yet I still wondered how it was possible to know people sufficiently to write about them? Could I ever learn about life and people? To me, with my vast ignorance, my Jim Crow station in life, it seemed a task impossible of achievement. I now knew what being a Negro meant. I could endure the hunger. I had learned to live with hate. But to feel that there were feelings denied me, that the very breath of life itself was beyond my reach, that more than anything else hurt, wounded me. I had a new hunger.

CRITICAL THINKING QUESTIONS

1. Have you ever wanted or needed something that someone in power denied you? If so, did the situation make you angry? Like James Baldwin and other African American artists, especially jazz musicians, Richard Wright spent years living in France. Look up the meaning of the word *expatriate*. Can you imagine situations that would lead you to leave your country?

2. After reading the excerpt from Richard Wright's *Black Boy*, read Langston Hughes's poem "Democracy," on page 515. Explain how the situation Wright describes illustrates Hughes's words "compromise and fear."

WRITING TOPIC

Wright wants a library card in order to read and grow intellectually. Perhaps today he would have been looking for access to a computer. Read about the computer divide. Seventy-five years later, are we still dividing access to knowledge according to wealth, if not race or ethnicity? Offer details to explain your viewpoint.

CHAPTER ACTIVITIES AND TOPICS FOR WRITING ARGUMENTS

1. Suppose you are a professional athlete who has just signed a multi-million-dollar contract. Assuming money is power, you certainly will have the power to do many things, but once you have bought Mom and Dad a nice retirement home and satisfied your own desire to trek through the Himalayas, what next? To what degree do you have responsibilities to your fellow human beings? Create a specific plan for using your assets, and argue that it is the best choice (literature suggestions: Brooks's "The Boy Died in My Alley" [page 509]; Milton's "When I Consider How My Light Is Spent" [page 520]; Kennedy's "Inaugural Address" [page 541]).

2. Here is a hypothetical situation: The United States is at war in the Middle East, and China has stepped into the conflict. Our government has stated that one objective of this war is to restore human rights to the besieged Middle Eastern countries. However, everyone understands that this war is also over oil: We win and life goes on normally; we lose and gas goes up to $6 a gallon while our economy unravels and depression looms. And in this ground war, fought by high-tech infantry, Americans are dying in large numbers. The draft has been reinstated, and your number is called. It's the front lines for you. But there is an alternative. The Scandinavian countries as well as Canada have denounced this war and openly accept conscientious objectors. What are your responsibilities? What do you do? Make a decision and support it (literature suggestions: Gurganus's, "Captive Audience" [page 538]; Schaeffer and Schaeffer's "My Son the Marine?" [page 552]).

3. Because we seem to share the desire to vanquish our enemies, revenge is sometimes called *sweet*. But is revenge sweet? When the person who has suffered unfair treatment finally triumphs, we often applaud him or her. And we ourselves cannot help but feel a twinge of joy when the court finally forces that unscrupulous car dealer to pay us back the money he unjustly took from us and to offer an apology. But is revenge always sweet? Situations

often are not as simple and clear-cut as they appear on the surface. Read the stories "Spanish Roulette," by Ed Vega (page 499), and the poem "Bully," by Martín Espada (page 510), and then write an extended definition of the word *revenge*. In your extended definition, you might include examples from history, literature, and personal experience, but also be sure to focus on the conflicts this impulse for revenge creates in people.

4. While Abraham Lincoln and John F. Kennedy were superior national leaders, everyday persons also take on the responsibilities and risks of leadership, as illustrated by Robert, the blind man, in Raymond Carver's "Cathedral" (page 436). On the other hand, Lieutenant Jimmy Cross in Tim O'Brien's "The Things They Carried" (page 482) believes he has neglected his duties as the leader of his platoon. If you were conducting a leadership workshop for your college or local community, how could you use these four individuals to illustrate key points of your presentation? What other examples—contemporary or historical, fictional or factual—might you use to illustrate leadership qualities?

5. The term "white lie" suggests that, in some situations, lying may be justified. Depending on the context, some persons may attempt to justify lies when they feel that the negative consequences of telling the truth outweigh the virtue of honoring the truth. For some people, however, lies are always unacceptable; to them, "white lie" is an oxymoron, a contradiction in terms that creates a **slippery slope**. Moving beyond the personal to the political arena, is a government ever justified in withholding information that directly affects its citizens? Recently, this issue has been debated in relation to national security and the war on terrorism. In an essay, take a stand on this issue; support your position with evidence from history and current events.

GLOBAL PERSPECTIVES RESEARCH/WRITING TOPICS

1. Hip-Hop, a Global Language for Youth

You may have seen the bumper sticker "Think globally; act locally." Such is the case with hip-hop music. While hip-hop artists share a rhythm and style, they create music that is deeply rooted in their local soil. Around the globe, hip-hop gives an identity and a voice to youth who often feel invisible within the mainstream culture and marginalized by the dominant power structure. Indeed, although in the 1990s hip-hop music arguably may have been considered an African American genre, today it is recognized as an international genre with its expressions as variegated as the individuals who are creating it. Do some research to learn about the hip-hop music in several countries, and then develop an argument that evaluates the significance of hip-hop. For example, is the music an authentic voice of oppression and resistance, or is it, as its detractors might argue, simply a purveyor of "dirty" lyrics, a crude expression of anger and violence?

2. The Case For and Against Sweatshops

The word *sweatshops* connotes images of individuals, particularly children and women, laboring long hours in unventilated, concrete-block factories for minuscule wages. These workers often are employed by large national or multinational corporations that, spurred by an increasingly competitive global market, have located their manufacturing "shops" in countries where the labor laws and standards are lax or nonexistent and where labor is "cheap." Globalization, however, has also sparked an international network of protest and a call for boycotting products of manufacturers who operate sweatshops. It would seem, therefore, to be an affront to ethical principles—a crass joke—to call sweatshops a "dream." But this is just what Nicholas D. Kristoff claims in his *New York Times* article "Where Sweatshops Are a Dream." Kristoff, whose "views are shaped by years of living in East Asia, watching as living standards soared…because of sweatshops," asserts, "Yet sweatshops are only a symptom of poverty, not a cause, and banning them closes one route out of poverty."[1] And Kristoff's is not a solo voice in daring to defend sweatshops. Defenders argue that sweatshops are a necessary growing pain for developing countries; they point out, for example, that child labor laws were enacted in the United States well after the dawn of the Industrial Revolution. Even so, others contend that "two wrongs do not make a right." After researching this issue, develop an argument that takes a position on the responsibility developed countries have to either sustain or terminate sweatshops in developing countries. As you develop your claim, keep in mind the creative problem-solving approach of Rogerian argument.

COLLABORATION ACTIVITY: CREATING A ROGERIAN ARGUMENT

For this activity, you will work in small teams to research, write, and present a Rogerian argument on a contemporary issue that has emerged from your exploration of readings in this chapter. The Writing Topics following many of the selections can help you identify an issue. For a discussion of the Rogerian argument and a suggested organizational approach to the assignment, please see Chapter 5.

---

[1]Kristoff, Nicholas D. "Where Sweatshops Are a Dream." *New York Times*. 15 Jan. 2009. Web. 22 Jan. 2009.

Following are guidelines for this collaboration activity:

- Identify an **issue**.
- Divide the research/writing responsibilities as follows:
  - Student one: introduction section
  - Student two: body section, affirmative position
  - Student three: body section, opposing position
  - Student four: conclusion, summation, and middle-ground position

Following are characteristics of effective collaboration. Each team member should:

- Contribute by collecting information related to the issue.
- Take responsibility by completing assigned work on time.
- Engage with other team members by listening to and considering other viewpoints.

SAMPLE ISSUE: THE JUSTICE OR INJUSTICE OF REPARATIONS

Acknowledging the injustice of the internment of Japanese Americans during World War II, in 1988 the U.S. Congress voted to issue a formal apology and to pay reparations. Today, some people argue that other groups, such as African Americans and Native Americans, also are deserving of payments for past wrongs and injuries. On the other hand, other people argue that wrongs done to these groups were committed in the distant past, and, therefore, reparations are not justified. Select one of these two groups and address the issue question: Should the U.S. government pay reparations for past wrongs and injuries?

Literature suggestions: "The Red Convertible," "In Response to Executive Order 9066," and "The Letter from Birmingham Jail" in Chapter 6; "Ballad of Birmingham" in Chapter 8; and "America" in Chapter 9.

ARGUING THEMES FROM LITERATURE

1. In what ways did Ichabod Crane surrender his power to his belief in superstitions? Search "The Legend of Sleepy Hollow" for textual support to argue for or against the idea that the schoolmaster fell victim, in some ways, to his own insecurities. In addition, offer your theories about Ichabod Crane's mysterious disappearance. Did he vanish under foul play or voluntarily? Explain.

2. If you notice, Raymond Carver never reveals the name of the narrator or his significant other in "Cathedral." In the text, the two refer to each other as "husband" or "wife." In what ways does this speak to the sense of power

and responsibility that each character feels (or lack thereof)? Do you believe couples sometimes take away and/or surrender their identities to each other? Use text from "Cathedral" to support your views.

3. In Gwendolyn Brooks's "The Boy Died in My Alley," why do you believe the narrator feels a sense of responsibility? Do you think the narrator is being too harsh on herself or fairly assuming some blame for the boy's death? In what ways can individuals exercise power to make their communities better places to live?

Glossary

Academic argument characterized by a reasoned, logical approach to debate over issues; the tone is one of respect and civility, and the goal is to move the discourse surrounding the issue forward through constructive dialogue.

Ad hominem the fallacy of personal attack. Instead of arguing with someone's position, one attacks the person. "Mrs. X has had two affairs and does not deserve our vote."

Ad populum the fallacy of substituting content with a "just plain folks" appeal.

Ambiguity intentionally vague meaning, sometimes leading the reader astray in argument or adding multiple levels of interpretation to literature.

Argument an essay or passage (written or verbal) with the purpose of persuading an audience to accept a conclusion.

Assertion sometimes called the *claim* or the *thesis*, it is the speaker's or writer's statement of his or her position in an argument.

Assumption in argument, an idea that the writer or speaker feels no need to support, prove, or justify because he or she believes that his or her audience will certainly hold the idea to be true. For example, in opposing abortion, pro-life advocates assume that life has human value from the moment of conception.

Authority an individual recognized as an expert within his or her field of study or occupation.

Begging the question to use an argument that assumes exactly what the argument attempts to prove; for example, gun control goes against our freedom because it takes away our individual rights.

Character the representation of a person in literature. A one-dimensional character is called a *flat* character, while one who is realistically complex is called a *round* character.

Claim in argument, the main point, thesis, or assertion of the argument—what the speaker or writer wants his or her audience to think or do about an issue.

Claim of fact a statement that argues something is either true or false.

Claim of policy a statement that argues for a specific action to take place.

Claim of value a statement that makes a judgment, labeling something as good or bad.

Concession   in argument, recognizing and acknowledging the validity of a portion of the opposition's point of view. In making a concession, the arguer can strengthen his or her *ethos* by demonstrating the character trait of fair-mindedness.

Conflict   the opposition that creates tension in literature. The opposing forces may be *external* when a character conflicts with other people, or they may be *internal* when a character faces conflicts within him- or herself.

Connotation   the emotional or social meaning attached to a word beyond its literal, objective meaning. See also *Denotation*.

Counterarguments   the opposition's primary and/or anticipated rebuttals to refute an arguer's stance on an issue.

Critical inquiry   an essential component in critical thinking; the habit of questioning one's own thinking, opinions, beliefs, values, as well as those of others.

Denotation   the dictionary definition of a word—its literal and explicit meaning. See also *Connotation*.

Diction   the speaker's or writer's choice of words.

Dramatic context   the interpretive implications of the setting, plot, characters/speaker within the literary work.

Dramatic monologue   a narrative told from the perspective of only one character which inadvertently reveals personality traits of that character.

Either-or reasoning   sometimes called the *black and white* or *false dilemma fallacy;* in argument, such reasoning is characterized by oversimplification that presents an issue in only two ways, either X or Y.

Electronic source   a document or image residing in a digital collection, including clouds, flash drives, and Internet resources.

Equivocation   in argument, the intentional use of a word that has more than one interpretation and thus misleads the reader or listener.

Ethos   the appeal first mentioned by Aristotle through which the writer or speaker evokes his or her credibility and trustworthiness; e.g., a teenager wishing to stay out past curfew might ask his or her parents, "Have I ever done anything to lead you to mistrust me?"

Evidence   in argument, there are many types of evidence, but the most common are personal experience, or first-person accounts; *logos*, or the use of facts and objective reports; *ethos*, or the use of character and credibility; and *pathos*, or the use of value-based and emotional appeals.

Explicit claim   a thesis in an argument that is clearly presented within the text of the argument. A single sentence usually can be identified as the claim within the introduction of the argument and/or in its conclusion.

False analogy   a false comparison, sometimes expressed as "comparing apples and oranges." People might say that like Rome, America is destined for destruction; however, modern America is quite unlike ancient Rome.

Figurative language language using imaginative comparison, such as *metaphor* and *simile*.

Foreshadowing a sign or hint of what is to come.

Hasty generalization moving from inadequate evidence to a broad generalization; jumping to a conclusion.

Imagery a reference in literature that calls to mind vivid details of sight, sound, smell, taste, and touch.

Implied (or implicit) claim a thesis in an argument that is not stated directly but can be inferred based on evidence provided within the text of the argument.

Inference S. I. Hayakawa defines it as "a statement about the unknown based on the known." Unlike a fact, an inference cannot be proven true or false since it is a probable explanation or an interpretation of evidence. An inference is reached through inductive reasoning.

Irony a humorous or sarcastic statement whose words mean the opposite of their usual use, or in literature, the contrast between a character's perception and the truth known to the reader or audience.

Issue a topic of argument that generates tension because both sides have some reasonable aspects to their arguments.

Logical fallacy illogical reasoning; often an intentional flaw created to manipulate the evidence and mislead one's audience, but sometimes an unknowing flaw in reasoning due to one's carelessness or ignorance.

Logos in argument, the rhetorical appeal that Aristotle identified as the arguer's use of reasoning and logic to persuade his or her audience to accept the claim.

Metaphor without using "like" or "as," this figure of speech describes something as if it were something quite different. "That man is an angel."

Narrator one who relates events to the reader. A *narration* is the recounting of a series of plot events in order to tell a story.

Pathos the quality in literature that arouses pity; in argument, an emotional or value-based appeal. When an emotional appeal replaces content, it is called the fallacy of *ad misercordium*, or appeal to pity and fear.

Personal experience a true story an arguer uses from his or her past as evidence to support a claim or position.

Plagiarism a writer's failure to give credit for words or concepts from another source.

Point of view the speaker or narrator of a work through which the audience or readers perceive the details of plot and character. The point of view may be omniscient, limited, or objective, as well as first, second, or third person.

Post hoc **fallacy** incorrectly attributing a cause and effect relationship; often called the false cause fallacy.

Prewriting the preliminary stages of drafting a writing assignment where the writer jots down ideas without worrying about technical, grammatical, and academic restrictions, but rather constructs lists and/or inventions that aid in planning, ordering, and writing the paper.

Propaganda information delivered in a deliberate, particular way to influence public opinion.

Prose written language in its natural form, without rhythm; not poetry.

Purpose a writer/speaker's motivation or reason for pursuing the study and presentation of a topic.

Red herring the fallacy of leading the reader astray by bringing up a different issue as bait to capture the reader's interest, thus distracting him or her from the real issue.

Refutation attempting to counterargue or prove an argument wrong.

Reports objective facts gathered from outside sources to support an argument.

Rhetorical appeals [See *Ethos, Logos, Pathos*]

Rhetorical device the precise use of language to persuade or evoke emotion in an audience; examples include alliteration, emphasis, anaphora, repetition, etc.

Rhetorical question asking a question as a way to involve the reader in the issue at hand. In this way, the writer sets him- or herself up to answer the question that has been planted in the reader's mind.

Rogerian argument named after twentieth-century American psychotherapist and communication theorist Carl R. Rogers, this argument strategy seeks to resolve conflict between opposing parties through a process of non-confrontational dialogue and negotiation. The goal of Rogerian argument is to find common ground on which to build a compromise.

Slippery slope a false appeal to fear; suggesting that a single event or situation will trigger a series of seemingly catastrophic effects.

Social context the events within society at the time the literary work was written that might have thematic implications related to the piece.

Symbolism a literary device where an object represents an idea; for example a rose can symbolize love.

Theme a recurring, unifying idea running through a piece of literature. To discover *plot*, readers ask the question, "What happens next?"; to discover *theme*, readers answer the question, "Why?"

Tone a speaker's or writer's attitude toward his or her subject and audience, often conveyed through diction.

Tragedy traditionally the fall of a great person through his or her own errors in judgment. In modern literature, the term is often applied to the downfall of less highly placed characters.

Two wrongs make a right a fallacy of logic that justifies a wrongdoing by pointing out a previous affront.

Value assumption a quality or belief that one assumes is shared by one's audience. For example, a value assumption underlying the argument for strict gun control laws is that the safety of the many trumps the rights of the individual.

Authors' Biographical Notes

Abbey, Edward (1927–1989) Although born and raised on a farm in Pennsylvania, Abbey lived in the Southwest from 1947 until his death. A passionate defender of wilderness, his book *Desert Solitaire* (1968) helped to launch the environmental movement. His novel *The Monkey Wrench Gang* (1975), about a group of environmental guerillas' plot to blow up Glen Canyon Dam of the Colorado River, is credited with influencing radical environmental groups such as Earth First!

Bacon, Francis (1561–1626) Bacon was an English author, a courtier, a philosopher, and an advocate of inductive reasoning in science.

Ballard, J. G. (1930–2009) Ballard was an English novelist and short story writer often recognized for his work in science fiction. His 1984 novel *Empire of the Sun* was made into a film by Steven Spielberg.

Ballou, Sullivan (1829–1861) Ballou was a major in the U.S. Army. A lawyer in Rhode Island at the outbreak of the Civil War, he volunteered for military service and was killed at the Battle of Bull Run. After his death, his wife, Sara, never remarried.

Bierce, Ambrose (1842–1914) Bierce was a master of the short story, but he was also a writer of poetry, news articles, and the satirical *Devil's Dictionary* (1906). He fought for the Union during the American Civil War. Later in life, he left for Mexico in 1914 to observe, and perhaps fight for, Pancho Villa and his revolution. He was never heard from again.

Blake, William (1757–1827) Born in Westminster, Blake became an apprentice to an engraver at the age of fourteen. Throughout his lifetime, he created engravings and poetry. Blake was an experimentalist as a creative artist and also a radical thinker for his time. His most famous books of poetry, *Songs of Innocence* (1789), *Marriage of Heaven and Hell* (1790), and *Songs of Experience* (1794), include his illustrations in hand-colored engravings. The poems in *Songs of Experience* center on topics of political corruption and social injustice.

Bradstreet, Anne (1612?–1672) Born in England, Bradstreet grew up in a Puritan household. At age sixteen, she married Simon Bradstreet, who had recently graduated from Cambridge. Sailing with Puritan John Winthrop's fleet to the New World in 1629, Bradstreet and her husband were among the settlers of the Massachusetts Bay Colony in the New World. Despite the harsh conditions in rearing a family in the wilderness, Bradstreet continued to pursue her childhood interest in writing poetry. A collection of her poetry, *The Tenth Muse*, was printed in England in 1650.

Brooks, Gwendolyn (1917–2000)
Brooks won the Pulitzer Prize for poetry in 1950 for her 1949 collection of poetry *Annie Allen*, thus becoming the first African American to win this award. After that, she continued to write and was named the Poet Laureate for the State of Illinois in 1969. Her poems reflect the diction and syntax of black street life. *The Bean-Eaters* was published in 1960, followed by *Beckonings* in 1975 and *To Disembark* in 1981.

Capote, Truman (1924–1984)
Born in New Orleans, Capote left for Manhattan and wrote for *The New Yorker*. He is best known for his novels, *Breakfast at Tiffany's* (1958) and *In Cold Blood* (1966).

Carver, Raymond (1938–1988)
Raised in a working-class environment in the Pacific Northwest, Carver worked at many jobs while writing stories about the lives of everyday working people who feel trapped by their surroundings. His writing is collected in *Fires: Essays, Poems, and Stories* (1989).

Chief Joseph (1840–1904) Following in the footsteps of his father, Chief Joseph led the Nez Perce Tribe of Native Americans in a struggle for permanent homeland territory in the United States. When Joseph the Elder died, Chief Joseph took his father's place in Nez Perce leadership. He, along with other Nez Perce chiefs, renegotiated a peace treaty with the United States with new reservation boundaries. But before the Native Americans could move, some warriors from White Bird's infantry attacked and killed several white settlers. Chief Joseph knew that the white man would demand justice, so he decided to retreat his people to Canada. However, the tribe was so tired by the time they reached the Bear Paw Mountains, just 40 miles south of Canada, that the Chief made his famous surrender speech there in 1877. He spent the next several years petitioning the U.S. government for his people's return to the Oregon Territory. In 1885, the Nez Perce were granted a return to the Northwest, but they were still miles from their original homeland area of the Wallowa Valley.

Chopin, Kate (1851–1904) In defiance of contemporary restraints, Chopin often wrote about strong, independent female characters. She also wrote frankly about her characters' sexual feelings and, for that reason, caused a literary scandal. Her novels, notably, *The Awakening* (1899), have recently found a sympathetic audience.

Cleary, Michael (b. 1945) Cleary grew up in upstate New York and now teaches college English in Fort Lauderdale, Florida, where he writes poetry. His first book of poems is *Hometown*, published in 1992. He has two more poetry collections: *Halfway Decent Sinners* (2006) and *Bearable Weight* (2011).

Corso, Gregory Nunzio (1930–2001) Corso was a poet who gained fame as one of the Beat poets along with Allen Ginsberg and Jack Kerouac. After a childhood in orphanages and foster homes, Corso became interested in literature while in a prison in New York. His book *Mindfield: New and Collected Poems* was published in 1998.

Crossley-Holland, Kevin (b. 1941) Crossley-Holland is an English, Oxford-educated poet, translator, and children's author. He taught in Minnesota at the University of St. Thomas, and he is a Fellow of the Royal Society of Literature and an Honorary Fellow of St. Edmund Hall, Oxford. He currently lives on the Norfolk coast in England.

Cullen, Countee (1903–1946) This African American poet, who graduated from New York University and later earned a master's degree from Harvard University, became an important part of the movement known as the Harlem Renaissance. His collections of poems include *Color* (1925), *Copper Sun* (1927), *The Black Christ* (1929), and *On These I Stand* (1947).

Davis, Lydia (b. 1947) Born in Northampton, Massachusetts, Davis is the author of the novel *The End of the Story* (1995) and several collections of short fiction. Her latest book is *Can't and Won't: Stories* (2014). She won the Man Booker International Prize in 2013.

Dickinson, Emily (1830–1886) Born in Amherst, Massachusetts, Dickinson rarely left her family home throughout her life. From a prominent family, she received more formal education than most of her peers, male or female. Dickinson's poems are noted for their syntactical and rhythmic improvisation, their conciseness, and their profundity. However, her poems were not published until after her death, first in the collection *Poems* (1890). Despite her lack of recognition as a poet during her lifetime, critics consider Dickinson to be one of America's most important poets.

Doyle, Arthur Conan (1859–1930) Born in Edinburgh, Scotland, Doyle is famous for his Sherlock Holmes stories and novels. Doyle also wrote science fiction, historical romances, and nonfiction on subjects like the Congo and World War I. He was educated as a doctor. In 1902, he was knighted for his pamphlet explaining and defending the Boer War.

Eliot, T. S. [Thomas Stearns] (1888–1965) Although born in St. Louis, Missouri, and educated at Harvard, Eliot immigrated to England and became a British citizen in 1927. *Prufrock and Other Observations* was published in 1917 during World War I. He won the Nobel Prize for literature in 1948.

Erdrich, Louise (b. 1954) Erdrich is the author of numerous novels, including *Love Medicine*, *The Beet Queen*, and *The Master Singers Butchers Club*. She has also written two volumes of poetry and is the coauthor with her late husband, Michael Dorris, of *The Crown of Columbus*. Her most recent publication is a memoir, *Books and Islands in Ojibwe Country*

(2014). Erdrich was born in Minnesota to Chippewa and German parents.

Espada, Martín (b. 1957) An attorney who was born in the housing projects of Brooklyn, Espada highlights the social inequities of urban America in his poetry. His book *Rebellion Is the Circle of a Lover's Hands* won the Peterson Poetry Prize in 1991. His most recent publication is a collection of poetry entitled *The Trouble Ball*. A previous collection, *The Republic of Poetry*, was a finalist for the Pulitzer Prize.

Forché, Carolyn (b. 1950) After attending schools in Michigan and Ohio, Forché moved to the Southwest, where she lived among Pueblo Indians. Later, she documented civil rights violations in El Salvador for Amnesty International. Her published books of poetry include *Gathering the Tribes* in 1975, *The Country Between Us* in 1981, and *The Angel of History* in 1994.

Franklin, John Hope (1915–2009) A history professor and an author, Franklin was awarded the Presidential Medal of Freedom and served as the chair of the President's Initiative on Race. His books include *From Slavery to Freedom: A History of Negro Americans* (1947), *Racial Equality in America* (1976), and *The Color Line: Legacy for the Twenty-first Century* (1993).

Frost, Robert (1874–1963) Frost was born in San Francisco but is best known for his relationship with New England, where he lived most of his life. *A Boy's Will*, his first collection of poems, was published by 1913, and Frost continued to write and publish poetry through 1962. He won four Pulitzer Prizes for his work and will always be remembered for reading his poems "Dedication" and "The Gift Outright" at the inauguration of President John F. Kennedy in 1961.

Gilbert, Jack (1925–2012) Gilbert won both a Guggenheim Fellowship and a grant from the National Endowment for the Arts but later chose to live quietly and away from publicity. He has published four collections of poetry: *Views of Jeopardy* (1962), *Monolithos* (1984), *The Great Fires: Poems 1982–1992* (1994), and *Refusing Heaven* (2005).

Giovanni, Nikki (b. 1943) Born in Knoxville, Tennessee, Giovanni is a poet, writer, lecturer, and professor of creative writing. She received the University Distinguished Professor Award at Virginia Tech in 1999. She has published many books of poetry as well as an autobiography, *Gemini: An Extended Autobiographical Statement on My First Twenty-Five Years of Being a Black Poet* (1971). Her most recent collection is *Chasing Utopia* (2013).

Glaspell, Susan (1876–1948) The work of this Pulitzer Prize–winning writer is heavily influenced by her rural Iowa upbringing. Glaspell embarked upon a career as a journalist at age 18, making an early impact in a male-dominated field. By age 20, she wrote her own column. Through the years, Glaspell wrote novels, short stories, and plays. One of her most famous works, *Trifles*, earned her widespread critical acclaim.

Grahn, Judy (b. 1940) After growing up in New Mexico, where she worked at several blue-collar jobs, Grahn moved to California and founded the Diana Press. Her work includes volumes of poetry and the nonfiction work *Another Mother Tongue: Gay Words, Gay Worlds* (1984).

Gurganus, Allan (b. 1947) A writer and an artist, Gurganus has taught fiction at a number of universities for the past thirty years. His most recognized work is the novel *Oldest Living Confederate Widow Tells All*, published in 1989. His fiction is most often set in the American South. Openly gay, Gurganus explores themes of homosexuality in his novel *Plays Well with Others*, published in 1997.

Hardy, Thomas (1840–1928) A major British novelist, Hardy also wrote poems throughout his career. *Tess of the D'Urbervilles* and *The Mayor of Casterbridge* are two of his many novels. At age sixty, he turned entirely to poetry, publishing *Late Lyrics and Earlier* in 1922. *Winter Words in Various Moods and Metres* was published posthumously in 1928.

Harjo, Joy (b. 1951) Born in Tulsa, Oklahoma, Harjo is a member of the Mvskoke Nation. She is an award-winning poet and musician. Her most recent work is her memoir, *Crazy Brave* (2012).

Hawthorne, Nathaniel (1804–1864) A Massachusetts author whose fiction draws on romance and psychological realism, Hawthorne found much of his material in New England's Puritan history.

Besides his many short stories, he is best known for his novels *The Scarlet Letter* (1850) and *The House of Seven Gables* (1851).

Hayden, Robert (1913–1980) Hayden was a professor of English at several universities, primarily Fisk University. During his teaching years, he published multiple volumes of poetry, including *The Night-Blooming Cereus* in 1972.

Heaney, Seamus (1939–2013) An Irish poet, Heaney won the Noble Prize for literature in 1995. *Government of the Tongue* was published in 1988 and *The Redress of Poetry* in 1995. In 1998, he published *Opened Ground: Selected Poems 1966–1996*.

Hemingway, Ernest (1899–1961) Hemingway, an author and journalist, wrote the novels *The Sun Also Rises* (1926), *A Farewell to Arms* (1929), *For Whom the Bell Tolls* (1940), and *The Old Man and the Sea* (1952). He won the Nobel Prize for literature in 1954.

Henry, O. (1862–1910) William Sydney Porter chose the pen name, O. Henry, and likely inherited his literary flair from his artistic mother, who died when Porter was three. Porter eventually settled in Austin, Texas, where he married and had a daughter. While working as bank teller, he pursued writing. Porter later moved his family to Honduras, only to be forced to return to Texas to face embezzlement charges stemming from his banking career. Found guilty, Porter wrote short stories while serving a five-year prison sentence. Details of his legal troubles were not made fully public until after his death. Popular collections of his short stories include *The Four Million* (1906) and *Options* (1909). Several volumes of his short stories were also published posthumously.

Horick, Randy (b. ?) Horick is a Tennessee-based writer whose editorials have been featured in diverse publications from the *Nashville Scene* to *The Tennessean*. His topics explore areas such as sports, politics, and religion. Horick owns Writers Bloc, Inc., and uses his journalism skills to work as a writing consultant.

Housman, Alfred Edward (1859–1936) A. E. Housman was an English poet and scholar. He became a professor at Cambridge in 1911, where he taught for the remainder of his career.

Hughes, Langston (1902–1967) Born in Joplin, Missouri, Hughes became a major force in the Harlem Renaissance. He was among the first successful African American writers in the United States and published poetry, novels, and plays as well as children's books and song lyrics.

Irving, Washington (1783–1859) Irving grew up a child of privilege, hailing from a wealthy New York family. He found himself fascinated with New York City high society and legends of areas upstate. After he studied law and dabbled in writing, Irving moved to England to run a family business. When that business dissolved, Irving opted to pursue writing full-time. He is most famous for his tales "The Legend of Sleepy Hollow," "Rip Van Winkle," and "The Spectre Bridegroom."

Jackson, Shirley (1916–1965) Born in San Francisco, Jackson began writing as a teenager. She pursued her interest when she moved to New York with her family and entered the University of Rochester. Though she withdrew from college in 1936, she spent a year practicing her craft by producing 1,000 words per day. By 1940, she had earned her college degree and met her husband, Stanley Edgar Hyman, with whom she co-founded the literary magazine *Spectre*. In 1948, Jackson rose to fame with *The New Yorker*'s publication of her short story "The Lottery." The piece is said to have generated more mail than any other story ever published in the *The New Yorker*'s history. Though most readers reacted negatively to "The Lottery," the story became one of the most famous short stories of the twentieth century.

Kelley, Robin D. G. (b. 1962) Kelley is currently Distinguished Professor of History and Gary B. Nash Endowed Chair in United States History at the University of Southern California; he served as William B. Ransford Professor of Cultural and Historical Studies at Columbia University from 2005–2007. Kelley is the author of numerous books, including *Hammer and Hoe: Alabama Communists During the Great Depression* (1990), *Yo' Mama's DisFunktional!: Fighting the Culture Wars in Urban America* (1997), *Freedom Dreams: The Black Radical Imagination* (2002), and *Thelonious Monk: The Life and Times of an American Original* (2009).

Kenan, Randall (b. 1963) Although born in Brooklyn, New York, Kenan grew up in North Carolina and received his bachelor's in English from the University of North Carolina in 1985. A former editor at Alfred A. Knopf, he currently teaches creative writing at the University of North Carolina. Kenan's literary awards include grant recipient for the New York Foundation of the Arts, 1989; MacDowell Colony Fellowship, 1990; and the Lambda Literary Award, Gay Men's Fiction, 1993, for *Let the Dead Bury Their Dead*, which includes "The Foundations of the Earth." In 1999, Kenan published *Walking on Water: Black American Lives at the Turn of the Twenty-First Century*.

Kennedy, John Fitzgerald (1917– 1963) Kennedy was the thirty-fifth president of the United States (1961–1963). Born in Brookline, Massachusetts, Kennedy graduated from Harvard University and served in the Navy during World War II. In 1953, he was elected to the U.S. Senate, and in 1955, his book *Profiles of Courage* won the Pulitzer Prize for history. Elected president of the United States in 1960, Kennedy became the country's first Roman Catholic president. Kennedy was assassinated in Dallas, Texas, on November 22, 1963.

Kincaid, Jamaica (b. 1949) Born as Elaine Potter Richardson on the island of Antigua, as a young woman, she studied photography at the New York School for Social Research and also attended Franconia College in New Hampshire for a year. She changed her name to Jamaica Kincaid in 1973. Since then, Kincaid has published a number of novels, including *Annie John* (1986), *At the Bottom of the River* (1992), and *The Autobiography of My Mother* (1996). Her most recent novel is *See Now Then* (2013).

King, Martin Luther, Jr. (1929– 1968) One of the most prominent civil rights leaders of the twentieth century, King was born in Atlanta and was the grandson and son of ministers. After receiving degrees from Morehouse College and Crozier Theological Seminary, he attended Boston University, earning his Ph.D. (1955) and D.D. (1959). In his decade of leadership of the civil rights movement, King was influenced by the example of Mahatma Gandhi, who led a bloodless rebellion against British colonial rule in India. King instituted training for his nonviolent campaign of protest. In 1963, King delivered his famous speech "I Have a Dream," and in 1964, "Letter from Birmingham Jail" was published. King received the Nobel Prize for Peace in 1964, but in 1968, at the height of his work for civil rights, King was assassinated in Memphis, Tennessee. Among his published works are *The Measure of a Man* (1968), *I've Been to the Mountaintop* (1994), and *A Knock at Midnight: Inspiration from the Great Sermons of Reverend Martin Luther King, Jr.* (1998).

Knight, Etheridge (1933–1991) Knight, who grew up in the South, was sentenced to twenty years in Indiana State Prison for a robbery in 1960. *Poems from Prison* was published in 1968, and he won the

American Book Award in 1987 for *The Essential Etheridge Knight* (1986).

Lawrence, D.H. **(1885–1930)**
David Herbert Lawrence, born the son of working class parents in England, battled poverty to become a highly respected twentieth-century artist. Lawrence is celebrated not only for his writing, but also for his paintings that became famous after his death. "Snake" is one of his most revered poems; *Lady Chatterly's Lover* is perhaps his most popular novel and one that was banned in both America and in the United Kingdom for a number of years due to its erotic content.

Lincoln, Abraham **(1809–1865)**
Born in a cabin in Hardin County, Kentucky, Lincoln became the sixteenth president of the United States. Shortly after his inauguration on March 4, 1861, the Civil War began. In 1863, he issued the Emancipation Proclamation, laying the groundwork for the passage of the Thirteenth Amendment, which outlawed slavery forever in the United States. Several weeks after he delivered his Second Inaugural Address on March 4, 1865, he was assassinated by John Wilkes Booth. Lincoln died on April 15, 1865.

Mansfield, Katherine (1888–1923)
A native of New Zealand, Katherine Mansfield achieved fame as a short story writer. She published two collections, *Bliss* in 1920, and *Garden Party* in 1922. Sadly, her career and her life were cut short when she died of tuberculosis at age 34.

Marquis, Don(ald) (Robert Perry) **(1878–1937)** A newspaper columnist, humorist, poet, playwright, and author of about thirty-five books, Marquis was born in Walnut, Illinois. He is best known for his books of humorous poetry about Archy the cockroach and Mehitabel the cat.

McKay, Claude **(1890–1948)**
Originally from Jamaica, McKay was an important figure during the Harlem Renaissance, when black writers found their voice in America. He wrote novels and plays but is best remembered for his poems. *Home to Harlem* was published in 1928.

Meinke, Peter (b. 1932) Meinke was born in Brooklyn, New York, and attended Hamilton College. He received his doctorate in literature from the University of Minnesota. His poetry has appeared in many magazines and journals since the 1970s. *Liquid Paper: New and Selected Poems* was published in 1991. He is Professor Emeritus of Literature at Eckerd College in St. Petersburg, Florida.

Merrill, James **(1926–1995)**
Independently wealthy, Merrill published poetry throughout his life, beginning with *First Poems* in 1951 and ending with *Selected Poems* in 1992. During that time, he won two Pulitzer Prizes and two National Book Awards.

Millay, Edna St. Vincent (1892–1950) Millay published many volumes of poetry during her lifetime and was also recognized as a dramatist, lecturer, short story writer, and actress. Although her reputation began to decline in the 1930s, a modern interest in feminism and women writers has allowed her work to regain a position of respect in

American literature. Her *Collected Poems*, edited by Norma Millay, was published in 1956.

Miller, Arthur (1915–2005) Although *Death of a Salesman* (1945) continues to be his most successful play, Miller had a long career as a playwright, winning both the Pulitzer Prize and the New York Drama Critics Circle Award. His play *The Crucible* (1953) grew out of his disdain for the anti-Communist fervor of the McCarthy-era House Un-American Activities Committee.

Milton, John (1608–1674) Milton worked for Oliver Cromwell during the civil war between the king and Parliament but was arrested when the monarchy was restored. During the last fourteen years of his life, he retired from public life and wrote his epic poems *Paradise Lost* (1667) and *Paradise Regained* (1671).

Morgan, Rhett (b. ?) Morgan reports for *Tulsa World*, a daily newspaper in Tulsa, Oklahoma. He has held the post since 1992. A graduate of the University of Missouri School of Journalism, Morgan has close to thirty years' experience as a journalist. His previous jobs include covering news in Jackson, Tennessee, and five years working with the *Tulsa Tribune* prior to accepting his current position.

Nye, Naomi Shihab (b. 1952) An American singer and writer with Palestinian roots, Nye has published children's books as well as poetry. Her poetry collections include *Hugging the Jukebox* (1982), *Words Under the Words: Selected Poems* (1995), and *Fuel* (1998).

O'Brien, Tim (b. 1946) After graduation from college, O'Brien served as an infantryman in Vietnam, where he won the Purple Heart. Upon returning home, he began to write about his war experiences. His Vietnam novel *Going After Cacciato* (1978) won the National Book Award for Fiction in 1979. His latest novel *July, July* was published in 2002.

O'Connor, Flannery (1925–1964) O'Connor was a Southern American writer of essays, novels, and short stories. Her writing contains elements of the Southern Gothic genre, examining religious and ethical issues through grotesque and often violent characters.

Okita, Dwight (b. 1958) An American of Japanese descent, Okita was born and raised in Chicago. His collection of poems is *Crossing with the Light* (1992); his novel is *The Prospect of My Arrival* (2011).

Olds, Sharon (b. 1942) A professor and writer, Olds is a much-published contemporary American poet. Her poetry collections include *The Father* (1992); *The Wellspring* (1995); *The Gold Cell* (1997); *Blood, Tin, Straw* (1999); *The Unswept Room* (2002); *One Secret Thing* (2009); and *Stag's Leap* (2012). Olds was New York State Poet from 1998–2000 and currently lives and teaches in New York City.

Oliver, Mary (b. 1935) Oliver was born in Cleveland and attended Ohio State University and Vassar College. She first published a collection of poetry in 1963, *No Voyage and Other Poems*. Oliver's collection of poetry *American Primitive* won the 1984 Pulitzer Prize for Poetry, and *New and Selected Poems* won the National Book Award for poetry in 1992. Her recent publications include *The Truro Bear and Other Adventures: Poems and Essays* (2008) and *Swan: Poems and Prose Poems* (2010).

Orwell, George (1903–1950) A writer and socialist, Orwell lived in poverty and associated with laborers early in his writing career. He later fought in the Spanish civil war and went on to write *Animal Farm* (1945) and *1984* (1949), both illustrating his distaste for totalitarian governments.

Owen, Wilfred (1893–1918) Owen was an English poet who died in France during World War I at the young age of twenty-five, before his career ever began. Twenty-four of his poems were published after his death.

Pastan, Linda (b. 1932) Pastan lives in Potomac, Maryland, and was the Poet Laureate of Maryland from 1990 to 1995. Her book *PM/AM: New and Selected Poems* was nominated for the National Book Award. Her latest publication is her 2011 book, *Traveling Light*.

Piercy, Marge (b. 1936) Piercy has written numerous novels and collections of poetry, as well as nonfiction. Her collections of poems include *The Moon Is Always Female* (1980), *Mars and Her Children* (1992), *What Are Big Girls Made Of?* (1996), and *The Hunger Moon: New and Selected Poems, 1980–2010* (2011). Piercy presently lives in Massachusetts on Cape Cod.

Poe, Edgar Allan Poe (1809–1849) An American writer whose name is synonymous with horror, Poe amassed an amazing trove of terrifying tales in his brief life. Some of Poe's best known works include "The Fall of the House of Usher"; "The Cask of Amontillado"; "The Raven," regarded as one of the best American poems; and "The Murders in the Rue Morgue," a story that credited him with inventing a new type of detective fiction.

Porter, Katherine Anne (1890–1980) A fiction writer who also played small parts in films and worked in journalism, Porter is considered a Southern writer. Her book *Collected Stories* won both the National Book Award and the Pulitzer Prize in 1967.

Pound, Ezra (1885–1972) Born in Idaho, Pound said he knew early on that he wanted to become a poet. After receiving his MA in 1906 from the University of Pennsylvania, he planned to support himself as a college teacher while writing poetry. After being dismissed from his first teaching position, Pound left the United States for Europe. Pound lived for a while in London, Paris, and finally Italy. During World War II, after numerous broadcasts attacking Jews and the United States, Pound was arrested and returned to the United States to be tried for treason. Found to be mentally unfit for trial, Pound was committed to St. Elizabeth's Hospital for the criminally insane from 1946 to 1958. Pound is known as the creator of "imagism," a new kind of poetry in which the poet attempts to present an object or situation directly. Pound also was significant in helping other writers to become published, including T. S. Eliot, Robert Frost, and Ernest Hemingway. In 1948, Pound's *Pisan Cantos* (LXXIV–LXXXIV) won the first Bollingen Prize for poetry.

Quiñoñez, Ernesto (b. 1966) *Bodega Dreams* is the first novel by Quiñoñez. He is an Associate Professor at Cornell University. He is currently working on two projects: *Taina's Song*, a novel, and *Botanica Tales*, a collection of short stories.

Randall, Dudley (1914–2000) Randall founded Broadside Press in 1965, where he published African American writers. His collected poetry is found in *More to Remember: Poems of Four Decades* (1971) and *A Litany of Friends: New and Selected Poems* (1981).

Rexroth, Kenneth (1905–1982) Born in South Bend, Indiana, Rexroth was a poet, translator, and critical essayist. Expelled from high school in Chicago, he began supporting himself with odd jobs. After hitchhiking around the country and traveling in Europe, he moved to San Francisco in 1927 and began publishing his first poems in small magazines. Rexroth's first collection of poems, *In What Hour*, was published in 1940. He is considered instrumental in launching the late 1940s San Francisco Renaissance, and in 1955, he organized and emceed the Six Gallery reading when Allen Ginsberg unleashed "Howl." In 1975, Rexroth received the Copernicus Award from the Academy of American Poets in recognition of his lifetime work.

Rich, Adrienne (1929–2012) Rich was a Phi Beta Kappa graduate of Radcliffe College in 1951, the year she published her first collection of poetry, *A Change of World*. Since then, she has won many awards, including the National Book Award for poetry in 1974. Rich published numerous collections of poetry, including *An Atlas of the Difficult World* (1992), *The School Among the Ruins: Poems, 2000–2004*, and *Tonight No Poetry Will Serve: Poems, 2007–2010*. In 2006, Rich was awarded the National Book Foundation Medal for Distinguished Contribution to American Letters.

Rilke, Rainer Maria (1875–1926) One of the most famous German poets, Rilke served as secretary to the French sculptor Rodin. He published *New Poems* in 1907. Later, living in Switzerland, he wrote *Sonnets to Orpheus* (1923) and *The Duino Elegies* (1923).

Robinson, Edwin Arlington (1869–1935) Robinson created psychological portraits of small-town citizens in his poems and received three Pulitzer Prizes for his work.

Rodriguez, Richard (b. 1944) His book *Hunger of Memory: The Education of Richard Rodriguez* (1982) focuses on the issues of education and ethnic identity. *Days of Obligation* (1992) was nominated for the Pulitzer Prize. His most recent work is *Darling: A Spiritual Autobiography* (2013). Rodriguez's essays have been published in *Harper's Magazine, Time*, and *Mother Jones*, and he has made regular appearances on the PBS show *NewsHour.*

Roethke, Theodore (1908–1963) Roethke grew up in Michigan and attended the University of Michigan and Harvard University. He won the Pulitzer Prize for poetry in 1954 for *The Waking: Poems 1933–1953.* He also won two National Book Awards for poetry.

Rukeyser, Muriel (1913–1980) Born in New York City, Rukeyser was a poet and social activist who published many books of poetry, including *Body of Waking* (1958) and *Collected Poems* (1978).

Sanders, Scott Russell (b. 1945) Born in Memphis, Sanders has published many essay collections, novels, and children's books. His collections of essays include *Hunting for Hope* (1998), *The Country of Language* (1999), *A Conservationist Manifesto* (2009), and *Earth Works* (2012). Sanders is a Distinguished Professor Emeritus of English at Indiana University.

Schaeffer, Frank (b. 1952) Schaeffer is an author, film director, screenwriter, and public speaker. He has written nonfiction books relating to the U.S. Marine Corps, including *Keeping Faith—A Father-Son Story about Love and the United States Marine Corps.*

Schalet, Amy (b. 1968) Schalet is an associate professor of sociology at the University of Massachusetts, Amherst and is a specialist in adolescent sexuality and culture. Her book *Not Under My Roof: Parents, Teens and the Culture of Sex* was published in

2011. She was born in Connecticut but grew up in Holland and is, thus, very familiar with the Dutch culture.

Setterberg, Fred (b. 1951) A native Californian and graduate of the University of California at Berkeley, Setterberg won a creative writing fellowship from the National Endowment for the Arts in 1982 and the creative nonfiction award from Associated Writing Programs for *The Roads Taken: Travels through America's Literary Landscapes* in 1993. His most recent work is the novel *Lunch Bucket Paradise* (2011). He lives in Oakland, California.

Sexton, Anne (1928–1974) Sexton was born in Newton, Massachusetts. She attended poetry workshops in the late 1950s in the Boston area and began writing poetry at age twenty-eight. Sexton received the Pulitzer Prize for *Live or Die* (1967) and taught creative writing and continued writing poetry until her death by suicide.

Shakespeare, William (1554–1616) Born in Stratford-upon-Avon, Shakespeare married Anne Hathaway in 1582. In the 1590s, Shakespeare began to establish himself as an actor and a playwright and became an owner in one of London's acting companies, as well as an investor in the building of the Globe Theater in 1599. Between 1598 and 1609, Shakespeare created a number of his great classic plays, including *As You Like It, Henry V, Julius Caesar, Twelfth Night, Hamlet, Othello, King Lear,* and *Macbeth.* Culminating this period of creative productivity was the publication in 1609 of Shakespeare's

Sonnets, including 154 sonnets, dedicated to the unidentified "Mr. W. H." a literary mystery that continues to elude scholars. From 1603 until 1616, Shakespeare divided his time between London and Stratford, where he died on his fifty-second birthday.

Snyder, Gary (b. 1930) Born in San Francisco, Snyder studied Asian languages at the University of California, Berkeley; worked as a logger; studied Buddhism in Japan; and shipped as a crew member on oil tankers. His poems draw on images from nature, Native American culture, and Buddhism. Of his many books of poetry, *Regarding Wave* was published in 1970, and his latest poetry collection, *This Present Moment: New Poems*, was published in 2015.

Song, Cathy (b. 1955) Song, who lives in Hawaii, published *Picture Bride* in 1983, for which she won the National Book Critics Circle Award. Her collection of poems *School Figures* was published in 1994.

Soto, Gary (b. 1952) Born in Fresno, California, Soto is the author of many books of poetry, two novels, a memoir, and numerous young adult and children's books. His most recent book is a memoir, *What Poets Are Like* (2013). His collection *New and Selected Poems* (1995) was a National Book Award finalist, and his memoir, *Living Up the Street* (1985), received an American Book Award. Other honors include the Andrew Carnegie Medal, the United States Award of the International Poetry Forum, and the Bess Hokin Prize and Levinson Award. Soto, who also

has received fellowships from the Guggenheim Foundation and the National Endowment for the Arts, lives in northern California.

Stevens, Wallace (1879–1955) Born in Reading, Pennsylvania, Stevens attended Harvard for three years and then received his law degree at New York law school in 1903. After briefly practicing law, he began to work for the Hartford Accident and Indemnity Company and moved with his wife to Hartford, Connecticut, which became his lifelong home. While prospering as a businessman in the 1930s (he became vice president of Hartford in 1934), Stevens also was fully engaged in writing and publishing his poetry. Placing the individual at the center of his poems—the self as observer and creator—Stevens is often considered to be the twentieth-century's modernist interpreter of nineteenth-century American transcendentalism. Many critics consider *The Collected Poems of Wallace Stevens* (1954) to be one of the most influential books of modern poetry.

Strand, Mark (1934–2014) Although born in Canada, Strand was named U.S. Poet Laureate in 1990. *Selected Poems* was published in 1980 and *The Continuous Life* in 1990. In 1993, he received the Bollingen Prize. In 1999, Strand won the Pulitzer Prize for Poetry for *Blizzard of One: Poems*, and in 2004, he received the Wallace Stevens Award for outstanding and proven mastery in the art of poetry. The American Academy of Arts and Letters awarded

Strand its Gold Medal for Poetry for an entire body of work in 2009.

Suárez, Virgil (b. 1962) Born in Cuba, Suárez moved to the United States in 1974, after four years in Spain. He is a poet, novelist, essayist, and short story writer. He also teaches creative writing and Latino/a Literature at Florida State University.

Swift, Jonathan (1667–1745) Swift was an Irish essayist, poet, and satirist.

Vega, Ed (1936–2008) Vega, a Puerto Rican fiction writer, published *The Comeback*, a novel satirizing ethnic autobiography and identity crisis in 1985. *Casualty Report*, his third book, was published in 1991. Vega made his home in New York.

Vest, George Graham (1830–1904) George Vest was an American politician and lawyer, serving as a U.S. senator and a Confederate congressman. He was known for his skills in public speaking. He also worked to protect Yellowstone National Park.

Villanueva, Alma Luz (b. 1944) Villanueva's fiction often appears in anthologies. Her novel *Desire* was published in 1998. *Weeping Woman: La Ilorna and Other Stories* came out in 1994. Her most recent works are the novel, *Song of the Golden Scorpion* (2013) and the collection of poetry, *Gracias* (2015).

Walker, Alice (b. 1944) Born in Eatonton, Georgia, Walker attended Spelman College and received her bachelor's from Sarah Lawrence College. A poet, writer, lecturer, and

professor, Walker also coproduced the film documentary *Warrior Marks* (1993). Walker has won numerous awards for her poems and novels, including the 1983 Pulitzer Prize for fiction and the American Book Award for *The Color Purple*. Other publications include *Revolutionary Petunias and Other Poems* (1973) and the novel *Possessing the Secret of Joy* (1992). Her most recent works are *The Cushion in the Road* (2013) and *The World Will Follow Joy: Turning Madness into Flowers* (2013).

Walker, Margaret (Abigail) (1915–1998) Born in Birmingham, Alabama, the daughter of college professors, Walker published *Jubilee* in 1966, a novel that imagines the Civil War and emancipation from the slave's point of view. Her collection of poetry *For My People* was published in 1942.

Wharton, Edith (1862–1937) Against all odds and societal norms, Wharton pushed back against established gender roles of her time to pursue her passion for writing. She was born into a family of wealth, and the privilege of travel ignited an intense thirst for education. Wharton's parents, particularly, her mother, discouraged her pursuit of a writing career, preferring her to concentrate on the role of rich debutante. Her nonstop pursuit of authorship led to some of the most famous American novels and short stories including *The House of Mirth, Ethan Frome, The Age of Innocence*, "Roman Fever," "The Choice," and a collection of ghost stories that includes "Mr. Jones."

Wilbur, Richard (b. 1921) Wilbur is a prolific poet who has taught at Harvard University, Wellesley College, and Wesleyan University. His many books include *The Poems of Richard Wilbur* (1963), *Waking to Sleep* (1969), and *The Mind-Reader* (1976). From 1987–1988, Wilbur was named Poet Laureate of the United States.

Will, George (b. 1941) A native of Champaign, Illinois, Will is a *Washington Post* columnist syndicated in more than 450 newspapers. The Pulitzer Prize–winning columnist earned a Ph.D. from Princeton. Additionally, Will served as a panelist on ABC's *This Week* from its premiere in 1974 until 2013, when he joined FOX News Channel as contributor and commentator.

Williams, William Carlos (1883–1963) A poet, novelist, playwright, essayist, and pediatrician, Williams is best known for his writing as an imagist poet. He won a Pulitzer Prize for his last book, *Pictures from Brueghel* (1963).

Wright, Richard (1908–1960) Born in Roxie, Mississippi, Wright graduated as valedictorian of his high school class in 1925, although during his youth he was often close to starvation. Fifteen years later, he published his novel *Native Son*, and in 1945 his autobiography, *Black Boy*, brought him much critical acclaim.

Credits

Photo Credits

cover: Exdez/Getty Images.

p. 42: Simmons, Graham. World War I Poster, The Army Isn't All Work © Imperial War Museums (Art. IWM PST 7686).

Text Credits

Author Index

Subject Index